The Secretary

The Secretary

Martin Bormann:
The Man Who
Manipulated Hitler

Jochen von Lang

with the assistance of Claus Sibyll

*Translated from the German by
Christa Armstrong and Peter White*

Random House   New York

First American Edition
Copyright © 1979 by Random House, Inc.
All rights reserved under International and Pan-American Copyright Conventions. Published in the United States by Random House, Inc., New York, and simultaneously in Canada by Random House of Canada Limited, Toronto. Originally published in West Germany as *Der Sekretär* by Deutsche Verlags-Anstalt, Stuttgart. Copyright © 1977 by Deutsche Verlags-Anstalt.

Except where otherwise indicated, all
photographs have been reproduced courtesy
Zeitgeschichtliches Bildarchiv Heinrich Hoffmann.

Library of Congress Cataloging in Publication Data
Lang, Jochen von.
The secretary.
Translation of Der Sekretär.
Bibliography: p.
Includes index.
1. Bormann, Martin, 1900–1945.   2. National
socialism—Biography.   I. Sibyll, Claus.   II. Title.
DD247.B65L3613 1979   943,086'092'4 [B] 78-57114
ISBN 0-394-50321-X

Manufactured in the United States of America

2 4 6 8 9 7 5 3

Foreword

Before he killed himself, Hitler called Martin Bormann "the most loyal Party comrade." Actually, he was more than that. Although his appearance —stocky, short-legged, with a bullethead and dark hair—was as far removed as possible from the ideal pure Nordic type who was to found the Greater German World Empire and rule over the "inferior races," his character, family origin and education made him a perfect example of the kind of German who sought to improve his self-image by putting on the Nazi uniform. It was no accident that for years Bormann stood at the head of the band of officials whom the German people nicknamed "the golden pheasants" (from the profusion of gold emblems on their uniforms) and both ridiculed and feared.

Some Germans feared Bormann especially—not the ordinary people; they did not even know his name, which was rarely mentioned in the Third Reich's controlled press, and often misspelled if it was, but ministers, high officials, judges, the big men in the Party, Hitler's court entourage, including his mistress, Eva Braun, generals, co-workers, even Bormann's own wife and nine children. Millions of others had reason to fear him had they but known it, beginning with "the grumblers and croakers" —the Party term for all who were critical of the Nazi regime—and including Christians, Jews, conservatives, intellectuals and Slavs. Bormann did not contribute a single idea to Party ideology, but he was a remarkably talented manager who steered the Nazi engine of corruption, duress, terror and crime so successfully that during the war years he became the secret ruler of Germany.

Born in 1900, he grew up amid the swagger and militarism of the Kaiser's empire. The German defeat at the end of World War I demoralized him, and the Weimar Republic failed to give him the sense of national pride that comes from being a citizen of a great power. As a member of the petite bourgeoisie he saw people of his own class reduced to bottom-line poverty during the depression and inflation of the 1920s, and this shaped his political objectives: Germany must become powerful again so that he could become powerful. He considered himself a revolutionary, but in fact he was far more attracted by tub-thumping nationalism and the belief that a firm hand would restore order to a world torn off its hinges by "Reds" and Jews. If these were the bad ones, then their enemies must be the good ones. It was as simple as that for a young man who prized deeds more than ideas and whose mediocre, half-educated mind accepted slogans and clichés as received wisdom.

Bormann was one of many who fell into the trap of these false conclusions. During the 1920s, elements of National Socialism were festering in the minds of countless Germans. This was, to be sure, true of other nations as well, but unlike the Germans, they were not being forced to the very margin of their existence. Democracy had manifestly failed in Germany. When Bormann was sent to jail for complicity in the Freikorps' summary execution of an informer, it gave him an additional reason for hating the system. He made up his mind to become a politician. Since he could not succeed on his merits and had no charisma whatever, he had to make the long, slow climb up the ladder of the Party machine. The qualities needed to accomplish this journey he either had or managed to develop to a quite extraordinary degree: diligence, perseverance, organizational talent, quick grasp of a situation, a stupendous memory, adaptability, obedience to superiors, ruthlessness to inferiors, tactical instinct and cunning. Careers can still be built today with these materials. Bormann's ambition, drive to dominate others, lack of scruples, and passion for intrigue would help a man to the top in any era. He did not have the slightest trace of creativity, the faintest spark of genius. But armed with the equipment he had, he made his way inexorably to the top of Hitler's bureaucracy.

The Bormann type is by no means peculiar to the National Socialist period. Among the Nazi Party leadership—that motley collection of sectarian preachers, bullyboys, adventurers, neurotics, idealists and patriots—Martin Bormann was, however, exceptional, and he found his place for precisely this reason. He became the "familiar" of Hitler, who styled himself a genius, like Wagner in Goethe's *Faust.* Yet history, unlike *Faust,* often gives men of Bormann's stripe an important part to play: the indispensable assistant, the sly instigator of policy, the executor of both details and dirty work. Such men renounce fame because they know they lack the requisite personality. Hence their enjoyment of secret power is all the more intense. Their fortress is built of laws, decrees and orders and buttressed by memoranda, files, secret reports and denunciations. Immune to attack, they rule invisibly, without assignable responsibility. Since they work mostly with documents and file cards, they find it easy to be inhuman. They meet their victims only as statistics on a printout.

Two circumstances enabled Martin Bormann to become so powerful in the Nazi system. The first was the utter confusion about the division of responsibility that Hitler deliberately encouraged. Inevitably this reserved a place for the bureaucrat uniquely capable of bringing order. The second was Bormann's sharp set of elbows which he used to shove any rival away from the center of power. He never attempted to become the chief authority because he needed a higher authority to give him commands. But he did become the sole guardian of the entrance to the holy of holies: the room where the idol with the small mustache and the hank of hair pasted on his forehead sat enthroned. No one could see the idol without Bormann's permission; to this extent he was more powerful than the man he guarded. During the last months of the Nazi regime, the Party's organizational chart was revised by Bormann and two of his closest colleagues in the Chancellery. According to the revised chart, the entire top echelon of Party dignitaries was superfluous. The Chancellery—headed by Hitler, of course—had gobbled up their responsibilities and authority like a spider with so many flies.

The grotesque irony of Bormann the bureaucrat was that, as his sphere of authority expanded, the actual physical area where that authority counted shrank. The more completely he got his hands on Hitler's domain, the smaller the domain became. Shortly before his death, he had thirty-six hours of glory as absolute regent and supreme commander of the Nazis, but his rule extended over not much more than one square kilometer of Berlin real estate. And immediately thereafter he was to disappear without a trace from that patch of ground.

The search for his missing person made his name more widely known than it had ever been in his lifetime. Jochen von Lang first became interested in finding Bormann, dead or alive. This detective work led him to examine the man's life, character, background and significance. It was, of course, satisfying when Bormann's bones were found exactly where Lang had expected them to be, but after working on the subject for several years Lang had become even more impressed by the astounding dimensions of Bormann's impact on the world of the Nazi elite and on the downfall of the Third Reich. He discovered that the man was in fact the manager who worked the levers of power in the regime's central headquarters—on orders from his Chief, to be sure, and in conformity with his Chief's wishes, yet with a degree of independence enjoyed by no one else in the Third Reich.

History does not repeat itself in the actual course of events, but there have always been parallels. There are no indications that Germany will regress into the barbarism of dictatorship. But who among us is sanguine enough to believe that the Bormanns in our midst no longer have a chance to get ahead?

CLAUS SIBYLL

Contents

The Secretary

1

The Unknown
Defendant

On October 18, 1945, Major Richard William Hurlstone Hortin of the British army was ordered to serve notice on Martin Bormann that beginning November 20, in the Palace of Justice in Nuremberg, Germany, there would be judicial proceedings against him. He was accused of war crimes, crimes against peace and crimes against humanity. If he presented himself to the International Military Tribunal, he could defend himself personally and through counsel. If he failed to appear, he would still be tried.

The court gave Major Hortin specific instructions on how to serve notice. Until the case came up for trial, the announcement must be broadcast once a week over the German radio and published in a newspaper in Bormann's hometown. Hortin realized immediately that the discharge of his duties would not be simple. Aside from the fact that no trace of the accused could be found, what was his hometown? Berlin?

He had had an office there, he was last seen there, and it was there that he disappeared. Yet during the twelve years of the Thousand-Year Reich he had spent only a minimum of time in the capital. The major had before him a report stating that the wanted man owned a large farm in Brandenburg, so that might be considered his home. But no one knew if it really was. Perhaps his hometown was still Halberstadt, where he had been born forty-five years before.

Major Hortin might have done better to choose Munich, "the Home Office of the Movement," or Berchtesgaden, the site of Hitler's mountain retreat and the whole Obersalzberg compound. For although Reichsleiter* Bormann had performed his duties in various places, his large family lived

*Highest Nazi Party rank.—*Tr.*

in Munich and Berchtesgaden, and he had offices in both places.

However, these facts were not mentioned in the dossier on Bormann, the least known of all the top Nazis. Always in the shadow of the Führer, he was familiar only to the members of Hitler's immediate entourage.

So Major Hortin gave the order that all German broadcasting stations and newspapers in the four Occupation Zones were to publish four successive times "the notice addressed to the defendant Bormann." He had two hundred thousand placards printed and displayed in all German government offices and Allied military posts. They were a sort of arrest warrant, without any exact description of the wanted man but with a photograph. The search for a suitable photograph had been hard enough, and the major doubted that anyone would recognize a man who looked so utterly commonplace.

Most Germans, still in shock from the magnitude of their defeat and full of hatred for those who had led them astray, would willingly have handed over a prominent Nazi to his well-deserved punishment. Before the war nearly all of them had voted for Hitler or worn a brown, black, gray or blue uniform with the swastika insignia. But now they were paying for their mistake, and they had no pity for those who had once occupied the seats of power and were answering for that on two hard benches in the Nuremberg Palace of Justice.

Since Adolf Hitler, Joseph Goebbels and Heinrich Himmler had committed suicide, only the second-rank Nazis were available for the "day of reckoning"; nevertheless, thirteen of the twenty-four defendants had held the rank of minister at some time. To be sure, some were on the list only because their names had a bad sound in their enemies' ears—for example, Gustav Krupp von Bohlen und Halbach, the traditional munitions baron and merchant of death, a geriatric case who proved to be too broken mentally to stand trial, and Hans Fritzsche, a section chief in the Propaganda Ministry, whose weekly radio news commentary predicting ultimate German victory had irritated the Allies.

Up to a point, however, the German people could see in the two dozen a crude representation of Hitler's brutal regime. Julius Streicher was the incarnation of the persecution of the Jews; Ernst Kaltenbrunner represented the terror of the Gestapo and the SS Security Service; Robert Ley, the meaningless hokum of National Socialism; Hans Frank ("Frank II" within the Party), the crimes against conquered nations; Wilhelm Frick, the soulless bureaucracy; Joachim von Ribbentrop, attacks on friendly nations; Alfred Rosenberg, the oppression of Christians; the military leaders, the instrument of war. But, most Germans asked themselves, who was Martin Bormann?

In Proclamation No. 1 of the International Military Tribunal, the names of the twenty-four defendants were listed without their former offices or titles. Why bother? Everyone in Germany knew them. If, however, Bormann had been listed as Reichsleiter of the NSDAP,* Reichstag deputy, Reich minister, chief of the Party Chancellery, Secretary to the Führer, head of the Volkssturm, and SS Obergruppenführer,† only a handful of Germans would have recalled ever having heard the name. The top officials of the collapsed system knew it well. But these men were nearly all behind barbed wire. Everyone in the camps—and they numbered over a hundred thousand—was interrogated and asked about his connections with the Party. What came out of all this to appear as evidence before the examining judge and the prosecution concerning the fate of Martin Bormann added up to astonishingly little. Only a very few of those questioned could remember ever having seen him.

There was ample evidence against him, however. The German trait of thoroughness—putting everything in writing, then storing the records in fire- and bomb-proof safes—delivered plenty of material for the prosecution brief: twenty-seven typewritten pages, almost all references to documents in the court record.

This evidence proved that Bormann had supported the Nazi conspirators, taken part in preparations for war and committed crimes against humanity. But no more than a few bare facts on the life history of the accused were included in the prosecution brief, and they were the kind of information that might be found in the morgue of any large newspaper. The prosecution stated that he was possibly still alive, and therefore the case had to be heard.

At that time indications that Bormann might be dead were somewhat feeble. There was a statement by his secretary, Frau Else Krüger, that late in the evening of May 1, 1945, just before he attempted to escape from the besieged Reich Chancellery in Berlin, he had resignedly told her that he would probably not get through. Hitler's chauffeur, Erich Kempka, was more precise. He said he had seen Bormann hurled sideways by the explosion of a German tank, which presumably killed him, near the Friedrichstrasse subway station at the Weidendamm Bridge. He had, however, not seen the body.

The man in charge of drafting and preparing individual prosecution briefs for the Nuremberg Trials was an American who must have been well known to old Nazi Party men. Until 1933 Robert M. W. Kempner had been senior counselor to the German government, legal advisor to the police department in the Prussian Ministry of the Interior, and an active opponent of the party that was then using every means to get itself into power. He made himself unpopular chiefly by the savage way in which he used the police power of the Ministry of the Interior to frustrate Nazi ambitions.

---

*Abbreviation for Nationalsozialistische Deutsche Arbeiter Partei (National Socialist German Workers' Party), the official title of the Nazi Party.—*Tr.*

†U.S. Army equivalent: lieutenant general.—*Tr.*

Six months later, when Hitler moved into the Reich Chancellery and Göring got control of the Prussian police, Kempner knew what was in store for him, and emigrated. Now he had returned as a United States citizen and a member of the prosecution. There was surely no one else on the Allied legal team so familiar with the fine points of not only Anglo-Saxon but also National Socialist law. When Göring and Kempner finally met face to face again, Göring asked coldly, "What can I expect from you, Doctor?" "Fairness, Herr Reichsmarschall," Kempner answered. "Because you fired me from my job, I have survived."

Kempner had never set eyes on Martin Bormann. When he fled the country, Bormann was still in Munich, a Party hack with no influence whose job it was to see that storm troopers injured in street fights and beer-hall brawls would not have to foot their medical bills. Yet the prosecutor was convinced that anyone clever enough and persistent enough to fight his way to the top through the internal bickerings of the Party must have known how to go underground when the Reich collapsed.

Kempner believed that Hitler's private secretary would have had no difficulty getting himself a new set of identity papers at the last minute. So the prosecution was not surprised when the search conducted by Major Hortin produced nothing but vague suggestions from busybodies whose leads all turned out to be figments of the imagination.

On November 15, a few days before the trial was to begin, Hortin's superior officer, Lieutenant Colonel Alexander G. Brown, reported to the prosecution that he had failed to find Martin Bormann. Two days later— it was a Saturday—the court assembled for "Preparation for Trial." At this meeting it had to be finally decided whether the action against Bormann should be pursued under the circumstances. Sir David Maxwell-Fyfe, deputy chief prosecutor for the British, a distinguished jurist and Member of Parliament, told the court that in the light of the information so far available there was no reason to assume that the accused was dead. He was less particular about the witnesses' statements. He maintained that Bormann had been seen *inside* a German tank, which exploded. Two out of three witnesses had stated that Bormann was killed in the explosion; only one had said anything about Bormann's having been wounded.

Yet this version satisfied the court, and when the prosecutor had verified through documents that all the conditions imposed by the court for the search for the accused had been fulfilled above and beyond the court's instructions, the judges, after a short pause for consultation, decided that "in accordance with Section 12 of the Statute, trial of the defendant Bormann *in absentia* shall be carried out," and announced that "defense counsel will be appointed for the accused."

This assignment went to Friedrich Bergold, who gladly would have done without it. To appear as counsel in a case the whole civilized world is following is every criminal lawyer's dream. But in this particular case, there was very little fame to be won. Who except the accused himself could help the defense attorney answer charges? Who could suggest where exculpating material might be found in the mountain of documents? Who could name witnesses for the defense?

Bergold was convinced that his client had lost his life in the fighting in the Berlin streets. He would have liked to have Bormann declared dead and the proceedings terminated on the first day of the trial. But it was too early for that. So at ten in the morning on November 20 he sat with the other defense attorneys a few feet from the defendants' benches and waited for an opportunity to give up his seat forever.

By the opening day of the trial two of the original twenty-four defendants had been dropped. Krupp, the industrialist, had been stricken from the list, and Robert Ley, Reich Organization Leader of the NSDAP and head of the Deutsche Arbeitsfront (German Labor Front), had hanged himself in his cell a few days after the indictment was handed down and his suggestion that if they let him live, he would cure the Germans of anti-Semitism was rejected. Bergold hoped the name Bormann would be the next to disappear from the list. On the third day of the trial he requested that the action against Martin Bormann be adjourned and prorogued because the defendant was uniquely unable to be heard in his own defense and because the defense counsel had had insufficient time to study the documentary material. Bergold did not see why he should have to go through the months of the trial—ten, as it turned out—working on a mountain of papers (5,330 by the end of the proceedings), all for a verdict that could never be carried out. But the court denied his petition. It merely recognized that he should be granted enough time to prepare his defense. For this reason the Bormann case would be heard last.

This sounded magnanimous, but only four weeks went by before U.S. Army Colonel Robert G. Storey brought up the subject of Bormann. "Though the defendant is not sitting on the bench with the other accused, the proof of his responsibility in the leadership and furtherance of the Nazi conspiracy lies here before us. As chief of the Party Chancellery directly under Hitler, Bormann was an extraordinarily important power factor in the governance of the corps of political leaders." He also controlled the Reich government, and through his double function as Party official and Reich minister, held a key position in the National Socialist organization.

It was shortly before Christmas 1945, which added emphasis when Colonel Storey, full of personal indignation, gave a detailed description of the savage way in which Bormann had oppressed the Christian churches. It also made it all the more awkward for Bergold, since for this aspect of his case there was no defense. Many documents bearing Bormann's signature gave unequivocal witness to the fact that even during the war he would have liked to eradicate Christianity.

During the Christmas recess the prosecution continued to keep its sights trained on Bormann. In mid-January a young U.S. lieutenant, Thomas F. Lambert, an assistant prosecutor full of zeal for his mission, was sent into the fray. With the energy of a man who wants simultaneously to save the world and to distinguish himself before a collection of high-ranking jurists, he vividly portrayed the way in which "the man in Hitler's shadow" secretly wielded power, committed war crimes, persecuted Christians and Jews, and carried out the annihilation of the civilian population in Eastern Europe.

Lieutenant Lambert loudly declaimed, "Everyone knows that Hitler was a wicked person. But without accomplices like Bormann he never would have been capable of seizing total power." Bormann, who had devoted his entire life to conspiracy, "was in fact an evil archangel at the side of the devil Hitler."

Discounting the rhetoric, Bergold was nevertheless obliged to deal with the concrete accusations in the indictment. The more power Bormann had gathered to himself in the last years, the more decrees, laws and orders went out over his signature. By the sheer volume of the documentary evidence, the prosecution, with its ample staff, was able to make its case without witnesses. How could a single lawyer with a small staff compete with that?

The twenty-one defendants were no help at all to Bergold. At the moment they appeared to be companions in misfortune. Actually, they were still enemies and competitors—just as they had been under Hitler. Hermann Göring presented himself as the Führer's successor. Karl Dönitz and Erich Raeder could not stand the sight of each other, despite or perhaps because of the fact that they had both commanded the navy. Almost everyone despised Julius Streicher. The military men, backbiting among themselves, quarreled with the Party men. They agreed on only one thing—and interestingly enough, their opinion coincided almost exactly with Lieutenant Lambert's: Bormann was Hitler's Lucifer. For whatever had been done that deserved punishment, Hitler's secretary bore the primary responsibility, after the dead Führer himself.

When Göring was interrogated in mid-March 1946 by the American prosecutor Justice Robert H. Jackson, he named Hitler, Goebbels, Himmler and Bormann as the individuals guilty of the crimes committed by the Third Reich. But, he added, "the decisive influence on the Führer himself during the war, and particularly from 1942 on . . . was exercised by Herr Bormann. It was a disastrous influence."

Ernst Kaltenbrunner, chief of the Reich Security Service and next to Himmler the most powerful man in the SS, maintained in all seriousness that he knew nothing of the millions of Jews murdered. "The people who did that are all dead: Hitler, Himmler, Bormann, Heydrich, Eichmann."

Alfred Rosenberg, author of the anti-Christian *Myth of the Twentieth Century,* refused to take responsibility for the Party's campaign against the churches. Because he had been unwilling to allow his departments to be used improperly as a "spiritual police," he said, the Führer entrusted Bormann "with representing the NSDAP policy vis-à-vis the churches." Bormann had also carried out Hitler's harsh demands in the "handling of the Eastern problem" (that is, the enslavement and decimation of conquered civilian populations). The defendant Baldur von Schirach stated that Bormann had harassed him because as Reich Youth Leader and Gauleiter of Vienna he had failed to make it sufficiently hard for the churches. Field Marshal Wilhelm Keitel, when asked by Bergold who had been responsible for the Volkssturm, that senseless *levée en masse* which prolonged the war and only created further bloodshed, answered that it was Bormann, who had "refused to advise, cooperate with or give any information concerning the Volkssturm to the military."

According to the defendant Hans Fritzsche, even Goebbels "was afraid of Martin Bormann." The Propaganda Minister—himself a Reichsleiter in the Party, of at least equal rank with Bormann in the Reich Cabinet and back in Hitler's good graces during the last two years of the war—had to justify to Bormann "every one of his operations susceptible to objections from radical elements in the Party." Whenever Bormann sent a telex, "the entire apparatus of Dr. Goebbels' ministry was immediately set in motion."

By the end of May the trial had been going on for six months, and Friedrich Bergold had made almost no headway with his defense. He hoped that one incriminating document or another might be made less damning, but what good would that be when there were more than enough for a verdict of guilty?

In desperation, Bergold attempted again and again to prove that his client was dead. He asked permission to call Hitler's chauffeur and Bormann's secretary as witnesses. Up to that time they had been interrogated only by Allied intelligence. The presiding judge, Lord Geoffrey Lawrence, allowed their testimony but immediately nullified its value by announcing, "It is unimportant whether the accused is dead or alive. The question is whether he is guilty or not guilty."

"Your Lordship," Bergold complained, "I am in an extremely difficult position. I have heard many witnesses and have taken great pains, but I can find nothing of an exculpating nature. The witnesses are all filled with rancor against the defendant and are eager to incriminate him in order to clear themselves." A few days before (it was the trial session of May 28, 1946), one of Bormann's associates, Helmut von Hummel, had been arrested in Salzburg. "I will go see him. Perhaps I will get some new information."

Hummel had in fact been one of Bormann's top men. He was in charge of the Obersalzberg compound, several farms in Mecklenburg, and Hitler's private funds. In addition, he had run a branch office of the Party Organization at Obersalzberg because Bormann wanted to have the most important files at hand when he stayed there with Hitler, sometimes for months at a time. Yet apparently Hummel was either unwilling or unable to get his former boss off the hook, for he never appeared as a witness at Nuremberg.

Fiascos such as this must have been discussed in the prisoners' dock as well as elsewhere, for in mid-June, Göring, who had good reason to hate Bormann, went up to Bergold before the court convened. Wearing a sanctimonious expression, he asked him if he had finally managed to find any defense witnesses. "He did have secretaries, after all," the former Reichsmarschall suggested. But the attorney had to admit, "None of them will testify in his favor." Triumphantly Göring said to his companions in the dock, "If Hitler had died sooner, I as his successor would not have had to worry about Bormann. He would have been killed by his own staff even before I could have given the order to bump him off."

At the end of June 1946 Bergold had to confess to the court once again that he had no witnesses. He had wanted to question Hitler's secretary Gerda Christian, but shortly before, she had been sent on home leave from the American internment camp at Oberursel and since then had been in hiding. The defense counsel had hoped to use her to prove that his client had done nothing on his own responsibility but simply followed Hitler's orders. Bormann's colleagues in the Party Chancellery might make the same statement, Bergold decided. Section chiefs Helmuth Friedrichs and Heinrich Walkenhorst could not be found, but shortly before the opening of the trial session of June 29, 1946, the Americans notified him that they had brought Gerhard Klopfer, State Secretary and Chancellery section chief, to the Nuremberg prison from an internment camp.

Bergold might have presented him on the spot, but he did not dare. After so many disappointments he did not want to go through another unpleasant surprise in public. He asked for a postponement of the Bormann case until he had had a chance to talk to Klopfer.

This was the moment at which the normally cool-headed and objective Lord Justice, who was actually quite sympathetic to Bergold, lost patience. "You have had many months at your disposal to prepare the case," he thundered, "and the court is of the opinion that you should proceed. If not with Klopfer's statement, then with other material." Bergold had no course but to plead, "My Lord, what I have is so meager I don't know myself whether it would hold up until I have interrogated the witness."

Bergold got his postponement in the end—but only for a couple of hours. Unfortunately, Klopfer did not feel that his ex-boss had been as devoid of power and influence as the defense counsel would have liked him to be; Bergold did not call him as witness. Instead he attempted, with the help of documents, to "establish a small proof to the effect that the defendant did not in fact play the legendary great role he is being credited with now after the collapse." Yet he felt poorly prepared for that, too, and after his presentation he apologized. "As a lawyer it goes against my grain to make something out of nothing," he said, "and for that reason I can present only very, very little. It is not neglect but inability to extract anything positive from the documents without the help of the defendant."

On July 3 he was finally able to bring forward his most important and last witness, Erich Kempka. Kempka, who had been born into a large working-class family in the Ruhr, was brought up to worship the Führer and for years served as his idol's personal chauffeur. In the final phase of the war he managed the motor pool in the subterranean garage of the Reich Chancellery. It was he who obtained the gasoline that was used to incinerate the corpses of Hitler and the woman he had just married. Administratively he was subordinate to Bormann, whom he referred to in court as "my indirect superior."

Kempka enjoyed a direct line to his superior, as is usually the case with personal chauffeurs and their employers. For this reason Bormann intrigued against Kempka, as he did against anyone who had access to Hitler other than through him. Kempka, on his part, resented Bormann's uncouth manner in ordering him around.

Under questioning by Bergold, Kempka told the court how he had met Bormann at the Weidendamm Bridge during the night of May 1–2, 1945, and how they and some other men from the Führerbunker had attempted to break through the Russian lines under cover of German tanks. Bormann had been walking alongside the first tank. "It blew apart, right where Bormann was walking."

Bergold asked, "Then, in the light of the flames bursting from the tank, did you see Martin Bormann fall?" Kempka, who had been temporarily blinded by the flames and knocked insensible for a few minutes by the explosion, recalled "a movement, a sort of collapse, one could also say a gliding motion," and he was positive "that Bormann was killed by the force of the explosion."

The judges were not satisfied. They asked if Kempka and Bormann had discussed the best way to get out of Berlin, and where he, Kempka, had been taken prisoner. "In Berchtesgaden," he said. When? "In the summer of 1945."

So this interrogation, too, failed to give Bergold what he needed. If Bormann, as Kempka testified, was wearing the uniform of an SS Obergruppenführer and had met his death at the Weidendamm Bridge, this particular corpse would surely have been noticed by the Russians. If he had merely been wounded, they would have taken him prisoner. Neither had happened. Besides, Kempka had not seen Bormann dead. Furthermore, he himself managed to slip through the ring of Soviet troops and make his way to southern Bavaria. If the Führer's chauffeur could do this, why not his secretary?

"I can swear that Hitler is dead," Kempka assured the court. And Bormann? He could not answer.

Bergold submitted the sworn testimony of Bormann's secretary, Else Krüger, that SS Brigadeführer (Brigadier General) Johann Rattenhuber, in charge of the police guarding Hitler, had told her of Bormann's death, though he knew that after Kempka's testimony this piece of paper was worthless. For Rattenhuber had disappeared just as Bormann had, and perhaps had made a similar escape.

On October 1, 1946, the verdicts were announced in Nuremberg. Three defendants were found "not guilty in the sense of the indictment" and were released. Seven were sentenced to terms of imprisonment from ten years to life. Twelve were condemned to death, among them Bormann. He was found guilty of war crimes and crimes against humanity. He was pronounced not guilty of crimes against peace.

As the verdict read, "there is no proof at hand that Bormann knew of Hitler's plans to prepare for and wage wars of aggression." Not until he became head of the Party Chancellery, following Rudolf Hess's flight to England in May 1941, did he attain access to the Führer's inner circle, by which time the attack on the Soviet Union had long since been decided.

The court erred in favor of the defendant on this point. But that was irrelevant for someone who would meet the hangman's noose anyway, if the Nuremberg authorities could ever catch him. When on the early morning of October 15, 1946, the death sentences were carried out, only ten of the twelve criminals were handed over to the executioner. One—Göring—had taken poison during the night; the other was nowhere to be found.

Neither the court nor the defense counsel knew at this time that in fact there was someone who had seen Martin Bormann dead. Records of interrogations stamped "Top Secret" and therefore locked in a safe were at the British-American military intelligence headquarters. Anyone privileged to read them learned a rather amazing story.

In late October 1945 a heavy snowfall drove a group of young men out of a peasant hut high up on a mountain pasture in the Bavarian Alps. They were former Hitler Youth leaders, and they turned themselves in to the Americans in Memmingen. Their leader was a young man who six months before had been the highest-ranking person in the Hitler Jugend, Reichs-jugendführer Artur Axmann, thirty-five years old. Many young Party members had believed he would be Hitler's successor.

He lost an arm early on in the Russian campaign. By the war's end he was a member of Hitler's intimate entourage in the Führerbunker, made the breakout with the others and was present at the tank incident at the Weidendamm Bridge. He told his interrogators—among them Major Hugh R. Trevor-Roper, an historian and Oxford don in civilian life—that immediately after the encounter he and some other men from the Reich Chancellery kept on moving, but subsequently the group broke up. Later, on a bridge near the Lehrter Railroad Station, he saw two dead bodies. One was Hitler's personal physician, Ludwig Stumpfegger; the other was Martin Bormann.

The Axmann report and the events of that night will be discussed in detail later. At this point the question is why Allied intelligence kept this information on Bormann locked up. Some possible answers can be found in Trevor-Roper's letters to colleagues. First, there was the contradiction between the Kempka story and the Axmann story. Who was mistaken—or who was lying? Possibly neither should be believed. The motive for a deliberately false story was plausible enough; nobody would go on searching for a dead man. The fact that both men maintained they were no friends of Bormann made their reports no more credible, for when it came to dealing with the occupying power, old Party comrades might well bury the hatchet. Anyone who was lying about Bormann could never be trusted. Both men were important witnesses to the fact that Hitler was dead and his body burned to ashes. How much truth was there in that?

The Russians maintained that they had found Hitler's corpse, and a pathologist wrote a detailed expert opinion on it, mantaining among other things that the Führer had been born with only one testicle. U.S. intelligence knew that this was not so. Hitler's physician Theodor Morell, a wreck of his former self, was in one of their internment camps, and naturally he had been interrogated about this in great detail. Were Bormann at this point to be declared dead by the court, and then to surface later on, die-hard Nazis would suspect that perhaps the Führer was alive too. Obviously a resurrected Bormann would destroy the credibility of Allied intelligence.

In *The Last Days of Hitler,* which is still a unique source for this period, Trevor-Roper writes that Axmann's statement "though available, was evidently overlooked." Since there was such a volume of documents, this is indeed possible, though the uncertainty of Bormann's fate had spurred both prosecution and defense to intensive research. Be that as it may, the question remains: Why did intelligence officers, who surely must have been following the trials with keen attention, never mention Axmann's testimony? Trevor-Roper apparently believed it to be true very early on; a few years after Nuremberg he wrote that Axmann's account, "apart from accidental errors of time . . . has proved accurate."

The court injected some concealed praise for Bergold in its opinion. Brigadier General Yola T. Nikitchenko of the Soviet Union read it aloud: "Bormann's defense counsel, who had to perform his duties under difficult circumstances, was unable to refute this evidence [of Bormann's crimes]. In the light of the documents bearing Bormann's signature it is hard to imagine how he could ever have succeeded in doing so, even if the defendant had been present. . . . His defense attorney alleged that Bormann is dead. . . . But no convincing proofs of death are at hand, therefore the court decided . . . to try him *in absentia.*" Should he turn up alive, then the sentence might be mitigated if there were extenuating circumstances.

The years that followed were to bring Friedrich Bergold further moral satisfaction. When he complained in the courtroom about the prosecution not supporting him in his attempt to verify Bormann's death, he prophesied that "this will give extraordinary impetus to the building of a legend." He had already been receiving mail from impostor Bormanns. This was only the beginning. In the next quarter-century two dozen alleged "Bormanns" were discovered, each with a new and more fantastic story. But, as we will see later, it was like the reports of the Loch Ness monster—whenever anyone investigated more closely, the evidence turned out to be a fraud.

At this point, let us try to see who Martin Bormann really was. How did he get started on a career that for a few years made him one of the most powerful men in Europe? Why did only a small number of people know him, and why did nearly everyone hate him? Everyone considered him a despicable character, but anyone who could rise from "unknown storm trooper" (the exalted phrase used by the Nazis to refer to the rank and file) to Hitler's right-hand man must have possessed some "capacities and elements of soundness."

2

Early Days

"My father must have been quite a man," Martin Bormann wrote in August 1944 from the Wolfsschanze (Wolf's Lair) Führer Headquarters in East Prussia to his wife, Gerda, in Obersalzberg. This burst of admiration was evoked by a photograph of his father which a family acquaintance sent to the son who had attained such high station in life. The picture was obviously taken before 1890. It shows the trumpet player Theodor Bormann in the uniform of the Halberstadt Cuirassiers with its splendid bandsman's epaulets on both shoulders, indicating that he had not only served the usual three-year hitch with the "heavy" cavalry but had stayed on voluntarily as a musician in this markedly aristocratic Prussian regiment.

When Martin Bormann wrote this, he and a number of Party and government offices engaged on his behalf had been working for several years on his family tree. Not that he particularly cared who his ancestors were—quite the contrary, in fact—but like every Party member, he was obliged to prove that his forebears were all Aryans without any taint of the Jewish "race." However, what he told his wife about his father and his origins was not strictly true. He used to embellish his account of his family considerably, perhaps because Gerda, the daughter of a former major in the imperial army, Walter Buch, might have been disappointed by a less impressive background.

Bormann always said that his grandfather had owned a stone quarry. In fact, Johann Friedrich Bormann, born in 1830 in Schöningen, near Brunswick, worked in a brickyard. His mother, Martin's great-grandmother, was the daughter of a farm hand and bore her first child before she was twenty —or married.

To explain the poverty in Johann Friedrich Bormann's family, grandson Martin had him die young when he told the family history; thus his son Theodor could not become a forester, as he had wanted, but had to start earning money early "to feed the family." In fact, Martin's grandfather was still alive and living in Hohendodeleben, near Magdeburg, when his twenty-year-old son enlisted in the Halberstadt Cuirassiers. Discovering that his musical talent could help him get ahead, Theodor built the foundation of his subsequent modest prosperity by blowing the trumpet; at the end of the service day the regimental bandsmen were permitted to play in the beer halls and cafés of Halberstadt. According to Martin, his father left the regiment because he had no chance for advancement as a musician, since in those days even the regimental bandmaster ranked far below the officers.

Theodor Bormann returned to civilian life in the summer of 1888, the year the aged Emperor died and the crown passed to his fatally ill son; three months later his grandson Wilhelm inherited the throne at the age of twenty-nine. A new era of youthful vitality seemed to be in the making, and perhaps this encouraged Theodor Bormann and some old friends from the regiment to start a band that played marches and dance tunes, first in Saxony and eventually on tours that took the group as far afield as the seaside resorts of England. In later years, when he was Foreign Minister, Joachim von Ribbentrop used to describe sneeringly how he had seen the father of the universally despised Reichsleiter on the conductor's stand at one of these resorts. It was a cheap fabrication, for Theodor Bormann had already changed his career to the postal service when Joachim Ribbentrop —he purchased the *von* later on—was still a child.

In 1891 Theodor Bormann married Louise Grobler, the daughter of a cavalry sergeant whose family was long established in Halberstadt. In the first five years of their marriage two sons (one of whom soon died) and a daughter were born. The postal worker—he was past thirty by then—won rapid promotions because he learned French and was hard-working and intelligent. In 1897 the family was able to buy a new house. Theodor's mother-in-law, recently widowed, loaned them the few thousand marks they needed for the down payment.

Frau Louise was not to enjoy the property for long. She died a year later, at the age of thirty. His children, house and garden prompted the widower to look around for a second wife. By happy coincidence a colleague in Wegeleben, near Halberstadt, had a daughter whom he wanted to marry off. At thirty-five, Antonie Mennong was no longer in the first blush of youth and not exactly a beauty, but she was spirited and strong-willed, and she had a dowry. Theodor Bormann married her seven months after Louise died. Not quite a year later her first son, born on June 17, 1900, was baptized in the Lutheran church and given the name of the Great Reformer. The next child, another boy, was born eleven months later but lived only a short time.

The third son, born in September 1902, was named Albert for a brother-in-law of his mother's.

These two Alberts played an important part when the Bormanns fell under the spell of the swastika and Hitler. But at the time, most Germans worshipped a different idol, the Kaiser, who promised he would lead them to glory. Naturally enough, in the Bormann house there was a framed color-print portrait of the Emperor with his upturned mustache.

Only the "proletarians"—the Reds, whom the Kaiser had declared his soldiers would be ordered to fire upon if necessary, even if it meant shooting one's own brother—had no portrait of the emperor but instead one of August Bebel, the lathe operator from Saxony whose speeches in the Reichstag were always creating a furor. Martin's grandfather, the brickyard worker Johann Friedrich Bormann, might have joined up with these *"Sozis,"* but his son Theodor very definitely belonged in the camp of the patriots. Not only had he served in the aristocratic Cuirassiers regiment, he was a government official with the title of senior postal assistant (Martin later upgraded him to postal inspector). Now that he was a respected solid citizen, he had more to lose than his chains, which did not weigh on him heavily enough to be noticed. The entire extended Mennong family was similarly nationalistic, with their master craftsmen, government officials, and brother-in-law Albert Vollborn, who was the branch manager of a bank in Halberstadt.

Oberpostassistent Theodor Bormann had been in failing health when his son Albert was born, and he died before the boy was a year old. Martin, barely three, lost his hero, whom he was just learning to admire. And it was twenty years before he found a surrogate father figure. He could not have had many personal recollections of his dead father. He depended on what he was told by his mother and half-brothers and -sisters when he created his idealized image of his untimely deceased parent.

Loss of the breadwinner was a cruel blow for his mother. There were four children to be cared for: two of her own and two stepchildren, Walter, just ten, and Else, eight. Mortgage payments had to be met. Theodor's post-office service had been so short that her widow's pension was very small. Yet with her love of life and ability to deal with it, she soon found a solution. Six months after her husband's death, she married again.

She had known her new husband for a long time, and the children knew him too; he had often been to the house when Theodor Bormann was alive. Albert Vollborn had become a widower when Antonie Bormann's sister died two years before, and he was looking for a mother for his five children.

Now and then it was whispered that the widower Vollborn had had more than a strictly in-law relationship with Theodor Bormann's wife even before her husband died, and that it was singular that dark-haired, thick-set Martin bore so little family resemblance to his slender blond brother, Albert. But there is nothing to verify these rumors. Certainly the fact that Martin never liked his stepfather and even hated him proves nothing. He always considered Albert Vollborn the stranger who had usurped his father's place. It remains an open question whether the marriage was founded on love or prudence. There were no children. Antonie, the widow Bormann, had just turned forty, and her new husband was thirty-seven.

In 1904 the house on Sedanstrasse was full of curious relationships. Besides the parents, who were in-laws before they married, there were four girls and a boy (also named Albert) from Vollborn's first marriage, a boy and a girl from Theodor Bormann's first marriage, and the two boys from his second marriage—making a total of nine children, with the oldest barely thirteen and the youngest under two. These siblings, step-siblings and cousins never grew into a proper family. Some were separated from the household early; others made their own way out of the nest and grew apart. When Martin was at the height of his power in 1943 and a sergeant major in the SS armed forces whose name happened to be Bormann asked him for a favor on the basis of family relationship, Martin's wife asked him what the degree of kinship might be. His reply was: "I don't care . . . I refuse to accept any more letters from that man." Why should he expose himself needlessly to the suspicion of nepotism? In later life, relatives reminded him of uncomfortable and apparently painful past experiences. This was true even of his brother Albert. His mother was the only one allowed to visit his family in Obersalzberg.

In August 1906, shortly before Martin entered school, Albert Vollborn moved his family to Eisenach, in Thuringia, and got a better job, still as manager of a bank branch. The two Bormann children from the first marriage, Walter and Else, remained with relatives of their late mother in Halberstadt. Strictly speaking, they were no relation to the Vollborn couple. Martin never missed these half-siblings. His relationship with his family must have been quite disturbed at this time, for he rarely talked about anything that happened in Eisenach in later life and always referred to himself as a native of Halberstadt.

Apparently Martin at six was not quite ready for regular school; he spent three years in a private school in Eisenach. And when in 1909 the family made its next move, to Oberweimar, his name did not appear right away in the records of the Registrar's Office. Possibly his stepfather placed him temporarily in a boarding school. The family could afford such expenses; they now belonged to the upper-middle class. Despite the not inconsiderable costs, all the children were given advanced schooling, and even the daughters of Bank Manager Vollborn—the occupation listed after his name in the city directory—were raised for a life in bourgeois society. Successfully, too, for one later married a doctor, and another became the wife of the director of a land-registry office.

Martin was almost ten when he came to Weimar and was enrolled in the fourth grade. In the school system of the time this was a student's last chance to be admitted to a program of higher education, since he began to study foreign languages in this grade. This instruction appears to have given Martin no pleasure. Although he had had at least seven years of a modern second language by the time he finished school, there is no indication in any of his documents, letters or speeches that he knew another language. Whenever he traveled outside Germany, which was rarely enough and only when he accompanied the Führer, he always had an interpreter. In the many questionnaires he had to fill out over the years as a Nazi Party official, he always drew a line in the space where one was supposed to list foreign-language skills.

The school's influence in shaping him as a German youth was somewhat more noticeable. Throughout the German empire, most teachers in a *Gymnasium* (high school) were fanatical nationalists who considered the French spineless lechers, the British avaricious shopkeepers, and the Russians drunken barbarians. Therefore the world was to seek its salvation in German ways, or as a popular jingle ran, ". . . *am deutschen Wesen soll, die Welt genesen* ("The world will be saved by the German spirit"). It was taken for granted all over Germany and especially in Weimar that German culture was superior to any other.

The time was past when men of intellect and genius were drawn to Weimar, the grand-ducal *Residenz* on the river Ilm, but Schiller could still be quoted on the subject of the Fatherland, and even Goethe, albeit with reservations. The teachers cited pithy sentences from Friedrich Nietzsche, although that philosopher had his foes in the nationalist camp. The Weimar atmosphere was quite different from Prussia's; in Weimar there was greater appreciation of art and science than of artillery, and the director of the court theater even staged Ibsen's *The Wild Duck*. This particular director, like many in the German dukedoms, was a former army officer, Carl Benno von Schirach, whose son Baldur, seven years Martin Bormann's junior, was to meet him later in the top circle of the Nazi Party. There were even some pre-Hitler germinations in Weimar. A group of fanatical Wagnerites fought vigorously in the spirit of their master against any Jewish influence in music. Adolf Bartels, a professor of literature, winnowed the Jews out of German poetry and condemned them as a corrosive influence alien to the German race.

This was all part of the atmosphere in which Martin grew up. The social class to which Bank Manager Vollborn's family belonged believed that it was living in the best of all possible worlds, where anyone who took the trouble could make something of himself. One only had to guard against the envy and ill will of the Reds at home who wanted to distribute the wealth to the poor, and those neighboring nations that were unwilling to allow Germany her place in the sun.

Eleven days after Martin's fourteenth birthday, a Serbian conspirator shot the heir to the Austrian throne in Sarajevo. On July 31, 1914, an officer accompanied by a couple of soldiers, a drummer and a bugler stationed himself before Weimar Castle and read an announcement of "the threatening danger of war." One day later the Supreme Commander ordered mobilization of the army and navy. Germans were in a state of jubilation, and there is reason to suppose that among the exulting crowd that marched through the streets and sang patriotic songs was Martin Bormann in his many-colored schoolboy's cap. One victory after another was celebrated with the pealing of bells, flags in the windows, newspaper extras, prayers of thanksgiving in the churches, and more pithy observations by the teachers in the classrooms. The boys in the senior class of the *Gymnasium* were afraid the war might be over before they had their diplomas in their pockets and could rush out to enlist as volunteers. As it happened, many of them were to meet their deaths soon enough.

Some exasperating things happened too. Martin's stepfather reported that the bank customers were storming the tellers' cages to withdraw their savings. His mother complained that so many people were preparing to hoard supplies that it was hard to find flour, sugar, rice or just about any nonperishable foodstuffs in the stores. Martin resented the fact that Albert Vollborn had not volunteered for service and was still wearing civilian clothes at the age of forty-eight. He was certain his own father, had he been alive, would have been back with the Cuirassiers. And when his stepfather, sitting at the family table at the end of September, calculated how much he had made on the first war loan, Martin's loathing for him knew no bounds. Later he was to describe him as a war profiteer.

At the time, however, Martin was still in need of Vollborn's help, the more so since he was not doing well in school. Reichsleiter Bormann later put in his questionnaire that he left school after *Obersekunda** and became a soldier. If that is so, he took at least eight years to get through seven grades.

He was diligent enough, but he could not keep up with intellectual concepts—either then or later. Baldur von Schirach, who knew him for almost two decades, once said, "As for his education, one can only say 'nil returns.' His knowledge of history was at best on the level of an *Untersekundaner*†—and he surely never went any further than that with it in school. Literature, fine arts, music, all zero." To be sure, some of the arrogance of an aristocrat toward an upstart lurks behind this harsh characterization, along with antipathy toward one who had risen too high in the Party. Nevertheless, it is essentially accurate.

As the NSDAP described itself even in its early phase as the stronghold of the spirit of the front-line soldier, Bormann would tell people later that in the first years of the war he volunteered several times for military service

*Roughly the equivalent of eleventh grade.
†Tenth grader.

but was never accepted. This may be true; however, when he joined the 55th Field Artillery Regiment in Naumburg in June 1918 he was just eighteen, and young men of that age were regularly drafted. His army career does not exactly support his claim that he had volunteered, either, or that he would have been eligible for officer training on the basis of his one-year service certificate. But he remained in Naumburg as an enlisted artilleryman long after the Emperor had fled to Holland and the government in Berlin had fallen into the hands of the despised Reds—the Social Democrats. Heinrich Himmler, who was approximately the same age as Bormann, enlisted in the last months of 1917 and worked his way up to second lieutenant.

Later the generals in Führer Headquarters told one another that Bormann remained on garrison duty as long as he did because he was a "polisher," an officer's orderly. Baldur von Schirach always maintained that Bormann was a coward, but the fact that he avoided front-line duty in the last months of a virtually lost war does not necessarily prove this. Everyone who could did the same. *Drückeberger*—the slang term for "slacker"—ceased to be an insult and became a term of approval.

The remarkable thing is how quickly the young man who had been so noisily patriotic learned to distinguish between theory and practice. The mustachioed old noncoms in the recruit training company helped him. As part of the process of transforming him from a civilian into a "real human being," they taught him that a smart fellow knows how to play up to the stronger—and he never forgot it.

In one respect, however, he was not prepared to follow this rule. When he turned in his uniform in February 1919, he had decided not to return to his stepfather's household. He began looking for a position as an apprentice on a country estate, farming being the only sector where jobs were available. He could have had only a minimal notion of farm work, as he had grown up in cities and none of his relatives had a farm, but he immediately got a roof over his head and—what was just as important in those days—three square meals a day. It was hard to find these advantages in other occupations. Conversion from a war to a peacetime economy was just beginning, and every day more demobilized soldiers were being added to the already large number of unemployed.

It is not clear whether or not Bormann ever learned to be a capable farmer. Surely he would have been happy only on a large estate with many employees to take orders from him. One of his favorite dreams later on was that Hitler would present him with such a property as a reward for faithful service. He did, of course, manage Hitler's land around Obersalzberg as a second occupation, always in a very businesslike way and with some enthusiasm. In any case, he came to farming propitiously because at this time it was decreed that the peasantry was the German people's source of life, the stronghold of German culture, and the preserver of the German heritage.

Bormann always claimed that he was an apprentice farmer in Mecklenburg, but his relatives said that the place where he worked was really a mill that made oil cakes for cattle feed. It may have been that and a farm as well, the two often went together. In any case, the next firm date in Bormann's life after his army discharge is August 1920, when he was, according to his own account, "general manager of an estate in Mecklenburg." This means that he must have learned everything about farming in a year and a half, and even if he showed remarkable diligence and a rapid grasp of the subject —as some witnesses report—it still seems improbable that so inexperienced and immature a beginner would be entrusted with the management of an estate so soon. He was still a minor and could not even sign a contract.

The name of the estate is known from court records, for there a man was brutally killed with Martin Bormann's help. It was Gut Herzberg, an estate some fifteen kilometers north of the small town of Parchim.

The owner, Hermann Ernst Wilhelm von Treuenfels, lived in the Herzberg manor house and lorded it over the town and the farm workers. When Bormann entered his service, the estate covered 800 hectares (about 2,000 acres), and von Treuenfels owned another 370 hectares [900 acres] in Muschwitz. His father owned an additional 2,000 hectares [5,000 acres] nearby. In other words, the family had the equivalent of some seventy-five medium-sized farms.

Three centuries earlier, independent farmers had owned the land, but the big landowners got title to their farms one after another. In 1938 the Mecklenburg journalist Friedrich Schmidt reported: "Even today the misery of the farm worker is much worse than the condition of the poorest people in the flop houses of the big cities." Farm workers had a higher rate of tuberculosis and infant mortality than any other group. "Often the peasant dwellings [owned by the landlords—*Author's comment*] lack the most elementary protection against bad weather. Often one goes from the road right into the kitchen without any entryway. The kitchen door has to stay open even in winter because there is no window. The heat from the fireplace goes directly to the outdoors. There is no protection for the fire, no baffle to catch the heat. The bedroom has nothing but a stone floor, no wooden planks. There is often less provision for drinking water in the farm house than there is in the landlord's cow sheds."

This indictment was written eighteen years after Martin Bormann went to work for von Treuenfels. "Of course," continued Schmidt, who was a member of the NSDAP district press office for Mecklenburg, "the Party and the government intervened immediately. Landowners were brought into court and sent to prison if they were guilty of violating the most basic rules of humanity in the treatment of their farm help."

It might be noted that nothing of this sort happened in the Treuenfels family. Perhaps conditions were not as bad on their farms, or perhaps they were, but they had a friend in court at the top of the Party who still felt the bond of "old times." For the rest of his life Bormann remained friends with Ehrengard von Treuenfels, *née* Baroness von Maltzahn. He learned a lot at Herzberg, and from there he was able to get into the business of politics, at which he proved so successful. He even named one of his daughters Ehrengard after the lady of the manor.

3

Rossbach and the Feme

Once when he was filling out a curriculum vitae questionnaire, Bormann put down under "Former Activity in the Party" that he had been a member of "an association against the arrogance of Jewry." When he wrote this he was already a Reichsleiter, and presumably no one dared ask such a high-ranking Nazi what sort of organization this might have been. Actually, the "association" was originally an offshoot of the Deutschnationale Volkspartei (German National People's Party), which remained so insignificant that Theodor Fritsch, the pope of the anti-Semites, never even mentioned it in his *Handbook on the Jewish Question.* Fritsch did, however, enthusiastically describe the Deutschnationale Reichstag members Reinhold Wulle and Albrecht von Graefe, who were behind the organization and who were supported primarily by the owners of the large estates in northern Germany.

The fact that the young farm supervisor at Herzberg joined the landowners' anti-Semitic organization only a few weeks after starting work was an indication not so much of his convictions as of the rapidity with which he learned to adapt himself to his new environment—and to the political beliefs of his employer. Nevertheless, it is certain that even at nineteen Bormann was no friend of the Republic. Education and background had made him a monarchist, so he had no need to dissemble when the Treuenfels reviled the government in Berlin as a band of Red traitors, and the state as a Jewish republic. Besides, the new regime could offer only a highly uncertain future to a young man who wanted to make a life for himself. The lost war, the harsh peace treaty, the bankrupt economy, hunger, rising prices, the black market—blame for all these things was heaped upon the individuals who had assumed responsibility for this evil inheritance when they took over the reins of government. They were quite obviously not powerful enough to maintain their position with their own resources. Whenever they were forced to use armed intervention—from the Spartacus uprising in Berlin to guarding the frontiers in Upper Silesia—they always had to call on the paramilitary Freikorps,* which sprang up after the Treaty of Versailles. And the Freikorps was anything but piously loyal to the government.

Before discharged artilleryman Bormann began his apprenticeship in 1919, he had spent a few days with his mother in Weimar and got a look at the top men in the new government who had come for the National Assembly: roly-poly Friedrich Ebert, President of the Reich for two days, who was said to be a former saloon keeper; Chancellor Philipp Scheidemann, who carried himself like an aging dandy; Defense Minister Gustav Noske, who tipped his floppy fedora in answer to soldiers' salutes; and Matthias Erzberger, already running to fat. These were not figures to impress a young man, as Bormann often told people later in Führer Headquarters.

Hermann von Treuenfels took the position that the Germans were not to be led by such *Schlappschwänze*† but by real men who knew how to command, rule and maintain law and order. Because under the new system one had to cooperate with the "hall of nonsense" of a Reichstag, one had to have a party, and the old conservatives, now united in the Deutschnationale Volkspartei, exactly filled the bill. Among one's own kind one felt for the first time part of a power group outside the government, a group which called itself the German People's Alliance for Defense and Defiance (Deutschvölkischer Schutz- und Trutzbund) and was already spinning its web over the entire country, making alliances with all nationalist groups and conspiring against the Republic no matter what course it took. As might have been expected, the Freikorps went along with it too—there were at times as many as four hundred Freikorps groups—whenever the Reds and the democrats were to be hounded.

The first coup, in mid-March 1920, was a fiasco. The Ehrhardt Brigade, led by Naval Lieutenant Hermann Ehrhardt, temporarily drove the legitimate Reich government out of Berlin to Stuttgart, and the former Director of Landscaping, Wolfgang Kapp, was able to put together a national government for a few days. A general strike, however, snuffed out the putsch.

A passionate debate about this miscarried action was still going on in the Treuenfels house when young Bormann took up his post. In Mecklenburg the insurgents had been especially effective. With the help of the Reichs-

*The Freikorps was nothing but armed, lawless gangs made up of "volunteers," ex-servicemen who were not allowed to join the Reichswehr (regular army) because the Versailles Treaty limited the army to 100,000 men.—*Tr.*

†Impotents.—*Tr.*

wehr they had been able to remove their district government, and a man known to nearly everyone had helped with his Freikorps. He was at that moment savagely suppressing the Reds' uprising in the Ruhr. First Lieutenant Gerhard Rossbach was a prototype of the young officer whose career was derailed by the war and the postwar situation. He was to have a decisive effect on Martin Bormann's next few years, although the unsoldierly, bureaucratic-minded farm supervisor had nothing in common with the leader of a country ruffians' band in search of adventure.

There was another man who had himself flown to the Kapp Putsch in Berlin in a fragile war plane, who wanted to "join" the affair, but whom nobody noticed—as indeed there was no reason why anyone should. Who outside of a clique of nationalists in Munich had ever heard of a painter called Adolf Hitler in March 1920? Six months before, he had turned up as an observer for the Reichswehr at a meeting of the German Workers' Party, and now he was making his first speeches before large gatherings. A year later, in the summer of 1921, the Junkers in the North could no longer afford to ignore him. He was by then chairman of a rapidly growing and extremely active political party.

The Soviet journalist Lev Besymenski doing research in Herzberg shortly after World War II found that Bormann had been hated by the farm workers for his abrupt and domineering manner, but that he had not tricked or deceived them. Apparently he drove them hard and got the greatest possible productivity out of them. There were also reports that he made crooked deals in foodstuffs and used the inflation for speculation. However, this was a time when a lot was done under the table, and illegal business deals were made by almost everyone who had the chance.

In one of his official statements Bormann confessed to having paid a fine of 3,000 marks (by then much devalued) "for violation of an agricultural ordinance," which, translated into plain language, means that he was caught in one of his black-market deals. Nevertheless, Hermann von Treuenfels was completely satisfied with his eager employee and soon entrusted the forceful young man with the supervision of the entire work force.

It was a tough job. It slowly dawned on the farm hands, many of whom had been working on the estates for years, that their employers were cheating them; when they were paid in money, the galloping inflation made it worthless by the time they received it. The estate owners, on the other hand, stored their produce in barns, where it grew more valuable every day. Many farm workers deserted the estates; others became rebellious. This gave the landowners the idea of offering the Freikorps shelter on their estates. They believed the men would welcome the suggestion, for since there was no more fighting on the frontiers in the East or against Communists inside the country, the federal government was not handing out any more pay. The landlords declared it was their patriotic duty to hold these nationalist fighting forces together for emergencies—meaning for the next putsch.

Until such time the military men would have to do farm work as well as stand guard in case hungry revolutionary riffraff threatened to pillage the farms. Thus Martin Bormann was told to turn a large stable at the edge of the village into a barracks. As it turned out, neither the Freikorps nor the landowners were happy with the arrangement. The latter complained that their new help preferred chasing girls and drinking schnaps to doing honest work.

In the NSDAP *Kampfzeit** it was useful for one's reputation and Party career to have fought in one of the Freikorps and thereby to have "kept the faith." So Bormann always put down that he had served two years as "section leader of the Rossbach Freikorps in Mecklenburg." This is true, but he never marched a single step or fired a shot in anger. At best he was a sort of paymaster, a bureaucrat for a group of volunteers. The Rossbach Freikorps was no longer a true military organization but simply a militant one with no fixed objective.

Bormann was not able to fool the NSDAP's "old fighters" *(Alte Kämpfer)* who had actually been in Freikorps organizations, but he loved to impress the lower ranks of the Party with stories of the beginnings of the Swastika Order. As late as the end of February 1945, two months before the Götterdämmerung, drinking French cognac with his secretaries in Hitler's bunker under the Reich Chancellery, he went into ecstatic reveries over the heroic days of the Kapp Putsch and how bravely the banner of the right-minded had waved. But he had no personal experience of it.

His first opportunity for active service came at Herzberg when some fifteen Rossbach men drew quarters in the former stable, and the farm-houses in the area were asked to supply billeting. Officially that particular Freikorps unit had been banned by the federal government as a danger to the state, but the leader had merely changed its name. For a while it was "Arbeitsgemeinschaft Rossbach," a sort of work-force partnership with headquarters in Berlin and a cashier's office in Mecklenburg. The inevitable second ban was followed by another name change, to "Agricultural Training Association." Hermann von Treuenfels, who was a former lieutenant colonel and a leading personality among the radical right, was assigned to arrange the billeting of the Rossbach men in the Parchim area, and he delegated the work to his capable young supervisor.

Thus Martin Bormann had his first experience of working with one foot outside the law without actually doing anything illegal himself. His duties were to report to association headquarters and pass on its orders to the individual groups on the estates in the area. He also had to manage the money that was withheld from each Rossbacher's pay and put in a savings account. This office work made him a sort of authority over the men of the camouflaged Freikorps—especially since through his employer he had a

*"Time of Struggle"—before the Party gained power, in 1933.—*Tr.*

direct line to the top leadership of the Deutschvölkische Freiheitspartei (German People's Freedom Party).

This party was founded in December 1922 by men who considered the German National People's Party not radical enough. Among them were Reichstag deputies Reinhold Wulle and Albrecht von Graefe, Theodor Fritsch and the writer Arthur Dinter (later Gauleiter for Thuringia). Taking advantage of the ever-increasing devaluation of the mark, the rising fear of Communists and Bolsheviks and outraged popular resentment over the French occupation of the Ruhr, the party rapidly won followers, chiefly in northern Germany. In the South and in Saxony it was less successful than Hitler and his NSDAP. Ostensibly the parties were on friendly terms— Hitler indeed let the Völkische party have the northern areas uncontested, since the NSDAP was prohibited in most of them. Secretly, however, they were at each other's throats. Graefe and Wulle thought of Hitler and his mostly Bavarian companions-in-arms as papists, anti-Prussians, imitators of Italian Fascism and un-German in every respect. Hitler on the other hand made fun of the idiotic political blunderers, reactionaries and Germanic fanatics in the North.

In these differences Supervisor Bormann naturally adopted his employer's prejudices, though he did not fail to notice that the people on the other side were ideologically less rigid. Lieutenant Rossbach, who after so many bans had camouflaged his headquarters in Berlin-Wannsee, as the "German Information Office," was a member of both Graefe's and Hitler's organizations, on the assumption that one of them would make the grade. There was actually not that sharp a line of demarcation between the many extreme rightist formations, fellowships and groups. They all hoarded weapons, painted swastikas on their army helmets and sang the same old British music-hall tune with different verses, the Ehrhardt song "Hakenkreuz am Stahlhelm, schwarz-weiss-rot das Band" ("Swastika on the helmet, an armband of black, white and red").

It can't have been easy for Martin Bormann to keep a tight rein on the Rossbachers in the environs of Parchim. Among the idealists who wanted to do something for the Fatherland were "confidence men, adventurers and scoundrels," according to the Stuttgart Freikorps officer Wilhelm Kohlhaas. People were beaten up, barracks mates stole from one another, and there were savage homosexual jealousies and betrayals.

In February 1923 a man by the name of Walter Kadow applied for membership in the Rossbach group at Herzberg. He was a schoolteacher who had headed a youth group of the Deutschvölkische Freiheitspartei in Wismar and been recommended by that party's officers. But the twenty-three-year-old recruit started passing himself off as a former World War lieutenant, adorned his tunic with decorations obviously never awarded him and borrowed money from his comrades without ever paying it back. Company Commander Georg Pfeiffer reported this to Bormann, and soon all those responsible for a decision—farm owner Bruno Fricke, the local group leader of the Völkische party; Hermann von Treuenfels; and Bormann, the liaison with Rossbach—agreed that the man must go. Before he left, he talked the estate bookkeeper into giving him an advance of 30,000 marks "for his mates," a sum then equal to about six hours' wages for a metalworker.

When the Kadow case turned into a criminal affair, Bormann maintained that he had been so incensed over the fraud that he told the cashier of the Völkische party in Parchim, a grocer named Franz Masolle, to let him know if Kadow ever showed his face in the vicinity again, so that he could be made to work off his debts. The motive was spurious, for the sum was minimal and growing more worthless every day with inflation. It is more likely that Bormann shared the widely held suspicion that Kadow was a spy and a traitor.

Bormann knew that traitors were usually subjected to the improvised justice of the so-called *Feme,* * a procedure that had developed during the time the Freikorps belonged to the "Black Reichswehr" and was secretly strengthening the regular army. Whoever belonged to such an organization and betrayed state secrets could not be tried in regular courts.

"This is how it started," one of the men involved in the Kadow case wrote two decades later, shortly before his execution by the Poles. "The *Feme* court was do-it-yourself justice, according to the ancient German practice in similar situations. Every betrayal was punished with death. Many traitors were eliminated this way." The man was Rudolf Höss, a Rossbacher and farm hand on Gut Neuhof, near Parchim, who later became commandant of the Auschwitz concentration camp and was condemned to death for mass murder.

Bormann set the trap in Parchim, and Kadow walked into it. On March 31, 1923, he looked up first the Völkische party official Theo von Haartz and then the party cashier Masolle, asking them for money, allegedly to get to the Ruhr and fight against the French occupation army. They did not give him much cash but ample amounts of schnaps to make up for it. He was already weaving when he walked out of Masolle's grocery store to the Louisenhof inn across the street, where the landowners and the Rossbachers in the neighborhood used to meet. Masolle sent a messenger with the news to the biggest single Rossbach group—about twenty-five men on Gut Neuhof, not far from the edge of town. He also tried to notify Bormann by telephone, but he could not get through and when he took his motorcycle, it broke down on the way. So he climbed on a borrowed bicycle and pedaled the last fifteen kilometers, arriving at Herzberg in the evening.

*A survival of old Germanic *Vehmgericht,* a form of secret tribunal which exercised great power in Westphalia from the end of the twelfth to the middle of the sixteenth century. Derived from an early German word, *Vehme* (also *Fehm*), now *Fehme, Feme,* meaning "judgment," "punishment."—*Tr.*

He had an easier and quicker trip back. Bormann ordered a horse-drawn hunting cart, called Company Commander Georg Pfeiffer and two Rossbachers, and sent all four of them back to Parchim. According to his later testimony, their instructions were to give Kadow a proper thrashing because he refused to work. By the time they arrived, the bar was full and most of the customers were drunk; Masolle and Haartz had passed the word that drinks were on them that evening. Kadow was lying on a sofa, not noticing that the men were going through his pockets. Allegedly they found a membership card in the Communist youth group, rubles and suspicious notes. When, around midnight, the innkeeper announced closing time, they told Kadow they would take him to a coffeehouse where there were women and continue the celebration. Two Rossbachers trundled him into the hunting cart and sat him down between them. Company Commander Pfeiffer and Rudolf Höss sat in the front seat. Two Rossbachers stood on the running board. When they got to the road leading to Schwerin, Kadow realized they were taking him away from town. He wanted to get out, but one of them held a pistol to his forehead. A few hundred yards on they went to work on him, first in the cart, pummeling him with fists, sticks, rubber truncheons. Then they pulled him into a meadow.

The blows came from all sides, six against one. Höss broke off a sapling maple and brought it down full force on Kadow's skull. Then they threw him in the luggage space in the cart, covered him with his cape and drove to Gut Neuhof. There they deliberated and decided that it would be best to give him the *coup de grâce* and bury him in the woods. One of the Rossbachers cut his throat with a pocketknife, and another pumped two pistol shots into his brain. Back at the farm the blood-smeared hunting cart was washed down and Kadow's effects were burned. The next morning the corpse was buried in a grove of pine seedlings.

Early that morning Bormann learned from Company Commander Pfeiffer what had happened. He called the district leader of the Völkische party, and they agreed that the affair had not gone as planned. Bormann always maintained that he had intended only to have Kadow beaten up, but that was certainly not the topic of this particular discussion. There had been so many accomplices, it would be hard to keep the matter a secret, but there was nothing to do except try to hush it up and say that Kadow had left on the early-morning train.

Bormann took Pfeiffer with him to Gut Neuhof to inform everyone involved of the cover story. Duty-conscious Höss had, however, already reported Kadow's murder to Masolle, and now he had to be cued in on the new scenario. As Bormann said, everyone who had had anything to do with it must disappear.

A couple of days later without Bormann's knowledge, two of the accomplices went to party headquarters in Schwerin and demanded to be billeted elsewhere. They were sent to an estate on the island of Poel, where one of them, Bernhard Jurisch, got into a fistfight, and from then on, believed his own friends were after him. Jurisch, who had spent some time in a Berlin insane asylum and had had a guardian appointed for him, was not exactly the right person to keep such a secret. Under cover of fog and darkness he fled the island and wandered about until the evening of June 22, 1923, three weeks after the bloody deed, when he sought asylum in the editorial offices of *Vorwärts,* the Berlin Social Democratic daily. There he described what had happened at Parchim, "anguished with fear, like a hunted-down animal," as the paper put it.

The police dug up Kadow's body, and Mecklenburg state prosecutors started an investigation. The six murderers, Jurisch included, were jailed pending trial, but there were only casual inquiries about those who had provoked and stage-managed the business. The Mecklenburg court would have preferred to dispose of the case as a fight between drinking companions in which a death had occurred, an unpolitical matter to be decided in a criminal court. Had it been left at that, no one would have been concerned with Martin Bormann's role in it. By the beginning of July, however, Superior Court Justice Ludwig Ebermayer had lost patience and called for further investigation under the Law for the Protection of the Republic. This brought the case under the Leipzig State Court's jurisdiction. Martin Bormann was arrested and brought to the Schwerin prison, later to be transferred to Leipzig. Years later in an article he wrote for the *Völkischer Beobachter* in August 1929, he described his transfer under heavy guard. His prison guards he said, were especially harsh and malicious because shortly before, Lieutenant Ehrhardt had been smuggled out of a cell there by the radical right. All the security measures were unnecessary, however, for he and his comrades "never thought of escape . . . we firmly believed, then as now, that we were not in the wrong, and that we deserved not punishment, but praise."

Such an expression of self-confidence could mean only that the "traitor" Kadow had received the punishment he deserved when he was put to death —and in 1929 Bormann could admit as much in this deliberately vague statement. When Rùdolf Höss was in the Cracow jail facing certain death, he set down openly what Bormann had only hinted at: "At that time I was firmly convinced that this traitor deserved death. Since in all likelihood no German court would have sentenced him, we passed sentence on him ourselves, because of the present exigency, according to an unwritten law we had made for ourselves."

In the summer of 1923 Bormann was probably not as self-confident as he makes himself sound in his newspaper article. He would not have been so outraged then over the irritations of prison life: that as a prisoner awaiting trial he had to wear tattered prison clothes and turn everything in, except for the shirt at the end of each day; that during the night he was checked every hour; that he got his first shave only after eight weeks; that his walking privileges in the prison yard were reduced. Demonstrably he was exaggerating, for Rudolf Höss, who was in the same jail at the same time, reported that political prisoners were given "every possible special consideration."

When Bormann was the only one of the prisoners released at the end of September, he was sure of vindication. In Leipzig he admitted to the examining magistrate what could not be disputed—he had issued the instructions to beat up Kadow, ordered the cart made ready, prepared the cover-up—and thus showed his good sense. After he returned to Herzberg he allowed himself to be celebrated as a young man of cunning who had borne sacrifices for the cause and had survived a criminal investigation. The landowners slapped him on the back, and whiskey and beer flowed at the Louisenhof. Let the police and the courts go through their clumsy motions—"It won't be long!" The march on Berlin and the end of the Republic seemed imminent. On October 1, 1923, in Küstrin, a hundred kilometers away from the capital, a Major Bruno Ernst Buchrucker from the Black Reichswehr actually did order his troops to stage a putsch. But the exultation was short-lived; the regular Reichswehr blocked it. In Hamburg, Thuringia and Saxony, the Communists armed themselves for an uprising; now the state would need every right-winger who could carry a gun, and they would no longer willingly give up their weapons.

The air was thickest in Munich. The word was that there even the local government would join in the putsch if it was against Berlin, so all the illegal soldiery with any kind of name and rank assembled there, including Rossbach and General Erich Ludendorff, the World War strategist, highly regarded by the Völkische party in the North.

What happened in Munich on November 9, 1923, is well known: Hitler's dilettantish musical-comedy revolt was a fiasco. The Völkische adherents in the North had a hard time suppressing their delight at his failure, but they feared that perhaps this had been the last chance for a coup. Most of the radical-right cliques had been banned. There were warrants out for the arrest of many Freikorps men, and their caches of weapons were constantly being uncovered. Four days after Hitler's arrest in the country house of one of his followers in the town of Uffing, something else happened that the Germans took for nothing less than a miracle—and which put a damper on the revolutionary ardor of many: the inflation came to an end. From the middle of November on, the Rentenmark became legal tender in place of the worthless paper mark. Suddenly prices and wages stabilized.

On March 12, 1924, Martin Bormann was back in the courtroom in Leipzig with the other defendants. During the four-day hearing before the political tribunal he presented himself as the lowly employee who had got embroiled in political affairs through adverse circumstance and naïveté. As a young man who dearly loved his Fatherland, he had been happy to support his employer Hermann von Treuenfels in his political activities, but there had been nothing illegal about it. Therefore he stood by everything he had done.

The only contrite defendant was Bernhard Jurisch, who had blown the cover on the foul deed. However, he had no way of knowing anything about the background and plans, since he had been in the Parchim clique only a short time and in a minor capacity, at that.

"Those who knew kept silent," wrote Rudolf Höss in his subsequent memoirs. "When I noticed in the course of the hearing that the comrade who actually did the deed could be effectively indicted only by me, I took the guilt upon myself, and he was released during the inquiry." It may be assumed with certainty that even with the gallows looking him in the face, he was still covering for Bormann as the instigator.

The master tailor Heinrich Krüger is still alive in Hamburg. In those days he lived in Parchim and was an eyewitness to the Rossbachers' drunken spree in the Louisenhof. He and a fellow worker had seen from the bar that Bormann was there that night. A Rossbacher showed Bormann papers that had been found in the pockets of the drunken Kadow: "I saw Bormann take a pistol out of his pocket and hand it to the Rossbacher." Krüger refrained from reporting this to the police at the time because he wanted to avoid any complications in his upcoming examination for master tailor.

Even if the judges had some notion that there was a lot more than met the eye about the crime, this was not taken into consideration when they handed down the verdict. From one point of view the verdict was deemed harsh. The public had demanded as much after new *Feme* murders were revealed. On the other hand, the judges knew that investigation of such crimes might lead to the area of state secrets. Every government since the Revolution in 1919 had made use of the nationalist paramilitary forces, which was of course illegal because it violated the provisions of the Versailles Treaty. So the gentlemen in the red robes were inclined toward clemency. In their decision they put it this way: "The defendants were in a state of extraordinary excitement while committing the act. It is therefore assumed that the slaying of Kadow was not premeditated."

Thus it was not murder, which could have brought a death sentence, but only manslaughter.

The court further ruled that "in the defendants' favor it must also be borne in mind that most of them were still youths; they had either no record of previous sentences, or none of a serious nature; they had fought in the war and were not only brutalized by this experience but had lost their former jobs, and in addition, they were not entirely sober at the time the act was committed. Finally, it was not without cause that they were filled with hatred and contempt for Kadow, in that they believed—in all probability correctly—that they had uncovered a Communist spy and traitor." Seen in this light, the deed was "motivated by attitudes not wholly dishonorable."

Despite this touching show of sympathy, the judges subsequently received scant mercy from Bormann. In his previously quoted newspaper account he called them "a collection of new-type Germans" whose political convictions gave them hostile prejudices against the defendants from the start. Only one could be counted in the nationalist camp, and he was Jewish.

"It seemed to me that what was going on there under the guise of justice was nothing but a farce, and I had to restrain myself from shouting it out to the learned gentlemen." He certainly did refrain from making any such remarks, for in those days he had no confidence in himself. He employed the same cautious restraint when he referred to the deed itself in a single sentence; otherwise he would have had to admit that he had ordered a man to be slaughtered like a beast. "After four long days of trial," he wrote, "we were all sentenced to long prison terms." This was true for the six executioners. The one who cut Kadow's throat got twelve years at hard labor; Höss, ten years; Jurisch, five and a half years. Bormann got off easily with one year. By making the hunting cart available he had been an accomplice— not to the killing, as the court neatly distinguished, but to the inflicting of serious bodily injury, since he had recommended only that the victim be beaten up. And his role as accessory after the fact—assisting in the cover-up —was also carefully considered. The court found he had been led to this course of action by considerations that were almost honorable, "partly by feelings of comradeship, partly by love of the party" to which he belonged, whose reputation he wished to keep untarnished.

At the same time, the failed adventurer Adolf Hitler was standing before judges in Munich who were filled with similarly sympathetic understanding. He, too, asserted that he had acted only out of love of the Fatherland. Bormann must have followed the newspaper reports on this case with the greatest interest, though hardly with sorrow. Up to that time, the National Socialists had been rivals, and the members of the Völkische party now exploited their advantage; since the NSDAP had been outlawed and Hitler thrown in jail, they went fishing for adherents in Bavaria as well as elsewhere.

When the verdict was announced, Superior Court Justice Ebermayer asked for a court order to have Bormann, the only defendant at liberty at the time, taken into custody too. Otherwise he might avoid serving out his sentence—by going to Bavaria, for example, where even "wanted" individuals with warrants out for their arrest like Rossbach and Ehrhardt were running around loose.

Bormann's defense attorney Karl Sack protested at length. He was one of the star trial lawyers of his day, and his fees were certainly not paid out of the wages of a farm supervisor. The Mecklenburg landowners assumed this expense—and surely they knew why they did. Sack's arguments impressed the judges, and they denied the request for Bormann's arrest. But the Superior Court Justice played his last trump card. He exercised his prerogative to have Bormann arrested in the courtroom and placed immediately behind bars. Like his fellow defendants he was loaded into the barred wagon known in Germany as the "Green Augustus." They all were still, or perhaps once again, confident that they would not be bereft of their freedom for long, so they sang their "defiant patriotic songs" as the wagon passed through the streets. In his article Bormann told how the Leipzigers "were so amazed it took their breath away."

4

New Beginning in Weimar

Credited with a month of confinement while awaiting trial, Bormann had to endure the monotony of prison life for only eleven months from the date of the verdict, March 17, 1924. Political prisoners could claim the privilege of a cell to themselves and also do their work there, insofar as the prison schedule allowed.

"I had to paste all sorts of paper containers together," he would say later, "for cigarettes, drugs, candy, gut strings for instruments . . . even for the purchasing cooperative of the Social Democrat Consumer Union." Fifteen hundred containers was the daily quota. A short count or botched work drew punishment. "The advantage of being in jail," Bormann observed, "is that one's thinking is not distracted by the peripheral matters of daily life," and one can see "further and more clearly into one's own ideas, especially political ones."

Since until then the young man, now just twenty-four, had not cared much for philosophizing over his political principles, he must have used the enforced period of reflection to only a very limited extent for a critical self-evaluation. He always came back to the conclusion that he had nothing to regret—it was just that he had been stupid enough to get caught. When the salvation of the Fatherland was at stake, one could not be squeamish.

It was clear in his mind what the character of this Fatherland must be in the future: as big, rich and powerful as it once had been, feared by all other nations, and giving each individual German a share in the wealth, power and respect. What must be done to achieve this remained to be seen until the crucial first step was taken: the "Novemberlings" (who took over the government after the 1918 Armistice) had to go!

Whatever happened, none of Martin Bormann's political principles would prevent him from participating. He had landed in "the dungeons of the Republic." Now he wanted to get going again properly. In typical bombastic Nazi style he later wrote: "Imprisonment did not crush us, it made us tougher; it did not teach us to love this so-called Republic and those who held power in it, rather it deepened and strengthened our love for our country, while it intensified our hatred against all those who thought they could play fast and loose with its people."

Bormann was released from prison in February 1925. The examining magistrate felt it necessary to give him a warning: he should think of his future and steer clear of the Völkische party. But the very next day, according to Bormann, "I traveled around the country on behalf of a comrade who had been arrested." The travel money came from Mecklenburg—the total of thirty marks he had earned pasting paper bags together would not have gotten him very far. Herzberg was the last stop. His job had been kept for him. Loyalty in return for loyalty was the watchword.

Yet the proper impulse was now missing. The wind had changed during the past twelve months. The attempt by the Völkische party to take over Hitler's bankrupt political estate after his unsuccessful putsch got off to a promising start because the Führer of the NSDAP kept issuing contradictory directives from prison as to who was to succeed him. It later became clear that he preferred to let his party disintegrate rather than turn it over to someone else. The Grossdeutsche Volksgemeinschaft (Greater German People's Community), led first by the ideologist Alfred Rosenberg, then jointly by Nuremberg Gauleiter Julius Streicher and Hitler's intimate friend Hermann Esser, had fallen apart and been absorbed by the National Socialist Freedom Movement, which then joined the Völkische coalition, in which the North Germans, with Wulle and Graefe, were predominant.

When the new Reichstag was elected on May 4, 1924, the extreme right jointly won 32 of the 427 seats. The Völkische party was able to get a foothold even in Hitler's Sturmabteilungen, the SA (storm troopers): Lieutenant Rossbach became their chief of staff, and when the SA was banned, Captain Ernst Röhm founded the Sturmbann as a substitute, under the protection of General Erich Ludendorff. But soon the North German National Socialists quarreled with their South German counterparts, and the Völkische party with both, and when on December 7, 1924, the prematurely dissolved Reichstag had to hold another election, the whole kit and caboodle fell apart. Only fourteen deputies from the Völkische coalition were re-elected, and this diminished group splintered still further when Graefe, furious over the incessant bickering, resurrected his old Deutschvölkische Freiheitspartei.

Bormann did not rejoin this party. By now he had acquired a sure instinct that told him that such a sectarian and exclusive organization, which saw universal salvation in a "North German king" and in the German peasantry, could never succeed. He stayed on at Gut Herzberg for a year and left in May 1926—a time of year when, normally, agricultural jobs had been set for the entire season. The dispute with his employer must have been serious because it ended a six-year relationship. The reasons could have been political differences of opinion. Bormann rejected the eccentric ideas of the orthodox Völkische party and had become fascinated by Hitler, who had been released from Landsberg Prison and was rebuilding his movement.

There might have been some unpleasantness too because the aristocratic landowners' snobbery kept the farm supervisor at a certain distance socially, despite his known sacrifice for Fatherland and party. Hermann von Treuenfels soon joined the "Stahlhelm," the Association of Front-line Soldiers, whose men looked down their noses at the National Socialist riffraff.

With tactical foresight, Bormann burned the bridges to his former political convictions only halfway; he took the step of reporting to the Sturmbann. Its chief, Ludendorff, was held in high regard by the Völkische party, while the real leader, Captain Ernst Röhm, was not only one of Hitler's few intimate friends (on such terms of familiarity as to use the second person singular *du* with him) but also enjoyed the confidence of most of the Freikorps officers. In the founding manifesto, written by Röhm, it was specifically stated that "Comrades are to give their unconditional allegiance to Hitler, Ludendorff and Graefe."

According to the Soviet journalist Lev Besymenski on the basis of his research in Herzberg, the real reason for the split was a love affair between Martin Bormann and the lady of the manor, Ehrengard von Treuenfels. She was thirty-five at the time, her husband forty-six, and Bormann twenty-five —an ideal situation for a romantic triangle in a bedroom farce or a Strindberg tragedy. It is certain that, in those days as later on, Martin Bormann was forever on the lookout for anything halfway decent in a skirt, but Besymenski does not name his informants, even though they, whoever they were, would not, as citizens of East Germany, have to worry about a libel suit from the Treuenfels family. What's more, Besymenski maintains that Bormann beat a hasty retreat from Herzberg under cover of darkness, because Hermann von Treuenfels had challenged him to a duel for adultery. This story is totally unbelievable, for an aristocratic landowner in archconservative Mecklenburg would never have fought a duel with an employee but would simply have had him beaten up and thrown out of the house if a scandal could not have been prevented.

On the other hand, it can be proved that later on, Bormann, dressed in his Reichsleiter uniform, used to visit Herzberg in a black Mercedes limousine. In conversation with this writer, Ehrengard von Treuenfels could not recall any of this, or the letters she exchanged with the former supervisor, although the correspondence extended over many years. At the end of July 1944, after the attempt to assassinate Hitler and the abortive officers' putsch, she wrote "an anguished letter" (as Bormann described it to his wife) because the nobility had come into the field of fire of the men in power. And as late as February 1945, when Bormann was in the bunker under the Reich Chancellery, she sent him a despairing note to tell him that the third of her four sons had just been killed in the war.

Occasionally Bormann, lost in reverie, nostalgically described his time in Mecklenburg the way a successful man looks back on his beginnings. He praised the blond, straightforward farm workers' families, so poor in earthly goods and so rich in children, who had followed Hitler's lead so eagerly that the National Socialists, to the aggravation of the landowners, won an absolute majority in their district government sooner than anywhere else in Germany. During one of Hitler's nocturnal "table talks," Bormann made fun of the Grand Duke of Mecklenburg's private railway. He tailored his own role at that time and place to fit his changed position in society; his participation in the Parchim murder was no longer in keeping with his top Nazi rank and station. Admitting ambiguously in his 1929 newspaper article that his time in prison had been served "on account of a *Feme* affair," he had turned this into "a year's jail sentence for political reasons" by the time he was made Reichsleiter in July 1933. And on his promotion to chief of the Party Chancellery in May 1941, he allowed himself to be represented in a newspaper article as a "militant of the earliest period" whose aversion to the "November system" had put him behind bars. A Nazi newspaperman he had known from the Mecklenburg period, the only journalist he trusted, was permitted to promote him to "general agent with full discretionary powers" for the Treuenfels property.

Be that as it may, in his final year of service in Mecklenburg he must have earned good money, for when he moved into his mother's house in Oberweimar at the end of May 1926, instead of riding a motorcycle he drove a car. It was an Opel, a two-seater convertible, known in the trade as a *Laubfrosch* (hoptoad) because it came only in green. A reliable small car and good value for the money, it was still very much a luxury, for in those years only one German in two hundred could afford to own a car. Bormann did not really need it, but he was then, and always remained, a "car nut."

At that time he had no idea what occupation to take up. There were hardly any large estates in the province of Thuringia, which was farmed mostly by small landholders. He did not have the money to buy his own piece of land, and his family was in no position to help. His stepfather had died in March 1923—unmourned by Martin—and what money he had left was wiped out in the final phase of the inflation. Despite the pretentiousness of her husband's title, Antonie Vollborn's pension was very small. She was able to hold on to the house because her son Albert Bormann, now twenty-three, was living at home and helped defray household expenses with his earnings. Unlike his brother, he finished school, and persuaded by his step-father, went into banking.

His first year back in the family, Martin did not work so much as "nosed around," as he put it, while he was getting ahead in the Frontbann.* Meanwhile, things were changing at the top. Ludendorff and Röhm had quarreled, and Hitler was pursuing certain plans of his own. He had assigned Röhm the job of building up and leading the SA on condition that the Sturmbann† would transfer its 30,000 members to that organization. This resurrected all the old rivalries. Hitler wanted a political arm of propagandists and bullyboys that he could command at his pleasure, whereas Röhm wanted to train troops to function as a people's militia, or if need be as an actual fighting force, thereby nullifying the Versailles Treaty. All troops were supposed to be subordinate to Röhm, and to Hitler only through him, and in no way to be under the authority of the Party *Bonzen,* as the Nazi top brass was called. Because Hitler rejected this plan, Röhm backed away and let Count Wolf Heinrich von Helldorf, a former Freikorps fighter, run the Frontbann.

When Martin Bormann, sturdy, self-confident and crafty, joined the Thuringian Frontbann, there was an old feud still to be settled. The Gauleiter of the NSDAP was the popular author Arthur Dinter, who wrote his books in the secluded village of Dörrberg. One of these, *The Sin Against the Blood,* had sold 250,000 copies. Like most of Dinter's work, it was anti-Semitic. While Hitler was in jail, Dinter had founded the Grossdeutsche Volksgemeinschaft as his own substitute party for the banned NSDAP and locked horns with the Sturmbann because its units refused to acknowledge his leadership.

There is no documentary evidence to show that it was actually Bormann who succeeded in reconciling these old antagonisms, but a photograph gives some indications it may have been. The picture was taken in front of the Hotel Elephant in Weimar at the second Party Rally of the NSDAP on July 4, 1926; that is, six weeks after Bormann had officially resurfaced. It shows Hitler standing in an open Mercedes, reviewing a parade with his closest circle of collaborators. Next to Hitler's car stands a formation of SA leaders, and the fifth man in the rank is Martin Bormann, dressed in a Brown Shirt uniform. This is noteworthy because by his own account Bormann did not join the NSDAP until eight months later, and the SA as much as ten months later. The privileged position on the reviewing stand and the storm-trooper uniform can be accounted for only as some sort of demonstration that the Frontbann in Thuringia was now unequivocally

*The Frontbann was a private army of former storm troopers (SA), raised by Röhm while Hitler was in prison. It was used by Röhm unsuccessfully as a bargaining chip for authority in the Party on Hitler's release from Landsberg Prison. Röhm resigned from it in May 1925. — *Tr.*

†The Sturmbann was a substitute for the SA founded by Röhm under Ludendorff's patronage when the SA was banned in 1924. The word later went into the SS vocabulary to designate a battalion-sized unit; thus, a Sturmbannführer was the equivalent of an army major.—*Tr.*

hewing to the Party line, and that Bormann had had something essential to do with it. It was a good opportunity to make a quick entrance into the limelight, for the Party leadership in Thuringia was in dispute.

Differences of opinion between Hitler and Dinter had been festering for a long time because the Gauleiter believed he had a further vocation as a religious reformer. Taking up where Luther left off, he composed 197 "theses" in which he rejected the Old Testament as Jewish, transformed Jesus into an Aryan God of Light and added spiritualistic overtones. He wanted to have the NSDAP formally pledged to this doctrine. Hitler believed that any religious commitment harmed the Party. Dinter was fair game to be shot down at that very Party rally, and Joseph Goebbels wrote disrespectfully in his diary: "Dinter and Streicher are talking crap." Six months later Hitler installed a new Gauleiter, Fritz Sauckel, a merchant seaman and anything but sophisticated, whom by the self-consciously refined upper crust of the Weimar Nazis accepted only with reservations. Twenty years later Sauckel ended up on the gallows at Nuremberg.

Being a determined nationalist was definitely *de rigueur* among the city's bourgeoisie at the time. On holidays one was supposed to hang a black-white-and-red flag from the gables. Since the Bauhaus school of art and architecture favored the un-German flat roof, and since Bauhaus painters had a high regard for multicolored ink blots, the Weimar bourgeoisie felt called upon to become guardians of German culture. Among these guardians was the writer and Deputy Gauleiter Hans Severus Ziegler, a relative of Franz Liszt, who was made much of in the Wagner and Nietzsche circles in town.

Ziegler survived the war and the postwar period. When he speaks of Martin Bormann today, the octogenarian has nothing but praise for Hitler's "most hard-working, honest and selfless retainer," toward whom he feels gratitude to this day. Whenever Ziegler needed a word from Hitler to settle something, Bormann would immediately take care of it. Bormann had reason to be kind to Ziegler, for it was Ziegler who smoothed the way for him in the Weimar Party councils. Since 1924 he had been editor of the weekly *Der Nationalsozialist,* virtually a one-man operation, and he was understandably glad when Bormann, who as an ex-convict was having trouble finding employment, offered him his help. Bormann was the right man for the job—reliable with money, firm with slow payers and lukewarm Party members, busy as a bee with the bookkeeping, functioning as cashier, advertising-space salesman, packer and truckdriver, distributing the paper in the villages in his own car. The job did not pay well. The chronic deficit of all Party papers ended only on January 30, 1933; until then wages were paid in installments.

It was also Ziegler who introduced to the former director of the Weimar court theater, Carl Benno von Schirach, and his son Baldur to Hitler. When on February 27, 1927, Martin Bormann joined the Party with membership number 60508, Baldur, seven years his junior, had already been a member for two years. They met many months later, when Schirach, still a student, came to Weimar for the holidays. As he told this writer, he was sitting with a friend in a café when he saw "a rather fat young man trying to force himself into a small Opel." His friend said that was *Parteigenosse* (Party comrade) Martin Bormann, who had got sprung from jail and as driver for the new Gauleiter Sauckel was taking him to meetings in the rural areas. At this time Bormann was already functioning as a Party official in addition to his work on the *Nationalsozialist.* As of November 1927 he was (by his own account) chief press officer for the Gau and then assumed the added duties of a district leader and general business manager. He also wanted to make himself useful as a speaker, for which there was always a need, because the NSDAP not only held meetings at election time but also inundated the countryside with floods of propaganda. In this capacity, however, Bormann was a total failure. Standing in front of a few dozen people, he would begin to stutter and blurt out incomplete sentences, turning purple with anger and facing his audience in helpless silence if he was interrupted by hecklers. When he became the laughingstock of the country bars, Sauckel took his name off the speakers' roster, friendship notwithstanding. To the day he died, Bormann never learned to speak in public.

As Gau press officer, his effectiveness was also modest at best. He almost never got a press release printed. But as Gau business manager, he was in his true element. Here he could work with written orders, form letters, lists of names, circulars, and rule over the various outlying district groups from his desk. Here he learned how to make an organization hum; here he got practice making plans and calculating tactics, on a small scale to be sure, but on a basis where real administrative experience could be gained. Here he learned that conviction and idealism are effective only if there is an organization to bind them together and steer them toward a goal. And here he discovered, along with everything else, who was intriguing against whom in the top Party leadership, and who belonged to which rival group.

Meanwhile, he never lost sight of his own career. Geographically, Thuringia was halfway on the National Socialist route from Munich to northern or western Germany. When the top brass stopped off in Weimar, the Gau business manager was always ready and waiting to greet them. Hitler came often; between 1925 and 1933 he made thirty-three speeches in Thuringia. On one of these occasions Ziegler introduced the promising young colleague to his Führer and to Rudolf Hess, who always traveled with him. Sometimes Bormann was sent on Party business trips to headquarters in Munich, and he never missed an opportunity to establish connections. Baldur von Schirach tells a story that illustrates how he did it.

They chanced to meet in the company of a Party member who also came from Weimar. "All three from Weimar," Bormann observed. "That calls for a celebration." When a bottle of wine was brought to the table, he raised his glass and addressed Schirach in the highly familiar second person singular. Taken aback ("I hardly even knew the man"), Schirach went along with it, and soon began to hear that Bormann was telling everyone they were old *du* friends from Weimar. As Schirach had just been appointed Reich leader of the National Socialist Student Association, this alleged intimacy could do Bormann nothing but good.

Now and again Bormann was made to feel that he was still pretty far down on the ladder of the National Socialist hierarchy. Once when Prince Friedrich-Christian zu Schaumburg-Lippe, a Party member of long standing, arrived late at Hitler's lunch table at the Hotel Elephant, all the seats were taken. Hitler looked first at Joseph Goebbels, a deserter from Gregor Strasser's *fronde* and newly appointed Gauleiter of Berlin, whose stock was high at the time; then he looked at Bormann and asked him to give the prince his place and go eat with the SS escort group. The prince reported: "I realized from the look on Bormann's face that he would never forget it." Presumably he never forgave Goebbels either; later on, when the opportunity arose, he always avenged every slight from the early period of his Party career.

In his memoirs the prince maintains that Bormann had been a follower of Gregor Strasser's. Deviating from Hitler's pragmatism, Strasser took the attribute "Socialist" in the Party designation seriously and demanded, for example, a co-determination as well as profit sharing for factory workers. But having just shouted down the officious North Germans at the Weimar Party Rally, Hitler did not wish to be bound by any program. He wanted, first, power in the Party, then, in the state—nothing less.

Bormann was still too insignificant to take a position in this matter, so it may be true that he had some connection with the Strasser group. At that point there was no way of knowing who would win. Still, at the end of 1926 Hitler appointed Captain Felix Pfeffer von Salomon, a West German Gauleiter and member of the Strasser *fronde*, supreme SA leader. When the former Freikorps commander came back to Weimar, Bormann proposed that a motorized SA be set up.

5

Bormann Moves into the Brown House

Bormann's call to Munich came at the end of October 1928 from Storm Trooper chief Pfeffer von Salomon. An employee in the SA Insurance Office had embezzled 2,000 marks, and Pfeffer needed a replacement who was not only trustworthy, honest and familiar with administrative procedure, but also able to work largely on his own. The new assistant was to be given an official title and rank, which had to be authorized by Hitler, just as the salary had to be authorized by Reich Party Treasurer Xaver Schwarz. Since they both agreed, Bormann took up his post on November 16 at a battered kitchen table in Munich's Schellingstrasse. A good, willing worker, he was soon given two additional sections to supervise.

SA Insurance was a sort of stepchild of the Party organization and seemed to offer no great opportunity for winning laurels. It had been set up when SA chief Viktor Lutze (Ernst Röhm's successor), demanded that his Brown Shirt bullies' medical expenses for injuries received in street fights and beer-hall brawls be covered. A contract was signed with an insurance company, though Bormann later recalled that "it worked badly from the very start." The SA chief had made the grandiose assertion that some forty thousand members would pay a monthly fifteen-pfennig premium per man, although the SA had no more than one thousand members at the time. Then it turned out that the insurance company would pay claims only if the injured storm trooper could produce a witness to prove that he had not been hurt as a result of an assault or provocation on his part. Since the SA was prone to committing assaults and provocations, this did not exactly fill the bill, and another company was approached. Disputes and lawsuits with this second company were under way when Bormann took over the job.

He discovered in a remarkably short time what had gone wrong with the previous efforts to negotiate a workable contract: according to the basic principles of insurance law, there was no way in which members of an organized band of brawlers could be indemnified for the financial consequences of their skirmishes. So a new contract was discussed with yet another company, whereby damages were to be paid only in case of death or permanent disability. Bormann published an announcement in the *Völkischer Beobachter,* studded with his own brand of bureaucratic jargon ("this inevitably caused a delay in processing which was increased by differences of opinion"), stating that injured Party members would henceforth get their money from a "Benefits and Relief Fund" run by the Party. To be sure, there was no legal redress. It was a bargain for the NSDAP inasmuch as only five of the now twenty-pfennig monthly premium went to the insurance company, instead of eighteen as in the previous arrangement.

This solved the problem for a short time. After a year the insurance company, Deutscher Ring, insisted on ten pfennigs a man per month. In a dramatic confrontation, Bormann reeled off figures to show that there could be no question of the company's losing money on SA business, because only two thirds of the total premiums had gone back to the insured. (Bormann apparently knew nothing yet about loss reserves.) When the Deutscher Ring thereupon canceled the contract, Bormann in February 1930 made a move which was to prove decisive for his career. He converted the insurance plan into a Nazi Party Relief Fund and raised the monthly contribution to thirty pfennigs. Those who paid it might receive help, but not necessarily.

Hitler issued an order that every member of the Nazi Party and its affiliated groups was to pay the thirty-pfennig monthly dues. With 390,000 members by the end of 1930, this added up to several million marks of cash flow, for which no one was accountable—a very handy situation for Hitler at a time when, due to a rapid succession of election campaigns, the Party was experiencing continual money troubles.

In a report prepared for the Party leaders, Bormann could proudly boast that "no difficulties of a financial or any other character" had resulted from this step, and that "despite increasing claims" against the fund, he was "entering reserves on the books." From then on he was regarded as a financial wizard by the clique whose Führer considered it beneath his dignity as an "artistic person" to have anything whatsoever to do with money and whose closest associates affected the life style of the bohemians from Munich's Schwabing district. To be sure, the contributers gradually began to realize that they had been euchred out of their rights by this coup. In September 1930 they read an announcement in the *Völkischer Beobachter* that "SA Insurance is not accident insurance in the legal sense." "To avoid all misunderstanding" it was to be known from then on as "the NSDAP

Relief Fund (SA Insurance)." "Payment of premium does not entitle anyone to sue the Party or the Relief Fund for compensation."

The announcement further disclosed that "Party Comrade Martin Bormann, Section Chief responsible for the Relief Fund," was the one to decide
who would receive compensation, and how much. Whoever felt unfairly
treated by him should present his complaint to the Reich Treasurer of the
Party, authority of next and last resort. Only one hurdle remained, and
though it presented no great challenge, Bormann's way of getting over it
was nonetheless impressive.

The Munich Federal Trade Commission wanted either to classify the
Relief Fund as taxable or to make it subject to the General Auditing Office
(Reichsaufsichtsamt); they felt it should at least have government approval.
Bormann countered by presenting the case for the fund's autonomy with
an expert opinion from Heinrich Heim, a young lawyer in the Munich office
of Hitler's lawyer, Hans Frank (later Governor General of occupied Poland). With this document he managed to persuade the authorities that
according to the new statutes, the Relief Fund had been deftly maneuvered
into a loophole in the law. According to the books, the government had no
right to exercise any supervision over Bormann's financial affairs. (Heim
continued as legal counsel to the rising star of the Nazi Party until the war,
when he was commissioned to take down Hitler's "table talks" at Führer
Headquarters.) Henceforth Bormann's reputation as a shrewd insurance
man was secure among the top Party bosses.

But work at the Relief Fund, however successful, offered Bormann no
opportunity to win the kind of public popularity other Nazi officials were
getting through speeches and public performances. Besides, since the Party
wanted the general public to know as little as possible about its finances,
it was not about to trumpet Bormann's praises. Only once, prior to 1933,
did the *Völkischer Beobachter* run a small picture of him with a brief resumé
of his career, as part of a series on Party members. The Nazi Old Guard
in Munich did not even notice the phenomenon of a man who, knowing
virtually nothing about the insurance business, had in a very short time
mastered not only the straight but the crooked ways in that line. Had that
malicious clique been aware of his performance and accurately assessed his
unscrupulousness, they would have realized sooner than they did that
Hitler would never let that fellow Party member out of his sight. Instead
they made condescending jokes about the proliferating bureaucratic machinery of the Relief Fund—by the end of 1932 Bormann, as Main Section
Chief, was in charge of over a hundred people—and failed to observe that
this was precisely what impressed their Führer. Although Hitler himself
never became familiar with the technical aspects of regulations, he always
had a weakness for organizational charts, squares denoting specific authority, diagrams, and so on.

Bormann had still another reason to be sure that he would remain in

Hitler's field of vision. When he first arrived in Munich the "glorious sun" of the Führer's special favor shone on former World War major and battalion commander Walter Buch from Baden, the scion of a highly respectable family of government officials. Buch had joined Hitler's party in 1922, and in the November putsch the next year he had marched in the parade as leader of the Munich storm troopers. He had never wavered in his loyalty since. His wife and children always came second to Fatherland and Party. In fact, his daughter Gerda complained later that after 1914 she never saw much of her father. "All the same," she wrote to Martin Bormann, "it was through him that we got to know each other, and everything was then right and proper."

"Then"—around the turn of the year 1928–29—Buch was chairman of USCHLA, the committee that arbitrated disputes within the Party. He was sitting with his family at a Nazi meeting in the Circus Krone in Munich when his nineteen-year-old daughter discovered the man who was to determine the course of her life. Gerda Buch was tall and slender, five feet eleven, with perfect racial German looks, and a mess of patriotic clichés about the Fatherland tucked under her coronet braid.

She was a kindergarten teacher and always felt at her best and most confident in the midst of a flock of children, so she did not mind the fact that Bormann was a good four inches shorter than she. Nor, as she picked him out among the uniforms of the storm troopers' top leadership, was she put off by the rather apparent bulge of his stomach. According to her brother Hermann, she annoyed her father by constantly begging that he invite comrade-in-arms Bormann to their house, for at first Walter Buch could not take his daughter's feelings about the man seriously.

Bormann had no thought of matrimony at this time. It was well known in top Party circles that he believed in taking his fun where he found it, which sat badly with the stern Protestant morality of the Buch family. Buch finally yielded to Gerda's pleading only because he hoped that the affair would evaporate by itself after the young people got to know each other better and saw for themselves how poorly suited they were to each other. On the surface, the raucous, boorish young man, given to fits of temper, seemed to have nothing in common with the shy, soulful girl who played the guitar, sang folk songs and preferred reading to any other pastime.

At first it looked as if Buch was right. Every Sunday, Bormann drove his Opel to Solm outside Munich, where the Buchs lived. But nothing happened. In April, however, while the family was taking a walk, Gerda and Martin lagged behind, and Gerda achieved her objective. Back at the house the prospective bridegroom formally asked for her hand. Mother Buch was pleased. "Soon we'll have a Martin in our family too!" she declared—that's how much she revered Martin Luther.

In September 1929 a regular picture-book, swastika-armband wedding took place, with Hitler and Rudolf Hess as witnesses, SA chief Pfeffer and assorted storm-trooper leaders as wedding guests, and a proudly smiling groom ceremonially clad in brown shirt, breeches, jackboots and the Nazi version of the Sam Browne belt (as indeed were all the Party officials, including his father-in-law). Gerda, all in white, with wedding veil and myrtle wreath, assumed a role that was already past history. Seven months later her first son was born, Adolf Martin, nicknamed "Krönzi" by his parents, a diminutive suggestive of the German word for "Crown Prince." The Old Guard Nazi militants took malicious and sneering cognizance of the date of the birth. The agronomist Walter Darré, who had just joined the Party and was immediately touted as the expert on peasants and race, heard from them that the upstart from Weimar had jumped the gun and seduced the foolish, trusting Gerda to make sure that he would "marry up." And there is no question that the Buch family had a great deal to offer to an ambitious young man who was making his way in the NSDAP.

Walter Buch was, after all, a member of the Reichstag, one of the twelve National Socialists to win a seat in the 1928 elections. Hitler had been a frequent visitor in his house even before the putsch, and as a schoolgirl Gerda had listened, enthralled, to his monologues. Shortly before the engagement she formally joined the Party (membership number 120,112), and to please her and her father, Hitler attended the wedding as a demonstration of his regard. This kind of family celebration was, however, utterly at odds with his mood of the moment. In 1929 he had suffered another attack of the indecisiveness that made him avoid taking a strong political stand. Since he had no firm program at the moment, he made himself unavailable, hiding out with friends, among them the Buchs. Consequently, anyone who belonged to that household, like a fiancé or son-in-law, enjoyed a direct line to the Party Chief.

It cannot be said that Gerda disliked her husband. A personable woman with genuine sweetness, she was obliging, cheerful, sometimes childlike and dependent, a total contrast to the robust realist she had married. He could be sure that his role as lord and master of the family would never be challenged and that he had won the ideal National Socialist wife: a faithful, obedient companion who would stay with him in good times and bad and devote herself entirely to children, home and wedded bliss. The Party clique ridiculed Bormann and claimed to be shocked by his pasha-like behavior at home, but that is no proof that he failed to appreciate his wife and did not, in his own fashion, love her. Their letters from the war years show how strongly he felt the bonds between them and how generously she tolerated his weaknesses. In one of them Gerda recalled the time "when our twins came." That was in July 1931, when, from what she wrote, the harmony of their union was troubled by financial worries. But it all worked out in the end.

Certainly the young couple was not blessed with riches. During the *Kampfzeit* the Party paid miserable wages, the Party Treasurer taking the position that idealists must make sacrifices. Even so, it was better to be earning very little than to be one of the 3.2 million unemployed who in 1930 had to subsist on a minimal dole. And once the Party came to power, it was argued, the idealists would reap the rewards of their sacrifices. It was natural for Bormann to bank on this eventuality. But neither he nor anyone else could have had any notion then how high he would eventually climb in the organization.

At that time Bormann was a member of the SA staff, which Hitler purposely kept small. He had no rank and no command, and in that society of marchers he was considered a deskbound paper pusher. Without intending to, he presented exactly the profile Hitler wanted. The Führer considered a show of legality valuable, so by the end of 1928 he had ordered that the SA's military games had to stop. The Brown Shirt gangs were to concentrate on intimidating and terrorizing political enemies, provide protection for their own gatherings, and make a show of order and discipline with their precision marching and resounding bands.

Hitler was therefore an open-minded and attentive listener when Bormann held forth in the Buch household about how the storm troopers needed more motor vehicles and suggested that all Party members place everything they had, from small cars to trucks, at the Party's disposal when the occasion demanded. In late fall 1929 he was asked to draw up plans for such an organization, and on April 1, 1930, the creation of a National Socialist Automobile Corps was officially announced. Bormann, the actual founder, remained anonymous, but he was accorded the honor of being listed right after Member Number 1 (Hitler, who offered his Mercedes-Kompressor to the corps only symbolically, of course). For the first few months Bormann managed the corps from his own desk. But the colorless bureaucrat was not even considered when, a year later, it had grown to such a size that it had to have a separate management. Hitler chose former Major Adolf Hühnlein, a veteran of the 1923 putsch who had served as motor-vehicle inspector with the Motorized Storm Troopers and who immediately christened his command NSKK (Nationalsozialistisches Kraftfahrkorps).

By this time Bormann was no longer on the SA staff. As head of the Relief Fund, he was a nameless functionary in the Party organization. This change had come about as Hitler put more and more of a curb on those storm troopers who as old-time revolutionaries and veterans of the putsch believed that nothing short of a march on Berlin could bring order to Germany and themselves within reach of the public trough. The politicians in the Party Organization had, they maintained, been using the same tactics for years without success. And it was true that Party slogans never inspired the people as long as the economy was halfway solvent. Then on October 29 and November 13, 1929, came the New York Stock Exchange crash with billion-dollar losses, which created an unprecedented crisis in the world economy. Hitler figured that unemployment and poverty would soon drive the masses to his side, and he could then make his revolution at the ballot box. The old militants, however, could not understand that they would no longer play first fiddle in Hitler's orchestra. They scoffed at the rapidly expanding body of Party functionaries, the PO (Political Organization), which they referred to as P-zero.

In mid-August 1930 the die was cast. Hitler learned that the top leadership of the SA was planning a putsch. Pfeffer von Salomon and his bullyboys had taken every precaution to conceal these plans from Hitler, and to this day it is not known who betrayed them, although there is reason to suspect that it might have been someone from the then very small top SA leadership staff. Hitler dismissed Salomon. Years later Gerda wrote her husband a letter addressed to Führer Headquarters asking if he was still alive. "Watch out for him," she warned, "and watch out for all men of his sort." This warning was triggered by "a frightful dream," in which they "all came back to Obersalzberg just when the smoke screen [for air-raid protection] was shrouding everything." She was afraid that the Freikorps veterans were going to do "something bad." Interestingly enough, this letter was written one month after the ill-starred July 20, 1944, officers' revolt. Bormann put his wife's mind at rest about Pfeffer: "Yes, he's still alive, but he has been in jail since July 21, 1944."

Bormann must have been Hitler's informant as far back as 1930. Indeed, when Pfeffer was fired, Bormann also disappeared from the SA staff, which put him out of the immediate reach of Freikorps veterans who were still in office. Reich Party Treasurer Xaver Schwarz, who had long lusted after the enormous sums in the Relief Fund, took control of all departments in the top SA leadership "that were concerned with economics." In an annual report Bormann described his change of heart—a change that plucked him from the doubtful career of SA leader of the middle echelon at just the right moment and put him into the camp of the more formidable battalions. "Countless times in the period that followed," he wrote at the beginning of 1933, "it was demonstrated how right this change of assignment turned out to be."

It does not matter whether he saw these advantages as favoring primarily the exercise of his office or his own career. The SA organization was thoroughly streamlined in the next four weeks. Hitler appointed himself Supreme SA leader, giving orders through a chief of staff, an office to which he soon appointed former Captain Ernest Röhm, recently returned from Bolivia. And in the national election of September 14, 1930, the Party Organization won its first major victory, of quite unexpected proportions. The NSDAP got 18.3 percent of all the votes cast and with 107 seats moved into the Reichstag as the second strongest representative body.

Neither Hitler nor the Party was prepared for such a success. In the weeks before and just after the election, applications for Party membership piled up in the central office in Munich. Now all the screwballs and dream-

ers, "big wheels" and revolutionary strategists on the staff at Party headquarters had to be replaced by hard-working organizers and planners. Many
a member of the Munich Old Guard who had felt secure in his position in
Hitler's entourage suddenly found himself crowded out by diligent, dependable bureaucrats.

The group Bormann landed in after his transfer was a motley crew.
Besides the punctilious bookkeeper Xaver Schwarz, who had given up his
job as administrative inspector of the City of Munich when he became Reich
Party Treasurer, there was a scarfaced character named Christian Weber,
who had first been a bouncer in a beer hall, then a horse trader, and who
was now a member of the city administration. Weber made up for his want
of education by his uncouth behavior and struggled mightily to gain access
to the public trough. There was Rudolf Hess, already confused and isolated,
a henchman from the first hour, with no office and no voice in the Party,
only a blind worship of Hitler, whom he served as secretary and general
factotum, and whom he addressed not with the familiar "Herr Hitler" but
as "mein Führer." And there was Hermann Esser, a frustrated man but a
brilliant talker who was one of the few to call Hitler *du* and who did not
hesitate to give the Führer a piece of his mind at times. Yet another member
of the circle was the photographer Heinrich Hoffmann, small in stature but
big on gossip, who liked to make jokes but saw nothing funny in any
challenge to the monopoly on picture coverage of Party affairs which had
been bestowed on him by Hitler.

Among this coterie of a few dozen men—the misguided do-gooders, the
fiercely ambitious, the coldly calculating, power-hungry operators, the patriots and idealists—there was a constant shifting of friendships and enmi-
ties, alliances and intrigues. The group met in the morning on Schellingstrasse, then a quiet residential area on the edge of Schwabing, where the
Party leadership and the men from the Party newspaper lived in houses
across the street from one another. They always ate together; Hitler,
Himmler, Röhm and Rosenberg favored the Osteria Bavaria, while
Schwarz, Max Amann and Gregor Strasser were more apt to go to the
Schelling-Salon. In the afternoon when Hitler made his way to the Café
Heck, his lieutenants gathered around the table, for often special jobs within
the organization were then assigned, Party titles awarded and absentees
dropped from the list of favorites. In the evening the game continued; the
clan would meet in the office or at a coffeehouse to listen while "the Chief"
conducted his monologues far into the night. But however much the clique
was torn by internal rivalries, it was unanimous in rejecting new faces.
Martin Bormann was made to feel this keenly.

After the wedding he and Gerda had moved to Icking, some sixteen miles
south of Munich, where their first children were born—after "Krönzi"
came the twin girls Ilse (named for the wife of their marriage witness Rudolf
Hess) and Ehrengard (after the *châtelaine* of Herzberg). Whether by train

or in the old Opel, the trip into town took a lot of time, so Bormann rarely participated in the nightly meetings. To win friends he had to take advantage of the lunch hour. He ate mostly at the Osteria Bavaria, where he could expect to find Hitler. The Nazi agricultural expert Walter Darré complained of Bormann, "However one tried to prevent it, he always found some reason to sit down beside you."

There were excellent reasons why Bormann made a point of seeking Darré out. Darré was in high favor with Hitler; he was also a newcomer in the inner circle, and perhaps Bormann could be helpful to him.

"That man repelled me to the depths of my being with his unctuous, sycophantic ways," Darré said later, explaining that he put up with him only "for his father-in-law's sake." Despite this, he and his wife accepted an invitation to the Bormanns' house in Icking in the spring of 1931, where he immediately noticed that Gerda was pregnant again.

"He behaved toward his wife right in front of all of us the way you'd expect some uncouth bum from the slums to carry on," Darré once said. He resolved never to set foot in the house again, and he never invited the Bormanns back, although he and his wife were on cordial terms with Gerda and the Buch family. To him, she had "the same refined, reserved manner as her father," whereas her husband was "extremely brutal . . . the kind of man who takes delight in humiliating his wife in front of friends as if she were some lower form of being."

Baldur von Schirach and SS Chief Heinrich Himmler, then still subordinate to Chief of Staff Röhm, both had the same reaction to Bormann's gross familiarity and coarse manners. For lack of more promising opportunities, the Relief Fund chief cultivated Hitler's new chauffeur, Erich Kempka, "with a catlike, overbearing friendliness." Kempka later recalled: "In those days he was still a very small man in the organization . . . He had an extraordinary ability to give his equals the impression that he was a good fellow and to make himself popular with his superiors." With inferiors, however, "he was brutal in the extreme. If there was anything at all good about him, it must have been his enormous capacity for work. One cannot deny that he worked day and night almost without pause."

The same quality was recognized in the highest councils of the Party. Schirach remembered that Bormann's "zeal and industry . . . were publicly praised by Hitler at a large gathering of Party leaders" where Bormann "had been singled out as an exceptionally reliable, hard-working, capable young man." The clique saw that recognition as good reason to keep its distance from the upstart. Powerful members like Göring, Gregor Strasser and the young Reich Propaganda Chief Goebbels took no notice whatever of him. Rosenberg later maintained that before 1933 he had hardly ever heard the name Bormann mentioned in Munich. Schirach downgraded his accomplishments with the Relief Fund as "a modest performance in a position of minor importance, no more than an insurance agency."

Nevertheless, Bormann was unassailable in his position, and none of the many job seekers in the Party envied him it. So no one held it against him when in April 1931 he brought his brother Albert from Weimar to work for the Relief Fund as chief of the Property Damage section. In fact, there was general astonishment that brothers could be so different. Handsome, reserved, polite, with good manners and an interest in culture, the younger brother quickly made friends, including some in the highest ranks of the Party leadership. It soon became obvious that the two could not pull the same wagon. Within six months, in October 1931, Albert transferred to the Private Chancellery of the Führer under the wing of the quiet, inconspicuous General Manager of the Party, Philipp Bouhler, whom Hitler later rewarded for his complete devotion with the rank and title of Reichsleiter.

In this way the younger brother got what the older had long been working for, access to the immediate proximity of Hitler, though the office had by no means the importance its name implied. The diffident Hitler was a long way from entrusting the management of his personal affairs to any agency of the Party. No one was to know that much about him. The Private Chancellery was in reality more an ornament of the Führer's magnificence than an instrument for effective political operations; its only important task was dealing with the flood of mail from followers and petitioners. A couple of years later Martin managed to make himself almost the only individual to deal with really delicate jobs and missions. At present, however, he was annoyed at Albert for having gone his own way, and from then on the two brothers avoided each other as much as possible, even though they met daily and occasionally had to work together. They did not show their hostility openly, but their antipathy gradually grew into contempt on the one hand and hatred on the other.

Just at the time Martin Bormann was leaving the SA to move into the corps of political leaders, the NSDAP came into possession of the Barlow mansion on Briennerstrasse, the imposing "home office" that Hitler and his Workers' Party had wanted for a long time. Hitler bought it despite the perpetually low level of the Party war chest. Actually the Relief Fund was often a last resort for short-term loans, which grew steadily larger. Bormann had no scruples about such transactions; he simply cut down on benefits for injured storm troopers.

Years later he wrote Gerda: "When I was still working for the Relief Fund, I found to my astonishment, honest fool that I was, that the good Party members who had fought so bravely against the Communists and had been wounded tried to stay on the sick list as long as possible to keep on drawing benefits."

In an official report he also complained that frequently claims were paid for injuries not traceable to Party service and that occasionally wounds were self-inflicted in order to get compensation. He found a physician, Gerhard Wagner, later to become Reich Surgeon General, who instructed the Party doctors responsible for each district to expose cheaters and get the bona-fide injured off the sick list as soon as possible. "Thanks to Wagner, the Relief Fund was able to refuse compensation in countless cases where claims were not justified and disability was not in fact the result of an accident."

This stance did not make Bormann exactly popular with the SA, especially in Berlin. Because he had transferred from their staff, they considered him a "Party *Bonze*" and a bureaucrat. Unemployment and poverty created special temptations to cheat; moreover, the young men resented the new Party policy of attaining power legally because it seemed to shift the Revolution, which they all understood was to be a *forcible* redistribution of property and jobs, into an ever more distant and vague future.

In Berlin, Bormann did a critical review of all Relief Fund cases with a Nazi doctor from the city, Leonardo Conti (later Reich Public Health chief and State Secretary), enraging the SA thugs and their friends, the unit commanders. In October 1930 there was a confrontation. Gruppenführer Walter Maria Stennes, a retired police captain and chief of storm troopers in northeastern Germany, wrote Bormann that he considered "bringing Dr. Conti into consultation for disciplinary purposes was out of order." And SA Oberführer Erhard Wetzel, who represented the storm-trooper units in Berlin, threatened that he was prepared "to take the matter up directly with OSAF [chief of the SA] and the head of the Party," if the Relief Fund was unwilling "to pay claims whose good faith is self-evident."

This threat was made good. Former chief of staff, ex-Captain Otto Wagener, must have reprimanded Bormann because on November 12, 1930, the Relief Fund manager sent a very humble letter of apology to Stennes, agreeing "naturally and without argument that further use of Dr. Conti as medical consultant is inadmissible." Five months later, however, this temporary defeat turned to victory. Stennes rebelled against "bourgeois-liberal tendencies" in the political leadership of the NSDAP, ordered his storm troopers to occupy Party offices and accused Hitler of bad faith. Hitler summarily expelled Stennes from the Party, together with the refractory Oberführer Wetzel. Once again Bormann could take credit for early detection of the traitors.

On September 25, 1930, Hitler had taken an oath in the Leipzig Superior Court that he would bring the Party to power by legitimate means. Since then he had been preparing for a takeover organizationally as well as otherwise. He created a shadow cabinet with departments modeled on the government organization, and in his New Year's address on January 1, 1932, he boasted of "the size of our National Socialist organization." The home office was moved in February 1931, but "it turns out that despite expansion and renovation, the Brown House is still too small. A new building is under construction, another is planned, and in December we moved into still another, adjacent to the Brown House." He hoped and planned that in the not-too-distant future this bureaucratic apparatus would supply him with the specialists needed for the various government agencies.

Not the slightest reverberation from the flood of appointments, promotions and plans reached the Relief Fund manager in his office. The *Völkischer Beobachter* regularly published the names of those who were being considered for prestigious assignments. Martin Bormann's name was never mentioned. He was not aiming for anything spectacular. He already knew that he was not the type that shone in public and had an immediate appeal.

No one who combined so little fascination with so much stodginess could expect to find success on the great stage; his place was behind the scenes. Moreover, he had learned how little staff appointments and titles could mean in Hitler's hierarchy. Many a position existed only on a letterhead and in ten lines of newspaper copy. It signified neither power nor activity; it had been created only to counter somebody else's long-standing claim to confuse areas of responsibility or to weaken someone who had grown too big in the Party. Whoever belonged to the top leadership had only as much power as Hitler would allow at that particular moment, and it often came to an end before its possessor had crossed the threshold of the office at the entrance hall of the Brown House. For though most of the offices in the Reichsleitung had something like branches in the Gauleiter offices, an instruction from Munich headquarters was binding only if the Gauleiter had no reason to oppose it. Bormann and his Relief Fund felt the effects of this situation, even though he was backed by the Reich Treasurer, who was in turn backed up by Hitler. Despite the Führer's orders, not all Party members paid their Relief Fund dues, and many of the units in the small localities had to be dunned as delinquents.

There was no indication at this time that the zealous young administrator —rude to those below him, submissive and solicitous to those above him —had any notion of playing a political role. He served the Party with a mixture of idealism and self-interest and rejoiced over its triumphs—when the Party placed one of its own as Minister in Brunswick or won more than a quarter of the votes in the municipal elections in "Red" Hamburg, or when it came out on top in the provincial elections in Hesse.

He followed political events only as an observer. He would tell people repeatedly how much he would prefer being in a Brown Shirt uniform, an SA commander or agitator, fighting in the front lines, but in fact he was much attached to his steadily growing bureaucratic organization, which was taking in ever larger sums of money. In 1932 this allegedly amounted to over 3 million marks. From this standpoint he could feel more important than someone like, say, the foreign-press chief, Ernst ("Putzi") Hanfstaengl, who had been given a tiny room on the third floor of the Brown House simply to receive visitors. Hanfstaengl later said of the Reichsleitung, the Brown House headquarters bureaucracy, that "outside of the purely administrative departments like bookkeeping, cashier, membership-card index," it was like "a machine idling, and turning out mostly waste paper." Presumably Bormann shared this view.

Twenty-five years after Bormann's death Hanfstaengl told the British historian Charles Whiting: "I always thought of him as an obedient, conscientious man who knew his business. He had nothing to do with politics. When he straightened out the Relief Fund, I was delighted that finally someone was paying attention to the money. Before that a number of people had filled their pockets with it, including Göring and Goebbels."

Only once did it appear that in spite of everything Bormann would get himself involved in the day-to-day political struggle. On a September day in 1931 his doorbell was rung by detectives from the Munich political police, who flashed a search warrant. Martin and Gerda were both at home and allowed the visitors to search for forbidden Nazi publications, leaflets, secret Party documents and address lists. Nothing was found in the house, but in Bormann's car—still the same green Opel—they turned up a book on *The Most Important Political Parties and Associations*. Rubber-stamped inside was a mark showing it to be police property.

Bormann was taken to police headquarters and questioned on how the book had come into his possession. Perhaps the police hoped to discover conspiratorial connections between one of their officers and the Nazis. To make Bormann more willing to talk, he was accused of possessing stolen goods and held temporarily. He was fingerprinted and had a mug shot taken for the file. Yet after two and a half hours the police lost interest in the case. Bormann was released and never heard anything more about it.

The very fact that the political police searched his home leads one to believe that by then Bormann was no longer an insignificant outsider. For years the Munich police had kept the Nazi top brass under surveillance. Apparently they must have decided that Bormann was in closer contact with the top Party leadership than his modest position in the organization suggested. Perhaps they hoped to get on the track of secret sources of funds for the NSDAP through him. The Relief Fund, which was accountable to no one, and beyond the jurisdiction of any law, was the best source when a Party project required the expenditure of large sums that needed to be kept secret. That sort of information was surely not to be extracted from Bormann. He was familiar with the tactics of police questioning, and the sound of a key turning and the sight of a cell did not frighten him.

People who witnessed Bormann's secret rise differ over whether it was the need for money, Bormann's zeal on the job or his aggressiveness that made Hitler draw him into his close circle. A characteristic scene was played out during the night of March 13–14, 1932. Hitler, Rudolf Hess, Bouhler, Hanfstaengl and Bormann were sitting in the large corner room on the first floor of the Brown House, where Lenbach's portrait of Frederick the Great hung on the wall over Hitler's desk, listening to the national election returns on the radio. The later it got, the greater their disappointment. Hitler was trailing Field Marshal Paul von Hindenburg in the campaign for President of the Reich. The men Hitler had called to his study to share these midnight moments of truth were by no means the most important in the Party. If they had a common denominator, it must have been their loyalty, which went all the way to blind veneration. Not a word of contradiction or reproach would ever be heard from any of them. There was a good reason why Goebbels and Göring had not been summoned: they were both in Berlin and made telephone calls of condolence in the course of the evening. But what about Röhm, Gregor Strasser, Rosenberg—where were they? They were not invited, because—whichever way the election went—Hitler wanted only yes-men around him during those hours.

Hanfstaengl later recorded that during that night the radicals in the Party badgered the Führer to call the SA to arms and win by a march on Berlin what the voters had denied him at the polls. Bormann, whom Hanfstaengl characterized as the "star of the bureaucrats," most certainly did not plead for civil war. He had no confidence in the top leadership of the SA, which he considered more a liability than an asset to the Party, since it had picked up a bad reputation with the public. Even during the campaign, Helmuth Klotz, an ex-first lieutenant and former NSDAP Reichstag candidate for Baden, had published an open letter denouncing SA Chief of Staff Ernst Röhm as a homosexual.

In a pamphlet distributed throughout the Reich, *We Build the Future Through Our Leadership Corps,* Klotz not only reiterated his attack on Röhm but supplemented it with a catalogue of the sins of a couple of dozen other more or less prominent Nazis. Bormann believed that the grounds for such accusations must be removed if the Party were to continue its gains at the polls. But he did not get through to Hitler with the idea. Since Hindenburg did not receive an absolute majority, there had to be a runoff election immediately followed by a series of provincial elections. For these contests the imposing processions of Brown Shirt columns were as indispensable as the marchers' readiness to engage political opponents with their fists. Besides, Röhm was useful because he had a good line to General Kurt von Schleicher, i.e., the Reichswehr, and thereby to the President of the Reich through Hindenburg's son.

So Hitler in a grand gesture published a declaration about his Chief of Staff: Contrary to the rumor "that I might plan to separate myself from my Chief of Staff . . . I declare expressly and for all time: Lieutenant Colonel Röhm stays on as my Chief of Staff now and after the elections." Not even "the vilest and foulest smears . . . will change that." Of course Hitler knew the truth; in his circle of confidants he observed that homosexuality must be judged differently in the case of a man who had lived in the tropics for years: "His private life does not concern me, as long as the necessary discretion is preserved." That, as we will see later, was also Bormann's feeling.

The Röhm case did not seem to be urgent, however. The second election, on April 10, 1932, gave Hindenburg an absolute majority, but Hitler and his Party could take comfort in 2 million more votes. On June 4 the Reichstag was dissolved by the new Chancellor, Franz von Papen, and new elections were called for July 31. The NSDAP won 230 seats, and 37.3 percent of the votes made it the strongest party in the election. Now it appeared to all Party adherents that at last there was a legitimate takeover of power. Hitler must surely now become Reich Chancellor.

There is no need to record in these pages why Hitler did not win that objective then, or how the struggle over who was to rule the Reich continued for another six months. It is, however, very much in order to relate how Bormann lived through these times.

Bormann was still a petty functionary, admitted to the circle of confidants, but without influence on ideas or decisions. Hitler found him handy to have around; he could always count on this competent, intelligent and reliable Party comrade to take care of casually mentioned requests immediately. The coterie of adjutants, chauffeurs and other listeners that Hitler needed about him as ornament and stimulus adjusted to this new face because of the benevolence being showered upon him from the highest quarter. In a way Bormann was the ideal type that Hitler wanted all his Party members to be: devoted, a true believer, willing to pledge his soul to a cause for better or worse, a little man who felt himself called to great things. His only supporter within the top leadership was Rudolf Hess, who considered himself the greatest idealist in the Party and who had the position of the Führer's private secretary without enjoying any of the prerogatives that come with such a post. Hess suffered from this situation but was too passive and too scrupulous to win any more influence amid the wolf pack of the power-hungry National Socialist leader corps.

Jubilant at first over the Reichstag election results, this corps was soon cast into bitter disappointment. For two years the Nazis had been winning at the polls. They had even won absolute majorities in local governments and were actually running them; but that was still not enough for the final victory. In the three months between the presidential election in April and the Reichstag election in July, a truly gigantic propaganda campaign had brought an increase of a mere 300,000 votes. Fear that the Party might destroy itself winning all these elections seeped through the Brown House and all the way down to the grass roots. True, 37.3 percent of the voters had opted for the swastika, but how could an additional 13 percent be won over? People were beginning to say they were not going to make it, after all, and if the Nazis were incapable of pushing through to victory, they would also be incapable of improving the sorry state the country was in.

Functionaries who lived off Party funds were the most nervous of all. Treasuries were empty, and debts at an all-time high. The papers were saying that if things ever started to go downhill, it would inevitably turn into a headlong plunge to oblivion. Everybody would lose not only their jobs but the chance of finding others, what with almost nine million unemployed, part-time workers and starving people desperately grasping at any straw. During the months of triumph, Nazis in the upper ranks had been jockeying for positions of responsibility. Now they were quarreling among themselves over who was to blame for the imminent disaster. On September 10, 1932, the Reichstag was once again dissolved, and a new election was scheduled. Perhaps there were some Party comrades who were nothing but a liability to the Party in public?

A grotesque episode that took place in the Brown House on the periphery of the political events was characteristic of the tense atmosphere. Internecine Party intrigues by Bormann, Buch and Reich Treasurer Xaver Schwarz had enraged Röhm. He poured out his heart to an old friend, former Captain Karl Mayr, describing the connivings of his enemies in the Party and asking if Mayr "had anything" on any of them.

Karl Mayr was anything but a harmless private citizen. As a Reichswehr officer in Munich in the early summer of 1919 he had commanded an "enlightenment battalion" whose mission it was to inoculate discharged soldiers with anti-Communism and imbue them with patriotic ideas. One of his propagandists and secret agents was Corporal Adolf Hitler. Mayr was later discharged because he wanted to use Bavarian Reichswehr units in the Kapp Putsch, and Röhm took over his post. By the time of the 1923 putsch, both captains, who had once been friends, had gone their separate ways. By 1932, Mayr had joined the Social Democrat Reichsbanner, the camp of an archenemy.

When the *Münchner Post,* the Social Democratic paper, ran a story on the cabals within the NSDAP, Röhm tried to get out of the affair by making a sworn deposition in court, but this gambit failed so miserably that Bormann saw his chance to go over to the offensive. He was able to do so all the more confidently because Mayr knew about Hitler's somewhat dubious role during the demobilization of the army and was therefore an uncomfortable eyewitness for the Führer to have around. Hitler's revenge eventually caught up with Mayr; he died in the Buchenwald concentration camp in 1945.

Bormann did not yet feel he could lodge a complaint against Röhm with Hitler directly. On October 5, 1932, he typed out a five-page letter "to the Private Secretary to the Führer, Herr Rudolf Hess." In this letter—given here in abridged form*—the once modest and almost submissive Bormann dropped his mask and made clear that he not only knew his business as an administrator but was also capable of a power play. His literary style is

*Since the full text of the letter is reproduced in the Appendix on page 387, no special indications are supplied on where cuts and abbreviations occur.

clumsy and simple-minded—and incidentally, always remained so. He wrote as he talked, in stereotyped phrases.

Dear Herr Hess:

It is only because of the pressure of events that I bother you on your vacation. The following, however, *has* to be said, in my opinion. You and the Führer must know the attitudes that prevail on the outside.

Let it be clear at the outset that I have nothing against the SA. Nor do I have anything against Röhm personally. As far as I am concerned, someone in faraway India can fool around with elephants, and in Australia with kangaroos. For me and for all true National Socialists, the only thing that counts is the Movement. Anything or anybody useful to the Movement is good; whoever does it harm is a louse and my enemy.

But the things that have been coming to light knock the bottom right out of the barrel. One of the most prominent leaders in the Party is complaining to an equally prominent leader of the opposition, and is insulting and reviling his own Party comrades.

Every SA man has it drummed into him, and this was especially important in the Röhm case, that he must cover for his comrades and leaders—and then the most prominent SA leader of all goes ahead with flagrant betrayal and slander.

If the Führer still stands by this man after that performance, then I and countless other people don't understand him anymore, and there simply *isn't* any way of understanding.

Let it not be said that the past services performed by Chief of Staff Röhm outweigh faults of that sort. The harm that R. has caused by his example cannot be outweighed by any amount of past services. To say nothing of the question: *What* services? Take a good look at all the orders Röhm has issued—you won't find a single *basic* innovation since Pfeffer's time.

They say Röhm is a personality, a "brain." One can certainly be of two minds about that. Besides, an accurate yardstick for judging a person is the quality of his co-workers. Brains? Take a look at the former Deputy Chief of Staff, Major Fuchs, and the present Deputy Chief of Staff, "Major and Gruppenführer" Hühnlein, and you will get some idea of how little gas there is in the tank. I am convinced that the post of chief of staff could be filled by any SA leader with an understanding of people and a talent for organization. I was never much of a soldier myself, but I'd bet my boots that even I could manage it. Take a look at the SS. You know Himmler and you know Himmler's capabilities.

It is said that the attitude against Röhm springs from the general resentment of the political leaders toward the SA. An outrageous insinuation, because after all, all we old Party members were once just plain SA men. In the Political Organization there is no bad feeling being fomented against the SA, as is the case the other way around. Who is only too ready to call our political leaders *"Bonzen"*? Personally I would rather be out in the field as an SA leader than be stuck behind a desk day after day, pushing papers around from morning to night. Furthermore, who spends more money, and more freely? Certainly not the man who brings in the dues and knows how reluctant most Party members are about paying up.

Does the Führer know about the "no confidence" attitude of Party members toward the elections? Does he know that a large number of SA men take the position that the best thing to do would be to vote Communist? When the Röhm correspondence was made public and the Führer let it be known that Röhm was to stay on as Chief of Staff, many Party members shook their heads. The idea of subjecting the Movement to the same trial by ordeal in the present situation seems to me extremely dangerous. There is practically no confidence in a victory in the Reichstag elections; the majority of the Party members are disappointed as a result of the exaggerated hopes aroused by responsible leaders (Röhm, Goebbels). *Trust in the Führer* still exists, and this must be preserved, for if it were ever lost, the Movement would be done for. *Certainly countless people will lose confidence in the Führer if the Führer continues to keep a man who betrays his comrades to a notorious political enemy, asks for and gets damaging material to use against them.* If I or some other Party members fail to understand political decisions, well and good, we don't know enough about the circumstances and conditions, the Führer is the Führer, he will straighten it all out in the end. But this is a question of the grave damage the Movement is suffering because of the behavior of one of its members.

Did Hess pass this letter on to Hitler, or at least tell him its contents? He did not like to go to his Chief bearing bad news; moreover, he—like so many others—could be paralyzed by an imperious gesture of Hitler's or a hard look out of those blue eyes. He knew that Karl Wahl, the Gauleiter of Augsburg, had learned about the latest putsch plans of the die-hard Freikorps men from two SA leaders in his district. He also knew that Hitler had intervened but had taken it for granted that the top SA leadership had cold-shouldered the two "traitors." He knew further from his experiences with Pfeffer von Salomon that Hitler considered a putsch not only politically wrong, but hopeless.

"Our formations are unarmed; insofar as any weapons are on hand against my wishes . . . they are ineffective against the police and Reichswehr with their modern equipment." Hitler said this some two weeks after Bormann's letter of complaint, but the Freikorps faction refused to believe that he had felt that way for years.

Bormann's remark about "no confidence in the elections" was proved right on November 6, 1932. The NSDAP lost 34 seats in the Reichstag elections. With 196 deputies, it still remained by far the strongest party, but it lost the aura of invincibility. The only silver lining was that the returns showed the Communists had won 100 seats. Now the voters could be more easily frightened by the slogan that the choice was between the swastika and the hammer and sickle.

The Relief Fund administrator could only observe the crucial events that ensued in the next three months. However much he was affected by each new incident, he had no influence over what was going on. If once in a while he picked up some information from powers behind the scenes not known to the ordinary reader of the daily newspapers, he did not get it firsthand. Only after the return to Munich would it be known whom Hitler would choose to be by his side in his dramatic struggle for power. Berlin was the stage upon which General Schleicher, Hindenburg, Hitler, Papen, Hugenberg and the politicians from the Center Party were negotiating.

No one was left in the Brown House but the administrative personnel, who were dependent on the meager fare from their rumor factory and thrown into renewed shock when in the provincial elections in Thuringia on December 6, 1932, the NSDAP lost nearly half the votes it had garnered in the Reichstag elections in the past summer. A few days later they were struck by another blow, the rebellion of a top man. Gregor Strasser, who as Reich Organization Chief was the hierarchical superior of every functionary in the Party Organization, had made a secret deal for a minister's post in the Cabinet with the new Reich Chancellor, Kurt von Schleicher.

Given Bormann's lack of imagination, he might well have been impressed by Strasser, who put his arguments together objectively and presented concrete programs. But that was all in the past. To Bormann, Strasser's flare-up at the Führer's conference in the Hotel Kaiserhof in Berlin was a bad breach of faith that inevitably suggested rats leaving a sinking ship. Yet no man of rank in the entire Reich leadership and no Gauleiter would have been prepared to follow Strasser's example.

Strasser's rebellion had consequences of unexpected magnitude for Bormann. The Party structure was reorganized. Just as Hitler had assumed personal leadership of the SA after Pfeffer's dismissal and appointed a Chief of Staff to do the work, he now put the whole Party organization directly under his command, and made former Gauleiter and Reich Inspector Robert Ley Chief of Staff.

At the same time he narrowed Ley's area of responsibility—a tactic he repeatedly used in similar situations—by dividing up the empire. The Office of Agrarian Policy under Darré became independent, and a newly created Political Central Committee, headed by Rudolf Hess, took over the departments where political decisions were made and carried out. Bormann's steady ascent began with his move into the Hess office six months later.

In the last weeks of the year 1932 it did not exactly look as if the Party was on the way up. All the Party bigwigs were crisscrossing the country, attending innumerable meetings to stem the collapse and draw money into the empty treasuries by charging admission—and sometimes just to be able to live for a few days on travel money and speaker's fees.

The articles in the anti-Nazi newspapers reviewing the past year assured readers that Hitler was politically dead. Hitler, on the other hand, spread confidence unperturbed. On December 18 he told Rudolf Jordan, the acting Gauleiter of Halle, "In a few weeks we'll have reached our goal; do call me."

He made the same promise to his functionaries in the Brown House before going into retreat for the holidays, as he always did, first in his Munich apartment, then in Haus Wachenfeld on Obersalzberg. The display of Christmas presents in the Bormann household—they had moved to Pullach—must have been rather pathetic, but the Bormanns had no doubts about the coming victory; they were politically so far gone that their certainty was now based on faith rather than reason.

Bormann's patron Hess was present when, on January 4, 1933, a meeting took place in Cologne at the house of the banker Kurt von Schröder. Hitler and Franz von Papen mapped out plans that led to the so-called power takeover. No one was to know of this discussion, but the press got wind of it from Schleicher's secret intelligence service and predicted that the Chancellor's downfall had been plotted. In this way the functionaries in the Brown House learned that their Führer was busy collecting ammunition for the next attack.

On January 17 the Führer moved his headquarters into the Hotel Kaiserhof in Berlin, together with a growing entourage of escorts and advisers. Only a few confidants knew with whom he was dealing, what had been decided, and who had been won over to support his chancellorship. Goebbels was one; when he traveled to Munich for a day to go to Reich Propaganda headquarters, he recorded in his diary that he could find there "no calm, while in Berlin, developments are moving forward irresistibly." Where it was all leading first became apparent to the Party members in the Brown House on Saturday, January 28, when Reich Chancellor Schleicher resigned. Who would take his place?

On Monday, January 30, a day that was to go down in history, the news arrived in the morning that Hitler had disappeared into the presidential palace with Papen, Hugenberg, Party comrades Frick and Göring, and various other gentlemen of potential ministerial caliber. In the Brown House the functionaries sat in their offices, their work untouched. Never had the Party been so close to victory. Anyone who sought distraction from the nervous tension by looking out the window saw on that damp, overcast winter's day how the passers-by went their ways as usual, unmindful that in these very hours their destinies, too, were being decided.

Finally at noon a call came through from Berlin, relieving the functionaries from their wavering between hope and fear: Hitler was Chancellor. They tramped in their jackboots from room to room, announcing the news with laughter and jubilation, embraced one another, and forgot personal animosities and rivalries. They were in business!

If we were concerned with the rise and fall of the Third Reich, we would have to begin a new chapter at this point, for that day proved to be the seed from which sprang a hitherto unimaginable growth. This book, however, is the record of the activity and fate of a single individual, a *Volksgenosse,* an "ordinary citizen" whose character, sense of values and goals in life were the same as those of millions of his fellow countrymen. No one knew then that he possessed capabilities that would lift him above the masses, that he was of greater consequence than the average man, so it is only natural that in the stormy months of the "national uprising," the Revolution, the administrator of the Relief Fund remained just as he was.

Naturally he, too, was gripped by the wild activity with which the Party comrades set about to change the world to suit their notions. At last the swastika insignia and the brown uniform gave everyone so outfitted as much omnipotence as he cared to claim for himself—at least momentarily. In the first weeks of their new-found glory the comrades hardly ever got out of their boots. They marched to election meetings, and unhindered by the police, staged demonstrations against the "system" that still continued to run things in Munich. They raised their flag on public buildings to the accompaniment of speeches and theatrically staged appearances.

The "old fighters" considered it only fair that they should now be indemnified for their lean years in Party service, for the slights, punishments and sacrifices they had endured. The simple-minded among them were content to wear a white armband on their brown shirts and for a small wage play at auxiliary police, exercising power and herding Reds behind the barbed wire of improvised concentration camps. The smarter, more ambitious ones demanded a decent living and a career. When some desirable job was occupied by a political opponent, they enforced *Gleichschaltung,** which, as they understood the term, meant that this job must be made available to them.

With Party membership number 60508, which automatically allowed him to wear the golden Party badge, Martin Bormann could easily have found himself a well-paid sinecure. For a number of reasons he refrained from doing this. Right up to the collapse of the National Socialist regime he always affected the stance of the committed idealist; in contrast to the

---

*"Coordination." This was the first phase of the Revolution, placing virtually all major civilian organizations in the political, economic and social life of the German nation under some sort of Nazi control.—*Tr.*

other old Party members who went foraging after money and possessions with both hands, he was in fact untouchable. This was partly due to his attachment to the Relief Fund; it was entirely his own operation. And as long as the Party did not have a firm hold on the government, it was something like a bird in the hand. But above all, Bormann was not ready to leave the Brown House.

Early in February a release from the NSDAP press office announced: "As is known, the headquarters of the National Socialist movement is to remain in Munich in the future." Sooner or later there would be a chance for Bormann to rise in the Party hierarchy. Reich Treasurer Xaver Schwarz was twenty-five years his senior, and when a successor was needed, there was an able money manager waiting in the wings.

However, Schwarz was not by any means tired of his job. Since Hitler, with his artistic temperament, refused to waste mental energy on vulgar money matters, Schwarz had had his master endow him with such wide-ranging powers that no one in the Party dared cross him. He thought of Bormann as a capable employee but was put off by his behavior, his oscillation between fawning submission and overbearing brutality. Besides, he had no intention of helping an ambitious rival on his way up. He felt the time had come to cut back the Relief Fund, its hundreds of staff members, and its chief.

In the Reichstag election of March 1933 the NSDAP, together with the German Nationalist Party, had cornered over half the total vote. The Communist Party was banned, and the Socialist Party dissolved itself. There were no longer any enemies left for the Nazi gangs to meet in bloody encounters. To be sure, Bormann complained in May that "there are many more claims being filed than before," and his office had "to handle three laundry baskets full of mail daily." But these were increasingly claims for accidents and property damage and hardly at all for injuries sustained in fights. The wife of the Berlin Relief Fund physician Leonardo Conti had written him in April that in her view "the need for the Relief Fund will gradually disappear during the winter."

Bormann had had discussions with her on whether his office should be turned into a medical-insurance fund for young people in the future Reich Labor Service. Elfriede Conti, who was a doctor, was now taking her elderly husband's place in authorizing payment of the service-connected claims of the Berlin SA men, but she had no desire to go on doing this work for an institution obviously on its way out. Moreover, she and her husband believed that they could now get along without Bormann's support. A year later they found they were mistaken.

On the very day after he wrote asking his Berlin colleague to continue her faithful service, Bormann arranged for his own resignation from the Relief Fund. Once again he sat down at the typewriter and wrote to Rudolf Hess, whose title was now Deputy Party Leader; a month before, Hitler had appointed him Deputy Führer for Party Affairs. This was newly created territory; a bureau had to be set up. Bormann wrote that the Reich Treasurer was planning to simplify the administration of the Relief Fund, in other words, to cut it down. "Herr Schwarz places no value on my opinions, I am . . . the employee who has to toe the mark . . . In view of this I ask you once again to employ me elsewhere in the *Political* Organization. I do not want to work in the Treasury." Schwarz, however, was not to be told about the request for transfer; he "would not understand and would break with me immediately and completely." (See the full text in the Appendix, pages 389-390.)

Bormann did not himself carry the letter to the reception room of the Hess office in the Brown House. That would have been too risky. He sent it on May 27 to the Reich Chancellery in Berlin, where Hess, a regular member of the Führer's entourage, was in the process of setting up a branch of his still rudimentary Munich office.

Organization had never been Hess's strong point, and he knew nothing about building up a bureaucratic apparatus. The letter from Munich must have come at just the right moment. On his next trip to the Munich he loved so well, Hess took the opportunity to talk to Bormann about his problems. Evidently Bormann's suggestions were acceptable, for they soon came to an agreement, with which Hitler concurred. In this way Bormann became a Stabsleiter, or chief of staff, in Amt Hess (the Hess Bureau).

6

From Unknown Party Member to Reichsleiter

Bormann moved into Amt Hess on July 3, 1933. When the *Parteikorrespondenz*, the Party paper, announced his appointment, many people in the Reichsleitung and even more in various Gauleiter headquarters wondered who he was. His high-sounding title was, however, misleading. The "staff" he was chief of did not yet exist. Hitler had never precisely defined the duties and responsibilities of Hess's office—nor was he ever to do so—and Hess himself was merely an appendage to the Führer, without the nerve to carve out an empire for himself in the jungle of conflicting departmental domains that Hitler had deliberately created. Hans Frank, who knew Hess well, once described him as "a good-natured but hopelessly dreamy weakling without any mental assets."

"Basically, Hess was a man of moderation and poise," but he watched with envy, anger and "false humility" while Göring, his rival for second place next to Hitler, amassed titles, power and wealth, although he didn't even have a Party rank. Hess hoped that one day his humility would be rewarded by the Führer. But this merely revealed how little he understood his idol, whose tactics were to reward his closest followers with the right to plunder, and thereby to involve them in disputes among themselves. As his Deputy, Hitler had deliberately chosen a man with scant ambition, limited views and no means to exert any influence.

When Bormann became part of Amt Hess, Hitler had been Chancellor for five months, and the new bosses had already divvied up the power among themselves. There were no more territories to conquer. The new office was set up chiefly to handle public complaints, but it was also supposed to supervise cooperation between Party offices and agencies and arbitrate the disputes between them so that Hitler could be protected from such picayune details. There was nothing much to be gained except aggravation and enemies, and Hess occasionally complained that he had been demoted 'to the post of the Movement's wailing wall.

When another duty was added, it seemed trivial enough. Amt Hess was to act as a sort of clearing house between Party and state, to prevent Party agencies from making contradictory demands on ministries, which might reveal internal Party feuds to outsiders. It was never clear to what extent Hess was empowered to settle a question himself; he always had to reckon with the possibility that the Führer would be called in as court of last resort and might overrule him.

The Hess office was definitely not a place to win laurels. It was more like a no man's land protecting the Führer's throne. Anyone who worked there had to be strong and unyielding, suspicious and canny, pragmatic and unscrupulous. Rudolf Hess, who liked to hear himself referred to as "the conscience of the Party," would rapidly have been swallowed up in this quicksand had it not been for his chief of staff. It was thanks to the exertions of Martin Bormann that he was able to stay in the job for eight years and that his office ever amounted to more than a set for Hitler's theatrical production.

Bormann, who was familiar with the operating procedures of the Party, quickly realized that the fuzziness about the parameters of authority made it possible for him to extend himself quite a bit—in fact, to meddle in everything and then to stick his neck out as far as seemed prudent. An appointed referee obviously had to be informed about the disputants and might even be courted by them, two procedures that would enable him to see through both sides and find out all about their transgressions; also, whoever served as a filter between Party and state could decide whether something should get through or not. In short, the conditions were ideal for a clever bureaucrat. Without drawing attention to himself, he could in the course of time work up to a position of real power in the monstrously proliferating Party organization.

This, however, involved taking over the domain that Robert Ley, chief of staff of the Party Organization, had long felt belonged to him. Ley, the successor to Gregor Strasser, had inherited from Strasser, in addition to the Reich Personnel Office and the Reich Training Office (Reichsschulungs-amt), the National Socialist Factory Worker Cell Organization (NS-Betriebszellen-Organisation), a sort of Party trade union, and the NS-Hago, a middle-class business association. When on May 2, 1933, the old trade unions were dissolved and their property confiscated, Hitler substituted the German Labor Front for "all who create with head and hand," and put Ley in charge of it. Ley was in the process of making this his own private empire, with a vast army of officers independent of the Party, with its own buildings seized from the trade unions, its own press, banners, even its own marching style—columns of workers in blue uniforms. At the same time he made it clear that, as Stabsleiter of the Party Organization directly under Hitler, he was to be regarded as the highest-ranking Party officer next to Hitler. Although he did not dare to insist that Hess, the Führer's Deputy (with "full authority to decide in all matters of Party leadership") was actually subordinate to him, he felt Bormann and all other top- and middle-management people in the new office should take orders from him.

There is no way of knowing for sure who thought up the trick to block Ley's power play, but there is some evidence that it may have been Bormann's first experience as director on a larger stage. Hess had been one of sixteen Reichsleiters holding office in the NSDAP. On September 22, 1933, Hitler decreed that from that date on Hess would drop "the titles of Reichsleiter and SS Obergruppenführer and henceforth use only 'the Führer's Deputy.' " With this dramatic gesture the idealist Hess suddenly soared above the entire Reichsleiter corps. Appropriately, he now wore a plain brown shirt with no insignia of rank at all—like the Führer. The next maneuver—which made the coup complete—followed three weeks later. On October 10 Bormann was named Reichsleiter. At a single stroke he had attained the highest rank in the Party. Now he was on the same level as Ley, which incidentally underscored the fact that the Führer's Deputy ranked higher still. In another month Bormann would catch up with Ley in yet another area: he was made Reichstag deputy. Hitler had dissolved the Reichstag because it included representatives of parties he had abolished. The next election offered a single slate of NSDAP candidates, with well over six hundred names.

Amt Hess was equally well armed for a power struggle in the administrative sector. Immediately after the takeover, Hitler had installed an NSDAP Liaison Staff as part of the Reich Chancellery. The rule was that "all NSDAP agencies wishing to contact Reich ministries or the Reich Chancellery . . . with questions, petitions, applications" must go through the Liaison Staff. Hess, the perpetual handler of trivia, managed to get control of that office. When he was given the right to attend Cabinet meetings, he and Bormann secured a bridgehead for themselves in Berlin.

There is good reason to believe that the Führer's Deputy was not personally behind the plans for extending the power of his office. A confirmed hypochondriac, he was intensely moody and so unsure of himself that he consulted astrologers. His Stabsleiter, on the other hand, was always ready to launch an attack, sooner or later. He restrained himself only because at first he would not have known what to do with more responsibility. Amt Hess had no trace of a structure. The lawyer Heinrich Heim, engaged on retainer by Bormann in August, found only two other colleagues, whose principal job, like his own, was to handle either begging or irate letters from individuals who saw in Hess a patron saint of justice. It was characteristic of the way Bormann visualized the duties and dimensions of the new office that he immediately brought in a lawyer, the first of many. Later, at his denazification, Heim stated that all he did was dispense helpful advice to aggrieved fellow citizens. Reminiscing in 1975, he told this writer: "The job was anything but promising. It was also wholly apolitical."

When Hess was made a Reich minister at the end of 1933 so that he could represent the Party's viewpoint in the Cabinet during legislative sessions, Bormann drew on his legal colleague's knowledge in the drafts he prepared for his chief. He and Heim were the same age. Heim came from a highly regarded family of Bavarian lawyers. His education, background and character were far above his chief's, but he could not compete with Bormann's aggressive drive. Despite Bormann's bad reputation as a boss at the Relief Fund, Heim found him "correct, realistic, energetic, and full of a sense of purpose" during the first year they worked together. Apparently it did not bother him that Bormann enjoyed playing the patron, handing out praise and promotion from on high with crude joviality. A handwritten letter to Heim was characteristic. "Dear Herr Heim" was first handed a compliment: "You write in a terrific style, really great!" Then he was told: "Hold on to your seat—I fixed it so you will be given the rank of Oberregierungsrat [Senior state counselor]. It wasn't easy, but I'm stubborn. It does not make any difference to *us* whether as our lawyer you are in or out of civil service. But I believe it is important for you because you never use your elbows for yourself, only for others, and something must be done to take care of your future. No objections: *The Führer has appointed you!* And when I am no longer around and you don't want to stay any longer, you can get yourself pensioned off any time."

As a further sign of his benevolence, Bormann had arranged for Heim, who joined the Party only after the takeover, to get a somewhat lower Party number, which would give the impression that he had joined early. The letter ended with a warning: "I must ask you not to say anything to anyone about the Party number or the reasons for your getting civil-service rank. What I have done for you does not go for others." (See the Appendix, page 391.)

Heinrich Heim will often be called as a witness in these pages, for he stayed with Bormann until April 1945. He worked up to the position of Ministerialrat (ministerial counselor) but his influence diminished from year to year—surely because of his weak elbows—and he was finally shunted off to a one-man department. As the office continued to expand, Bormann had civil-service rank given to other colleagues. By filling organizational slots in the Reich ministries, they saved the Party money, since the government paid their salaries and Bormann did not need to extract the consent of the niggardly Reich Treasurer for each new appointment.

In the course of the years, Robert Ley lost one stronghold after another. Bormann baited him by harmless intrusions into his domain. In November 1933, for example, Bormann complained in a circular to Reichsleiters and

Gauleiters that Party officers were wearing olive-green overcoats, which were regulation only for SA men; Party officers, he ruled, should wear brown overcoats. He later fired off a circular ending an argument over whether Party members were to greet one another with "Heil Hitler" or just "Heil," by ruling that both were acceptable. In another announcement Bormann decreed that the right arm should be raised only for the national anthem and the "Horst Wessel Song," but not for songs of the Hitler Youth or other organizations.

Bormann was furious when in September 1933 Ley appointed district inspectors to monitor the Gauleiters, making sure they kept to their authority and cutting down on their general omnipotence, which Hitler still tolerated. These "tribal princes" had to be made subordinate to the Führer's Deputy. Hess contrived to have the monitors brought under the control of his office, but although he changed their title to Commissars of the Party Chancellery, the ploy made him nothing but enemies. It was Bormann who smoothed the ruffled feathers of the Gauleiters in a letter which assured them that he had no wish to check up on them but only to back them up in their burdensome tasks. After a six-month interval for face-saving, the monitors were abolished. Bormann had recognized—more quickly than Ley had—that for the time being he was still dependent on the good will of the regional Party leaders.

There was another test of strength in September 1934 over what seemed to be an issue of no consequence. Up to that time Ley had used a Party letterhead which read "Die Oberste Leitung der PO [The Supreme Directorate of the Party Organization]—Der Stabsleiter." Bormann objected to this, and Hess complained to Hitler about Ley's presumptuousness. Backed by Hitler's decision to support him, Hess announced that Ley did not have authority over all departments of the Party Organization and ordered him to use the title "Reichsorganisationsleiter" (Reich Organization Leader) in the future. This had been Gregor Strasser's title, but Ley was not given anything like the same range of command. In several top departments he had merely bureaucratic authority, while Amt Hess held the political. Hess also tried to institute an intra-Party court action against Ley, but Party Judge Buch let the matter die—to the great irritation of his son-in-law.

The Führer's Deputy and his Stabsleiter were feeling unassailable in their position because of the role they had played ten weeks previously as accessories to one of Hitler's most nakedly atrocious acts, the so-called Röhm affair. Whatever the real reasons behind it may have been, historians agree on one point: the SA Chief of Staff never had any concrete plan to mount a putsch against Hitler. It is true that many of the Brown Shirt marchers were mightily discontent with the way the National Socialist Revolution was actually working out and how little it had done for them. The street fighters—glorified in so many speeches as "the unknown SA man"—felt the effects of the socialism they had been promised only in the drop in unemployment. Few of the middle echelon were rewarded with jobs and sinecures. The carpet knights of the Party Organization always moved faster when there was something attractive up for grabs. The *Uralt-Kämpfer* (the earliest fighters), who had belonged to the Freikorps, were the ones most seriously disenchanted. They had never really known what they wanted beyond the vague sense that those at the bottom ought to be on top. The Weimar Republic had effectively prevented them from working this change, and now they felt cheated once again. They had fought for victory, and now the *Bonzen*—instead of Reds they were "Browns"—were right back in there again taking all the spoils.

In his strike against the SA, Hitler was aiming primarily at winning over the Reichswehr, but he also welcomed the opportunity to start with a clean slate; that is, to settle accounts with the Freikorps and other untamed elements that might turn against him. In December 1933 he had sent out letters of commendation to a dozen "old fighters" for "the year's end of the year of the National Socialist Revolution." The letter to Röhm was especially cordial—the second-person singular *du,* which they used in conversation with each other, appeared in a published communication. But Hitler may already have been speculating on how he could rid himself of this disreputable gang, for by January 1934 he told Gestapo chief Rudolf Diels to begin collecting material on terrorist acts by the SA and on "Herr Röhm and his friendships."

In his self-justifying speech after the morning of June 30, Hitler maintained that it had been mostly Hess's warnings that had alerted him to certain conditions "which I myself with the best will in the world could no longer disregard."

The star witness, whom everyone trusted, had been well chosen. In fact, Hess and his Stabsleiter had long been fomenting opposition to Röhm and his clique. No one in the Party was considered more upright and ethical than Hess—though there were whispers that he was such a prude because he was sexually impotent. Be that as it may, the strange, introverted Hess must indeed have been revolted by the noisy guttersnipes, a repugnance also felt by his Stabsleiter.

Bormann had several reasons for this. First there was the corrosive effect homosexuals had on the Party's image. Second, a number of high-echelon SA officers, chiefly former Freikorps members, had accused Bormann of supplying the material that led to the ouster of Pfeffer von Salomon. These men—Heines, Heydebreck, Hayn, Schulz and their friends—had always brushed him off when he tried to pose as a Rossbacher and *Feme* veteran, making it very plain that they considered him nothing but a low-grade bureaucrat and not a soldier by any stretch of the imagination. Now they were all eager for the Night of the Long Knives, and he—Martin Bormann —might be one of the targets they had in mind. On November 9 at the celebrations held in Munich for the anniversary of the 1923 putsch, he watched, as a guest of honor, while former Freikorps units handed over their battle standards for safekeeping by the Movement—a symbolic gesture that their time was past. Germany no longer needed rebels, only government authority.

No one knows which confidants Hitler let in on the plan for the massacre. Apparently he made the irreversible decision and decided the details between June 23 and 26 at Obersalzberg. On June 25 Hess declared in a broadcast: "Woe to him who breaks the faith by believing the Revolution can be served by a revolt!"

Was he preparing the public for the coming blood bath with his unctuous tones, or was this meant as a warning to Röhm? If the latter, it was too late, for on June 27 Hitler was back in Berlin. There he told those concerned: Göring, who was charged with the plan's execution in Berlin; Goebbels, who was to accompany Hitler to Westphalia, Godesberg and Munich; SA Obergruppenführer Viktor Lutze (who was also Oberpräsident of the Prussian province of Hanover) because he was to be Röhm's successor; Heinrich Himmler, an interested party because with Röhm out of the way his SS could get back its independence; and also, of course, the Reichswehr top command. The generals would no longer have to fear competition from an SA militia.

There is no evidence that Bormann had been told before June 27. He always carried a notebook with him, and his entries of important matters served him as a cue for future action. There is mention of a Gauleiter conference at the end of May, then, under June 28, the item: "The Führer inspects the Reich Labor Service." The next entry is June 30: "Röhm plot uncovered: Schneidhuber, Count Spreti, Heines, Hayn, Schmid, Heydebreck, Ernst shot." The wording is almost the same as a press release drafted by Hitler himself. It is striking that these troubled times did not produce more detailed entries, especially since by then Bormann was in Hitler's closest entourage, attended all Party functions, shuttled from the Reich Chancellery to the Brown House and already managed Hitler's private affairs. The course of events suggests that Bormann and Munich Gauleiter Adolf Wagner were operating behind the scenes, just as Bormann had done in the Parchim *Feme* murder, so the drama would unfold without a hitch on the Bavarian stage.

On the night of June 29 Wagner gave the signal by phone; the Führer, then staying at the Dreesen Hotel in Godesberg, on the Rhine, was told that storm troopers were marching through the Munich streets, alerted by putsch-minded SA officers. About four-thirty the next morning Hitler landed at the Munich airport and immediately sped to the Ministry of the Interior, where he demoted and arrested two senior SA officers. Then he, his adjutants, SS bodyguards and plain-clothes men drove on in three black Mercedes limousines to the town of Wiessee, on the Tegernsee, where the

SA leaders had assembled. There is no need to retell the whole chain of events in these pages. Bormann's role in the affair is, however, a matter of substantive interest.

He certainly did not believe the fabricated story of a putsch forestalled in the nick of time, but he felt the summary liquidations were justified. Eyewitnesses can no longer recall with certainty whether he was at the airport on Hitler's arrival in the early morning and among those running from room to room behind a wildly excited Führer at the Ministry of the Interior. But after the bloody deed was done when Hitler returned from Wiessee and made his entry into the Brown House, Bormann and Hess were on hand to summon all the Party officers into the Senate Chamber. There Hitler announced that he had removed Röhm and appointed Viktor Lutze to succeed him—a suggestion Bormann had made in his letter to Hess in 1932. Then Hitler delivered a speech Hess believed would "go down in history."

As Hess told it, "Sitting in his study, the Führer pronounced the first death sentences." There was a list of the arrested SA officers drawn up by the officials of the Stadelheim Prison, where the men were confined. Now that list was in Bormann's hands, and he knew better than anyone else how to go to work with a document. He did not mind that the summary procedure dispensed with indictments, witnesses, defense counsel, judges of any kind. In blind obedience he simply crossed out one name after another as Hitler reeled them off.

The man to carry out this operation, SS Gruppenführer (Major General) Sepp Dietrich, commander of the Leibstandarte SS Adolf Hitler (bodyguard regiment), was kept waiting in the Adjutants' Office while Hitler in a mad frenzy dictated page after page of public announcements and press releases, whipped on by a compulsion to assuage his own guilt. It was Bormann's job to see that these texts were typed, corrected and delivered. After the final opus, an order of the day for the new SA Chief of Staff, had been signed, Sepp Dietrich was called in. Bormann pressed the list of the condemned into his hand, and Hitler ordered that a firing squad of six noncoms and a company commander take the men whose names were crossed out, line them up in front of the prison wall and shoot them. As in Parchim, Bormann did not actually commit the murders; he was an accessory, following orders, presumably for the good of the Fatherland. And he had shown his Führer that he could keep his nerve in a sticky situation.

By now it was nothing new for Bormann to perform his duties in Hitler's immediate presence. Rudolf Hess had progressively lost interest in the day-to-day office routine; he could no more adjust to the bureaucratic work of the legislative machinery, which was part of his responsibility as Party minister, than he could accept the work habits of his Führer, which forced him to sacrifice his own private life and hobbies—folk medicine and flying.

He lacked the split-second reactions needed in the daily game of tactics. Years later at the Nuremberg Trials, psychologists assessed his IQ as 120, considerably above average. But it was not in him to reduce a problem to an abstract principle that could be stated in two sentences. This was precisely what Hitler demanded of his closest collaborators so that he could cut off every objection at the start. He once said of Hess, "I only hope he will never be my successor. I don't know which I'd be sorrier for, Hess or the Party." It got to a point where Bormann complained to Heim: "It can't go on like this. Hess gets called in only after the decision has been made. If that doesn't change, there isn't any future for our office!"

Hess soon saw that his Stabsleiter was smarter than he was and achieved more. This did not upset him. His very inability to hold his own in the policy-making hassles reinforced his notion of himself as the decent, straightforward person the Germans were meant to take him for. Despite warnings, he refused to worry about the possibility that Bormann might be crowding him out. And for whatever reason, Bormann really was loyal to him. So, more and more, it was Bormann's job to brief the Führer in terse, concise summaries. Sometimes Bormann did his work at the NSDAP Liaison Office in Berlin, right next to the Reich Chancellery, but more often in Munich. He traveled a lot. He had to make an appearance at each meeting of the Party elite—over thirty are marked in his 1934 appointment book—to show off his status as Reichsleiter, get to know the influential men, especially the Gauleiters, and be on the lookout for potential allies. He was not yet part of the Führer's permanent entourage. Adjutants Julius Schaub and Wilhelm Brückner; Heinrich Hoffman, who was in charge of providing publicity photos and gossip; Julius Schreck, who drove the Führer's supercharged Mercedes, did not yet have to be afraid of him. In March 1935, during the celebration of the Saar plebiscite, he put down in his notebook for the first time: "Drive with the Führer." Later this became an everyday affair.

But that was still in the future, and Hitler made no move to support Amt Hess in its bureaucratic wrangles with its adversaries. Before Hess was accorded the privilege of speaking as the Führer's Deputy in the Reich Ministers' Cabinet, Minister of the Interior and Reichsleiter Wilhelm Frick had already prepared his protest. He argued that the duties of a Party minister should not be permitted to become topics of dispute with other Reich ministries. His fellow Reichsleiters in the NSDAP also refused to confer specific prerogatives of authority on "the Führer's Deputy for Party Affairs," particularly since the structure of the Party hierarchy made them virtually powerless themselves. At the end of 1933 Bormann sent around a letter objecting that his office was getting its first news "of decrees, ordinances, enactments and promulgations from the newspapers." Again in April 1934 Hess was driven to issue an order (never obeyed) that Reichsleiters "must inform [him] on all questions of special concern to the Party," and that "all significant ordinances . . . must be submitted without fail prior to their promulgation."

Instead of showing him the deference he craved, the Gauleiters treated him with a kind of condescending familiarity. They all reported directly to Hitler and never bothered with orders emanating from Reichsleiters except when they were useful to them. Amt Hess and its Stabsleiter annoyed them chiefly because any complaints or requests they wished to submit to Reich ministries or the Reich Chancellery now had to go over Bormann's desk. In practice they always circumvented this, and even ten years later, Bormann had to needle them into compliance. By December 1934 they went so far as to call a Gauleiter conference in Berlin on their own so they could meet without any supervision from the Brown House.

Bormann heard about it only after it had happened, and he succeeded in arousing Hitler's fury over this overt insubordination. In a circular Hess told them in no uncertain terms: "No Reichsleiter and certainly no Gauleiter has the right to call a conference on his own initiative or to conduct business with agencies of the Reich government without my permission."

And that was in fact the last time the provincial bosses, even small groups of them, were to meet without a summons from above. Their meetings which had been fairly autonomous became merely occasions for receiving orders; Bormann, always in charge, nipped in the bud any attempt at discussion. That is how the Führer wanted it after he was enraged by some rambunctious backtalk from one Martin Mutschmann, Gauleiter of Saxony. Moreover, it was carefully spelled out to whom the Gauleiters were to defer to in the future. Immediately after their meeting they got a questionnaire from Bormann which they had to fill out each month from then on. This "Report on Activity and Morale" called for information ranging from Item 1, "Organizational Questions," to Item 42, "Particular Incidents." However, the "subjugation" of the Gauleiters was never accomplished in Hess's time. Not until the last convulsions of World War II would they finally if unwillingly dance to Bormann's tune. But that was a short-lived triumph.

Bormann continued to try to act as a spokesman for Hitler at the Party summit. In the fall of 1933, he informed a meeting of Reich state governors that they were forbidden to engage in any public discussion of possible changes in the territorial divisions of the Reich, because they would inevitably get into a fight.

At the same time, he sent out a circular stating that the highest circles deemed it undesirable that veteran Party members attempt to form an elite corps. He was not at all bothered by the fact that he was thereby directing a blow at his own father-in-law; Supreme Party Judge Buch had for a long time been working hard on this very plan because he wanted a counterpoise in the party itself to Hitler's all-powerful despotism. In February 1934

Bormann not only chaired the Gauleiter conference in Berlin, but was picked to draft the Party's official protocol for Hitler's speech. The man singled out for such duties—as Bormann was more and more often—could no longer be ignored.

Moreover, there were times when the Gauleiters needed to cooperate with him. In the never-resolved dispute over which took precedence, the party or the state, the Gauleiters and Bormann found themselves in the same camp. Hitler felt no need to get involved; he was boss, no matter what, as Führer, as Chancellor and later as head of state. So the argument was essentially over whether the more radical Party officeholders or the more conservative civil servants in the government were to have the last word in decisions at the lower levels. At the 1934 Party Rally, Hitler gave the impression that he had decided the question when, before 200,000 cheering employees of the Party Organization, he announced: "It is not the state that commands us, it is we who command the state." This was instantly interpreted by leaders of the local Party groups to mean that now they could tell the mayors what to do. But in practice the guerrilla skirmishes between them continued unabated.

Although civil servants from Reich ministers down to office clerks hastened to join the NSDAP, and Jews and political adversaries were ousted from government posts, the spirit of National Socialism made only feeble headway in the government agencies. When Bormann took spot checks in individual departments, he discovered to his annoyance that in the police headquarters in Prussia the "Old Party Members" made up a mere 10 percent of the senior civil servants.

After Hindenburg's death, when Hitler became head of state in addition to everything else, all civil servants came under his ultimate jurisdiction. Without his signature no one in the higher ranks could be hired or promoted. Amt Hess was given the task of assessing the political reliability of such candidates. Bormann's circulars to the local Party organizations that checked on individuals made it clear to the Gauleiters exactly what was expected of them and what their options were. "In handling civil-service appointments I have to depend almost entirely on the cooperation of the Gauleiters," Bormann explained. He suggested that it would therefore be useful to keep a file on all civil servants in the Gauleiters' offices.

National Socialist Reich ministers did not see why individuals they favored had to have Bormann's seal of approval. Reich Propaganda Minister Joseph Goebbels, who was Gauleiter and Reichsleiter as well, refused to allow Party members in his ministry to accuse their colleagues of lack of Party loyalty. He made it known that whoever he hired had been adequately checked out, and that anyone who informed against anyone else in the office would be fired.

Goebbels could afford to take such a stand because he was in a strong position on both the government and the Party level. He could look with amusement at Bormann's exertions to get more clout for the Party (and incidentally for the Party Minister's Stabsleiter).

In February 1936 Bormann accused Otto Meissner, chief of the Presidential Chancellery and one of the most senior bureaucrats in the government, of disrespect for the Party. The charge was particularly grave because Meissner made civil-service appointments. Bormann was not, however, taking much of a risk; Meissner had had the same position under Presidents Hindenburg and Ebert, and he was considered something of an opportunist in Party circles. His department had drawn up an official list of precedence for German dignitaries, to determine how they were to be invited and placed on state occasions. Bormann discovered that in Meissner's order of precedence "leaders of the Party . . . were ranked, if at all, in a way that was utterly out of keeping with the Party's image with the public."

Bormann lodged his complaint in a "Strictly Confidential" letter which was hand-carried to Wilhelm Frick, who managed the administration's bureaucracy. He also sent copies to a carefully screened list of Party bigwigs, hoping to marshal a broad front of similarly outraged Nazi brass. Most of them reacted tepidly, however; they had no desire to give Bormann a leg-up in his power play, and some even tried to harness him to ploys of their own. Reichsleiter and German Labor Front chief Robert Ley, for example, went along with the intrigue by pronouncing Meissner's order of precedence "an insult and a provocation to the NSDAP" and asking Bormann to intervene with "all the necessary pressure." But he also took the opportunity to suggest that certain Reichsleiters ought to be sacked because, considering the dwindling importance of their departments, they no longer merited the dignity of the title.

The briefest and most sensible response came from Goebbels. Bormann, addressed as "Dear Party Comrade," was informed that the Reich Propaganda Directorate of the Party and the Reich Ministry for Public Enlightenment and Propaganda had long had its own "ranking order," according to which Party people "were assigned their proper position, beginning with Reichsleiters and Reich ministers in alternate succession." Nevertheless, Goebbels' letter continued, he was "very much interested in having all these questions straightened out soonest." There was not a word of censure of Meissner or any encouragement of a joint protest. In Goebbels' eyes, Bormann was merely a stupid Party primitive with whom no man of reputation and character would ally himself. And indeed the affair worked out as Goebbels had foreseen: Meissner quietly adapted his list to the new order, stayed in office and a year later was promoted by Hitler to Reich minister.

Inspired by fear that the state was getting too powerful and might crowd out the Party, Bormann produced a nineteen-page "Memorandum regarding the Establishment and Position of a Reich Sport Flying Corps and State

Youth." He maintained that "according to strict orders from the Party Directorate" (for which read Amt Hess) it was no longer proper for "individual officers of the NSDAP to give orders to individual civil servants," yet civil-service officers "still seem to be making a deliberate effort to avoid cooperating with the Party." Recently, in fact, it had been "almost impossible for the National Socialist Movement to proceed with the political education and guidance of the German people" because civil-service officers insisted on taking over areas "that are the Movement's responsibility."

Then in typical German officialese, he delivered himself of what was really on his mind. Were one to believe him, the very existence of the Party was at stake; government agencies were siphoning off the Party's young talent. "Since the German is *a priori* a soldier," the best young men joined the army while others went into the Labor Service, railway police, postal guards, customs, Reich Air Defense League. Many of those who were left had professional obligations, duties as officers of various groups and associations, or interests in sports and cultural pursuits that left them no time for the Party.

And as if that were not enough, the German Labor Service retained its hold on those who had finished their term of duty with the Arbeitsdank-Verband, as the army did with its reservists in the Soldatenbund, and the navy in the Marinebund. "The notion that joining these organizations is purely voluntary exists only on paper; anyone who does not want to get a bad reputation, anyone wanting to be promoted" must join.

Now—and here was the crux of Bormann's concern—instead of finding out "whether all these organizations are really necessary," there were plans to create two more: the Reich Youth Leader of the NSDAP was organizing a "State Youth," an opposite number to the Hitler Jugend (of which he was head), and Air Transport Minister Göring wanted to set up a Reich Sport Flying Corps as a state-run paramilitary formation. According to Bormann, a "State Youth" was unnecessary because in a few years 90 percent of all ten-to-eighteen-year-olds would be in the Hitler Jugend anyway. Furthermore, it was absurd because it would assign the actual work of training youth in National Socialism to government officials and employees, who "are quite incapable of performing this task."

Göring's plan was even more pernicious. He insisted that any young man who hoped to join the Luftwaffe must first have been a member of his Reich Sport Flying Corps. Bormann held that members of such an organization would no longer be able to take part in "the political life of the nation. The army and the navy would try to play the same game." And as a result, Bormann bleated in his conclusion: "The fate of the very existence of the NSDAP—and this is no exaggeration—would be doomed."

No one knows who got copies of this memorandum; certainly not Göring or Schirach, but undoubtedly many big shots in the Party did. Since everyone in the inner circle was fiercely jealous of anyone else's expanding his domain, Bormann could be sure of the support of those who stood to forfeit something to the new organizations. That was the real reason behind his protest. The more Amt Hess asserted its claim to be the clearing house for all Party agencies, the more it had to protect itself against the encroachment of the state and strive to acquire an influence over the government apparatus.

In the spring of 1936 Bormann should have had no difficulty handing the memorandum to Hitler personally; he was already his financial manager, construction superintendent and discreet confidential clerk. Nevertheless, this piece of bureaucratic draftsmanship must have earned him little more than the indulgent forbearance one might extend to well-intentioned but simple-minded servants. Hitler was not the man to be impressed by such banal plotting. A year later Göring got his flying corps. It was not quite as grandiose as what he had had in mind, but it was independent of the Party and reported only to the Ministry for Air Transport. Schirach's wish was also granted: the State Youth was legally established that December. It turned out to be nothing but a Hitler Jugend beefed up by government authority. And despite Bormann's dire prophecies, the Party remained unscathed. The organizations increased—but that had always been one of Hitler's most effective ploys when he wanted to play his paladins off against one another. At the time, Schirach and Göring were his favorites. The envious saw the former as a possible successor to the Führer; the latter, who had been promoted straight from ex-captain to general and chief of the Luftwaffe, was heading for control of German industry and appointment to Number Two man in the government.

Bormann knew of course what he was getting into when he sent out the memorandum—even greater hostility from two men who had never cared much for him in the first place. Did he take this upon himself because he wanted to protect the Party—and, as he saw it, Germany—from harm? Or did he hope to apply the brakes to the careers of the two court favorites and accelerate his own? But the most important thing to him was to prove himself the guardian of the true Party doctrine, in the spirit of his immediate superior.

With the same recklessness and puritanical fanaticism, he drew a bead on three men in Hitler's permanent entourage. They were the Führer's adjutants, ex-Captain Fritz Wiedemann, SA Obergruppenführer Wilhelm Brückner and SS Brigadeführer Julius Schaub, all-purpose companions from way back. A short while before, the Duke of Coburg had honored them with a decoration his family had traditionally been entitled to confer. Bormann heard about it by chance in the Reich Chancellery mess hall. A man in his office was immediately dispatched to deliver them "on behalf of the Reichsleiter . . . for your information," copies of a 1933 Hess ordinance prohibiting Party members "from accepting decorations as a reward for services in Germany's Revolution and the like." Since Brückner had distinguished himself chiefly by his enormous bulk, and Schaub had more experience waging bar fights than formulating a cogent statement, Wiedemann took on the job of composing a reply. He wrote that he had asked Hitler's prior permission and Hitler had allowed "myself, Brückner and Schaub to accept the decoration."

Bormann did not give up that easily. He wrote back by return mail that his action was not aimed at the adjutants, and he had always assumed Hitler knew about it. However, "erstwhile potentates" had long been prohibited from handing out "decorations." This ruling had become necessary, Bormann wrote, because the duke "had promptly distributed a great number of additional decorations." Even "Gruppenführer Ernst, since executed by a firing squad," had worn one. The reason why good National Socialists should pass up such "honors" as a matter of principle was explained in two paragraphs, which are here quoted verbatim as characteristic of Bormann's style and way of operating.

> We take the position that in this day and age it is sheer presumptuousness if an erstwhile potentate thinks he still has the prerogative of handing out decorations. The assumption behind this privilege can be traced to none other than the divine right of our former monarchs. Furthermore, we take the position that it is out of the question that the so-called "family" decorations of these erstwhile potentates should be bestowed on officers in the NSDAP. The badge we should strive for is the intensity of our commitment on Germany's behalf, above and beyond all other fellow countrymen's, and if anyone award us a decoration, it can only be the Führer. If the former Duke of Coburg considers himself entitled to decorate an SA Gruppenführer, he must feel that he stands above that Gruppenführer, and by parallel reasoning, the Gruppenführer will consider the duke of higher station than himself. And ultimately such an erstwhile potentate might come to believe that since he had been able to decorate the Führer's highest-ranking lieutenants, that places him on a par with the Führer, or even higher!

Wiedemann refrained from pursuing the matter; he put the letter in his out-basket marked "For the files." A couple of weeks later he was back in Bormann's field of fire. At a Reichsleiter conference in Munich some of the officials objected to having SA Chief of Staff Lutze referred to in print as "Chief of Staff to the Führer." Lutze refused to be censured; he pointed out that it was not he who had usurped that title, but that the Führer's adjutants' office had recently begun to use it. Bormann sent Wiedemann a registered letter marked "Personal" warning: "I must ask you most urgently to see to it that use of this designation is discontinued" because "first of all it is inaccurate, and second, for that very reason, has provoked a lot of resentment." As this letter is also typical of the Party apparatchik, some passages are quoted:

> If Party Member Lutze is designated Chief of Staff to the Führer, that would signify that he is Chief of Staff in all the Führer's domains of activity; that is, Party Member Lutze would be Chief of Staff of not only the SA but also of the whole Party, and all that goes with it; moreover, Adolf Hitler is also the Führer for the Labor Service and the army! Furthermore, were this factually incorrect designation to be used, we would see countless other designations and titles with "to the Führer" tacked on! For find me the National Socialist who does not want to be something or other "to the Führer"? Every SA man could style himself "SA man to the Führer," every SS man, every NSKK man, every political leader, etc., as well. Reichsführer Himmler and Korpsführer Hühnlein in particular are opposed to this designation, because it creates the impression that they in turn have given up some of their own independence again, and rank below Party Comrade Lutze as Chief of Staff to the Führer.

In the last paragraph of the letter Wiedemann is once again warned to correct the error. "If you do that," Bormann hinted heavy-handedly, "then will not have to bother the Führer." His secretary evidently garbled this sentence, which of course should have read "then I will not have to bother the Führer."

Bormann was to provoke encounters like this with the adjutants more and more often. It galled him that their immediate access to Hitler allowed them to introduce individuals and documents that interfered with his plans. Wiedemann was the easiest of the lot to impress; he had won no Party honors when the Führer made him adjutant. Hitler and Wiedemann had known each other in the war, when Officer Fritz Wiedemann was regimental adjutant and Hitler, a dispatch runner, used to have to click his heels and stand at attention before him. Now the ex-corporal made the ex-captain kowtow to him. Wiedemann had resigned himself to this, but he was sick and tired of Party intrigues. Shortly before the outbreak of World War II he asked to be relieved. He was appointed consul general in San Francisco.

The documents quoted frequently in this book rarely make for entertaining reading. However, Martin Bormann and his legendary rise to power can be explained only by written testimony. He was never the hero of dramatic scenes; he never stood in the limelight. He deliberately remained in the shadow of a bigger man. Thick-set, with a broad back and hunched shoulders, his round head bent slightly forward on a short, thick neck, he was always in a servant role, first on the German stage and soon on the stage of world history. Figures like him are easily overlooked. Some found him a typical sergeant major—in fact, that is how he saw himself: top sergeant to the nation under Company Commander Hitler. Among the Nazi top brass there were few who did not go out of their way to avoid him.

Of course, there were exceptions. Ernst Hanfstaengl, NSDAP foreign-press chief, wrote in his memoirs: "He was orderly, modest and frugal, and in my view a good influence. He and Hess battled tirelessly against corruption in the Party."

It is true that Bormann did not participate in the wholesale amassing of personal wealth after the takeover. Wherever he fought it, however, he worried less about moral issues than what it did to the Party's public image. When he heard about a crooked deal, he often just filed a document in the steel cabinets of the Brown House—to be retrieved when needed. The frugality Hanfstaengl praised was a rare virtue among the Party elite, and Hanfstaengl had reasons of his own to appreciate it; scion of a wealthy family, he had often advanced money to the Party during the *Kampfzeit*. Later he was criticized by Party members for being avaricious when he wanted it back.

He could observe Bormann's activities only up to 1937, however, because he left Germany that year. The Party said he left because he could not take a joke. According to Hanfstaengl, it was because they tried to kill him. Bormann was part of the attempt to lure him back because he knew so many Party secrets. He sent a letter to "Putzi" couched in the tone of a well-disposed superior (Hanfstaengl's department was under Amt Hess), promising to restore his confiscated fortune, forget all the legal penalties he had incurred and even refund him the expenses of his stay abroad, as soon as he returned to Germany. If Bormann thought he would catch his former department head through cupidity, he was wrong. Hanfstaengl did not go back until after the war. Bormann was not grateful to him for his good opinion of him. During the war Hanfstaengl anecdotes still caused general merriment at the nightly "table talks" at Führer Headquarters. Every time Hitler told some, Bormann would add a few more.

Baldur von Schirach's judgment of Bormann is more discriminating:

At first we Reichsleiters had no reason to complain about Bormann. He dealt with matters needing Hitler's attention more quickly than Hess, who was always vague and slow. Originally Hess was supposed to be present at every conference between Hitler and the Party leaders, but he soon passed that duty on to Bormann. From then on, whether Hitler was in Berlin, Munich or Obersalzberg, without Bormann there would be no conference. He would pretend to be your good friend, innocent of any self-serving, who represented the interests of the Party leaders. It took quite a while before I saw through him and realized how dangerous he was.

When the Nazi agricultural expert, Reich Minister of Food and Reich Leader of the Peasantry Richard Walter Darré was interned by the Allies after the war, he wrote character sketches of the top Nazis for them under the pen name "Merkel." Of Bormann he said:

> His personality was an unreconciled mixture of personal ambition, hunger for power, pragmatism in questions of organization and administration, including money management, and a pronounced inferiority complex because of his subordinate position. As a cold-blooded gambler on his own behalf he resembled Stalin, i.e., he recognized the merit of a rigid party dictatorship and systematically built up the Party accordingly. Hitler was the beginning and the end of his work, and except for temporary alliances of convenience, he was not interested in winning support from anyone else.

Darré neglected to mention that he himself once entered into an alliance of convenience with Bormann. Darré had at the time created a department for "race and resettlement" policy, following the slogan that the peasantry was the nation's treasury of racial strength. Inevitably this impinged upon the private Nordic preserve of SS Reichsführer Himmler. After his commercial failure as a chicken breeder, Himmler elected to become a breeder of human beings, a problem he solved in his own way. Darré, like anyone in the Party's office for agricultural policy, or anyone who had something important to say about the peasantry, was given honorary rank in the SS. At first he liked it, but soon he felt boxed in by black uniforms. Knowing that Himmler and Bormann mistrusted each other, he came to Bormann for help. Bormann was a chain-smoker in those days, and as a permanent reminder of their alliance, Darré gave him a cigarette case. At the end of March 1935, after a long private conversation with Darré, Bormann recounted in a handwritten letter to "Dear Darré" that "this evening I went home with joy in my heart, since God knows present conditions demand close cooperation between National Socialists." From now on, Bormann suggested, they should see each other more often "to assess the situation," or else "you may feel the same way about a certain person that I do, but for the sake of expediency you might want to stroke him as the ant strokes the aphid while I am doing the very opposite!" (See Appendix, page 390.)

Grateful for such cooperation, on the 7th day of Scheiding, 1935 [neo-Germanic for September] Darré made "Agriculturist Martin Bormann, Reichsleiter of the NSDAP," a "regular (i.e., lifetime) member of the Reich Peasantry Council." This was an affiliation that, aside from a membership document, a numbered badge and a ceremonial oath-taking in the Goslar

Palatinate, must have meant so little to the recipient (who had already "arrived") that Darré felt he had to sweeten it by making him a member of the organization's Court of Honor besides. Yet according to his report for the Allies, late in 1935 he had by pure chance discovered "that all the threads of political intrigue came together in Bormann. For the first time I noticed that Bormann passed [ultimate] judgment on leading personalities in Berlin." Having learned this, Darré did the stupidest thing imaginable: "I warned Himmler first of all, and he was taken aback."

In his political innocence it never crossed Darré's mind why the Reichsführer SS and head of the entire German police force should have been taken aback. Bormann and Himmler had as little love for each other as ever, but they had found they could be useful to each other. For a year, an order from Hess had prohibited offices of Party agencies from spying on and keeping files on their countrymen; this was exclusively the business of the SD, the Security Service of the SS. Many Gauleiters ignored the regulation, and some even forbade their political officers to cooperate with the SD; they wanted to avoid any dependency on the high-riding local SS dignitaries, rightly suspecting that these characters were shadowing the Party big shots too and would include damaging evidence about them in their reports to the SS. Bormann's ordinance in mid-February 1935 directing the Party Organization "henceforth to cease all mistrust of the SD" was therefore grist for Himmler's mill. The ruling continued: "Since the SD's work benefits the Party, its operation must not be hampered by subjective opposition by individuals such as refusal of cooperation, but should rather be encouraged with all due effort."

The two men drew closer together during Hitler's triumphal tour through the Saar, which had opted for return to the Reich by plebiscite in March 1935. Now it was Himmler's turn to bestow a token of "friendship" (in the case of these two, it is necessary to add quotation marks to the very end). He took Bormann to visit strategic points in the empire he was building for himself. Verden an der Aller was the first stop. Here Charlemagne, whom the SS called the "slayer of Saxons," had reportedly had several thousand Germanic nobles massacred for their rebelliousness, and a memorial was to mark the ancient atrocity.

The next day Bormann and Himmler examined a contemporary atrocity; they visited the SS-operated concentration camp at Esterwegen. The climax of the tour was a visit to Wewelsburg, south of Paderborn, where the Reichsführer planned to establish the main research center on Germanic tribes. In September, Bormann reciprocated by issuing an ordinance directing the political leaders to cooperate with the Gestapo if anyone was heard criticizing the Party and make sure that such "impertinent" individuals would land in a concentration camp. The following May he offered a special attraction to the Reichsleiters and Gauleiters attending the conference he was chairing in Munich; together with Himmler he took them on a tour of the Dachau concentration camp, hitherto off limits to even the highest ranks in the Party. In Dachau "at that time everything was in good order. The prisoners were well fed, well clad and well housed," as Rudolf Höss, who then wrote up the camp reports, later recalled—the same Höss who had been Bormann's accomplice and fellow defendant in the Parchim murder. After several years in jail he was given amnesty and became a career soldier in the SS Death's Head units. He had a cordial conversation with his two well-wishers, the Reichsleiter and the Reichsführer, and soon after, thanks to a warm recommendation by Bormann, he could sew a third star on his collar to mark his promotion to SS Untersturmführer (second lieutenant).

At the time, the Bormann-Himmler alliance was not perfect, but everyone knew they were working together. Darré, gullible and ineffectual in day-to-day political infighting, first noticed the relationship on New Year's Day, 1937, when he visited the Himmlers and ran into Bormann's whole family, who had been driven over to reinforce the "friendship." A month later Bormann was appointed SS Gruppenführer. Darré's influence continued to diminish until during the war, when he lost even his Reich minister's post—to a Himmler man.

According to Darré, he also warned Reich Party Treasurer Schwarz about Bormann, and was laughed at for his pains. Perhaps the Party's top moneyman distrusted him because he was known to be friend of Bormann's. Hans Frank, then Reichsleiter of the Party Rechtsamt (Department of Justice) and head of the Rechtswahrerbund (League for the Preservation of Justice), in which judges, lawyers, state prosecutors and public notaries were brainwashed into good National Socialists, said that back in 1935 Schwarz had told him in confidence, "Bormann is the most pernicious egotist around and an enemy of the old Party. I wouldn't put it past him to have them all killed someday—à la Stalin." However, Frank was not an unprejudiced witness; Bormann intrigued against him for years and finally got him fired. When they first met, Frank, an ace lawyer and Hitler's defense counsel, might scarcely have noticed the low-ranking Party hack in an insignificant job until Bormann stole Heim from his firm. As Frank describes it, "Bormann hated me from the very depths of his being, a mutual revulsion which was to cause me untold suffering."

Frank brought the vendetta upon himself because after 1933 he repeatedly tried to make the Reichsleiters the leading body in the Party capable of imposing boundaries on Hitler's omnipotence. He therefore refused to recognize Amt Hess as a higher authority. He failed to notice that Hitler did not want a truly functioning body of Reichsleiters that might interfere with him and never really understood that Hitler basically despised all jurists and their laws because he alone was to decide what was right and did not want to have to bother about any law.

Bormann could be certain that his Führer would never interfere with his own operation of checkmating the Reichsleiters. Bormann's method was simple and resourceful. He set up sections in his office for certain domains, ostensibly to serve as liaison with the various offices of the Reichsleitung. Frank, who would have liked to control the entire legislative process was the first to realize what their real job was. "More and more lawyers were added to the staff," he complained, "and Bormann created his own department of justice . . . By the end of 1933 the Reich Party Law Office had been rendered completely powerless." In the cases of other Reich Party offices, it took a little longer before Bormann's rival bureaucracy was operational, but nearly all of them were eventually successfully crowded out.

Before paying the death penalty he accepted as just, while he was in jail in Nuremberg, Frank wrote his memoirs, *In Sight of the Gallows.* Here he gave full vent to his hatred of Bormann. He accused him of ruining the Führer and corrupting the Great Idea, heaping upon him such epithets as "Hitler's lackey," "boot-licking slave," "Secretary Wurm" (referring to the villain in Schiller's drama *Cabal and Love*), "arch-scoundrel."

"Boot-licking slave," though only part of the picture, is close to the mark. There is a photograph (see Illustrations) by Heinrich Hoffmann showing the Führer seated and some of his court standing in front of him. Closest of all to him is Martin Bormann. Hitler is talking. All the faces show close attention, but Bormann's face and stance betray an ecstatic devotion normally seen only at religious services and the look of prostrate subjugation regularly observed among the participants in Hitler's mass meetings. The solid figure in Reichsleiter uniform, already running to fat, Hitler's ideal Party man: fanatic and unconditionally devoted. He possessed "the mixture of slimy sincerity and cold viciousness" that Klaus Mann, who served in a United States Army propaganda unit at the end of the war, found to be true of so many Nazis.

The Stabsleiter who perhaps just a moment before had stomped through his office in his jackboots, roaring threats at the slightest provocation, could, in Hitler's presence, instantly transform himself into the boot-licking slave. Obsequiously he would present his file of documents all complete and in perfect order, ready for a decision. He never forgot that it was only in his first weeks as Chancellor that his boss had disciplined himself to work at a desk at all and that he had always hated to work systematically on papers. Now at least on Party matters, faithful Bormann—dependable, selfless, always well informed and able to give a concise explanation—did it for him. He carried a note pad and pencil at all times. Every order, every question, even every passing remark was noted down. Should Hitler in the course of the briefing request information about some event or individual, Bormann's staff would be alerted by a note from their boss and even in the middle of the night would get to the phone and the teletype machine to come up with the answer. A parenthetical phrase, a thought of the Führer's casually thrown out in conversation would be recorded with the date and precise wording, and might blossom into a completely formulated directive. No request was too trivial; if Hitler expressed interest in a book, it would appear on his desk the next day. The difficult assignments Bormann attacked with dogged persistence.

In the summer of 1934, while Hindenburg was fading away at his Neudeck estate and Hitler needed to know when the end could be expected, Bormann was told to produce the attending physician, Dr. Ferdinand Sauerbruch, immediately and in complete secrecy. After hasty phone calls and orders to hold up express trains in defiance of timetables, Bormann managed to bring the doctor to Bayreuth, where Hitler was listening to Wagner.

Baldur von Schirach observed that even at the lunch table in the Reich Chancellery, Bormann had his note pad on his lap, "all ears and all scribbling" as he took down the Führer's words. Asked why he did it, Bormann explained that his notes served him as a guideline. "Then we know that the Führer said thus and so on that day, and we can take a proper compass reading." Hitler's pronouncements were classified in a card file of cue phrases. He changed his mind so often that some of the entries were contradictory, and Bormann in his directives could choose whichever suited him. Whenever there was a rumble of criticism from the Party big shots, Bormann got his cards out of the safe and garnered special praise from Hitler, who was convinced of his own infallibility. With his enormous capacity for work, industriousness and phenomenal memory, Bormann had made himself indispensable within a few months. So willing and capable a worker must inevitably move on to tasks of greater moment.

7

Idyll at Obersalzberg

When the Führer spent the night in Schloss Grevenburg near Detmold during the fateful provincial elections in Lippe only seven weeks before the takeover, his adjutant Brückner, who paid the bills, had no idea where to find the money. There was no point asking Hitler, who never had a pfennig and thought it beneath his dignity to bother about finances. Otto Dietrich, a journalist acting as Reich Press Chief for the Party, finally bailed them out. Once again Dietrich had found a backer. Hitler boasted later that during that crisis he had signed great quantities of promissory notes, fully aware that he could pay them off only if he became Chancellor soon. Had he failed, all would have been lost, he would say—not only the money, but Germany too.

Six months later, Hitler still carried no wallet and no change in his pocket, but he had more than 100 million marks at his disposal which did not have to be accounted for to anyone. On the initiative of steel magnate Gustav Krupp von Bohlen und Halbach, the Reich Association of German Industry and the League of German Employers' Associations decided that an extraordinarily generous cash present to the new Reich Chancellor would help to make the point that National Socialists must refrain from slaughtering the cow they expected to go on giving milk. Big business set up a "German Industry's Adolf Hitler Fund," which called for employers to make quarterly contributions based on their payroll. Hitler was pleased to accept this permanent flood of millions. He made it known that he would use the money primarily to promote cultural affairs and supply relief to old comrades who had fallen on hard days through no fault of their own. He would not consider the money his property, therefore it should not be managed by either his adjutants or his personal office. Artistic people like himself should have nothing to do with filthy lucre, or they would lose their freedom. Before he came into office, he used to tell the world that he was not struggling simply for bread and butter. To maintain the image of frugality, the millions had to be assigned to someone who was known to be aboveboard and incorruptible.

Many of the "old fighters" had joined the Party only because they had failed in civilian life. There were not many of them who knew how to handle money and could be trusted with it. Hess, for many years the Führer's secretary who had also taken care of his financial affairs, seemed ideal, except that the staggering sums involved were a little too much for his Puritanical soul. Fortunately he had a Stabsleiter who was experienced in handling money, utterly trustworthy, a demon for work, discreet, and, by his office, already close to the Führer. So Hess was officially appointed fund administrator, but the real dragon guarding the hoard was Bormann.

Hitler had always kept his wallet hidden by this kind of camouflage. Party comrades had always wondered what he lived on. In 1921 Rudolf Hess, then a student, assured Bavarian Prime Minister Gustav von Kahr in a letter: "Herr H.," whom he knew well, was sacrificing himself to the general welfare "in a selfless way, never taking a penny for it. He lives on lecture fees."

Hitler was not quite so penniless as propaganda made him out to be. On his 1933 tax return he declared an income of 1,232,335 Reichsmarks apart from the 60,000-mark Chancellor's salary he first refused to draw but finally accepted, at the Treasury's insistence—to say nothing of the millions in the Adolf Hitler Fund. Moreover, it was a gross-for-net income situation, because when on the basis of it he received a tax return to file he evidently felt he was doing more than his share for the Fatherland and refused to pay a single cent, and arranged to have himself ruled exempt for life. Karl Anders, a journalist who covered the Nuremberg Trials, collected records of Hitler's personal expenditures and established that in the twelve years of his dictatorship, Hitler had disposed of 305 million Reichsmarks. Anders assumed that many millions more had been spent by Party and state to fulfill the Führer's private wishes.

No one asked any questions as to what became of the money in the Adolf Hitler Fund. Schirach recalled: "Whenever Hitler needed money for something, Bormann always paid, even for gifts for Eva Braun." Painters and sculptors, of course, got commissions, although only if they produced honest-to-goodness Aryan German art. Party big shots and government servants were rewarded with vast sums, and as the word got around that Bormann kept the key to the cashbox, he was carefully courted by such people, especially when they found themselves in debt. Frau Winifred Wagner wrote him letters soliciting and thanking him for money; he also not only sent her Hitler's contributions to the Bayreuth festivals, he financed a team of researchers commissioned to certify that Richard Wagner's father was not Jewish, as had been alleged. The directors of many opera houses got generous contributions for spectacular productions of *Die Fledermaus* and *The Merry Widow,* since the Führer loved these operettas almost more than he did the heroic music dramas of the Bayreuth master.

In 1938 Bormann bought Hitler the house in Munich on Prinzregenten-platz where he lived as a tenant, and paid for it out of the privy purse. High prices were disbursed from the Adolf Hitler Fund for the paintings Hitler hung on the walls. These were supposed to be donated to museums later on but it is an open question just how much this would have done for the museums. However, it was no concern of Bormann's. The master chose, and Bormann made out the check. It was all the same to him whether it was a Makart, a Spitzweg, or something by Party Comrade Ziegler, whom even the Nazis called "the master of German pubic hair."

The Dragon Hoard was a continual irritation to Treasurer Schwarz. Since he had to meet the payroll for all full-time executives and employees of the Reichsleitung, he had hitherto been able to object to any financial arrangements in excess of the budget. Now he was complaining: "I have no idea where they get their money from. My auditors are not allowed to show their faces there." Bormann could expand his office at will because he could always pay salaries out of the Adolf Hitler Fund if he had to. Schwarz no longer had the power to apply the brakes when Hitler demanded colossal sums for some project, because he knew Bormann would not hesitate to give it to him. When Austria was taken over in the Anschluss, Hitler grandly promised the Gauleiter of Linz that he would make the city where he had lived for part of his youth into a world metropolis that would compete with Vienna. There was to be a splendid office building for the Party, an assembly hall for meetings and ceremonies, and so on. By his own account, Bormann later said at one of the table talks that he had spontaneously offered to make the necessary funds available. But since Schwarz had meanwhile decided to finance the projects, Hitler did not need to accept Bormann's offer. Nevertheless, he appreciated it.

This anecdote is significant; it shows the complete independence with which Bormann could dispose of millions of marks. After all, he was only offering money that belonged to Hitler anyway. So what was all the fuss about? Why did his offer of the money meet with such appreciation? Was it because he had been carried away by one of Hitler's pet projects? Or because he could read in Hitler's eyes what he wanted? It is possible that Hitler found the episode especially gratifying because it enabled him once again to play off two of the faithful against each other. The clever Bormann fellow, with his quick offer which in the end cost Hitler nothing, had euchred huge sums of Party money out of the niggardly Schwarz.

Hitler also had a way of handing out money without consulting his private banker. He went to the Augsburg City Theater in 1935, found it in poor repair and told the local Gauleiter: "Wahl, we'll rebuild it and make it better than before. I'll assume the expense." The expense came to some million marks, and Bormann paid, as always. And once he got going, Hitler also sketched a plan for a new city center, a second theater, a Party palace, an assembly hall, a showpiece boulevard—to the tune of 140 million Reichsmarks. The project was to be the responsibility of the Augsburg municipal government, which, however, had no way of raising that much money. It had nothing to go on but a passing remark of Hitler's that he would take care of the financing. He may later have regretted his generous offer, or Bormann, who had always considered Wahl too lax, may have contrived an intrigue—the details are past finding out. In any event, it all blew up when the burgomaster of Augsburg humbly asked Hitler for a commitment in writing before the work began. Albert Speer says Bormann presented the request on the Berghof terrace in a mock detached tone and promptly reaped the outburst of fury he had deliberately provoked: "Isn't it enough that I give him my name as a guarantee?"

"Wahl has always been a jerk; now he's letting himself be talked into something by that damn fool burgomaster." The Gauleiter got a telex from Bormann: "By the Führer's order, Oberbürgermeister Mayer is to be removed immediately and replaced by someone with more initiative."

Actually, it did not come to that. Wahl managed to conciliate the Führer.

Whoever has his hand on the till has it on everything is a truism that the pursekeeper to the most powerful man in Germany must have noted early on. For this very reason he was anxious to keep the treasury well filled at all times. He instructed the various Gauleiter headquarters to make sure that legacies, which Hitler received now and then from citizens who remembered him in their will, got channeled to the proper place, i.e., to him. Until then Reichsleiter Max Amann, the official Party publisher, had settled book royalties with Hitler every six months in a private tête-à-tête he always exploited for special privileges. Now Bormann collected the money, which was steadily increasing, since the marriage registry offices were now presenting *Mein Kampf* to newlyweds at the town's expense, and new volumes of Hitler's speeches were always appearing.

Speer has described how Hitler got royalties in fractions of a pfennig for each postage stamp bearing his image. Hitler stamps first appeared in the spring of 1937. A Munich art professor drew the original from a Hoffmann photograph. And Hoffmann, who held exclusive rights to the Hitler pictures, made sure he got a large fee. Bormann was not about to let such a source of revenue get out of his control.

Still, it cannot come to as much as Speer says, because before World War II the Hitler profile appeared mostly on stamps promoting public charities, which were issued in small printings. Not until 1941 was the Führer's likeness put on stamps of all denominations and in permanent series. And by then Bormann no longer needed to go after little fish. He could help himself from the government treasury at will. Hitler, the all-or-nothing gambler, no longer worried about a few billions—he believed then as before that a victory would cancel out all debts, and in case of defeat, all would be lost anyway. So even in the last years of the war Bormann could go on spending millions on the most exorbitant of all his projects, Obersalzberg.

It had begun in a small way. In 1925 Hitler, just out of prison, wanted to get away from his strife-ridden following and let them stew awhile in their own hostile juices. So he rented a cottage in the remote Bavarian village of Obersalzberg over three thousand feet above Berchtesgaden. Haus Wachenfeld was a vacation home built by a business lawyer from Buxtehude near Hamburg.

When Hitler bought the property and filed title in the name of his half-sister Angela Raubal, it was a modest country house in Bavarian style with the typical wooden balcony on the upper floor and a shingle roof weighted down with rocks. After the takeover it was shown this way on postcards for the public captioned "The little cottage of the People's Chancellor." Bormann was assigned to adapt it to the new situation.

At this point the quiet mountain village of Obersalzberg was drawn into the turmoil of world politics. The beginning was harmless enough, even idyllic. Germans made mass pilgrimage on fine summer days to what the Munich Gauleiter called the "Holy Mountain of the Germans." When their beloved Führer was in residence, he would come to the meadow, wave cheerfully and cordially, and suffer his enthralled countrymen to walk past him in long queues. This created a need for permanent housing for a detail of SS and police guards, and barracks were built. But what about accommodations for Hitler's guests?

Rooms needed to be added for Eva Braun, Hitler's mistress since 1932, so that she could stay in the house without drawing attention to herself. An architect named Delgado was brought in to rebuild and enlarge the house, now called the Berghof, without noticeably changing its outward appearance. This still did not solve the problem of putting up all the other people. The nearby inns and guesthouses were not enough, as became immediately apparent when all the Reichsleiters and Gauleiters assembled in August 1933 for an economic conference. Bormann had to adjust to the fact that his master would occasionally move the seat of government from Berlin to the mountains.

To this day the inhabitants of Berchtesgaden consider Bormann a despoiler of nature, and his insane building spree did indeed destroy one of the prettiest mountain landscapes in the area. But despite his far-reaching powers, one may safely assume that the responsibility was not his alone. His boss, forever conceiving designs for monstrous buildings and sketching plans for changing big cities, would hardly have given free rein to a man who lacked any artistic talent for the construction at Obersalzberg. Bormann got the job because he would have to finance the project and could supervise it from Munich. Besides, Hitler was sure of him as a tractable and energetic assistant. Bormann's first move was purely commercial: he bought up all the land.

The actual Berghof property consisted of only adjacent fields and a few small woods. Eventually it was completely surrounded by the lots Bormann acquired, registering all titles in his own name. He assembled a parcel of ten square kilometers (six square miles), mostly woodland, and some eighty hectares (200 acres) of farm land, a respectable working farm in those days. And he was generous with the sellers. Many a mountain peasant, many a homeowner was glad to get rid of his property at such a good price. But if anyone refused to sell, out of attachment to his ancestral lands or for whatever reason, he was told the Führer needed the peace and quiet up there. Whoever still failed to get the point was threatened with eviction. The all-pervading might of National Socialism made the most obstinate capitulate—even city people who owned vacation homes.

According to Erich Kempka, Hitler's chauffeur, "the Chief" instructed his agent to avoid coercion in his transactions. Bormann is supposed to have replied that people were swamping him with offers, since he could afford to spend money freely. Indeed, in the summer of 1938, when Bormann already had title to the entire countryside, there was an episode that supported this claim. Gazing at the wide panorama, Hitler regretted that a humble cottage far below the Berghof spoiled the view. Then he left for a day. Bormann had already bought the house and land, but he had been obliged to assure the owners, an elderly couple, that they could stay for the rest of their lives. By handing them an incredibly large check, he got them to move at once. Bulldozers and a crew of workmen were waiting. When Hitler looked down a day later, cows were already grazing where the cottage had been.

Two years earlier Bormann had proved his devotion and ability as an organizer in a similar operation. The Führer had complained that when he reviewed the procession of citizens in front of the Berghof terrace the bright sunlight hurt his sensitive eyes. When he returned from a trip a few days later, he found he could stand in the shade of a linden tree with a trunk as big as a man's. Bormann had had it trucked up the mountain and transplanted, disregarding the expense.

Before any such extravagances were possible, before workmen and machinery could be moved to the high plateau, the steep road up the hill from Berchtesgaden had to be improved and a second approach built through Oberau across some sections of valley. Bormann soon fell out with Delgado, the architect; he said the man was all right for designing a small post office (this had actually been his last assignment at Obersalzberg), but he was wrong for the big jobs coming up. The Munich professor of architecture Roderich Fick replaced him. A huge construction site soon materialized, first with several hundred workmen, later with several thousand, for whom barracks had to be built. Bormann had offices for himself and his building staff put in Haus Hudler, one of the older properties. He could see the workers out the window and make sure that nobody was loafing. Whenever the din of the pneumatic hammers let up, he would run out and demand to know why.

By the summer of 1936, after more than a year of work, the Berghof, the first of the new buildings, was completed. There was no longer any talk of "alterations," as the project had been described in a grotesque understatement. By now hardly anything was left of Haus Wachenfeld. The new structure covered four times as much ground, not counting a long wing that had been added on the side; there were now two stories above the ground floor, and thirty rooms. Just behind the entrance hall was a living-and-conference room with a huge picture window whose glass could sink into the floor. On the second floor Hitler had a living room, bedroom and office, and a few yards to the rear were quarters for Eva Braun when her presence was wanted. Hitler, the architect *manqué,* had drawn all the plans himself, but they hardly turned out to be a work of genius. In his memoirs Albert Speer, a real professional, takes savage delight in cataloguing all the mistakes in the elevation—enough, he claimed, to have failed any architecture student. No expense had been spared; the hall columns were of Untersberg marble, the windowpanes were framed in lead, the porcelain stoves had custom-made tiles, and the furniture was a combination of genuine antiques and classic copies. It was all totally out of key with the myth of the Führer who contented himself with so little.

While the work was in progress, Hitler rarely came to Obersalzberg. Building debris, dust and noise kept him away. In the first months of 1936 he was on the road a great deal, always with Bormann in his entourage. In Munich there were meetings of Reichsleiters, Gauleiters and the National Socialist Student Association on successive days; the Winter Olympics opened in Garmisch-Partenkirchen; in Schwerin there was the funeral and burial of the leader of the Swiss Nazis who had been shot to death in Davos. More and more often Bormann's notebook shows "M.B. trip with Führer," in the special train, the oversize Mercedes or in a vehicle of the official convoy.

On July 5 the Nazi leaders celebrated in Weimar the tenth anniversary of the first Party rally, and Bormann noted: "18:45 left with the Führer for Obersalzberg." As the entry for the next day shows, this was premature, for they spent the night in Munich. But the day after, the great moment finally arrived. "Arrival at Berchtesgaden with the Führer; the Führer's new house, the Berghof, is ready," he wrote. He was able to show his god around his up-to-date Valhalla.

Two days later, at the official housewarming, a huge crowd of select guests congratulated the beaming householder and his construction superintendent. The Berchtesgaden Christmas Rifle Brigade marched to the terrace and fired a salute—incongruously, as summer had just begun. The top Nazis took nearly a week to look around, then the public was permitted to see its Führer's accommodations from the outside. "First 'march past' at the new Berghof," Bormann noted. It was an agreeable conclusion to a tense period of deadlines, disputes with construction workers, and threats to those whose work was behind schedule. With this success under his belt, there was now no way to keep Bormann from top responsibility for all construction at Obersalzberg.

It was only logical that Bormann should have his own permanent residence there. Before being made Reichsleiter, he had moved from Icking to a colony in Pullach built by the Party for its officers. But this had become too small for his own needs and his fast-growing family. Nor was there room for them all in Haus Hutterer, where he had his office. He chose one of the finest houses in the village, built by a physician, Dr. Richard Seitz, as a children's convalescent home. It had three stories and was located not far from the Berghof, high enough above the village for Bormann to see the construction sites from his window. Practically all that was left of the original after renovation were the bare timbers of the outer walls, preserved to give the impression of a rustic simplicity that was conspicuously absent within.

"From the cellar to the tiniest room in the attic," reported Josef Geiss, of Berchtesgaden, "there was nothing but luxury and the best of everything. One could truly say that no parvenu who ever lived treated himself to anything like it." The children's bathroom, for example, had a washbasin that covered twenty square feet. Although it was a rarity then, it was a perfectly practical idea for a family with a lot of children and not that much of an extravagance, considering that Reichsleiters had the same pay as Reich ministers. More important, the master of the house received all this feudal magnificence as a present; the bills were paid out of the Dragon Hoard.

Of course the Party Chancellery had to have its mountain branch, too, so the Führer's wishes could be acted on quickly. First it occupied a former boarding house, until its steady expansion demanded a new building. The staff had to have quarters. The RSD (Reich Security Service) bodyguards needed barracks, as did the guard detail from the Leibstandarte. A huge garage was erected for all the Führer's cars and those of his entourage, and a whole network of roads was constructed on the hilly terrain, where each foot was many times more expensive than it would have been in flat country.

The plan also called for a comfortable mountain hotel for guests. But when Bormann had an enormous movie-set cutout mounted at the chosen site to see how it would fit into the landscape, it turned out that seen from below, it demeaned the effect of the Berghof. So the Platterhof, a mountain inn, was torn down, and the new building on its site was well along when

Hitler inspected it and asked where they were putting the bar. No bar had been planned; Bormann assumed that Hitler, for whom alcohol was anathema, would not serve hard liquor. But he did not want to admit his mistake and he pretended the bar was to go in the cellar. And it did—after a huge area of concrete ceiling was demolished and the pipes and water supply were expensively rerouted. The man who could order such costly changes became known locally as "Our Lord of Obersalzberg."

Bormann recorded various stages of the operation in his notebook. On September 30, 1936, we find: "The Führer approves plans for the Moosland teahouse." And on November 3: "M.B. conference with Dr. Todt on road to Kehlstein." The first entry concerned a pavilion fifteen minutes' walk from the Berghof. In later years Hitler used to take strolls to the spot with his party after lunch, always walking ahead with someone especially picked for that day beside him. Since the rest kept a respectful distance, the brief walk offered a fine opportunity for a private conversation which Bormann often seized. More time-consuming topics were brought up with Hitler in the car, on drives to the Hintersee, the isolated lake at the foot of Hochkalter Mountain. What was discussed on these occasions was recorded not in the notebook, but rather in the extensive records Bormann kept in his office safe. The talk with Autobahn-planner Todt was the first step in the most extravagant and inane of all the Obersalzberg projects: the teahouse on the rock called the Kehlstein. Bormann needed confirmation from the road-building expert that an access for motor vehicles was feasible. This absurd plan was originally conceived as his birthday present for Hitler. But before we come to that, there was the present Bormann gave himself: the Obersalzberg farm.

At a time when all farmers were being exhorted to increase their yields and Nazi organizations were even going around from house to house collecting garbage to feed the pigs, the Obersalzberg fields and pastures could not lie fallow. The former estate supervisor, whose ID card still listed his occupation as farmer, eagerly seized the chance to show off his agricultural capabilities. It was not entirely his fault that this did not work out well; the soil was stony, the climate raw, and the growing time too short. There were eighty head of cattle in the sheds, and a hundred pigs, but the crop yield was so small that large stores of feed had to be bought, especially for the horse farm, which had over sixty Haflinger brood mares, mountain horses from the South Tyrol, which were supposed to put the whole operation in the black.

Hitler had very little interest in the working of the farm. On one occasion when Bormann was showing him around, Bormann fatuously praised the cleanliness of the pigs in the tiled sty. "I hope," said Hitler sarcastically, "that every morning the pigs are washed with soap and then rubbed with eau de Cologne." This was typical Hitler humor, sarcastic and counting on the fact that no one would dare answer back. Bormann would not only join the laughter on these occasions, but actually felt honored to be the butt of the dictator's wit. But the day when Hitler asked for the farm ledgers, he had a few bad moments. According to his valet Heinz Linge, Hitler pored over the figures for a long time and finally declared, "Excellent! Not nearly as expensive as I thought; a liter of milk costs me only five marks at the most." Neighboring dairymen would have delivered twenty for that amount.

Nevertheless, Bormann was allowed to go on playing the farm manager with no apparent control from above. After all, the farm did not have to show a profit. He could afford to operate a greenhouse that produced hothouse flowers for the Berghof daily and fresh vegetables all year. He had a little difficulty at first with his attempts to provide mushrooms and honey. The mushroom cellar had to be transferred to a Bad Reichenhall brewery, and the apiary with a hundred hives rebuilt with better shelter. The bees were always an expensive hobby. They had to be fed sugar all winter to keep them alive, which required the services of a special beekeeper who had to have still another house built for himself and his family. The only item that turned a profit was a cider mill attached to the farm. This was, of course, a seasonal affair, and there were so few home-grown apples that most of the fruit had to be bought.

Bormann was conspicuously more successful as major-domo. When state guests came—and increasingly Hitler chose to receive them at his new country seat—Bormann was in charge of all arrangements. Erich Kempka reported that he was an arbitrary boss to those under him: "At one moment he would be friendly and courteous . . . [and] minutes later he would curse at the same people in a really sadistic way . . . He threw such fits of rage you couldn't help thinking he was crazy."

Was this the result of being overworked or was it a lust for power? It could have been both, but perhaps stronger than either was the compulsion to be a perfect servant to his master. According to Kempka, at the Berghof "he could hire and fire at will. Woe to the subordinate who . . . fell from grace. Bormann's hate pursued him as long as he was within reach." Any-one Hitler liked, Bormann treated with a catlike amiability so that nothing but good would be said of him on high. When there was no reason for him to watch himself he would fly into rages; once he smashed the model of the hotel bar to pieces because he did not like it, even though it had cost several thousand marks to make. Yet if Hitler felt like listening to a duet from *The Merry Widow* late at night, Bormann put the records on himself. Since Hitler, who loved animals, prohibited hunting at Obersalzberg, Bormann banned all cats and dogs in the compound because they might attack the game.

Bormann's mornings at Obersalzberg were spent hurrying up the build-ing projects, checking on the menus (even in SS barracks' mess), keeping things moving at the Party Chancellery, and reading reports. His duties at court never began before noon, the hour at which Hitler, who was a night person, got out of bed. If Bormann had a new set of architectural drawings to show, he could count on being let into the Presence immediately and getting right to the documents Hitler so hated. Meanwhile, the luncheon guests were assembling in the anteroom: adjutants; physicians; secretaries; some important Party member or other; Albert Speer, for whom Hitler had ordered a house with an architect's office built; Eva Braun and her girl friends; Heinrich Hoffmann, in whose photographer's studio Eva Braun was still listed as an employee. And, of course, Martin Bormann. This was the nucleus of Hitler's private entourage at Obersalzberg.

Bormann knew very well how to sustain his image as the tireless man in charge of everything. Occasionally, to look important, he would excuse himself from lunch at the last moment, explaining he had been unexpectedly called away somewhere on urgent business. But if young, good-looking women had been invited, he always managed to be present. He could not, like his master, kiss the ladies' hands with a sentimental Viennese flourish, make small talk in old-fashioned flowery phrases, but he made up for that by rushing around the house on his conspicuously short legs and showing great solicitude for the ladies' comfort.

In the dining room he had his fixed place: next to Eva Braun, whom he always escorted to the table and who sat on Hitler's left. On Hitler's right there was a different woman each day, selected by rotation from among the guests. It was an open secret that Eva Braun and Bormann did not like each other, but since they were careful to keep out of each other's way, the hostility never came out in the open. She knew that for her, politics were taboo; Hitler once observed in her presence that a truly intelligent man should have only a stupid woman so that she would not influence his decisions. Eva found it easy to meet these specifications; her interests focused almost exclusively on movies, movie stars, pleasant company for dancing and skiing, and other unproblematic pastimes. No doubt she loved Hitler very much; in May 1935 she tried to kill herself with sleeping pills because she felt neglected. In her diary at the time she wistfully wrote: "He only needs me for certain purposes"—which fits perfectly with Hitler's biological convictions on the essence of human nature and his withdrawal from close relationships. Bormann had no need to fear her influence, so she was the only member of the court against whom he plotted no intrigues. Of course, Hitler would have taken any insult on Bormann's part to his mistress Eva as an intolerable intrusion into his private life.

So they had to get along, especially since Hitler had replaced his half-sister Angela Raubal, who was hostess and housekeeper at the Berghof until 1936, with the large staff of servants his position now demanded. Eva Braun became the lady of the house, but only unofficially. Bormann was quick to see how this superficial young woman could be won over. She never acted the great lady, but there were things she wanted that she could not get with

her own money. Hitler liked to pass her an envelope full of bank notes every so often—a charming touch—but he evidently never bothered to find out how much she needed for her cosmetics and wardrobe. When he wanted to give her a piece of jewelry, he went to a small shop run by an old Munich Party veteran and bought the kind of thing one might have found in the jewel case of any small-town businessman's wife. The keeper of her lover's cashbox understood her better. He would take her to the jeweler and let her pick things out without looking at the price tag. When she wanted money she could always go to him in confidence. In the beginning she was flippantly disdainful of him, but later her manner changed—to the astonishment of the rest of the entourage. It is not really surprising, however, since Bormann was always on his best behavior with her, always at her service. Nevertheless, when he was not around, she occasionally made fun of his clumsy bowings and scrapings, his ostentatious officiousness, and the offensive way in which he chased the secretaries.

At the lunch table Bormann made no effort to entertain her. As long as Hitler was talking, the entire table maintained silence anyway, and when he stopped, one was expected to utter only a few words in a low voice. Hitler was a vegetarian, but he did not require the same of his guests. From time to time, Bormann made a point of choosing the vegetarian menu, then told everyone how powerful and full of energy this diet made him feel. But there were hams and sausages from the farm hanging in his larder at home, and when he got back from Hitler's table, he would often carve himself a few good thick slices. He never missed the afternoon stroll to the teahouse, however, for the chief would often call him to his side, and he had to be on hand at that hour for the daily ritual of tea and cakes, even though Hitler often dozed off in his chair. After that he had two hours left in which to dart around inspecting building sites ("Push them, push them" he wrote in his notebook on January 7, 1937), dictate, telephone and check off the things to be done he had scribbled on his ever-present pad. A little after eight o'clock he was back at his place next to Eva Braun, always with the same people, always alert for whatever orders his Führer might care to give while consuming hard-boiled eggs, curds and potatoes in their jackets.

After that everyone took a seat in the big living room to watch the same movie that was playing in the public cinemas. It is reported that during this interlude Bormann liked to go off in a corner and take forty winks. He must have needed it. He was not required to contribute to the critique of the actors that always followed the show, because that was not his field. But the next few hours could make great demands on him. The Führer might indulge in a monologue, or slap his thigh with laughter at the gossip being spread about the absent. In either case Bormann was wide awake, scribbling notes for his records. Sometimes, long after midnight, Hitler would think of some information he needed—like the market price of eggs in 1900—and Bormann would rush to the phone and the teletype, even if dozens of people had to be routed out of bed. An hour later he could proudly tell the groggy Führer the fruits of his zeal. Speer later described how this nearly identical daily routine at the Berghof, this constant preoccupation with doing nothing, paralyzed his own working capacity and frayed his nerves. But for Bormann, who was essentially uncreative, each day of this sort was a further corroboration of his own self-image as an important person. He was like a steam engine under excess pressure, which had to be left running to keep it from exploding. His strong constitution enabled him to be up early the next morning after only a few hours' sleep, chasing from one construction site to the next, throwing a fit here, praising there, giving out orders to keep guard details, construction foremen, drivers, dairy hands, Party officers and cleaning women all moving at the same swift pace.

The construction of the teahouse at the Kehlstein on a rocky peak 6000-feet high with almost vertically descending rock surfaces, provided him with a large amount of work and challenge. The memoirs of the leading Nazis all tell how Bormann started this project as a birthday present for Hitler. But there was never any question of making it a surprise; whenever there was building, Hitler wanted to be part of it and therefore had to be consulted from the start. Apparently this happened in the late fall of 1936, though the detailed planning did not begin until the following spring after the thaw. It was around this time that Bormann went up the Kehlstein with Todt, who was to build the roads, and the architect, Fick. In August they worked ceaselessly for two days because a landslide weakened the road. By mid-October, well before the onset of winter, the tunnel leading into the mountain's interior had been bored so that the elevator shaft leading up to the top could be worked on during the winter months.

The first half of the fateful year 1938, the year in which the expansion of the Greater German Reich began, left Bormann very little time for building projects. In January, Hitler summoned him to Berlin, where the government was preparing several legal actions. Commander in Chief of the Army, Generaloberst (General) Werner von Fritsch, was being investigated for alleged homosexuality (this was actually an unfounded accusation and a vicious plot), and Minister of the Reichswehr Werner von Blomberg had compromised himself by marrying a woman beneath his station. At the same time, Reich Foreign Minister Konstantin von Neurath, several ambassadors and a dozen generals were relieved of their posts. Bormann's nominal chief, Rudolf Hess, on the other hand, was promoted: henceforth he was to drop "without portfolio" from his Reich minister's title because he had "important government duties to perform as adviser to the Führer and Reich Chancellor."

Two days later it became clear that this promotion was really for the office and its Stabsleiter. When Hitler met with Austrian Chancellor Kurt von Schuschnigg at Obersalzberg, Hess was not brought along, but Bormann was, and he had duties other than playing major-domo to perform.

Hitler wanted to intimidate his adversary from Vienna as much as possible, and he not only "put on display the two most brutal-looking generals" for the reception in the anteroom, but Bormann also had to see to it that Schuschnigg felt surrounded by compatriots he had prosecuted as National Socialists, who had had to flee to the Reich. Several thousand were living in training camps in the Bavarian mountains, wearing SA uniforms and receiving board, lodging and a modest soldier's pay as part of the "Austrian Legion." The money presumably came from Bormann's inexhaustible coffers. He had also put in a word for the Austrians at Party Organization headquarters and had a number assigned to his construction staff at Obersalzberg—to the Führer's great gratification. On February 12, 1938, Bormann had a hundred of the uniformed émigrés transported to the Berghof to take over the guard duty normally performed by SS bodyguards. The Austrian Chancellor was to realize that he was in the lion's den.

In March, Bormann had no time at all for the Kehlstein project. He was still needed in Berlin. Schuschnigg's plebiscite had to be forestalled, and Hitler gave the orders for the march into Austria. "Flight with the Führer to Munich," Bormann wrote in his notebook for March 12. Around ten in the morning they got out of the plane at Oberwiesenfeld Airport, took a field-gray military vehicle to Mühldorf-am-Inn, the headquarters of VII Army Corps, and in the early afternoon rolled on to Braunau, Hitler's birthplace. The customs barrier pole was raised high to let them through, and they were welcomed by the pealing of church bells and the cheers of tens of thousands. It took them four hours to drive the seventy-five miles of highway to Linz because the masses were reluctant to make way for the convoy. By the time Hitler gave his first speech on Austrian soil, from the little town-hall balcony, it was already dark. Newspaper stories about this event list the names of the Party elite who stood next to him or behind him. There is no mention of Reichsleiter Bormann. Two days later nobody noticed that he was one of those looking down from the balcony of the Vienna Imperial Palace at the sea of enthralled followers below, listening to Hitler's speech. For all his rank, Bormann was still an unknown.

All the well-known Party big shots had been assigned roles in this operation. Göring was to represent the head of state in Berlin; Goebbels was to read the Führer's proclamation over the radio; Hess had already gone to Vienna on March 11 as symbol of the Third Reich's honorable intentions —and so had Josef Bürckel, Gauleiter of the Palatinate, who had picked up some Anschluss experience in 1935 when the Saar was reintegrated as part of the Reich. At the same time, Himmler appeared in Vienna complete with police and Gestapo detachments.

They all basked in the glow of popularity fired by the general enthusiasm, and they were made to believe that they had writ their names large on the pages of history.

Bormann was content to watch all this in the shadow of the Omnipotent, where he was at the very center of power. He was given no spectacular assignments, but some that required a high degree of discretion. It was important to Hitler that nothing emerge about his youth, his relatives and his years in Vienna that contradicted his own account in *Mein Kampf.* To ensure this, documents had to be removed from government offices, eyewitnesses rounded up or even eliminated—especially one Reinhold Hanisch, who had peddled Hitler's watercolors in 1910 when he was trying to establish himself as a painter and had lived with him in the Meidling "Home for Men," which was actually a flophouse. Hanisch had once been stupid enough to try to threaten Hitler with embarrassing disclosures. Now Bormann ordered the Gestapo to arrest him. In a memo for his files Bormann later recorded: "After the takeover of Austria, Hanisch hanged himself."

Not until mid-April, after the great victory celebrations in Berlin, the dissolution of the Reichstag, a series of election speeches and the new elections, did Hitler return to Obersalzberg. Bormann showed him the new construction which had been finished while he was away. The Berghof had another wing, the greenhouses and barracks had been expanded, the farm buildings completely renovated. Hitler spent three days inspecting. The teahouse on the Kehlstein was not ready to be shown, and if Bormann had ever hoped to dedicate it by Hitler's birthday on April 20 he must have misjudged the difficulties. There is some evidence that Hitler had lost interest in the building. He did not bother to inspect the access road—nearly four and a half miles, with tunnels cut through the rock, and a hairpin turn. He forbade blasting (the only way such work could be done) during morning hours because it disturbed his sleep. At table he made lame puns about Bormann being well named because he bored through the mountains. He once complained to his adjutant Julius Schaub that the construction work and concrete-pouring at Obersalzberg were so distasteful to him that he was going to look for a more peaceful spot for his later years. If so many millions had not already been spent on all this foolish building, he said, he would like to blow up the whole kit and caboodle.

So Bormann took extra pains to protect him. The "pilgrims' parade" was immediately abolished. A six-foot wire fence was put up around the entire area of Obersalzberg mountain, with two circular enclosures inside it. The gates to the outer one, where most of the construction was going on, had security guards who stopped anyone without a valid pass. The guards at the inner enclosure were employed by the SS but got their orders not from their organizational chief, Himmler, but from Bormann. It was he who decided who might pass through—except for invited guests—and he used to remind the guards, "A minister's uniform is not a credential."

During the summer of 1938, Hitler went to the Wagner festival at Bayreuth as usual, inspected troops, saw a naval review, visited the fortifications on the West Wall and, at the beginning of September, spent eight days at the Nuremberg Party rally being fêted by millions of worshipers. On all these occasions he was accompanied by the shortish bullnecked Reichsleiter whom only a few people could recognize and no one in the National Socialist hierarchy could place accurately.

At the rally the Führer told the world of his claim on the Sudetenland, which he was resolved to separate from Czechoslovakia ("one way or another," as he used to say). Three days later British Prime Minister Neville Chamberlain came to Obersalzberg, hoping to fend off the threatening war.

That was on September 15. The world—including most Germans—worried about peace. Bormann and Hitler chose this day to amuse themselves by inspecting the luxurious appointments of the Kehlstein. On September 16, before Chamberlain's plane had completed its return flight, Hitler and Bormann were driven up the steep, winding road, past vertical rock walls and over high viaducts, 5,600 feet above sea level. A double-winged copper-and-bronze gate set in the rock opened in front of them. They drove through a wide, brightly lit tunnel with natural walls cut into the rock. A shiny brass elevator took them up 400 feet to the teahouse entrance. "Teahouse" was something of an understatement: there was a big kitchen, a dining room, a study, a guardroom, bathrooms, cellars, a sunbathing terrace, and as the central showpiece, a circular room built around a huge fireplace which revealed a magnificent panorama through its picture windows.

Bormann's "birthday present" is said to have cost 30 million Reichsmarks, equivalent to some 200 million today, yet he received no more than nominal recognition for his efforts from Hitler. Some chroniclers maintain that Hitler went up there only a couple of times, but this is not true. The very next day he showed off his teahouse to Goebbels, Himmler and the noted British journalist Ward Price, who described it in his papers and must thereby have planted the wartime rumors about Hitler's "Eagle's Nest" and the "Alpine Redoubt." (German papers were forbidden to report on the Kehlstein house, and this ban included quotes from Ward Price's newspaper stories.) Two days later, another tour took place, this time for a whole group of more or less important people, among whom Bormann noted: "Ribbentrop, Bouhler, etc."

Only the Sudeten crisis interrupted these showings. Hitler met Chamberlain at the Hotel Dreesen on the Rhine, and in company with Bormann went on to Berlin to whip up enthusiasm for a possible war. In Munich he signed the agreement that sealed the fate of the Sudetenland and took Bormann with him on trips to these regions newly added to the Reich. As soon as he returned to Obersalzberg in mid-October he resumed his invitations to see his latest toy. The guests included the Gauleiter of Munich, Adolf Wagner; the Prince of Hesse, who as a relative of the Italian royal family was worth cultivating; French Ambassador André François-Poncet, whose bright conversation Hitler enjoyed; the entire Goebbels family, who were photographed together to demonstrate a reconciliation after Goebbels' affair with movie star Lida Baarova had almost led to a divorce; Generals von Brauchitsch and Keitel; and Unity Mitford, the sister-in-law of the British Fascist leader Sir Oswald Mosley who was widely believed to have been Hitler's mistress at one time and who tried to kill herself with a pistol in Munich when war broke out in 1939.

By November the succession of trips to the Kehlstein fell off; the play-thing had lost its novelty. Bormann, who proudly recorded each visit in his notebook, only rarely put down that a meal or a discussion had taken place at the lofty heights. Schirach says that Hitler did not enjoy going up there because the rapid altitude change caused him discomfort. "He disliked the mountain house from the very start," according to his valet. Only to please Eva Braun or Bormann did he occasionally let himself be talked into going up there, and he was always afraid that a bolt of lightning might destroy the elevator cable while he was in the cabin, or that an assassin would draw a bead on him from the rocks above the roadway. Apparently Bormann's extravagant present was not quite the right thing.

Yet this misdirected "generosity" in no way impaired his standing with the birthday boy. And Bormann never hesitated to use the teahouse himself. He would bring people up whom he wanted to impress or single out for special honor, and when he had an opportunity to indulge in a love affair he could be sure nobody would disturb him there. Linge reports that on New Year's Eve of 1938–39 Hitler and Eva Braun went to bed soon after midnight, while some thirty guests who wanted to go on celebrating went down to the ground floor. There Bormann ordered champagne and weiss-wurst served for a late snack. Already full of wine, Bormann was inspired to move the party to the Kehlstein. Scarcely anyone wanted to drive up the snow-covered mountain road that late, but only the military adjutants refused. As Linge observed, "Those gentlemen knew Bormann could not affect their careers."

All the others piled into a convoy of automobiles. Bormann took the wheel in his own car. Linge had to sit in back with an enormous radio on his lap because there was talk of dancing at the teahouse. With engine roaring almost full throttle, the host began speeding up the road. His chauffeur, exiled to the passenger seat, vainly pleaded caution. On a sharp curve, the car knocked down the safety barrier in front of a precipice. Only a snowdrift stopped it from going over. With the radiator steaming it reached the teahouse parking lot, but the riders could not open the gates to the tunnel until they had shoveled a huge snowdrift out of the way. By then they were so exhausted they had no desire to celebrate. There was a general feeling that the New Year had gotten off to a bad start. But Bor-mann did not feel that way: the entire court had danced to his tune.

8

Hard Work with the Elbows

The Party dignitaries first noticed how far Bormann had got in the organization at the "Greater Germany Party Rally." Gleaming with the gold-and-silver embroidery of their insignia, they took their places in the reviewing stand on the morning of September 11, 1938, to watch the parade on the Adolf Hitler Platz in Nuremberg. As usual, the Reichsleiters had filled all the places in the front rank. Suddenly Bormann appeared and as if by chance moved into the position at the extreme right. This was a place of honor which had always belonged to Robert Ley, Reich Organization Leader and *primus inter pares*. Ley gave Bormann a black look. Wilhelm Frick and Hans Frank, the Reichsleiters next to Ley, were amused.

In this particular instance there was not a word of objection any of them could have raised about their pompous colleague. Bormann was where he belonged, sizing up everything with his critical sergeant major's eye. He was the man in charge of the whole eight days of the celebration, responsible for every last detail in the bombastic "Hitler spectacular." This responsibility had begun back in August 1935, when Hitler brought him along to the initial planning sessions for that year's rally. At the music rehearsal, Hitler missed the sound of an organ, and Bormann managed to have one installed in two weeks. Now he was always with Hitler on inspection tours of the models for the massive constructions used as stage settings at the Nuremberg rallies.

When the Reichsleiters lined up on that autumn day in 1938 they already had good reason to distrust the man on the right: he was locked in fierce competition with nearly every one of them. In 1934 Bormann had created his own personnel office, which was parallel to the Main Personnel Office of the Reichsleitung. He was always inviting high-ranking Party officers from the Gaus to occupy temporary guest positions in the office "to strengthen mutual confidence" and "as a better way of keeping in touch." Actually, he was suborning them into extensions of his power structure, and in order to prevent them from dispersing, he quickly pointed out to them that his files on them would determine their careers. This was no empty threat. In a "Stabsleiter's Note to the Deputy of the Führer" dated February 20, 1939, Gauleiters and other top-ranking Party officials were moved about like so many chessmen on a board. One section dealt with "Changes in the *Ostmark,*"* another with firing two Gauleiters who had fallen from grace. Both were Party veterans of long standing, but they did not shape up to suit Bormann. Reich Education Minister Bernhard Rust, who doubled as Gauleiter of South Hanover–Brunswick, was a rock-solid Lutheran, and Josef Wagner, Gauleiter of South Westphalia and Silesia, was a devout Roman Catholic. Bormann's plans called for Wagner to be relegated to Price Commissioner—a post he already held in addition to his other responsibilities—where his Christian convictions could do no harm. As it worked out, Bernhard Rust remained a minister—for the time being. By 1941, both men were out.

Basically, Reich Organization Leader Ley would have to put up with having Hess as his intermediary with Hitler. However, he found it incompatible with his own station that he should have to depend on the concurrence of Hess's Stabsleiter in important political questions. In June 1939 he complained bitterly in a long letter to Hess that "the demarcation lines between the various jurisdictions within the Reichsleitung are in urgent need of comprehensive clarification." Hess, he continued, had authority over Reichsleiters, "but this is not something that can be delegated to your subordinate Stabsleiters. Matters I bring to your attention for a decision or authorization are intended for you personally, and should not have to be checked out by political officers who are equal or inferior to me in rank."

It also nettled Ley that Bormann "has set up an office within your staff to correspond to each office in my staff." He had shrewdly guessed that there was an effort to build a super Reichsleitung, which was all the more threatening since Bormann hired qualified specialists wherever he found them—they did not even have to be Party members. Ley hoped to stem the rivalry by asking for job descriptions and for the organizational chart of Hess's office. But though he made these suggestions directly to Hess, it was Bormann who answered him two weeks later.

Bormann wrote that since the Führer's authority was unlimited in all domains, this was true in Party matters for his deputy Hess, and Hess's staff. In short, no one but Hitler and Hess could tell him, Bormann, what to do. He therefore refused to give the Reich Organization Leader the job

---

*Nazi geography for Austria.—*Tr.*

descriptions and organizational chart he asked for. He wrote scornfully that the men in his office "who have special knowledge in particular fields" were so well known that the requested directory was superfluous. The directory did indeed exist, but it was kept in a safe and stamped "Top Secret." Ley's remonstrations did not affect him. "What can you expect?" he would say. "He's the son of a cattle dealer." In Bormann's book, that was almost as bad as being Jewish.

If Reichsleiter Hans Frank, head of the Reich Department of Justice, could still make jokes about Bormann's pompousness at the rally, his humor must have been wry indeed. Years before, the busy lawyer had provoked the upstart's enmity when Bormann—who was then Relief Fund manager —stopped by Frank's imposing office near the Frauenkirche in Munich seeking legal advice, and as we know, Frank passed him down to a young associate in the office named Heim. Bormann's pique burgeoned into outright hatred when Frank, the brilliant Party speaker who had risen to become Bavarian Minister of Justice and head of the Rechtswahrerbund (League for the Preservation of Justice), still refused to take any notice of him. Too late, Frank found that the wind had turned against him; Hitler considered all jurists an impediment to his caprices.

But at that rally Frank did not know what he was to put in writing years later, just before his execution at Nuremberg, that "a certain Stabsleiter, Martin Bormann, embarked on a program, which became increasingly obvious as time went on, to eliminate all the other offices in the Party." Easygoing Rudolf Hess even encouraged this, "stupidly believing that . . . he would win . . . more power for himself in the process. Bormann, the sophisticated exploiter of all the Führer's moods . . . always managed to trim the sails of his little ship of power to the wind of Hitler's inclination, never setting a course of his own."

It may have been true that in the last years of the Nazi regime Bormann acted as a seducer, but Frank's interpretation suggests that Hitler at least had a course of his own. "The Führer actually never felt himself bound to the Party program in any way," Frank lamented in hindsight, when he realized too late how successfully a lieutenant can make himself the secret master of a despot if both of them are entirely without principle. He learned what he had brought on himself by provoking Bormann's wrath in 1942, when he was stripped of all his titles and his old department was transferred to the Party Chancellery, which Bormann ran.

There is also some question as to whether Wilhelm Frick still felt entirely safe from Bormann's waxing ascendancy at the time of that rally. They had both been awarded their Reichsleiter insignia on the same day in October five years before. But as Reich Minister of the Interior, Frick already occupied one of the most important posts in the government, and as Reichstag deputy he was the National Socialist Party floor leader. A participant in the 1923 putsch and a Nazi official of long standing, he had made a name for himself inside as well as outside the Party. So how could a newcomer with no previous training and no administrative experience constitute a menace to him?

Bormann took his first swipe at Frick's authority where it seemed most impregnable: among the civil servants. Without Bormann's seal of approval, no one could hope for a government career. Back in 1936 Bormann's office colleague Walter Sommer had warned all government employees that "from assistant school principal and lowest-ranking court clerk up, no civil servant shall be promoted without the prior inspection of his personnel file by the Führer's Deputy." In the same year Bormann upgraded the importance of the training camp for civil servants he had founded: "In the future no one will be given tenure who has not been through the camp."

In rating civil servants, Amt Hess got its information from local Party agencies. Inevitably, personal vendettas crept into the assessments. The official who was thus given black marks usually never learned to whom he was indebted for his poor rating. But if he ever did, and sued the slanderer, he could not expect to clear his reputation in court. Bormann advised the Reich Minister of Justice that such lawsuits not be accepted; Party members should be able to pass information on to higher authority with impunity. It was recommended, therefore, that civil servants take care to keep their noses as clean with the Party—i.e., Bormann's office—as they did with their superior at the office.

Frick also had regular tussles with Party officers who encroached on the government's areas of authority. When Hitler announced at the Party rally in 1934 that the NSDAP gave orders to the government and not the other way around, the local Nazi leaders in the towns thought they could now depose the mayors; those on a higher level tried to boss their district presidents; and Gauleiters overruled the decrees of the provincial governments and their Oberpräsidenten, or chief executives. Naturally, Bormann always took the side of the Nazi politicos, who then felt that they owed him something. And so he penetrated more and more government agencies. After the war began, Göring and Frick tried to end the everlasting hassle over jurisdiction. As Chairman of the Ministers' Council for Reich Defense, Göring ruled that Party officials, at least from Kreisleiters (district leaders) down, were to "refrain from interfering in regular government business." Four weeks later Bormann sent all Gauleiters and Kreisleiters a "Secret Directive" saying that Göring's ruling lacked final authority.

In higher-level conflicts between Gauleiters and Oberpräsidenten he had already carried the day. A few Gauleiters complained to him that they had been overruled by government decisions on political matters, and the dispute went all the way to Hitler. Frick got his ruling in May 1939 in writing —from Bormann. It stated that since Gauleiters were responsible for public morale in their areas, political measures could be implemented only with their concurrence. If the representatives of the government and the Party people could not agree, "then a decision must be requested from the Führer's Deputy, as the government officer in charge of public guidance."

With this ruling Bormann won Hess the right—and for all practical purposes himself as well—to control Frick's top executive agencies. He also got his hands on all the Gauleiters, who now depended on him in conflicts with the government. Frick was unable to check on whether Bormann had passed down Hitler's verbal orders accurately, or whether he had edited them to suit his plans. Frick could barely get to Hitler anymore. Cabinet meetings had been abolished, and he was never summoned for a briefing. Bormann, on the other hand, was with Hitler every day.

It was no problem for Bormann to find fault with Frick, the top administrative executive. Government officials in general were a red flag to Hitler. He despised systematic, thorough work of any kind; a dossier threw him into a fit. He fretted because he could not, as head of state, give government servants arbitrary commands or send them packing at will. The very fact that their position and their work were defined by law made Hitler, an anarchist at heart, regard them all as reactionaries.

So Bormann could always be sure of a sympathetic audience when he criticized something like the pay scale, job tenure or pension claims of civil servants. It was not enough for him if a state servant faithfully did his job; he demanded quasi-religious submission to Nazi ideology as well. He gave the order that anyone not prepared to follow Nazi principles in word and deed must be fired. And in July 1938 Hitler did indeed notify all government agencies "to see that civil servants for whose activities there is no longer room in the Third Reich are dismissed."

Yet Bormann was not about to forgo the services of government employees in his own shop. Since Amt Hess collaborated in drafting legislation and assigning personnel within the state organization, he created a Section III to deal with questions of legislation, and he had specialists from various government departments transferred to his office on detached service. He saw much sooner than Hess did that Hitler was playing state and party off against each other so that neither would grow too strong, and he realized that he could keep the game going better if, along with his Political Section (II), which handled Party matters, he also had his own bureaucratic instrument for the government sector. Characteristically, the organization of that office was also a secret. No one was to know that a shadow control over each ministry had covertly been created. In mid-October 1938 one of the top men in his office wrote a memorandum for the record, doubting the usefulness of "informing a ministry in writing that in our office a government counselor [Regierungsrat] or assistant judge does the same work as a ministerial counselor does in a ministry." Bormann endorsed the memo with "I agree completely" and ordered it distributed throughout the office as a directive. He could boast to Hitler about how much work he got out of the government employees under his thumb, and how small his payroll was compared to Frick's "hydrocephalic" apparatus. Eventually Hitler got on the bandwagon which was attacking Frick's administration, and Frick was moved to another post. That happened in 1943—not quite five years after his disdainful smile when Bormann upstaged Ley at the rally.

But in September 1938 the Reichsleiters must have wondered why their Führer was so blatantly bestowing distinctions on this man. The ideologists among them liked to remark that the upstart had not contributed a single new idea to the National Socialist *Weltanschauung.* However, this very lack of originality made him ideal for following orders. Administrators under the Reichsleiters—Treasurer Schwarz, for instance—might point to their own accomplishments and ask if this Bormann fellow could come up with anything comparable. But they misjudged the engine that drove him, the exhaustive zeal that made him appear to be a man who could do everything. No assignment from the Führer was too small, too large, too unusual or too unpleasant for him. After Hitler seized total power, the Reichsleiters became merely an irksome appendage from the past, and he needed an indefatigable executive built to the specifications of the ideal Party comrade: loyal, reliable, authority-minded, always ready to serve, ambitious, with a highly developed practical sense and no scruples of any kind when an order had to be executed.

There are many examples of the manner in which Bormann served his master. In the course of one discussion on the role of the mayors in the Third Reich, Hitler happened to mention Carl Goerdeler, whom he had removed as Price Commissioner in the fall of 1936 but then appointed Chief Mayor of Leipzig. He recalled that Goerdeler had dragged his feet in setting up a new monument to Richard Wagner in his birthplace, although Hitler had personally approved the sketches. In a rage, he said that if Goerdeler didn't come around, he would be fired as mayor too. "Remind me of this six months from now," he told Bormann. The following year Leipzig had a new mayor.

Hitler used to say that Bormann was the only person in his entourage who never forgot anything, and he appreciated Bormann's discretion and devotion as much as his good memory. He trusted him more than anyone else, even with his most private affairs. As we have seen, Hitler was very careful about what he wanted to have known about himself—everything must fit the image of the leader—and he was highly sensitive about his origins, his past, his relatives and his relations with women. "People mustn't know who I am, where I come from, what family I'm descended from," he is supposed to have told his nephew Patrick Hitler, who was living in England.

Bormann was allowed in on these secrets because part of his job was to obliterate unwanted traces of the past and make sure that useful mementos were shown in the right light. When Hitler crossed the Austrian border at

Braunau on March 12, 1938, the day of the Anschluss, he did not bother to stop at the house where he was born. But since inevitably it would become a shrine, Bormann was told to buy the property, including the bar and restaurant on the ground floor. To have hordes of visitors full of liquor on the premises would have been a sacrilege. The owners, two brothers named Pommer, were quite aware of the value of what they had, and they did what they could to drive up the price. The brothers had risen in the world and joined the Party, but Bormann's agent complained that they haggled like oriental Jews. He paid them 150,000 marks, a considerable price in those days for an old building in an unimportant location. The closing was in May, and title was recorded not in the name of either the Party or its Führer, but in Martin Bormann's. Evidently Hitler wanted to avoid both appearing rich and having the property listed as a possession of the NSDAP, which was a corporation under the law and had its financial statements audited by government officials, which might have encumbered his rights of ownership at some future date.

The house Hitler's father had bought in 1899 in Leonding, at the southern end of Linz, also became a shrine administered by Bormann, who had a lot to do in Linz. Hitler wanted to make the city of his school years into "the new Pearl of the Danube." The top architects of the Third Reich—Hermann Giessler, Roderich Fick and Albert Speer— were commissioned for the job, and Hitler himself sketched the plans for representative buildings. Bormann was to provide the funds from his Dragon Hoard. Hitler also told him to buy paintings to hang in a future Linz art museum.

But there were other things in Linz people were not to know, like the rather tangled stories of the women in the life of the Führer's father, Alois Hitler, who married three times. There were relatives still living in the nearby village of Spital in more or less respectable homes, and there were family secrets they might tell. After the march into Austria when some enterprising journalists tried to locate the family and write a story, they were forbidden to publish anything.

Hitler found out that someone had placed a plaque on a house in Spital stating that he had once lived there as a youth—he had stayed there with an uncle to recover from an illness. Greatly agitated, he summoned Bormann and snapped at him that the plaque must be removed immediately. He had given orders time and again that his name should not be linked with that village.

Hitler had last seen his Spital relatives in 1918 when he was on furlough. Once he began his political career, he discarded them. The more successful he became, the more he cut himself off from his immediate family. His half-sister Angela Raubal, who had been his housekeeper in Munich and Obersalzberg for many years, was packed off after Bormann renovated the Berghof. She was not good enough for the great house suitable to a head of state. She did not see the Berghof again until March 1940 when, on a word from Hitler, Bormann invited her and showed her around while her half-brother was in Berlin. By Hitler's standards, looking after his relatives was a highly confidential job. The Führer wanted as few people as possible to know anything about them.

9

The Domestic Tyrant

When the American prosecutor at Nuremberg, Robert M. W. Kempner, interrogated Supreme Party Judge Walter Buch after the war, he asked him if his missing son-in-law had been "a dreadful person." Buch's answer was: "I think he went insane." Buch suggested that it was because he could not stand the thin air at the pinnacle of power. There may have been some truth in this, but Buch could not have missed the lust for power, and the abuse of power, that was inherent in Bormann's character from the very beginning. He was the kind of underling who obsequiously obeys every order given him and turns into a tyrant as soon as it is he who gives the orders. After the spectacular swastika wedding, the staff at Party headquarters in Munich never took their eyes off the couple thus honored by the Führer, and soon they were muttering about what a sorry choice of a husband the young wife and mother had made.

Walter Darré, Reichsleiter of the Peasantry and sometime witness to the lord and master's bad behavior *chez* Bormann, pitied her. According to him, she was constantly "tormented by this extremely brutal man . . . who [took] delight in humiliating his wife . . . in front of strangers."

This comment dated from Bormann's days as Relief Fund manager, but his ascent into the Nazi stratosphere changed nothing in that respect. The Berghof coterie used to be mortified when Bormann called his wife by whistling through his fingers, always insisting that she "hurry up" (one of his pet phrases)—that is, get going "on the double." Supposedly not only his wife but his children and servants sighed with relief whenever he left the house or was away on a trip.

But for all that, the marriage could not be called unhappy, thanks to

Gerda Bormann's personality. As her husband said later, by the time they married she was already "a dyed-in-the-wool National Socialist woman." Her father had brought her up that way, and she had always followed his example. As a schoolgirl she had listened raptly to Hitler's tirades at home, absorbing Hitler's idea of the role suitable to a nubile German girl: companion to her husband, guardian of the hearth, mother of many children. She needed a masculine authority to rule over her.

For a while she may well have seen the trinity of her authority figures in Führer, father and husband. Only that can explain why she never fought back against the constant oppression and mental cruelty in her marriage. It must have made her feel good when Hitler addressed the Frauenschaft (the National Socialist Women's Organization) at the Party rally in 1934. "The words 'women's emancipation,' " he roared into the microphone, "are a phrase invented by the Jewish intellect." A man's world was the state; a woman's, "her husband, her family, her children and her home." Gerda Bormann could not be there in person to hear him; she had just had her fourth child.

Housework was not her strong point. In a letter to her husband she even acknowledged that his mistress of the moment (there were several over the years) might be a better housewife. Her brother Hermann said that his sister had no special talent for practical things and always lived in a dream world. Her father, as a former army officer, felt that he was basically an educator, and for some time after World War I he planned to open a boarding school. It was with his example in mind that Gerda became a kindergarten teacher. Martin praised her cooking now and then, saying it had put several pounds too many on him, but actually that happened when she had a cook. Gerda always felt at her best sitting with the children, telling them fairy stories, teaching them folk songs, keeping them busy with drawing pads and linocuts. She had no trouble accepting the family order of things and staying in the background, yielding undisputed primacy to the master of the house. As he described it to his mother: "The management of the household, dealing with the servants, the education of the children—everything goes according to my instructions, which Gerda must follow!"

During the first six years of their marriage, this pompous domestic hierarchy would have sounded absurd. At least until the summer of 1933, the household had to be modest, and their first house in Icking was a small one. Even the Sonnenweg house in the Party colony at Pullach, which was assigned to Bormann before he became Stabsleiter, did not have much room. But the steady, parallel growth of his responsibilities and the number of his children soon convinced the Party that he needed more space. The family moved to another Party-owned house, on Margarethenstrasse in Pullach.

When their fifth child was born, workmen were already laying the foundations for their next home in Pullach. Heinrich Bormann, born in mid-

June 1936, was named for his father's new friend and ally Heinrich Himmler. Each birthday and Christmas thereafter Himmler sent a present to his godchild, which the SS Reichsführer secretariat duly recorded in the files—the first year a silver pusher and a teddy bear, later, during the war, a submarine, a gun, a tank.

In mid-September 1936 Bormann treated the workers on his new house to the traditional "raising the bush" celebration for having completed the frame. The beer and sausages cost him as little as the land and construction had. The Party was paying for everything, and Hitler had given the word not to be niggardly; after all, the house was for public relations as well. It took so much time to finish the interior that the family did not move in until late the following year—almost at the same time that the Bormann house at Obersalzberg was completed. Now the family had the choice of living in the mountains or just outside the city of Munich. But the decision was never left up to Gerda. Whenever Hitler was at the Berghof, Martin wanted to be within calling distance. Sometimes Gerda was banished to Pullach as punishment for disobedience or neglect, like forgetting to send Martin's favorite dress shirt to the laundry on time.

He almost never took her to the large receptions and festivities in Berlin and Munich, though Reichsleiters usually brought their wives. The fact that she had a child regularly every two years is not sufficient explanation. Did he feel uncomfortable having a wife who was so much taller standing beside him in a reception line? Or was he bothered because she was unable to project herself socially? Even in a small group of people, she only listened and never joined in the conversation.

Speer writes that despite her husband's career she remained "a modest, rather intimidated housewife." Schirach confirms this: "One saw her only at Obersalzberg, and there she would often sit by the fireplace among the wives of Hitler's closest staff, not saying a word all evening. She was all 'Mommy,' and for that reason Hitler treated her with special respect." The Führer showed his feelings by faithfully sending her a big bunch of roses every year for her birthday.

Hitler found out, either from his photographer Hoffmann or from Eva Braun, that Bormann was not faithful to his wife. Whenever young movie actresses were invited to the Berghof, Bormann would proposition them—often with success, for a Reichsleiter had a lot of clout in that society. Yet whoever informed on him was mistaken if he thought he could thus shake Hitler's confidence in his solicitous servant. Hitler was not overly fond of men who were paragons of domestic virtue; they were that much harder to blackmail. But he never realized that Gerda, too, knew all about Martin's escapades—from Martin himself. She accepted them as natural to the male and was always sure that he would come back to her because of the children. And as it turned out, she was right.

With a father like Martin the children had no easy time of it. In May 1936 he joined the Reich German Family Association, a group to promote the National Socialist population policy of encouraging larger families. By then he had four dates and places of birth to put in the membership file, although he cheated a bit and moved his wedding date back six months so the records would not show that the Reichsleiter's bride was already with child when she appeared at the registry office. Soon the Bormann family was an example to the whole membership; they had six children by the beginning of the war, and nine by the war's end (one child had died).

As far as Gerda was concerned, her contribution to the Fatherland—for so Hitler counted each birth—meshed perfectly with her own inclinations. She could never have enough children around her. At Obersalzberg she always had an extra flock of little houseguests around.

It is doubtful that her husband loved the children as much as she did. But in his defense, he had little time to give them. Even before the war they hardly saw him for weeks on end, because he was needed in Berlin or was traveling from one Party function to the next. Later he spent most of his time in Führer Headquarters. But the children did not miss him very much. When he was home they had to keep quiet so that he could relax his strained nerves, and were punished if they failed to carry out his instructions instantly. They were not allowed to talk to strangers or play with children they did not know because he was afraid they would say too much and get him in trouble. Given to sudden rages and always arbitrary, he would beat them over trifles—with a dog whip, according to one eyewitness and with a riding whip, according to another.

He beat two of his children while they were on an outing because they were scared of a large German shepherd. When one of his sons stumbled in a puddle, he punished him with kicks. Yet he would be concerned about the children during his absences, and he used to write Gerda telling her what she was to teach them: never play with matches, never accept candy from a stranger, never get into a stranger's car. He was very proud when he was asked to bring them to the Berghof to call on Hitler, who always patted their heads and seemed diverted by their ingenuous talk.

Before Bormann surrounded Obersalzberg with fences, the dictator was able to indulge himself with a wider choice of children. Once during a "citizens procession" he singled out a little girl with brown curls and had her and her mother sit with him at the coffee table. They were both invited to come back and visit him often, which they did, several times. Then Bormann had them checked out and discovered that the little girl's father was not "Aryan" according to the Nuremberg laws. He forbade either of them to appear at the Berghof ever again. Since he made the arrangements for such invitations, he saw to it that there was no competition for his own children. Speer's and Linge's children were the only ones he could not prevent from coming.

Bormann's children were kept from all contact with Christian ideas and practices until they started school in Pullach and in Berchtesgaden, when it became impossible. "Krönzi" (Adolf Martin), the eldest, was nine when the war started, and Ilse, whose name was later changed to Eike, was eight. Of course, they did not attend the religious-instruction classes, but their schoolmates, who were nearly all Catholic, gave them glowing accounts of First Communion celebrations and processions. When the children talked about these things at home, their father was furious. Christian books and publications were not allowed in the house or Gerda was told to keep them hidden from the children.

If Bormann had had his way, there would have been no Christians at all at Obersalzberg. When he had a group of houses built there, mostly for the staff of the local branch office of the Party Chancellory, applicants were admitted only if they had left the Church. Obviously this kind of repression, like their severe upbringing, was bound to trigger rebellion in the Bormann children eventually. "Krönzi" started giving trouble when he was only ten. Because Martin had to be away so much and did not trust Gerda to raise the boy as a tough Nazi militant, he sent him as punishment to the NAPOLA (National Socialist Education Institution) in Feldafing where the sons of Party and SS leaders were given Spartan training.

Bormann's irritation with his progeny was trivial, however, compared to the exasperation his ancestors caused him. Ordinary Party members had to prove by documents (such as extracts from church records) only that there was no Jew in the family tree back to the great-grandparents, but the rank Bormann held demanded that two more generations be researched. This was a time-consuming affair, further complicated by the fact that many pastors who actively objected to National Socialism deliberately sabotaged the search. So Bormann, who had a great deal to do, decided to turn the whole thing over to Party agencies and professional genealogists.

In January 1932 he tried to get the National Socialist Information office in Party headquarters to take the assignment and willingly paid the 100-mark fee, but the results were meager. Later, when government offices had to take orders from the Party, the race-research specialist in the Reich Ministry of the Interior got the job. The Reich Peasant Council was also pressed into service. But two hurdles stopped them all: Bormann's illegitimate grandfather, whose father could not be traced, not even by the court papers of a suit for child support; and the Mennong family on Bormann's mother's side, whose records went back only three generations.

H. Bormann, a tax adviser from Frankfurt, sent in a promising report stating that in the eighteenth century a family of that name in the Wittenberge area had been "almost exclusively professional men . . . such as clergy, physicians, professors," but the gratifying illusion of having uncovered hitherto unknown distinguished ancestors eventually dissolved into nothing, as did the hypothesis that Martin was descended from a Westphalian peasant family named Bormann "whose ancestral records go back to 1508."

He told his eldest son a fanciful story about how the Bormann ancestors had migrated from Germanic Flanders to Westphalia, where they owned large farms, and how their descendants had spread throughout Northern Germany as men of learning and important government officials.

He kept hoping that at least the Mennong branch of the family tree would have something more interesting to offer than small-town folk and agricultural workers. Someone tried to tell him that the name ("perhaps it was once 'Mennon' ") was of French origin, so the family might have been Huguenot, perhaps even aristocrats. But all research stopped with the grandfather, a humble glovemaker who married and settled in the Halberstadt area and who could have come from anywhere. The Secretary of the German Huguenot Society in Berlin wrote that he was sorry, but "Mennong unfortunatley does not appear in any of the material to which I have access."

Still, the Party insisted: tracing one's forbears was mandatory. In January 1936 the Office for Ancestry Research in the NSDAP reported its scanty results:

"Despite the greatest efforts" the ancestry of both grandfathers was lost in obscurity. Under these circumstances, it was difficult to comply with one of Himmler's wishes—to collect the heraldic shields of all the high-ranking SS members and hang them decoratively around the great hall of some SS fortress. SS Gruppenführer Bormann had nothing of that sort to offer. A Party official who specialized in just such embarrassing situations advised him to commission the design of a coat of arms. Bormann decided to wait, hoping something choice and noble might still turn up after more research.

From 1934 on, the director of the Reich Ancestry Bureau, a Party member named Kurt Mayer, was put to work on the Bormann pedigree. He searched for years on end and found nothing, even though with each request for information he stressed the fact that his commission came "from high up," and even though Bormann promised "not only to pay the private expense, but to give proportional financial support to the agency from state funds."

During the war, church registries and registrar's offices refused to give out information because their records were stored in bombproof cellars. So Himmler became the ancestorless Bormann's last hope. He mobilized the chief of the SS Race and Settlement Office, SS Gruppenführer Harald Turner, and was soon able to write "Dear Martin" the good news that now there was an excellent chance "of completing the family tree." Turner's office issued avalanches of requests for information. Even Bormann's mother was formally instructed to verify her baptism. And this battle of documents was going on at the end of August 1944, when the Red Army was at the gates of Warsaw and the Western Allies were deep in France. Air raids drove the SS office concerned with the search to a little town in the Harz Mountains, but it refused to give up. As late as January 1945 it demanded, "despite the difficult situation possibly prevailing in the Saar at this time," that the Saarbrücken district court supply information on the Mennong family, on orders "from the highest authority."

Still the problem remained unsolved. A few months later Martin Bormann made the journey to where his ancestors were waiting—without knowing whom he would be meeting there.

By 1936, when his career really began, Martin Bormann had already severed contact with most of his living relatives. His younger brother Albert, known as "the kid" both in the family and in the Hitler coterie, even though he was a head taller than Martin, first held a fairly unimportant position under Reichsleiter Philip Bouhler in Hitler's private secretariat, of which he was later put in charge. High-ranking Party members found him dependable, cooperative, straightforward and civilized. Lacking both great ambition and lust for power, he was one of the few in the palace guard who believed that they were serving a good cause and who did not pursue their own advantage.

Hitler needed just such a man in his close circle. In 1938 he had Albert assigned to the group of adjutants who were not subordinate to Martin Bormann. But Martin had felt entitled to the first-born's right of primacy ever since he was a little boy, and he saw Albert's independence as a diminution of his own authority. As Albert became increasingly popular with Hitler and at the same time resistant to his brother's wishes, Martin began to see him as a serious rival.

At Obersalzberg, in Berlin and later in various headquarters, their paths crossed several times a day, but there was never any display of family feeling. An eyewitness reported: "They had nothing to do with each other except in the line of duty."

For Martin's children, Albert was a distant uncle. When Albert fell in love with one of Hitler's secretaries, Martin is supposed to have prevented the marriage by an intrigue, lest his brother get still another direct line to the center of power. And when Albert then married the widow of an officer killed in the war, Martin showed his displeasure because the bride did not measure up to Martin's standard of the North German woman. Contemptuously he referred to his brother as "the man who holds the Führer's coat."

To Martin, the description seemed appropriate because Albert never tried to exercise the slightest influence on Hitler's decisions. Their mother tried vainly to make peace between the two. Forced to live side by side in a narrowly circumscribed area and an almost closed circle of people, they grew further and further apart psychologically. When I wanted to talk to Albert about his brother, Albert said, "As long as Martin was alive, he never spoke to me, and now I am not going to talk about him. During his lifetime my brother said he had no brother. Now I can say the same."

Martin's mother often had reason to complain about him. He had resented her since his childhood for putting another man in his father's place. The name Vollborn, from her second marriage, and the house in Oberweimar, bought in 1909, were reminders of it. What he considered his strong points—his sense of duty, industry, perseverance, mental agility—he considered his biological inheritance from his father. When Gerda once dared to criticize him for being undisciplined and arbitrary, he blamed these traits on his mother. He allowed her to visit her grandchildren in Pullach or Obersalzberg only on his invitation. When she tried to give him advice or lecture him, he told her to "stay away from such things."

He complained that she had "restless blood" and traveled too much. During the war he sent her a reproving letter telling her to stay home, and he reprimanded her severely in February 1943 when she suggested to Gerda that in response to Goebbels' call for total war at least one of the maids in Pullach or Obersalzberg should be released for work in a war plant. "You cannot possibly judge how many servants I need in my position," Bormann wrote. "That is my decision and mine alone . . . Once again: Don't mix in my affairs. Stop these critical comments, especially at a time like this, and do not bother about things that are none of your business."

Visits from Gerda's parents were totally unwelcome. It no longer counted for anything with Bormann that he owed the start of his career to his father-in-law. The two men were too different in character to be able to stand each other. The former major, as his friend Darré said under interrogation, "with his dignified, relaxed style simply did not belong in the Party circle." He was also far from the unconditionally devoted Party officer Hitler would have liked him to be; he was not ready at all times to tailor his judicial opinions on command. He was often so stubborn that the top Party coterie wondered why "the old fool" had not been thrown out of office. But he served as a useful bit of window dressing to give a false impression of probity. Beyond that, Hitler had a perhaps sentimental loyalty to his old comrades in arms from the early days. When they made him uncomfortable, he preferred to cut off their power bloodlessly rather than fire them. He had invited Buch to be one of his adjutants in 1933 because he wanted a man of integrity for his front office; at the same time, Buch was an officer with a will of his own, and Hitler wanted him where he could be kept on a tight rein. Buch, however, declined the appointment.

At first Bormann had been delighted with his in-laws. It was useful for a Stabsleiter in Amt Hess to have a family connection with the official expert on Party comrades' quarrels and misdemeanors. But he was affronted to see how the totally undiplomatic Buch disobeyed the dictates of the Party chief. Buch saw himself as an independent judge who took orders from no one —either for initiating a court action or for reaching a verdict. Hitler, then as later, wanted to be the sole arbiter of who was to be indicted and who was to be punished.

It also galled Hitler that Buch had been promoting a plan among the

Party leaders to have the Senate Room of the Brown House, with its red upholstered chairs, used at last for its original purpose, as a real senate, along the lines of the Fascist Great Council in Italy, where the best men in the Party could be assembled to advise and consent on important issues. Buch wanted the top leaders to be trained to the moral concert pitch of the Prussian officer corps, with strict concepts of honor and self-discipline. But this was not at all what the dictator had in mind.

At the end of November 1935, Bormann and his father-in-law flew to Königsberg. The Gauleiter of East Prussia, Erich Koch, had pushed despotism and corruption to such extremes that the Supreme Party Judge could no longer be restrained from bringing the matter to trial. But Hitler had nothing against letting his princes in the Gaus fill their pockets. Since he valued Koch's ruthlessness and energy more highly than a clean record, he ordered Bormann to put the brakes on his father-in-law's zeal to administer justice. As a result the Party action against Koch misfired, and Koch and Bormann even became friends. But Buch would not let the matter drop, which, as he soon learned, worked to his disadvantage.

"If back in 1935–36 your father had followed the instructions I gave him in the Führer's name," Bormann wrote his wife years later, "he would have spared himself and others a lot of trouble." Buch, still trusting the Führer as a man of integrity, simply refused to believe that Hitler had knifed him in the back. He accused Bormann of lying and becoming too close to Koch.

After that, Hitler hardly ever received Buch again. Since no proceedings could be started against prominent Nazis without Hitler's consent, this was the simplest way to cut a man off who refused to realize that the Führer was always right. In protest, Buch walked out of his office one day and went to the United States for a few weeks, naïvely assuming that this would demonstrate how indispensable he was. Hitler must have been secretly pleased to be at least temporarily rid of the irksome moralizer whom he could use as a scapegoat should anyone complain about the Party's justice department not doing enough to keep everything on the right path.

Buch expected to be given a free hand to perform his duty when he returned. He set before Hitler a voluminous dossier of incriminating material against Robert Ley, the massively corrupt Reich Organization Leader, and demanded that he be removed from office. Hitler screamed at Buch and sent him away. Ley had remarried, and his second wife was good-looking young woman with whom Hitler was quite infatuated. Buch finally blew his last bit of credit after the *Reichskristallnacht* (the Night of the Broken Glass) on November 9, 1938, when synagogues and shops owned by Jewish businessmen were systematically destroyed all over the country. A number of vandals took the opportunity to enrich themselves. As a safety valve against the widespread indignation this provoked among decent citizens, the Party courts were ordered to proceed against the looters. Buch was ready to go ahead on condition that the instigators—of whom Goebbels was first in line—were also brought to account. When this was refused, he took another trip, this time to South America.

It now became impossible for his ambitious son-in-law to have him around any longer. Buch was banished from the Bormann house, and so was Frau Buch, since she sided with her husband. In a partisan abandonment of principle which is hard to explain, unless it was some sort of sexual dependence, Gerda took her husband's side and complied when he forbade her to visit her parents, with or without the children. But it is clear from one of her letters to Martin that this act of obedience did not come easily.

"When a child gets married," she wrote, "it is lost to its parents. I think I will cry myself sick when my daughters get married . . . They will stick by their husbands and go along with them through thick and thin." She was, however, allowed to telephone her parents. But as she wrote in the same letter, "When I called Ammersee [where the Buchs had a house] I did it when I was sure I would get only Mother on the phone."

If there was one thing Bormann envied his father-in-law, it was a small silver medal which he could wear on ceremonial occasions. Dangling from a shiny red ribbon attached to the buttonhole of his right breast pocket was the *Blutorden,* the "Blood Order" with which Hitler had decorated all those who marched in his abortive 1923 putsch. Bormann wanted no other medals, or so he pretended. As an artillery private in a home-based regiment in the World War, he had had no chance to earn any. At the Führer's meeting with the Duce, two Italian decorations were hung around his neck, but he never wore them. He probably considered them not good enough. As he wrote his wife, anyone who was trusted by the Führer needed no further decoration. But he would have liked to have the *Blutorden,* the emblem of a militant from way back. And he got it. In May 1938, after the march into Austria, the Austrian Party comrades had to be rewarded for having endured struggle and persecution, and Hitler decreed that the order would also be given to those who "in the fight for the Movement" had spent not less than one year in jail. The time factor, which was perfect for Bormann, suggests something tailor-made, and one suspects that Bormann had a hand in drafting the decree. It was, to be sure, stretching a point to interpret the *Feme* murder in Parchim as something done in the service of the Party. Bormann had been a member of the Völkische party at the time and no way a follower of Hitler's. But he got decorated just the same. He received the medal and a citation from his Führer on September 5, 1938, at the beginning of the Party rally ceremonies, before all the top Nazis assembled at Nuremberg. It was a kind of consecration to a higher order of knighthood for him—and besides, his unloved father-in-law was now no longer one-up on him.

Bormann allied himself with Buch one more time, in the case of Gauleiter Julius Streicher. The Frankenführer ("leader of the Franconians"), as he styled himself, had always been one of the most repulsive characters in the entire NSDAP—a brutal sadist with a shiny bald head, who, like Hitler in the Kampfzeit, always carried a leather whip attached to his wrist, and who promulgated an obscene anti-Semitism in speeches at public gatherings and in his weekly magazine *Der Stürmer*. He was always going on about Jewish sensuality, lechery and avarice while pursuing every female in sight, and he exploited every opportunity offered by the "Aryanization" of businesses to fill his own pockets with windfalls from the ruin of others.

Complaints about this monster were piling up in the Party to such a degree that Rudolf Hess felt he had to put an end to the scandal. Though Hitler deliberately allowed his Gauleiters open season for any kind of robber-baron activity, on the theory that the laws of nature gave the strong the right to whatever they wanted, Buch and Hess put pressure on Bormann to get the Führer's permission to hold a Party trial. On January 10, 1940, he wrote in his notebook: "Führer conferred with M.B. and Liebel on Streicher." M.B. is his abbreviation for his own name; Willy Liebel was Chief Mayor of Nuremberg and an enemy of Streicher's.

In this case Bormann cared less about justice and the Party image than about the opportunity to show refractory Gauleiters his power. It would make clear to them that even Streicher, who had repeatedly been put on a pedestal by Hitler himself, could not escape Bormann's long reach. A Party court with Buch presiding actually did strip the Frankenführer of his post and honors. But Hitler had not wanted that, either. He considered overturning the verdict and removing "the old fool" Buch. Bormann blocked both measures. They would have cost him some of the prestige he had won with the Gauleiters. (His notebook entry for February 17, 1940, reads: "Briefing for Führer on proceedings against Streicher ended on February 16 in Munich.")

By 1942, relations between the Buchs and the Bormanns were so icy that Martin fought shy of asking even small favors. The line of Aryan forebears had to be checked out on not only his family tree but his wife's as well. Rather than ask his in-laws for the documents they had already assembled for their own clearance, Bormann asked the director of the Reich Ancestry Office, who had been working on his case, to see if he could put the Buch family tree together too. If he could, Bormann would be grateful "if you could send me a transcript of all the material you have processed." Soon after, he was able to deal the *coup de grâce* to his father-in-law: Hitler decreed that Buch could initiate proceedings and pronounce judgments only with Bormann's prior approval.

When Frau Buch died at the end of October 1944, Bormann had not a word of condolence for her husband. He wrote Gerda to take care of this duty on his behalf, since, he said, he had never been very close to his mother-in-law. In his next letter, written two days after the death, he didn't even mention it. He did not attend the funeral, although a fast courier plane was at his disposal at Führer Headquarters in East Prussia.

10

Against Christians and Jews

At Christmastime the Bormanns always took particular care not to have their children contaminated by what Martin, in a letter to Gerda, called "a poison that it is almost impossible to get rid of." By this he meant the Christian religion. Yet paragraph 24 of the NSDAP's 1920 program, which was never amended and remained supposedly binding for all Party members, stated: "The Party as such stands for positive Christianity."

The author of the program, Gottfried Feder, who even by 1933 had faded into anonymity, was never authorized or able to explain in any detail what he meant by "positive Christianity." And by the time the Bormanns moved to Obersalzberg, paragraph 24, like many others, was accepted as nothing more than propaganda. But in those days of apparent national euphoria, not too many Germans worried about that. True, there was concern among the Christians, but wasn't Hitler a member of the Catholic Church? He even remained one to the end, and he always paid his church taxes on time. But many of his entourage and leading members of the Party left the Church and had themselves listed simply as *"gottgläubig"* (believing in God) in the registrar's and internal-revenue offices.

The newly coined term represented one of the devious ways by which Party members tried to get around paragraph 24. Ostensibly they were fighting against the ungodliness of Marxism and protecting the faith against the dissidents' subversive immorality.

Every so often Hitler would invoke the "Almighty" in his speeches. When, after 1933, Augsburg's Gauleiter Karl Wahl, a devout Catholic, challenged him on his religious beliefs, the Führer repudiated the neo-pagans in the Party: "I'll take care of those people, slowly but surely."

Like most of his promises, this was a blatant lie. At the very moment he made it, he had given full rein to Bormann, the rabid anti-Christian who had no intention of establishing a new faith; on the contrary, he wanted to destroy the existing one. And since no one knew better than he what the Führer believed (or rather didn't believe) in, Bormann never needed to be afraid that Hitler might put a stop to his activities. At the most, he would blow the whistle on him if at some point his ruthless methods happened not to suit the political trend of the moment.

Bormann described himself and his family as Protestants when he joined the Reich German Family Association. He still professed this faith in a biographical sketch written late in 1933 for the Reichstag Directory when he became a deputy. The reference *"gottgläubig"* appears for the first time in September 1937 in a questionnaire for the SS leaders card index. He was certainly never a practicing Christian, and it is easy to see why he and his wife left the Church, probably in the summer of 1936.

At that time a heated argument was going on inside the Protestant Church, in the course of which a letter reached the Führer's desk from the church leadership protesting against "the practice of venerating the Führer's person in a way that should be reserved for God alone." Meanwhile it had become obvious that the Party could not simply take over the Protestant Church and that neither the Gestapo nor the concentration camps could silence Protestant enemies of the Nazi regime. Despite the fact that he had official NSDAP support, Reich Bishop Ludwig Müller's following was dwindling. This marked the end of the closed season on Christians, no matter what their denomination.

It was time for Bormann to get busy behind the scenes, although for the time being an appearance of harmony had to be maintained in a country that was ruled by a "Peoples' Chancellor." A typical example of his method of operation was the case of Catholic Bishop Alois Hudal, a Bohemian by origin, who, as an ethnic German, was very much taken by the ideas of National Socialism. In 1936 Hudal published a book in Austria, *The Basic Elements of National Socialism,* which he dedicated to Hitler. Franz von Papen, the former Vice-Chancellor and Hitler's "house Catholic," then serving as ambassador in Vienna, presented the Führer with a copy at Obersalzberg and asked that the book be authorized for publication in Germany. "Every time I felt I had convinced him," Papen later recalled, "the door would open and Bormann would plug himself into the conversation." Thanks to these efforts, the book was made available only to a limited number of leading Party members. It is one of the ironies of history that it was a Catholic priest who, after the collapse in 1945, looked after the Bormann children, stranded in the southern Tyrol, and that Catholic organizations helped many Nazis who were "wanted" by the Allies to escape from Germany.

In 1936 Bormann, who had only just switched from being a nominal

Christian to a neo-pagan, was suspicious of any cleric. He instructed the Party Organization to hunt down "pastors or other Catholic subleaders who are taking a stand against party or state" and "report them to the Gestapo through official channels." To undermine the reputation and credibility of this opposition, the Gestapo was urged to uncover currency violations committed by church authorities or—worse yet—sex offenses in convents and monasteries.

Under the auspices of the Reich Minister of Propaganda, the newspapers were allowed to report colorfully on such incidents in the style of the otherwise-scorned yellow press. Whereas in former years clergymen (mostly Protestant) had regularly spoken at Party rallies, especially in areas with a religious population, they were now looked upon with suspicion. In February 1937 Bormann's office advised all Party divisions "to refrain from admitting members of the clergy into the Party," allegedly "in order to prevent ecclesiastic controversies from seeping into the Movement." But the real reason was revealed the following year in one of Bormann's inter-Party decrees; it was a declaration of war on Christianity which proclaimed the National Socialist ideology as the one and only true faith. Party speakers were advised to avoid remarks implying that life after death was the business of the churches while the here and now was that of the Party, for "actually the clergy knows no more about the afterlife than we do." Ministers should therefore no longer be called "servants of God" but church servants or church officials. "By the same token, church service in our day and age can no longer be regarded as a service to God." Nor should the clergy be the established authority on spiritual welfare; it could devote itself to it, but it did not have a monopoly and could not guarantee people's salvation. Anyone closely affiliated with a denomination should be described not as religious but as a church person. Bormann usurped the term *Weltanschauung* for National Socialism exclusively; Christian ideologies were to be known as "Christian confessions, or something along that line."

Thus, confidentially for the time being, the order of procedure was laid out. When the chief of the German Labor Service forbade his units to attend church services in groups or to provide the brass bands at church events, Bormann gleefully passed the word on to the Gauleiters (several of them ignored it, however, and, as true believers, kept on working with church organizations). He reprimanded Reich Youth Leader Baldur von Schirach, certainly not a man favorably inclined toward the clergy, for having instructed his Hitler Youth groups not to schedule Party activities on Sundays during the hours of church services.

Inside the Party Organization, where he was able to issue direct orders, he laid down the law. Late in July 1938 he ruled ("not for publication") that "clergymen holding rank in the Party . . . should immediately be relieved of their Party office," i.e., they should not be allowed to continue as local branch leaders or in higher-level offices. Where they held minor ranks, in the National Socialist People's Welfare Organization or as SA troop leaders, they were to be phased out "gradually, as suitable substitutes become available." Henceforth, clergymen could not be appointed "to Party offices, divisions or organizations." Shortly afterward they were no longer tolerated even as ordinary Party members: "clergymen and other citizens strongly committed to religious affiliations are unacceptable for Party membership." Bormann subsequently amended this order by directing that "in the future, Party members entering the clergy or pursuing theological studies must resign from the Party."

In his attempt to discredit the churches, Bormann brought all his perseverance and bureaucratic pressure to bear on every minor issue. Following Hindenburg's example, Hitler always acted as honorary godfather to the tenth child born to any German mother. Bormann discovered that the application forms the parents had to send in asked for the date of baptism. In November 1937 he wrote in a formal letter to the Führer's adjutant Wilhelm Brückner (whom he saw several times a day) that "the Church is trying to suggest to Party members and citizens who have left the Church" that an honorary godfather cannot be had without baptism. Brückner should therefore immediately see to it that the Presidential Chancellery, which was in charge of such matters, print new application forms eliminating this question and discontinue the old forms at once. Brückner, who was not overly bright, missed the point; two months later Bormann read the new version: "Date of baptism, if baptism is envisaged or has taken place." This called for another letter. "I suggest," Bormann wrote, "that the question of baptism be dropped altogether from the forms."

In November 1938 Bormann remembered that the case was still open and wrote a third, even more urgent formal letter, despite the fact that he could have gotten Hitler to rule on the matter at any time. He was gathering material which would someday make it possible for him to prove that Adjutant Brückner was losing his grip and should be replaced. Which was what eventually happened.

Whenever, in the Third Reich, a prominent Party member acted outrageously, the ordinary citizen would remark in righteous indignation, "If only the Führer knew!" In the case of Bormann's anti-Christian policy, even government ministers were convinced that it was all happening behind Hitler's back. When he was a defendant at Nuremberg, Franz von Papen still believed that "at the time, Hitler was quite willing to keep his peace with religion, but the radical elements in the Party"—and here he named Bormann and Goebbels—"urged him time and again to launch attacks against the policy of the churches."

Goebbels' one-time aide Werner Stephan, on the other hand, has reported that the Reich Minister of Propaganda opposed Bormann's persecution of Christians, that he warned his staff not to leave the Church, that he always emphasized his personal affiliation with the Church in conversation with Party officials in his department, and that he had all his children baptized.

Albert Speer, a regular at the Berghof round table, has described the method by which Bormann got his Führer worked up about the churches. Although, in general, politics were not to be discussed at table, someone in the group might let drop a few words about a troublesome clergyman. Hitler would pick up the remark and ask for more details. Bormann would at first play down the case, thereby whetting Hitler's curiosity. Fully prepared, Bormann would then pull a telex message from his pocket, read it aloud and promptly trigger the desired emotional outburst from the Führer. "Once I have settled my other problems," Hitler announced, "I'll have my reckoning with the church. I'll have it reeling on the ropes."

Martin Bormann had long known from private conversations that Hitler never considered religion more than a means to an end; if the churches had adjusted to his objectives, the priests would have become his friends; since they refused, they became his enemies. He would have put up with their faith as long as they supported his power. As it was, he was determined to get rid of them just as soon as the war was won. Words to this effect were ready and waiting in the Party Chancellery's steel cabinets; Bormann had noted them down personally. They were arranged by key phrases and could be produced if anyone accused Bormann of playing his own political game. If need be, he could even use them to convince the Führer that only his will be done and that his faithful servant had been guided by the best intentions, even where he might have committed a tactical error. Being occasionally called to order by Hitler did not diminish his devotion; it was a maneuver they both winked at, which made the servant all the more indispensable. He was the bloodhound to be chained or unleashed as the occasion demanded, and for whose ferocity his master could not be held responsible. Reich Press Chief Otto Dietrich, another regular at the round table, confirmed the fact that Hitler never restrained Bormann but rather egged him on. And while the Führer himself remained a Catholic and attended religious-holiday services, "official pressure was brought to bear on Party functionaries" with his approval "to sever their ties with the churches."

Reassured by this knowledge, Bormann felt it was his duty to shape government policy along the same line. For a number of years he had watched with increasing annoyance as the long-suffering Reich Church Minister Hans Kerrl was dealt one rebuff after another by the Protestants, and as prominent Catholics—such as Württemberg's Bishop Sproll, who had conspicuously stayed away from a staged yes-or-no election—openly defied the Party. If new blood for the priesthood could be stemmed at the source, Bormann speculated, the churches would eventually dry up. In a lengthy correspondence he demanded early in 1939 that Reich Minister for Education Bernhard Rust phase out the theological departments at the universities. Theology, he argued, was "not so much a branch of liberal knowledge as a discipline serving the purpose of certain denominations." Where obligations established by concordats and formal agreements with churches stood in the way, "a special legal situation" had now been created by the general change of circumstances, since young people should in the first place attend to their military duties now and work for the country's economy. Even if the theological departments "could not be abolished altogether," they should at least be cut back substantially.

The letter was marked "Secret" not only because it was an invitation to breach of contract and violation of the law; it also would have been unwise to let the public in on this plan. Even Germans with only nominal ties to a church had no sympathy for the radicalism of the neo-pagans. By negotiation and staff studies, Minister Rust tried to postpone the decision. He knew that Göring, for one, was on his side, and so, to some extent, were Goebbels and several members of the Party elite's second echelon.

Bormann therefore sought the assistance of Alfred Rosenberg, a man he normally looked down on. In April 1939 he told Rosenberg that Rust had agreed to close down the theological departments at Innsbruck, Salzburg and Munich (where no concordat stood in the way), and to merge others or let them die out gradually. But the operation did not go quite according to plan. A few months later World War II broke out; other problems became more urgent, and Bormann was advised not to put undue strain on the morale of the German people.

A five-page letter on "The Relationship between Schools and Churches," sent to Rust on March 20, 1939, reveals how much the Reich Minister for Education was already under Bormann's thumb. Though Bormann did not himself write the letter—he did not write all that well—and had obviously edited it from a draft prepared by one of his specialists, it is typical of the way he dealt with government ministers and of his anti-Christian fanaticism. In it Bormann recommends to the young generation of, by now, the Greater German Reich what he had prescribed for his own children: total renunciation of the Christian idea.

In demanding, for instance, that religious instruction—a voluntary course for which no grades were given—not take up more than two classroom hours a week and be scheduled only as the first or last period of a school day, he hoped to lure the students away from denominational influence by offering them free time. Given the author's conviction, his insistence that religious instruction should "conform . . . to the Party's ideology" could mean only that the Christian religion should no longer be taught at all. In the end, he quite candidly stated his position: religion would be tolerated in schools only because of existing government agreements with the churches; it was quite unnecessary for the education of the young and their *Weltanschauung*. Actually Bormann considered religion counterproductive; although he never said it in so many words, his many directives and prohibitions on the subject make it clear. Religious instruction outside of school was permissible only if it did not put too much strain on the students. School prayers were abolished. Caritas (a German Catholic charity organization) was no longer allowed to send children to areas with parochial schools. Crucifixes had to disappear from the classrooms—provided this could be done without causing "political problems . . . disproportionate to the importance of such a move."

Rust, less radical and therefore hesitant, was repeatedly given to understand that too much talk had been wasted on the matter and that Bormann would now like to see action. "Without delay" the minister should submit the draft for a decree, to be followed up "soonest" by a second one; local police headquarters should be brought into the act; and Rust was given subtle warning that the Gestapo was already at work in this area. It was made clear to the minister that he had no right to rule on these matters but was expected to act merely as the Party's executive assistant. And the Party spoke to him only through Bormann, which meant that in the future Rust should "refrain from consulting with other Party offices on the subject."

As for Reich Church Minister Hans Kerrl, Bormann had long since ceased to take him seriously; in his attempts to strike a balance between the anti-Christians in the Party, the Nazi-inspired "German Christians" and the refractory Confessional Church, Kerrl had fallen between several stools. His ministry had been downgraded to a mere administrative office; he was no longer able to get anything done at all. Still, he was not willing to give up. Denied access to speaker's platforms and newsprint, he wrote a book for a small publishing house, entitled *Weltanschauung und Religion.* Bormann heard about it. In October 1939, not having read one word of it, he dictated a letter to Kerrl: the theme of the book "impinges on the domain of the Party in the strongest possible way," since it obviously attempted to draw the line between what should concern the Party and what should be reserved for the churches. It would be a mistake to publish such a book, which was clearly directed against the Party. Bormann requested that he be shown the draft—by which he obviously meant the manuscript. It would be for the Führer to decide whether or not it should be published. (See the Appendix, pages 391-392.)

Predictably, Hitler had it banned. But by then it was too late for Kerrl to stop the printing and distribution. Bormann spotted the book in the Christmas catalogues of Protestant bookstores. Himmler was told to have it confiscated. Goebbels, as Reich Minister of Propaganda, was reprimanded in writing—and thereby for the record—because his officials had not been on the ball. (See the Appendix, page 392.) No one bothered to bring it up with Kerrl; to all intents and purposes he was politically dead already. When he died two years later, still a Reich minister, Hitler gave him a state funeral but departed for his headquarters a day before the ceremony.

Before he died, however, Kerrl had one more chance to be useful to

Bormann. In the fall of 1939 Rosenberg felt the moment had come to have himself appointed pope of Nazi ideology, an extension of his position as "The Führer's Commissioner for the Supervision of the NSDAP's Instruction in Matters of Intellect and *Weltanschauung.*" He was anxious to increase his prerogatives and raise them to government level. The title he had in mind was "Commissioner for the Protection of National Socialist *Weltanschauung.*" This would have infringed on Bormann's domain. At first, in keeping with his usual tactics, Hitler allowed Rosenberg to go ahead. Reich Chancellery Chief Hans Lammers was instructed to prepare a draft announcing the functions of the new office. On December 20, 1939, all departments concerned—nine altogether—received copies. By the next day they had turned into so much wastepaper, for Bormann objected, and Lammers had to rush out a new draft. It was discussed in a conference on February 10, 1940, by the senior officers of, by now, fifteen different departments. Kerrl warned those present that Rosenberg was considered an exponent of the anti-Christian faction and that his appointment would "cause grave concern" among the public. There was also some dispute as to how far Rosenberg's sphere of responsibility should extend. Eleven days later Bormann had his triumph; Rosenberg was defeated. As far as matters of *Weltanschauung* were concerned, Bormann would continue to play his part. As Lammers wrote him: "The Führer is concerned about the objections raised by the Reich Minister of Churches" and had therefore refused to sign the decree. And why should he? Bormann, unknown to the public and therefore not suspect in any way, could keep a watchful eye on the Christians and always advocate whatever *Weltanschauung* suited his Führer at a given moment.

There were other reasons for suppressing Christianity besides the obvious one that a religion based on kindness, compassion and trust in God was bound to antagonize an unscrupulous dictatorship. To fanatical anti-Semites, Christianity had the added stigma of its Judaic origins. The attempt to transmogrify Jesus into an Aryan was merely a cover for Nazi atheism, but it also had the advantage of making it possible to saddle the Jews with the responsibility for the death of Jesus; simple-minded Christians had always regarded them as the people "who crucified our Savior." Certainly this argument had not turned Bormann into an anti-Semite, nor did he ever mention any event or experience to explain his hostility toward the Jews. Obviously, all he needed was the slogan "The Jews are our misfortune," which the Party kept repeating over and over again like a Tibetan prayer wheel.

As a Party officer who had risen from the ranks, he of course knew by heart the whole catalogue of allegations against the Jews: "lice-ridden peddlers from the East" and "exploitationist" Wall Street Jews, Zionists and assimilated Jews of the National Liberal Party, the Talmud and the teachings of Karl Marx, were all lumped together in an absurd synthesis designed to prove the existence of a secret plan for world domination. To be sure, Bormann did announce in a Party circular that Julius Streicher's yellow sheet *Der Stürmer* was not an organ of the NSDAP, but this was not because he wanted to dissociate himself from the pornographic publication. All he objected to was the crude methods by which the paper solicited subscriptions and thus encroached on the preserves of other Party publications.

One wonders if Bormann ever had a good look at Professor Hans Günther's "race bible" and found out that his rounded skull and stocky torso made him a member of the Eastern, supposedly inferior race rather than the Nordic-Germanic. Probably not. In his later letters to his wife he never mentioned the Jews, although Gerda, with terrifying naïveté, brought up the subject several times. Did he fail to answer her because he was afraid to give away the awful state secret of the "final solution"? More likely, he was never really interested in the basic facts of the Nazi regime's racial policy.

To him, this was a fact like any other, an order to be obeyed. In his various résumés he never failed to mention his early membership in an anti-Semitic organization, although only as a means to worm his way into the category of militant Party old-timers. Whatever he knew about race, and particularly about the Jews, he had learned from *Der Stürmer* or the newspaper *Völkischer Beobachter.*

During his first two years of service as chief of staff in Amt Hess, he had hardly given the matter any thought. He was still a minor official, in charge of the Relief Fund, when a Jewish boycott was called in April 1933 to stop the "terror campaign" of the foreign press. His name was first linked with Nazi racism when the Party began to deliberate on how to prevent the Jews from changing their family names in the files of the registrar's offices, together with the reverse problem: "Aryan" citizens with Jewish-sounding names.

A peasant family named Wolf, for instance, had lived for many generations in the vicinity of Stuttgart. In keeping with their Pietist traditions, they still were partial to first names taken from the Old Testament. Shouldn't they be protected from being mistaken for Jews? Always the pragmatist, Bormann had the bright idea that the Jews should be labeled in their identification papers by a legally assigned supplementary first name —which actually happened some years later. He suggested "Yid." For years the Ministry of the Interior, which was in charge of the matter, stalled on a decision, but in 1941 Israel and Sarah became obligatory first names assigned to male and female Jews, respectively.

Bormann was also involved in the anti-Semitic Nuremberg Laws, which were promulgated at the Party rally of September 1935 in a meeting of the Reichstag especially convened for the purpose. As a deputy, he naturally voted in favor. The ministries in charge were allegedly taken by surprise;

they later maintained that Hitler and his Party officials had secretly drafted the texts of the "Reich Citizenship Law" and the "Law for the Protection of German Race and Honor," by-passing the ministries' bureaucracy. Even if this was only a way of unloading responsibility, there can be no doubt that the bulk of the work was done by Bormann and his legal staff and the repercussions of those laws kept him busy for months to come.

At Nuremberg, Hitler had ordered his top leaders to "abstain from single-handed acts against the Jews," but that obviously was not enough. Bormann followed it up with a decree that Party members should not participate in "autonomous actions against provocative Jews" and that members of the Wehrmacht "unwittingly and unintentionally entering Jewish-owned stores" should not be reprimanded. But lest anyone get the idea that the Party had become more lenient, he later issued a regulation on "Contact of Party Members with Jews," which all but ruled out both personal and business relations.

Ironically enough, soon after this, Bormann himself was accused of having Jewish family ties. Buch's Party court was hearing a case against Wilhelm Kube, Gauleiter of Brandenburg, a loud-mouthed anti-Semite who, as deputy in the Prussian State Assembly, had made himself conspicious by the use of his fists and his powerful voice. In an attempt to get back at the Supreme Party Judge, Kube maintained in an anonymous letter that Frau Buch was half-Jewish—which by the Party's rigid rules would have called for Buch's dismissal from office, labeled Gerda Bormann and her children *Mischlinge* ("of mixed race") and thereby jeopardized Bormann's position. But devoted as Hitler was to Kube, that good old roughneck, it was Bormann's influence that prevailed.

In August 1936 Kube was removed from office. But he did not suffer; during the war, as district commissar in the Occupied Eastern Territories, he again held a fat sinecure until he was killed in 1943, by a bomb his Russian mistress had put under his bed.

During the years before the war, Bormann's record of anti-Semitic activities was relatively insignificant compared to that of other Party big shots; he left such matters to his friend Himmler, i.e., to the Security Service and the Gestapo, which were able to conduct unpopular business under a cloak of secrecy. He went into action only when he discovered a bureaucratic loophole in the system that was closing in ever more tightly on the Jews. He was annoyed, for instance, that government officials were still consulting Jewish doctors and buying prescriptions from Jewish pharmacists. But he was even more outraged by the fact that they were able to collect the usual government indemnity on these expenses. Minister of the Interior Wilhelm Frick, advised that taxpayers' money must not be made available to Jews, hastily issued an instruction to that effect. It was so all-inclusive that even the services of Jewish morticians were listed as not refundable.

Bormann did not participate in the *Reichskristallnacht*. But it is hard to believe that he was not informed of the allegedly spontaneous action which, in fact, had been organized down to the last detail. Members of the SA, SS and the group of political leaders, dressed as hoodlums in civilian clothes, were the actual perpetrators. Goebbels and Himmler, or rather the latter's Security Service Chief Reinhard Heydrich, pulled the strings with Hitler's consent, without which they could never have staged an operation bound to rouse world-wide horror. In other words, Hitler's "left hand"—Bormann would only later become his right hand—was well aware of the plan.

On the evening of November 9, 1938, i.e., forty-eight hours after the assassination of Ernst vom Rath in Paris, Bormann sat with the Party leaders in the assembly hall of the Old Town Hall in Munich. They were attending the traditional ceremony marking the anniversary of the 1923 putsch when word came through that all over the country the hunt for the Jews was on. The news took most of those present by surprise. Late at night Goebbels announced that "strong popular action" had developed which government and Party should not oppose, even if this was recommended by "formal juridicial considerations." The police were not to intervene, and the fire brigades were to fight fires only if it was a question of protecting German property.

At first Bormann saw no reason to get involved; he let the terror run its course. Not until long after midnight on November 10, at 2:56 A.M. to be precise, did his tickers issue instructions to all Gauleiter offices forbidding them to set fires to Jewish stores. Unlike the synagogues, these contained raw materials and merchandise which had to be protected, and which a national economy geared to an imminent outbreak of war could not do without. In his notebook Bormann did not mention the spectacular incident at all; he merely listed the official events of the Party ceremony. The journal page for the next day was left blank. He felt uninvolved in every respect. Probably he did not even envy Goebbels the job the Führer had assigned him. Being in the "Reich doghouse," thanks to his affair with Lida Baarova, the Reich Minister of Propaganda badly needed a chance to prove himself. Only three weeks before, his marriage had been barely saved by Hitler at Obersalzberg in Bormann's presence.

Gauleiter Rudolf Jordan of Dessau, who had attended the ceremony in Munich, was told on November 10 that Reichsleiter Buch would bring Party court proceedings against all participants in the pogrom. The Party's inner circle felt that that was going too far, but there was no way of stopping this law-and-order fanatic altogether. He was therefore sent a token group of the worst offenders for sentencing. In a matter of a few weeks a special judicial senate with two chambers tried sixteen cases of the most atrocious excesses. Out of thirty Party members who had been indicted, four were expelled from the NSDAP and taken into custody, not because they had raped Jewish women (among them a thirteen-year-old schoolgirl), but because they had thereby committed *Rassenschande;* they had defiled the German

race. Two others were reprimanded and deprived of their Party rank because they had committed murders in violation of expressly issued orders.
The rest had also committed murders, but according to the Party court's
summary report, the proceedings were either "dismissed out of court or
minor sentences were imposed," which meant that the defendants need not
fear further action from the government court system.

Despite all this clemency, Hitler and his cronies must have been barely
able to control their anger when they read Buch's report. The acquittals
were justified on the premise that one cannot hang the little fellows and let
the big ones go scot-free. The report even named the guilty party most
responsible. On November 10, around 2 A.M., Reich Minister of Propaganda
Goebbels had been informed that a Jew had been killed and "concern was
expressed" that "if nothing was done, the operation might get dangerously
out of hand." Goebbels had "replied to the effect that the person reporting
the incident should not get excited over one dead Jew, since thousands of
Jews would die within the next few days." The court concluded that "the
results of the operation had been intended or had at least been considered
a desirable possibility." If anyone was held responsible, it should be the
instigators. Needless to say, nothing was ever done about it.

On November 10, when the Germans stood in horror or at least in
shocked disbelief at the night's work of their political elite, Bormann—on
Hitler's instructions—wrote a letter to Göring. The Führer was still holding
himself aloof from the events. It was now up to Göring, the letter said, to
"take on the Jewish question as a whole" and "to settle it one way or
another."

On November 12 there was a meeting of all dignitaries concerned with
the matter: Göring, Goebbels, Economic Minister Walter Funk, Finance
Minister Count Lutz Schwerin von Krosigk, several State Secretaries, Chief
of Security Service Reinhard Heydrich and officials from the Reich Ministry of Air Transport. They discussed ways and means to deprive the Jews
of their property and what to do with them after that.

Meanwhile the Hitler-Bormann team spent the day in private consultation at the Berghof. Two days later the two left via Munich, Nuremberg and
Berlin for Düsseldorf to attend the funeral of the embassy official who had
been shot in Paris. Contrary to his custom of sounding off at grave sites,
Hitler kept silent on this occasion.

Other problems were now taking priority. On November 10, with the
pogrom still in full force, Hitler had addressed the publishers and editors
of the leading German newspapers in an off-the-record speech, preparing
them for what was in store. For years, he said, he had talked peace for
appearance's sake, but there were things that "could be settled only by
force." The German people should now be prepared for such an eventuality,
namely war, to which he geared his traveling schedule during the first week
of December.

On his special train he and Bormann went to visit the Czech "Maginot Line" (as Bormann called it) in the Sudetenland, which had been "conquered without a shot." Their next stop was Hillersleben Proving Grounds near Magdeburg. Wherever they went, they inspected troops and armament. Two days later they were in Kiel for the launching of the aircraft carrier *Graf Zeppelin,* a novelty in German naval equipment which, however, was never completed. Mars, the god of war, stood waiting in the wings; and Bormann was ready.

When on February 1, 1939, the SS Personnel Office sent him a questionnaire marked "Confidential"—he had meanwhile been promoted to Gruppenführer—asking him whether he had a "mobilization assignment" or whether, in the case of a mobilization, he was exempt from such assignment, he scribbled in his own handwriting: "Unnecessary, since I shall be in the Führer's company in the case of a mobilization." The fact that the statement could mean that the Führer was about to accompany him into war should not be taken as a Freudian slip; it was just that Bormann did not know how to write very well.

11

The War Profiteer

While Hitler savored the collapse of a mythical order in *Götterdämmerung* at Bayreuth, Bormann worked on his papers in the guesthouse of the Wagner family. Operas bored him, and Wagner's lengthy music-dramas most of all. His required attendance at *Die Meistersinger* at the beginning of the annual Nuremberg rally more than satisfied his needs. He knew then what few of his countrymen even suspected: the fateful drama of the German people was also heading for a climax. It was the beginning of August 1939.

The next day the Führer's convoy drove to Nuremberg. Bormann, who was in command there, in addition to his other duties, gave Hitler a tour of the superstructures already rising from their foundations at the rally grounds.

The next morning they started for Obersalzberg. When the mountain peaks began to appear, the dictator reached his most fateful decisions. It was war or peace, or more precisely, whether the war he had already planned at the beginning of his political career should begin now or later.

The year seemed to have started peaceably. In Berlin there had been the formal dedication of the new construction on the Reich Chancellery, with its enormous halls. At the solemn ceremony enacted before eight thousand workers in the Berlin Sportpalast, Bormann was not among the inner circle of the Führer's retinue. News reporters spotted him on the dais for guests of honor, and in listing them, they printed his name at the top, ahead of Robert Ley.

In mid-March Hitler raised the temperature of the already seething

cauldron of world politics by a series of moves. He occupied the rest of
Czechoslovak territory, assimilating it into the Reich as a protectorate. He
made the Lithuanians give up Memel. The Poles loomed as the next victims.
Hitler plotted their fate at the Berghof and put together his directive for
Operation White.

Shortly before, he had launched the battleship *Tirpitz* and inspected
troops in Austria. Bormann was always with him. In May they drove for
seven days through the West Wall fortifications, then watched a live-ammu-
nition exercise by a division of SS Verfügungstruppen (later the Waffen SS
combat troops) at Munsterlager Training Ground. In Bormann's Pullach
house, Hitler held a secret conference at the end of July in which he
prepared his closest Party colleagues for the possibility of a treaty with
Stalin. Two days later, the Luftwaffe demonstrated its latest achievements
at Rechlin Test Airfield. On August 7, the Gauleiter of Danzig, Albert
Forster, got instructions to fan the crisis with the Poles into a conflagration.
On August 24, at about one o'clock in the morning, Hitler received confirmation that his devil's brew was now mixed and ready: the German-Soviet
Nonaggression Pact had been signed in Moscow. Bormann, incapable of so
sudden a switch from anti-Bolshevism, ashamedly noted it down in his
journal as a German-Russian pact.

After lunch they drove to Ainring Airport, about thirty miles away and
reached Berlin at 6:40 in the evening. "Starting August 25, German mobilization is silently going forward," he noted on the next day, adding: "The
Reichstag session planned for August 26 is canceled; the Party rally will not
be canceled, only postponed." It had been billed as the "Party Rally for
Peace"—by way of camouflage. The decision was still open. If England was
willing to throw the Poles to the wolves, Hitler could accept congratulations
in the Reichstag for the peaceful conquest of Danzig and the Polish Corri-
dor.

Reichstag deputies had been summoned to Berlin for August 25. The
most prominent tried to get some information from Bormann, but Hitler
himself had not yet arrived at a clear decision. They were all quartered in
hotels around the Kroll Opera House, where the Reichstag met. They were
allowed to absent themselves for only a few hours at a time after checking
out with a security officer appointed by the commander of the Reichstag
guard. On August 27, in the late afternoon, they were summoned to the
Ambassadors' Room in the New Reich Chancellery. Hitler appeared with
Bormann, Himmler and Goebbels. He declared that if his demands were not
met, war was inevitable, and he would be "in the farthermost front line."
General Franz Halder, Chief of the General Staff, noted in his diary:
"Applause as ordered, but faint."

Meanwhile the deputies were allowed to go home. Negotiations continued, and Göring in particular took pains to prevent the diplomatic

threads of communication from being ripped apart. Bormann noted on August 29: "German mobilization goes silently forward despite all negotiations."

Rudolf Hess, and indirectly his Stabsleiter, were assigned additional functions on August 30. A Reich Defense Council for "unified control over management and business" had been created, and the Führer's Deputy had a seat as one of six on this committee. It sounded impressive, as it always did when Hitler created offices and handed out assignments. However, when it got down to everyday business, it usually proved to be pure ornament, because Hitler always kept the most important decisions for himself and arranged things so that his lieutenants would have running disputes with one another over spheres of jurisdiction. Bormann put no record of the new agency in his book. He did note: "On Thursday, August 31, German mobilization will be completed."

Hitler did not make his decision until that day. At 12:40 P.M. he signed "Directive No. 1 for the Conduct of War," the order to attack the next morning. He made the decision alone; no one from his entourage was consulted. He needed no advisers, only people to execute orders. Bormann had to see that the Reichstag deputies, who had meanwhile been recalled, appeared in as full force as possible. A session was called for 10 A.M. the next day, but announced in the hotels only after midnight. Just before six in the morning, the deputies might possibly have learned that the die was cast when a proclamation of Hitler's was read over the radio. But because they had all gone to bed so late, many heard the news for the first time in the Opera House lobby outside the auditorium that served as the Chamber. Bormann, who was also a deputy and had moved up to eighth place in the Reich Seniority List in the 1938 elections, did not enter the Chamber with the rest; he went in with Hitler's party. Hitler wore "field gray" cut in the style of a Nazi Party uniform. He spoke of the front soldier's tunic, "that was most sacred and dear to me. I will not take it off again until victory is secured—or I will not survive the outcome."

Going through the archives, one is struck by the incongruity that Bormann, normally in such a hustle, was feeding fewer papers than usual into the Party machinery during those critical days. Like the Chief of the General Staff, he had made every organizational preparation for a war situation beforehand. So he was free to remain at Hitler's side in the Reich Chancellery.

Around noon on September 3, he was waiting in the anteroom with most of the Reich ministers and the top Party members. In the office next door, Chief Interpreter Paul Schmidt was translating the ultimatum delivered by the British government. It contained a Declaration of War; another was expected momentarily from France. When Schmidt announced this in the anteroom, everyone realized that the invasion of Poland had turned into a world war. They had nearly all been afraid of this, but except for Göring, not one of them had made any attempt to stop it. Bormann is not on record as having taken any position; he trusted the Führer's genius.

All who had been chosen to accompany Hitler to headquarters received an order: "Have luggage ready. Departure tonight." A special train stood waiting in the Stettiner Bahnhof (one of the Berlin railway stations), in which Hitler, according to one of his proclamations, was to leave "today for the front."

The train remained Hitler's headquarters until the end of September. Bormann had his mini-office in one of the ten railway cars. They were pulled by two locomotives and protected by armored cars with quadruple-turret artillery. Hitler's living room, sleeping compartment, bathroom and the compartments for his adjutants were in the first car. After that came the command car, with a conference room and signals section, outfitted with teletype machines, radiotelephone and other radio equipment. Bormann was in the next car. Reich Press Chief Dietrich, also on board, placed Bormann's name far down under "Others" on the passenger list in his victory release on the Polish campaign. He claimed that Bormann was in charge of the "execution and transmittal of all orders from the Führer . . . that fall within the Party's jurisdiction." Shades of professional jealousy!

During the trip Bormann also served as liaison to the government sector, since Ribbentrop, Lammers and Himmler were on another train and Göring remained at Luftwaffe headquarters.

Using the train as his fixed base, the Supreme Warlord and his retinue made reconnaissance junkets through the conquered country, sometimes driving within close range of the advancing front. Together with the armored reconnaissance cars commanded by Major General Erwin Rommel, it made an awesome convoy. It was joined by the cars of high-ranking military officers, government officials and Party officers, all following in Hitler's footsteps. Bormann felt he was being pushed around by them and complained about it to Rommel, who yelled back at him, "I'm not your nurse—if it bothers you so much, go straighten it out yourself!"

At this time Hitler was getting ready to slip into the role of the great strategist. He followed the operation of the military machine with undivided attention; politics had become peripheral. It was Bormann's business to keep the home front intact by his messages from the signals car. In Hitler's last speech, he had warned: "Let no one report to me that morale is bad in his Gau!" The Party machine had to be kept moving; the drumfire of pep talk could not slacken; vigilance against "grumblers and gripers" must be intensified. The Reichstatthalters, the state governors, who had been appointed Reich Defense Commissioners, must have their backbones stiffened so they would not let themselves be ignored as the "executive branch" by the military men in the army district commands.

The first time Bormann was again able to involve himself in a top-level government policy action came on September 18. Hitler had entered Danzig as a triumphant conqueror and declared in a speech that the war in Poland was over after eighteen days—though the fighting still continued.

At this moment Hitler decided to deal with a problem he had been carrying around in his head for a long time. His own codeword for it was "Euthanasia," which actually means helping terminally ill people to die if they wish. Hitler's plan, however, was "destruction of unworthy life," which meant mass murder of the incurably insane. While the public's attention was on the war, the Reich must be rid of useless consumers of food, who were also a burden on hospitals and their staffs. According to Hitler's notions of racial biology, if men of precious German blood had to go out and get killed on the battlefield, then those of inferior racial heritage must not survive.

Bormann had known about these plans for some time. Back in 1935, Hitler had shared them with Reich Surgeon General Dr. Gerhard Wagner, a member of Bormann's staff, who had since died. And a few months before, Dr. Karl Brandt, Hitler's physician, had authorized doctors in Leipzig to kill a child born blind and hopelessly retarded. The parents had pleaded for this "mercy death" in a letter addressed to Hitler. Through channels the letter came to the Führer's Secretariat and the desk of Reichsleiter Philipp Bouhler. Now the decision was to be made in a luxury hotel in Zoppot as to who would get the same operation going on a vast scale, and then run it.

Bormann had always thought of Bouhler's office as irksome competition for the Führer's favor, the more so as his brother Albert worked there. Whoever got the secret "Euthanasia" assignment would gain distinction. He therefore suggested that Reich Director of Public Health Dr. Leonardo Conti, Wagner's successor, with whom he had been friendly since Relief Fund times be put in charge.

The assignment was not given out immediately. Reich Minister Hans Heinrich Lammers, head of the Reich Chancellery, who was responsible for the legal end of it, was called in. His arguments must have provoked thoughts on Conti's part; he insisted on a law specifically empowering physicians, heads of institutions and hospital personnel to kill, otherwise they would all be liable to prosecution. Hitler did not go along with that, nor did he like Conti's plan to do the victims in with overdoses of drugs; he considered this method too time-consuming.

The decision came at the end of October; Bouhler and Dr. Karl Brandt got the assignment. To legitimize their authority, they were given no more than a couple of typewritten lines on Hitler's private stationery, with his name and a gold eagle on the letterhead. The text, classified "Secret," gave Bouhler and Brandt the right to authorize the killing of the incurably ill.

The competition for the job of mass murder—according to Dr. Brandt's later confession there were some 60,000 victims—is characteristic of the individual's total subjugation under the catchwords "The Führer commands, we follow." Reichsleiter Bouhler with his "Führer's Private Chancellery" had been practically unknown to the public until then. He had had to accept the perpetual chipping away of his area of responsibility by Bormann's Party Chancellery. Now he felt it was his turn to make a contribution to historic events. While competing for the job, he had assured himself of the support of Göring, Himmler and Frick. After the war his deputy, Dr. Viktor Brack, told the court as a defendant at the Nuremberg Trials that Bouhler and Brandt had competed only so that Bormann and Conti would not get it, for in the hands of those men, "euthanasia . . . would never have been confined to the incurably insane." This may have been the usual self-exculpating defense put forward in hindsight ("to avoid something worse"). But it is also certain that Bormann would have carried out every order of Hitler's in this respect without any qualms.

Whether he really wanted the assignment at all costs remains an open question. He would have had to pass it on to Conti, and he had begun to have reservations about Conti's loyalty. Perhaps he wanted to drive up the competition, like prices at an auction. It would not hurt to have Bouhler involved in such a nasty business. And soon Bormann had the satisfaction of being called in to help after all, because there had been foul-ups in the operation. They had made the mistake of using the same form letter to notify all the victims' families. This declared that the patients had died of appendicitis, although the relatives of some of them knew that they had had that organ removed long before. Bishops protested, and the Stuttgart district attorney intervened with the Reich Minister of Justice on "cases of unnatural death in hospitals and asylums."

What was happening in the insane asylums leaked to the public. The regional Party offices all over the country sent queries to Amt Hess to ask what was going on and how they were supposed to handle the situation.

District Leader Zimmermann, who was managing Franconia in Streicher's place, wanted to know the purpose of a doctors' committee then active in the Neuendettelsau Asylum. Bormann naturally could not tell him in black and white that candidates for death were being selected. So he wrote—at the end of September 1940—that the committee "is under the control of Reichsleiter Bouhler, and is acting on his orders." In answer to Zimmermann's report that the numerous deaths had caused public unrest, he wrote that "notifications of relatives . . . are being phrased differently," but there might be one or two cases "in which two families living close together have received letters with the same wording." Even when the churches opposed the action, it was still to be clearly understood "that all Party offices give their support . . . to the committee's work." (The full text of this letter is given in the Appendix on page 393.)

Naturally, Bouhler was blamed for the way he had botched the job. Brack's deputy, Party Comrade Blankenburg, was sent on a tour of all the

Gauleiter offices to try to save the situation. What he said was taken down by the clerk at one such conference in the beginning of October 1940. The key phrases tell the story: "Hardly any errors so far. 30,000 out of the way. An additional 100,000 to 120,000 waiting. Keep number of people informed down to a minimum. When necessary tell district leaders in time. If possible, supply list of candidates: 1) Institutions; 2) Attitude of doctors; 3) Location of institution?; 4) Who is the district leader? The Führer has given the order. Law already enacted. At present only clear-cut cases being processed, more to be included later. Notification will be handled more adroitly from now on."

Meanwhile, however, the public had found out what was happening. It was for this reason, and by no means on any grounds of conscience, that the liquidations were terminated in August 1941 by Hitler's verbal order to Brandt. Bouhler had not made a desirable track record for himself; he had mismanaged at the very moment Bormann was approaching the apogee of his power.

At first it looked as if the war might drive Bormann out of the competition. At the onset, he had proudly written to Lammers: "I will continue to be part of the Führer's staff, therefore after the Führer leaves Berlin, I will be unable to represent the Führer's Deputy at the conferences of the Council of Ministers for the Defense of the Reich." Apparently Bormann's presence at these meetings had become the rule. The other members of the council, especially Göring, Frick, Lammers and Minister of Economics Funk, were surely not sorry that Bormann would be detained elsewhere. They had been given full authority to run their shop working together— without having to clear anything through Hitler, who was now totally absorbed in the war, and without having Bormann's power-hungry shadow around. But nothing much came of the council. Göring was too easygoing, Frick too much of a dried-up bureaucrat, Lammers too timid, and Funk not ambitious enough. Since they always had to reckon with the possibility that Hitler might overrule them, they decided to table all decisions not important to the war, so as not to make any mistakes.

Their independence soon diminished. On October 6, 1939, the whole headquarters moved back to Berlin. The next day Bormann proudly recorded in his notebook that the Führer's new Condor airplane had been put at his disposal for an excursion to Obersalzberg. He was chiefly occupied with the new Gaus of Danzig and the Wartheland. Gauleiter Forster continued to rule in the old Hanseatic town, but a new man had to be found for the former Prussian garrison town of Posen, in the newly created Wartheland Gau. Following Bormann's suggestion, Arthur Greiser, president of the Danzig Senate, was appointed Gauleiter there, and both Gauleiters were directed to fill their Gaus with "German blood" as rapidly as possible, i.e., to get rid of Poles and Jews. How they did it was up to them. As long as they reported a 100 percent success, no one would ask any questions. The means to carry it out were explained, and made available to them. SS Einsatzgruppen (task forces) had already begun their work of murder and deportation.

Generaloberst Franz Halder, Chief of the General Staff, began to get reports from horrified army officers. On October 5 he wrote in his diary: "Murders of Jews—discipline." On that same day Hitler and Bormann heard complaints from Forster that the Wehrmacht showed no understanding of his "measures in connection with population policy." Not quite two weeks later, Hitler informed the Chief of the Wehrmacht High Command (OKW), Generaloberst Wilhelm Keitel, that a civilian administration would relieve the military in Poland. Present at the conference were Hans Frank, who had been appointed Governor General, Frick and Bormann. It was plain enough what Hitler wanted: "The implementation requires a harsh struggle between national identities, which will not allow for any legalistic inhibitions." The Wehrmacht was unsuitable for such an operation.

For Bormann and the new Gauleiters the conquered country was to become an experimental testing ground. Laws that would have interfered with the program in the Reich were often considered not applicable to Poland. In the new Gaus, and most particularly in Nazi-occupied Poland, there was an opportunity to implement programs that "served the people" according to the Nazi definition. From his personnel files Bormann unearthed especially fanatical and unscrupulous Party comrades to set up an administration. The fact that these men enriched themselves and—unlike other citizens in Reich territory who were on reduced wartime rations—lived high on the hog did not bother him at all. What was annoying was that so many of these well-fed Party hacks shacked up with Polish women. Hitler heard about that in the spring of 1940, and Bormann was instructed to tell Minister of the Interior Frick that all such officials, who had no national pride, were to be "immediately removed from government service and their pensions forfeited."

This was not possible under existing law, however, so Frick tried equivocation. He pointed out that if this were to go through, sexual intercourse with Czech women would also have to be prohibited, and the ban would have to include soldiers as well. Konstantin von Neurath, Reich Protector in Prague, and Hans Frank, Governor General in Cracow, were told to take a position on the issue. The move eventually gathered dust in the files without anything concrete being done. Nothing was heard from Bormann, who was usually so punctilious about following up any unfinished business. Could he have sympathized with his Party comrades? It is more likely that he filed their sins away in the archives, because a guilty person might be more pliable.

These incidents were not earth-shaking affairs, certainly, and Bormann's role in them was relatively modest. But since he had so many opportunities to discuss matters with the Führer, it must be assumed that he could also influence decisions. When Frank called him a yes-man and a toady, it was only half the truth. The other half was the unbounded worship and total submission of a lowbrow in thrall to a brilliant psychopath. Hitler could not tolerate opponents in his entourage; he had to have positive feedback of everything he said as a stimulus. This Bormann supplied. All the same, Bormann must have been less influential between the outbreak of the war and the spring of 1941 than he ever was before or after. For during this time Hitler was occupied with the planning and strategy of his campaigns, and Bormann, his brown shadow, was out of his element in military matters.

Bormann, of course, had to make an appearance at the traditional anniversary celebration of the Munich putsch. On November 7, 1939, late at night, he boarded the Führer's special train in Berlin. A few days before it had still been an open question whether the big show would take place. Against the advice of the generals, the offensive on the western front would be launched in the next few days. In Munich, Bormann accompanied Hitler on a visit to a hospital. He was quite right in accepting this as a proof of his master's trust in him. There lay Unity Mitford, who had shot herself in the head with a pistol in despair at the outbreak of war against her country and was now being treated by the best surgeons in the city on Hitler's orders.

Punctually at 8 P.M., Bormann trudged with the first group of the Führer's retinue to the seats reserved around the speaker's platform in the Bürgerbräu cellar. At 9:07 Hitler brayed out his concluding *"Sieg Heil!"* The patriotic anthems had scarcely died away when he hastily went back to his car. The scheduled express train for Berlin was due to leave Munich at 9:31, and special cars had been attached for Hitler and a few men in his party. The train was still standing in the station when, at 9:20, a bomb exploded in the Bürgerbräu cellar behind the wooden paneling around a walled pillar behind the speaker's platform. The exact times are important, because this assassination attempt was viewed in many quarters as a put-up job. A good deal of evidence counters this hypothesis, but the controversy has no place here. Bormann's notebook entries, presumably written the next day and never intended for the public, indicate that he had known nothing of the bomb. He wrote: "In Nuremberg a report reached us on the train that eight minutes after we left Munich, the Bürgerbräu cellar was destroyed by an assassination attempt with explosives; 8 dead, 60 wounded." All the figures are wrong. Had the entry been intended to conceal complicity in a staged event, the figures would have been correct. A scene that took place late in the afternoon after the party had reached Berlin supports the theory that the attempt was genuine. Hitler's chauffeur Kempka had ordered a heavily armored Mercedes sometime before, but his master had refused even to look at it. Now he inspected it and found it would do nicely. He told Bormann that from then on he would use only that vehicle. "How can

I tell if some idiot might not throw a bomb in front of my car?"

Because that day Hitler postponed the attack in the West to an undetermined date, the "phony war" continued for the time being. Bormann commuted with Hitler on the special train for the rest of the year and the first quarter of the next, shuttling between Berlin, Munich and Obersalzberg. During the Christmas holidays they visited troops near the front. With appropriate folksiness, they celebrated with Christmas trees and candlelight the birth of the founder of a religion they were in the very act of trying to demolish. "Christmas celebration" is written three times in Bormann's notebook, if one includes the visit to the SS Leibstandarte bodyguard unit at Bad Ems where, as Himmler had ruled, a "Yule festival was being observed."

Bormann busied himself a good deal with the Christian faith and the churches during the uneventful early months of 1940. Hitler had more time for the Party now; the Wehrmacht had been given its instructions. He finally allowed the Party court to proceed against Gauleiter Streicher. Rosenberg, in his capacity as training director in National Socialist *Weltanschauung* for the postwar period, was commissioned to make preparations for an "institute of advanced education" as "a central facility for National Socialist research." Ley was instructed to develop plans for a "comprehensive, generous social security system for the elderly." Occasionally Party big shots were invited to meals in the Reich Chancellery. There, as at Obersalzberg and later in the various headquarters, Bormann had his place opposite the host. The meals were plain, often a single-course casserole as an economy measure. The guests handed in their ration cards as they would in a hotel, and the kitchen had to get along on the regular rations. Shop talk was rare; Hitler did not want it, and his followers avoided it because they mistrusted one another.

A typical table conversation occurred at the end of January 1940, in which Hess, Rosenberg, Lammers and, of course, Bormann, took part. Someone told a story about a ship's captain in the merchant marine who after an absence of many years put in to Odessa and discovered that, unlike previous occasions, this time there was not a single Jew among the officials of their new Soviet friends. Hitler declared that if this was a new trend, it could lead to a terrible pogrom, and the West would end up begging him to come to the rescue of human rights in the East. The company found that idea very droll, especially when the host, trying for more mileage, went on to say that he, as president of a congress for the protection of the Jews, would appoint Rosenberg executive secretary.

Continuing the conversation, Hitler described a motion picture being shown in the Soviet Union that dealt critically with the Vatican's influence in Poland and asked if there would be any way of getting hold of a print. With mock sternness, Rosenberg declared, "We're not allowed to show anything about the Vatican here." Bormann, roaring with laughter, interrupted him, "Then things like that can be seen only in Russia—too bad!" Like Ribbentrop when he signed the Moscow Pact with the Communists, if Bormann had gone to Russia, he would have felt that he was among old Party comrades.

Two entries of Bormann's from those February days in 1940 are noteworthy. On February 24 he and Hitler had taken the special train to Munich for the annual ceremony to commemorate the founding of the Party. In the Hofbräuhaus beer hall Hitler delivered the usual speech to the Nazi veterans, then went on with his close circle to Café Heck, where the original group had met in the old days. Bormann noted: "Dispute between the Führer and R.H. on healers and *Magnetopaten.*" He was unfamiliar with the last word and should have written *Magnetopathen* (mesmerists). But R.H.—the initials stood for Rudolf Hess—knew all about it. He was the patron saint of chiropractors, homeopaths, nature freaks, astrologers, clairvoyants, and so on. When any of them were harassed by narrow-minded Party bureaucrats wedded to simple rationalism, they always turned to Hess for intervention and relief. Bormann sometimes made fun of this side of his boss. But since in his official capacity he was always loyal to him, it cannot be assumed that he was trying to undercut Hitler's regard for him by such wisecracks. On the other hand, it is not impossible that these barbs made a dent and that Hitler was seizing the rare chance for a meeting with Hess in a private place to read him a lecture. Perhaps his Hofbräuhaus speech, in which he compared himself to a magnet "always playing over the German people" and inducing new currents of power, had served as an impetus. The word Bormann used, *Disput,* implies that Hess defended his convictions. He could be very stubborn and most likely resisted any attempt to change his mind.

When Hitler took his special train back to Berlin the next day, he was still working the topic over. In his parlor car there was, according to Bormann's notebook, a long "Conversation of the Führer with M.B. on the theme of 'superstition and medicine' and prominent Party men." Bormann was able to contribute a fair amount to that conversation. In his personal card file on top Nazis and in the Security Service records available to him, there were notes on many bizarre idiosyncrasies of Party men in high places. The choice crackpot of them all was, of course, Himmler, who swore that much ancient folk wisdom could be found in the practices of shepherds and female herbalists. In any event, this conversation did not put Hess in Hitler's bad books because two months later, on Hess's forty-sixth birthday, Hitler called at his Berlin residence to offer congratulations, a very special honor by Third Reich standards.

Nevertheless, Bormann found it necessary to put in the *Reichsverfügungsblatt* (Reich Ordinance Bulletin) of the NSDAP a "clarification" marked "Confidential" and "Not for Publication" for the benefit of the political leaders, to refresh their memories on the prerogatives and importance of his office. It informed them that the papers composed by his specialists were not to be interpreted as "opinions expressed by the Führer personally," but that "in all questions concerning the leadership of the Party," he was "the Führer's Deputy"—and Bormann really was, for all practical purposes—"the highest and last instance under the Führer." The leaders were instructed to forward "proposals and suggestions for legislation" to the ministers of the departments concerned only through his office. Moreover, in the appointment of officials, no other Party agency needed to be consulted.

This ukase is dated May 9, 1940, but it surely had been on Bormann's desk ready for signature before that. For on that day he boarded the special train at 4:38 P.M. with Hitler and the retinue. As the departure was supposed to be secret, it was arranged from the outlying Berlin-Finkenkrug railway station. According to the entry, the train went "first, for camouflage, in the direction of Hamburg, then by way of Uelzen-Celle to Euskirchen." The destination was concealed from most of the passengers, but Bormann, one of the few in on the secret, knew where he was when he got off, though all station signs that read "Euskirchen" had been carefully removed. The next morning, punctually on time for the launching of the offensive set for five-thirty, the convoy of cars arrived at the "Felsennest" (Nest in the Rocks), a headquarters equipped with concrete bunkers, anti-aircraft guns and quarters for troops, built on a hill within the boundaries of the village of Rodert near Münstereifel.

Not until late the previous evening, after getting the last weather reports, had Hitler sent off the code word to begin the attack in the West but he had told Bormann days before. Apparently Bormann's ukase to the Party Organization was intended to remind the top level that they must faithfully observe all the ground rules even if Bormann was away for a long period. This was all the more important since Hitler would have no time for Party matters in the turbulent weeks to follow. And that is just how it worked out. For many days there were no entries in Bormann's notebook; he had so little to do that not until he had been at the Felsennest a whole twenty days did he take a pencil and note that it had rained for the first time.

Bormann sprang into activity again when a civil administration had to be established in the conquered territories. That had been true before in mid-May, when Josef Terboven, Gauleiter of Essen, was appointed Reich Commissar for occupied Norway, and again, after the capitulation of Holland, when the Austrian Anschluss specialist Arthur Seyss-Inquart got the same post for the Netherlands. On May 25, Bormann had a conference with him, Police Chief Himmler, and Fritz Schmidt-Münster from Amt Hess. Bormann used a favorite word for that meeting: *Rücksprache,* consultation, implying that he, Bormann, was issuing the orders. A month later, when all fighting ceased after the armistice, he had his own day of triumph when he summoned the Party "war profiteers" who had made a good thing out of the victory in the West to a conference at headquarters in the Black Forest (code name "Tannenberg"). Besides Seyss-Inquart and his staff, there were the Gauleiter of Baden, Robert Wagner, now proconsul in Alsace as well; Baldur von Schirach, who was taking over as Gauleiter of Vienna; and Josef Bürckel, recently of Vienna and transferred to his native Gau of Saar-Palatinate, which had recently been enlarged by the conquest of Lorraine. Bormann had worked out the suggestions for these shifts weeks before, and Hitler had signed the paper.

During those weeks Bormann spent many days traveling—by plane, car, special train. Whenever Hitler left headquarters, he was always along with pad and pencil in his pocket. He allowed himself only one private excursion: two days after the capture of Paris he drove to the French capital with Adolf Wagner, Gauleiter of Munich, but he refrained from sampling any of that city's pleasures. In the evening he reappeared opposite Hitler at the headquarters dinner table. He went to Munich with Hitler for the meeting with Mussolini, accompanied him for the signing of the armistice in the historic railway car in the Compiègne Forest, flew to Paris with him and his favorite architect, and tagged along when the Führer showed his buddies from World War I some of the old battlegrounds. Bormann regretted moving out of the advanced headquarters (code name "Wolfsschlucht"—Wolf's Ravine), a transportable barracks camp near the Belgian town of Bruly le Pêche. "Sorry to leave," he noted in the book, and added, "Huge slaughter of chickens and pigs." After many weeks on lean army rations supplied only from what was available at home, the retinue had received special permission to help themselves to whatever the cellars and barnyards in enemy country could provide.

On July 9, exactly two months after the departure from Berlin, the special train pulled into the main railway station in Munich. The day before, Hitler had praised his soldiers in a Reichstag speech. Now he was to honor his vassal with a favor granted to only a few: he gave a party in Bormann's house at Pullach and invited a lot of Munich artists. What followed amounted to gilding the lily—after the victory, which had been splendid in itself, there were receptions, state ceremonies, a series of trips between the Berghof, Linz, Munich, Berlin, and once to Essen for the seventieth birthday of munitions king Krupp, to whom Bormann, on Hess's behalf, presented a bust of Hitler.

During this peaceful period Bormann, like all Party big shots, was making his own plans to exploit the vastly expanded area Hitler now dominated. Himmler came forward first, with a paper written by his alert staff of young manager types entitled "Staff Study on the Treatment of Non-German Nationalities in the East." In his covering letter to Bormann he boasted that "The Führer found it very good . . . but gave instructions that only very few copies should be made available." It was treated as classified material (*Geheime Reichssache,* a very high security label) and shown only to the

Gauleiters in the East—Erich Koch (East Prussia), Albert Forster (Danzig-West Prussia), Arthur Greiser (Wartheland) and the Governor General of Poland, Hans Frank. Bormann got his copy. It suggested that the "racially valuable" people from Polish territory be removed and Germanized. The masses were to be at the Reich's disposal as "a leaderless nation of common labor." Until the end of time these people were not to be taught anything more than "simple arithmetic up to 500 at the most, how to write their name, and that it is God's commandment to be obedient and honest, hard-working and well-behaved toward Germans." There was no need for them to learn to read.

Despite Himmler's assurances, Bormann was not going to accept this document as an authentic expression of the Führer's intentions; he knew better than anyone how easily and casually Hitler handed out compliments. Besides, the manuscript came from his rivals in black. Therefore, at the beginning of October 1940 he took advantage of a "consultation of the Führer's with Governor General Dr. Frank" to inject his own thoughts on this general theme into the minutes of the meeting. Accordingly, Poland was to be reduced to a "work camp," whose inmates would be seasonal workers employed in the Reich only temporarily. Interbreeding with Germans should be prevented. The Poles were to earn enough so they could send some money home to their families, but the "lowest German peasant must still be ten percent better off than any Pole." They were to keep their Catholic priests so they would always remain "dull and stupid." All intelligent Poles were to be exterminated, because "that is the law of nature."

A few months later Hans Frank complained that the Poles were being treated intolerably badly—even worse than these slave regulations called for. Fearful that he might not be able to fulfill the economic production targets imposed on him, he reminded Bormann of the Führer's guidelines during that conversation. Frank had no copy of the minutes, however. So Bormann could brush him off by saying that as a participant in the conversation he knew for a fact that "no such decisions were ever arrived at," that on the contrary the Führer took the position that the Poles were not Europeans at all, but Asians, to be handled with a knout. Frank refrained from calling another guest at that table as witness, knowing he could not expect any support from Gauleiter Koch, of East Prussia, who was one of the most ferocious operators in the eastern territories and a conscienceless mass murderer, whose Gau had been substantially expanded by parts of conquered Poland. Bormann had had frequent disputes with him before because he used to ignore all orders from Munich as a matter of course. But now Koch and Bormann were friends.

As it turned out, Hitler's slave plan proved problematic in one respect. The Poles sent to work in factories and on large estates came in contact with not only race-proud National Socialist women but also women of different ages who would not put up with the shortage of men created by the draft.

Women who thus forgot their "racial identity" were sent off to concentration camps by the Gestapo—at least for a few months. Worse befell their imprudent lovers. On Himmler's orders, these unfortunates were hanged without trial; but first he had photographs sent him of the delinquents, for any who looked Germanic enough were to be reprieved and Germanized.

"Prohibitions and threats of punishment," Bormann wrote confidentially to the Gauleiters in December 1940, "are of only limited effectiveness, and because of political considerations cannot be promulgated in all cases." He then referred to a decree from Minister of the Interior Frick which he himself had inspired, ordering "the establishment of special houses for prostitutes." Here, however, "general racist principles are to be taken into consideration." The Gauleiters were directed "to give special attention . . . to the question of establishing bordellos for foreign workers . . . In case difficulties arise, I request an immediate report." (See the Appendix, page 397.)

He was much more concerned over Reich Minister of Justice Franz Gürtner's plan to introduce German criminal law in the assimilated eastern territories—i.e., the Gaus of Danzig–West Prussia and Wartheland, and parts of East Prussia and Silesia. In a way, this would have ended the wanton arbitrariness and terror being visited on the Polish population by Party officers, because the atrocities would then have to be investigated and punished by German courts. Bormann protested against this plan in a seven-page letter to Lammers. He signed the letter, but he surely did not write it; he had neither the legal knowledge nor the requisite language skills. The content, however, reflects his conviction: a regular criminal code would prevent the Gauleiters from fulfilling the Führer's command to make their regions "German—and that means pure German"; only martial law would enable them to bludgeon the Poles into total submission or even extirpate them, without any juridical restraints.

This product of bureaucratic inhumanity (reproduced *in toto* in the Appendix on pages 394-397) gives us the first evidence that Bormann did more than pass down or interpret orders from above. It reveals him as an executive who originated actions from his own desk. He personally saw to it that the directives he formulated on November 20, 1940, were implemented. In May 1941 the Reich Ministry of Justice agreed in principle to place the Poles under a special criminal law. Bormann was still not content. In another letter to Lammers he demanded "a special criminal trial procedure for Poles, differing fundamentally from the procedure applicable to Germans . . . and which, in order to serve its purpose more usefully, should be enacted in the form of a police-type martial law." Besides the death penalty, "introduction of corporal punishment . . . should be considered."

Bormann made clear what he had in mind for this martial law in another letter written a week later. In it he told Lammers about an incident in Wartheland. A policeman of German ancestry was stoned in a Polish village. Gauleiter Greiser took the guilty ones and an additional twelve hostages from the village and had them hanged in the presence of the entire population, which had been rounded up. Bormann's comment: "Since the Gauleiter . . . lacked the proper legal authority for such proceedings," he asked that "the Führer renew his authorization for setting up martial-law courts," which in this case would be a Party officer as court president and two police officers as members. Bormann asked that the verdicts of these courts be restricted to either concentration camp or death. Hitler gave Greiser "the desired authority" and ruled in addition that commutation of the death sentence imposed on Poles was no longer the province of the Reich Minister of Justice, but would be decided by the local Gauleiter.

Almost as significant as the content of this letter are some concomitant circumstances. Lammers, head of the Reich Chancellery and the official responsible for the phrasing of laws and coordination with the Reich minister concerned, learned from a Reichsleiter, i.e., a Party officer, what the chief of state had decreed over the heads of all the organs of government —in flagrant violation of all existing law. At the same time the individuals responsible for this decision—Hitler, Lammers, Greiser and Bormann—all happened to be at Obersalzberg, so the letter marked "By Hand! Personal!" could have been handed directly to each addressee. Thus began a practice which more and more became the rule: Hitler reigned, in authoritarian fashion, from his throne; Bormann shielded him from objections and recommendations, and so became the sole adviser, interpreter and proclaimer of the supreme will.

On December 4, 1941, the "Edict on Criminal Law Practices against Poles and Jews in the Incorporated Eastern Territories" was published in the *Reich Law Bulletin.* Bormann had achieved what he was after: police-type martial law.

Historians argue over whether Bormann moved into this role more or less out of necessity, whether he seized it, or whether he obtained it by false pretenses. All three versions are correct. For years Bormann had worked at undercutting the reputation of other competitors for Hitler's favor, partly by intrigue, partly by the strength of his elbows. At the same time he succeeded, by a combination of humble adoration and almost superhuman capacity for work, in winning Hitler's almost total confidence. But in the long run his role could never have become so all-embracing and above all so effective without an event that raised him overnight to heights above all the rest of the Führer's retinue. It was an event that deeply shocked all Germans—at a moment when their soldiers had subjugated half of Europe and they no longer harbored any doubts that a victorious peace was just around the corner.

On May 11, 1941, at around ten o'clock in the morning, two of Rudolf Hess's adjutants, Dietsch and Leitgen, appeared at the Berghof. Greatly agitated, their faces white, they announced that they had a personal letter from their superior to deliver to Hitler. The addressee was still asleep, as usual at that time of the morning, and they had to wait in the anteroom. When Albert Speer appeared with architectural sketches, they asked him if they could go in ahead of him because their mission was urgent. Finally Hitler emerged from his private rooms on the second floor and came down the stairs. He summoned Dietsch to the adjoining living room. Speer reports: "While I began leafing through my sketches once more, I suddenly heard an inarticulate, almost animal outcry. Then Hitler roared: 'Bormann, at once! Where is Bormann?' "

What had upset Hitler so much and brought on his scream for his closest confidant was the written message from his Party Deputy that he had flown to England, hoping through friendly connections with influential people there to end the war with the British Empire before Hitler started the now carefully planned campaign against the Soviet Union. Bormann was told to summon Göring, Foreign Minister von Ribbentrop and Luftwaffe General Ernst Udet, ordnance chief of the Air Force, immediately. The facts of the case were soon clarified.

In the late afternoon of the previous day, Rudolf Hess, fighter pilot in World War I and a successful private flier since, had taken off from Augsburg's Hanstetten Airport in a Messerschmitt 110 in the direction of the North Sea, with extra fuel tanks for increased range, maps and the latest weather reports. Udet was supposed to give an opinion on Hess's chances of reaching England. He reported back by telephone: due to navigational difficulties, as good as none at all.

Clinging to hopes, Hitler exclaimed, "If only he would drown in the North Sea! Then he would vanish without a trace, and we could take our time working out some harmless explanation." In fact, Hess had after an astounding aeronautical feat reached his destination in Scotland nearly twelve hours before all hell broke loose at the Berghof.

Hitler was surely not afraid that Hess might betray state secrets. But he was enormously concerned over how to explain to the German public and to his allies the disappearance of his Deputy Führer, who had stood next in line in the succession behind Crown Prince Göring. Conferences on this went on for hours, and finally Bormann's suggestion was accepted that Hess should be declared insane. Reich Press Chief Dietrich had to contrive an official Party statement to that effect. According to the release, issued on May 12, despite the Führer's order prohibiting Hess from flying because of an advancing illness, he had been able to get hold of an aircraft and had not returned from the flight. A letter left behind betrayed mental disorder. Therefore, unfortunately, it must be believed that Hess had crashed.

Propaganda expert Goebbels was not consulted in this affair. He found the post facto explanation quite idiotic. Just how idiotic, events very soon showed. The BBC broadcast that Hess was in British custody. Now a second announcement had to be made. It asserted among other things that

Hess, in a state of great physical suffering (he was, in fact, perfectly healthy) might have been thrown into mental confusion by "mesmerists, astrologers, etc.," and an investigation was about to be initiated to ascertain "to what extent these individuals might be responsible."

Bormann's journal entry on the already mentioned "debate" in the Café Heck on February 24, 1940, suggests that he might have contributed an idea or two to this announcement. But there are no facts to prove that he knew of Hess's plan or even encouraged it, to make way for his own progress, although that suspicion turns up occasionally among historians. It could not have seemed a very promising idea to get rid of the man behind whose good reputation and vast despotic powers he had been hiding until then. Before Hess's flight, Bormann had already been able to manage and command as he pleased, and to the day he died he never felt any need to be fêted in public. Besides, if there had been the faintest trace of evidence of any such machinations, it would have been his ruin. Hess's adjutants, who were only fragmentarily in on the secret, were immediately sent to a concentration camp by Hitler, and anyone who had been in contact with Hess in any way was cross-examined or arrested.

There is more weight to the theory that the introvert Hess was driven to the flight because he felt increasingly shorn of his power by Bormann's unremitting ascent. Baldur von Schirach suggested: "Perhaps it was in protest against this silent degradation that Hess took himself off on his mystery-shrouded flight to England." In Spandau Prison, where Hess and Schirach were together for twenty years and were actually friends at times, the former Reich Youth Leader tried to get Hess to confirm this theory. But his taciturn jailmate immediately asserted that he could not recall anything about Bormann. He had already used the same tactics to duck questions at the Nuremberg Trial. He ended by refusing to talk to Schirach at all on this subject, on the ground that it made him angry.

Speer had long suspected that Bormann's ambition drove Hess "to this desperate move." Yet after twenty years' shared confinement in Spandau Prison, he was no longer quite so sure, inclining instead to the idea that Hess really believed he could get the pressure off Germany's back for the war against the Soviet Union. Europe as far as the Urals for Germany and the rest of the world for Britain was Hess's offer when he landed in Scotland, and also exactly the bait Hitler hoped would win the British over. Immediately after the Reichstag session of May 4, 1941, a week before his flight, Hess had verified in a private conversation with the Führer that his offer to divide the world into the two spheres of power still held good.

This interpretation is not invalidated by the eye- and ear-witness story of Hitler's valet Linge that "within a few minutes" Bormann pronounced his superior a traitor, someone he had always thought would eventually prove to be not genuinely devoted to the Führer. This statement rather reflects Bormann's fear that he, as Stabsleiter in Amt Hess, might be suspected of having been in on the secret. Linge believes that he read in Bormann's face during this scene proof that Hess's flight took him completely by surprise. But it was also obvious that "the turn of events secretly filled him with gratification and glee." This can mean only that during those two days Bormann saw how his chances had improved by his apparent innocence, his prompt reviling of the now utterly disavowed escapee, and his protestations of undeviating devotion. It is completely in keeping with his character and pathological lack of empathy that on the evening of May 10 he actually threw a party in his home. There is no way of knowing whether Hitler had already told him of his promotion or whether the news came to him on the second day. On the third day Hitler announced it publicly, first to the Reichsleiters and Gauleiters, who were hastily summoned to the Berghof. But it was done in such a way that many of them only half understood the significance of the proceedings. Bormann himself made very little of it. He put in his notebook: "4:00–6:30 P.M.: Führer consultation with all Reichsleiters and Gauleiters." This display of Hitlerian stage-management will be analyzed at greater length in the next chapter.

12

The Favorite Cleans Up

Almost as soon as the BBC flashed the news on May 12, 1941, that Hess had landed in England and was in custody, Hitler ordered all Reichsleiters and Gauleiters to come to Obersalzberg the next day. Bormann's telex worked efficiently; in spite of the distances, nearly all of them arrived on time. All they knew was what was in the first announcement, and they bombarded Bormann with questions when he received them at the Berghof. But Bormann was taciturn and indicated by his officious preoccupation that he had more important things to do than answer them: The Führer would explain everything. A few select individuals forced their way through to Hitler; Bormann managed to fend off the rest.

Göring, who had not yet fallen from grace, asked Hitler how he proposed to fill the vacancy and warned him against Bormann, who had nothing but enemies in the Party. Ley, long since outmaneuvered by Bormann, saw the moment for revenge. Standing at attention, he told Hitler that despite his many offices he was prepared to assume the additional burden of Deputy to the Führer. There was no way, he suggested, that the Stabsleiter of a traitor could become that traitor's successor. Hitler assured both Göring and Ley that under no condition would he make Bormann his Party Deputy. Instead he would himself take over responsibility for the political leaders and abolish Amt Hess. Once again he used the truth to palm off a lie.

Around four in the afternoon, some seventy men gathered in the Berghof living room. According to eyewitnesses, Hitler, Göring and Bormann entered looking deadly serious. Bormann had the honor of reading aloud the letter Hess had left for Hitler. Thirty years later, one of the Gauleiters admitted that the language of the letter "made a deep impression on us and would have had tremendous effect if Hitler had not immediately delivered a harsh verdict." Asserting that this was one of the blackest days in his political career, Hitler excitedly shouted that Hess had "abandoned trust and discipline" at the very moment "when our divisions are alerted along Germany's eastern borders . . . and might at any time receive the order to launch the greatest military operation of the war." The last bit of information came as a shock to most of those present; until then they had not known that war with the Soviet Union was imminent.

One person present was frightened out of his wits by Hess's letter: Ernst Wilhelm Bohle, Gauleiter of the Party Auslandsorganisation, responsible for the supervision of all Germans abroad. He had been born and raised in England and knew the language perfectly. And, unlike the other Gauleiters, he reported to Amt Hess. Now he nervously recalled that a few months before, Hess had summoned him to his residence in Berlin late at night and asked him to translate into English a letter addressed to the Duke of Hamilton. The letter had contained the same thoughts, very nearly the same sentences, that Bormann had just read out to the group.

Bohle decided to tell the whole story. He moved to the front and asked Bormann to arrange for him to have a private conversation with the Führer. He got it sooner than he wanted. Hitler caught his eye and demanded, "And didn't *you* know anything about it?" He had just begun to speak when Hitler descended on him with raised fists. Bormann refrained from intervening, but Göring suggested that Hitler hear Bohle out.

One of the Gauleiters present wrote later: "Without anybody saying so, one could already sense who was to succeed Hess. Martin Bormann . . . began to show a revolting officiousness that complemented the repellent picture one already had of him. The boss who had flown the coop did not worry him at all; he was going all out to worm himself into favor with the new one."

It should be noted that this eyewitness, Augsburg Gauleiter Karl Wahl, was in poor standing with the Hitler coterie and therefore had rarely observed Bormann at close quarters. He had no way of knowing that Bormann's subservient solicitude toward Hitler was normal and that he no longer needed to "worm himself" into the Führer's favor.

Wahl says it was no surprise to him when he got back to Augsburg late at night and found the most recent Party announcement in the papers:

> The Führer has issued the following decree: The former office of Deputy to the Führer henceforth is to be known as the Party Chancellery. It is to be under my personal orders. Its chief executive officer is, as before, Reichsleiter Martin Bormann.
>
> May 12, 1941   Adolf Hitler

As he had promised, Hitler had not actually appointed a successor to Hess. But if some of the Party elite had hoped there would be one less competitor around, those hopes were dashed. The organization and authority of the bureau remained as before, and it grew in size faster than ever. Hiding behind the office of "Party Chancellery" there was, unknown to the public, a bureaucrat more obsequious to Hitler than his predecessor and also much more ambitious, who was shrewdly and ruthlessly pursuing the position of Number Two man in the government.

Characteristically, Hitler's decree made no mention of Hess, although he had been gone only two days. One of Bormann's first acts of office was to erase the name from the collective memory of the German people and avenge the betrayal. This gave the Gestapo a lot to do. From Obersalzberg came the cues for the next moves: all photographs of Hess were to be removed from Party and government offices, all "accomplices to this act of insanity" were to be mercilessly punished. One man implicated, the "geopolitical fantasist Professor Haushofer" from Munich University, had been a friend of Hess's from his student days. Details of the operation were left to Bormann, who was certain of one thing: a lot of cleaning up had to be done to eliminate all suspicion that he might have been involved.

He demonstrated his righteous revulsion by changing two of his children's names. Hess had stood godfather to Rudolf, born August 31, 1934, and Frau Ilse Hess was godmother to Ilse, born July 9, 1931. After the flight to Scotland they became Helmut and Eike by court decree.

Bohle was interrogated by Heydrich and Müller but managed to clear himself and was left alone. Under interrogation at Nuremberg Bohle said that "there is no doubt that the persecutions were instigated by Bormann, and were carried out in the most vindictive way possible."

Ilse Hess maintained that she had known nothing about her husband's plans. When she was given no peace, she complained to Hitler about Bormann—and the brakes were applied. As proof that she was not hiding anything, she let Hitler know whenever she got a letter from her husband in England. Perhaps one of her reasons was that the style and content of the letters were clear evidence that Hess was by no means out of his mind. Bormann instantly reprimanded the postal censors—the letters should never have been allowed to reach Frau Hess. Hitler ordered him to stop the surveillance and directed that she be given a pension in place of Hess's minister's salary, which Bormann had instantly stopped. Bormann retaliated with pinpricks, as he had often done before. He delayed a long time before releasing the bedroom furniture Hess had bought for his Berlin home, which had been confiscated. He moved only after a lengthy exchange of letters, and he made her pay twice for her husband's property—the second time to the Party treasury.

He also went after the seventy-two-year-old geopolitician Karl Haushofer and his son Albrecht with special ferocity. Both were arrested, and the son was held for a long time. The father's scientific publications were banned. After the officers' plot to kill Hitler, Albrecht ended up in the hands of the Gestapo as a member of the resistance. He was put to death shortly before the end of the war.

Bormann ordered a collective persecution of all individuals the Party organ designated as "mesmerists, astrologers, etc.," although there was no evidence that any of them had influenced Hess in his decision. To be sure, Hess was a hypochondriac, suffered from complexes and totally discounted orthodox medicine, trusting in the powers of nature and various kinds of faith healing. He—and also Himmler, incidentally—was treated by Felix Kersten, a healer and masseur who reached the conclusion that sexual impotence was the key to Hess's disorders. When Bormann heard this, he wrote to Himmler that Hess was only trying to prove his masculinity when he made the flight to England.

Bormann, a simple realist, had long been uncomfortable with his superior's sometimes bizarre trains of thought, which did not quite fit into the framework of National Socialist ideology. It is possible that he may already have considered lowering the boom on these notions as unacceptable to Party orthodoxy. At any rate, three days before Hess's flight, Bormann sent a "Strictly Confidential" letter to all Gauleiters on "Superstition, Belief in Miracles and Astrology as a Means for Propaganda Hostile to the Government." It was directed against "confessional and occult circles" that were attempting "once again and more than ever to spread uncertainty and confusion among the public." Like the clergymen who were frightening people with sermons about the end of the world, "soothsayers, clairvoyants, astrologers and card readers" were taking advantage "of the natural tension over the political and military developments of the war." If some Gauleiters felt that the war did not give them enough to do, they should work on "developing the people's ideology and enlightening them" so that the "slogans of politicking soothsayers" would bounce off "the solid National Socialist *Weltanschauung* founded on a scientific knowledge of the laws of race, life and nature."

Two weeks later Rosenberg, the Reichsleiter in charge of ideology, received Bormann's circular ordering him "to take measures to foster ideological training, which the events of the past week have made more urgent than ever." The Party Propaganda Office and the Reich Propaganda Ministry were also pressed into service to clean up the book and magazine market, "to remove all printed matter relating to astrology and similar hocus-pocus" and to suppress any displays or entertainments that might reinforce belief in the supernatural.

Thanks to Bormann's hectic zeal, this turned into a major operation that lasted for several months and wasted inordinate amounts of paper, ink and office time. Magicians and illusionists performing in variety shows or engaged by the government's Kraft durch Freude (Strength through Joy) organization to entertain troops and civilians were forbidden to appear on the stage. They could get their work permits renewed only after specially designated officials of the Party and the Security Service had certified that they revealed to the audience the secrets of their acts, from card tricks to sawing a woman in half, to destroy any belief in the supernatural. However, perhaps not surprisingly, shows promoted by the Party Chancellery in which "illusions and the subsequent demonstration of how they are done are used to show the public that there is no such thing as magic," were prohibited by unwitting bureaucrats on the local level.

One incident in his occultist hunt took Bormann down a blind alley. In May 1943, Reichsleiter Rosenberg called his attention to a man named Hermann Kritzinger, who called himself professor and was allegedly performing supernatural acts. The Party Chancellery discovered, however, when they checked, that it was not the right moment to go after him. In February of that year the *Völkischer Beobachter* had announced that Kritzinger, "together with other deserving men of science working on solutions to war problems" had been awarded the title of professor by Hitler himself. As Bormann wrote Rosenberg, he had actually been recommended for the honor by the Naval High Command. "Kritzinger and a whole staff of so-called 'pendulum-danglers' are supposed to have been busily engaged in dangling pendulums over maps to locate convoys!"

By his exclamation point Bormann indicated what he thought of people who located enemy ships by swinging a pendulum on a thread over an ocean map until they got a "signal." He dared not interfere, but he kept an eye on the matter. "I shall try to ascertain if this pendulum stuff is still going on now, after the change in navy command [Karl Dönitz had relieved Erich Raeder as Commander]," he wrote Rosenberg later. "By the way, Herr Kritzinger is said to be a good friend of Admiral Canaris." Canaris, chief of military intelligence, had long been on Bormann's voluminous blacklist of people to be "shot down" and was marked on it—correctly, as it happened—as an enemy of the regime.

But that was not until long after Bormann had become an authentic despot. When he was first made head of the Party Chancellery, he had to fight for authority for himself and his department and outmaneuver his rivals. He knew, of course, that he had scarcely any friends among the Reichsleiters and Gauleiters, and that the new appointment had increased the number of his enemies. His first order of business was to reassure and at the same time instruct the top-level Party officers, making it clear that he had something to offer them—a carrot and a stick. Those who attended the meeting of May 13, 1941, in Obersalzberg were hardly back at their desks when they got a circular dated May 15,—"Personal—Strictly Confidential" —by fast messenger from Bormann in Führer Headquarters.

The wording and content of this circular are so typical of Bormann the hustler and shifty tactician that it deserves careful study (see the Appendix, page 398). It begins by asserting that the Party Chancellery will go on operating as before, "but now under the supervision and protection of the Führer." Next come a few hints on how close Bormann is to the Führer and how useful it is that no matter at which headquarters, he can keep the Führer abreast "of all important issues." One sentence reminiscent of the familiar structure of Hitler's speeches begins: "Since 1933 I have . . . ," and presents a rundown of successful achievements. Fifty-eight words later the sentence grinds to a halt with the assertion that he, Bormann, "worked like a horse" to accomplish these things. "Indeed, more than a horse, since a horse has its Sunday off and its night's sleep," both of which he had often had to do without.

He obviously was so sure of Hitler's backing that he challenged his enemies to "tell the Führer at once" if anyone was better suited to the job than himself. He also pretended to offer each senior officer free access to Hitler: they were all welcome to lunch at the Reich Chancellery—after previous notification that they were coming. But every one of them knew perfectly well that the ever-present Bormann had his say when the guest list was being drawn up.

Just two weeks later, on May 29, Hitler signed a decree giving Bormann "the authority of a Reich Minister" and appointing him "to the Council of Ministers for the Defense of the Reich as a member of the government." It also provided that "all competences pertaining to the Führer's Deputy by laws, ordinances or decrees will be transferred to the chief of the Party Chancellery." This gave Bormann Hess's former prerogatives. All he lacked were the titles Deputy and Minister, so that Hitler could keep his promise that he would not appoint a successor to Hess. Bormann cared no more for titles than for decorations. All he wanted was power.

His most dangerous enemies at that time were the two top Nazis who had warned Hitler against him: Robert Ley and Hermann Göring. Instinct told Bormann not to lock horns with both of them at the same time. The Führer's May 29 decree made him safe in the government sector, but Ley was gathering allies in the Party, in the belief that, now that Bormann was no longer backed up by Hess, he, Ley, could recapture lost territory.

On June 4, 1941, Bormann had his driver take him from his Obersalzberg house to Göring's, where he had requested a meeting. In a memorandum to his two closest associates, Helmuth Friedrichs and Gerhard Klopfer, he later summarized the occasion: "The Reichsmarschall stressed repeatedly that he was aware that a lot of people thought they could by-pass the Party; of course he, the Reichsmarschall, was not one of them." Bormann pointed out that "several Reichsleiters had sought the Party's collaboration in drafting laws, ordinances, etc., for their own domains." This Göring rejected as "completely unworkable." After an hour and a half they reached an agreement. Bormann wrote that he had "also asked the Reichs-marschall several times to always send for me immediately if he had anything in mind with respect to the Party." He instructed Friedrichs and Klopfer to "continue to work closely with the Reichsmarschall's departments." (See the Appendix, page 399.)

This nonaggression pact was only temporary, directed as it was against common foes. Göring, with no rank or influence in the Party Organization, wanted to curb the Reichsleiters and Gauleiters with the connivance of the Party Chancellery. Bormann needed assurance that the governmental sector of his office would remain undisturbed and he not have to wage a war on two fronts. Now the campaign against the insurgents could begin. The time was right, too. During the first weeks of June, Hitler was completely absorbed with preparations for the attack on the Soviet Union. He would soon be playing supreme warlord behind the barbed wire of the Wolfsschanze Führer Headquarters in East Prussia, out of reach to almost everyone—except Martin Bormann.

Meanwhile, Bormann had made sure of a second ally whom Hitler held in high regard, Reich Minister Fritz Todt, who was in charge of armaments and head of the OT (Organisation Todt), the paramilitary team of workers and engineers that built fortifications, mostly along the Atlantic Coast. Bormann had spoken to him about the "negative attitudes that Dr. Ley is currently provoking and encouraging among the Reichsleiters." His alliance with Todt was actually a windfall. The dispute over jurisdiction between Ley as head of the German Labor Front and the Todt Organization was so basic that they could not even agree on who was to manage the workers' canteens at the big construction sites. Bormann recorded for his two lieutenants: "Dr. Todt, in answer to my question, said that Ley's plans were practically unworkable, as they would lead to complete disruption within the Party, and eventually cripple government operations."

Ley was trying to achieve his long-time objective: power over the political corps, and with it over the entire Party and its ancillary organizations. He could never approach the Gauleiters with any such proposal, since each was a territorial despot in his own right and was dead against any central authority. So Ley tried to lure the Reichsleiters, who were suffering from the same chronic lack of power, by promising them he would firm up their areas of responsibility. By formal Party regulations, he would prevent the Party Chancellery from poaching on everybody else's preserves. He had already won the support of several Reichsleiters, among them Frick, Frank and Rosenberg. He opened hostilities by demanding that his personnel office and not the Party Chancellery should decide on the careers of Party officers. This was the keystone of his strategy; if he could win this round, he saw victory in his grasp. As it turned out, it was his Waterloo.

Bormann was all set for a red-tape campaign. But he needed a third decree added to the two that defined his position, one that gave him specific, far-reaching powers. He had already written a draft and given it to Friedrichs and Klopfer for comment. The former urged caution "since there is no compelling need for it yet" and it would "provoke unnecessary unrest among the Gauleiters." Furthermore, Hitler would insist on discussing the draft with Ley. Obviously he intended, Bormann answered in a memo for the record, "to inform the Führer at length about the present tendencies among some of the Reichsleiters." He would keep the draft until he was called upon for an opinion. It was his duty to brief Hitler on these matters —and here he was secretly covering himself against suspicion of intrigue: "I have no independent office of my own; I am, rather, a specialist for the Führer in particular areas, and the Party Chancellery is no longer a structure more or less separate from the Führer; it is an office directly under the Führer."

In the end he deemed it more prudent to leave the draft in his desk drawer and refrain from fanning the flames of Party quarrels. Ley got no rulings or responsive answers to his letters and memoranda, only the notification that everything would be laid before the Führer. On July 1 he lost his patience and wrote Bormann, "in the spirit of quiet reasonableness," explaining once more that "the processing of proposals and the maintenance of personnel files on the political leaders appointed by the Führer must be the responsibility of my office." "So there may be peace at last," he went on, the "personnel records kept in the Party Chancellery must be surrendered."

This letter reached Bormann at Wolfsschanze headquarters, at a moment when Soviet losses in the Minsk pocket were being counted and all speculations concerned what victories might come next. Hitler was fully occupied with the greatest military campaign in history; the Party and its business would have to wait. He agreed with Bormann that matters should go on as before. In a communication to Ley, Bormann gave a generous interpretation of this lapidary decision. On July 15 he wrote: "The Führer orders me to inform you that the previous arrangement is not to be changed; now as before, personnel policy decisions will be referred to the Party Chancellery." Only personnel statistics, the monster card index on several million Party members, would stay in Ley's Central Personnel Office. "The Führer stressed that processing of proposals on personnel could be done properly only by someone constantly in his company."

This established the position of the one "constantly in his company" as the ultimate maker and breaker of careers. The offensive had been shattered and important territory taken from the enemy. There was no need for a new decree. A year later, by a legalistic flank movement, Bormann was able to ascribe to himself whatever Party prerogatives he wished. He could refer to an existing regulation he had composed jointly with the chief of the Reich Chancellery, Lammers. The "Regulation of January 16, 1942, on Implementation of the Führer Decree on the Position of the Chief of the Party Chancellery" grandly assigned competences and domains Bormann had accumulated over the years as master of the locks in the canal that ran between government and Party. As sole representative of the Party in the government sector, he had the right of consultation in the civil-service apparatus, the right of collaboration in drafting legislation and regulations down to the level of Reichsstatthalter, and the exclusive right to forward requests and complaints from the Party to the government.

Sensibly, nobody mentioned that in practice, he had long been overstepping the boundaries herein described.

In April 1942 Bormann made use of this self-tailored regulation to hoist himself by his own pigtail, like Baron Münchhausen, over the heads of the Party officers. All he had to do was send one of his circulars to some hundred Party comrades in leading positions. It announced that he had been ordered "by the Führer to handle, in accordance with his basic instructions, all internal Party planning and all vitally important questions for the preservation of the German people within the Party's purview, as well as to adapt all suggestions from Reichsleiters, Gauleiters and chiefs of organizations to overall political exigencies." On four typewritten pages (see the full text in the Appendix, pages 400-402) he used the authority established in his custom-made regulation to construct a second channel which gave him sole control of communications between Hitler and the Party. For years he had had the job of keeping the Gauleiters off the Führer's back; now he generously extended the assignment to include Reichsleiters and chiefs of organizations too. Henceforth they were obligated to keep him "up to date on the development of the Party's work," while he promised to keep them "up to date on all the Führer's decisions, directives and wishes." To make a travesty of a Biblical quotation, if everything had gone according to plan, Bormann would have been able to declare: No one comes to the Führer but by me!

Robert Ley was the first to learn what sort of teeth the new regulation had. As head of the German Labor Front he had asked that the Reich Minister of Finance be allowed to work with him on Ministry legislation. His request landed routinely on Lammers' desk. Lammers referred him to the new regulation, on which the printer's ink was not yet dry—and turned him down. With quiet malice Lammers added that he had forwarded a photostat of Ley's proposal to the head of the Party Chancellery.

Ley sought to make up for the prestige he had lost at the top Party level by gaining favor with the public, hoping that by giving speeches he could prove that he was still a big shot. At "staff gatherings" held at the large industrial corporations, he roared out in patriotic ecstasy that victory was assured if everyone served Germany and the Führer by doing his job at his post. But exhortations of this sort drew less applause than a few words of criticism about shortages of various kinds. Ley liked to use such occasions to shoot holes in his enemy Todt, the Minister of Armaments. When he began doing this in newspaper articles as well, Bormann had printed evidence to show Hitler. After Hitler moved back to Berlin, Ley was summoned to the Reich Chancellery. First Bormann peppered him with "harsh reproaches"; then, as Goebbels, who happened by, later reported, Ley was ushered into the holy of holies, where the Führer administered a further reprimand.

Nevertheless, Bormann encouraged Ley in his speechmaking; that way he kept him away from where the action was and channeled his energies to less important areas. Ley bragged about his speeches to improve his standing with the Party elite. He once told Schirach: "There is a very curious relationship between Bormann and myself. I get the feeling he is jealous because I am always out making speeches while he sits in headquarters and scribbles. I offered to get him some audiences so he could be more in the public eye. After all, as the Führer's Deputy he is"—here Ley confessed his thralldom—"the man at the top of the whole Party. But he said he couldn't do that, he was completely incapable of speaking before a group. That was for me to do. It was my big job in the war."

Next in line for the Bormann treatment was Hans Frank. During the Party's *Kampfzeit* he had supported a never precisely defined "Germanic code of law," and after the takeover he was made Bavarian Minister of Justice, the senior of all Nazi lawyers and president of the Academy for German Law. As head of the Party Department of Justice he wore the Reichsleiter collar tab on his brown Party uniform. But this office no longer had any clout or significance. Bormann's own legal staff worked out and decided all important matters. Frank had been almost forgotten when to everyone's surprise he was appointed Governor General of the occupied territories in Poland in September 1939. Now he sat in the ancient palace fortress of Cracow, pompously holding court, although in fact he had no power at all. Himmler and his Einsatzgruppen actually ruled the country with terror, wholesale roundups and executions, and no more than an indulgent smile for any orders that might come from the Governor General.

Himmler and the SS were delighted to serve as Bormann's eyes and ears. They reported that the Governor General and his staff did not take the Nazi commandments of decency and restraint at all seriously, and that on every trip to Munich, Frank filled his parlor car with furs, expensive jewelry, gems, paintings—including a Rembrandt—for his home. After accumulating enough evidence, Bormann summoned Frank to one of his "consultations," with Lammers and Himmler present. But the showdown did not work out as planned. Frank could prove that he had paid for everything out of his own pocket. Since Hitler rarely demurred at any corruption that was even halfway camouflaged, Bormann pressed no further. He had found out all he needed to know.

Bormann was very careful about his own reputation. In March 1943 he admonished his wife by letter to see to it in their home that in view of his position of trust with the Führer and his position as head of the Party Chancellery, "we give no cause for criticism." Goebbels had complained to him about Party *"Bonzen"* buying food on the black market. With a positively schizoid avoidance of reality, he chose to overlook the fact that he and his family were not obliged to make do with the official rations. They had the produce from the Obersalzberg farm to draw on. And by then he was running a huge farm of his own in Mecklenburg.

Bormann the petty bourgeois resented the "King of East *Frank*-Reich" [a pun on the German word for France], as the Governor General was nicknamed in the Party because of his huge parties and ostentatious living, just as Bormann the lowly fund manager had been irritated by the prestigious figure of lawyer Hans Frank in Munich. Frank was no longer a dangerous adversary, but Bormann's list of black marks had been building up for over a decade, and he was now ready for a reckoning. The wind was with him. Hitler was expressing more contempt for lawyers than ever before, they were not making enough heads roll to suit him. In one of his midnight monologues at the end of March 1942, he announced that he was about to "discredit the study of law as much as I possibly can" and to throw nine out of every ten judges off the bench. A month later he had the Reichstag confirm his legal right to dismiss "judges who obviously fail to heed the commandment of the hour." This incriminated Frank by profession alone. He was also giving speeches studded with phrases like "police state" and the "anarchy of absolute power." All his published writings were confiscated, and he was forbidden to speak in public anywhere in the Reich. Bormann needed to give him only a slight nudge, and he would fall.

If this happened now, Bormann would have an opportunity to promote some of his own favorites to high office. The position of Reich Minister of Justice had been vacant ever since Gürtner's death at the end of January 1941. Roland Freisler, a veteran Party hack who wanted the job in the worst way, was turned down because Hitler considered him a "Bolshevik." Bormann's candidate was Otto Georg Thierack, president of the People's Court, who was willing to take Bormann's lawyer, Klemm, into the Ministry of Justice and promote him to State Secretary.

But Hitler had his eye on Curt Rothenberger, a senator from Hamburg and president of the Superior State Court there. Rothenberger, at his Gauleiter's suggestion, had sent the Party Chancellery a memorandum on a proposed reform of the German judicial system, and Klemm asked him to come to Munich for a conference. When Rothenberger got no further reaction, he gave another copy of his memorandum to one of the Führer's adjutants he knew, SA Brigadeführer Albrecht. It got to Hitler's desk through Albert Bormann, and the Führer liked it so well that Lammers was told to give its author the position of State Secretary in the Reich Ministry of Justice.

The fact that Hitler could be approached through the Adjutants' Office, by-passing the head of the Party Chancellery, annoyed Bormann to the end of his life. Anyone who tried to sneak in that way became immediately suspect. Rothenberger was soon given to understand this, but by then Thierack's appointment to Minister of Justice and Rothenberger's to State Secretary could no longer be prevented. Both happened on August 20, 1942. All Bormann could do was take some small satisfaction from reporting to the Führer that in preliminary talks, Rothenberger had made it a condition that he should never be made to work with Hans Frank.

Frank's demotion came four days later, and his legacy was divided up. Thierack was given charge of the Rechtswahrerbund (League for the Preservation of Justice) and the Academy of German Law; the Party Chancellery swallowed the remaining functions of the NSDAP's Department of Justice. Frank's name was eliminated from the list of Reichsleiters, but he was allowed to remain Governor General of Poland. On the other hand, Bormann and Thierack gave State Secretary Rothenberger such a hard time that within a few months he longed to be back in Hamburg.

Frank realized that he had not yet been brought low enough to satisfy his worst enemy, but he had no idea how thoroughly he was being watched. When, soon after his downfall, he invited members of the French embassy to his castle at Cracow, they asked him whether he would like to see Paris again some day. Gladly, he said, but not until his romantic memories were no longer offended by the sight of German soldiers. Shortly afterward Bormann wrote him that the Führer had taken violent exception to this remark which, moreover, bordered on treason. Having hardly ever succeeded in being received for a talk at Führer Headquarters—and, if he was, "always in the presence of the watchdog, Bormann"—he now saw Hitler only at a distance on official occasions. When in February 1944 he was once again summoned to headquarters, it was such a surprise that he checked back to make sure that he was really expected.

Over and over again, Frank offered his resignation in writing. Had it been up to Bormann, it would have been accepted every time, so that his friend Himmler and the SS could take exclusive charge of Poland. But Hitler did not release his former attorney from duty until Frank himself, terrified of the advancing Soviet armies, relinquished his castle and recommended that the governor-generalship be dissolved. Bormann kept tabs on Frank even after his flight. When, in January 1945, he learned that his despised and humiliated enemy was throwing elaborate parties with the remainder of his former staff in Silesia, feasting on the supplies of food and drink they had taken out of Poland, he decided that this hotbed of asocial elements had to be cleaned out. But before he had a chance, it was scattered to the winds by the soldiers of the Red Army.

It took little effort for Bormann to get back at Reichsleiter Alfred Rosenberg; he was able to enjoy his revenge in small doses. Rosenberg, the originator and proclaimant of an abstruse cultural philosophy, had always been a loner without a following. Inside the Party his speeches were ridiculed as soporifics. Despite the positions he had occupied since the

Party's early fighting days—most of which boasted high-sounding names—
he had never succeeded in establishing a clearly defined area of responsibilities. The title Reichsleiter was a relic from the past, attached to his Aussen-
politisches Amt der NSDAP (Foreign Policy Office of the NSDAP). He had
never risen above a low level, nor was he ever allowed to influence the Third
Reich's foreign policy. He was responsible for the "supervision of the Party
members' ideological education," but the amount of paper wasted in this
department was considerably larger than its effectiveness.

Early in 1940 he had succeeded in having Hitler appoint him "commissioner for safeguarding National Socialist ideology," but hardly anyone
inside the Party organization took any notice of his pronouncements, since
neither their contents nor his position made any impression on them. Hitler
once remarked during one of the late-night talks at the Wolfsschanze that
Mythus, * his seminal book, did not represent the official Party view and that
even its title was misleading. He said he had read only the beginning, and
finding it heavy going, had put it aside.

There has been much speculation as to why, three weeks after the beginning of the Russian campaign, Hitler made this theoretician, who shunned
decisions and was out of touch with reality, Reich Minister for the Occupied
Eastern (Soviet) Territories. Some said it was because of his Baltic origins.
Others felt it was a consolation prize for not getting the Ministry of Foreign
Affairs, which he had been promised. There is some evidence that Bormann
put the idea in Hitler's head and that it was he who provided these two
arguments. But his own motives for intervening on Rosenberg's behalf must
have been of a different nature. To assess them properly one has to go back
to the events before the invasion.

Walter Schellenberg, chief of Himmler's espionage department, has described a dinner conversation at the Reich Chancellery during which Hitler,
tortured by doubts before the invasion of Russia, was urged by Bormann
to follow the call of Providence, which had chosen him for this crucial
conquest. Nothing could go wrong, and no one knew better than he, Bormann, "how much concern and trouble you, my Führer, have devoted to
the smallest detail." It was blatant flattery, which Hitler loved and Bormann never failed to supply from the reservoir of his blind devotion. Among
the higher ranks of the SS, it was assumed that Bormann was thinking of
the gigantic empire in the East as a future Lebensraum for his own career
when he recommended a policy of brinkmanship. Whoever became its
viceroy after the final victory would by necessity be the second largest power
in the Reich, and eventually succeed to the Führer's throne.

Ever since April 1941 there had been discussions about how the areas to
be conquered could best be dominated and exploited. The Wehrmacht and
the SS agreed that a wide strip behind the front would have to be adminis-

The Myth of the Twentieth Century.

tered by the military, and that the SS would try to pacify the hinterland, whatever that meant. Bormann insisted that the Party also be given a slice of the pie. The Wehrmacht and the SS would become overwhelmingly powerful unless a civilian government "representing the political aims of the German people" were established. The two partners in the deal suggested that the duties and responsibilities be defined in a joint conference with Hitler, but Bormann saw to it that each partner was called in to report separately, after which the Führer would announce his decision. At this time Rosenberg was authorized to prepare for his new office.

A letter written by the head of the Party Chancellery to Lammers on June 16, 1941—i.e., a week before the attack—shows the close cooperation between Bormann and Himmler during this phase. It recommended that Himmler be given extended powers "to carry out the necessary police actions in the eastern territories." "Particularly during the first weeks and months," it read, "the police must . . . under all circumstances be kept unencumbered by obstacles arising from possible disputes over prerogatives." More precisely, no one should be permitted to prevent the execution of Hitler's orders to kill, which defied all international agreements. When Himmler saw the carbon of this letter he had personally requested, he dictated his "best thanks" to "dear Martin."

The reason Bormann, of all people, sponsored his enemy Rosenberg was that he "preferred a crackpot Minister for the Occupied Eastern Territories to an intelligent one," as Goebbels' crony in the Ministry of Propaganda, Wilfried von Oven, found out. Rosenberg's office could easily be made a burden to him. All one had to do, Bormann thought, was to assign a few energetic and practical people to this unrealistic theoretician. Such persons were picked by Hitler on July 16, 1941, at a Wolfsschanze "Führer Conference" attended by Rosenberg, Lammers, Göring and Keitel. As usual during meetings on secret affairs of state, Bormann kept the minutes. He had in fact already compiled a list of Party comrades he considered suitable for a despotic regime in the East.

The program announced at this conference will be described later in greater detail. For the moment it should be noted that from the start Rosenberg was unable to get his way when the commissars for the various areas were chosen. The northern region consisting mainly of the Baltic States and renamed Ostland, was given to Gauleiter Hinrich Lohse of Schleswig-Holstein, a man "of natural intelligence," according to Rosenberg, who was, however, inclined "to be extremely stubborn about trivial matters" and who "out of sheer pigheadedness" turned into an enemy, with Bormann's enthusiastic support. Rosenberg agreed reluctantly to the appointment of East Prussian Gauleiter Erich Koch as area commissar of the Ukraine when Bormann and Göring insisted. Bormann, who was a friend of Koch's, wanted to put a trusted man in Ostland; Göring, as head of the wartime economy, knew he could trust Koch to squeeze the rich territory like a lemon. In Rosenberg's eyes, Koch was a "petty bourgeois and a braggart," and nothing but "a front for Martin Bormann."

Bormann observed with a certain amount of satisfaction that other agencies were also giving the Reich Minister for the Occupied Eastern Territories a hard time. As Minister in charge of the Four-Year Plan, Göring demanded enormous deliveries of foodstuffs and raw materials. The Minister Plenipotentiary for Manpower, Fritz Sauckel, who had originally been Gauleiter of Thuringia, rounded up an army of slave labor and deported it to the Reich. Heinrich Himmler's security forces terrorized the vanquished peoples while Himmler, as Reich Commissar for the advancement of the Germanic race, determined which areas the "inferior" Slavs would have to evacuate at some point to make room for German settlers. Finally, there was the Wehrmacht, which needed airfields and lines of communication.

Soon the Party Chancellery was talking about the "Cha-os(t) Ministry." In mid-February 1942 Bormann complained to Goebbels, who had been Rosenberg's enemy from way back, that Rosenberg's department was in utter confusion, and he was now "picking fights with everybody and his brother." Rosenberg had plenty of reason. Koch, for instance, drafted lengthy memoranda criticizing his superior's mistakes, and whenever Rosenberg tried to find out what the complaints were, Bormann refused to reply to his inquiry. Rosenberg's adjutant, stationed at Führer Headquarters to provide a permanent liaison with Hitler, was summarily dismissed by Bormann on the ground that he had too little to do. Rosenberg complained that the last time he had been able to talk to Hitler alone was late in 1941. The next year he was received only three times, each time in the presence of Bormann. Actually he was no longer needed at all; whatever was to be done in Ostland was determined by others.

Shortly before his death Rosenberg wrote that he had wanted to create a new European order in the East, but that "the leading officials had been otherwise influenced by Bormann and Himmler, which, unfortunately, the Führer did nothing to prevent." Aside from the fact that this remark is a defense of the despotic system, it also reveals that after twenty-six years of political activity by Hitler's side, Rosenberg still had no idea of his leader's character, methods or aims. Whatever Bormann and Himmler undertook against him was done with blessings from on high and was thoroughly in keeping with the Darwinian principle that the strong must swallow the weak.

This was another reason why Bormann was never prevented from crippling Rosenberg even in areas that had always been close to his heart. Rosenberg considered himself the Pope of National Socialism and had irritated Christians by the ideology he proclaimed in *Mythus.* So his disappointment was great when Bormann announced in a letter to the Party organization that henceforth he alone was in charge of church policy. To Christians this meant going from the frying pan into the fire. As will be described later, Bormann fought them more radically and brutally than Rosenberg would ever have been able to.

The only consolation Rosenberg, the "scholar," had was that his nonintellectual rival would never be able to confront Judaeo-Christian ideas with new principles. To prove how much better suited he was for such a purpose, he decided to write a sequel to *Mythus*. He must have talked about it prematurely, for Himmler's Security Service got wind of it, and in October 1942 "dear Martin" received a five-line note marked "Secret! Highly Confidential! Personal!" from his friend Heinrich, saying that "it would be advisable . . . to show the book to the Führer before it is published." It never was published; the mere thought of having Bormann as a censor was enough to frighten off the author.

Nevertheless, Rosenberg still had the Führer's instructions to prepare the ground for an "Academy" where after the war Nazi ideology would be studied and evidence against its opponents would be collected. Rosenberg had already hired university professors. Now material on the opposition was to be collected from all the areas under German domination, from the North Cape to Salonika, and soon perhaps from the Atlantic coast to the mountains of the Ural. Inside the Reich it was mainly a matter of searching through the libraries of monasteries that had been closed; in the occupied countries, synagogues, freemasons' lodges, museums and academic institutions would supply additional material. This would also provide a good opportunity to confiscate art works owned by ideological enemies.

But here Reinhard Heydrich, chief of the Reichssicherheitshauptamt, raised objections: when it came to books by ideological enemies, they were to be confiscated by the Gestapo. And if such material required scholarly study, it could always be turned over to Rosenberg's scholars "after the police had done its political work."

Bormann had no intention of getting himself in trouble with Himmler or the SS over this issue. The Führer had decided, he wrote to Rosenberg, that no books or works of art should be removed from the monasteries throughout the Reich except by the Gauleiters. There would be ample time after the final victory to make a careful study of existing material. "Under no condition, however, should the libraries become centralized, as the Führer has repeatedly pointed out."

The letter also put a damper on Rosenberg's art "collectors." So far they had been admitted only to the occupied countries in the West, but now that Yugoslavia and Greece had been conquered, they were eager to loot the Balkans too. But here, as Bormann interpreted the Führer's wishes, "it won't be necessary to bring in your experts, because there are no art works of any kind to be confiscated in that area." Whatever needed to be done would be done by Heydrich, anyway.

Rosenberg tried to use confiscated works of art to make himself popular. There were 20,000 items, after all, according to his department's catalogue.

Needless to say, Göring helped himself immediately, and he did not take the cheapest pieces. In March 1943 Hitler was given a folder with photographs of the most valuable items from which to choose a birthday present for himself. Instead of a thank-you note, a letter—ironically dated the day after Hitler's birthday—arrived from Bormann instructing Rosenberg to hand over the entire collection at once to the Party Chancellery, where it would be administered from now on. After that Bormann no longer found any need to bother about Rosenberg. The man was now on his own—off to one side.

He had even less trouble putting Reichsleiter Bouhler offside. Bouhler had once been Secretary General of the Reichsleitung, another high-sounding title for a nebulous function. He had not been called to Berlin until November 1934, after Hindenburg's death, when Hitler insisted on having a private "Chancellery of the Führer of the NSDAP" in addition to the official Presidential Chancellery of the head of state. Most of Bouhler's men came from the Party's old guard. One of them was, of course, Bormann's brother Albert, who, as head of Hitler's Private Chancellery, was in charge of one of Bouhler's departments and at the same time acted as adjutant to the Führer. As usual, Hitler had avoided defining the responsibilities of the Chancellery of the Führer of the NSDAP and those of its subdivision, the Private Chancellery. Disputes with the other chancelleries—the Reich Chancellery, the Presidential Chancellery, the Party Chancellery—on who was in charge, were purposely inevitable.

Although Bouhler, as the head of the Party's Investigating Commission for the Protection of National Socialist Literature, had still another official function, he did not overexert himself. Nor did his secret activity as head of "euthanasia" operations occupy much of his time; most of his work was done by his aide Viktor Brack. The Reichsleiter himself spent a large part of his time at his country estate, in Brannenburg near Rosenheim, and made only occasional brief appearances at his Voss Strasse office in Berlin. He was tired of the constant bickering over who was in charge of what.

When, after the outbreak of the war, Hitler became inaccessible to him and he was able to correspond with him only through Martin Bormann, he looked around for another job. He had lived abroad and spoke several languages, and since the claim for German colonies had not yet been abandoned, he fancied he might have chances overseas. In June 1940 he traveled to the Wolfsschlucht, the Führer's headquarters in the Eifel mountains. The situation seemed favorable; France was all but defeated and if, as Hitler presumed, peace negotiations with London were soon to begin, a redistribution of Africa appeared imminent. On June 23, 1940, Bormann noted: "Reichsleiter Bouhler asks the Führer for colonial mission; the Führer declines."

This was probably not quite the way Bormann had wanted it, for if Bouhler's "general store" had been liquidated, quick action might have gotten him a few "bargains," such as, for instance, control over the "euthanasia" commissions. He might also have been tempted by the prospect of having his brother as a subordinate and giving him a hard time. By helping himself to the Department for the Protection of National Socialist Literature, he might have captured yet another position in the constant bickering over what the Nazi *Weltanschauung* was to be. For the moment, however, he could only sit tight and needle Bouhler with small dirty tricks.

Early in March, Bormann warned Bouhler once again in a matter-of-fact letter not to interfere with basic principles; the "Chancellery of the Führer" should concern itself only with the problems of individual citizens, which left Bouhler with virtually nothing but the processing of appeals for mercy. Again he asked for permission to start at least on the preliminary work for a takeover of colonies. This time Hitler agreed. Bouhler was authorized to assemble a staff for Operation Sisal—the code name for East Africa—and could pretend that some day he might rule there as Governor General.

But he had to resign himself to the fact that at the same time, a lower-ranking Party functionary was preparing Operation Banana for a takeover in West Africa. This was embarrassing inasmuch as the Party comrade was a subordinate of Gauleiter Ernst Wilhelm Bohle's of the Auslandsorganisation and thereby indirectly under Bormann. Both men were already laying claims to "moral leadership" in the colonies.

Having Bormann as a superior was totally unacceptable to Bouhler. But here they were dividing the skin of a lion that was never shot. Since Hitler refused to oust Bouhler, who had worked in the Party for fifteen years, Bormann had to find him another field of action. It occurred to him that by a clever move the underemployed Reichsleiter might relieve the enfeebled Rosenberg of his new project. Such a move could even be justified as a necessary step to tighten up the Party organization in wartime, for which Bormann had general instructions from Hitler.

Late in January 1943—to quote from the files of Rosenberg's department —"Reichsleiter Bouhler came to see Reichsleiter Rosenberg and offered to put himself and the official Party investigating commission under his authority. Protocols were signed on the matter." This would have removed one of the many rivalries purposely created by Hitler; in addition to Bouhler's official "Party Investigating Commission for the Protection of National Socialist Literature" there was Rosenberg's "Central Department of Literature of the Führer's Deputy for the Supervision of the Spiritual and Ideological Education of the NSDAP"—an inflated title that only a pompous busybody like Rosenberg could have dreamed up. It was agreed in the protocol that the two Party agencies should be merged into a "Department of Literature of the NSDAP" headed by Bouhler. The combined agencies, however—and here was the hitch—were to be integrated into Rosenberg's department.

No sooner had the ink dried on the signatures than a fight erupted between the two Reichsleiters. Ostensibly it arose over a question of personnel; Rosenberg refused to accept in the new department one of Bouhler's officers who had expressed favorable views on astrology. Both men complained in lengthy memoranda to Bormann, who thus found himself in the position of superior arbiter. Rosenberg fumed that it really seemed "a bit much" if Bouhler was to have "a free hand in firing my aides if he so chooses." Bouhler, on the other hand, insisted that as a Reichsleiter he had to have a free hand in questions of personnel.

For months Bormann gleefully watched the bickering, in which both parties would inevitably lose face, and wisely refrained from taking sides. Only once, in mid-April, did he lecture Rosenberg in a brief interim note. Rosenberg had claimed that there was nothing unusual about a Reichsleiter being placed under the authority of a colleague of equal rank. But Bormann, a long-time authority on the structure of the NSDAP, shrewdly proved that Rosenberg did not know the finer points of the Party organization. In reference to the dispute he assured him that "I shall deal as soon as possible with the other items in your letter." But he took his time over it, even when, in a conversation in Berlin on May 20, 1943, Rosenberg tried to get a verbal decision from him.

Nevertheless, the conversation must have left Rosenberg under the impression that Bormann was on his side, for a letter of his a few days later expressed his "satisfaction with this far-reaching concurrence of our ideas." He must therefore have been hit all the harder by Bormann's letter dated June 29, 1943, which said that "the Führer, to whom I recently reported the present state of affairs," had instructed him, Bormann, "to inform you that there can be no question of having two NSDAP departments of literature at this time." Henceforth Bouhler alone would handle the job. With the surrender of the last German soldiers in Africa, Bouhler's colonial dream had just gone up in smoke anyway. "In view of your immense responsibility in the Occupied Eastern Territories, which in itself is a lifetime occupation," Bormann wrote, Hitler suggested that Rosenberg should stand aside.

The loser tried to reverse this decision by a whole stack of memoranda, and since he was unable to obtain an appointment for himself at Führer Headquarters, he sent one of his best people to the Party Chancellery in Munich to see Oberbefehlsleiter Helmuth Friedrichs. Friedrichs said he felt "Reichsleiter Rosenberg was already fighting his battle as a withdrawal operation." As Rosenberg's emissary phrased it to his boss, he advised that "we should fight for our interests." Since it was unlikely that Friedrichs would have dared to undercut his superior, the remark leads one to believe that he had been instructed to add a little more fuel to the conflict so the two fighting parties would expose themselves even more. This was exactly what happened, until a letter from Bormann later in July informed Rosenberg of his final defeat. The letter never said a word about the negotiations between the two functionaries. As an added humiliation, its text was identical to the note of June 29.

This relatively trivial incident has been described in such detail because it is so typical of Bormann—of his talent for exploiting his opponents' weaknesses, of his method of striking out from behind and always under cover of the Führer's will. He never gave Bouhler a chance to enjoy his triumph.

The Department of Literature provided less and less work for him as the wartime economy put ever-increasing restrictions on book publishing. The only area where Bouhler was "still" allowed to have full responsibility was in the barbaric experiments the medical profession conducted on the inmates of concentration camps. But they were a government secret and could hardly improve his image. In the last year of the war his department was finally dissolved and integrated into the Party Chancellery. Bouhler was left with only his rank and his uniform. It is said that he was eventually reduced to being Bormann's messenger boy. But he was no longer needed even for that, and therefore nobody noticed that he was missing at the great twilight of the gods in Berlin. He attached himself to Göring's coterie, hoping to be safe there from Bormann's threats to hold out to the last. When the Americans tried to arrest him at Zell am See in Austria, he and his wife committed suicide.

Bouhler's Private Chancellery of the Führer had been irksome to Bormann mainly because he was unable to control or censor what was being brought to Hitler's attention from that end. His instructions to put a screen around the Führer so that he could concentrate on the large tasks of his office coincided with his own ambition to become the dictator of the ante-room and thereby the most powerful person next to Hitler. Probably Hitler never had any fears that such exclusive influence might one day enable the director of the ante-room to exert his rule over his chief as well; as he had with Hess, he trusted Bormann's loyalty. Nor would it ever have occurred to Bormann to rebel. His method was to influence the one who gave the orders to such an extent that his wishes became identical with his own intentions. Part of these tactics was that he remained in the background. He once wrote to his wife that Robert Ley might be known to the masses by his many speeches, but that he, Bormann, was the more successful of the two; although his words might not reach the masses, they reached the men at the top.

Hitler was not bothered by the fact that Bormann sometimes acted high-handedly and often brutally. "I need him to win the war," he once told a trusted aide. For this period of time at least, Hitler was prepared to let Bormann put up a wall around him. But he always kept a window to the outside world: the Adjutants' Office. This was a relic from the time of the royal courts; it consisted of not only the adjutants for personal services and office transactions but also the deputies of ministries and organizations. These observers were meant to provide a liaison between the head of state and their superiors. While most of them were without influence and served more or less as extras at the late-night monologues, they could still bring visitors, memoranda, verbal information and gossip to Hitler's attention, and on occasion ruin Bormann's plans. Bormann had tried for a while to win one or the other adjutant over by being excessively friendly. When he failed, he shifted to a war of nerves, thinly disguised as a cool cooperation.

One of his favorite targets was Wilhelm Brückner, who accepted the decoration from the Duke of Coburg as already described and was the most popular of Hitler's adjutants. Apart from his feelings of competition, Bormann resented Brückner for qualities he found lacking in himself. Tall and well-built, Brückner had been an army officer in World War I, and took part in the Munich putsch of 1923, had been convicted with Hitler and had served a sentence in Landsberg Prison. He knew more about Hitler's private past than almost anyone else. When he appeared in the uniform of an SA Obergruppenführer, he was unquestionably the pride of the Führer's entourage. The fact that he had hardly any political ambitions and was too phlegmatic and too modest to lend himself to intrigues did not make him any more acceptable in Bormann's eyes. Hitler loyally supported his old comrades in arms as long as they served him faithfully, even if they made mistakes. In Brückner's case he overlooked many a blunder. Bormann, on the other hand, eagerly made a list of them so as to be able to present them at the right moment. That moment came on October 18, 1940, the day on which he was able to record in his notebook: "Dismissal of Chief Adjutant Brückner over differences with Kannenberg."

Hitler had gone on his special train from Berlin to Obersalzberg to receive a distinguished guest, the Crown Princess of Italy. As usual when he had ladies visit the Berghof, he was anxious to be the perfect host. He had brought Artur Kannenberg, his major-domo, from Berlin especially for the occasion. Naturally, Hitler took the princess to see his house on Kehlstein, as Bormann proudly recorded in his journal. Naturally, tea was served in the teahouse. But it was too hot and burned the mouth of Her Royal Highness. Hitler liked to pride himself on the fact that things always functioned like clockwork in his house; he apologized profusely and felt humiliated.

When reproaches came crashing down on him, Kannenberg ducked the responsibility, maintaining that Brückner had taken over the tea kitchen. Presenting the case to Hitler, Bormann argued that Brückner's age and the effects of a former skull fracture, which now seemed to become apparent, indicated that the strenuous position of chief adjutant should be filled by a new appointment. He said he had enough evidence to prove that this *faux pas* was not an isolated incident. He suggested as successor Adjutant Julius

Schaub, another of the old guard, coarse, blunt, not very attractive and anything but a Germanic prototype in spite of his high rank in the SS. Bormann believed that he could win Schaub over and manipulate him later.

After the war Schaub recalled that Bormann always acted as if he were afraid "someone might pull something on him without his noticing." There were certainly reasons enough why this might be so. On the other hand, as head of the Party Chancellery, Bormann was so firmly established in his seat that there were few people left who would have wanted to pick a fight with him. He could be threatened only by those who enjoyed as much of Hitler's trust and favor as he did. There was no one who could claim this among the political leaders, but there were such men in the SS, which was all the more suspicious because there was evidence of increasing rivalry between them and the Party Organization. Since Hitler had played the various Party agencies against each other all along, it was quite conceivable that some day he might strip the political leaders of their power and put Himmler's SS leaders in their place.

Himmler was certainly not the man who could bring about such a change, but there was always Reinhard Heydrich, whom the navy had ousted years before because of an affair with a woman but who, as chief of the SD (Security Service) had thereupon become an SS officer. In his dual function as head of the Security Police and SD chief—i.e., invested with both government and SS authority—presiding at the Berlin headquarters of the Gestapo on Prinz Albrecht Strasse, he was privy to more information than any other German and had, at the same time, control over law enforcement. Hitler described him as the "man with the iron heart" and, tall, blond and blue-eyed, he looked like the perfect Nordic prototype.

Heydrich and his SD were unpopular with the political leaders, who were, rightly, afraid that the SD files contained records of not only the activities of political enemies but also their own sins. It was because of this reservoir of information that Bormann had on occasion supported the SD and collaborated with Heydrich. He used Heydrich's regular reports on public morale to get—as he put it—the Party functionaries "off their asses." And whenever wrongdoings of individual Party members were brought to his attention, he used them to enlarge his personnel file. The ambitious and inscrutable Heydrich was however constantly trying to expand his powers. Bormann became nervous when, immediately after the Hess flight, there was a rumor that Heydrich, who had been charged with the investigation, would recommend himself for a post close to Hitler. In September 1941 Bormann found an opportunity to switch his potential rival onto a sidetrack.

Karl Hermann Frank, a Sudenten-German hostile to the Czechs who was acting as State Secretary to Reich Protector Konstantin von Neurath at Prague, complained to Hitler at the Wolfsschanze that his superior was much too soft on the increasing acts of sabotage against the Protectorate's armament industry. The next day Himmler was called in, and the following day, September 23, 1941, Neurath was summoned. In the presence of Bormann and Goebbels he was informed that he had failed and that although he was not being dismissed officially, he would have to leave the control of Bohemia and Moravia to a deputy. As that deputy, Bormann recommended Reinhard Heydrich. Himmler agreed; he, too, was beginning to find this all-too-efficient young man somewhat sinister.

In Bormann's appointment calendar, which faithfully records all of Hitler's important visitors, Heydrich's name pops up in October 1941, and then never again. But he must have been summoned to the Wolfsschanze once more before his death, for he told his aide Walter Schellenberg, who partially succeeded him, that he had been called to Führer Headquarters to report on the economic problems of the Protectorate. He was made to wait for a long time outside the Führer's bunker; finally Hitler emerged with Bormann, but he only eyed him with displeasure before Bormann ushered him back. The next day Bormann informed Heydrich that the Führer had already made up his mind and no longer needed to be briefed on this matter. Quoting what Heydrich had told him, Schellenberg said that "outwardly Bormann remained extremely polite, but his icy coldness was clearly evident."

Heydrich blamed Bormann for having intrigued against him, but he was never able to prove it. In May 1942 he complained to Schellenberg that his relationship with the head of the Party Chancellery and with the Reichsführer SS had deteriorated so badly that he was thinking of planting an observer in Führer Headquarters to find out why he was in disgrace. But it never came to that. On May 27 Heydrich was fatally wounded in an attempt on his life. He died on June 4. As Bormann noted: "Obergruppenführer Heydrich dead. At night Führer consults with M.B. on Heydrich's succession, memorial service, etc. (It was on my suggestion that Heydrich was named Deputy Reich Protector at the time!)"

Does the exclamation point mean that he felt guilty? It might also be a sign of triumph. Schellenberg speculates in his memoirs that Heydrich may not have fallen victim to a Czech assassin but to "the secret *Feme* of the Führer's innermost circle (Hitler-Bormann-Himmler)." The evidence he produces is not convincing, however. Another contention might be closer to the truth: Heydrich was so far superior to him in intelligence and imagination that "one day [Bormann] would inevitably have got caught in the trap" of the SD chief and "fallen from his proud heights." But the head of the Party Chancellery was probably not the only one to whom Heydrich's death came at a very convenient moment.

Ironically, it was Bormann of all people who was assigned to look after the welfare of Heydrich's widow, among other reasons because she was a so-called bearer of secrets. This was not a special assignment; whenever prominent Party members died, his department took care of and kept tabs on their families, who often needed to be reminded that they had to give up their social position and accustomed life style after the dignitary's death. Gerda Bormann, who saw all of her husband's duties in the glow of unquestioning admiration, once begged him in a letter to take care of his health because "we all need you so much," naming, aside from her own family, "Frau Todt, Frau Heydrich, Frau Kluge and many more." The first was the widow of the Minister of Armaments who died in a plane crash; the last, the widow of author Kurt Kluge, whose novel *Herr Kortüm* graced Bormann's bedside table.

Frau Heydrich caused him some embarrassment, since she found it hard to resign herself to the modest role of a private person. The same problem arose when Victor Lutze, the SA Chief of Staff, died after a car accident and his widow refused to move out of his official residence, although the Party offered her a choice of several large apartments. In order to guard once and for all against complications of this sort, Bormann had Hitler authorize him to issue a general rule; he informed all prominent Party members by letter that in case of their death, their widows would have to leave the official residence.

"That goes for you too," he wrote to Gerda. At that time, in July 1943, when hundreds of thousands of German families had already lost their homes in air raids, he kept up three houses: in Pullach, at Obersalzberg and in Mecklenburg. His fourth home, the confiscated Jewish property at Schluchsee in the upper Black Forest, was just being remodeled for him. Although officially the deeds to two of these—Obersalzberg and the estate in Mecklenburg—were in his name, they actually belonged to Hitler, or rather to the Dragon Hoard. In a letter he warned Gerda that if he died, "you will have to move out of Pullach as soon as possible," and even if the Führer left her the house at Obersalzberg, Eva Braun might make life difficult for her, for example by cutting off the vegetable supplies from the greenhouses. In that case it would be better for Gerda not to expose herself to such humiliations.

He was not telling her this, he said, because he was tired of life or had premonitions of death, but because he took "an entirely realistic view of such matters." He might die "in an accident, in an attempt on my life, or some such thing." What he thought of death and what a true National Socialist was supposed to think of it he put down in an office memo to one of his aides whose job it was to read and review books, and on the basis of the digests he made, to enable Bormann to appear the well-informed reader. Bormann criticized this aide for having recommended *Reflections on Life and Death* as a book worth sponsoring, when its author, Bruno H. Bürgel, whose popular-science books were widely read at the time, did not share the Nazi ideas on the nature of death. Bormann let the reviewer know that man lived on through his works and—even more—through his kin and his ethnic stock. The individual might be mortal but not the nation. This was obviously the faith that might inspire the Germans to die on the battlefields for Hitler's plans for global power. Any other religion therefore had to disappear.

13

Hitler
Was His God

When Martin Bormann's mistress, the actress Manja Behrens, was afraid of the air raids in Dresden, he reminded her in a letter of her religious convictions: people of her faith should actually be glad to be transported to heaven out of this vale of tears. The "sensitive" patriot wrote this at a time when hundreds of thousands of German soldiers and tens of thousands of civilians had been massacred in the war. His approach to the Christian faith was primitive, demagogic, and drew heavily on the antireligious Communist propaganda of the early 1920s. Challenging Christian doctrine with spiritual arguments was not his line; it would have been too time-consuming. Those whose faith was lukewarm were to be intimidated by dirty tricks, restrictions and threats; steadfast believers could ultimately be isolated in concentration camps. Rather than believe in Jesus Christ, the Germans were to worship Adolf Hitler.

But Bormann could not duck the confrontation of ideas completely. On a few occasions he circulated long-winded memoranda prepared by his aides as his own thoughts. Evidently he did not feel as secure preaching his faith as he did organizing and conducting the fight against "ideological enemies" —his classification for Christian believers. He therefore never professed his nonbelief in public. But in August 1942 Hitler authorized him to announce the Party's point of view on all "religious matters." Bormann's anti-Christian activities had multiplied after the the war began; he assumed people would now be distracted by greater concerns. He was always most active when moments of victory and special radio announcements seemed to prove that the Almighty, so often invoked by Hitler, was fighting on the German side.

His simplistic notions about the nature of the Christian churches convinced him that he could cripple them by robbing them of their financial assets. Soon after the beginning of the war he requested Reich Minister of Finance Count Schwerin von Krosigk to stop the internal revenue service from levying church taxes, thereby forcing the churches to raise their own funds—a request he repeated in vain several times over the next few years. At the same time he tried to squeeze the churches in other ways. In order to finance the war, cities, communities and corporations were obliged to make defense contributions to the Reich, and the churches were not excluded. The Protestant Church was required to raise 1 million Reichsmark a month, the Catholic Church 800,000. On January 18, 1940, Bormann had Gerhard Klopfer, head of his constitutional-law section, draft a letter to the Minister of Finance informing him that Bormann considered the sums too low. It seemed "entirely appropriate" to him that "the churches, too, should pay a higher rate." Should this necessitate a cut in personnel expenditure —in other words, in the salaries of priests or ministers—this seemed "perfectly reasonable" to him. "Contrary to all other Germans eligible for military service," continues the letter, "no Catholic priest is serving at the front; nor do Catholic priests take up the burdens every German who is head of a family must carry."

The newly fixed, considerably higher defense contributions were to be raised from all denominations, and it should be left to them to collect the money from their organizations. In case of forcible collection, however, it should be left to the government "to draw on the assets of the various individual bodies at its discretion." As became evident in due course, Bormann wanted at all costs to get his hands on the property of the monasteries.

The day before this demand was sent off, Bormann had signed another letter drafted by Klopfer, this one addressed to Rosenberg. In it he fumed that "both Catholic and Protestant churches are still extraordinarily attentive to members of the Wehrmacht." From the clergy of their home communities, soldiers regularly received religious booklets which "have a certain influence on the morale of the troops." The Wehrmacht's officers' corps, which was religiously inclined, rejected Bormann's complaint about this on the ground that censorship could stop only printed matter containing attacks on the government or the Party. Nor would or could Reichsleiter Max Amann, who was responsible for the allocation of rationed paper, prevent the printing of religious tracts. Police action appeared to Bormann "unsatisfactory and rather dubious as to its ultimate effect." As a result, he ordered Reichsleiter Rosenberg to turn out Party tracts which would "appeal to all members of the Wehrmacht, regardless of their background."

Only a day later, Rosenberg was urged to deliver these tracts "promptly" and was chastised for having praised, in Hitler's presence, a book written for soldiers by Reich Bishop Ludwig Müller (nicknamed "Reibi"), a one-time Protestant minister with the Reichswehr in Königsberg who now had only a negligible following among the splintered Protestants.

"I could not disagree more," Bormann raged. "Soldiers who have left the Christian faith may through this book become reacquainted with semidisguised Christian ideas." At the same time, Reichsleiter Amann was urged "in the case of . . . new paper allocations to see to it that politically and ideologically deserving literature is given preference over religious publications which, judging from past experience, have dubious value in strengthening the people's resistance against the outside enemy."

In the eyes of the churches, Alfred Rosenberg was the Antichrist personified. Only a few churchmen knew that he was not their worst enemy in the Party and that he was constantly being put down as too soft by the largely unknown Bormann. A ten-page letter to Rosenberg, dated February 22, 1940—which was signed by Bormann, but judging from its style and content, certainly not written by him—would have made them recognize their most dangerous opponent earlier in the game, had they been able to see it. Under the heading "Guidelines for Religious Instruction in the Schools," Bormann explained for the first time why he rejected a compromise between Christian *Weltanschauung* and his own, and also revealed the tactics by which he meant to destroy the churches. The letter was motivated by a rumor that Rosenberg had assigned Reich Bishop Müller to work out guidelines for religious instruction in schools.

Typically, Bormann never tried to get to the bottom of this (as it happened, false) rumor in a face-to-face conversation. As far as the much despised Rosenberg was concerned, he was notified in writing of "the grave doubts I must raise against such an assignment." It was "not for the Party" to create such guidelines, since they were based on the premise of "a synthesis of National Socialism and the Christian doctrine" which "I consider inconceivable. . . . Both are basically so different from each other that it would be impossible to evolve a Christian doctrine that could be fully accepted on the level of National Socialist *Weltanschauung.*" No compromise, he lectured Rosenberg, could replace this antithesis, only a new *Weltanschauung,* "whose coming you yourself have predicted in your works." A compromise would make "the soul of the German people sink back once again into Christian dogma," after it had only just been "liberated by National Socialism."

Religious instruction, Bormann announced, could continue as before, provided the teachers presented "this subject matter as Biblical and not as German or National Socialist ideas." Later it should be supplemented by "a manual for a German way of life to be compiled by the Party" so that in addition to the "highly inadequate Ten Commandments, every German boy and girl" would be made to observe, "for instance, the commandment of bravery, the taboo of cowardice, the commandment of love of nature in all its forms . . . the commandment for maintaining the purity of the race."

"Confirmation classes" would thereby "lose importance." "Young people brought up on our moral code" could be trusted to make their own decision on "whether or not to bring up their children in the inferior Christian faith."

Needless to say, in his long-range pursuits Bormann did not forget the day-to-day practices which could give the churches a hard time. Albert Speer, who was in charge of remodeling the Reich capital, had been negotiating with the local ecclesiastical authorities on building sites for churches in the new sections of Berlin. As a result, he was harshly reprimanded by Bormann, who forbade him to set aside real estate for such projects. Later, when the cities crumbled under the bombs, some overeager Gauleiters ordered that damaged churches be torn down. Having learned from bitter experience, Speer, wherever possible, declared the ruins "historically and artistically important monuments," and asked Party Comrade Bormann in a letter to prevent their demolition "until the Führer himself has definitely decided on reconstruction plans for the cities . . ." And when, a few months later, Speer was chastised again by the head of the Party Chancellery for having decontrolled scarce building material to repair churches, he again hid behind the excuse that these were "national monuments of historical and artistic value." Bormann had to pass; this was an area about which he knew nothing.

Other church-owned monuments Bormann artfully planned to expropriate, if possible to the Party's advantage. The reputed wealth of the monasteries attracted him particularly. On January 13, 1941, he sent all Gauleiters a "Strictly Confidential" telex message which, in actual fact, was an invitation to loot. It deserves careful study, because in just a few lines it reveals a great deal about the author's practices. "Experience has shown," he wrote, "that the public has expressed no indignation when monasteries were converted to generally accepted useful purposes. Examples of generally accepted useful purposes are hospitals, rest homes, national-political educational institutions or Adolf Hitler Schools, etc. These possibilities should be exploited to the largest possible extent."

The telex did not mention a law or decree covering the confiscation of the property; nor did anything of the kind exist. It should also be noted that uncharacteristically, Bormann did not refer to the Führer's wishes. It may therefore be assumed that Hitler had been informed about this move but thought it best to stay out of the game so as to be able, if need be, to disown the illegal exercise as a high-handed act of some busybodies.

In March the Gauleiters received an additional tip—marked "Secret! Personal!"—on how to justify their raids. There had been a great deal of confiscation in Ostmark (Austria) "as a result of violation of wartime economy regulations (such as hoarding of foodstuffs, textiles, leather products, etc.), in other cases because of violation of the *Heimtückegesetz*

(Treason Law*), and frequently also ownership of arms." Accusations of this sort could be fabricated quite easily: the secret sale of a few quarts of milk, a critical remark about the Party or a few shotguns hanging on the wall for decoration were sufficient incriminating evidence. In all such cases, Bormann pointed out, there could, of course, be no question of compensation to the churches.

This Bormann message also carried Hitler's indirect approval; the Gauleiters supposedly informed him ex post facto after they had carried out such requisitioning operations. When this was done on March 1, 1941, during his visit to Vienna, Hitler actually expressed the desire—although by no means issued an order—"that he wished the confiscated property to be designated to the respective provincial governments." Bormann wrote this to Lammers, since the now-awakened Reich Ministry of Finance was claiming the loot as property of the Reich.

The booty was handled according to Hitler's usual tactics: whoever was able to rob had the right to do so. This offered Bormann a welcome opportunity to recommend himself to the Gauleiters as the well-meaning Reichsleiter. He was present in Vienna when the rule was passed, and his letter to Lammers gave the Gauleiters added support. Whoever denied the Party's provincial governments the right to own property, he wrote, on the "childish argument" that they might thereby become too independent of the Reich's central power, was "actually trying to deny the Gauleiters and Reichsstatthalters independence." This was also a sideswipe at Reich Minister of the Interior Frick.

The action against Klosterneuburg, one of the largest and most beautiful monasteries in Austria, is an example of how such confiscation procedures were prepared and carried out. A few days after Bormann's invitation to loot, the Party big shots in Vienna met to decide where they could make the biggest killing. They focused on the Augustinian monastery on the outskirts of the city. With its nearly 9,000 hectares (roughly 22,000 acres)—about the size of a hundred large farms—and other scattered pieces of land, elaborate buildings, twelfth-century church, art treasures, coin collection, 120,000-volume library and famous wine cellar, it particularly appealed to them. In order to make the action urgent, they designated the monastery as one to be converted into an Adolf Hitler School—to serve the Party's rising generation. They felt that "its size and the nearby playing fields" made it especially well suited to this purpose, but quick action should be taken or the school would be based in Hamburg.

A day later a dossier arrived from the Vienna Gestapo. It established, among other things, that there had earlier been—obviously false—suspicion

*A special law designed to punish wartime offenders. It was intended to control political dissenters, many of whom were arrested by the Gestapo and sent to concentration camps.

of illegal currency deals; that the prelate had had friendly relations with followers of former Chancellor Kurt von Schuschnigg; that monastery inmates had been convicted on morals charges; and that legal action was pending against others for subversive activities. That did it. On February 22, 1941, only a month after the Party leaders had met, Gauleiter and Reichsstatthalter of Vienna Baldur von Schirach signed the confiscation order, under the heading of "Lawful Requisition for the Accommodation of Public Institutions."

The statistics of the [German] Institute of Contemporary History in Munich give an idea of the extent of the action Bormann had instigated. By early May 1941, the inmates of thirty-five monasteries in West Germany alone had been expelled; the diocese of Breslau reported over sixty acts of requisition, Austria over two hundred. Protesting to the courts did not do the victims much good; only in rare cases did their objections have any delaying effect, and the hearings before the civilian judges dragged on forever. But in July 1941 something occurred that Hitler had wanted to avoid at all costs: the action turned into a public scandal. It was started by the Bishop of Münster, Count Clemens August von Galen, in whose diocese eight monasteries had been requisitioned by the Gestapo. In three sermons he accused the National Socialists of persecuting Christians and churches, as well as of multiple murders of mental patients in the course of their so-called euthanasia operations. This was reported in the foreign press, and the texts of the sermons were circulated at home in underground leaflets. On August 15, 1941, Bormann wrote: "It remains to be seen what steps the Führer will take against the bishop. The death penalty would certainly seem appropriate; but in view of wartime conditions the Führer will hardly resort to such a measure."

Bormann had to defer his revenge: Galen was merely put under house arrest and forbidden to leave his palace. The head of the Party Chancellery, however, was obliged to inform his Gauleiters by a circular that the Führer had ordered "confiscation of church and monastery property to be discontinued for the time being." If "in special cases" it proved absolutely necessary, "the cases must be brought to the Führer's attention through my office."

As usual, Hitler wriggled out of the whole business: once again he had known nothing about it. When during a visit to Führer Headquarters some weeks later his former Vice Chancellor, Franz von Papen, brought the conversation around to Galen, Hitler professed indignation and insisted that he had put a stop to the "nonsense" by issuing a stern order—Bormann's circular. Lammers, however, confided to Papen that Bormann had added a phrase to the Führer's order, telling the Gauleiters not to take it all that seriously. In such cases Bormann considered it an honor to serve his Führer as a scapegoat; he knew that it made him all the more indispensable.

The experiences of Augsburg's Gauleiter Karl Wahl demonstrate how much Hitler shunned getting directly involved in the action against the monasteries. When an emissary of Bormann's tried to impress on him that it was time for him to get busy in his Gau, Wahl asked him "whether his chief [meaning Bormann] has gone out of his mind" to want to upset the country's morale now of all times when a war was going on. The emissary pointed out that "the fight against the church organizations" was "Bormann's pet project." Wahl stood firm, even when a second request ominously implied that it would be "in his own best interest" to comply. He was not urged again after that, even though Bormann would have proceeded against him with the greatest pleasure if he could have obtained authorization to do so. Hitler decided to postpone getting even with Galen until after the war. Here he followed Goebbels' advice that the arrest of the bishop would mean that the regime would have to "write off Münster and all of Westphalia for the duration of the war."

Münsterland, which was predominantly Catholic, had always been poor soil for Nazi ideology. Gauleiter Alfred Meyer would have felt better holding office in that clerical stronghold if Bormann had chosen a project other than the fight against Christianity. When the pseudo-Protestant Reich Bishop Ludwig Müller tried to set up a Reich Church, thereby infuriating the Protestants, Meyer suggested a compromise. This time Bormann—as pope of the Party, so to speak—felt called upon to proclaim what a National Socialist was supposed to believe or condemn. Meyer received a detailed reply, dated June 7, 1941, on the "Relationship between National Socialism and Christianity." And since it concerned itself with basic principles, all the other Gauleiters were also mailed a copy of the text, marked "Secret!"

The introduction of this incredibly banal treatise repeated the premise that National Socialism and Christian ideas were irreconcilable. The churches, Bormann insisted, were banking on the ignorance of the people, for this was the only way they could "maintain their power." "National Socialism, on the other hand, is based on scientific principles" and "far superior to the concepts of Christianity, which were essentially taken over from Judaism." Theology was branded a "pseudoscience." He, Bormann, could recognize God at any time—one look at the nocturnal sky was enough: "What we call the Almighty or God is the power of nature's law by which all those innumerable planets move throughout the universe. The allegation that this universal power could concern itself with the fate of each individual being, each minute earth microbe . . . is either naïve or a commercial fraud."

Whatever might strengthen the Christian churches should be rejected "without discrimination, for the Protestant Church is just as hostile toward us as the Catholic Church." For the first time in German history the state was now independent of the churches. "Only the Reich government and, by its order, the Party . . . have a right to lead the people. Just as the damaging influence of astrologers and other frauds . . . is suppressed, the influence of the churches must be totally eradicated."

Proud as Bormann must have been when he rushed this product of petty-bourgeois thought through the telex wires, he was given little chance to enjoy it later. Without going into detail, Goebbels, who knew a thing or two about propaganda, gently lectured him on how unwise it was in time of war to provoke the churches in this way. Rosenberg remarked condescendingly in conversation that official Party communications of this kind were unacceptable and noticed with satisfaction that Bormann sheepishly kept silent. At the Nuremberg Trials, Hamburg's Gauleiter Karl Kaufmann testified that Bormann had been forced, on Hitler's orders, to retract his elaboration—and that all copies had to be retrieved. Rosenberg also stated that the author of the text was not Bormann but an aide of his from the Party Chancellery who, as a penalty, had been obliged to change from his brown uniform into field-gray—in other words, had been sent to the front. However, the pasted-together Party slogans, the clumsy language, the primitive arguments and the distorted ideas are so characteristic of Bormann's style that there can be no doubt about the authorship.

At this point Bormann obviously did not feel like sticking his neck out ideologically again. He withdrew to an unassailable position where he was protected by the power of his office—to his role of manager. He directed that the invocation still customary in some schools at the beginning of classes should be "cut down more and more and ultimately abolished." Instead, "National Socialist aphorisms" should be read out or occasional morning services might be held. Rosenberg's Party poets were called upon to submit samples. Bormann also wondered to what extent the political reliability of religious sisters serving in hospitals and field hospitals ought to be investigated. He finally decided that "in view of the current shortage of nurses" it had not yet reached an "intolerable" level. In a circular the Gauleiters were warned against the pathological desire for ceremonies among Party members who were still floundering ideologically and searching for a substitute religion. It would be wrong to try to replace religious customs—to have an ethnic ceremony instead of a christening, for example, or a coming-of-age party instead of a confirmation. National Socialism was a way of life based on scientific principles. Without resorting to cults and mysticism, its ceremonies should serve only to shape political conviction. Jointly with Ley, this vest-pocket Robespierre even succeeded in seeing to it that the families of soldiers killed in the war no longer received the news from their priest or minister but from the local Party representative.

"Why shouldn't the priest be the harbinger of death?" Goebbels argued. In matters of church and faith he was Bormann's toughest opponent in the Party—partly perhaps in memory of his boyhood dream of becoming a priest. Nevertheless, he, too, was in favor of a showdown with the unruly clergy. In private he remarked to Werner Stephan, one of his aides in the

Ministry of Propaganda, "Contrary to the Party Chancellery, I was always against provoking the churches to a fight . . . and tried to keep up the appearance of loyal cooperation. There will be no problem after the war to deprive the churches of their material basis and thereby break their backs."

Goebbels gave in when Bormann, supported by Himmler, demanded at Christmas 1941 that the radio refrain from broadcasting the traditional hymns on the birth of Christ. Only the noncommittal "O Tannenbaum" was acceptable. Bormann recommended instead light music and popular tunes. Perhaps Goebbels bowed to this demand only so that he could report to the Führer after the holiday how violent the public's reaction against the ban had been. Hitler was not going to submit to that a second time; the next year Bormann had to resign himself to the customary "Silent Night."

The hassle between the Reich Minister of Propaganda, who was responsible for public morale, and the fanatical head of the Party Chancellery about issuing a statement that would keep the Party out of all religious disputes dragged on from early December 1941 until February 1942. Goebbels was disturbed by American newspaper reports about a book entitled *God and People,* written by a dedicated neo-pagan, which had appeared in Germany, and by a brochure, "Our Faith in the Next World," which stated among other things that National Socialists would proudly forgo "the next world as promised by the Christian faith."

If he were an agent of the Allied secret service, Goebbels declared, he would "do nothing but write such books and brochures," because nothing could do worse damage to the German people at home and abroad. He had his aide Walter Tiessler of the Reich Propaganda Directorate ask Bormann naïvely, and slyly, whether it was un-German "to believe in the next world in some form or other." Also, was it really the job of National Socialism to determine this question or wasn't it more important "to let everyone find salvation in his own way"? Tiessler suggested a basic announcement by the Party stating that National Socialism was responsible only for life here on earth; questions concerning the next world must remain "each individual's personal affair." "Whoever deals with such questions—positively or negatively—should not refer to the NSDAP or National Socialism."

If he had allowed such an announcement, Bormann would have disavowed himself ex post facto, for his letters had done just that. Since he was at the Wolfsschanze headquarters, he did not have to get involved in an argument with Goebbels, but he had to listen to Tiessler. Goebbels subsequently received Bormann's decision in writing. Bormann had no intention of confiscating neo-pagan writings, because "Germany enjoys the same freedom of conscience as exists in the democratic countries." He agreed that the Party should not "burden itself with writings of this sort," and declared that he had ordered "only a few days ago that a brochure written by Hauptbefehlsleiter Schmidt should be withdrawn from circulation and pulped." Since Party Comrade Fritz Schmidt was head of the NSDAP's

Hauptschulungsamt (Central Training Office), which was part of Ley's bailiwick, Bormann found issuing this order no hardship. He took over a month to comment on the announcement suggested by Tiessler. Then he simply swept it off the table. The Führer had repeatedly decided, he wrote in a memo to Tiessler, that everyone should find salvation in his own way. "There has been no official Party announcement, nor will there be one."

Bormann could act so peremptorily because during the past few weeks his Führer had made clear to him that he was on the right track. Hitler had given him the Reichsgau Wartheland as testing ground for anti-Christian experiments. Gauleiter Arthur Greiser, who operated out of Posen, was authorized to introduce a special church regulation for his territory which Bormann's legal advisers had drafted. Since all the agreements Poland had signed for this area had become null and void after Poland's collapse, this was legally possible. Bormann was able to develop a model for religious life in "Greater Germania" in a legal wasteland.

The model provided for perfect separation of church and state. In the eyes of the law, the religious societies were mere clubs, forbidden to estabish any ties outside their local affiliation. Those who wished to join had to submit an application in writing. Minors were not admitted. Anyone moving to Wartheland from the Reich had to renew his membership application. Religious organizations of any kind, such as youth groups or charitable organizations, were strictly forbidden. The church tax was abolished. The societies were allowed to collect dues but could not accept donations. There were to be no more full-time priests or ministers; they were required to have another profession by which to earn a living. Except for a "cult hall" (church building), the associations were not allowed to own any real estate.

It was certainly an evening of triumph for Bormann when, on July 4, 1942, at the Wolfsschanze headquarters Hitler announced during an almost endless late-night monologue his conditions for the churches, and these turned out to be almost identical to the ones Bormann had just meted out to Wartheland. And, Hitler promised, they would settle their account with Bishop von Galen, Bormann's archenemy, "to the last penny."

Bormann was obviously satisfied with his victory, for in the months and years that followed, his anti-church activities dwindled. He had done what he could; now it was the Gestapo's turn to attend to the details. He therefore directed his energy and aggressions toward the Jews and the "subhumans" in the East.

14

The Armchair Assassin

"All the people who did it are dead: Hitler, Himmler, Bormann, Heydrich, Eichmann," Ernst Kaltenbrunner, the regime's last chief of the Secret Police and Security Service, told the War Crimes Tribunal at Nuremberg, when the mass murder of the Jews came up for trial. He was wrong in assuming that Eichmann was no longer alive, and he forgot to list Goebbels as one of the instigators. But the roles were indeed divided among these men. Himmler, Heydrich and Eichmann operated the switches of the death machinery. Goebbels, with simulated fanaticism, kept fanning the terror. Hitler, the actual driving force, issued the secret extermination orders to his Party comrades in casual conversation, without compromising himself as a killer.

The role played by Martin Bormann is best illustrated by an incident that occurred toward the end of 1940. Governor General Hans Frank had been summoned to the Chancellery for discussions on the occupied areas of Poland that had been designated to become collecting centers for Jewish deportees. Bormann, of course, attended the meeting, while East Prussian Gauleiter Erich Koch and Vienna's Gauleiter Baldur von Schirach joined the party for dinner. As usual, Hitler talked and talked after dinner, and his guests responded with adulation and approval like loyal henchmen. Bormann sat quietly, taking notes and recording the main points in a detailed memorandum.

Frank was bragging that many parts of Poland, including his own residency of Cracow, had been almost completely cleared of Jews. More and more were being herded into ghettos. He objected, however, to rushing in shipments of Jews from other areas, warning that they would cause overcrowding. Besides, if additional Polish districts were to be incorporated into the Reich, he was not going to have enough land on which to establish Jewish reservations. But Koch insisted that he would get rid of the Jews and Poles in his province, and Schirach demanded that the 60,000 Jews remaining in Vienna be deported to German-occupied Poland.

Bormann, the meticulous rapporteur, lost no time transforming the conversation into action. A few days later he reminded Hitler of the Jews of Vienna, rekindling the youthful hatred Hitler had manifested in *Mein Kampf.* The Führer's decision was succinct: in view of Vienna's housing shortage, "the 60,000 Jews still residing within the Reichsgau of Vienna" were to be deported to Poland without delay; that is, while the war was still on. Bormann conveyed this to Lammers, who in turn relayed the order to Schirach and the heads of the SS and police, as official routine prescribed. The timing of the operation—the letter was dated December 3, 1940—must be understood in context. Hitler and his entourage were obviously counting on a victorious peace in the coming year. Hence a postscript was added that "the deportations . . . be started by early next year."

In the persecution and extermination of the Jews which now sprang up in all directions, Bormann's part was always that of the bureaucrat, the signer—generally in conjunction with others—of decrees and laws, the converter of the Führer's will into action, the computer who ensured that no one was overlooked by the killers, Hitler's informant and pace-setter.

He showed hardly any originality of thought in these activities, nor does he seem to have been nearly as involved as he had been in his passionate campaign against Christianity. Hitler found him the ideal front behind which he could hide, from the public and from posterity, the killer instinct he had focused on the Jews. What's more, Bormann was proud of his function. Often a few anti-Semitic phrases from one of Hitler's dinner monologues were enough for him to work into yet another decree. And he was encouraged by the fact that in this sector his zeal could never go wrong as long as he was ruthless enough.

Characteristically, he managed to turn even the pettiest matter into a political affair. Certainly it would never have occurred to him personally that the Gothic letters of the alphabet, venerated from time immemorial by German chauvinists, might be of Jewish origin. When this allegation was brought before Hitler in the early days of January 1941, Party publisher Max Amann and "Herr Adolf Müller," the owner of a printing press and of the other facilities used by the Party's central publishing office, were summoned to the Berghof. Hitler informed them that henceforth the Antiqua type— the ancient Roman alphabet—was "to be known as the standard script." To this Bormann added a memorandum that the Schwabach Jew-letters were to be abolished as soon as possible in schools, printing presses, on street signs, documents, everywhere. Those in charge of the wartime economy were appalled at the waste of manpower and raw material that resulted from this directive.

The prosecution at Nuremberg accused the absent Bormann of having co-signed almost all the anti-Semitic laws after 1941; that is, after Hess's flight to England. Yet it never examined the extent to which he shared in the making of these laws above and beyond the routine signature of his office —for example, in enforcing racial laws in the areas newly incorporated into the Reich or in a decree concerning government seizure of property left by Jewish émigrés. Bormann or his associate Gerhard Klopfer participated in the planning and wording of all objectives, although he and those he authorized distinguished themselves less by their perfidious actions than by the bureaucratic perfectionism with which they closed even the smallest loophole in the network of inhuman legislation.

Although he did not play a prominent part in it, Klopfer attended the so-called Wannsee Conference on January 20, 1942, chaired by Police and SD chief Heydrich, which developed the program for the extermination of the Jews. Bormann stayed behind at the Wolfsschanze, although he was hardly needed there at the time; Hitler was so preoccupied with attempts to stop the Soviet breakthroughs at the middle section of the front, which was already weakened by retreats and icy temperatures, that he could not be bothered with other matters. Bormann left for Berlin two days after the conference and immediately went on to Obersalzberg. His indifference suggests that he knew what had been decided but wanted to leave the action to Himmler and his men.

Even before the conference he had carefully not overstepped the amount of anti-Semitism standard among Party members. He urged the Gauleiters to put Jews into concentration camps if they "failed to follow certain orders instantly." But this could also be done to an "Aryan." He was also among those responsible for the directive that as of September 5, 1941, no Jews in Germany, including children above the age of six, were to appear in public without wearing the yellow Star of David. Years before, he had proposed such an identification, but now it was no longer his sole doing. Unlike his activities in other areas where his energies were always in high gear, in hunting down the Jews he obviously restrained himself for months. Did he, at this time, already know of Hitler's decision; did he know before any other Party official of the plan for a "final solution"? Was this why he felt it was no longer worthwhile bothering about details? Presumably so.

Hitler's army adjutant, Colonel Gerhard Engel, recorded a monologue the Führer delivered in the Chancellery on February 2, 1941, in the presence of Bormann, Speer and Keitel. After the war, Hitler predicted, there would be no Jews left in Germany. The only question was what to do with them. He had mentioned the matter before, and the Foreign Office had drafted plans to deport all the Jews to the African island of Madagascar. But this, he reminded them, would be impossible now with the war going on. Besides, in the meantime the Jews from the conquered areas had been added. "If I only knew where to put those few million Jews," Hitler said; "there aren't that many, after all." At that point he had stopped talking about a resettlement, a permanent Jewish home in the East.

Bormann knew that Heydrich was preparing the mass deportations and that he had indeed been deporting Jews since October 1941; that is, months before the Wannsee Conference. For the time being there was talk about the East being made a roundup area and transit territory, but Bormann had learned from Hitler that it was to be their final destination. He was constantly around the Führer and as Hitler in private conversation weighed the pros and cons of the various options, he may have served as catalyst in the decision for mass extermination.

During the Wannsee Conference it was decided that Jews should be used as forced labor in the East, where "a large number will be eliminated by natural decimation." The rest, the more robust, would have to be "handled accordingly," since "if they went free, they would form the nucleus for a comeback of the Jewish race." The German public was not unaware of the deportations, even though the police called for the victims at dawn and took great care to keep the action secret. One day in the middle of May, Hitler expressed annoyance during lunch at the Wolfsschanze that the "so-called bourgeoisie was weeping crocodile tears for a Jew being deported to the East." At the same time, reports from soldiers on leave from the eastern front began filtering through at home; rumor had it that the Jews were being systematically slaughtered out there.

As a result, in October 1942 Bormann felt obliged to provide his Gauleiters with some, albeit wishy-washy, directions on how to respond. The civilian population should be reminded of the two thousand years of warfare between the Jews and the Germanic people. If the Jews were now locked in concentration camps and forced into labor service, it was "in the nature of things that these very difficult problems . . . can be solved only with ruthless severity." The text is revealing, since, after much twisting and turning, it finally, in its last words, hints at the terrible secret in a phrase borrowed from the standard Nazi vocabulary.

But Bormann continued to react rather than act. In October 1942 he did make the Reich Food Minister Herbert Backe, who had taken over Darré's position, drastically cut the food rations for Jews. But this measure was not his idea. A month earlier Goebbels had barred the Jews of Berlin from all special food distributions, had prohibited them from keeping pets and denied them the services of "Aryan" hairdressers.

However, Bormann still handled "petty cases" with bureaucratic fervor. In one of these the Army High Command had decided that in exceptional cases, a soldier could be granted permission to marry a woman who had previously been married to a Jew. Bormann submitted the case to Hitler. A circular informed the Party Organization of his decision. "A German woman who has lived in marital communion with a Jew has proved such lack of racial instinct that a later union with a soldier cannot be considered."

A somewhat bizarre situation evolved when Bormann was informed that a check into the antecedents of Hitler's dietary cook had revealed that one of her grandmothers was Jewish. The excitement was all the greater since Hitler had often praised his cook's culinary art and, on occasion, had even invited her to the dinner table. Everyone agreed that a quarter Jewess must not cook for the Führer. Yet, when Bormann brought this up, Hitler shied away from a decision. Bormann the steward mailed her the fatal letter while she was away on vacation. But that, again, did not suit Hitler. He was not going to do without his good vegetable soups. And so the dismissal was rescinded.

To Hitler, Bormann became increasingly the specialist on the Jewish question, or at least the staunch advocate of the tough line. He was, for example, given the responsibility for teaching Nazi anti-Semitism to a Hungarian government delegation, led by a Cabinet minister, which was coming to Germany on a visit. The Hungarian ally had always been lax in this respect and had left the large number of Hungarian Jews as undisturbed as Big Brother in Berlin would permit. But if Europe were really to become free of Jews, no exception could be permitted in Budapest. On the evening of March 7, 1943, Bormann left the Wolfsschanze and traveled to Obersalzberg via Berlin. At the Party's main office in Munich he was greeted by a telex which the Reich's Foreign Minister, who was responsible for the visitors, recommended as "guidelines for such talks." Bormann must have considered it presumptuous that Ribbentrop, a vain numskull and upstart in the eyes of the Party's old guard, wished to have a say in ideological matters. Nor was there anything new to him in Ribbentrop's argument that the presence of "100,000 Jews in Germany or a German-allied country has about the same effect as if 100,000 Secret Service agents were to be admitted into the country." Jews, according to Ribbentrop, were spreading Anglo-American news and defeatism and, for ideological and practical reasons, must be given "special treatment." So far, Jews of Hungarian nationality residing in Germany had been deported to the East only if they failed to return to their homeland, but this would have to be changed.

It was Bormann's task to make it clear to the Hungarian visitors that they, too, would now have to begin persecution "along the lines of the German laws against the Jews." As practical measures, Bormann demanded that Jews be excluded from Hungary's cultural and economic life, that their property be confiscated immediately, that they be identified to the public, i.e., by wearing the Star of David, and that their evacuation to the East be started.

The guests arrived at Obersalzberg in the early morning. They were fed and shown around, and attended a performance of *Die Fledermaus* in

Salzburg. Bormann was able to bask in the glory of playing host and representative of the Greater German Reich. Next day he took them in a motorcade of gleaming black Mercedes cars along the autobahn to Munich. Following a tour of Party headquarters, they were given lunch at Bormann's house in Pullach, to which, after more sightseeing, they returned for an evening of further entertainment. On the third day they visited armament factories and buildings on the Nuremberg rally grounds. The results, however, were disappointing. The Hungarians feigned enthusiasm and support, but two months later, at a conference of Gauleiters in Berlin Hitler complained that the Jewish question was being handled "in the worst possible way by the Hungarians" and that "the Hungarian state is totally contaminated by Jews."

Some months earlier a law had been prepared against the Jews remaining in Germany, depriving them of the last of their rights. It had been touched off indirectly by a speech Hitler gave before the Reichstag late in April 1942 in which he blasted the jurists because the courts were still refusing to carry out the decrees of government terror. At this point Roland Freisler, then State Secretary in the Ministry of Justice, tried to prove his loyalty by drafting an anti-Semitic law. There was already a model for such a law. The decree Bormann and Gauleiter Artur Greiser had issued for Wartheland, which robbed the Poles there of all legal protection and delivered them to Himmler's police.

Inspired by this, Freisler sent off a special-delivery letter early in August 1942 to all the ministries concerned, as well as the Party Chancellery, with a "draft for a decree limiting legal means of redress in criminal cases against Jews." The covering letter did not name the author of the draft. Freisler did not like to claim sole responsibility, for he emphasized that *"he"* had advocated "the wartime importance of the decree, since indirectly it serves the country's defense." Many Germans, he claimed, were grumbling because Jews still had the right to call on judges when they were indicted by the police and to appeal against convictions and such. The new decree was to deprive them of all such privileges.

Freisler soon received suggestions for amendments. The officers of the Ministry of the Interior thought this might be a good opportunity to deprive the Jews of all civil rights in administrative matters as well. The Food Ministry proposed that Jews should be denied the right to appeal in cases where farmland was consolidated or water supply was involved. Elsewhere it was felt the Jews should be denied a hearing under oath. This, however, raised new problems, since an unsworn and untrue statement could then not be punished as an act of perjury. Bormann also contributed proposals for amendments. Among other things he demanded that Jews accept without protest financial charges from government agencies as well as judicial writs, and that they not be entitled to appeal a sentence. Himmler demanded that the estate of a deceased Jew be declared government property. He also complained that the legal machinery was working too slowly and insisted that they discuss means to speed it up.

The meeting was called at the end of 1942, and the decree, initially intended to consist of a single paragraph, burgeoned into nine. It was subsequently held up in the Ministry of the Interior; "in view of developments in the Jewish question," Frick considered it "no longer necessary." Dead people, he presumably told himself, can no longer be deprived of their rights by anyone. But in March 1943 Chief of Security Police Ernst Kaltenbrunner put him in his place; it was much too time-consuming, he said, to argue cases over the estates of Jews without a general precept. Besides, there were still heirs around who, being Jews married to Germans, had not been deported. It was only after Bormann, the coordinator, had put his foot down, however, that the decree became final, on July 1, 1943. It now plainly bore his signature and ruled that criminal acts committed by Jews could be assessed and punished only by the police. Like the Poles, the Jews were now deprived of the right to due process and delivered to the mercy of Himmler's terror machine.

It was also ruled that subsequent to the death—or rather the murder—of Jews, their property would go to the Reich unless non-Jewish relatives were present to claim it. In actual fact, the decree merely confirmed an already accepted practice. More than a year earlier, on May 12, 1942, 1,500 Jewish men, women and children had been sent to the gas chambers in Auschwitz—the first mass killing to be dated precisely. In April 1943 Himmler compiled statistics on "The Final Solution for the Jewish Question in Europe." To make the report acceptable to be submitted to Hitler, Bormann requested that the words "liquidation" and "special treatment" be avoided. Himmler obliged and had it rewritten. Therefore, by the time the report was issued, 1.45 million Jews had been deported to the East, out of which 1.27 million had been "processed through the camps," as the term for the killings was made to read so as not to offend the Führer's "delicate feelings."

This was an interim count; the death machine kept churning. Three months later Bormann, on behalf of the Führer, issued a secret directive to the Party executives—Reichsleiters, Gauleiters, heads of agencies—on what the increasingly wary German public should be told about the disappearance of the Jews: "In dealing with the public on the Jewish question there should be no discussion of a future overall solution. It is permissible to mention, however, that the Jews as a group are being employed in appropriate labor services." The card indexes of the Party agencies listed this memo under "Treatment/Jews."

Hitler almost certainly never read Himmler's report. To be more precise, he did not wish to read it. In April, Bormann had got it back for submission at a later date. In June he was once more obliged to carry the sixteen sheets, typed in the oversize letters of the Führer's typewriter, away from Hitler's room without their having been acted on. The situation was still unchanged when, on October 2, 1943, Bormann arrived at the field headquarters of Himmler, who had meanwhile become Reich Minister of the Interior. According to a memorandum, "the head of the Party Chancellery felt that at this point the Führer did not wish to receive the report." The two men agreed that the matter should therefore be tabled and submitted again in a year's time. This, according to the ways of the bureaucracy, meant postponing it indefinitely. Dead Jews, no matter how many, were of no interest to Hitler. But the Gauleiters wanted to know what exactly had become of the Jews in the East; the rumors spreading among the people were beginning to bother them. At the very least, they wanted an official Party statement with which to counter the "slanderous propaganda."

However, as Schirach testified at the Nuremberg Trials, Bormann forbade them to approach Hitler about the final solution or to appeal to him on behalf of individual Jews.

Bormann no longer needed to worry about Himmler's extermination activities. He had found a new task for himself: the so-called *Mischlinge,* persons whose one parent or even grandparent was descended from a Jewish family. Bormann knew how gravely this problem concerned his Führer. In December 1941, holding forth for hours after dinner on his theories of racial biology, Hitler had touched on these *Mischlinge.* They were, he claimed, so Jewishly oriented that most of the second and third generation married Jews. Even an Aryan marriage partner could not prevent the Jewish blood from contaminating the family up to the ninth generation; only beyond that could it be considered "Mendeled out"—bred out genetically according to Mendelian law. Hitler had belabored the same subject at lunch on July 1, 1942, citing the alleged semi-Jew Roosevelt, President of the United States, as an example "that total amalgamation of racially foreign blood is inconceivable." *Mischlinge,* Hitler declared, should therefore be barred from service in the armed forces, lest they be rated equal to pure-bred Germans. "Further tainting of our blood by racially foreign elements is unacceptable."

Bormann had instructed his colleague Henry Picker to make a record of Hitler's table talks. During one of these, an orderly slipped him a note: "Dr. Picker, please note accurately and in particular detail what the Führer has to say about the treatment of our Jewish *Mischlinge* and the threat they represent, why these *Mischlinge* are to be barred from service in the armed forces and why they must not be treated as equals. B." Two days later— and here Bormann's method of operation becomes obvious—the Gauleiters were advised by a memorandum to refrain from taking an "absurdly mild attitude" toward Jewish *Mischlinge* who had remained outside the Nuremberg racial laws.

How doggedly he worked on his project can also be deduced from a study Heydrich had been ordered to undertake on behalf of the Party Chancellery a few months before his death in June 1942. He was to examine the feasibility of compulsory sterilization of about 70,000 *Mischlinge* of first and second degree. His conclusion was that each case would require a ten-day hospitalization, a prohibitive expenditure in wartime. Bormann thereupon suggested that all *Mischlinge* be screened by a board of Nazi race researchers who would carefully segregate those who appeared to be German from the Jews, at which point there would be tacit agreement as to what should be done about the latter. But Hitler declared the procedure too costly, and the problem remained unsolved.

Himmler had one helpful suggestion. The department head of his Race and Resettlement Office, SS Hauptsturmführer (Captain) Bruno K. Schultz, was commissioned to work out a plan to speed up racial screening. At the end of May 1943 Himmler wrote to his "dear Martin" that in his opinion such screenings were essential. "In this respect—although this is just between you and me—we must proceed along lines similar to those followed in the propagation of plants and animals. Descendants of families with mixed heritage must undergo racial screening for a minimum of several generations; in cases of racial inferiority, individuals must be sterilized and prevented from continuing the race." But this plan, too, proved unfeasible.

By February 1944 Hitler had realized that no one but Bormann could take on the complex task of solving the problem of the *Mischlinge*. A dual order was issued, one advising the government agencies, the other going to the Party organizations. Each made the head of the Party Chancellery responsible for dealing with "applications for special permissions from persons of Jewish or racially foreign blood." As usual, both versions had been prepared and submitted for signature by Bormann's office. Furthermore, Bormann was authorized to reopen all cases that had previously been processed and decided by other agencies. Presumably, the agencies that Bormann had tried to by-pass launched protests against such far-reaching powers, for on April 1, 1944, Hitler issued yet a third decree, which curtailed Bormann's overall authority. Lammers and Keitel were given a say in cases concerning civil servants or soldiers. But they were not able to give the Aryan seal of approval without Bormann's consent. Once in the early days of the Nazi regime Göring had boastfully announced, "I'll say who is or isn't a Jew!" It was Bormann now who had the say.

Some weeks after the first directive was issued, Bormann revealed how serious he was about his office of racial arbiter. He informed the Gauleiters that marriages between Germans and *Mischlinge* of the second degree (i.e., persons with one Jewish grandparent) were not yet prohibited but were undesirable. Descendants from such marriages could never be accepted as Party members and would be excluded from certain jobs, regardless of whether or not the German father had distinguished himself for outstanding bravery at the front.

It was because of such rigid principles that, in January 1944, he forbade all Party leaders to continue "personal relations" with the composer Richard Strauss. Although the maestro had never voiced political opposition to the regime and for a time had even served as a willing cultural symbol, he had in the course of his artistic career commissioned a number of Jews to write librettos, and his son was married to a Jew (who, incidentally, as the great man's daughter-in-law, was not harmed and survived the war). If Bormann had had his way, Strauss's eightieth birthday in June 1944 would have passed without official recognition. But Baldur von Schirach, who always fancied himself a sponsor of the muses and who in cultural matters occasionally diverged from the Party line, ignored all official instructions and, traveling to Bavaria on a good-will mission, invited Strauss to his palace residence in Vienna for a ceremony in his honor. "He kissed the hand of a Jewess," Bormann snorted.

Three months later his wife wrote him a letter. The power of Jewry was horrible, she said, and not even the war would weaken this race, which fought its battles with money rather than blood. "Neither disease nor filth will ever eradicate this vermin," Gerda wailed. "How on earth can we get rid of them wholesale?" Her husband knew, but her question indicates that he had not taken her into his confidence. Nor did he ever give the slightest hint in any of his letters. In matters of secrecy, too, he was his Führer's ideal henchman.

15

Slavs Are Slaves

On June 23, 1941, when he left Berlin with Hitler and his entourage on the Führer's special train, heading for the Wolfsschanze headquarters, Martin Bormann was convinced that this was at last the beginning of the gigantic Germanic migration to the eastern plains which *Mein Kampf* had proclaimed as the Third Reich's most important mission. Nobody knew at this point where the conquest would end and the borders of Greater Germania be drawn. The far side of Moscow? At the foot of the Ural Mountains? Or up along their crest? War and victory would decide. There were many plans for the future. Hitler, Göring, Rosenberg, Himmler—to name only the top—let their fancy soar, playing with the vast mass of land and its peoples. Bormann stayed aloof. He lacked the imagination, creative impulse and, indeed, the basic knowledge and was therefore not even tempted to join in the planning at this early stage. Being a realist, he waited until assignments were brought to his desk, where he would deal with them, directing his administrative apparatus by telephone and telex machine.

Long before the invasion of the Soviet Union, Bormann had often heard and carefully recorded how Hitler wished to handle the people in the East. There had been that lengthy discussion dealing with the status of the Poles in the future Greater Reich at the Reich Chancellery in October 1940, which Frank, Schirach and Koch had attended. Hitler had pronounced the Poles "lazy by nature," people who had to be "pushed to make them work," obviously "born to perform menial labor." There could be "no question" of self-improvement, and "their level of subsistence should be kept low." Bormann's minutes faithfully recorded these and other Führer guidelines.

He could safely assume that Hitler would not think any better of the "subhuman Bolsheviks."

The question of which of the various plans Hitler would adopt once the country was conquered remained, however. There were the Wehrmacht's ideas, picking up where the Kaiser's imperialists had left off, of a rigid dictatorship controlled by the army and big business. There was Himmler's concept of a strict division between the master race and its minions, with the ultimate aim of wiping out inferior races and dividing the country among the Nordic supermen. And then there was Rosenberg, the Baltic émigré, burning with contempt for the Russian Bolsheviks and obsessed with the idea of reviving the Ukrainians' revolutionary fervor.

Even before the German armies stood poised for the attack on Russia, Bormann had decided to exploit the rivalry among the planners as long as possible and to make sure that they gave one another a hard time. Since the early days of the Party, this had always been Hitler's formula, and Bormann was a clever disciple. He gave moral support to Rosenberg by warning him that he should firmly defend the Party's point of view against the military, who were out to bring the largest possible territory under their rule, and also against the police and the Waffen SS, who did not wish civil servants to hamper them in their acts of terror. Even before taking office, the Reich Minister of the East therefore demanded that Himmler submit all basic regulations to him for approval. The Reichsführer SS managed to turn down this request by calling Bormann to witness "that the Führer . . . has announced that in my area of responsibilities I am not to be under Rosenberg's orders." Confidentially Himmler complained to his "dear Martin" that working with Rosenberg, let alone under him, "is certainly the toughest assignment in the Party."

On July 16, 1941, Hitler started out at the Wolfsschanze to—as he put it —cut the giant pie into proper slices. For the moment he actually held only a sliver although the enemy had been badly weakened by encirclement operations. But the six conquerors of the East assembled at headquarters were confident of victory. Those invited were Rosenberg, Lammers, Keitel and Göring, and again Bormann kept the minutes, which were later stamped *"Geheime Reichssache"* (Top Secret State Document) and thereby given the highest degree of confidentiality. To some extent at least it was left to the rapporteur to decide what should be included as a resolution and how it should be phrased. The other participants, insofar as they later received a copy at all, could make no changes, since by that time Hitler, the final authority, had already initialed it. At the Nuremberg Trials, Göring and Rosenberg claimed that Bormann's minutes presented the planning in a crude unqualified light. The accusation may have been justified, for he certainly would not have missed an opportunity to produce a document he might want to use at some time to stir up trouble. He also allowed his own views to creep into the minutes—i.e., by stating that Rosenberg thought highly (meaning, too highly) of the Ukrainians. The conference lasted for five hours, including a coffee break; no doubt Hitler spoke most of the time, but whatever the others may have said, Bormann reduced in the minutes to occasional questions and marginal remarks.

It is easy to explain why Himmler was not invited: a court does not summon the executioner at the time the sentence is passed. His special train, Heinrich, which contained his field headquarters, was standing only a few miles away on a siding in a wooded area; he must have felt terrible anger at being left out. But in the party of six nobody missed him, least of all Rosenberg, though neither Bormann nor Göring minded having the Reichs-führer SS reduced to second rank. Bormann's protocol carefully described Himmler's area of responsibilities: while for the sake of the indigenous population "apparent steps will be taken to restore peace and assure food supplies and communications, this need not prevent our taking all necessary measures—shooting, resettlement, etc." Besides—according to Hitler—"this guerrilla activity has an advantage for us; it enables us to exterminate everyone who opposes us." To nip resistance in the bud, the SS brigades were to be equipped with armored cars, and the Luftwaffe was to shift its training fields to the East, for even the clumsy transport planes of the JU-52 type could always be used to drop bombs on a civilian population in revolt. To dominate, to administer, to exploit: this was the order of priorities.

Since the defection of Hess, Bormann had been Göring's ally against the clique of Reichsleiters. Long before the conference the two had obviously agreed who in the administration should assign the key posts—i.e., the Reich commissars of the eastern provinces. They stubbornly demanded that East Prussian Gauleiter Erich Koch administer the wealthy Ukraine, despite Rosenberg's predictions that Koch would go his own way and never submit to his authority. Rosenberg personally picked Gauleiter Hinrich Lohse of Schleswig-Holstein to administer the northern region, renamed Ostland; Bormann saw to it that he would regret this bitterly. The Crimea was to become the domain of Austria's former Gauleiter Alfred E. Frauen-feld; and the former Gauleiter of Brandenburg, Wilhelm Kube, was marked down for Moscow, rather, Byelorussia. Without exception, these were men who through their Party affiliation depended on or maintained friendly relations with Bormann. He and Göring therefore could afford generously to allow one of Rosenberg's men to rule over the Caucasus at some future time. But that, of course, never happened.

Toward the end of the conference the somewhat weary participants remembered the absent Reichsführer SS. As Bormann's minutes recorded, there was a lengthy discussion about the range of his future duties. A phrase, both telling and bland, remarked that "in the course of the meeting the participants also considered the future responsibilities of the Reichs-führer SS." "The Führer, the Reichsmarschall, etc., repeatedly emphasized that under no condition should Himmler's responsibilities extend beyond those he holds in the Reich." This casual remark seemed to comply at least halfway with Rosenberg's demand that in his domain the police should be put under his jurisdiction. On the other hand, Bormann's reference to Hitler's order of "shooting, resettlement, etc." gave his friend Himmler the necessary freedom of action. Göring should also have been pleased with the text. The emphasis on his superior position (as chairman of the Ministerial Defense Council and head of the economy) put Himmler in his place.

At this time the Reich Minister for the Occupied Eastern Territories was so new in office that he did not even have a building of his own. At the conference he ventured to ask Hitler for the former premises of the Soviet trade representative in Berlin. He was given the buildings, which meant a victory for him, since his special enemy, Ribbentrop, had hitherto steadily denied him occupancy, maintaining they were extraterritorial. Bormann, too, must have been pleased with this choice of domicile: it meant that Rosenberg and his staff would now reside so far away from their area of responsibility that the Gauleiters who had been appointed viceroys would be able to do pretty much as they pleased, or rather as Bormann pleased, since his contact with them was much closer geographically, and firmer, thanks to Party affiliations.

In the occupied East, Bormann achieved instantly what he had managed to attain in only a rudimentary way in the occupied countries in the West: he became part of the ruling body. Whenever he brought Hitler's wishes to bear, everybody fell in line: the Reich commissars and their subordinates; Himmler's security organization; Gauleiter Fritz Sauckel, who had been appointed chief slave driver, rounding up millions of men, women and adolescents to be shipped to Germany as forced labor; even Hitler himself came more and more under Bormann's influence, since he was the only one of the Party top brass to be constantly in attendance. Hitler's habit of condoning conflicts among his followers made it easy for Bormann to encroach on matters outside his own domain. The "pie-slicing" conference had been another case in point, although, according to the minutes, "the Führer had emphasized that the conflict would subside once the plan was put into practice." In actual fact it became permanent—much to Bormann's advantage. As the interpreter of the Führer's will he was always called upon to act as referee, which, in turn, gave him the chance to get his own plans approved.

As a result, he had a much greater influence on the policy for the occupied East than his position might suggest, regardless of the fact that he lacked the necessary qualifications. What, after all, did he know of the huge land masses between the Baltic and the Black Sea? The vast forests, the impassable swamps, the fields of black earth reaching to the horizon were to him merely symbols and names on a map. And besides his conqueror's egotism, prejudice and arrogance, his lack of personal contact prevented him from understanding the people of the country.

Bormann's world was that of the desk—his own and Hitler's—in wooden shacks at first, later in windowless, air-conditioned bunkers with reinforced-concrete walls. At the various headquarters his and Hitler's bunkers were always in the center of the camp, in a special security zone surrounded by an eight-foot fence of meshed wire, its gates guarded by SS sentries and plain-clothes men of the Security Service. This area was in turn surrounded by two more safety zones, secured by high-voltage barbed wire, machine-gun positions, automatic quadruple-turret anti-aircraft guns, land mines and sentries. General Alfred Jodl described the Rastenburg headquarters as "a cross between a monastery and a concentration camp," although the Wolfsschanze wasn't even in enemy territory but inside East Prussia, twenty-five miles from the Soviet border.

Nor did the monotonous daily routine, adapted to Hitler's particular life style, offer Bormann much of a view beyond this enclosure. There was no point getting up before nine o'clock unless work had been left from the day before—which was against the rule. The courier plane from Berlin did not arrive until ten, bringing mail, new documents, newspapers. Hitler never got up before ten, usually much later. After breakfast he would take a fifteen-minute walk along the paths of the little pine forest, accompanied by an adjutant and often by Bormann, who, in a semiprivate, semiofficial way, would seize the opportunity to discuss a few matters. The military briefings usually began after twelve o'clock. Since the generals did not appreciate his presence, this was the time for Bormann to devote himself to his papers. At the joint lunch he had to be in his place, diagonally across the table from Hitler, next to Keitel. When Hitler pushed back his chair and left, he often took Bormann back with him to his study. But their talks seldom lasted for more than a half-hour—which shows how carefully the papers had been prepared and how concisely the various issues had been condensed.

The next two hours were usually marked "private" on the calendar by Hitler's valet, Heinz Linge, Hauptsturmführer (Captain) in the Waffen SS. It was his way of saying that during that time his boss stretched out on his cot trying to sleep, often until dinner time. Occasionally, however, Hitler would summon Bormann, who had to be on call, particularly after the evening briefings at eight, which often lasted until midnight. After that there was "tea," according to Linge, the night session marked by general exhaustion and tiresome Führer monologues which might drag on until dawn. With casual questions and little anecdotes on recent events Bormann would use the hour to recall those table talks and dinner decisions that he subsequently consolidated into actual Führer orders. "4 A.M. closing time," Linge would often note. After that Bormann had to digest what he had heard. Less than six hours of sleep became his routine. Only a rugged constitution could stand this way of life year after year, without physical exercise and, most hours of the day, without fresh air or daylight. Aside from routine journeys to Berlin, Munich and Obersalzberg and occasional side trips to attend official functions, he hardly ever left this quarantine station, except when Hitler took some time off at the Berghof. Bormann actually set foot in conquered country on only the two occasions when Hitler temporarily moved his headquarters to the Ukraine. At that time Bormann even slipped away once from the protection (and confinement) of the barbed wire and the security guards.

Whatever knowledge he had of the conquered country before this outing he had acquired mostly from men who hardly knew it any better—at least less well than any infantry soldier forced to a halt and retreat by stages before Moscow at the beginning of the winter of 1941. All the head of the Party Chancellery had learned from Hitler's table talks was that the Slavs were lazy, anarchistic, uncivilized, Asiatic and incapable of any great achievement. The German police had better keep their hands on their holsters at all times, Hitler had warned. Never once did Bormann come face to face with the dead on the battlefield, the mass graves of the murdered, the sufferings of the wounded, the torture of prisoners. To him, they were abstract figures. His reality was Hitler's recital of how he visualized the future of the country. German peasants in "eminently beautiful land developments"; "magnificent building projects"; "governor's palaces"; German cities surrounded by well-kept villages, connected by superhighways; space for a hundred million Germans; and far in the distance the Russians— destitute, scattered, dominated and exploited.

Party colleagues who could not believe in a rapid and complete victory were defeatist in Bormann's eyes—Goebbels, for instance, who in the late fall of 1941 sent a twenty-seven-page memorandum to headquarters, urging that the eastern peoples should be promised liberation from Bolshevism and won over as allies with assurances of a better future. How stupid and short-sighted Rosenberg seemed with his ideas of granting special status to the Ukrainians and perhaps even the Balts through cultural institutions, such as a university, better living conditions, landownership and possibly even permission to establish their own military units to fight the Moscow Communists. And how feeble-minded were those generals who allowed Russsian Orthodox priests to resume religious services in the conquered areas after decades of atheism, just because the military were hoping that this would make the faithful turn against Stalin as the devil. Whatever news of such intentions reached headquarters Bormann carefully kept away from Hitler, and wherever that seemed too difficult he played off one author's memorandum against another: Himmler was against the clergy; the military against any plan of giving arms to the vanquished; and when it came to granting special privileges to the Ukrainians he needed only to call upon Göring or Gauleiter Koch, whom Hitler regarded highly.

At times even Rosenberg was inclined to open the East to the Christian doctrine. On February 15, 1942, he submitted to Hitler the draft of a resolution offering religious freedom in his eastern domain. He expected it to have a strong propagandistic effect. But Bormann went over the text and voiced misgivings. Might not a newly established Eastern church turn into a resistance movement? If, on the other hand, the faithful were split up into individual congregations, they would be hard to supervise. Much the best thing—Bormann and Hitler agreed—would be for every village to have its own God.

When on his next visit to headquarters, in May, Rosenberg submitted a revised plan, Hitler suggested that he listen to Bormann, who had had a lot of experience dealing with Christian churches in the Warthegau (Wartheland) and the Ostmark (Austria). At this point, however, Bormann was no longer dead set against freedom of religious practice; what he objected to was a public statement of tolerance. If word got back to the Reich, he warned, the German churches would inevitably make their own demands. For practical purposes, therefore, Rosenberg had better refrain from making any statement at all, leaving it to the Reich commissars to issue directives for getting the new trend under way. And that was how it was done. But it did not have the desired effect on the people.

There was no doubt in Bormann's mind that the country and the people should be ruthlessly exploited. But he was not alone in this. Göring boasted about his looting policy in public speeches. Koch bragged of his ruthlessness, and in the local administrations down to the Party bosses it was routine to buy up food by the truckload at ridiculously low prices and ship it home to Germany. Quantities of consumer goods went the opposite way, mostly junk articles which fetched high profits in local barter deals. As a matter of fact, the Party officials were merely following the example of the government back home, which paid rock-bottom prices for the products of the eastern territories and passed them on to the German consumer at colossal markups while charging exorbitant prices for shipments of German goods to the eastern areas. Late in March 1942, referring to an observation of the Führer's, amateur economist Bormann made a special point of condensing this principle into a memo to serve him as a reminder. In due time, it said, the slush funds from this exploitative policy would pay for the war and the defense production.

The first to feel the low regard the new rulers had for the lives of the vanquished were the prisoners of war, mainly those who fell into German hands in unbelievably vast numbers during 1941. They were rounded up in improvised camps, and in the absence of operable railroads, shipped off to the West at such a slow rate that with the onset of winter tens of thousands died in their frigid barbed-wire enclosures. Fuming with indignation, Rosenberg wrote to Keitel calling the "stiffening resistance of the Red Army" a direct result of such inhumanity and therefore "a contributing factor to the death of thousands of German soldiers." Keitel was in a tight spot. During that harsh winter there were not sufficient lines of transportation to keep up even the supplies for the armed forces and ship soldiers with cases of frostbite back to Germany. Our own people must take precedence, he argued, and Bormann supported him against Rosenberg, whom he berated in a letter of November 28, 1941, for not treating prisoners of war harshly enough. There were too many of these "subhumans" anyhow, he thought.

Bormann's callousness is fully revealed in a circular he sent to the political executives early in November 1941, advising them how to dispose of the bodies of Soviet prisoners who had died in Germany. The corpses should not be placed in coffins but wrapped in tar paper or oilcloth and whisked away in army trucks. Only after a sufficient number of bodies had been assembled were they to be laid in mass graves side by side, though not necessarily head by head—obviously to have the bodies stacked as tightly as possible. During this procedure no ceremonies were to be permitted, nor were the graves to be decorated later on.

When in July of the following year Hitler moved his headquarters (code name "Werewolf") for three months to Vinnitsa in the Ukraine, Bormann ventured to take a closer look at the "subhumans." He did so on only one occasion, during a drive with Dr. Karl Brandt, Hitler's attending physician. For a whole day, on July 22, 1942, they drove from village to village, from collective farm to collective farm, where German agricultural commissars proudly showed their distinguished guests the vast expanses of undulating wheat fields. In the evening Bormann reported to his Führer what he had seen in those twelve hours—with the hard, cold eyes of the conqueror whom not even the idyllic rural scenes had managed to soften.

He had seen children, far too many children. His concern was that "someday they may give us a lot of trouble," because they belong to a race "brought up in a much more rugged way than our own people." Further observations: no one wore glasses. Most had perfect teeth, were well fed and apparently kept in good health from childhood to a ripe old age, in spite of the fact that they "drink unpurified water which would make us ill." These "so-called Ukrainians" (to Bormann they were all Slavs) were apparently immune to malaria as well as spotted fever, even though lice were part of their daily life. Most of the villagers were blond and blue-eyed, true, but of the East Baltic type, which meant that the faces of the adults were flat and coarse—in other words, Slavic. Under the well-organized German system these people would multiply even faster—which after all, was hardly desirable, "for we want to have all of this country settled by Germans someday."

The portly office worker, who was already given to shortness of breath, could hardly conceal his admiration for this breed of people. He and the rest of the group that evening had to admit that according to their own racial theories, they were facing their future conquerors, a stronger, tougher, more dynamic race. But since Hitler could not very well denounce his own gospel, he reacted to Bormann's report with peevish anger. Someone had actually suggested the other day, he sneered, that there should be a ban on the sale of contraceptives in the eastern territories. Anyone who tried that he would "shoot down personally." On the contrary, these items should be pushed vigorously, "but apparently it takes a Jew to get such things going." It would be sheer madness to introduce a health-care program based on the German pattern. However, it might not be a bad idea to spread the rumor that vaccination "is actually harmful."

Once he got started Hitler rambled from one subject to another. He carried on about future schools, city planning and housing projects in the newly conquered country—always with the idea of turning the vanquished into full-time slaves. Instead of using the Cyrillic letters, the Ukrainians were to learn the Roman alphabet and just enough of the German language to understand orders. "Under no circumstances" should they "be entitled to a higher education." Those who wished to go to school would have to pay for it but "should not be allowed to learn anything beyond, at the most, the meaning of traffic signs." Henry Picker, whom Bormann had assigned to take notes, dutifully recorded this in particular detail.

The very next day Bormann condensed these minutes into instructions for the Reich Minister for the Occupied Eastern Territories, consolidating the Führer's views in an eight-paragraph *"Geheime Reichssache."* Among other things, Alfred Rosenberg learned that abortions in the eastern territories "are favored by us and should under no condition be opposed by the German legal profession." "A flourishing trade in contraceptives" should be encouraged. Vaccination of "the non-German population and similar preventive health care are out of question." Since "living conditions under German rule are bound to be better and more secure . . . we must take the necessary precautions to prevent the non-German population from multiplying." No higher education: reading and writing will be enough. No fraternizing between Germans and the indigenous population.

The letter struck Rosenberg's headquarters like a bomb. With good reason, it was taken not as an opinion expressed in a sudden fit of anger but as a reply to the ministry's *"Grosse Denkschrift"* (final document) which Rosenberg had left at Führer Headquarters some time before. This document had once again stressed the importance of granting the Ukrainians some independence, at least in cultural and administrative affairs, as the only way of winning them over to the German cause and eventually perhaps to the crusade against Bolshevism.

The situation leads one to suspect that Bormann's trip through the villages was designed less to satisfy his curiosity or provide a change from office routine than as a move in his tug of war with Rosenberg. The blond hair and the many children could not have surprised him as much as he professed in his report at the evening session. For even though this was his first and almost only contact with the country and its people, he must have heard a few things from others before. But now he was in a position to present his personal impressions in conversation, and by his tried-and-true method, to extract from Hitler, usually aggravated by the day's irritations, a statement that could later be fashioned into an announcement of the Führer's will.

The letter broke Rosenberg's back. In his written reply the Reich Minister for the Occupied Eastern Territories conceded that naturally the Führer's will be done and that, in fact, he had already initiated the requested measures. As he later stated at Nuremberg, he did this only to relax the atmosphere so as to be able to present his proposals again at a more favorable moment. Even his staff urged him to take action, most of all Georg Leibbrand, the head of his political department, and Leibbrand's colleague Markull. In September 1942 the latter compiled a memorandum on the harm Gauleiter Koch and like-minded Party officials had wrought in the Ukraine. Markull found a "striking resemblance between Koch's views and the instructions in Bormann's letter." "A ministerial resolution along the lines of the Bormann letter," he wrote, would be regarded by most department heads "as a complete reversal of previous policy" and bound to cause "profound consternation and disillusionment."

But still the minister under criticism did not find the courage to launch a new effort to change the Führer's mind as made up by Bormann. Early in December 1942, therefore, Markull wrote another warning in the light of the Stalingrad debacle he was already anticipating, under the rubric "New Regulations for the Eastern Territories." In the long run the conquered areas could obviously be held only "through use of the eastern peoples," but so far "everything has been done to make [them] bitterly resent our rule. In particular, Bormann's letter of July 23, 1942, whose contents have spread alarmingly, has seriously damaged our policy and morale in recent months. It should be made clear to the Führer that responsibility for the current trend can no longer be accepted." But Rosenberg ventured nothing of the kind; he sought to regain Hitler's, i.e., Bormann's, interest and confidence by giving in. Thus, when the Party leaders (read: Bormann) released Leibbrand, who had been responsible for the two memoranda, for service in the armed forces, he let it happen without protest.

In fact, the Reich Minister for the Occupied Eastern Territories soon deteriorated into a figurehead. He was not even allowed to participate when, early in September 1942, a group of Party and government dignitaries met in Berlin to discuss better ways of using and exploiting the female population in his territory. The secret minutes of these discussions specifically state that "Reichsleiter Bormann sees the solution for the problem of domestic help"—which must have become acute in his own multiple household—in the mass deportation of Ukrainian women to Germany. The idea must have occurred to him during his trip through the villages, and it was probably a result of his report that—as the minutes said—"the Führer ordered the prompt admission of 400,000 to 500,000 female domestic workers, aged between 15 and 35, from the Ukraine." Fritz Sauckel, who was in charge of labor allocation, was given three months to complete the operation. In addition, Bormann directed that "illegal imports of domestic help into Germany by members of the armed forces or other departments should be sanctioned ex post facto . . . and not refused in the future." However—and here again the results of Bormann's observations six weeks earlier are evident—"only those women are to be recruited against whose permanent stay in the German Reich no objections can be raised with regard to their attitude and appearance." The Party district officials were ordered by Bormann to assign the Ukrainian help to farms and households.

In addition to nonvaccination, sanitary neglect, promotion of contraceptives, and mass killings, yet another idea was introduced to decimate the Ukrainians. "For," the document continued, "it is the Führer's particular wish that a large number of these women should be Germanized." Hitler and Bormann had obviously recovered from the shock of finding that these strong, healthy people were part of the Slavic race. With no further ado the Führer therefore decided in the course of a tea session to revise "our academic knowledge of the great migration," converting the blond, blue-eyed Ukrainians into "peasant stock descended from Germanic tribes which settled down . . . whose re-Germanization was only a matter of time." According to the minutes of the September 1942 meeting in Berlin, this method, which the Romans had already tried successfully in the rape of the Sabine women, would "allow 250 million German-speaking people to live in Europe in another hundred years."

For the men of the eastern territories Bormann had prescribed a fate common in the days of the Old Testament after a successful campaign: slavery or death. On August 19, 1942, he wrote that "they should work for us" and "where we have no use for them, we shall let them die." To the very end of the war he never stopped demanding that the prisoners of war should receive harsher treatment. The Wehrmacht's guards were always too humane for his taste. When, finally, in January 1943—and partly as a result of his urging—the High Command of the Armed Forces issued an order permitting corporal punishment and the use of arms against insubordinate prisoners, Bormann lost no time in bringing it to the attention of the political leaders of the Party. He wanted them to see to it that truly drastic measures were applied from then on. In November of the same year Bormann circulated a notice announcing that certain Gauleiters had complained of too much leniency on the part of the guards. They felt the prisoners were protected rather than guarded. He wrote to the High Command of the Armed Forces that the hard-working Germans could not understand why the prisoners of war, who were and always would be enemies, should live better than they did at a time when the Fatherland's existence was at stake.

Bormann urged the Party functionaries to send in regular reports on the prison camps in their areas, and for their information furnished them with the full text of the regulations by which the Wehrmacht tightened controls in the camps. Six months before the end of the war, he finally managed to have the camps removed from the Wehrmacht's authority and handed over to the SS, which had developed efficient methods of exploitation, torture and liquidation in the concentration camps.

But Bormann's hard-nosed policy found less and less scope in the East. The fall of Stalingrad in early February 1943 marked the beginning of the retreat. From then on, an increasing number of voices were heard among the Party leaders, advocating a more conciliatory course in the eastern territories. In a meeting on March 5, 1943, Goebbels confidentially told his staff that he had discussed the bad treatment of foreign workers with Göring and other leaders. They felt "that we cannot keep the eastern peoples in line if we continue with our current methods." He planned to issue explanatory regulations making it impossible for "anyone to hide behind the myth that abusing and mistreating the peoples of the East is a particular virtue of National Socialism."

This was a swipe at Bormann, but he acted totally unconcerned. When, two months later, Goebbels in a joint action with Himmler's Reich Central Security Office issued a pamphlet "On the General Principles of How to Treat Foreign Labor in the Reich," Bormann incorporated the text in a memorandum he relayed to all Party departments, down to the local branches. In a covering letter he stated that "Party and public should be duly advised of the necessity for strict but fair treatment of foreign workers." He was not all that anxious, however, to have the full text become too widely known, and therefore barred it from publication.

Needless to say, the pamphlet did not do much to improve the fate of the 12 million "foreign workers," most of them forced labor in Germany at the time. Of course it stated the necessity of humane treatment if "the full working capacity" of these people was to be "maintained . . . or, it is to be hoped, increased in the long run." Calling them "bestial, barbaric and subhuman" was not going to win their active cooperation for a new idea. But at the same time the Germans were warned to keep "the necessary distance between themselves and the aliens as a matter of national responsibility. Any German disregarding the racial principles of National Socialism"—i.e., concerning sex relations—"will be subject to severe punishment."

But on this issue Bormann showed himself flexible, in procedure if not in principle. In the current situation, after Goebbels' announcement of the total war effort, he could not interfere very well with measures that were supposed to strengthen Germany's economy and defense production. Besides, a semipublic controversy, which he shunned in any case, might have branded him a bloodhound. In addition, Hitler's state of health was no longer the best. Were Bormann to lose his leader's protective hand, he had better not be surrounded only by enemies. Allies might become important in the future, and Goebbels seemed the best possible choice, since he had obviously reaffirmed his position. In this precarious situation Hitler needed someone to beat the drum for him, and extremists were now much in demand. On the other hand, Goebbels was not strong enough to stand up to Bormann. He never succeeded in issuing the regulations prohibiting corporal punishment of "foreign labor"; one remark from Bormann was enough to make the Propaganda Minister drop his plan. For the same reason he also never followed up on his intention to abolish the discriminating patch of cloth that "foreign workers" from the East were obliged to wear at all times.

Goebbels had been forced to pull in his horns on several previous occasions in matters of eastern policy. Not knowing what had been resolved at the secret conference of July 16, 1941, he had been a long-time sponsor of Ukrainian autonomy. Late in April 1942 he regretfully noted in his diary that contrary to the situation in the early months of the war, Hitler was no longer regarded there as the liberator and savior of Europe. "Hitting people over the head is not always a convincing argument," he complained, "and that also goes for our dealings with the Ukrainians and Russians." But if after all these years on the shelf he was to make a comeback in Hitler's graces, it could be done only with Bormann's permission.

Goebbels did not mind subjugation all that much because it enabled him to join the ranks of those opposing his old adversary, Rosenberg. Late in 1941 Goebbels had developed a plan on how to win "all-out sympathy with the peoples of the East," which was completely on the wrong track. Hitler wished to disperse them, deport them, or if there was no other way, have them all liquidated. Collaboration was not his idea at all. One night in May 1942 there was a long discussion at the Wolfsschanze on the extent to which the population of the conquered territories could be made into German citizens. Danzig's Gauleiter, Albert Forster, who attended the late tea party, reported that Professor Günther, an authority on racial questions, had found after a ten-day trip through West Prussia that most Poles deserved to be given German citizenship. And if in certain rural districts the Germanic racial heritage did not seem quite up to standard, SS garrisons might be stationed there in the future to revitalize the race. But Bormann was loud and clear in his protest: the German race should not be contaminated by "Polacks" of Slavic blood who might affect its genes unfavorably. Like Hitler, he was dead set against making common cause of any kind with the conquered. As he had often done before, Hitler was gambling for all or nothing; if he wanted allies, he had to offer them something. But he wanted the very things for himself that might have won them over—their land and their liberty. That was why he had rejected Rosenberg's plan for the Ukraine. When the Reich Minister for the Occupied Eastern Territories proposed a statute promising the Baltic States autonomy—needless to say,

The Secretary
to the Führer
in his
SS Obergruppen-
führer uniform.

As supervisor on an estate near the town of Parchim in Mecklenburg, Martin Bormann was responsible for the work and wages of mercenaries disguised as farm hands. When they murdered one of their members as a "traitor" in 1923, Bormann participated at least in the planning of the crime. The murder was plotted in an inn—today a shop (marked **x**, *opposite page*). The judges could prove only his complicity; for this he spent one year in prison. This murder began his career in politics.

Flotsam and jetsam from
World War I: soldiers of the
Rossbach Freikorps (with
swastika armbands).

The debut: Bormann was there when the National
Socialists held a Party rally in Weimar in 1926. Hitler
reviewed the troops outside the Hotel Elephant.
Behind him is Rudolf Hess; fourth from the left is
Göring (in black shirt). To the far left is Bormann,
in SA uniform.

Bormann was moved to the Party's central office in
Munich in 1928—as manager of the Party's Relief
Fund. Here he stands to the far right in a group of
functionaries around the Reich Party Treasurer
Xavier Schwarz.

Wedding in 1929.
Hitler was a witness to the marriage.
The bridal couple went to the church in his automobile. To the bride's
right is her father, "old comrade" Walter Buch.

Bormann's wife,
Gerda
—in a painting
done
several years
later.

A Swastika Wedding.
Behind the bride and groom stands the Nazi upper
crust (*from left to right*) : Hitler's secretary Rudolf
Hess; the SA leader in Munich, August Schneidhuber,
who was liquidated in the Röhm putsch in 1934;
Supreme SA Leader Franz Felix Pfeffer von Salomon;
the bride's father, Party Judge Walter Buch; Hitler;
Bormann's brother Albert.
The bride in white; the groom in brown. The
Protestant minister had to get special permission to
perform the wedding in uniform.

Hitler and his entourage provide the background in
this family portrait. To the far right is Bormann's
mother, Antonie; behind her stand the bride's parents.

1930 in Munich.
Bormann's sponsor, Reich Party Treasurer Xavier Schwarz, and Hitler's
secretary Rudolf Hess in conversation with the Führer in front of the
Party's office building in Schellingstrasse.

1935 in Nuremberg
Hitler and staff discussing plans for the parade at the
Party rally. In the center is Martin Bormann in his
Reichsleiter uniform; at the time, he was right-hand
man to Rudolf Hess

Hitler pontificating in the old Reich
Chancellery before his adherents,
who are listening with rapt attention
to his every word.
First row, from left to right:
Luftwaffe Captain Hans Baur;
Minister Franz Seldte;
Rudolf Hess;
Minister Wilhelm Frick;
Martin Bormann;
SA leader Viktor Lutze.

Above: Visitors to the Hohenlychen sanatorium: Hitler, Hess, Bormann and SA Adjutant Wilhelm Brückner.
The owner, Dr. Karl Gebhardt (in white coat), was condemned to death at Nuremberg for experiments on human beings.

Right: Get-together of Hess staff members. Bormann (*bottom, right*), who was a smoker, would do without in Hitler's presence.

Below: Party Rally in Nuremberg. Hitler's adjutant Brückner beats Bormann to it: he gets to hold Hitler's flowers. To Hitler's right is Hess, then Bormann; to his left, Reichsfrauenführerin Gertrud Scholtz-Klink.

Berlin was going to be Europe's capital and would be called Germania. Convinced that his megalomaniac plans would materialize, Hitler outlined the magnificent buildings for his seat of government as far back as 1925.

Hitler, Bormann and staff before the triumphal arch.

During the war, however, shelter for bombed-out citizens became of greater urgency. In 1944 Hitler inspected the model with Bormann.

Bormann always made it plain that he was Hitler's closest confidant. As all-purpose functionary he managed Hitler's private funds, as well as his Berghof estate at Obersalzberg. There he had to accommodate himself to Hitler's constant companion, Eva Braun (*below*). The two of them couldn't stand each other, but here Bormann exudes feigned amiability. She distrusted him to the last day of her life.

The erstwhile Adolf Hitler disciple Adolf Martin Bormann (*left*) joined the Catholic Church after the war. His comment: "Father would have had me shot for that!" Almost all his siblings followed his example. He became a priest. *Right:* Here, at his first divine service, he blessed his brothers and sisters. All of them achieved respected positions in postwar society.

Gerda Bormann (with her back to the camera) and her children and their nurses as guests of Hitler and Eva Braun. In the center of the picture is Hitler's godson Adolf Martin Bormann, the eldest son.

stern-

Bormann's mistress Manja Behrens in the film *Susanna Bathing* (1936).
Today she is an actress engaged by the state, in East Germany.

In 1944 the Führer's Secretary planned a *ménage à trois* with his wife, Gerda, and his mistress Manja Behrens. After the victory he was going to issue a decree telling each German to take a second wife so that the birth rate, which had declined during the war, would rise again. *Above:* Future mothers visiting Bormann and Hitler. *Below:* On the special train with Hitler's secretary Gerda Christian. Typical Bormann gesture—playing with his wedding ring.

Above: Christmas 1943 at Obersalzberg—a great party! Bormann the arranger, in boots and country-style clothes, gazes with satisfaction at Hitler, who has linked arms with Eva Braun and her girl friend for this group photo. Guests: the Speers, Morell, Brandt, Hoffmann, adjutants.

Above right: Wedding at Hitler's. Eva Braun's sister Gretl became the wife of the much-decorated SS General Fegelein, who thereby advanced to Hitler's "brother-in-law." Along with Hitler, Bormann is selecting his wedding gift.

Right: With his pal Heinrich Himmler, the Reichsführer SS, Bormann was witness at the Fegelein wedding in Salzburg. At the time of the collapse, Bormann saw to it that Himmler's friend was eliminated "because of cowardly treason" and, in Hitler's name, had him shot.

In May 1941 Hitler's Deputy Rudolf Hess flew to England, which rendered the road to power clear for Bormann. He achieved minister rank and became the Führer's Secretary.
Henceforth he alone had continuous access to Hitler. The Party had to obey his command, and he snatched more and more power in the government sector.

After the defeat at Stalingrad, the bad news multiplied. Bormann, Hitler and Foreign Minister von Ribbentrop studying new messages at the Wolfsschanze headquarters. On July 7, 1944, Count Stauffenberg's bomb exploded here.

At the scene of the crime: Bormann (*left*) and Göring (in light uniform), rivals to the end.

Bormann behind the slightly injured Hitler. Next to General Jodl (with head wound) is Bormann's brother Albert (*third from right*).

Artur Axmann, who fled with Bormann.

Eyewitness Herbert Seidel (*right*) with the author.

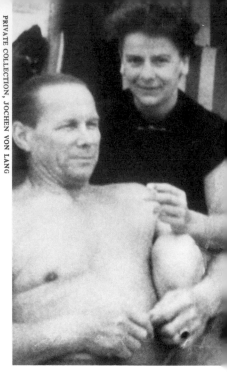

Ernst Ott, who found Bormann's diary.

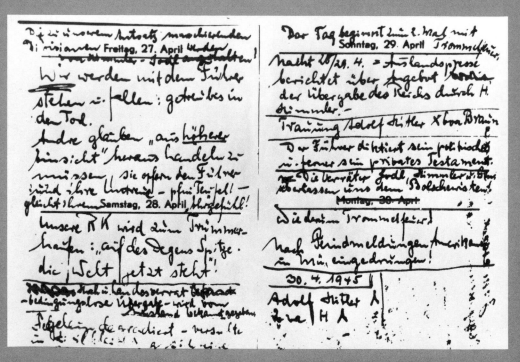

Ott's girl friend Inge Schwandt (*top right*) brought it to the Russians. Not until 1974 did they release it for publication. Above are entries from the last days: Adolf Hitler and Eva Braun's wedding; the Führer dictates his last will and testament; the deaths of Adolf and Eva Hitler; etc.

Disinterment of Bormann:
Albert Krumnow (in hat).
The political career of Martin
Bormann ended during the night of
May 2, 1945, and all traces of him
were lost in the streets of Berlin.
In 1946 in Nuremberg the victors
condemned him to death *in absentia.*
Since then his ghost has roamed
through the world press; he is
supposed to have appeared in South
America, Saudi Arabia, Tibet,
Australia—even in Moscow. Until
1972—twenty-seven long years—
his fate remained undetermined.
Then some workers found a
skeleton in Berlin, and forensic-
medicine experts agreed that it was
Bormann's. Thus a legend came to
an end.

The digging in 1965 in Berlin was unsuccessful. In 1972 the skeleton
was found thirteen yards from the site of the first digging.

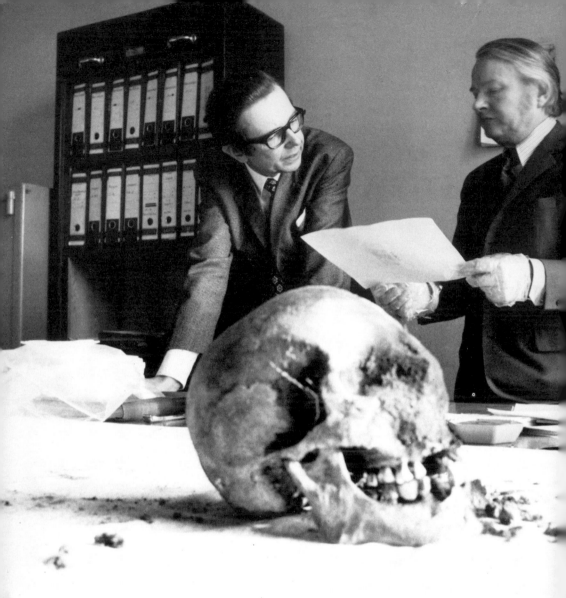

Twenty-seven years after World
War II it is established that
Bormann is dead. He died on May 2,
1945, in Berlin.

Above: The author (*left*) and dental
technician Fritz Echtman (*right*)
at the identification.

Right: First Public Prosecutor
Joachim Richter displays a photo to
the international press that shows a
reconstruction of the head made
from the original skull.

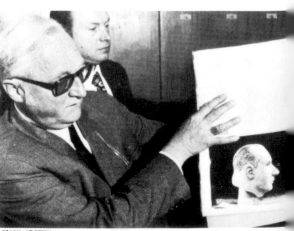

under German rule—Bormann knew that this also was doomed to fail. For a starter he sent Reich Commissar Hinrich Lohse, a man who furiously resisted any curtailment of his viceregal powers, into the arena. Then he himself got into the act, with complaints about the confusion in the Reich Minister's ideas and appointments. In dealing directly with Rosenberg, Bormann pretended for a while that his plan for the Baltic States was open to discussion. But in the fall Hitler announced that he would never give up the Baltic States; they were to be incorporated into the Reich.

This could not prevent Himmler from recruiting the Estonians and Letts for the Waffen SS. Having already raised a few battalions on the sly, he immediately set out to draft several age groups at a time. When it came to fighting and dying together, he was not all that particular about race. Ruthenians, Ukrainians, Cossacks, Tartars and other ethnic groups, 50,000 altogether, were already in his services. Now, he argued, reinforcements were needed, because his divisions, engaged in fighting partisans in the eastern territories, were constantly called upon to stop up the holes along the front. Moreover, he felt fully justified in grabbing the Estonians and Letts because the Wehrmacht was in the process of quietly recruiting auxiliary troops of eastern origin—in addition to the hundreds of thousand *Hilfswillige* (helpers; known as "Hiwis") who were already serving in the armed forces as drivers, auto mechanics and kitchen help at the front and in the communications zones. Himmler smelled competition.

"Dear Martin," he wrote early in March 1943, "please inform the Führer that the Wehrmacht has encouraged and established a Russian Committee as well as a Russian Liberation Army. This clearly runs counter to the Führer's recent guidelines. Please advise me on the Führer's decision."

Himmler's jealousy was not unfounded. Keitel and Jodl were in favor of authorizing Soviet General Andrei Vlasov, a prisoner of war since 1942, to set up Russian units. Goebbels also supported this plan, with the reservation that promises made for propaganda purposes need not necessarily be kept at a later date. But Hitler, backed by Bormann, remained adamant. "We will never build a Russian army," he announced at the briefings. "This is pure fantasy." The more Russians shipped to Germany as forced labor, he argued, the more Germans could be drafted into the armed forces. By mid-May a highly satisfied Bormann was able to put the Führer's will on paper; any announcement to the eastern territories, i.e., specific promises, could be made only with Hitler's permission, which he would never give. To Bormann it seemed more important to suppress and exploit the people of the East than to win their allegiance, let alone their friendship. "The only valid policy," he argued, "is the one that guarantees us the largest amount of foodstuff." He urged drastic action against any resistance. He recommended the most fanatic SS generals for guerrilla warfare, maintaining that things were extremely unsafe where "those wise-guy Wehrmacht generals" were in charge.

Anyone suspected of favoring a soft line was kept away from headquarters. An exchange of telex messages between members of his staff and Rosenberg's department shows how Bormann accomplished this. In mid-September 1943 the Reich Minister for the Occupied Eastern Territories asked for an appointment to report to Hitler. The Party Chancellery in Munich thereupon requested "telex information on the issues to be discussed . . . for advance briefing of Reichsleiter Bormann," giving him time to procure the necessary documents and making sure that "the meeting produces profitable results." Rosenberg's department chief replied the same day that Bormann had received a telex copy of the agenda at headquarters days before, but that another copy would be sent to the Party Chancellery. When Rosenberg finally received an answer, it came from Hans Lammers, chief of the Reich Chancellery, to whom Bormann had referred the matter as part of his responsibility. The Reich Minister for the Occupied Eastern Territories was told that four of the items on his agenda were premature and could not be discussed with Hitler at this point, since the comments of other authorities had not yet been received. "The remaining part of Rosenberg's agenda," Lammers wrote, "had to do with Party affairs obviously," which were outside his domain. If Rosenberg wanted his appointment with Hitler, the whole procedure would now have to be started over again. He would have to ask Bormann for a date and once again face being made a fool of.

At this time Rosenberg was also engaged in a bitter power struggle with Goebbels, who for months had insisted that all propaganda in the eastern territories be transferred to his department. As usual, Hitler had made an ambiguous decision which had launched the two contestants into yet another series of arguments. Again Bormann was asked to mediate in the case, but he carefully avoided taking a definite stand. Thus he managed to keep the quarrel alive into December 1943. In view of their growing common interests he finally went over to Goebbels' side and, together with Lammers, who had meanwhile been demoted to hanger-on, once again saw that the matter landed on Hitler's desk. Hitler's decision was made in accordance with whatever Bormann had suggested, which once again reminded all parties concerned that nothing could be achieved any longer except through Bormann's intervention.

Neither Goebbels' propaganda machine nor the pathetic fraternization efforts of the Rosenberg outfit were liable to instill confidence in the people of the East. Besides, these ventures were started only when German victories had stopped and large parts of the conquered land had to be abandoned in a series of withdrawal operations. Only in the summer of 1944 did Hitler and Bormann agree to having auxiliary forces recruited in the East—albeit without specific confirmation and always with the mental reservation that promises made by other Nazi authorities need not necessarily be kept by them. Himmler was given permission to do what had been denied to Rosenberg and the Wehrmacht: to negotiate with General Vlasov. At the time, the Reich Minister for the Occupied Eastern Territories was unaware of this.

When in August 1944 the Red Army had practically reached Warsaw and the French and Italian front lines drew closer and closer to the borders of Germany, Rosenberg felt that the precarious situation might obtain him a hearing on his previous plans. By now, however, he was more or less a king without a country and thus deprived of a people he might have called into battle. Of all his glory only the bureaucratic apparatus of his Berlin office remained, anxiously trying to justify its existence by giving aid to displaced persons and voluntary labor from the eastern territories. Hence Rosenberg was extremely eager to finally get a free hand for an agreement with Vlasov. But when he asked Bormann for an appointment with Hitler in August 1944, he was promptly informed that the Führer's time was completely taken up by military problems.

On September 7, 1944, Rosenberg wrote to Bormann again, more specifically this time. He listed what in his opinion had been neglected in the East "for reasons I won't go into at this point . . . But even now we might still explore whether we can constructively activate the able-bodied millions of the East who are by and large in the same boat with us." According to his figures there were 4 to 5 million people, after all. He had worked out "certain basic guidelines" which he "wished to present personally to the Führer." There was only a gentle hint of the fact that Bormann himself was one of those responsible for the failure of eastern policy: "I believe . . . that by your intervention you, too, have assumed part of the responsibility."

Rosenberg did not send this letter to Führer Headquarters through normal channels. For months most of his letters had gone unanswered into the files of Bormann, who had no desire to waste his time with the shopworn Reich Minister for the Occupied Eastern Territories. Lammers, who happened to be in Berlin, took the letter to the Wolfsschanze, and through him came the reply, dated September 18, saying that Lammers and Bormann had "agreed to urge the Führer to receive you at his earliest convenience for a joint briefing with the Reichsführer SS." Before that, however, Rosenberg was requested to provide the two guardians of Hitler's inner sanctum as soon as possible with a written copy of the "guidelines you have worked out for the treatment and control of the eastern people," so they could follow up on "the issue" in case "your appointment with the Führer does not materialize within the next few weeks."

Having been fooled too often, Rosenberg this time recognized that Lammers, on Bormann's instigation, was trying once again to pick his brains and then give him the run-around. He did not send his guidelines and promptly received word on September 22 that the Führer found it impossible to see him in the near future. In an effort to appease him, Lammers assured him "that the treatment of the eastern people within the realm of the Greater German Reich will follow the principles and guidelines advocated by the Reich Minister for the Occupied Eastern Territories." But as he soon found out, that also was a trick. When he addressed a "report to the Führer" to headquarters, listing the activities of his departments and once again condemning the disastrous effects of the hard-nosed policy, it landed once more in Bormann's files instead of on Hitler's desk. In view of the latest intrigue it was nothing but scrap paper anyway.

Two days earlier, on September 26, the Party Chancellery had sent out a memorandum "Re: General Vlasov" in which the Party leaders were informed of the agreement signed with the renegade Russian general by Himmler—of all people the very Party leader who had always opposed Rosenberg's policy for the East as too mild and who had considered himself too Germanic for any cooperation whatever with the Slavs. Rosenberg must have felt doubly cheated, since the Bormann memorandum no longer even mentioned him as the minister in charge. On October 17 he indignantly requested Bormann to refrain from sending the Party specific information for the time being, before the situation had been cleared up, and "in the future to consult me about announcements to the Party regarding eastern policy or the eastern peoples." Furthermore, Bormann was to circulate another memorandum among the Party leadership, pointing out that the Reich Minister for the Occupied Eastern Territories had always wanted the right things and had been hampered in his efforts by nefarious intrigues.

Bormann ignored these requests. When in mid-November the representatives of the eastern migrants, who had long been completely demoralized and hopelessly at odds among themselves, were summoned to Prague for a joint pledge of allegiance to the Nazi regime, Rosenberg was not invited. On this occasion the SS was allowed to run the show. In a twenty-page memo—the irascible fusspot rarely managed to issue anything less elaborate —Rosenberg complained bitterly about this latest rebuff. He was doubly hurt, of course, because Himmler, Bormann and Hitler had now switched to the line of a conditional agreement which he had recommended in the first place. As if that were not enough, Bormann, in search of a scapegoat for the sins of the past—exploitation and terror—discovered that there was no one better suited than the very Alfred Rosenberg who as minister in charge was responsible for what had happened in the eastern territories. In Prague he was therefore ambiguously but distinctly accused of having pursued a "colonial policy" by plutocratic methods, for which reason he could not possibly be trusted with the mass movement.

This time Rosenberg sent his elaborate lament to headquarters "through strictly personal channels," i.e., by-passing Bormann. To justify such deviation from official routine he enumerated all those missives to Hitler that in the past years had been held up by Bormann. This time the sheets written on the large-type "Führer typewriter" actually reached the addressee.

Rosenberg complained that the charge of the Reich Minister for the Occupied Eastern Territories being responsible for "the colonial policy in the East" had been deliberately introduced by his enemies. "The Reich Minister for the Occupied Eastern Territories has a duty to protect his reputation and honor against such accusations. Since government consideration forbids him to demand public satisfaction, he puts his trust in the Führer's justice."

After more than twenty years of experience with the man, Rosenberg should have known that such trust in Hitler was misplaced. Nothing was done to restore his honor. On the contrary, Hitler was grateful to Bormann for having presented him with a man on whom all the mistakes and sins of omission in the east could be blamed.

16

Secretary
to the Führer

For better or worse, the fate of the Party leaders, the ministers and the entire elite of the Third Reich depended on Hitler alone. His withdrawal, therefore, behind the barbed wire of his headquarters was a blow to all those who had to remain outside. But they were hit even harder by the fact that there Bormann held him virtually in confinement. It is almost impossible at this point to evaluate the extent to which Hitler merely tolerated this, whether he himself possibly wanted this isolation or whether, like the gambler he was, he was so obsessed with his great game that he no longer even noticed the walls Bormann had put up around him. Probably all three theories hold some degree of truth.

First of all, there was Hitler's idea that he would rapidly win and end the war if only he could conduct it with undivided energy, leaving all other problems to managers who would follow general instructions. To control the various areas of responsibility, often assigned in an ad hoc fashion, and to guard against undesirable encroachment on his time, the "Committee of Three" appeared to him the ideal structure. This was a mammoth secretariat with Minister Hans Lammers in charge of the government sector, Field Marshal Wilhelm Keitel in charge of the military sector, and Bormann in charge of Party affairs. At first the committee was simply a mini-version of the Reich Council for National Defense, but the more unwieldy and inactive this institution turned out to be, the more important its offshoot grew.

Bormann did not like the term "Committee of Three"; an unpleasant name, he wrote to his wife. But he knew very well how to make use of it. In due time it became the control panel of his power. Although the committee's activity was at first limited to only a few areas, the three men, by virtue of their rank and office, managed to get their hands on all sectors of government, and constantly invoking the Führer's will, had the potential to develop into a shadow government. Keitel, whose thinking was limited and who was at home only in military affairs, was merely an extra in this show. Lammers, a cautious civil servant, shirked responsibility and was anything but a fighter by nature. Neither of them was a match for Bormann, who was more brutal, more primitive, more crafty, more dynamic, more obsessed with power than either of them. And, above all, more trusted by Hitler than anyone else.

During the Nuremberg Trials, Göring told his attorney, "Bormann was privy to the Führer's most intimate affairs. At certain tea sessions, only he and a few secretaries were allowed to be present, and that was where the most important matters were often decided." Such trust must have been earned. One of Rosenberg's aides, Werner Koeppen, whom Bormann's intrigues edged out of headquarters, gave him credit for having been present at all times. "He was not talkative, not anxious to make contacts, and he gave his time only to work for Hitler. No sooner had Hitler voiced an idea than Bormann would formulate it . . . into an order."

He knew all that went on in the Reich Chancellery and wangled his way around everybody. Tailoring himself to his special status, Bormann observed the most minute details. He was a chain-smoker, but whenever Hitler was around he never touched a cigarette or he went to the men's room for a smoke when a meeting recessed. He liked schnaps—and not in small quantities—but he never touched a drop whenever he thought he might still be wanted on duty. No service was too trifling for him. He recommended and procured books, got Hitler the food for his special diet, checked on the Führer's behalf whether the movie on Bismarck, which was made in 1942 and highly praised by Goebbels, was suitable for public viewing without adverse political effects, and fired the manager of the mess at the Wolfsschanze for having failed to examine a case of wine for bombs before it was taken to the storeroom.

Hans Severus Ziegler, who had been Bormann's mentor at Weimar when he first started as a Party functionary, followed his career with the pride and satisfaction of a successful talent scout and, a high Party official in Thuringia himself, always kept in touch with him. Ziegler, an authority on the inner workings of the Nazi scene, believes to this day that Bormann's greatest achievement was "to have kept the twelve paladins [the Reichsleiters] . . . and also some of the Gauleiters away from A.H. during the war insofar as possible." In doing so, "Bormann certainly may have used his elbows quite ruthlessly to get his Führer some breathing space and spare his nerves from undue strain."

But Speer saw the situation in a different light: admittedly, Bormann did keep the paladins away; on the other hand, he bothered and burdened Hitler unnecessarily with an incredible amount of trivia. Nevertheless, Hitler himself once mentioned in a teatime conversation how glad he was to have such a watchman who kept people off his back. The fact that this meant that it was Bormann who decided who should brief him and obtain a decision from him, Hitler obviously accepted without a qualm as part of the bargain.

It was also Bormann's job to protect Hitler's creative genius from the harsh winds of reality. Wherever possible, unpleasant news was to be kept from the Führer, particularly reports on the disastrous effects of the air raids at home lest, as Speer put it, he lose his "unerring somnambulist touch." The protective screen suited Hitler well; he refused to have hard facts destroy his faith in the mission that Providence had chosen him for. He shirked visits to bombed cities and during the war avoided rallies where he had to meet the public face to face. To be sure, Bormann was able to rise to power only in Hitler's shadow, but Hitler had an equal need for this lackey whose broad back blocked everything he did not wish to see.

Bormann would have had to be a model of unselfishness not to exploit the situation. Henry Picker reported that by 1942 his Minister and his State Secretaries in the Ministry of the Interior were "no longer able to contact Hitler in person by either letter or telephone." Goebbels was made to submit his weekly editorials for the intellectual magazine *Das Reich* to Bormann, who brought them to Hitler's attention—not without personal commentary, of course. The Reich Minister of Finance had his last personal appointment at headquarters in 1942, and having reason to suspect that Bormann would not even let his memoranda get to Hitler's desk, he implored Lammers to look after his interests. Reich Minister of Economics Walther Funk complained that it was "incredibly hard . . . to have a reasonable conversation with the Führer because Bormann butts in all the time. He cuts me short and constantly interrupts."

Bormann gladly chimed in when Hitler complained about an address Goebbels had given to the Wehrmacht, remarking that someone who had not served in the army could not possibly speak the soldiers' language. For Hitler's benefit Bormann collected all the jokes and nasty cracks about Göring and other Nazi big shots that were circulating among the Germans. He enjoyed asking Hjalmar Schacht, the former Reich Minister of Economics, to return the Golden Party Badge which he, along with all the other members of the 1933 Cabinet, had received in 1937. In both cases he felt the upstart's delight in humiliating people he had once been obliged to look up to.

Whenever Hitler had one of his fits of rage, Bormann seized the opportunity to act as the mouthpiece and executor of the Führer's wishes—even in cases that did not concern him at all as a Party representative. When, in September 1942, the advance on the Caucasus bogged down and the generals countered Hitler's reproaches by referring him to his own orders, "the greatest strategist of all time" retired to his bunker to sulk. Profoundly shaken, Bormann noted in his journal: "Since September 5, the Führer no longer takes his meals with the staff at Führer Headquarters." Two days later: "The Führer requests that stenographers be present at the military briefings." Bormann had them brought over from Berlin, put them under oath and told them—they had hitherto recorded only political speeches— to take down every word of the rather differently structured military discussions. Needless to say, their transcripts, intended by Hitler to serve as an alibi, went through Bormann, allowing him to get a foot in the door to a sector that had previously been closed to him.

At this time he also intervened in a dispute between the recently appointed Reich Minister of Justice, Otto Georg Thierack, and top police chief Himmler. The feud had evolved from Hitler's rabid attack on the "subversive" judges who were not generous enough with death sentences. The new minister was perfectly willing to employ executioners to the desired extent, but Himmler felt that even the court procedures, though no longer routine by any means, had become an unnecessary luxury. "Special police treatment," by now the accepted procedure in the conquered eastern territories, could considerably cut down the work of his liquidation program in the concentration camps and make it less conspicious. He had already sent Bormann regular reports on court sentences that he felt needed to be revised by the police. Now it had to be decided whether Thierack or Himmler would be the Third Reich's supreme arbiter of justice.

The two antagonists met at Himmler's field headquarters in Zhitomir. On Bormann's advice they agreed on the most important points after five hours of negotiation. As might have been expected, the penal code—and this included Germany proper—was inhumanly and unlawfully tightened. Thierack had previously written to Bormann that unfortunately the Ministry of Justice could contribute only in a minor way to the liquidation of offenders serving long terms and now sponging on the German people. The agreement with Himmler relieved him from this concern. Germans and Czechs sentenced to more than eight years in prison were taken over by the Reichsführer SS "for liquidation through labor." In the case of Jews, Gypsies and people from the eastern territories, even a three-year sentence was sufficient. Bormann emphasized that it was most important to him to spare Hitler any aggravation arising from misplaced leniency on the part of the judges. He therefore urged that the Minister of Justice revise such sentences on the spot by requesting "special police treatment" for the offenders. In cases where Thierack and Himmler were unable to agree, Bormann as the mediator had final jurisdiction, i.e., over the life and death of a human being. He bluntly announced that "in principle the Führer's time will no longer be taken up by matters of this kind."

Yet another of the many instances where, especially in 1942, the head of the Party Chancellery infringed upon the powers of the government sector was the *lex Krupp,* the act by which Hitler intended to safeguard the continued existence of the munitions factory at Essen as a family holding. Twice already Bormann had been the guest of the company's president at Villa Hügel. He had been instructed to look into the problems of the industrial clan, particularly with regard to the tax burdens a takeover by the next generation might bring about. They had reached rather friendly terms, for around mid-November 1942 the chief executive wrote a long letter, starting "My dear Herr Bormann" and ending with an assurance of "ever grateful admiration." According to the text, three months earlier Alfried Krupp, junior executive and successor to his father's title, had negotiated with Bormann at headquarters, and since then the sender had put their agreement into the terms of a law to be authorized by Hitler. In December, Bormann dictated the reply, addressing the recipient as "Dear Herr von Bohlen" and winding up by hoping "to be pleasantly remembered." He had informed Lammers, he wrote, that "the Führer favors a *lex Krupp.*" The head of the Reich Chancellery would be "glad to come to Essen" for further discussions, "since he has never seen the [Krupp] Works." As it turned out, Hitler did not ratify the law until November 1943. But meantime Bormann made every effort not to lose touch with the big-money aristocracy; he had discovered that in expanding his power he had for far too long neglected the economic area.

By now Reich Minister Lammers had got accustomed to receiving his Führer's orders through Bormann, as well as to the fact that the clear division between the government on the one hand and the Party on the other had been abolished to his disadvantage. In the first years of their side-by-side existence the experienced civil servant may occasionally have smiled at the novice Bormann charging through the bureaucracy like a bull in a china shop. But he soon found out that the newcomer's uncouth manners, combined with a talent for condensing entire stacks of documents into a few pithy phrases, made his recently arrived colleague a formidable competitor.

Lammers was further hampered by the fact that he considered it beneath his dignity to accept just any kind of job, like an all-purpose secretary. Unlike most of the ministers, he was not left behind in Berlin, but he did not figure as part of Hitler's personal entourage either, and instead of being assigned rooms at headquarters, he was billeted somewhere in the neighborhood. And although Hitler praised his common sense at the nightly sessions, his relationship to the boss remained distant. In February 1943, before headquarters were temporarily moved to Vinnitsa, Bormann wrote to his wife: "Tomorrow morning he [Hitler] is flying there with a small group of trusted friends. . . . Keep this strictly to yourself. Lammers, Himmler, Ribbentrop, etc., are to remain in their winter quarters for the duration."

Bormann had taken early precautions in case Lammers objected to being patronized in this fashion. Along with dossiers on all important personalities, he kept a special file on Lammers in his safe. A telex he sent from

Obersalzberg on April 29, 1942, to Adolf Scheel, Gauleiter and Reich Governor in Salzburg, reveals how he collected such material. He had received word, Bormann wrote, that on April 26, the day after the Reichstag session, Scheel had traveled with Lammers in his private parlor car from Berlin to Munich, and that matters had been discussed which would be of interest to the Party leadership. Scheel should report these to him at once.

He did, the very same day. As a Gauleiter in the immediate vicinity of the Berghof, Scheel was directly under Bormann's thumb. He reported that Reich Minister Otto Meissner, head of the Presidential Chancellery, and several top officials had also taken part in the conversation on the train, and that the discussion had centered on the Führer's speech and the newly enacted law by which Hitler had assumed authority to fire judges and revise court sentences. But having been involved in a lively conversation with one of the other officials, he had been able to hear only snatches of what Lammers and Meissner had said. According to Scheel, Lammers had not been exactly enthusiastic about the new law, but his information was too vague to serve as incriminating evidence. A physician in civilian life, Scheel had nevertheless had some experience with tricky situations of this sort in his capacity as senior officer in the Security Service and in the SS. Professing to have not the faintest recollection of the actual words Lammers had used, he managed to wriggle out of the whole business.

A year later it was made abundantly clear to Reich Minister Hans Heinrich Lammers that in the future he was to play second fiddle, with Hitler as well as with the Committee of Three. Emerging from Hitler's study at the Berghof, Bormann carried in his folder a sheet of paper of a kind used only for the most important documents. Printed in gold, the capital letters in the upper left-hand corner spelled DER FÜHRER. Underneath, the text, typed on the Führer typewriter with its quarter-inch letters, announced:

> As my personal assistant, Reichsleiter M. Bormann will bear the title "Secretary to the Führer."

Führer Headquarters
April 12, 1943

The event was sandwiched between two state visits. Two days earlier Italy's Duce had visited Obersalzberg, and only hours after Bormann's appointment the Rumanian head of state, Marshal Ion Antonescu, arrived.

Brockhaus' Dictionary defines the word "Secretary," which is derived from the French word *"secret,"* as "a scribe, secret scribe, the title of medium-level civil servants." But Hitler could hardly have had that in mind when he chose it. Being partial to historic pomp and circumstance, he may have thought of the secretaries to Renaissance princes and Baroque kings who rose to fame, custodians of secrets who manipulated their master's state and love affairs from the murky twilight of their chancelleries. The title was not badly chosen, for if it was thus defined, it granted its bearer virtually unlimited authority to act in the name of the boss at all times and under any circumstances.

How Bormann came to be honored in this fashion will be described later in this chapter. What the title meant he personally explained to the Reichsführer SS in a letter he dictated a few days later at Obersalzberg and gave to a courier who was on his way to Himmler's field headquarters. The paper it was written on—without the swastika, and with the new title placed here, too, in the upper left-hand corner—appeared to be private stationery, but its self-conscious matter-of-factness was enough to fill any recipient with trepidation. This time Himmler was not addressed as "Dear Heinrich" but as "Dear Comrade Himmler," and the familiar *Du* was replaced by the official *Sie*.

Bormann wrote that apart from other considerations, Hitler's action had become "necessary for technical reasons." He went on to say: "For years, as you know, I have almost daily been given assignments outside the range of the Party Chancellery's duties. Hitherto I have dealt with such assignments on stationery with just the 'Reichsleiter Martin Bormann' letterhead to indicate that they were not part of the Party Chancellery's responsibilities. But since more definite clarification has been required in a number of cases, the Führer issued the enclosed instructions on April 12. This does not mean that a new office with a new set of duties has been created."

What Bormann himself announced on the Party level, deliberately underplaying it for tactical reasons, Lammers was forced to communicate a month later by a circular to the top government agencies and to the departments under the Führer's immediate authority. The text is considerably more detailed than Bormann's letter to Himmler but remarkably similar in content; it even uses some of the same phrases. His memorandum of May 8, 1943, reveals that Bormann dictated most of the text to Lammers, who, left to himself, would hardly have advertised the fact that he had been demoted to the rank of a minor assistant. Among other things it says: "As a rule, Reichsleiter Bormann will relay the Führer's instructions through me to the Reich ministers in charge or others concerned."

Everybody in the Third Reich elite gnashed their teeth when they read the news. For years, and particularly within the past few weeks, they had tried, individually or as a group, to stop this careerist or push him back into second rank. But they had underestimated his perseverance, craftiness, servility, zeal and ambition, not to mention the effect of those dark, trusting eyes which had enchanted Gerda at their first meeting and in which Hitler read boundless devotion every day. Now at last it dawned on his opponents that they would not have an easy time trying to topple this man, that being on the wrong side of him was dangerous, and that it might be wiser to seek his friendship. A plot they had hatched against him crumbled like a mud wall.

The seed for the plot had been planted on the very day, May 12, 1941, when the office of the Party Chancellery was created after Hess's spectacular flight. Practically nobody in the Führer's entourage wanted Bormann to have it. But, as mentioned earlier, he had been wise enough to curry favor with Göring, who at the time ranked second in the succession of power. He had no need to fear Himmler, since they were in the same boat. Speer had not yet advanced to top rank, and whoever else was around was of secondary importance, to be feared only in conjunction with others. Goebbels was the one exception, but his standing with Hitler was still suffering from his tiresome bygone affair with movie actress Lida Baarova. It had not improved when, while successfully beating the drums of war, the Minister of Propaganda had on occasion indicated in private that he would have preferred a less martial and hazardous rise to world power. Consumed with ambition, the power-hungry, intellectual Goebbels hardly fancied playing a supporting role in the long run, but he recognized that he could improve his image only by involving himself more deeply in the events of the war and overcoming his unsoldierly appearance by excessive revolutionary zeal.

On March 20, 1942, after a long interlude, he once again met Hitler face to face at the Wolfsschanze. It was actually a three-way interview, since Bormann too attended the meeting, silent and wary. After the retreat of the German forces advancing on Moscow and the Wehrmacht's disastrous failure to provide the soldiers with proper winter clothing, Hitler was still full of resentment against the generals. Now Goebbels urged that the war be drastically stepped up and all forces mobilized. "The Führer was in a frame of mind," he noted in his diary, "that caused my proposals . . . to meet with an absolutely favorable response on his part. . . . Everything I proposed was accepted item by item and without objection by the Führer." But that was all that happened. The Committee of Three was instructed to deal with Goebbels' proposals, and they became just another pile of documents.

Furiously Goebbels turned on Bormann, Lammers and Keitel, accusing them of "setting up a sort of kitchen cabinet and erecting a wall between Hitler and the ministers." As far as he was concerned, it was all Göring's fault that matters had come to this pass, because as chairman of the Reich Council for National Defense he had been a failure and "had made extremely grave mistakes in the past three and a half years." The "Three Wise Men from the East," as Göring called the Committee of Three, were only secretaries, after all, and had no right to "exercise plenipotentiary power of their own." This was all quite true, but the reason for the shift in power was not just Göring's laziness or Bormann's ambition, but also the deliberate confusion about areas of responsibility created by Hitler, which resulted in never-ending rivalries among his followers.

Needless to say, a man of Goebbels' intelligence knew this, but he wisely refrained from confiding the knowledge to his diary. He acted with logic. If the paladins agreed among themselves and stopped letting Hitler play them against one another, they would be able to join forces and demand from Hitler freedom of action for government and Party. The three secretaries would thereby be reduced to their former role of office managers. Goebbels first approached Speer, Minister of Armaments and War Production; in the summer of 1942 Goebbels had used his propaganda to promote him to celebrity status, and it was common knowledge that Speer and Bormann disliked each other intensely. Minister of Economics Walther Funk and Robert Ley, head of the German Labor Front, were amenable to joint action. Goebbels invited them all to his house for a fireside chat, and they soon agreed that this "primitive GPU type"—Goebbels was ranking Bormann with the infamous Soviet state police—had to be deposed.

Their plan was to set off an all-out war effort by demanding "total war" from the German people, at the same time blaming the "Three Wise Men from the East" for the fact that this had not been done much earlier. They hoped they would have little trouble winning the support of Göring and others. Early in October, Goebbels and Speer had occasion to discuss the first phase of the plan—all-out mobilization—but they were unable at this early stage to set the bomb to destroy Bormann. It was not a good day because three enemies of Bormann's who were in Hitler's bad books and thus apt to aggravate him by their mere appearance—Gauleiter Baldur von Schirach from Vienna, Governor General Hans Frank from Cracow, and Party Judge Walter Buch from Munich—had also been summoned before their Führer. All the same, Hitler promised he would soon give the signal for total war.

He gave it on December 27, 1942, at the Wolfsschanze—to Bormann. On this date Bormann's journal shows an entry which is unusual if only for its length: "After a number of consultations with Hitler, M.B. travels to Berlin to discuss, on December 28, with Dr. Lammers and subsequently with Dr. Goebbels the all-out mobilization of the German people for the purpose of increasing the war potential."

This was not exactly what the conspirators had had in mind. They found they had in fact strengthened Bormann's position, for their decisions now required his approval more than ever. That day he instructed Goebbels to draft the declaration of total war—"all-out mobilization of able-bodied men and women for national defense." The draft was to be ready for further discussion in January.

On the night of December 30, 1942, Bormann traveled back to the Wolfsschanze. After New Year's he noted—and all his pride shines through the few words: "December 31. M.B. alone with the Führer until 4:15 A.M." And although in those hours of the waning year Hitler probably did all the talking while his companion faithfully listened, the hitherto unheard-of distinction revealed how close their relationship had become.

Since the text of the announcement and additional plans had long been ready and waiting in Goebbels' desk drawer, the next discussion took place on January 8, 1943, again in Berlin. Goebbels called in Speer and Funk for support. Stressing the importance of the Committee of Three, Bormann arrived with Lammers and Keitel. They quickly agreed in principle. A large number of small and medium-size industries were to be closed down since they were not of strategic importance. Their employees would be reassigned to the defense industry, which could then release its able-bodied workers for service in the armed forces.

Reverting to his pre-1933 radical phase in proletarian Berlin, Goebbels also urged a ban on luxuries of any kind. Bormann, who had repeatedly circulated letters urging the Party leadership to adopt a simpler life style, found it hard to oppose him. He may also have been looking forward to the resulting troubles Goebbels would soon have to face. Sure enough, Göring protested the closing of Horcher's, his favorite gourmet restaurant in Berlin. Eva Braun intervened on behalf of the cosmetics industry and objected to the ban on permanent waves. Hitler actually made some concessions to her on the ground that soldiers on leave were entitled to come home to attractive women. In this context he may have been thinking of Napoleon's remark, which he quoted on occasion, that one night in Paris made up for the casualties of a battle.

Bormann used his stay in Berlin for a sideswipe at Goebbels. He summoned Goebbels' aide Tiessler to the Reich Chancellery and complained that the fight against Bolshevism had lost momentum "in domestic as well as foreign propaganda." The neutral nations, in particular, needed to be convinced "by means of first-rate news and picture documentation" that in this struggle "our whole culture" is at stake. In Germany each and every citizen in all walks of life should be reminded what his fate would be in the event of a Bolshevik victory. (The full text is quoted in the Appendix on pages 402-403.)

Although it will put us ahead of events, in view of the changing rate of value in the Bormann/Goebbels relationship it might be interesting to note at this early stage what resulted from Bormann's intervention. Late in April 1943 he instructed a member of the Party Chancellery to remind Tiessler that "so far the Reichsleiter's wishes have not been complied with." The ministry, for instance, had not sufficiently exploited the discovery of a mass grave in Katyn Forest, near Smolensk, where several thousand Polish army officers, murdered on Stalin's orders, had been buried. Since Goebbels' aides knew that their boss had a fit every time Bormann took him to task, Tiessler promptly countered with a rebuttal. He pointed out that "Allied propaganda is constantly taking the anti-Bolshevist line" and its success in the Katyn affair had been greater than even Goebbels had anticipated. The Party Chancellery would certainly not have left it at that, but meanwhile

—it was by now the early part of May—friendly cooperation between the two bosses had become advisable.

In the main arena, however, things were different. On January 13, 1943, Bormann had flown back to headquarters and the same day reported to his Führer on the Berlin agreements. Hitler promptly signed the resolution Bormann had brought with him, and by the end of the month an amendment was added recruiting all German males between the ages of sixteen and sixty-five and all females between seventeen and forty-five for special duties upon future draft orders. But Goebbels and his friends were not satisfied. Speer complained: "After a few meetings at the Chancellery it was clear to Goebbels and me that armaments production would receive no spur from Bormann, Lammers or Keitel. Our efforts had bogged down in meaningless details."

Himmler was equally annoyed, for other reasons. He arrived at headquarters on January 16, fussing and fuming that he had not been included in the action and that he felt left out in general. "It was quite unpleasant," Bormann told his wife. Himmler complained that apparently all he was good for now was to produce more and more new divisions. He had been so harsh and violent in his criticism, Bormann wrote to Gerda, that under different circumstances he would have had no choice but to make Himmler relinquish his uniform and dismiss him from the service. He had refrained from doing so only out of consideration for Himmler's overwrought nervous condition. If the Führer treated them unjustly, people just had to bear it. "Considering that all of us lose our tempers every once in a while, it is only natural that the same thing happens to the Führer, whose burdens are superhuman, after all. He towers above us like Mount Everest. When all is said and done: the Führer is the Führer! What would we be without him?"

At this point Goebbels felt that it was of the utmost importance that Hitler speak to the people. There were reasons: the Sixth Army had been savagely crushed at Stalingrad, and now the Germans were expected to rally their forces for an all-out war effort. But Hitler refused, as he always did, when a defeat had to be explained. Besides, he felt the generals and their soldiers had disgraced themselves after they took leave of him on the banks of the Volga; they should have committed suicide or let themselves be killed instead of choosing to be taken prisoner. Goebbels should therefore make the speech. For the purpose he had a unique backdrop built for himself at the Sportpalast. The rally went down in history as an example of mass hysteria and public deception. "Do you want total war?" he asked on February 18 in his clear, resounding voice. The ear-splitting cheers of thousands of people were his reward. Meanwhile Hitler sneaked off to the front, to Zaporozhye in the Ukraine, and almost got caught in the firing line of advancing enemy tanks which had broken through.

Bormann heard the speech over the loudspeaker at the Wolfsschanze. He must have noticed that in a subtle way it was also directed against him. Only four days earlier he had bragged in a letter to his wife that it was he who had given the signal for the mobilization about to get under way and that he was responsible for its success. That was why he had so much on his mind and not enough time for personal correspondence. But on the day after the speech he heard from his wife that his mother, for one, had reacted with alarm and had advised her daughter-in-law to relinquish one or two of her domestic servants to the defense industry. Rudely and with obvious pique he told his mother to mind her own business.

Goebbels was determined to fight. The night after his speech he entertained Speer, Funk, Ley and other Nazi celebrities at his house. Among them were Göring's confidant and World War I comrade Field Marshal Erhard Milch, Minister of Justice Thierack, and several state secretaries. This time there was joint agreement that there had to be an end to the chaos of conflicting responsibilities and that the Reich Cabinet must be restored to action. Speer and Milch offered to mediate between Party comrades Göring and Goebbels, who were at odds once again. As a result, on March 2 the Minister of Propaganda was able to travel to the Reichsmarschall's country house at Obersalzberg. The air was "clear" up there. Hitler and Bormann were at the Werewolf headquarters in the Ukraine.

For one solid hour Goebbels and Speer presented their plan and the motives behind it, and Göring jovially endorsed it with genuine conviction in his voice. But Goebbels was skeptical. "It seems to me that Göring has been standing aside too long from the political factors that do the real driving." Besides, he had become somewhat "tired and apathetic." "It is therefore all the more necessary to get him straightened out."

"As regards Bormann, Göring is not quite certain about his true intentions. There seems to be no doubt that he is pursuing ambitious aims." "Depend on it, "Goebbels assured Göring, "we are going to open the Führer's eyes to Bormann and Lammers. . . . I believe we shall render the Führer the greatest possible service by our action." Speer predicted that Bormann was aiming straight at being Hitler's successor.

A few days later Goebbels passed on the information to Ley and Funk in Berlin. They were "very happy" about the result. But in the typical fashion of the alcoholic when he happens to be sober the Reich Organization Leader started to whine. Bemoaning "the inactivity of the Party," Ley said that "that is chiefly due to the somewhat bureaucratic conduct of Party affairs by Bormann. Bormann is not a man of the people. He has always been engaged in administrative work and therefore has not the proper qualifications for the real tasks of leadership."

The plot seemed to be taking shape; everybody who was anybody joined in, with the exception of Frick, whom everybody disliked, and Himmler, whom Goebbels promised to win over in due course. But this was not to be, for on March 9, 1943, a unique opportunity for attack seemed to present itself. Two days earlier Speer had been with Hitler; according to Goebbels,

"As always, he did wise and clever spadework." Bormann was traveling around Bavaria with the Hungarian government delegation, which he was tutoring in anti-Semitism. When Goebbels arrived at the Werewolf headquarters around noon, Hitler received him for a discussion which lasted four hours. Assisted by Speer, Goebbels was able to unburden himself of everything that had been on his mind. The trouble was, he said, that there was a total lack of leadership in Berlin. "The Führer is not yet well acquainted with the working methods of the Committee of Three," he observed in his diary. Goebbels' visit had been meant to remedy that, but, as the diary reveals, it was not all that easy. "Bormann still has the Führer's confidence to a considerable extent, whereas Keitel is already on ice."

Praise from the Führer is recorded in detail in Goebbels' diary. "My measures concerning total war meet with the Führer's full approval." His speech at the Sportpalast was hailed as "a psychological and propaganda masterpiece." In spite of Bormann's criticism, "the Führer fully endorses my anti-Bolshevik propaganda." In the second part of the discussion the subtle drilling operation of giving Hitler advice began. In church matters (Bormann's pet scheme) the Party had better go easy and mark time. The morals of the Party big shots needed to be shaped up; he complained about "a number of Reichsleiters and Gauleiters, whose standard of living is very much out of tune with the times." Only one-dish meals and nonalcoholic beverages should be served at Party rallies. Moreover, there was corruption, even in Bouhler's "private Führer's chancellery." It stank, in other words, even in the Most Supreme's own entourage.

Goebbels and Speer had a hard time during the tea hour late that night when they tried to resurrect their ally Göring's reputation. He had lost the war in the air against England, was unable to fend off the air raids over Germany, and despite his boastful promises, had failed to supply the encircled troops at Stalingrad from the air. But there were excuses. Then, just when Goebbels and Speer were certain they had aroused Hitler's sympathy, the news arrived that Nuremberg had suffered a severe air attack. Hitler ordered General Karl Bodenschatz, the Reichsmarschall's deputy at headquarters, out of bed and, in Göring's absence, gave him a lecture on air defense. Goebbels tried to come to the aid of the Luftwaffe's portly supreme commander, "for his authority must be maintained under all circumstances." But it was to no avail. Hitler was in a rage. In view of the prevailing mood, the all-out attack on Bormann had to be postponed.

By mid-March a long-festering canker inside the Party burst wide open. In a lawsuit against a black-market operator, the names of high-ranking Party members came up who had supplemented their rations in the black market and reinforced their domestic staffs by faking work contracts. Among them were Reich Minister of the Interior Wilhelm Frick, Reich Minister of Education Bernhard Rust, Reich Minister of Agriculture Walter Darré, the head of the Reichsarbeitsdienst (State Labor Service) Konstantin Hierl and, on the military side, Field Marshal Walther von Brauchitsch and Grand Admiral Erich Raeder. In some respects the scandal suited Goebbels well, for it proved once again that his call for drastic measures and total order had been justified. On the other hand, some of the people thus exposed were traditional enemies of Bormann's, and he would have liked to include them in his plot. In a meeting of the Committee of Three he presented his case, condemning the laxity which had developed because of the lack of strong leadership.

This tipped off Bormann, who suddenly felt something was brewing against him. On the day the Committee of Three met, he wrote a letter to his wife, warning her that under no condition should they be open to criticism. Since he always kept urging others to be model National Socialists and observe the rules, his own house should be run impeccably, particularly in view of his "special position with the Führer."

On March 18 his opponents met again in Berlin. Goebbels, Speer, Ley, Funk and Göring conferred for three hours. In a moment of self-criticism they agreed that the "Three Wise Men from the East" had proceeded much more cleverly than they had in taking account of Hitler's psychology and shifting moods. Bormann, they felt, was the most dangerous of the lot. In order to prevent him from driving a wedge between the Führer and the ministers, the Reich Council of National Defense should be not only put back in action but also reinforced by a few strong men such as Speer, Ley and Himmler. "Of course we must proceed very carefully," Goebbels wrote in his diary, "so that the members of the Committee of Three won't catch on to our scheme prematurely." Göring promised to get the thing started at his next talk with Hitler.

Everybody assumed this would be soon, as Hitler was just about to return from the East to spend a few weeks in Germany and, above all, at the Berghof. But Göring's intervention never came about. One reason may have been that in the following weeks Hitler's schedule was filled with travel and state visits. It is also possible that Bormann, again in charge of appointments, simply took Göring off the list. Speer suspected that Göring had quietly defected from the alliance, since just at that time Bormann had presented him with an endowment of 6 million marks from the Adolf Hitler Fund.

The gang did not meet again until the funeral of SA Chief of Staff Viktor Lutze, who had been killed in an automobile accident on the autobahn—on an illegal trip, incidentally, with his entire family in an official car in spite of the ban on private driving because of the gas shortage. On this occasion Hitler spoke to several of his top executives. Göring was not among them. But he talked to Goebbels three times in a row, which convinced the Minister of Propaganda that he had backed the wrong horse by including the fat, lazy Reichsmarschall in his scheme. On the afternoon of May 9 he, Ley and Bormann—who had arranged the meeting—had another opportunity "to discuss the necessary official appointments" with the Führer. Goebbels was proud to note this in his diary, for it had been years since he was invited to attend such confidential discussions. In summing up, he rejoiced: "Bormann acted exceedingly loyally. I must say that the criticism leveled at him is for the most part unjustified. When you compare what he keeps in the way of promises and what Göring keeps, Göring is undoubtedly at a disadvantage. There is no longer any real dependence on Göring. He is tired and somewhat washed up."

It was easy for Bormann to be loyal; since April 12 he had been Secretary to the Führer, entitled to assert his power in every department. Goebbels wisely took this into account. He knew that only with Bormann's approval could he secure a place close to Hitler for himself. As Speer reports, Goebbels promised from here on in to approach Hitler only via Bormann and no longer to solicit decisions on his own. The drafts of his speeches that Hitler wished to see before they were delivered also reached the Führer by way of Bormann. When on June 5 the Minister of Propaganda in a joint effort with Speer wanted to step up popular support of total war by another mass rally in Berlin's Sportpalast, Hitler promptly eliminated entire paragraphs with a wide marker and later, partly by marker, partly in ink, revised individual phrases. He obviously went through the draft once again with Bormann; several hard-to-read corrections were made more legible and others inserted in Bormann's handwriting. Moreover, Bormann summed up the Führer's comments on a covering page: "Too many repetitions, too long, needs a lot of cutting. Please submit future speeches only as final draft after finishing touches have been added."

That was only one of the bitter pills Goebbels had to swallow. Now and then he would mention talks with Bormann in his diary, most of the time with a critical undertone, but he never dared to oppose him openly. Late in November 1943 they discussed in Berlin "a number of personnel problems," i.e., they arranged between themselves who was to come under fire next. There was first of all Ribbentrop. "Bormann, too, is worried about German foreign policy," Goebbels noted after the talk. "Ribbentrop is too rigid . . . But I don't believe the Führer is ready to part company with his Foreign Minister." The thought was touched off by the Minister of Propaganda's own desire to become Ribbentrop's successor. When he felt the time was right, he sent a forty-page memorandum to Bormann for Hitler's attention. In view of the military defeats, he advised a peace treaty with the Soviet Union, offering personally to negotiate with Stalin.

For weeks he waited for a reply from headquarters. When he checked back, Bormann blandly told him that he had not even submitted the memorandum, since the proposal would not have the slightest chance of Hitler's approval. Nevertheless, when Goebbels referred to it at his next meeting with the Führer, Hitler knew about it, but the carefully prepared papers had been buried in the files. Both Hitler and Bormann preferred a Foreign

Minister without initiative and without a mind of his own.

Bormann did not dare to be quite as boorish with Speer, the second man in the plot. No one knew better than he how highly Hitler regarded Speer. He therefore "appeared amiable," according to Speer, "intimating that, like Goebbels, I should be on his side." But whenever he could get away with it, he put obstacles in Speer's way: late in August 1943, for instance, when the Minister of Armaments and War Production presented his Führer with an already approved draft of a law by which the entire German industrial production was to be put under Speer's command, Hitler did not sign; Bormann had advised him not to, he said, because Göring and Lammers had not been consulted. "I am glad," he explained, "that at least Bormann watches faithfully over me." By quick action, Speer managed to obtain the requested approvals and to abort the intrigue.

But the law did not give Speer what he had expected from it. Many Gauleiters objected to having industrial plants in their region converted to wartime production. Bormann encouraged this opposition, and he had yet another instrument that he used effectively: the Gauwirtschaftsberater (district economic counsel). For a long time this office had existed as part of each Gauleitung, but it had remained ineffectual for years because no one in the Reichsleitung took an active interest in it. Bormann had discovered this vacuum when he was chief of staff under Hess and had secretly started to develop it. As a result, he was able to penetrate an area where the Party Organization had had difficulty in getting a foothold. Only Ley with his German Labor Front had managed to man a few economic outposts. Beginning in 1940, Bormann had more and more frequently called the district economic counsels to conferences, and since he bolstered their reputation on those occasions, they gladly became his loyal followers. Should the need arise, he could always put them to work against Göring's Four-Year Plan agencies, Minister of Economics Funk, their own Gauleiters, and now also against Speer.

In the past he had restricted himself mainly to secretly supporting Speer's opponents, such as the architect Hermann Giessler, who regarded his colleague as a threatening competitor. Now direct confrontations multiplied in proportion to Speer's fall from Hitler's graces. Bormann shrewdly submitted cases to the All-Powerful that were bound to provoke his anger. This happened, for instance, when, in view of the wartime economy, Speer proposed to cut down the production of Hitler's pet industry, Nymphenburg porcelain. For old time's sake Hitler also patronized a frame maker at Munich. When his workshop was ordered to close, Speer was advised by Bormann that the frame manufacturer's work was "under the Führer's special protection." Speer's request "not to bother the Führer with such trivia in the future" fell on deaf ears. Needless to say, he also made himself unpopular when Bormann saddled him with the chore of decontrolling a villa for State Actor Johannes Riemann which had been confiscated from a Jewish owner in the west section of Berlin, and Speer regretfully had to inform him that he had no more real estate at his disposal.

Speer realized how much his reputation with Hitler had been undermined by such incidents when he presented his armaments program for 1944. It proposed that forced labor should no longer be drawn from France, Belgium and the Netherlands, but that local production should be stepped up in those countries instead. Both Keitel and Himmler were in favor of this plan, lest there be an increased enlistment in underground organizations in the occupied countries. But Bormann objected to the plan, as did his flunky Sauckel, who was in charge of labor allocation. Bormann made sure that Hitler's emotional barometer was indicating stormy weather before the meeting got started. Speer was rudely put in his place, and Sauckel was given a free hand to round up forced labor. As Speer wrote later: "From now on we had to deal with, at first covert, but soon with more and more overt, attacks upon my aides in industry. More and more frequently I had to defend them at the Party secretariat against suspicions . . ." Bormann even went so far as to suggest that the Ministry of Armaments was harboring a whole nest of political opponents and enemies of the system.

But Speer did not give in all that easily. When in the spring of 1944 he was once again given a moment in the light of the All-Merciful, and Hitler received him as a distinguished guest at the Berghof, going out of his way to do him honor, Bormann realized that he would have to change his tune. He assured Speer that he "had not had any part in the grand intrigue against me." A few days later he invited him to dinner at his house at Obersalzberg with Lammers, toasted him profusely and toward midnight even addressed his two guests with the intimate *du.* Speer promptly dropped it again the following morning but, he wrote, Lammers stuck with it.

In his official position, the malleable head of the Reich Chancellery profited less and less from such familiarity. He was by-passed with increasing frequency. Bormann assured Lammers that "as a rule" he would take him along to briefings with Hitler, but in actual fact he reduced him to the role of his office manager. At the Nuremberg Trials, Lammers testified: "Bormann was able to see the Führer every day. I saw him only once every six or eight weeks. Herr Bormann would communicate the Führer's decisions to me. He reported to him in person. I did not."

When a month after Bormann's promotion to Secretary to the Führer they returned from a joint briefing, Lammers timidly commented in Hitler's ante-room that the new title had already caused quite a stir. Triumphantly Bormann relayed the interchange that followed in a memorandum to his closest associates, Klopfer and Friedrichs. According to Bormann, he replied to Lammers, "I don't understand this at all, because in reality I have been acting Secretary to the Führer for years." But without the title there were bound to be misunderstandings and feelings "that I concerned myself with issues that were none of my business." The memo continues: "Lammers replied that people had tried to get his goat by saying Dr. Lammers might now be superfluous. The Reichsmarschall had . . . told him that in the future he had better stand at attention whenever he received a letter from me as Secretary to the Führer. In the end Dr. Lammers pointed out that Dr. Goebbels, in particular, had been far from pleased with my appointment as Secretary to the Führer."

By the end of May 1944 Lammers once again—for the umpteenth time, it seems—was obliged to remind all top government authorities by memorandum that he was not in charge of anything. Bormann alone with his Party Chancellery represented the Party. "Direct communication of the top government agencies and top agencies of the *Länder* [provinces] with other Party agencies is . . . not permissible."

But familiarity paid off in the private sector. When Lammers turned sixty-five at the end of May 1944, he found among his presents a document making him the proud owner of a hunting lodge with thirty-three hectares (about eighty acres) of land, building annexes and "existing furniture." Initially the plan had been to present Lammers with a large gift of money, which Bormann had already requested from the Reich Minister of Finance. But then the birthday boy had expressed a desire for some inflationproof real estate offering. Bormann was delighted to oblige, particularly since what he was giving away was part of the so-called Schorfheide Foundation, and as such, government property, which Göring had always made use of as though it belonged to him. Here the Reichsmarschall had built his baronial residence, Karinhall, and here he held court with hunting parties, glamorous banquets and a standing battalion as bodyguard. He would hardly welcome his new neighbor. To make sure that Lammers would actually settle there later and be able to "construct suitable residential and farm buildings on the given property after the war," Bormann obtained for him an additional tax-exempt cash endowment of 600,000 Reichsmarks.

On the other hand Robert Ley, deserted at this point by all his allies, was subjected to constant humiliation. A typical example is a memorandum Bormann dictated after a talk with the Reich Organization Leader on August 23, 1943. It was triggered by a prospective order through which Ley had meant to underline the power of the Reichsleiters over the Gauleiters, making the provincial and regional subdivisions more dependent on the respective Reichsleiters. The idea was based largely on an old rule to which the Gauleiters, anxious to preserve their independence, had paid little attention. But Hitler and Bormann objected in principle to strengthening the Reichsleiters' position; there was to be no authority besides the Führer and his Secretary on the Party level. Ley was therefore denied permission to pass the order.

More humiliating than the actual refusal, however, was the way in which Bormann informed his colleague—he was monosyllabic, angry, condescending, and cut short all discussion. An appointment for Ley to see Hitler was canceled on short notice. Ley's building plans, which the architect Giessler had been commissioned to carry out, Bormann countered with a design by Speer. Bormann must have known why Ley's weekly pep-talk article had been stopped at the editors' desks, but he professed ignorance. There had been trouble with some of the Gauleiters, but the head of the Party Chancellery would not talk. The only piece of news Ley received was that Himmler had replaced Frick as Reich Minister of the Interior, but he might have read that in the papers two days later.

On reading the account, one can virtually see the fat little Reich Organization Leader, desperately uneasy even under normal circumstances, sitting meek and small in an armchair sweating profusely as he faced Bormann's desk. The memorandum also reveals how Bormann relished this hour of revenge. For even greater enjoyment he marked it "Secret" and circulated it for days among his closest aides before filing it away in his safe. They should all know how their boss dealt with his enemies.

In July 1943, having quashed all quarrels and intrigues, Bormann made a list of "the responsibilities of the Secretary to the Führer," which he sent to all Party and government agencies. In it he proclaimed himself the sole mediator between the dictator on the one hand, and the government, the Party and the people on the other. Only the Wehrmacht remained outside his range of power. He listed as his prerogatives: "(1) to manage the Führer's numerous personal affairs; (2) to attend meetings with the Führer; (3) to report to the Führer on incoming items relating to the duties of the Secretary to the Führer; (4) to relay the Führer's decisions and comments to the Reich ministers, other top government authorities or agencies of the Reich." He deliberately refrained from defining the range of his actual jurisdiction too precisely, leaving it as open as Hitler's own. With the right to "(5) settle disputes, jurisdictional controversies between Reich ministers, etc." he netted himself yet another power that hitherto had been reserved for the Führer as the ultimate authority and that, in the interminable quarrels among the paladins, allowed him to intervene in whatsoever domain he chose.

Equipped with the full powers of these five points, the Secretary to the Führer was now as strong in the government sector as he was, as head of the Party Chancellery, in the Party. The remaining three items on his list of responsibilities could therefore be modest. They gave Bormann full rein in developing Hitler's favorite building project, the city of Linz; entitled him to supervise Hitler's household at the various headquarters, at Munich and at Obersalzberg; and gave him control over the stenographers at military briefings. A ninth claim he deliberately omitted from the list. Under a "Secret" label Bormann announced to the Chief of Security Police Ernst Kaltenbrunner, who in turn informed his boss Himmler that the Secretary to the Führer was to be responsible for "all matters concerning the protection and safety of the Führer and his entourage." Whether he liked it or not, the Reichsführer SS was obliged to place the agents of the Reich Security Service and the sentries of the Waffen SS, assigned to protect the Führer, under Bormann's command.

Bormann had assured everybody that the appointment did not create a new agency. But it inevitably inflated the Party Chancellery's staff, which already numbered over five hundred. The interplay of the two functions now clearly revealed how strong and all-encompassing the power of the still virtually unknown official had grown by the second half of 1943.

In September 1942 the German newspaper published in Lemberg (formerly the Polish city of Lwow) had printed a lengthy tribute to Bormann with his picture. It maintained that he was "advocate with the Führer for everybody whose cause is just," and the "champion of comradeship," the usual phrases from the Nazi vocabulary, albeit totally inappropriate in this case. The report made no mention of Bormann's actual duties and responsibilities. Back home in the Reich only a few copies of the paper were read. To Bormann it was more important to sign his name to orders, decrees, regulations: they made him stronger than any form of notoriety. Nor had he any use for decorations. He certainly could have had any medals he wanted from Hitler. "I have accomplished more than can be expressed in decorations," he wrote to his wife. As the reader will recall, on two occasions, during Hitler-Mussolini meetings, the Italians hung a medal around his neck, but later no one ever saw it or even its ribbon on his uniform. The only ribbon he wore constantly was the *Blutorden.*

He ruled over his departments from wherever he happened to be stationed with the latest technological means of communication. When in August 1944 the Reichsbahn (State Railway Agency) gave him a new command car with telephones, telex machines and radio equipment, he proudly showed it off to Hitler. "Now I shall also be able to work on long train trips," he raved to his wife, meaning that now he would be able to hound, push, reprimand and abuse his staff even while he was on the move. His wife once wrote to him that on the whole, people were selfish and needed to be kept on their toes by threats and severe punishment. He had drummed this belief into her, and he treated his aides accordingly. Once when Hitler happened to witness Bormann shouting and ranting at a subordinate over the phone, the cynical Führer, who seemed to enjoy the performance, gleefully remarked, "Quite some fireworks!" Nor did he object when his Secretary ordered a government counselor to leave the room "On the double, quick!" But Hitler the charmer would have protested had he caught his boorish Secretary at his usual habit of telling the female telex operators to get a move on by kicking them in the rear. Everybody on Bormann's service had to be on call day and night. Out of the blue and unannounced, he would sometimes inspect his departments, expecting to find feverish activity. Yet it escaped his notice that in the complex setup, many a busybody comrade merely shuffled papers to avoid the draft. On the other hand, anyone caught smoking a cigarette on duty was promptly fired.

He did not spare himself. "Having to sit constantly at a desk gives me dreadful backaches," he complained in a letter to his wife. "And after a sixteen-hour work day, my ears buzz all night." And again: "Between the two of us, Müller [one of his aides] and I keep five secretaries busy day and night." Or: "Our life here is quite a rat race. Nobody else could stand it for any length of time." Gerda responded with childlike admiration. "I cannot imagine," she wrote, "how the Führer would manage without you." And elsewhere: "What would the Führer do without you? There is no one as selfless and completely familiar with everything as you are. As far as the others are concerned, it is just a matter of ambition and vanity, more or less." At times she begged him to take a vacation and get some rest at home. But he felt he was indispensable—and to a certain extent he was.

17

The Stick
for the Gauleiters

Each time the Gauleiters were called before their Führer, Martin Bormann
had his hour of triumph. He invited them, received them with tempered
friendliness or somberly, as the case might be. He assigned them their
quarters and briefed them about the program. Once they were assembled,
he welcomed them with a few, always identical remarks, announced in six
words the next speaker on the agenda ("Now we will hear Comrade X")
and finally, at the end of the conference, belted out the threefold *Sieg Heil!*
To him, the three and a half dozen Party potentates were his personal
troops, the executors of his power. But although he achieved a great many
things on his way to the top, the Gauleiters never became the devoted
followers he wished them to be. His Führer had told him often enough that
getting this gang of high-handed territorial rulers under control was one of
his most important duties. But it did not really bother Hitler that Bormann
never quite succeeded. It enabled him to bring home to Bormann the fact
that his authority was, after all, only secondhand and that it was he, Hitler,
whom the Gauleiters obeyed without a murmur.

But however faithfully Bormann copied his master's tactics, he was never
more than partly successful with the Gauleiters. With the tough old-timers,
the seasoned veterans of the 1920s pub brawls and streetfights, he lacked the
clout of seniority. The more intelligent ones were put off by his primitive
ways; the few decent ones, by his vicious intrigues. Whenever their Führer
addressed them, they were invariably under his spell, even up to the very
last months of the regime. Bormann, on the other hand, had not a trace of
personal magnetism. The regional administrations sometimes modified his
orders or simply failed to carry them out. As Augsburg's Gauleiter Wahl

commented: "For a long time I put a good face on it and tried to mitigate his orders, until one day I just cut loose and threw everything that had Bormann's name on it into the fire, unread." Needless to say, that was only in the late phase of the dictatorship when many ties between the center and the regional agencies inside the Party organization had been severed and reports of local disobedience no longer reached the head of the Party Chancellery.

But even in earlier years, Bormann had to put up with willfulness from the Gauleiters. His only recourse in such cases would have been an appeal to the Highest, but Hitler was not inclined to put his foot down every time Bormann ran into opposition. Besides, he regarded people who were unable to command respect as weak and incompetent.

This was another reason for Bormann not to get involved in overt conflicts with the Gauleiters, especially since they would always forget their individual jealousies and join forces whenever the independence of one of them was infringed upon. Furthermore, many of them were Reichsstatthalters (governors) as well, and since the beginning of the war, Commissars for the Reich's Defense, which endowed them with government authority they could always bring to bear on any claim Bormann might have in that sector. The situation changed only when Bormann's appointment as Secretary to the Führer gave him legitimate access to this area.

For a long time, therefore, he was obliged to treat them much more cautiously than the weak Reichsleiters or those ministers who were no longer heard at headquarters. As late as November 1943, when he was firmly in the saddle and riding high, he still avoided ordering them around. Always anxious to strengthen the Gauleiters' position, he constantly offered them new prerogatives—admittedly with the thought in the back of his mind that someday Hitler would appoint him the head of the Gauleiters and all this accumulated power would come to him. But that never happened. As Hitler had solemnly announced after Gregor Strasser's defection in December 1932, the Gauleiters "as deputies of the Movement's supreme leader" remained "solely responsible to him."

Along with the carrot, Bormann also used the stick to get the herd used to his authority. To the regional bureaucracies he added the position of Gaustabsleiter (regional chief of staff), a kind of office manager who supervised the various Amtsleiters as well as the Gauleiter himself and his deputy. Since these watchdogs were not, on the whole, very popular at their seats of office, they had only Bormann for support, and as a result, were devoted to him. He was even more effective in his efforts to get a hand in the appointments, transfers and nominations of Gauleiters and their deputies, having already worked in this particular field under Hess. Their personal files, which were kept in the Party Chancellery, gave him the information he needed.

Back in 1939, he and his aides had devised an elaborate game of strategy:

"shuffling the Gauleiters." Among proposals for "possible switches of personnel in the Ostmark," he devoted several pages to two German regional potentates who were particularly odious to him, Gauleiters Josef Wagner and Bernhard Rust. In the course of the next couple of years he managed to get them both out of the way. Another "list of eligible Party comrades," compiled in September 1939, consisted of suspended and currently unemployed Gauleiters and Party officials from regional and district agencies whom Bormann wished to promote. Among them were a few who had lost their jobs because of boozing—a popular pastime in Party circles—pub brawls or controversies with enemies of Bormann's. From this pool he gradually siphoned a number into the Party Chancellery, some for good, some with a view to sooner or later elevating them into positions in the provinces, where they might promote their own as well as their benefactor's welfare.

To the bitter end, the chess game with the Gauleiters remained a pastime Bormann indulged in with relish. Every few months he compiled yet another list of proposals, sometimes for a pressing reason, when for instance a death made a new appointment necessary.

The case of Gauleiter Josef Wagner beautifully illustrates the tactics he used. Wagner was one of the Party's old guard, a schoolteacher by profession, like so many of his colleagues. In his original bailiwick at Bochum in Westphalia, he had worked hard to win the miners and the deeply religious Catholic rural population over to the swastika. When the local Gauleiter in Silesia was fired after a scandal, Wagner was given the post in addition to his own. He was also Price Commissar, charged with introducing price controls to cover up the sneaking inflation brought about by forced armament production. All in all, he was a man toward whom Hitler had been well disposed for many years and whose abilities he valued highly.

In Bormann's mind, however, Josef Wagner had a serious flaw: he and his family were devout Catholics. What had gained Wagner the trust of the Westphalians and Silesians was a sacrilege to National Socialism in the eyes of the bigoted Reichsleiter. On December 5, 1939, after having urged Hitler several times to take at least one of the two regional administrations away from Wagner, Bormann was allowed to dictate a message from the Führer ordering the churchgoing Party comrade to resign himself to Bochum and relinquish the Gau Silesia, which meanwhile had been enlarged by conquered Polish territory. One half of divided Silesia was to become the domain of Wagner's deputy, whom Bormann praised for, among other things, having no religious ties whatever. The other half was given to Karl Hanke, hitherto State Secretary in the Ministry of Propaganda, who was dispatched to the farthest Prussian province because the handsome comrade had been attentive to his minister's wife at the time of Goebbels' affair with Lida Baarova.

Hitler obviously felt somewhat uneasy about this decision, and for the time being nothing was done about it. In mid-April, Bormann reminded his Führer that things were still as they had been. Furthermore, Wagner was digging in his heels and refused to return to Bochum unless his department, which had meanwhile been divided in two, was given back to him in its original form.

"The Führer declares," Bormann wrote in his journal, "Josef Wagner must restrict himself to South Westphalia." A week later he had aroused Hitler, whose nerves were on edge by preparations for the campaign in the West, to such anger against the obstinate Gauleiter that the entry in the journal could be stronger: "The Führer repeats that there can be no question of a Ruhr Gau; I am to ask Josef Wagner for an apology; if he fails to oblige, Wagner is to be removed from office." This massive threat probably brought forth the requested apology, because Wagner returned to Bochum. Bormann's first assault had misfired, but his opponent was beaten. In January 1941 Hitler officially decreed the partition of the Gau Silesia and appointed new Gauleiters in accordance with Bormann's proposal.

A few months later a Gestapo file offered Bormann the ammunition with which to blast Wagner from Bochum as well. Wagner's daughter Gerda had fallen in love with Klaus Weill of the Leibstandarte (SS Bodyguard Regiment Adolf Hitler). When the two young people wanted to get married, Gerda's parents refused to give their consent. Her suitor's reputation was not the best. Moreover, he had left the Church, which particularly upset Frau Wagner. No divine blessing could rest on such a marriage, she wrote to her daughter. If she chose to get married regardless, she would no longer consider her her child. This poison-pen letter, as Bormann called the document, made its way up the ranks inside the Leibstandarte and finally landed with SS Gruppenführer (Major General) Heinrich Müller, head of the Gestapo, who summoned Klaus Weill to Berlin for questioning, pumping him for other charges that might be pinned on enemy-of-the-state Wagner, who wore the Golden Party Badge and the insignia of Gauleitership. As it turned out, there was quite a lot which a conscientious local Party executive might have frowned upon even in the case of an ordinary citizen.

In the fall of 1941 Bormann was presented with the list of sins. Josef Wagner was blithely ignorant of the storm gathering above his head. Nor was he supposed to know; Hitler planned to release his pent-up wrath in a dramatic scene that would end any rebellious urges within the Party leadership. Bormann was delighted. In recent years Wagner had not only barred all antireligious measures in his own area but also criticized such policy among the Party leaders.

On the evening of November 8, 1941, the entire Party elite gathered as usual in Munich for the anniversary of the 1923 putsch. This time Hitler made his speech at the Löwenbräu beer hall, since the Bürgerbräu had not yet been restored after the attack two years before. Along with his usual abuse of the Allies, he wove into his speech a passage that belittled the opposition within Germany. Anyone who schemed to "disrupt our front" —regardless of what camp he came from—would be under observation. "You know my method. This is the probation period. But when the moment comes, I strike like lightning . . . and then there will be nothing to hide behind, not even religion." With these phrases Hitler may have been allowing himself a foretaste of the coup he had planned for the next day. Bormann certainly must have heard the threat with particular relish, since it forecast, in terms understandable only to him, his triumph in the drama about to unfold.

When the Reichsleiters and Gauleiters assembled the next afternoon in the Führerbau on the Königliche Platz in Munich and Hitler entered the hall with Bormann, the scene was set for what Gauleiter Wahl called Bormann's "carefully planned assault on Wagner." As he had done at the time of Hess's disappearance, Bormann read out a letter, the very "poison-pen letter" Frau Wagner had sent to her daughter. Then Hitler spoke briefly, announcing in a cutting voice that he would not stand for such intolerance in the Party. He asked Wagner to leave the hall and the premises instantly. The assaulted official firmly requested the floor to defend himself against the accusations, which infuriated Hitler even more. He repeated his command in even harsher, more threatening tones and announced that he had already expelled Wagner from the Party leadership. Wahl later reported that with the exception of Bormann and Himmler, the entire audience sat frozen with shock, no one daring—"more's the pity"—to come to their unfortunate colleague's defense. With great satisfaction Bormann noted in his journal: "The Führer dismissed Wagner from office; Deputy Gauleiter Paul Giesler becomes Gauleiter of South Westphalia."

While the meeting was still in progress, Supreme Party Judge Buch was ordered to prepare proceedings against Wagner. At the hearing he was charged with having remained in the Catholic Church despite the fact that its bishops had only recently taken a stand against the Nazi Party. Worse still, he had clearly joined the opposition by sending his children to convent school in Breslau, whereas their presence in the Hitler Youth had seldom been noticed. Judging by his wife's letter, he had not been able to enforce the Nazi *Weltanschauung* even in his own family, and his wife had genuflected to the Pope at a Vatican reception.

But Wagner defended himself ably by citing the doctrine of "positive Christianity" to which the Party had pledged itself in its original program, which had never been officially revised. He had known nothing of the letter, or of his wife's genuflection. Neither the presiding judge nor the six members of the jury, all of them Gauleiters, felt that Hitler's expulsion order was justified, and in February 1942 they reversed it. In a letter to Bormann, Himmler angrily observed that he had certainly been surprised at the verdict. But his annoyance was short-lived; Hitler refused to ratify the court's aquittal with his signature. Buch speculated that "the rat"—by which he meant his son-in-law—had prevented it.

On the same occasion, the head of the Party Chancellery was able to boot yet another intimate enemy. The proceedings against Wagner had revealed that the Gauleiter had leaked remarks made by top Party members at the Berghof, on the occasion of Hess's defection, to the former SA Chief of Staff Franz Pfeffer von Salomon, who until August 1930 had been Bormann's boss when he was administrator of the Relief Fund. After his discharge, which Bormann had engineered, Pfeffer was named "head of the Party's Department for Cultural Peace"—an honorary title and basically a sop to pacify and silence a man who knew too much and therefore could not be dropped right away. Later, however, the post was put under the jurisdiction of the Führer's Deputy and, consequently, under his chief of staff. Subject to constant pressure by Bormann, Pfeffer had finally resigned in October 1934. But he had not allowed himself to lose touch with the Nazi old guard, or, for that matter, with Hess. After Hess's flight to England, Bormann had added Pfeffer's name to the list of those to be arrested.

Since his release, Pfeffer had criticized Hitler's policy in letters to his old comrades in arms and protested against the injustice that had been done. Several of these letters had found their way to Bormann's desk. On December 10, 1941, he wrote in his journal: "On the Führer's behalf, I notify former SA Chief of Staff Franz Pfeffer, who was arrested in connection with the R.H. [Rudolf Hess] case, that Pfeffer has been expelled from the NSDAP; he had better stop writing letters or he'll be arrested again." (Sure enough: in the next big wave of arrests, after the attempt on Hitler's life on July 20, 1944, Pfeffer was again included. Bormann was not going to loosen his grip on his former sponsor ever again.)

Only six months later, in May 1942, death disposed of another of Bormann's opponents among the Gauleiters: Carl Röver, who had been in charge of the Gau Weser-Ems since 1929. Röver's stubborn opposition had annoyed Bormann as much as his constant speaking invitations to Rosenberg.

On the night of May 13, 1942, Röver announced that the next day he was planning to fly, first to Führer Headquarters and then to see Prime Minister Winston Churchill in order to make peace. Before this he wished to have a four-hour speech recorded. An SS medical authority, hurriedly called in, diagnosed progressive dementia paralytica, the late stage of syphilis which the patient had supposedly contracted in Africa, where he had been in business before World War I. The president of the Oldenburg provincial government, Röver's seat of office, and the Gauleiter's chief of staff spirited the sick man away to an isolated cabin.

Bormann ordered that the nature of the disease be kept secret. From Munich he dispatched two agents to Oldenburg who, on May 15, were able to report to him that Röver had died, officially from heart failure. Another of Bormann's favorites became Röver's successor—and that was all that mattered to him.

During the first half of 1942, Death seemed to have been added to Bormann's payroll. Heydrich, whom he had feared as a rival for Hitler's favor for a while and who, as head of the Security Service, knew too much about the head of the Party Chancellery, died after an attempt on his life early in June. Next on the bier, in mid-June, was Adolf Hühnlein, corps commandant of the NSKK (National Socialist Motor Corps). The former major was one of the old SA militants who had always remained hostile to Bormann. Bormann also held against him the fact that years before, he had been given the leadership of the NSKK, which Bormann had founded. A man with little support in the Party organization became Hühnlein's successor. To make clear who was boss right from the start, Bormann, according to his journal, "informed the leaders of the NSKK of the new corps leader's nomination" even before Hitler had announced the promotion to the new dignitary himself.

With Adolf Wagner, Gauleiter of Munich–Upper Bavaria, Bormann always appeared to be on friendly terms, but only because this tough old Party man, who shared not only Hitler's first name but also his dialect and tone of voice, always had access to the Führer. In fact, Bormann found it rather inconvenient to have this powerful figure at the head of so tradition-laden a Gau and at the seat of the national Party leadership. He can hardly have been inconsolable when in mid-June he was called to Traunstein, where Wagner had suffered a stroke. On arrival he found a very sick man whose speech had been impaired and who was hardly able to move. When a few days later, after a bedside visit, Hitler confirmed the patient's incapacity, Bormann was allowed to fill the important post. He chose Paul Giesler, whom he had only just enthroned at Bochum, enabling yet another of his pets to assume that office. To everyone's embarrassment, however, the invalid was unwilling to relinquish the power he had wielded for so long. Months later, Bormann still had to block government and Party agencies in Munich against orders from the not-quite-compos-mentis Wagner and to issue instructions that he "should abstain from taking any part in the management of his former office."

With the newly appointed Gauleiters, however, Bormann was the jovial superior officer. At a dinner party at his home in Pullach, he presented Wagner's successor Giesler to the Nazi publisher, Reichsleiter Max Amann, to the Reichsstatthalter of Bavaria, Reichsleiter Franz Xaver Ritter von Epp, and to the provincial president. A few days later he introduced him and the new corps commandant of the NSKK to Göring. He honored two newly nominated Gauleiters, Scheel (Salzburg) and Lauterbacher (South Hanover–Brunswick), who had replaced Rust, by inviting them to the Rastenburg headquarters and introducing them to Hitler. Let the stubborn old mules who never fully respected him die out. He would bring order and discipline, the full Party ethic, to the giant machinery of the NSDAP and its organizations with the help of the younger generation who had served their apprenticeship in the Party Chancellery, where they had learned strategy and management.

Hitler seemed to approve. In his late-night monologues at the Wolfsschanze, he praised Bormann for providing the Gauleiters with "the necessary instructions" and for training them uniformly. Always preferring many small potentates to a few big ones, Hitler even wanted the Gauleiters to have wealth of their own. He felt there was no danger that this would turn them into independent sovereigns, since they could be deposed at any time. He also agreed with Bormann when he pleaded that the Gauleiters be given more time for long-term operations. In actual practice, however, the head of the Party Chancellery wanted to have this principle apply only where his favorites were concerned. One man whom he could not stand and would have liked to sell down the river after he had been in office only a year was the Gauleiter and Reichsstatthalter of Vienna, Baldur von Schirach. He could never forget that in the early days at Weimar and later at Munich he had had to kowtow to him.

When, early in 1940, Schirach succeeded Gauleiter Bürckel in the Austrian capital, the sun that had been shining on him from the Berghof was already going into eclipse. All the same, he was still influential, and when late in September he waited for an interview at the Reich Chancellery, Bormann again spoke to him in the familiar *du*. On this occasion Schirach confessed that he had overextended himself financially. Bormann immediately offered to help. Just one word from him to Hitler, he said, and a gift of a quarter million or more would be approved.

Schirach thanked him but declined the offer. "Perhaps," he told the author, "I made it too obvious to him at the time that I would not let myself be bought by him. For from then on I noticed that he was working against me in the Party and with Hitler." That was not difficult. With his youthful arrogance, the Gauleiter of Vienna let the simple-minded, petty-bourgeois functionaries know that he considered them philistines. A patron of the Muses, he felt called upon to launch a new golden age for the indigenous Danube culture. This annoyed not only Hitler, who never forgave the Viennese for having failed to recognize his genius in painting and architecture, but also Göring, who was fiercely competitive and wanted to turn Berlin into the metropolis of the arts. When Schirach, with blatant self-assurance, finally tried to cast himself as the independent political leader of the younger generation and digressed from the Party line in all directions, he opened himself up to criticism from his many opponents time and time again.

Speer was a witness once when Bormann deprecated Gauleiter von Schirach during Hitler's tea session. Almost casually he told more or less typical tales from Vienna, which promptly triggered the usual snide remarks from

Hitler. Then Bormann would say how lucky it was that there was such an efficient Gauleiter in charge there who would eventually turn the Viennese into good Germans, deliberately laying it on so thick that Hitler had to disagree. "After about a year of this sort of thing," Speer relates, "Bormann had brought Hitler to the point of disliking Schirach and often feeling outright hostility toward him." In the Party, Bormann let it be known that Schirach was the ideal choice for Vienna, where everybody was always plotting against everybody else. This was the signal for other Party leaders to get even with Schirach for his past snubs and high-handed behavior. When in September 1942 he organized a European Youth Congress in Vienna, where, with much pomp and circumstance, he elevated himself to the role of sponsor of all the youth organizations in the occupied and allied countries, Ribbentrop prevented prominent politicians from attending and Goebbels would not let the German press report on it. Bormann busily spread the word that the Viennese were talking about "Baldur's children's party."

With almost inconceivable short-sightedness Schirach stumbled into situations that were bound to lose him the last vestiges of Hitler's favor. Early in 1943 he organized an exhibit in Vienna under the title "Young Art in the Third Reich." It displayed pictures that by Hitler's standards—the Third Reich's sole criterion—were bound to be labeled "degenerate art." Schirach was summoned to Obersalzberg. Hitler did not even offer him a chair, and Bormann opened a copy of the Hitler Youth magazine *Wille und Macht* (Will and Power) with an illustrated review of the show. Quietly and icily, according to Schirach's account, Hitler remarked, "A green dog! With this you are mobilizing all the cultural Bolsheviks against me. It is a call to opposition!" He ordered the show closed.

Nevertheless, Schirach and his wife were asked to Obersalzberg at a later date, this time as guests. Bormann sourly acknowledged their presence. Eva Braun received them coolly; relations between her and Henriette von Schirach, the daughter of Hitler's photographer Hoffmann, had always been tense because for a while the Hoffmanns had dreamed that Hitler might marry Henriette. But she obviously did not know the idol of her youth very well; during the fireside chat after dinner she indignantly related how she had seen Jewish women being driven through the streets of Amsterdam on their way to deportation. Hitler's loud, furious reaction was: "What are those Jewish females to you?" Soon afterward the Gauleiters received a telex from Bormann forbidding them to approach Hitler on behalf of Jews or to protect Jewish individuals.

On such occasions Hitler felt threatened in the very areas where he considered himself infallible—art and the Jewish question. It proved to him that Bormann's warnings had been justified: Schirach had become "Viennized." "I made a mistake in sending you to Vienna," he shouted at him. Goebbels, newly allied with Bormann, remarked in his diary that "the

Führer has nothing big in mind" for Schirach. "He would sooner or later like to shove him off into a diplomatic career . . ."

As a last straw, Schirach also refused to toe the radical antireligious line. He warned Vienna's Hitler Youth leadership not to snub the clergy. Viennese who had been drafted into military service received from the Gauleitung a book of religious pictures and texts, plus a poem with religious overtones written by Schirach. His adjutant later testified that Schirach had contemplated entering into conciliatory talks with Cardinal Theodor Innitzer, the primate of the Catholic Church in Austria. But an order from Bormann stopped him. And from the spring of 1943 on, the Party Chancellery's attacks on Schirach multiplied. He was accused of having grossly neglected Vienna's civil air defense and was investigated by an expert, who, however, gave him a good report. The Gauleitung was called a hotbed of rumors; "influential men from the Alps and Danube region" were "leaking information on planning to unauthorized personnel."

At the top of the Party Chancellery the Gauleiter chess game had long since been revived. In November 1943 Bormann wrote several memoranda on appointments. By the middle of the month he presented Hitler with plans to "reshuffle the Vienna Gauleitung." The Party chief of the Lower Danube area, Dr. Hugo Jury, whose offices were also in Vienna, was to be given the top post, at least provisionally, in addition to his own. But here Bormann did not win. Hitler was afraid that such extension of power would strengthen the capital's influence over the rest of Austria and someday result in a "Reichsgau Ostmark" that would include the whole country. Bormann wrote this—in longhand so as to prevent a secretary from knowing anything about it—to his top aides Klopfer and and Friedrichs, adding: "For these reasons, the Führer suggested that I think of a better solution. I [underlined twice] request your proposals soonest." He was in such a hurry to overthrow Schirach that only two weeks later he offered Hitler a new strategy: Why not send either the Gauleiter of Cologne or the Gauleiter of Weser-Ems to Vienna? He had trouble, however, proposing the right man for the gap that would thus be created, and there was always the question of what to do about Schirach in the future.

In the fall of 1944 Hitler was still hesitant to give in to his pressure to appoint a new man in Vienna, so Bormann sent two emissaries to Austria. One was his top aide Friedrichs, the other Heydrich's successor, Ernst Kaltenbrunner.

Afterward both delegates submitted separate memoranda stating what their employer expected them to say—namely, that Schirach was doing a terrible job. But even that did not win the condemnatory verdict from Hitler. For one thing, Hitler shrank from the publicity that would follow the dismissal of a man who as Reich Youth Leader was well known not only in Germany but abroad. For another, Schirach still had both the power of the Hitler Youth and an ally against Bormann, Artur Axmann, his next-in-succession in the youth organization. Sometimes their joint ventures were even successful. "In six consecutive cases," Himmler was told by one of his informants, Axmann and Schirach were able to prove that "Reichsleiter Bormann had wrongly informed Hitler and had caused the Führer to make decisions which, being based on such misinformation, they would consider invalid. Both intend," the report continues, "to call on Hitler in person in the near future and ask for reappointment elsewhere unless the situation is remedied." Needless to say, their action could not shake Bormann's position, but though he was longing to see overthrown the man who had known him as an insignificant functionary and had treated him condescendingly, he was obliged to put up with Schirach to the very end.

He did succeed in shortening the list of the old-guard Gauleiters by three more names. The first, Karl Weinrich, fell through his own incompetence. When his provincial capital of Kassel was bombed in October 1943, he happened to be out of town at a get-together of Party comrades. And there he stayed until the bombs stopped falling. Then, when he returned to the half-destroyed city, his first concern was safeguarding his own possessions instead of attending to the fires, other damage and many victims, which was his duty as Reich Defense Commissar of his province. Goebbels heard of the scandal in Kassel. He reported it to Bormann, who decided that Weinrich had to go. One of Bormann's protégés, whose name he suggested at every opportunity, became his successor. Even though Weinrich had ruled the Gau since 1929, he had remained such a nonentity in Bormann's mind that the Party Chancellery's personnel list had him down as "Weinreich." However, he had one virtue: he had always obediently carried out what he was ordered to do from above, so Bormann did not want to relegate him to poverty and disgrace; he was to be given a farm where he could retire and live a quiet life. Himmler's SS, which was in charge of "land settlement," was to procure the farm. However, Weinrich made demands— "unconscionable demands," as Himmler wrote to Bormann in a letter suggesting that "Herr Weinrich be drafted into the labor force together with his esteemed lady and his even more highly esteemed daughter." But Bormann had a soft spot for the harmless, fat ex-official. In his reply he explained that Weinrich was "discontented, like so many people who have nothing to do." Everything would turn into "blissful serenity . . . once Weinrich is settled on his farm, putting up curtains and such; he simply loves housework, you know."

Bormann did not have to move much more than a finger to get rid of Hinrich Lohse, Gauleiter of Schleswig-Holstein. Lohse, who was also Reich Commissar for Ostland, i.e., the conquered Baltic States and the Baltic region of the Soviet Union, had gradually managed to fall between all the available stools. He shipped back to the Reich whatever he could extract from the country, but it was never enough. He was always at odds with Himmler and his SS organization, with the Wehrmacht and even with his superior, Reich Minister Rosenberg, who had once regarded him as a member of his coterie. Worse still, Lohse, in an indignant letter, had protested against the mass murders of Jews by *Einsatzgruppen* detachments, asking whether this was not much worse than the Katyn Forest massacre. A simple farmer's son from Schleswig-Holstein who had always prided himself on having Hitler's special confidence, he was hopelessly entangled in the jungle of big politics. And then he had the misfortune to get sick at the most inconvenient time.

In mid-August 1944 there was, according to Hitler, only "a hole" where Army Group Center had been holding the eastern front. In the breakthrough of the Red Army, twenty-eight German divisions with a total of 350,000 soldiers were lost. Enemy advances had struck close to the East Prussian border. Ostland was in danger of being cut off. Lohse took advantage of a visit to the supreme commander of Army Group North to get a physical checkup by Wehrmacht doctors. They diagnosed a case of "stress" and recommended a few weeks of rest in a sanitarium; "however, there is no urgent need for treatment at this particular moment." Army physicians, after all, are never too anxious to send people on sick leave. Lohse thereupon consulted a civilian doctor and had himself committed to the internal-medicine department of the St. Elisabeth Hospital in Königsberg, where he was put to bed for an attack of phlebitis in his lower right leg, inflammation of the lymph vessels and a kidney infection. He reported this to Bormann in a handwritten note: "I arrived with an acute thrombosis just in time to prevent something worse." The attending physician certified—not quite as dramatically—that "immediate hospitalization" had been necessary, "or the case might have taken a serious turn."

Bormann suspected that Lohse had sensed acute danger in the military situation rather than in his state of health. Instead of get-well wishes he sent a telex ("Secret—Deliver in a Sealed, Double Envelope") from the nearby Wolfsschanze via the Königsberg Gauleitung, advising Lohse "in view of the current situation not to proceed to Ostland," but to return "to your Gau." This order passed through the wires at 5:10 A.M. on August 28, 1944. But after Hitler had held the morning briefings, Bormann obviously submitted the case again, at which time he succeeded in obtaining a tougher decision than that of the night before. In a second telex, at 4:50 P.M., he forbade Lohse to return to his seat of office in Kiel. "I shall advise the agencies concerned," he wrote, "that due to serious circulatory disorders you are unable to continue in office as Reich Commissar and Gauleiter until further notice."

A month later the third of the old guard was erased from Bormann's lists. Josef Bürckel, by Nazi standards one of the most deserving Party comrades, died. After the 1935 plebiscite he had been able to report to his Führer that the Saar had been returned to the Reich; after the invasion of Austria he had resided in Vienna as an "Anschluss specialist," and in 1940 he had returned home to his Gau to "align" Lorraine, which had just been conquered. On Hitler's orders, manipulated by Bormann, he had organized a housecleaning operation late in the fall of that year, pushing a hundred thousand "Frenchies" in a raidlike action across the border into unoccupied France. They were allowed to take only what they could carry. In Metz he occasionally governed from the prefectural palace, but by now the city had been recaptured by the Western Allies without the Gauleiter's having risked his life leading the defense, as Bormann had ordered as a matter of principle.

The official word was that Bürckel had died of pneumonia in his hometown of Neustadt. Rosenberg, who had been asked to give the eulogy, mentioned heart failure, which he said Bürckel had suffered after he became "violently agitated over Bormann's action" of assigning a deputy as a watchdog to supervise the Gauleiter. But even Rosenberg knew this only from hearsay. According to the latest historical research, Bürckel is supposed to have committed suicide after he was censored for his flight from Metz. Ex-Gauleiter Wahl also testified that Bürckel was driven to his death by Bormann.

The fact that he died unexpectedly and that nothing was known of an illness in Party circles is made clear by a letter Gerda Bormann wrote to her husband on September 29, 1944, the day the news of Bürckel's death was announced. "Is all this legitimate?" she asked. She suspected that Saar separatists might have killed Bürckel with bacteria. Her husband gave a monosyllabic answer to her question; he was in the habit of returning Gerda's letters to Obersalzberg with marginal comments. In this case he limited himself to putting a terse "yes!" after the question. He had already picked the successor—an aide from the Party Chancellery.

During the past two years at least, the Gauleiters had been given ample proof that they had reason to be afraid of Bormann. The rather insouciant Schirach had instructed his adjutant to read every one of Bormann's letters and then throw it away immediately. But he later confessed to the author: "When speaking to a leading Party comrade, you would still be very careful never to say anything negative about Bormann; you could risk it only with people who made no bones about where they stood and openly criticized him to others. There weren't too many of those. They spoke about the desk clerk, called him a bootlicker and often a pig. If cartoonists had drawn his picture, his shape, bulk, short legs, mug—it actually would have turned out to be a pig."

But when push came to shove in Hitler's ante-room, all the Gauleiters knuckled under because the head of the Party Chancellery ruled on not only their careers but also their life or death.

18

The Volkssturm

"Now the gentlemen would like to have their memos back. But I shall keep them in the safe for future reference." These words of the Führer's were grist to Bormann's mill; the keys to the safe were in his custody.

The "gentlemen" thus sneeringly referred to were the generals, and the remark was made in the months after the blitzkrieg in the West which, contrary to all the military's gloomy predictions, had ended in a victory unprecedented in European history. Bormann, the simple gunner of World War I, had never had much sympathy for the military caste, but he had been confident that at least the generals knew their business. Now the successes of the amateur strategist Hitler had disposed of that myth. What remained was the distrust the radical members of the Party had always felt toward the military. Had not the Reichswehr as late as 1930 discharged young officers simply because they had connections with the the NSDAP? Had not Chancellor-General Kurt von Schleicher at the very end tried to block the road to power with military weapons and by declaring a state of emergency?

In their "Horst Wessel Song" they sang not only of the comrades whom the Red Front had shot but also of those done in by the reactionaries, the social class to which the predominantly monarchist army officers belonged. Like so many of the Party's old guard, Bormann was convinced that the upper ranks of the Wehrmacht harbored many a pocket of reactionary elements which the National Socialist revolution had not touched.

Of course, these people were hard to get at as long as they were in uniform. Their esprit de corps protected them. There was no way of making them pledge their allegiance by joining the Party, since soldiers were barred from Party membership. Party functionaries and unit leaders who served in the Wehrmacht had complained often enough that their allegiance to the Movement prevented their promotion. At headquarters, Bormann was surrounded by officers and generals; most of them, like Heinz Guderian, for example, and Franz Halder, hardly took notice of him or openly showed their dislike. Others fell in by necessity, like Hitler's military adjutants, who saw him day and night. Only a few—the sycophants and the buddy types —now and then drank a bottle of schnaps with him. To the rest he remained the Party functionary, the civilian in disguise, who had no business in their area of responsibilities regardless of his Obergruppenführer's uniform with the SS-general's insignia.

It seemed to him all the more important, therefore, that he and the Party —which to him were identical—should be given a say in Wehrmacht affairs. As usual, he avoided a direct confrontation, starting out with minor advances on the periphery and attacking the enemy wherever justice and morality seemed to be on his side. Thus he made a modest but regular protest to the leading Wehrmacht authorities whenever it was reported to him that agnostic soldiers had been ordered to attend church services or had been assigned KP or cleaning duties on Sunday morning as a punishment for the ungodly. He would have liked to abolish the military chaplains but gave up after a few feeble attempts, for no matter how little Hitler thought of the Christian religion, he still clung to an institution that might alleviate the soldiers' fear of death on the battlefield.

Bormann demanded that the High Command of the Wehrmacht consult the Party whenever the political status of Wehrmacht members was to be evaluated. He instructed his aide-in-charge to work out details with the head of the Wehrmacht Personnel Office "on the problems of the Party's participation in the promotion of Wehrmacht personnel." He temporarily restricted himself to sending just one aide to reconnoiter the situation, and he did not openly reveal what he had in mind, but his goal was already evident. As it did in the case of high-ranking government officials, the Party was to decide on the careers of army officers.

Needless to say, Bormann knew that it was still too early for his Führer to comply with this request, but at least he went on record as saying that, like Hitler, he regarded many of the opinions held by the officers' corps as reactionary and outdated. In mid-May 1942 the two became indignant over a minor scandal in the navy: a career officer had asked permission to get married, but when the moralists in blue found out that the bride was pregnant, they denied his request, stripped him of his career officer's status and shifted him to another post. In their view, an officer's wife had better be a virgin when she got married, or at least appear to be. Bormann summed up Hitler's personal comments on the case to serve as basic guidelines in the future. The ten points condemned several "unwritten laws" of the officers' caste as "morally corrupt." The relish Bormann's petty-bourgeois mind took in being able to berate the arrogance of a feudal creed while having the "people's sound judgment" and the Führer's decision on his side can be felt throughout the text.

On the other hand, he had to put up with quite a few pinpricks from the military. It did not bother him that they would not admit him to their briefings, since he kept Hitler's copy of the stenographers' transcripts on file anyway. But he was furious when, in July 1942, he arrived at the Werewolf headquarters to find that his sleeping quarters did not have running water, to which all high-ranking officers were entitled, but just a pitcher and basin, both of which were brown to boot. The Wehrmacht detail in charge was ordered to install the missing convenience without delay.

Not unjustly, but without concrete evidence, Bormann suspected the Abwehr, the Wehrmacht's counterintelligence service, headed by Admiral Wilhelm Canaris, of being a hotbed of subversives. In his letters he occasionally referred to the admiral as "our special friend." There could not have been two more dissimilar characters than the civilized, sophisticated Canaris and the vulgar, unsophisticated Party Chancellery official. It therefore suited Bormann very nicely when, late in 1942, Gauleiter Ernst Wilhelm Bohle, who was in charge of the NSDAP's representatives abroad, complained to him that the Abwehr had recruited all the Party functionaries in Switzerland as intelligence agents behind his back. If the Swiss counterintelligence organization made a fuss, this might lead to a ban on the Party in Switzerland and mess up diplomatic relations. Bormann protested to Keitel, somewhat hypocritically, since SD chief Walter Schellenberg, head of the SS espionage, was already waiting in the wings to take over the intelligence network. As the pseudofriendship between Bormann and Himmler was still in bloom at this time, the Party comrades in Switzerland found that only their employer's nameplate had changed, not their job.

But there were some generals whose attitude came up to Bormann's expectations. One of them was Eduard Dietl, the hero of Narvik, commander in chief of the forces in northern Norway. Whenever he had any news of him, Bormann immediately wrote to his wife, who had also taken Dietl to her heart. The general was sympathetic to the fact that in the cold regions thousands of miles away from home his soldiers needed the comforts of a warm bed at night. He had no objection to temporary fraternization with Norwegian girls, but he considered them unsuitable as marriage partners. The daughters of the country were by no means as blond and Aryan as the Nazi race theoreticians had believed the people of the Germanic sister nation would be. Nevertheless, quite a few of Dietl's soldiers put in applications to marry their wartime sweethearts. Since an overall ban would have challenged the theory of the Northern race's high quality, Dietl restricted himself to issuing a warning to his own troops: German women were racially superior to Norwegian women.

Bormann welcomed this decree all the more because the military commanders in the occupied Western countries had shown much greater indulgence in this matter. He sent Dietl's text to the Gauleiters, using it as propaganda within the local Party organizations to drum up public feeling against infiltration of foreign customs or undesirable blood. He recommended that functionaries should offer soldiers on leave social get-togethers, where the Frauenschaft (the Nazi women's organization) and the older age groups of the Bund Deutscher Mädel (the female Hitler Youth) would participate and represent the home-grown variety of superior femininity.

One of the generals considered a reliable Nazi early in 1943 was Walter von Unruh. In the total war effort now getting under way, he had been assigned the role of *Heldenklau* (hero snatcher). The title had been bestowed on him because he was combing the communications zone and the Wehrmacht units stationed at home to find able-bodied soldiers who could be transferred to front-line duty. From experience, however, Bormann did not trust the general. In 1935 Unruh had been one of the founders of a *Soldatenbund* (soldiers' league) and had tried to make it compulsory for all veterans to join. "SA, SS and other Party organizations in need of recruits," Unruh had announced to army officers at Würzburg, "must address themselves to the Soldatenbund."

Thanks to the forceful protests of Hess and Bormann, among others, these plans had come to nothing, but the general, now sixty-six, still believed that a soldier's creed was more important than the Nazi *Weltanschauung*. At this point the regime could have used his energy and rigor, but Bormann urged that the entire Wehrmacht at last be aligned to Nazi ideology. Reichsleiter Rosenberg, who was in charge of ideological indoctrination, had been thinking about this for some time. In the course of his drive to collect books for army libraries he had made a number of contacts, and his office had been approached now and then by army posts requesting speakers to preach the Nazi catechism.

In mid-May 1943 Rosenberg happened to be at the Wolfsschanze again, first with Hitler for the usual hassle with Koch and Bormann, and on the next day, with the Secretary to the Führer to discuss Party affairs. The two quickly agreed on the necessity for giving soldiers more Nazi ideas, and Bormann did not say a word when his visitor outlined how he was planning to go about it. Confirming the agreement, Rosenberg wrote a few days later: "We have always complained that National Socialism has not taken root in the Wehrmacht to the extent we had hoped for. Now the declaration of total war has opened up an opportunity for bringing Party and Wehrmacht to ideological unity."

But there were not enough preachers. Rosenberg's apostles were either on active duty or no longer young enough for long-term service in the armed forces, even if their fight was only to be conducted verbally. It was therefore decided to recruit for the project those men who "after having fought on active service and being loyal National Socialists" could be made "ideological supervisors." "We also agreed," Rosenberg confirmed, that these people "would be trained by my department and that their assignment to the Wehrmacht divisions would be subject to joint agreement between the Party Chancellery and myself."

It was fortunate that soon thereafter Hitler's former orderly, Hans Junge, now an SS officer on the eastern front, came to headquarters on a visit. He informed Hitler of the black-white-and-red-edged leaflets of the National-komitee Freies Deutschland (National Committee for a Free Germany), an anti-Fascist organization of German prisoners of war sponsored by the Russians and under the leadership of Stalingrad generals. Hitler felt that faith in the swastika needed to be bolstered in the face of this, the "worst danger threatening the eastern front at the present moment."

This gave Bormann a good start; he was able to assure the Führer that preparations for such action were already being made. Rosenberg, however, heard nothing from him for a number of weeks. When he grew restive, Bormann had him talk to Keitel and his department, and members of training groups Rosenberg had established, most of them professors, were given permission to lecture at officers' meetings. But since most generals considered the swastika only an insignificant and superficial part of their uniform, the talks progressed slowly. Finally, in mid-November 1943, the ideological expert was able to report "satisfactory progress" to the Führer. In fact, he said, the only thing pending and therefore subject to Hitler's decision was the official title to be given to the Nazi preachers in uniform. The choice was between "National Socialist Education Officer" and "Ideological Education Officer." With his typical know-it-all attitude, Hitler decided on a cross between the two proposals and came up with "National Socialist Ideology Officer." But that was not to be the final version either.

All this time Bormann had been kept posted on the negotiations in writing by Rosenberg. But he had not let on by a single word that at the same time he was building up an organization of his own. In a series of conferences and discussions he had already worked out a program and recruited a staff. And he had not even bothered to request the officers Rosenberg had proposed from their respective army units. He had got the cooperation of Goebbels and Himmler. Now all he had to do was find a trick by which to wipe out his rival's prior claims.

To begin with, he voiced misgivings to the Supreme Commander about the title "National Socialist Ideology Officer;" he claimed it did not cover the full range of duties, since this new type of soldier was not supposed simply to preach principles but also to rouse the troops with daily pep talks on current issues. Rosenberg, whose reputation as a dull speaker was a joke everywhere in the Party, could certainly not be trusted with such a job. The last time Rosenberg came for a briefing at headquarters, Bormann had been away on a trip. "After my return," he now wrote, "the Führer spoke to me, among other things, about the prospective title and the overall duties these officers ought to have. The Führer decided on this occasion that the final title should be 'Offizier der nat. soz. Führung' (abbr. NS-Führungsoffizier)."

Obstinate and small-minded, Rosenberg went for the bait hook, line and sinker. On November 26, 1943, he sent a "notice to the Führer," written in oversize type, to headquarters, arguing that these officers were meant to educate but not to lead in battle. In fact, in its present form the title could be conferred only by division commanders. In spite of his many years in Hitler's service, he still did not understand that the Führer was not basically interested in ideology but only in power and that the urgently desired indoctrination was needed only to make the soldiers go to their death more willingly.

Neddless to say, Rosenberg's "notice to the Führer" got stuck on Bormann's desk. After Rosenberg had been hopelessly defeated, Bormann asked him sarcastically "whether after all these explanations you still want me to submit your notice of November 26, 1943, to the Führer." There was no need for it now. But just in case, Bormann had a report handy which one of his Gaustabsleiters (regional chiefs of staff) had sent him, in which one of Rosenberg's functionaries was criticized for the "dry and irrelevant" lectures he had given at the Wartheland military academy. Besides that, the speaker had driven "wedges into the community" by "touching on religious problems and discussing . . . the racial inferiority of the population in certain regions of Germany."

A letter from Bormann on November 30, 1943, finally made Rosenberg realize that the whole operation had been snatched away from him. "For some time now," it said, "the Party Chancellery has concerned itself with this military rank, which was created and developed on its suggestion. *One part of its duties . . . is ideological education, another considerable part is practical political enlightenment . . . current issues.* In dealing with the Wehrmacht, the Party Chancellery will be the sole representative of *all* agencies of the NSDAP. Where would we be if, apart from you, Reich Minister Dr. Goebbels, Reichsleiter Dr. Ley and other Reichsleiters concerned, Reich ministers and leading political agencies were to enter jointly or, as is too often the case, competitively into negotiation with the Wehrmacht!" Toward the end of the five-page letter Rosenberg finally learned to what extent he had been defeated. Bormann wrote: "In agreement with the Oberkommando der Wehrmacht I have asked the Gauleiters to submit the necessary documents for the applications of suitable officers from the leadership of the movement. The incoming applications will subsequently be put at the Wehrmacht's disposal."

Since Rosenberg still refused to give up, a few more angry letters were exchanged in which Bormann concealed how craftily he had planned his game. In mid-October 1943 he had introduced his plan and his crew to a select assembly of generals at the Wolfsschanze, and he had already found the man in the Wehrmacht whose general's uniform was to lend authority to the project: Hermann Reinecke, chief of the Allgemeines Wehrmachtsamt (Armed Forces General Office), who toed the Party line so faithfully that the People's Court appointed him a member of the jury. On December 22, 1943, Bormann's new position of power was confirmed by an order from the Führer authorizing the formation of an "NS Führungsstab" (National Socialist Operations Staff) within the Oberkommando der Wehrmacht. Reinecke was appointed head of the NS Führungsstab, although for all intents and purposes the actual control went to the Party Chancellery.

Bormann had reassured the generals that he was not going to put Party orators in uniform but that he would choose officers who had shown special valor and whose National Socialist convictions were beyond reproach. He did not want apparatchiks and commissars like those in the Red Army. But the actual picture was quite different. By late spring of 1944 he had appointed NS propaganda officers to 201 army posts. Typically enough, over a hundred of these Party whips had left the Church. Many of them did not, as regulations prescribed, regard the Oberkommando der Wehrmacht as their supreme authority but sent their reports straight to the Party Chancellery. When Bormann tried to use this information to put the heat on the military, a massive tug of war erupted between him and General Guderian, who objected to having his officers spied upon and threatened to penalize the authors of the reports.

On the other hand, hardly any of the NS propaganda officers succeeded in playing the part Bormann had assigned them. Unlike the commissars in the French revolutionary army or the early Red Army, they were unable to intimidate the faint-hearted by sheer terror, and they were forbidden to criticize the generals. By the sixth year of the war, heroism and fighting spirit could no longer be drummed up by either threats or inflammatory speeches. The propaganda officers came into their own only in the last weeks before the regime's collapse when, with cocked pistols instead of arguments, they stopped the retreating soldiers of the exhausted regiments in the hinterland and drove them against the enemy—or had them hanged as deserters. Thus they finally carried out what Bormann had requested two years earlier in a letter circulated among the Gauleiters: "Any doubt about a German victory or the justice of our cause must be silenced immediately by massive action, true to the example of the *Kampfzeit.*"

As the situation deteriorated, the words "radical" and "brutal" became Bormann's leitmotifs. Since the courts of the Wehrmacht were not forthcoming enough on capital punishment, he was going to turn all political charges against soldiers over to Reich Minister of Justice Otto Thierack. If Admiral Dönitz had not protested to Hitler, he would have succeeded in doing this in the summer of 1943.

As it was, he had to contain himself for another year: the People's Court was given jurisdiction over the military only after the attempt on Hitler's life on July 20, 1944. Radical and brutal was Bormann's idea of what all Germans should be, including those back home in a country that was being more and more devastated by air attacks. Since the Luftwaffe was no longer able to fend off the raids, Bormann, Goebbels and Himmler, with the rage of the powerless, decided to answer "the terror from the air" with another kind of terror. The idea was to create an outlet for public exasperation and at the same time weaken the attackers' morale.

In April 1944 Ernst Kaltenbrunner announced that "in certain cases," shot-down enemy pilots could be killed when captured and that the police should not be permitted to protect their prisoners when an understandably outraged public resorted to lynching. Goebbels promptly seconded the move in an editorial published in the press and broadcast over the radio. But except in a few cases, the desired public outrage failed to emerge. To remedy the situation, the Party adopted a formula that had already proved successful in the Jewish programs. Late in May 1944 Bormann issued a memorandum, stamped "Secret," which even the district leaders were to receive. Its very title, "Justice Exercised by the People against Anglo-American Murderers" revealed its purpose. (See the Appendix, page 411.) Referring repeatedly to women and children who had been strafed by low-flying planes, it drummed up hatred and then pointed out that bomber crews who had parachuted or made emergency landings had been lynched "by the outraged public" without punishment to "the citizens involved." The district leaders were, however, allowed to relay this instigation to murder to the local branch leaders by word of mouth only. Still, the desired effect failed to materialize; many functionaries recognized the instruction as an invitation to crime, and a number of Gauleiters forbade it to be passed on to the district leaders.

Bormann invaded the military sector from other angles as well. Since March he had been with Hitler at Obersalzberg, far away from the events of war. But since the Allied invasion in the West would no doubt take place in the summer, he set out to prepare the Party. On May 30 the Gauleiters received a *Geheime Reichssache* (Top Secret State Document) with instructions on "Party Action in Case of an Invasion"—a great many pages with very little concrete information but a lot of Party-line clichés and pep talk. It informed them that the Supreme Command did not exclude the possibility of an enemy advance on the borders of the Reich; according to Bormann's text, "it may therefore become necessary to enlist women for auxiliary services, such as trench digging and leveling among other things, in the immediately affected areas." A week later enemy forces landed on the Atlantic coast of France.

In mid-July, Hitler amended Bormann's orders with a decree "on collaboration between the Party and the Wehrmacht in an operational theater inside the Reich." In case enemy forces advanced into German territory, "the agencies of the NSDAP, their divisions and subdivisions" should carry on with their activities and report to the military commanders, who, in the event, would be given executive power. A "Gauleiter for the operational theater" would be in charge of Party action. The paragraph most important to Bormann stated that he was to draft "the necessary instructions for the enforcement of this decree," which would then also apply to the military.

The reason why he was so persistent in pushing for these prerogatives is revealed in a letter he wrote to his wife on July 15, the first letter from the Wolfsschanze after a month's stay in the Bavarian Alps. Their return had been "absolutely necessary because, astonishingly enough, this war has made it increasingly evident that it is not the officers—the higher the rank, the more obvious—who are the fiercest champions of fighting and resistance, but the Führer and his Party men."

By now the generals were having a hard time believing in victory. Contrary to Himmler's boastful predictions, the Allied invasion had not collapsed within the first eight hours. In fierce battles, American and British forces were steadily broadening their base in France; in the East, Soviet advance units had reached the East Prussian border. On July 18 Bormann wrote to his wife: "At the moment everything is at sixes and sevens. If the Russians break through with tanks and enough armored personnel carriers, etc.—which at the moment may not be too difficult—there are no effective weapons to stop them farther on, behind our thin front line." The Führer's nerves, he reported, were understandably very tense.

Things were also going badly behind the front line, in the communications zones and at home. In May, Bormann had sent the Gauleiters a sixteen-page report on the deplorable condition of the "internal front," warning them to take drastic action and to insist on flawless conduct inside the Party leadership. Black marketeers and profiteers were undermining the people's morale and the soldiers' fighting spirit and stamina. Defense projects were sabotaged by large-scale corruption; huge quantities of raw materials, foodstuffs, luxury items and other commodities were being traded on the black market. In the occupied countries, army officers were heavily involved in such deals. In the military subdistricts, corrupt officers were protecting draft dodgers from active service. "We must create strong defenses," Bormann warned, since it was a matter of "not just winning the present war but also the future peace."

What happened at 12:24 P.M. on July 20, 1944, during the military briefing at the Wolfsschanze, finally confirmed to Bormann that the officers' caste had to be decimated and rendered powerless. There is no need to describe here the assassination attempt, in the course of which a bomb Colonel Claus Schenk Count von Stauffenberg had smuggled into the shack exploded next to Hitler under the thick oak top of the map table. Bormann was not in the room; he heard the explosion at his desk. When he arrived, Hitler, bleeding and with torn clothes, was being led to the Führer bunker, supported by Keitel. Soon thereafter he learned from the doctors Morell and Hasselbach that the Führer had suffered only superficial, minor wounds.

A half-hour later, Hitler and Bormann were walking along the fence of the safety zone. The agents of the Security Service had not yet discovered how the attempt had been made. It was Bormann who found the clue. A sergeant of the signal corps told him that a severely disabled colonel had left the shack just prior to the explosion. This struck Bormann as suspicious, and he immediately took the witness to see Hitler, disregarding the Wehrmacht officers present, who loudly protested the monstrous insinuation brought against one of their peers.

Thus Stauffenberg, who was now on the plane headed for Berlin, became a suspect.

By 4 P.M. it became evident at headquarters that a far-reaching conspiracy was behind the attempt, that in Berlin the code word "Valkyrie," issued from the office of General Friedrich Fromm, commander of the Replacement Army, had alerted his units to internal riots, and that the military subdistricts had been ordered to obey a new Supreme Commander of the Armed Forces, Field Marshal Erwin von Witzleben. Himmler was the first of the Party crew to profit from the defamation of the army generals: he replaced Fromm, on whose staff Stauffenberg had been. The man with the pince-nez was suddenly the commander in chief of a colossal power machine: as Minister of the Interior he ruled over the entire police force; as Reichsführer, over the units of the Allgemeine [General] SS, its special units at home and in the conquered countries; the concentration camp guards; the divisions of the Waffen SS, nominally at least; and now over all the units of the armed forces stationed inside the Reich and in the Protectorate (Nazi-occupied Bohemia and Moravia). Together with his police chief Kaltenbrunner, Himmler boarded the plane to put down the revolt in Berlin.

He did not head straight for the center of the plot, which was Fromm's seat of office in the former War Ministry at Bendlerstrasse, but first took his bearings—as he put it—by observing the enemy from the periphery. At 6 P.M. the conspirators were still able to send telex messages to all military district posts, ordering them to arrest at once all Reichsstatthalters, Gauleiters, ministers and chiefs of police, and to occupy all communication centers. But except for a few cases, this never came about. Half an hour later all radio programs were interrupted and the public was informed by special announcement that Hitler had survived an attempt on his life almost unharmed. This disposed of one of the basic objectives of the plot. Nor did the rebels succeed in occupying Berlin's government sector.

While most communications at the Wolfsschanze were temporarily disrupted—the head of the army signal corps was a member of the conspiracy—Bormann's telex network remained intact. But he did not use it until evening. For two hours after the radio announcement the functionaries in the Gauleiters' offices and in the Reichsleitung in Munich waited in vain for information and instructions. It seems that in the heat of events he temporarily lost his nerve, which would account for the tenor and content of the series of telexes he rushed out to the Party organization after 9:30

P.M. He dictated them straight into the telex machine to his trusted secretary, Else Krüger, who, infected by his nervousness, not only made a lot of typographical errors but left out words and jumbled names.

The first two telexes, sent five minutes apart, could only have caused confusion. The Gauleiters were first warned of the attempted plot and then instructed "immediately to act according to what the situation demands," while "observing extreme caution" at the same time. What they were to do, or not do, in the provinces, Bormann obviously had only a vague idea of himself. They were advised that "only the orders of the Führer Adolf Hitler or his men . . . are valid," and "not the orders of renegade, reactionary generals." Jointly with the local police chiefs, the Gauleiters were "to arrest immediately all persons conspiring with the reactionary criminals: Fromm, Hübner, Witzleben, Baron von Stauffenberg" and "under all circumstances to keep . . . your region firmly under control."

A third telex, dispatched at 9:30 P.M., showed no clearer thinking. It reported that General Olbrich (instead of Olbricht) was also part of the conspiracy, established a totally absurd connection between the "clique of generals" and the Nationalkomitee Freies Deutschland in Moscow and assured everyone twice in nineteen lines that the Führer's survival was also the survival of Germany. Twenty minutes later another message in Bormann's usual swashbuckling style indicated that he was at last back to normal. "A certain General Beck has had the audacity to try to take over the government. General [an error in dictation], former Field Marshal von Witzleben is posing as the Führer's successor. It goes without saying that National Socialist Gauleiters will not be deceived by or take orders from these criminals, who are actually very small potatoes. Heil Hitler. M. Bormann."

By this time the coup had collapsed. Long after midnight Bormann realized that he owed his Party comrades a summary of the events. At 3 A.M., on what was now July 21, twenty-nine lines went through the telex machines. They contained little more information than Hitler's speech, which had meanwhile been broadcast over all radio stations. But they were marked "Secret." The Party elite was being reassured; Himmler had the Replacement Army "firmly in hand" and "a steady flow of pledges of allegiance is pouring in" from all army units. At 11:35 that morning Bormann was obliged to modify his first orders. On Himmler's advice, he notified the Gauleiters via telex "to refrain from any further action against officers whose attitude suggests or even proves they should be classified as enemies . . . and to forward all documents of cases which in your opinion should be investigated." Himmler wanted to be the only one to present the booty from his raid.

In listing the conspirators, the telex messages, unlike all the official news reports, mentioned General Fromm several times and always first. In fact, Fromm was not involved in the coup at all; he got word of the attempt only that afternoon, in the course of a telephone conversation with Keitel, when he asked, apparently innocently and with concern, whether his aide Stauffenberg was among the victims. When the conspirators asked him to join the revolt he refused, whereupon he was confined to his quarters "on his word of honor." After the action had failed, he resumed his duties and had five leading resistance officers shot by a firing squad in the courtyard of his office building. Although he seemed not to be incriminated in any way, he was arrested on Hitler's special order on July 21. The People's Court sentenced him to death in March of the following year—not for high treason but for cowardice; he should have taken up arms against the conspirators.

How did Fromm get onto Bormann's list of conspirators the evening after the attempt? Hitler's naval adjutant had noticed earlier that the Reichsleiter distrusted Fromm particularly, maintaining that he knew him from way back. Admiral Karl Jesko von Puttkamer, Dönitz' deputy at headquarters, remembered that the acquaintance went back to World War I when Fromm was attached to the 55th Field Artillery Regiment stationed at Naumburg/Saale, where Bormann was permitted to extend his abnormally long basic training to the end of the war, working as an orderly for an officer who obviously rewarded his zeal and devotion by saving them both from being transferred to active service at the front. For months Bormann shined his boots and was said to have been deeply troubled by the class distinction between officers and enlisted men, which was still very marked in the Imperial Army. Some of his friends even suggested that during this period he developed a "boot complex"; he later owned some three dozen pairs of boots—brown ones, to go with his Party uniform, black ones for his SS uniform—and they always had to be shined to a high gloss.

Perhaps this explains why he had an aversion to General Fromm. The upstart never liked to be reminded of the days when he had been a nobody, and he hated people who at one time had made him feel small and humble —like SA leaders Pfeffer von Salomon and Röhm, like Rudolf Hess after his flight to England and, as we will see, like Hermann Göring. Driven by resentment, he finally succeeded in persuading Hitler to have Fromm arrested, an act from which Bormann also profited in the Party sector. Now, he observed to Hitler, all the forces of the NSDAP must be consolidated and put into action. As a result, he obtained his leader's signature on a decree that empowered him to bring all the Party organizations "into the total war effort," to "shut down Party agencies and areas of responsibility completely or partially . . . and shift the personnel thus made eligible to other areas of strategic importance." With this power he became the master of the entire Party organization down to the smallest Blockleiter (block warden) and of all its parts like the SA, SS, NSKK and associate organizations. He could close down the office of any functionary who opposed him and send him on active duty to the front.

During the hectic night of July 20, 1944, Bormann got only ninety minutes of sleep. He was therefore too tired to tell the whole story in a letter, he wrote to his wife, but he would make up for it when he came to Obersalzberg sometime soon. Meanwhile he sent her carbon copies of his telex messages to give her an idea of what he had accomplished. Her answer brought him the praise he had hoped for. "You are working too hard," she warned him, "much harder than others." He had no time to spare himself now, he replied. "The assassins of July 20 must be tracked down."

But he was obliged to withdraw some of the sweeping insinuations he had made during his moments of fear and rage. The revolt had to appear to be the work of a tiny, ineffectual group, which was despised by the people. In a telex message, sent at 4 A.M. on July 24, he warned the Party executives that no one should get carried away and "attack or offend the army officers' corps, the generals, the aristocracy or Wehrmacht units as a whole." After all, the army had not carried out "the conspirators' orders to arrest the Gauleiters or Kreisleiters." And he offered another piece of good news: the Führer had made it clear that the executive power in the Gaus "is not to be transferred to the Wehrmacht or to individual generals but in times of crisis must . . . remain more firmly than ever in the hands of the Gauleiters." To the man who ruled over all the functionaries, this assurance was particularly important. Another telex he distributed the next day forbade the Gauleiters to take "any individual action against suspects," in order not to interfere with the investigations of the Reichssicherheitshauptamt and to prevent people from being tipped off in advance.

On July 26 Bormann had to resign himself to the fact that the Reich Minister of Propaganda, who as a result of the Berlin putsch again enjoyed Hitler's high regard, was appointed Minister Plenipotentiary for the Total War Effort, which gave him control over virtually the entire government apparatus. But the bureaucratic way in which the nomination was made indicated that the title promised more than it actually held. First of all, an order from the Führer instructed Göring as chairman of the Reich Council for National Defense to "align every area of public life to the needs of the total war effort." But the very next sentence requested him to propose for the "execution of these duties" a Minister Plenipotentiary for the Total War Effort—namely Goebbels, who was given office by a second order from Hitler. Bormann also played a part in this game of confusing prerogatives: not only did the first order establish that the head of the Party Chancellery "due to the powers conferred on him" could not be touched by orders from Goebbels where Party affairs were concerned; it was signed by Bormann together with Hitler and the inevitable Lammers, who had to be present at all governmental endorsements. Bormann sent copies of both decrees to his underlings. To make sure they did not underestimate the part he had played in this development, he promised them that he would hold a conference in a week's time "to explain the necessary measures." And early in August he summoned them to Posen and to the Wolfsschanze.

Another memorandum, also dated July 26, indicated that he still was the functionaries' guiding star. Stamped *"Geheime Reichssache,"* he sent each Reichsleiter, Gauleiter and unit leader a numbered copy of his "first report on the background of the attempt." Compared to the earlier telex messages, the text was relatively free of abuse, moderate in tone and factually accurate, even though it constantly referred to a "clique of conspirators." The choice of words suggests that Bormann did not write the report himself or at least that he availed himself of the help of a more skillful stylist. Nine conspirators were mentioned by name and even military rank. Five of the names were marked with a cross; these men were already dead. In four cases a (v) signified that they had been arrested *(verhaftet)*. General Fromm was not on the list.

In a memorandum he circulated on August 12, Bormann scoured the scene for further "traitors, defeatists and other tools of the enemy." The German people had a right to demand that they be "ruthlessly wiped out." In order to apprehend everyone involved in the plot, "all suspects or contacts must immediately be reported to me." Beyond that, he must have information on all persons who in the past or at present" had given anyone reason to doubt their National Socialist beliefs or ideological convictions." It was the signal for the great witch hunt. Bormann himself was on the lookout too. When Franz von Papen, the former Vice Chancellor who was then ambassador in Ankara, was called to headquarters, he met Bormann in Berlin at the Stettin Railroad Station. Papen took Bormann's cynical smile for an unspoken threat: "You too are up for the big purge."

Bormann kept an eye on everyone who was being hunted down. Kaltenbrunner reported to him regularly on the results of the Gestapo's interrogations. His aides from the Party Chancellery were sent to attend the hearings of the People's Court. He was also being informed by Reich Minister of Justice Thierack, who reported that the presiding judge of the People's Court, Roland Freisler, had shouted down the defendants. "This created a very bad impression," he felt, "particularly in view of the fact that the president [of the court] had permitted about 300 people to attend the hearings. Such procedures" were dubious, to say the least. Nevertheless, Goebbels wanted to have the documentary film, *Traitors before the People's Court,* which had been shot during the hearings, made available to the Gauleiters. Bormann objected and prevailed on the ground that this would enable a larger audience to watch the hearings, which might lead to "disagreeable discussions on how they had been conducted."

"Our investigations concerning July 20 are still far from being complete," he wrote to Gerda in October. The enemy had gone underground, and more bitter disappointments were to be expected. "In the future they will arrive not just with briefcases but with grenades and poison." To him, the revolt of the officers was a standing issue. The Führer's adjutant Günsche knew why. "In some quarters," he said after the war, "people were anxious to drag these things out in the open, especially the political leaders who wanted to blow all this up in a big way."

When Field Marshal Günther von Kluge, commander of the armed forces in the West, came under suspicion in August, Bormann joined in the witch hunt. By a bold fabrication he tried to prove that Kluge had steadily kept the conspiracy alive. He explained in a memorandum to his three top aides why Kluge was being relieved of his post. "According to present testimony," he must have been in on the plans of the various conspirators and failed to report them. Moreover, he was suspect as a "long-time commander of Army Group Center (Russia)," almost two dozen of whose generals had joined the Nationalkomitee Freies Deutschland in Moscow when the army group collapsed in June and July.

What Bormann presented in his August memorandum as likely, he communicated as a fact to Gauleiter Joachim Eggeling at Halle a month later. "There actually are connections between the collapse of Army Group Center and the events of July 20, 1944." The traitors had gathered there under Kluge's command, according to Bormann. "Tresckow, the Chief of Staff, is one of the main conspirators. His defeatist attitudes influenced a lot of generals." Eggeling had asked how the conspiracy could have remained undiscovered. Bormann replied that the officers' incredible sense of comradeship had been responsible, and "no one could have imagined the amount of intrigue and treachery that went on." As a result, there was no longer any "social contact" between the officers of the Army High Command and the Führer's trusted followers. The latter simply didn't have the time, for everybody was working "from early morning until late at night to attend conscientiously to their duties."

Such confidential information was not meant for public consumption. The lower-ranking Party officials read quite a different story in the *Reichsverfügungsblatt,* the official newsletter of the Party Chancellery: "Generalizing from individual cases is not only contrary to already issued instructions but also casts doubts on the devotion and loyalty of hundreds of thousands of brave officers." Bormann's special pets, the NS propaganda officers, were fed the same line to give to the troops. Referring to the collapse of Army Group Center, their newsletter said: "The few, whether generals or enlisted men, who turned traitor and after succumbing to the enemy, are now collaborating with him, will be court-martialed. The conspirator's kin will be held responsible for his actions." Bormann adopted the last sentence from Himmler, who, early in August, had announced this monstrous verdict at the meeting of the Gauleiters in Posen.

Now he was faced with the bitter surprises he had predicted in the letter to his wife. "Just imagine," he wrote to her late in September, "the assassination attempt on the Führer and on the National Socialist leadership was planned as early as 1939." In a safe the Gestapo had found documents belonging to Canaris which incriminated more members of the resistance.

Gerda replied: "I hope nobody got away, who could then go on working in secret. Oh, Papi, it is inconceivable what would happen if you and Heinrich [Himmler] were not there to uncover these things. The Führer could never do everything by himself."

For weeks now Bormann had kept a watch on the house of Erwin Rommel at Herrlingen, near Ulm. Rommel, the most popular German field marshal, was recuperating from grave injuries incurred in an automobile accident during the invasion operations in France in mid-July. From the reports of Kaltenbrunner's investigation Bormann concluded that the legendary Desert Fox had apparently been part of the plot. When he submitted his report to Hitler, he obtained permission to have Rommel arrested; in a meeting, attended by Keitel, Himmler and Hitler's chief adjutant, General Wilhelm Burgdorf, and, of course, Bormann, they decided how to go about this inconspicuously. The field marshal was to be lured to Berlin on the pretext that he was to be given a new command. But on his doctor's orders, Rommel declined to make the trip and asked to have an authorized officer visit him. On October 14, 1944, Bormann sent Burgdorf and another general to Herrlingen. They offered the field marshal two alternatives: the People's Court and disgrace, or suicide with the right to a pension for his family and an appropriate burial with military honors. Rommel chose suicide, shot himself and was given a state funeral. His "treason" remained a secret. The official announcement said that he had died from his injuries. Thus the fact that the Wehrmacht had lost face at headquarters and that its areas of responsibility were now at the disposal of the Party elite was kept secret.

Late in July, Hitler had ordered the construction of a defense system to be built in the foothills of the Alps, reaching from the Swiss border to Venice, as protection against the enemy forces advancing from Italy. The Gauleiters of the Tyrol and Carinthia were to supervise the operation. Shortly thereafter the Gauleiters in the western provinces of the Reich received similar orders. Bormann explained to his chief aides in the Party Chancellery how he had snatched this assignment away from the Wehrmacht: "In view of Gauleiter Koch's achievements, the Führer has charged the Gauleiters instead of the OT [Organisation Todt] or the army engineers with the operations."

After the collapse of Army Group Center and the advance of Soviet units to the borders of his East Prussian Gau, Koch had forced the people in his area to dig trenches. Late in August, Bormann proudly wrote the Party functionaries: "The construction of field fortifications was given to the Gauleiters instead of the Reich Defense Commissars, i.e., to Party members and not to government officials."

They were actually the same people, but to Bormann the distinction was important because it made him head of all the trench diggers and shovelers, a builder of fortresses. "This involves an enormous amount of additional work for me. The Gauleiters must report to me daily on their progress in the construction of fortifications and on any complications. My secretaries have to cope as well; right now, three of them are typing away."

He did not spare himself or others, and the Gauleiters were pushed too. "The first reports from the provinces which came in last week show that the construction work does not come up to the Führer's expectations at all," he declared. "If the Gauleiters simply let the OT or the army engineers work for them, the Führer might as well have given them the job in the first place."

Not until September 1, 1944, i.e., long after the operations had started, did Hitler actually sign the documents that legalized the project. He obviously wanted to see results first. This explains the hectic pace at which Bormann pushed operations ahead, often creating intolerable conditions in the process. Many sites lacked dredges and graders, and where they existed, there was a shortage of fuel, which was already hard to come by for automobiles and aircraft. Hundreds of thousands of women, adolescents, members of the Labor Service and foreign slave labor were supposed to carry out massive excavation work with pickaxes and spades while they were fed meager rations and billeted in miserable lodgings. In the end, the fortifications were practically no use at all.

Hitler needed divisions even more urgently than he needed dugouts and trenches. Since late July, Himmler and Goebbels had drafted any men from industry who were even halfway able-bodied. They recruited "people's divisions" which to the seasoned troops at the front were more frightening than the enemy, since they represented an uncertain factor. If Bormann was to keep up with the competition in the final dash for the Führer's favors, he, too, needed to find soldiers. Never having any ideas of his own, he once again borrowed some.

When, in August, Russian forces were approaching East Prussia, General Walther Wenck, chief of operations on the General Staff, urged that all men be called to arms. General Guderian supported the plan, but Gauleiter Koch was even faster in picking it up and creating a personal force for himself, which he did not put under the command of the army but kept solely under his personal orders. Guderian suggested to Hitler that such a reserve should be organized in all border provinces and that the SA should take over the recruiting and training. With a reference to the Röhm affair and to the Gauleiters' unbroken loyalty, Bormann successfully stepped into these plans.

In 1937, when he addressed the Kreisleiters at Vogelsang Castle, Hitler had described a national guard as a "totally worthless crowd"; he had also condemned popular uprisings along the lines of the French Revolution because "drumming up enthusiasm" could never produce soldiers. But the Volkssturm was truly the bottom of the barrel.

On September 26, 1944, Bormann wrote to his wife: "Today, after some labor pains, the Führer consented to the Volkssturm order. I feel like a new mother, exhausted but happy." He could not quite exclude Himmler, the commander of the Replacement Army, from the project, but Himmler's accumulated duties would hardly allow for an extensive involvement. Ever suspicious, Hitler did not want to make the Reichsführer SS stronger than he already was. The Führer's decree, dated the day before, prescribed that "the Gauleiters should assume the recruiting and leadership in their provinces," while Himmler was to be responsible for "the military organization, training, armament and equipment." Bormann's name popped up only in the next-to-the last paragraph: he was to issue the rules for "political and organizational procedures."

But Bormann's first telex revealed that he did not regard his role as quite that modest. Three days before the "birth" of the decree, his people had already got together a working staff made up of representatives of the various organizations; and the Party leadership was requested to send all the material it had on "previous experiences in this area" to the Berlin office of the Party Chancellery. To his wife, Bormann spoke of "my" Volkssturm.

For him and for the Gauleiters, the question now was who would have power by the end of the war. The Führer? It was more evident to Bormann than to anyone else that his state of health was deteriorating. On September 28, after having had the shakes for some time, Hitler took to his bed with an attack of stomach cramps. The question of a deputy—if not of a successor—had to be taken into consideration. Irrevocably, the first candidate for the top government job was still Göring, who had, however, completely lost face with the German people. Goebbels had moved up far within the past year, but he had no following, either in the Party or with the ministers or the Wehrmacht. His extensive powers made Himmler a likely candidate, but to a small circle of insiders the man to watch was Bormann.

On October 18, 1944, the anniversary of the Battle of Leipzig, the army Bormann had built up with the help of the Gauleiters was officially initiated. But experienced soldiers found it pitiful. Its considerably more than a million men were impressive only in number. What had entered the ranks were the rejects of several siftings of male Germans between the ages of sixteen and sixty—the sick and the weak, the very old and the very young, most of them without any military training and, understandably enough, without either enthusiasm or any confidence that they of all people would be able to save Germany at the risk of their lives. By necessity it was a spare-time army; production was not allowed to drop, and the Volkssturm units were seldom able to meet in the evening because of the long hours. Sunday was the only day available for military training. Since there was a shortage of arms, basic training was conducted mostly with dummies. For emergencies, there were only captured rifles in most cases and very little ammunition to match. Clothing was so scarce that the Gauleiters sent their combatants off with air-raid victims' cards to buy textiles and boots in neighboring provinces, or they scoured the black market in northern Italy.

When the Reich Ministry of Economics complained to Lammers, and Lammers relayed the complaint to Bormann, the founder of the Volkssturm reacted rudely. "This army of idealists," he wrote, was the Party's concern and none of Lammers' business.

Bormann allowed the Wehrmacht to interfere least of all. At the Nuremberg Trials, Keitel testified that "Reichsleiter Bormann rejected all advice, collaboration and information . . . from military departments." Since the Volkssturm battalions could be sent into action only in the vicinity of their hometowns, the Wehrmacht was able to do without them most of the time. In emergencies the majority of the Volkssturm's older age groups would silently creep away. But the Hitler youths, brought up to be fanatics, all too often were cannon fodder. As a result, Bormann's letters to his wife no longer contained references to his army, which had been started with so much advance fanfare. Only a military amateur like Bormann, who did not see his first battle until shortly before his death, could expect that the Volkssturm would contribute anything to help turn the tide. But in the fall of 1944 he still firmly believed that it would. In a letter to Himmler late in October—still "dear Heinrich" in spite of growing rivalry—he berated him for his negligence as a co-sponsor of the Volkssturm. Himmler's aide, the devious Obergruppenführer Gottlob Berger, dealt "mainly with organizational affairs which are my responsibility, whereas no instructions on military training have been issued." If this did not happen soon, Bormann threatened, the Gauleiters would make "the necessary arrangements" with General Guderian, i.e., with the Wehrmacht, and "inevitably things will take a completely wrong turn." The dictatorial tone indicates that after his victory over the generals, the Secretary to the Führer also felt equal to the Reichsführer SS.

19

The Morality of the "Golden Pheasants"

The Reichsführer SS and the Secretary to the Führer were friends as long as appearances needed to be kept up; and either innocently or consciously, their wives played the game. The cordial relationship was actually based on the fact that Heinrich Himmler, though married, was sharing his life with a woman who did not share his name. Hedwig Potthast had been his secretary for some time, and she was the reason why he was separated from his wife. Her parents criticized her severely for the improper relationship, but the Reichsführer SS wished to avoid a divorce scandal.

Since Hedwig had a child by him—her son, Helge, was born in February 1942—he wanted to offer her at least a house. But typically, he, the master of vast business areas in the concentration camps, did not have the money to build one. So he knocked on the door of "dear Martin," from whom other members of the Nazi elite had obtained large sums of money before.

Himmler got 80,000 Reichsmarks not, like the generals and ministers, as an endowment, but as a loan, at—unless SD chief Schellenberg exaggerated—an outrageously high interest rate which the debtor, saddled with two families, found hard to carry in spite of his minister's income. "Häschen" (Bunny), as he called his sweetheart, got her little house in the Schneewinkel-Lehen near Berchtesgaden; and since Gerda sent several gifts from her collection of toys and baby clothes on the birth of Hedwig and Himmler's daughter, the two women began to visit each other. Bormann wrote that he thought it "very nice that you are in touch with Häschen, and Himmler is happy that the two of you get along so well."

Bormann, as we have mentioned, was not against extramarital pleasures, and his wife tolerated or even encouraged his escapades. Not that she was indifferent to his philandering, but she believed family harmony was better served by her putting up an amiable front. Aside from many fleeting acquaintances, there was an affair early in the war with an actress in Berlin. There was also a liaison "with that little Swedish girl who died later," as his wife reminded him in a letter in which she took exception only to the fact that at times her husband had slept with this companion in the very house she herself used to visit on occasion—moreover, one supervised by a "narrow-minded" housekeeper. But the climax was the affair (on his part) and friendship (on Gerda's part) with Manja Behrens, the actress at the Dresden State Theater and at the state-owned Tobis Film Production Company in Munich, where she had starred in movies like *Susanna im Bade* (Susanna Bathing) and *Stärker als Paragraphen* (More Powerful Than Paragraphs).

When she started her movie career in 1936, Manja Behrens was twenty-two years old. Since in those days the Party elite of Munich frequently cruised around the Tobis studios at Geiselgasteig, more or less genuinely looking for talent to sponsor, Manja Behrens and Martin Bormann might have met there even before the war. Later she may possibly have been a guest at the Bormann house in Pullach, where the Reichsleiter, like Hitler, would occasionally invite artists. Her permanent scene of action, however, was the national theater of her birthplace, and there she lived—as she does today. It is irrelevant how and when the initially casual contact between the Bormanns and Manja Behrens became closer, but toward the end of 1943 Gerda discovered that her friend Manja was really a terrific girl because she had convinced Martin, who had lately added another ten pounds to his already portly frame, that he needed to go on a diet. At this time, twenty-nine-year-old Manja—Gerda was five years older—had on several occasions stayed with the Reichsleiter's family at Pullach as well as at Obersalzberg, each time for a number of weeks.

In October 1943 Bormann visited her, probably in Dresden, and described what had happened—enthusiastically, proudly and without a trace of guilt—in a letter to his wife, written on New Year's Day 1944. Until that meeting, he said, he had found Manja merely attractive, but this time he had been immensely taken by her, he had roused her with his kisses, and she had become his mistress in spite of her reservations. "You know my will power," he bragged to Gerda; "in the long run M. just could not resist. Now she is mine, and that is why I feel so incredibly happily married." Admittedly, his mistress felt very bad about Gerda. "But that's nonsense, because it was I, after all, who simply had to have her." There was no need for Gerda to write him how she felt about it: he knew her well enough, didn't he?

"*Ach,* my sweet," he assured her, "you cannot imagine how happy I am with the two of you." How kindly fate had treated him: a wife with many children and a mistress to boot. "Now I must be doubly careful to look after my health and keep up my strength."

This remark, referring purely and simply to the biological side of a love affair, was not meant to be frivolous and perhaps not even funny. A coarse, beer-hall type, Bormann had little use for the poetic and romantic sentiments of love in song and story. Baldur von Schirach testified that at raucous parties with the functionaries, Bormann used to hand porno photographs around; these were so rare in the Nazi era that he could have got them only from his friends in the top echelon of the police department. By the same token, the jokes he told on such occasions were crudely off-color. Thus the rise of his sudden passion is easily explained, especially by looking at his appointment calendar. Since the end of June 1943 he had been at headquarters almost without interruption, always among men, and in September, Gerda had given birth to her tenth child, which meant that she had been very pregnant on his rare, brief visits. The way he raved in his letters after the birth about how slim and pretty she was again reveals how little she had attracted him at the time. The Secretary to the Führer simply craved a sex object when he saw Manja Behrens in October.

In the spring of 1944, when Martin spent months at Obersalzberg with Hitler, she stayed with the Bormanns for some time, playing her part. But after that, Bormann let the affair peter out. In midsummer of 1944 only the two women were keeping up the relationship, by letter and telephone. Through Gerda, Martin heard that Manja was complaining that he had not written to her in months. He passed in silence over her remark that she was looking forward to her next visit to Obersalzberg, and he never lifted a finger for her in September when, after all the theaters were closed as part of the total war effort, she was sent to work in an armament factory at a tedious ten-hour-a-day job on the assembly line. But he flared up in a fit of jealousy when she wanted to join the Wehrmacht Nachrichtenhelferinnen (women's auxiliary signal corps); many of those girls, he moralized, were nothing but "mattresses" for the home-front soldiers. In February 1945 he became even more indignant at Manja's brother for not being at the front but gallivanting around Prague on obscure intelligence missions with Manja's approval. "He and M. take it for granted," Bormann raged in a letter to his wife, "that others fight and risk their lives, even for them! Nope, Gerda baby, those aren't our kind of people."

The course the affair took is too revealing of Bormann's character to let it go unmentioned. Besides, strange as it may seem, the story also had a political aspect. It might serve as a typical example of how a person at the levers of power can evolve maxims for general application from personal situations: after the war, the Secretary to the Führer was going to make the *ménage à trois* he treated himself to on occasion, with the more or less voluntary approval of his wife, a duty or at least a moral obligation for as many German men as possible. The bloodletting at the front was bound to result in a shortage of men and a surplus of women, but for the further extension of its power the Greater Germanic Reich needed as many births as possible in the immediate future.

Perhaps it even was Gerda who gave her husband the final push for such planning. During the second half of January 1944 she wrote that the affair with Manja and her husband's twice-blessed happiness suggested that there should be a law after the war allowing every man worth his salt to have two wives. "The condition is, of course, that the two women tolerate each other; in most cases, that will be difficult. And Manja is so talented that in the long run she would not find her role of concubine satisfactory."

In her next letters Gerda Bormann continued to spin the thread and even designed an official form by which the spouses could sign an agreement to a "people's emergency marriage" as a threesome. Gerda felt that women like Manja were really too valuable—in a racial and biological sense, obviously—not to have children. Gerda suggested to Martin: "You can certainly be helpful to Manja, but you have to see to it that Manja has a child one year and I have one the next, so that you always have one woman around who's in good shape." The children, she felt, could all grow up together on the Bormann property at the Schluchsee in the Black Forest, looked after by the pregnant wife while the other attended to social and marital duties with their mutual husband in Berlin or at Obersalzberg.

Bormann reacted skeptically. Such a marriage arrangement could never work out, but he agreed in principle and as usual noted his reply in the margin of Gerda's letter. "The Führer contemplates something like it." Hitler, in fact, had pondered for a long time how to make up for the wartime loss of human lives, and Bormann had notes on this in his safe. At a late tea session, he therefore had no trouble at all bringing up the subject Gerda had suggested. On January 29, 1944, shortly after Gerda's initial observation, he drafted a "Note Re: Safeguarding the Future of the German People," which in ten typewritten pages summed up the latest Führer monologue and "earlier discussions and reflections."

In typical Nazi-German, inspired by Hitler's speeches, he wrote: "Our racial situation will be *disastrous* after this war . . . There can be no doubt that we will win the war militarily, but we will lose it racially unless we make drastic readjustments." And further on: "Now, it is a fact that women who find themselves without a man after this war cannot have children by the Holy Spirit but only by men who have survived." Consequently: "It is desirable that wherever possible, women who do not have or find a husband after the war enter into a marriagelike relationship which will produce as many children as possible." (See the Appendix, pages 406-410.)

For his own purposes, Bormann did not want the relationship to be quite as permanent as his human-breeding schedule pictured the three-way marriage to be; as usual, where the Nazi *Bonzo*cracy was concerned, there was a wide gap between theory and practice, between publicly proclaimed maxims and personal conduct. Unfortunately, this did not escape the notice of the general public. On the ground that scandals were bad for the morale of the German people, Bormann and Goebbels competed with each other in intra-Party warnings, urging the Nazi demigods to observe some discretion; under no condition must they attract attention by their extravagant life style.

But although in the past two years most Germans had moved closer together inside their houses, taking in the air-raid victims assigned to them as subtenants by the authorities, Bormann, who already had houses at Pullach and Obersalzberg, remodeled two more domiciles for his family— the villa at the Schluchsee and the country house in Mecklenburg. The Black Forest house, he advised his wife, should be stocked with "ample amounts" of potatoes, vegetables, fruit, juices and fuel coke from the Obersalzberg estate; bringing these roughly 250 miles, the trucks used up strictly rationed fuel. And during her stay at the "House on the Lake," his wife was given a car and driver for her personal use.

But his concern for his loved ones did not develop his understanding of the small transgressions of others. He fired one of his drivers over a few heads of lettuce the man had stolen from the hothouses at Obersalzberg. And he wanted Himmler to send a chambermaid to a concentration camp because she had been pilfering over a period of time. But Himmler decided it was enough if the thief spent a few days in the local jail at Berchtesgaden and was given a dozen lashes by "extra discreet men of the Security Service." Nor did Bormann wish to see the taboos of bourgeois morality that stood in the way of his breeding program abolished in his own house. He did not allow his eldest daughter to see a harmless enough movie with a love story, and he urged his wife, if he should die, not to live anywhere near army barracks, where young girls could easily end up with illegitimate children.

With obvious *Schadenfreude* he followed the marital drama of Reichsleiter Max Amann, whose wife, because of her husband's constant infidelities, had tried to drown herself in the Tegernsee but was saved in the nick of time by a Polish slave laborer. Apparently the thought never entered Bormann's head that he was saved from a similar scandal only by his wife's generosity. Indeed, the incident inspired him to circulate his instructions for a second time: "Re: Conduct of Wives and Relatives of Leading Party Members," which stated, among other things: "The longer the war lasts, the more important it is that leading Party members set an example for other comrades of fighting spirit, trust in victory and modesty in their personal conduct."

The instructions were published for the first time in February 1944. They should therefore have been observed by Bormann himself when, early in June, he arranged the wedding of Gretl Braun, the youngest sister of Hitler's mistress, and SS Gruppenführer (Major General) Hermann Fegelein at his house at Obersalzberg. During an earlier party Eva Braun had insisted on an elaborate wedding to make up for the fact that she herself would never have such a glamorous show. Committed to his austerity act, Hitler —with Bormann's assistance—chose an expensive tiara for the bride and invited the pair to a frugal lunch, but everything else was arranged by his all-purpose Secretary. The feast went on for several days, partly at the Bormann house, partly in the "aerie" at the Kehlstein, and local gossip had it that incredible amounts of costly delicacies, champagne and liqueurs from France were consumed. At some point Bormann addressed the arrogant, alcoholic Fegelein with the intimate *du*. Only Gerda ran into bad luck amid the boozy gaiety: this was the time when her husband found that his best dress shirt was still unwashed from the day before and penalized her by banishing her to Pullach for several days.

In spite of the wartime shortage in manpower and construction material, Bormann's building craze continued unchecked. He ordered two housing developments, Klaushöhe and Buchenhöhe, to be built on the most difficult terrain imaginable at Obersalzberg. By the standards of the time, the apartments were very comfortable and the rents ridiculously low, since the building costs were largely met by the government. But prospective tenants needed more than proof that they were employed at Obersalzberg. Members of a church had no chance at all; Party membership was obligatory, as was a favorable report from the local head of the Party Organization. Throughout the rugged, alpine winter the masonry work continued, and preheated concrete was poured. By 1943 air-raid shelters were given priority. An extensive system of tunnels and cubicles was constructed for Hitler and his immediate entourage, and a second, smaller one for the Bormann family and a few aides. The shelters were built deep into the mountainside, protected by 170 feet of solid rock, equipped with air conditioning, kitchens, a water supply, marble tiles, parquet floors and machine-gun positions by the entrances. The floor space of Bormann's subterranean home, including the offices for several aides, measured roughly 1,000 square feet.

Speer reports that Hitler had called a halt to the housing construction at Obersalzberg by March 1942, but Bormann paid no attention. While pretending that the air-raid shelters and other safety installations were only for the protection of the Führer's precious life, he went right on employing the crews of large construction companies on several building sites. When, in September 1944, Speer, the minister in charge of production and manpower, got on to his tricks and in the course of an inspection summoned the building engineers for questioning, Bormann indignantly wrote to his wife: "Instead of sticking to routine and coming directly to me, the architectural superman forces my people to report to him." But since material and workers could be obtained only through Speer, Bormann sent his Obersalzberg manager Helmut von Hummel to negotiate, and he, as Bormann noted with great satisfaction, eventually reached a favorable compromise. When "Our Lord of Obersalzberg" returned home in December 1944, the air-raid tunnels for Hitler, Göring and his own family were finished except for minor interior jobs.

The inappropriate extravagance of these projects and the costly adjustments of errors in planning aroused criticism in Party circles. But late in October 1944 Bormann lectured the critics in a memorandum saying that this part of his work was none of their business. "It is a gross misconception that the Obersalzberg administration is part of the Party Chancellery." It merely happened that he was head of the Chancellery and "at the same time in charge of all matters concerning Obersalzberg." The only connection between the two offices was that he held them both. "There is no legal or financial connection between the Obersalzberg administration and the financial administration of the NSDAP," even though for the "purpose of simplification" and "to make things easier for myself," Party employees were brought in to "handle certain projects." Enterprises like Obersalzberg's agricultural estate or the Hotel Platterhof were "managed strictly as private ventures."

With equal extravagance Bormann oversaw an area in eastern Mecklenburg known as "Agricultural Estate North," which he had acquired on the sly and which was operated practically unnoticed by the general public. By deed it was the property of the Obersalzberg administration, which, in turn, was in Bormann's name, but in the last instance belonged to the poor, unworldly head of state. The original seven country estates now formed an almost unbroken area of 10,000 hectares (roughly 25,000 acres)—equal to more than a hundred large farms—with farm buildings, stables, tenants' houses and baronial manors, including a castle, Schloss Stolpe, and its surrounding land.

Whenever Bormann and his aides were questioned about the purpose of this gigantic agricultural enterprise, they replied that it was there to "guarantee the Führer's food supply." But surely an area of such dimensions produced more than a vegetarian with chronic stomach ailments could consume even if he fed a retinue one hundred strong.

According to Bormann's plans, this area, located about sixty-five miles away from the capital, which was to be called Germania, would be the site of a "Sans Souci" for Hitler. The Reiherberge had been chosen for the Führer's future residence. But first of all Bormann had Schloss Stolpe renovated and the manor at Möllenbeck remodeled on a grand scale, the former for possible Führer visits, the latter for his own personal use. The administration and agricultural management were entrusted to "first-rate agricultural experts," he said in a letter to State Secretary and later Minister of Agriculture Herbert Backe.

The country estates also served Bormann as a secret hideaway whenever he wanted to slip out of Berlin with a female companion. But much more important to him, they allowed him to pose before Hitler as the super agronomist who could boast yields far above those of his predecessors. He constantly pressed Backe for larger allotments of chemical fertilizer, diesel fuel, machinery, vehicles and equipment. Occasional reminders that his enterprises were already favored with higher allocations than others he bluntly dismissed with the statement that the Agricultural Estate North "needed to be put in order and as quickly as possible; I simply cannot tolerate dawdling." In another letter he threatened Backe: "In order to avoid any kind of trouble, I suggest you increase our current contingent as requested." The neighboring landowners complained in vain about such favoritism. Backe did not dare refuse the powerful lord of the manor anything. But in his anger he turned to someone he considered to be a stronger force, his friend Heinrich Himmler.

"Dear Heinrich" would have liked to take the opportunity to turn against "dear Martin," but his investigators could not produce any evidence, since Bormann and his aides refused to give any information. A final remark by one of Himmler's staff members read: "All in all, I have concluded that things are handled here in a way that cannot be justified to the general public. The Party should set an example . . . particularly now in wartime, which it does not insofar as the furnishings and equipment of the Agricultural Estate's administration are concerned." On second thought the author of the report obviously found the matter a little too hot to handle, for in the last sentence he suggested that his observations "had better be destroyed."

One of the estate's agricultural supervisors later testified that productivity was only a small factor in the enterprise. Mecklenburg potatoes were first shipped to Obersalzberg, where they were stored before being sent to headquarters with the daily vegetable transports. Besides, all planning was directed toward the long-term goal of a "Sans Souci" for "Old Adolf," modeled after that of "Old Fritz."* Hitler never visited Schloss Stolpe. But just in case the castle should at some point become the Führer's country residence, Bormann had already chosen his own spot. Aware of the fact that a successor would have no use for him, he needed to prepare a place for himself close to his great protector. Even more than the manor of Möllenbeck, the neighboring estate of Krumbeck caught his eye. In letters to his wife he fantasized on several occasions that "when everything is over, the Führer might possibly give me Krumbeck or another estate in Mecklenburg as a bonus and ancestral manor."

In January 1945 Gerda Bormann was in Stolpe once again, obviously in order to collect some private possessions in view of the approaching front. In March, Hummel inspected the estates for the last time. Shortly before the Russians took it, Schloss Stolpe was burned down by an SS detachment on Bormann's orders.

*Popular name for Frederick the Great, King Frederick II of Prussia. He was one of Hitler's idols.—*Tr.*

Ever since the summer of 1943, Bormann had been plagued by fears that the war might injure his family. In his letters he constantly gave his wife new instructions—for instance, on how to behave during attacks of low-flying planes or even poison-gas alerts. At times Obersalzberg struck him as a particularly vulnerable bomb target, and he would send his family to the house at the Schluchsee. "The Black Forest will always be the safest region, no matter which turn the war takes." When a bombproof shelter for occasional Führer visits was completed at his Pullach house, his wife and children were moved there. But only a few days later, reports of the extensive fires and devastation the air raids had brought to Hamburg made him order his family back to Obersalzberg. Here on clear days and whenever enemy aircraft were reported approaching southern Germany, the whole alpine valley was camouflaged by artificial fog. In case of a threat from the air, two Mercedes limousines of the "Nürburg" luxury type had to stand by at all times to drive the Bormann family to the air-raid shelters still under construction.

In the summer of 1944, the Schluchsee again seemed to him the safer place. Gerda was told to arrange their trip discreetly, "or people will criticize the automobile ride again." But there was enough talk, nevertheless, for the Bormann children told their schoolmates at Berchtesgaden that they were going to the Black Forest, where the war would never come and from where, if need be, they could even fly to Japan with their father.

At the same time Bormann was anxiously trying to make the foothills of the Alps and the mountains themselves unattractive for air attacks. On the pretense that the Führer did not wish to have the scenic beauty marred by industry, he forbade the evacuation of businesses to the area. Reich Treasurer Schwarz was criticized for having allowed a section of the Bavarian Motor Works (BMW) to move into an empty Party building on the Starnberger See; the bombs had started falling there immediately afterward. Minister of Armaments Speer was forbidden to build workshops for aircraft manufacture behind a wall of rock near Salzburg. By May 1944 Bormann had closed the districts of Berchtesgaden, Reichenhall and Traunstein as well as the entire Gau Salzburg to any additional influx of government authorities and Party agencies; let them find shelter from air raids elsewhere. In February 1945 he renewed the order in even stricter terms. Now not even "the families of leading Party and government dignitaries were to to be housed there . . . if only because the area is particularly vulnerable to attacks from the air." This was pure hypocrisy, for until then there had been hardly any air raids in the vicinity, which was the main reason why he kept his own family at Obersalzberg. He chose a place on the Starnberger See for the Party Chancellery's "Confidential Records Office," where copies of all documents were stored. It was given the code word "Übersee" (Overseas), a name that later caused considerable confusion.

Thus, even in the sixth year of the war, the Bormann family lived in relative security and did not suffer any of the deprivations the average German had to endure. But to its head, the family continued to be a constant source of worry. In almost every letter he gave instructions on what they were to do or not to do, even going so far as to warn the children not to eat poppy seed because they might die from it. The large number of foreign construction workers at Obersalzberg made him fear that some men might invade his "women's quarters" at night; his wife was given a pistol and ordered to take shooting lessons.

In the fall of 1944 Gerda began to ail. On the whole she had always been in good health, so he worried, although initially it appeared to be nothing but a cold. "You better watch it," he told her. "You must stay in good shape so you can have many more children and live to be at least a hundred." Blithely she replied that she had already planned to have the next child, "when the situation in the West is all right again." If he stopped smoking and stayed away from liquor, she was sure they would produce a healthy boy, in spite of his being constantly overworked. But at Christmas time she was no better.

She also suffered in silence over the ever worsening relationship with her father. Since late in 1942, Supreme Party Judge Buch had no longer been allowed to conduct a hearing without his son-in-law's written approval, and every sentence had to be validated by him. In his humiliation, Reichsleiter Buch did not hide his chagrin; the entire Nazi elite knew about the family dispute, which late in August 1944 even became the cause of a hearing before the SS Supreme Court. It concerned a conversation in the course of a *Kameradschaftsabend* (comrades' evening) at the officers' academy of the Waffen SS in Tölz. The chief of the Race and Resettlement Office, Gruppenführer Harald Turner, was drinking with members of his staff who had been called up for active service. Sitting next to Turner was the adjutant of the school, Hauptsturmführer Hermann Buch, Martin Bormann's brother-in-law. A month later Hermann Buch reported the conversation to his boss, Reichsführer Heinrich Himmler.

"Very quickly" the talk had turned "to my father's relationship to Martin Bormann." Since Turner, whom the Wehrmacht had eased out of his chief administrator's job in Serbia because of his rabid Nazi conduct, assumed that Buch's son would be on his father's side, he praised the Party Judge and criticized Bormann for giving Hitler bad advice and even lying to him. The friendship between Himmler and Bormann, he said, was "just for show." Inevitably, after the war, there would be a power struggle between the SS and the political leaders of the Party. Bormann was already preparing it.

Whether he liked it or not, Himmler was obliged to have the incident investigated, or Bormann might bring the matter before Hitler. An SS judge questioned Turner, who denied everything and maintained that except for some vague rumors he did not know "a thing about Reichsleiter Bormann's family life. . . . But I do know that he is a truly dynamic personality and totally devoted to the Führer." Nevertheless, Turner was suspended from office until further notice.

The fact that Himmler turned such heavy guns on his trusted supporter, who had been a Party member since 1929, shows how embarrassed he must have been by the thoughts the alcohol had unleashed. Of course he knew that Bormann and Buch were mortal enemies, and on the whole he must have been pleased that the fact was being discussed among the Nazi leadership. On the other hand, he could not afford to ignore the remark that the head of the Party Chancellery was misinforming his Führer, since that implicated Hitler himself, who always reacted violently if his authority was challenged and it was implied that he did not notice immediately that he was being misled. The reaction might become explosive, if a blabbermouth who predicted a struggle between the Party and the SS, i.e., between Himmler and Bormann, went unpunished. As long as Hitler held the reins and Bormann enjoyed his unlimited confidence, such a confrontation was not to be mentioned under any circumstances.

Turner and Himmler were lucky. Ostensibly, none of the other participants at the get-together had heard any of this gossip. Young Buch stood alone with his allegation. By mid-October 1944 SS Judge Breithaupt sent his summary to Himmler, simply stating that the testimonies were contradictory, the reason probably being that Hermann Buch had looked upon the evening as a strictly military occasion, while Turner and the rest, all of them members of his staff, had felt totally relaxed, and that therefore such remarks had passed unnoticed in the general conviviality.

20

"Uncle Heinrich"

Top-level Party members had been anticipating the inevitable showdown between Bormann and Himmler, between the "golden pheasants" and the NSDAP's Black Corps, ever since 1941. After the murders of Röhm and his followers discredited the SA, after the degrading of Robert Ley's German Labor Front, which Bormann had engineered behind the scenes, and after the Party Chancellery had systematically curtailed the Reichsleiters' authority, only these two groups remained powerful. As long as there was no victory over the outside enemy, both contestants realized the feud could not be brought into the open. But they were biding their time, enlarging their positions and establishing favorable lines of action.

To the casual observer Himmler seemed to be obviously the stronger. He ruled over an almost omnipotent police force; commanded the elite divisions of the Waffen SS; headed a variety of SS agencies, some of which were invested with government authority; was supreme commander of the Replacement Army; and master of all prisoner-of-war and concentration camps. Bormann appeared to have hardly anything to match this, only a corps of political leaders, most of them potbellied bigmouths quite unwilling to risk their lives for Germany, let alone for the head of the Party Chancellery. Besides, they were ruled by three and a half dozen Gauleiters, who acted like sovereign tribal lords and mostly looked after their own interests.

All the same, Bormann never had to fear that the nominally superior force might dispose of him in a coup. In his tried-and-true tactics of maintaining a balance of power, Hitler needed this dualism; the demands of the two power machines always canceled each other out. Moreover, Himmler never managed to get a firm foothold in the entourage of the dictator he feared—neither at the Berghof nor in the Reich Chancellery, neither in peace nor in war. At the Wolfsschanze headquarters, Bormann lived within a few yards of Hitler's bunker, while Himmler's field post was thirty-five miles away. Whenever and wherever the Reichsführer SS called on his Führer, he fared like the fabled hare: hedgehog Bormann was already there.

SD chief Walter Schellenberg provided another zoological parallel to that of the fat, sly, prickly rodent versus the simple-minded, scrawny runner. He saw Bormann as a feisty wild boar in a potato field, Himmler as a spindly-legged stork in a salad patch. According to Schellenberg, Himmler "would never have been able to oust his opponent." The SD chief considered the two men total opposites physically as well as psychologically. And the differences were, in fact, almost grotesque. Tall and narrow-chested, Himmler resembled Don Quixote, both in appearance and in his susceptibility to absurd ideas and blindness to reality. Bormann, on the other hand, was Sancho Panza in body, craftiness and realism. This explains why, during the first years of their joint activities in the Party, they had remained indifferent and even strangers to each other, although they worked together in the top leadership of the SA, were the same age and bragged equally of merits earned as Freikorps fighters—one with no justification at all, the other only nominally, since Himmler had never actually taken part in any of the action. Not until after the murders of the SA leaders were they brought closer together; both were on the winning side and both rose from anonymity to top leadership. Soon afterwards they began to collaborate on a give-and-take basis.

In 1935, for example, Bormann instructed the political leaders to work closely with the SD's intelligence service. On January 30, 1937, when Himmler had begun bribing men of influence with honorary ranks and handsome uniforms, Bormann, although he was never a member of that service, was given the rank of Gruppenführer (major general) with, to make it look better, the predated SS serial number 555—very special digits to the Party's old guard, since they had been on Hitler's first membership card when he joined the party of Anton Drexler. On Hitler's birthday in 1940, Bormann was promoted to Obergruppenführer (lieutenant general). Needless to say, he thereafter was quick to be helpful when Himmler asked him for small tokens of friendship.

Whenever the unequal champions met, their encounter was marked by an almost Wagnerian ceremony. They always walked toward each other with measured steps, reached out with both hands and looked deep into each other's eyes in true Teutonic fashion. A buff for anything Germanic, Himmler had introduced this ritual. From him, Bormann and his wife got their hatred of Charlemagne; to them, the founder of the Frankish empire was the butcher of the Saxons. In Hitler's presence, however, Bormann kept this view to himself; the Führer had little use for rebels against the authority of the state.

On the other hand, Hitler had no objections to Himmler's plans for reviving Germanic ways of life in the conquered areas as a means of preparing the way for a reunification with the Reich. In Denmark, Norway, Belgium and the Netherlands, the SS was ordered to work toward this goal. This led to an agreement in November 1941 between Himmler and Bormann, who induced Reich Treasurer Schwarz to finance the SS action from Party funds. In August 1942 Himmler finally received his official Teutonization order from the Party at Bormann's request.

In The Hague the Senior SS and Police Commander* Hanns Rauter, was thereby made responsible for the Teutonic put-on in the Netherlands. In an enthusiastic letter he congratulated his Reichsführer for having been solely and exclusively appointed by Bormann "to enter, in the name of the NSDAP, into negotiations with the country's Germanic ethnic groups. The news," he said, had "hit like a bomb."

Fragments of this bomb, unfortunately, struck, among others, the Commissar General of the Netherlands, Fritz Schmidt, who as deputy of the Party Organization had hitherto collaborated with the Dutch Fascists and their leader, Adrian Mussert. He favored a "soft" plan by which the Netherlands would retain a vestige of independence. The SS, on the other hand, took a hard line, aiming at the total annexation of the country and its integration into Greater Germania. As a result, Rauter and Schmidt were now enemies. In a letter to Himmler, the SS officer wrote triumphantly: "Certain problems have come up regarding Hauptdienstleiter Schmidt who, as you know, has gone on a three-week vacation and does not know where he stands. He was planning to get instructions from Reichsleiter Bormann."

Schmidt had worked in the Party Chancellery as a Hauptdienstleiter, but he had not been aware of the internal developments that were making a farce of his collaboration with Mussert. Now he felt not only useless in his post but threatened by the SS. Bormann persuaded him to continue in office; he would support him and see to it that the Party Chancellery kept the political lead in these matters. In December, Rauter protested to Himmler about Schmidt's continued activity; there could be "no doubt" that because of him "the SS has been largely edged out of the political arena." The Reichsführer's gray eminence, department chief Gottlob Berger, immediately threatened to give Schmidt "a hard time."

But Bormann had no desire to get himself involved in a major fight with Himmler over a zealous colleague. When Schmidt-Münster (so called after his hometown) had problems again and went to Berlin, Bormann noted for his files: "On 6/21, I had a very friendly talk with Schmidt on the way to

*A high-ranking title (Höhere SS- und Polizeiführer). A senior SS and Police commander was Himmler's personal representative in each defense district and the commander of all SS and police units in his area.—*Tr.*

my office from the Propaganda Ministry." "Somewhat unhappily, but not unduly so" Schmidt complained that now he was in for even greater trouble.

After this conversation Schmidt left Berlin on a special train heading west; the Party Chancellery was giving a number of high-ranking Party members a tour of the Atlantic Wall. On the return trip he mysteriously fell from the window of his sleeping compartment as the train approached Chartres. His body was found lying by the tracks; and the side of the railroad car had traces of blood. Bormann's top aide, Helmuth Friedrichs, the tour conductor, reported the incident by priority telex to his boss at Obersalzberg. He presumed that Schmidt, in a "state of nervous exhaustion" had committed suicide by jumping out of the window, "in the belief that due to differences of opinion with other agencies in the Netherlands he was under surveillance and would have to face charges."

Bormann was not concerned by the death. The memo drafted for his closest colleagues does not contain one word of mourning or regret, merely an attempt at self-justification. He had "searched his mind over and over again in the past few days for any reasons that might have driven Party comrade Schmidt-Münster to take such an unfortunate step." Surely he, Bormann, could not have been the cause. In a handwritten note he ordered that "all matters pertaining to Schmidt's last days" should be locked away in the safe. In his chess game with Himmler, he had sacrificed a pawn. Officially he announced that Schmidt had lost his life in an accident. He ordered the burial in Münster to be a minor state ceremony, complete with the parade of an SA unit, Wagnerian music and a death vigil. He himself stood silent by the grave, wisely leaving it to others to do the talking. In the news reports his name (spelled Bohrmann, with an *h*) headed the list of mourners.

By this time Bormann knew that he would soon cross swords with the Reichsführer SS in another, much more important arena. Late in August 1943 Himmler's appointment to Reich Minister of the Interior was announced. There are indications that at some point Bormann himself had aspired to this office. But the fact that it would have meant leaving his place by Hitler's side probably made it easy for him to pass it up. Besides, he could always be sure that Himmler, with his notoriously clumsy tactics, would get himself in trouble regardless of, or even because of, this addition to his power. Almost inevitably the new minister would make the same mistakes that—with a little help from Bormann—had been his predecessor's undoing. Frick had aimed at a tight central administration, and as a result, had collided with the Gauleiters, to whom Hitler, always opposed to any rigid order, had granted extensive autonomy. Despite their honorary rank in the SS, they were not favorably inclined toward the Black Corps, having been annoyed too often in the past by the arrogance and elitist attitude of the top-level SS officers in their provinces. Himmler had been in office barely two weeks when Bormann lectured him in a condescending letter on what to do and not to do in his proposed reform of the internal German administration.

If the Minister of the Interior was to assert himself all the way down to the regional authorities, he needed to get the Gauleiters on his side. This would have taken years, and he could not wait that long. Besides, he was under pressure from his own outfit, the senior SS and Police commanders in the provincial capitals who now hoped to be the local big shots on the spot at last. Some of his regional commanders had already let their Gauleiters know who was now running the show. The Gauleiters complained to Bormann, and because he quickly came to their rescue, they rallied to him more strongly than ever.

By briefing the Führer on each individual case, Bormann also managed to work up Hitler's annoyance with the SS. Himmler had been in office just a year when Ernst Kaltenbrunner drafted a report on the discrepancies between Party and government. He noted an increasing shift of power in Bormann's favor because the Gauleiters, although they were government officials in their capacity as Reich Defense Commissars and Reichsstatthalters, "preferred to work through the Party Organization, making the administration feel left out." Wearily Himmler told Schellenberg that the Führer had got so used to Bormann and his *modus operandi* that his influence could no longer be curtailed, even though there was every reason to "edge him out of his position."

There was plenty of occasion for discord. After Minister of the Interior Himmler had driven the Gauleiters into Bormann's fold, Bormann felt the time had come to dispose of the SD's domestic intelligence service, which had long been troublesome to him and the tribal lords. Originally this institution, headed by Otto Ohlendorf, had been a combination of a public-opinion institute and a Party-owned private-investigation agency. Its function was, on the one hand, to observe and report on public morale, and on the other, to gather information on persons indifferent or hostile to the regime. The network of investigators worked on an honorary—i.e., unsalaried—basis. Every government agency, every business enterprise, every organization was spied on by trustworthy Party agents. As long as Bormann was building up Amt Hess, he had gladly turned to this outfit in cases where, for instance, the political reliability of high-level civil servants had to be ascertained. But since he had no desire to be dependent on the SS in the long run, he built up a personnel file of his own which was supplied with material by the Party Organization, down to the smallest local branch. Now he no longer needed other information and felt spied on himself. Understandably, therefore, he was anxious to put the SD out of commission.

The *Meldungen aus dem Reich* (Reports from the Reich) newsletter, published by Ohlendorf and available only to a select group, was branded a "mouthpiece of defeatism" by the Secretary to the Führer, who maintained that obviously the "informants of the SD" moved "only in negatively oriented circles." The reports no longer reached Hitler's desk, and since most of the influential functionaries disapproved of criticism, Ohlendorf was complaining by January 1943 that he was working merely for Himmler's wastebasket.

Late in April, Bormann brought in heavy artillery. "Dear Party comrade Himmler"—the form of address always varied with the mood of the hour —had to swallow the admonition that his espionage system had once again trespassed on territory belonging exclusively to the Party Chancellery: the screening of high-level civil servants. "Since your appointment to Minister of the Interior," the letter writer remarked sarcastically, such efforts were obviously "directed at putting stronger emphasis on political considerations in the choice of government personnel." The screening of "personnel for government jobs" was not, however, the SD's job but that of the Party Chancellery. "In preparing my decisions I always avail myself of the SD's data," Bormann wrote. But he "set final store by the Gauleiters' reports," since they were able to judge civil servants by their performance on the spot. The letter ended with an open threat: there was the question of "whether and on what terms the political leaders should perform honorary services for the SD."

By mid-June the threat had turned into reality. Bormann forbade all Party functionaries to supply the SD with any further information or reports. Obediently Robert Ley and officials of his German Labor Front followed suit. And without protest Himmler allowed himself to be deprived of a weapon he could certainly have used in future altercations with his rival. Ohlendorf complained to Himmler's masseur, Felix Kersten, that there were bound to be further counteroffensives. He was fully aware of the fact that the seemingly strong arm of his Reichsführer could not protect him —this was in the summer of 1944, when Himmler had reached the peak of his power and Goebbels believed that he would be his ally for all time. In those days Goebbels was convinced that with Himmler controlling the Wehrmacht and him conducting the war on the home front, Germany would soon be saved. Not long thereafter he was made to realize how much he had overrated the partner of his dreams.

On July 20, 1944, as a result of the attempt on Hitler's life, Himmler was given control over at least part of the Wehrmacht, the Replacement Army. During those weeks he toyed with the idea of having Bormann arrested. That he refrained from doing so can be only partly explained by the fact that Hitler would never have stood for it. In thought and to some extent in deed, Himmler had already betrayed his much proclaimed loyalty to the Führer. All that was needed was a push and he would have had to jump off the Third Reich's sinking ship. Although he had the SS slogan "Our Honor Is Loyalty" engraved on his belt buckle, he had already spun his web, which reached enemy forces inside and outside Germany through his secret service, the overseas SD, and through private channels. In case of an emergency he planned to weave the threads into a safety net that would prevent him from falling into a void.

He started his plotting very much in private. In the villa next to his official residence in Berlin lived a lawyer named Carl Langbehn. They often had neighborly talks, and the lawyer indicated on those occasions that he was not a friend of the regime. Langbehn, who belonged to a resistance group, believed, like his friend Carl Friedrich Goerdeler, that the regime could be overthrown only if the Party could be split by playing its opposing factors against one another so that one of them would help to bring about the change in power. According to Goerdeler's analysis, there were four groups inside the NSDAP: a Hitler group, a group around Ley, another around Bormann, and the SS. A pact with the last seemed the most expedient solution, since this was the only one of the four groups under arms. Once the regime had been overthrown, the SS would have to be disposed of, too. Through their foreign contacts, the conspirators vaguely knew that Himmler and his SD chief Schellenberg were in touch with the enemy in Stockholm and Zürich. It therefore did not strike them as all that much of a risk to take the Minister of Police a little way into their confidence. Late in August 1943 Langbehn arranged for a meeting between Johannes Popitz, the former Prussian Minister of Finance, and Himmler. In the course of it the Reichsführer indicated that he had no basic objections to a joint action. A year later, in his speech to the Gauleiters at Posen after the attempt on Hitler's life, Himmler described his contacts with the resistance as a trap he had set for the traitors, and maintained that Hitler had always been informed about them and had approved.

The truth was somewhat different. Hitler did indeed know about the contacts, but he never even suspected what his loyal Heinrich had in mind. There is no telling how far the Reichsführer would have gone in his double-dealing if the Gestapo had not decoded an Allied radio message concerning Langbehn's relations to the U.S. intelligence service in Switzerland. Gestapo chief Heinrich Müller did not report his discovery by the usual official channels; he sent it straight to Führer Headquarters. If Bormann had been previously unaware of Himmler's overseas contacts, this report was bound to put him on the alert, but most likely he already knew more from Müller, who was scheming against Schellenberg and who, in the last phase of the war, openly collaborated with the head of the Party Chancellery.

Now Himmler had no choice but to have Langbehn arrested. All he could do for his neighbor was to protect him for a few months from the Gestapo's worst methods of interrogation. The fact that he arranged to have the prosecution of his interlocutors take place practically behind closed doors is proof of how he felt about his own dubious role in the affair. From now on he was hiding a skeleton in the closet, and Bormann knew it. This is the only explanation of why, even in the months of his greatest power, the Reichsführer never tried to oust his rival Bormann and why, as a friend of the family, he still let Bormann's wife serve him his favorite rice dish. After the attempt on Hitler's life, Bormann and Himmler vied with each other in giving visible proof of their devotion and concern.

For example, having assumed responsibility for his Führer's safety and being in charge of his guards, Bormann informed the Minister of Police that he had also taken intensified precautions against poisoning. Henceforth the food for Hitler's diet was to be bought in bulk and constantly tested. All personnel who had access to the stores must be beyond reproach politically. Himmler demonstrated his concern by outdoing these instructions. He made Kaltenbrunner and Reich Physician of the SS Ernst Robert Grawitz responsible for testing all Hitler's food and medication "by ever-varying, constant random checks."

But such joint action was becoming rare. Bormann still avoided open confrontation. Whenever he wanted to put pressure on Himmler, he had the Gauleiters bring charges against the SS. Erich Koch, the "Duke of East Prussia," was ideally suited to this; although he was "dear Erich" to Himmler, he never missed an opportunity to show the Black Corps that in his domain (which for a time included the Ukraine as well as his original bailiwick) the Party alone—the Gauleiter, in other words—was boss. Bormann ignored Himmler's protests.

Outwardly for the Gauleiters' benefit, but actually for the sake of expanding his own power, Bormann went into action in August 1944 when another decree from the Führer had to be prepared. This was to announce who should have "executive power" in case of internal riots or an advance of enemy forces to the borders of the Reich. Since Bormann never budged from Hitler's side at headquarters, Gerhard Klopfer, the head of the constitutional-law department, negotiated in Berlin with the top-level government agencies assigned to participate, above all with the Reich Ministry of the Interior, which was in charge of the police. Himmler had instructed his State Secretary Wilhelm Stuckart to make sure that not only was his jurisdiction in this matter preserved in principle but that it was established from the start that he would have central command of all action and could, in turn, delegate regional authority to senior SS and Police commanders. The Party Chancellery, on the other hand, demanded that the "executive power"—that is, all power of action, including that of martial law and the right to court-martial—should be given to the Reich Defense Commissars, i.e., the Gauleiters. The Führer had instructed him along these lines, Bormann maintained, "after the events of July 20."

The negotiating parties were unable to agree. Himmler's man felt that Bormann's plan was shutting out the top-level government agencies— which indeed was true. "It is inconceivable that the Reich Defense Commissars should take steps, each according to his own judgment, without the guidance and authorization of the Reichsführer SS, who is responsible for order and public safety inside the Reich." He should be given central authority, "since the Führer cannot possibly concern himself with everything." But Bormann's deputy remained adamant. Klopfer reported back to Stuckart: "It must be stated beyond any doubt that in case of an invasion, executive power will rest with the Reich Defense Commissars," and "in reference to the Führer's clearly expressed wishes" the term "'executive power' must be included in the decree." Himmler could be allowed at most to prescribe general guidelines for the Reich Defense Commissars, but delegating jurisdiction to a Himmler man was out of the question, since Himmler "as Reichsführer SS . . . has no general deputy" for his many offices.

In the face of such strongly opposing views, it was once again left to Hitler to settle the dispute. As it turned out, the contestants were fighting over the skin of a lion which had not even been released for shooting. In actual fact, a decree had been in existence since July 13, 1933, providing that in case of an invasion, executive power should go to the military, as had been the custom in the past. Only under the shock of the attempt on his life had Hitler contemplated a change early in August. When, in mid-September, Himmler and Bormann confronted him with their dispute over jurisdiction, his distrust of the generals had not diminished, but his first burning anger had subsided. Returning to his favorite method of playing the powers against each other, he merely modified the existing decree. The Gauleiters' authority was somewhat enhanced, that of the military slightly curtailed, and Himmler got nothing at all. For Bormann it was not a great victory; all the same, his rival had suffered a defeat at the height of his power.

"Last night Heinrich Himmler departed for the West Wall," Bormann reported to his wife early in September 1944. "We are in daily contact by telephone. He has tackled his job as commander of the Replacement Army with splendid energy." Inspecting the fortifications in the West was not exactly part of this job, but Bormann had convinced Himmler that there was no one better equipped than he to take a look at concrete bunkers. It kept the Reichsführer busy for well over two weeks. Bormann welcomed such eagerness; it made him the one to issue the orders, which meant that he could fortify his own position merely by the way he phrased the instructions. But he was also doing Himmler a favor; the Reichsführer dreaded any meeting with Hitler and was grateful to Bormann for saving him from awkward moments.

There was still another reason why Bormann had no need to fear that Himmler might contest his position at headquarters. Late in September the Reichsführer, who was something of a hypochondriac, confessed that he could not stand a life as unhealthy as Hitler's working habits demanded. He could not work until 4 A.M.; he needed to be asleep by midnight at the latest.

This was certainly not the man who could bring down "a wild boar in a potato field." In his jovial way, department chief Gottlob Berger tried to rouse him to action by reminding him in a letter that "the soldiers and those at home" believed in only "Adolf Hitler, Heinrich Himmler and Dr. Goebbels," although the last had by that time abandoned his trust in the Reichsführer and had begun to align himself with the now obviously inevitable Bormann. Himmler's bureau chief, Rudolf Brandt, complained to masseur Kersten that Hitler saw the Reichsführer only if Bormann permitted it.

Himmler was given more than his share of assignments. "At my request Uncle Heinrich goes to the Ruhr on November 3," Bormann wrote to his wife. "He must get that situation under control." Finally Himmler was even allowed to appear as Hitler's deputy at the traditional ceremony in memory of the 1923 putsch where he read a long-winded proclamation of the Führer's. Bormann did not envy him the job. To him, it was more important to impress on the Gauleiters that they were fighting for their lives, but that final victory was at hand if they forced men into the Volkssturm and made women dig trenches.

Did Bormann the agriculturist know that hypertrophied growth may lead to death? He helped his "dear Heinrich" to ever new assignments and positions, as though their rivalry did not exist. He knew that the World War I second lieutenant dreamed of being a military leader. When in November the Allies had conquered almost all of Alsace, he recommended that the Reichsführer be appointed commander of a newly established Upper Rhine army group. Early in December Himmler was given the title. Greatly pleased, he nosed his special train southwest and established his field headquarters between Freiburg and Donaueschingen on the tracks of the Black Forest railroad, where a number of tunnels offered shelter during air raids. This removed him again for some time from Hitler's immediate entourage, which also suited the Führer's plans. The Ardennes offensive, spearheaded by SS divisions, was about to begin, and the Great Strategist had no desire to be bothered by suggestions and interference from the Reichsführer SS.

On November 20 the Führer and his entourage left the Wolfsschanze, never to return again. At first Hitler stayed in Berlin. Bormann seized the opportunity to have his wife join him at Stolpe for two weeks, spending as much time with her as his duties allowed. On the night of December 10, Hitler's special train headed for a new location, a number of high-rise bunkers near Schloss Ziegenberg in the Hessian district of Friedberg. Immediately on arrival, Bormann raised hell; the space assigned to his department was inadequate, the office furniture insufficient, and worst of all, the telex machines were unsatisfactory. They were the guns with which he conducted his war, and when he stomped around between the two rows of machinery, giving orders, dictating and reading, he was in truth the "telex general" they called him in Party circles. He had induced Reich Treasurer Schwarz to place the entire network under the Party's authority.

Four days later Himmler arrived from the Black Forest to make his first appearance. He needed to replace a supposedly incompetent general of his army group, and above all, he refused to be under orders to Field Marshal Karl Rudolf Gerd von Rundstedt, the commander in the West, because he wished to plan and fight his own battles. Bormann promised him his support. General Heinz Guderian, the Chief of Staff, was convinced he did this only so that the Reichsführer would fail and thus be easier to remove. But even for Bormann, things were not quite so simple; he could not wish for a failure at the front, because his own existence depended on the final victory. But Himmler should not be allowed to win it. Himmler's crony Gottlob Berger saw another danger. In a letter he warned the Reichsführer: "I urge you to shorten your assignment as commander of the Upper Rhine and return to Führer Headquarters," to squash rumors of being in disgrace which "certain parties are eagerly spreading around." An even more explicit warning came from the SS war correspondents, urging Himmler to break Bormann's "monopoly" with Hitler.

The Reichsführer felt strong enough to turn a deaf ear to such advice. He promised to recapture Strasbourg. For this purpose he placed two more experienced divisions under his command. But after some successes, the attack bogged down and the recaptured territory was lost again.

Another assignment, which he again owed to Bormann's intervention, got the Reichsführer off the hook: on his return to Berlin the Führer appointed him commander of Army Group Vistula, which for the moment existed only on paper. As of January 12, 1945, the Red Army had advanced to the Oder near Frankfurt; a new line of defense had to be established at the northern flank of this gigantic wedge. Guderian had no desire to entrust the job to Himmler, but Hitler maintained that he had shown himself tough and therefore successful on the Rhine, and that as commander of the Replacement Army he could quickly dispatch new troops to the front. On January 24, 1945, Himmler took office. At first his only success was the slogans he invented. It began to dawn on the more ambitious of his followers that riding on his coattails would no longer help their careers. Gruppenführer Fegelein therefore attached himself more closely to his drinking partner Bormann. Kaltenbrunner openly speculated on Himmler's succession, and Bormann encouraged him by giving him an opportunity to brief Hitler in Himmler's place.

Now and then Himmler came to Berlin from his command post and joined Bormann and Fegelein for lunch, but the reception he got was less friendly than it used to be, although he was allowed to attend the military briefings in the bunker of the Reich Chancellery. During one of them, on February 13, he was the cause of a noisy argument between Hitler and Guderian which lasted for almost two hours. The Chief of Staff insisted that Himmler's knowledge was inadequate for his position as the head of an army group and that General Walther Wenck, an experienced army commander, should be assigned to his staff. Hitler threw a fit but finally gave in. But Wenck was incapacitated in an automobile accident after only one day in office. The offensive which was to have cut off the wedge of the enemy advance was unsuccessful; Himmler's divisions got stuck. With a mixture of distress and *Schadenfreude,* Bormann wrote to his wife on February 20: "Uncle Heinrich's offensive did not work out, i.e., he did not properly organize it, and now his reserve divisions must be assigned someplace else."

The Russians were now launching their offensive—successfully. When Guderian received nothing but vague reports from Himmler's field headquarters, he went there himself in mid-March and learned that the commander had been at the Hohenlychen nursing home for some time with the flu. Guderian found him in bed, "in relatively good shape, which made me feel that a slight cold would certainly not have prompted me to leave my troops in such a precarious situation." Through Guderian, Himmler asked Hitler to relieve him of his command on the ground that he was overburdened by the large number of offices he held. He did not have the courage to approach Hitler personally on the matter.

In January 1945 Hitler's progressive physical deterioration prompted Minister Hans Lammers to ask Bormann whether he could find out whom the Führer had in mind as his successor. Surely it could no longer be Göring. Bormann waved the matter aside. "If the question has not been settled already," he said, "the Führer will certainly not appoint the Reichsmarschall now; but I do not believe that once the decision has been made, he will change the appointment. Let's drop the subject."

Did he believe that the office would almost automatically fall into his lap? His self-confidence was considerable; nevertheless, he must have felt some doubts about his ability to stand on the Reich's highest pedestal in the sight of everyone, to represent the government and to make the big speeches expected from a popular leader. His ambition had always been to work in the background and secretly hold the reins of power. The man best suited to succeed Hitler was, in his opinion, someone without a base in the Party, which meant that it could never be Himmler. But Bormann no longer needed to worry about him. On April 20, 1945, when the Reichsführer arrived for Hitler's birthday reception at the already badly battered Reich Chancellery, he was able once again to shake his Führer's trembling hand, but he was not admitted to a more intimate conversation, and there was no reaction to his request that Hitler should lead the defense of the Alpine Redoubt at Obersalzberg as the last German bastion.

21

The Secret Ruler

There were many leading Nazis who feared Bormann as the future ruler of Germany; with some figurehead at the bow, he would be able to set the course. Around Karinhall, his residence and Luftwaffe field headquarters, Göring kept a division of paratroopers ready for fear Hitler's brown eminence would instigate a coup to remove him from office and have him assassinated. Alfred Rosenberg discovered a group of young men among the leaders of the Hitler Youth who, in silent agreement with Reich Youth Leader Axmann, were planning ways to prevent Bormann from succeeding Hitler—if need be by an attempt on his life. And although Bormann was in Bavaria, far from the scene of action, Reich Treasurer Schwarz suspected that he would wipe out the Party's old guard the day he took power.

Others like Ernst Kaltenbrunner and Gestapo chief Heinrich Müller attached themselves to Bormann's coattails. Gruppenführer Hermann Fegelein; the Führer's chief adjutant, General Wilhelm Burgdorf; and the last Chief of Staff, General Hans Krebs, addressed Bormann by the intimate *du* and were always ready to bend an elbow with him. Reich Organization Leader Robert Ley, whom the Party had trained to blind obedience, kowtowed to him every time he visited headquarters.

The impression the Führer's right-hand man made in the last months of his life was vividly described by Cavalry Captain Gerhard Boldt, who early in February 1945 attended military briefings on two occasions where he saw for the first time "the man who is supposed to have such crucial influence on Hitler." He described him as "about forty-five years old, barely medium size, stocky, thickset and bull-necked. He seems almost like a heavyweight. The round face with its strong cheekbones and flat nose suggests energy and brutality . . . His dark eyes and facial expression reveal cunning and cold ruthlessness."

During those final months it was these qualities above all that made the man more indispensable to the Führer than ever before. On July 4, 1944, Hitler had admitted in a speech to industrialists at Obersalzberg that he was playing for "all or nothing," as he had done ever since he first entered politics. His exact words were: "Gentlemen, should the war be lost," the economy would no longer need to readjust to peacetime. In that case, his listeners had better worry about their "personal adjustment to the transition from this world to the next," given the choice between the gallows, a shot in the head, death from starvation, Siberia or suicide. During the speech Bormann sat in the front row. At least from that day on, he knew he was fighting for his life.

His formula for victory was as simple-minded as most of his thinking: where the Führer's genius and aura failed to work, he would step in and exert power. He must force the whole population to give its entire strength to the fight. And he must protect the Führer from anything that might distract him from the larger issues, diminish his determination or undermine his faith in Providence. The attempt on Hitler's life had proved that there was treason all around. Bormann no longer trusted anyone but himself and Hitler. Everyone else, from the ordinary citizen up to the top leaders, simply wanted to save his own skin. But they would all have to die so that Germany—i.e., Hitler and Bormann—could live. Stubborn and apparently oblivious to the steadily approaching catastrophe, he constantly proclaimed in announcements, actions, telex messages, conferences and letters to his wife that final victory was imminent. From week to week his activities became more hectic, his orders harsher. In the end he was driven not by courage but by the rage of despair. But not until quite late in the game did he reveal in his letters to Gerda that there were moments when he no longer believed they would be saved.

To get an even firmer grip on the public, the Party had to be on its toes at all times. On August 16, 1944, Bormann's two co-champions, Klopfer and Friedrichs, had received handwritten orders to "immediately compile and submit as soon as possible secret lists of possible replacements of persons in prominent positions, such as Reich Minister, State Secretary, Gauleiter, head of organization, Reichsleiter, should such persons become incapacitated." He added a postscript: "For the sake of secrecy, the lists must be submitted in handwriting." Now and then they were brought up to date. The last one, compiled on March 10, 1945, is quite revealing. In comparison to the many departments of the Party Chancellery, the rest of the Party cuts a modest figure. Marginal comments indicate how Bormann envisaged its further development. For example: "In case Reichsleiter Bouhler should be incapacitated, I feel that most of the duties pertaining to the Chancellery of the Führer of the NSDAP could be assigned to the Party Chancellery."

To all intents and purposes the same procedure was planned in case Reich Organization Leader Ley dropped out. Bormann already saw himself as the future Secretary General in command of the entire Party, like his secret idol, Josef Stalin—for whom Hitler, too, had a hidden admiration. In such a position he, like Stalin, could safely leave representative government offices to others and attend to the actual power.

Commuting between Hitler's desk and his own, he slaved for eighteen hours a day to get the awkward, improvised machine that was the Party into high gear. His instructions invaded the private lives of his employees. He was determined to make Party hacks into national examples.

The Wehrmacht was given its lecture too. Late in August 1944 he distributed a treatise on the conduct of "Party and Wehrmacht in Occupied Poland," written by a puritanically minded Party member. The area behind the lines, it said, was a disgrace to the front and to the people at home: "It is totally inconceivable that while soldiers at the front are fighting a battle to the death and people at home are living in Spartan frugality and working themselves to the bone, in the communications zones people are living it up, boozing, eating, whoring to their heart's content."

In September 1944 he zeroed in on hunters, circulating a letter in which he preached that every true National Socialist must forgo the pleasure of hunting in times as grave as these. In December it was the turn of the chicken and rabbit owners. The local Party functionaries were instructed to investigate rabbit hutches and chicken coops. Wherever they found more animals being kept than were needed for the family's own consumption, they were to kill them and distribute the meat. In the second week of February 1945 he urged his wife to pick as many wild greens as possible that spring. A month later the Party, too, was sent out to grass with eight pages of instructions. The Führer, he said, would be informed of the picking operation's progress "at regular intervals." His own family was not all that dependent on those greens; he often sent them food—obtained at headquarters or ordered for himself as rations for his trips—in the official metal suitcases of the daily courier, who commuted between Berlin and Obersalzberg.

While he kept warning his wife not to overexert herself and to keep away from danger, he constantly thought of new ways to put women into harness. In September 1944 he proposed that 80,000 young women replace soldiers in the searchlight units of the anti-aircraft batteries. On November 16 he wrote to Goebbels that it was now "up to the Party . . . to prepare the German people for the fact that in the future an even larger number of women will be called up, possibly even into active service." When late in November an auxiliary corps of female signal operators was founded to release another 150,000 soldiers from offices and communications centers for active service at the front, Bormann hailed it as a "service of special distinction for German women." "The political, ideological and cultural training" of the women who had been drafted into service was conducted by the Frauenschaft organization under his guidance.

In late November he announced that "in general women should be kept out of the combat zones," and should therefore not be drafted into the Volkssturm. But early in December he requested the High Command of the Armed Forces to forward to his department all applications "in the original" of women volunteering for active duty in the armed forces. On February 28, 1945, Hitler approved—with Bormann's help, certainly—the draft of a women's battalion. Should this task force prove successful, other units would be formed later on. "The Führer expects," Bormann noted, "that this will have a certain effect on the attitude of the men." But for the moment things remained in the planning stage. In March, however, when large parts of the Reich had already been invaded by enemy troops, Bormann remembered the women warriors. "To perform special missions behind the enemy lines," he set up the Werewolf partisan organization and urged "determined, courageous men and women of all ages" to apply. The wives of the Party elite were exempt from such sacrifices.

Ever since the attempt on Hitler's life, most officers and generals were reactionaries and enemies of the state in Bormann's eyes. In late September 1944 he succeeded in getting the Wehrmacht to consider not only the *Hoheitsträger*—i.e., the Party's upper level—but also the lower Party officials as officer candidates upon enlisting.

Wherever Bormann detected a crack in the structure of the Wehrmacht, the Party squeezed in. After he had badgered the Wehrmacht for the longest time for its undue leniency in the treatment of prisoners of war, the High Command of the Armed Forces issued a statement—"at my suggestion," Bormann declared triumphantly—which he sent to his functionaries in mid-September to inform them of their new prerogatives. As Bormann's covering letter states, the officers guarding prisoner-of-war camps must now work in "close cooperation with the high-level Party functionaries," and camp commandants must appoint liaison officers with the district leaders. This enabled the Party to check on whether or not the prisoners were whipped into work forcefully enough.

Bormann was particularly incensed over the "extremely important problem of catching deserters." In his opinion there were more than a million men in uniform with marching orders and illegal IDs roaming around the country evading combat duty. Late in February 1945 he conferred with Friedrichs and Klopfer, on how to dispatch these evaders to the front. "If those men," he argued, "could be grabbed and again made into soldiers with soldierly convictions, etc., we would have not only enough people at the front but even the necessary reserves to launch another offensive." The men should be rounded up in raids. One aide suggested that deserters be hanged in public and their bodies left to swing on the rope for a while as a deterrent to others—which was exactly what happened.

The head of the Party Chancellery, who officiated in a bombproof bunker and had never been startled by an actual shot, finally sent an open letter on March 9, 1945, to inform all high-level Party members of his formula "for strengthening the front and rounding up stragglers." Actually, he said, he did not see how there could be any stragglers. Any soldier who lost contact with his unit needed only to head toward the sound of battle and there join up with another unit, or he would be court-martialed as a deserter and executed. In another open letter on the following day, he meted out the same punishment to all those "who shamelessly pretend they are wounded."

In late March 1945 Bormann finally managed to get what he had wanted all along: he was given exclusive control over the National Socialist propaganda officers. But Hitler delayed signing the order to dissolve the staff in question at the High Command of the Armed Forces for another two weeks. Meanwhile the finished draft of yet another, more extensive order was waiting for him in Bormann's desk drawer. This was to establish "the Party Chancellery's Responsibility for the Political Indoctrination of the Wehrmacht," and thereby the Party's rule over the military. The order had been approved by Hitler, but it was obviously never signed.

To Bormann's constant annoyance, the Party comrades were not nearly as determined as he wanted them to be. On September 5, 1944, he was obliged to rush his first pep talk on endurance to the Gauleiters in the form of a telex message marked *"Geheime Reichssache."* When the Western Allies advanced on Aix-la-Chapelle and Trier, the local functionaries had evacuated villages in the area. Now there was not enough manpower to dig trenches. Any exodus, he ordered, must be approved by headquarters, by him, and whenever anyone acted on his own in an emergency, he should be informed immediately. At the end of the year he called on the Party dignitaries, urging them to be on hand at all times "wherever the situation is grave and difficult to handle," in order to maintain public trust in the Party. During the first hours of 1945 he wrote to Gerda from the Ziegenberg headquarters that the fateful year was about to begin. Thanks to the Luftwaffe's negligence, it would be even tougher than the one before—a premonition which had come to him as he stepped out into the bright moonlit night and realized that on the next cloudless day another offensive against the British and Americans would be launched in the West virtually without air cover. "Still, we must stand by our cause," he continued, "for our destiny, like that of many families, depends on the outcome of this war." An hour earlier, during a New Year's Eve party with French champagne in Hitler's company, he had been more optimistic. "We shall win in the end," the Führer had predicted, to which the party remained silent; only Bormann agreed enthusiastically.

Five days later he blasted the Gauleiters for letting the defense positions behind the front deteriorate in the winter weather. Women and Volkssturm troops must be sent immediately to repair the damages. Even greater was his concern about "the conduct of Party leaders in enemy-occupied territory." His instructions on this issue show that many functionaries were already rating their own skins above Hitler's. Under no condition, they were warned on January 23, were they "to leave their homes before the civilian population." In case of an evacuation, those under the age of fifty-one were "to present themselves immediately after their mission was accomplished to the Wehrmacht or the German Volkssturm for active duty." Barely three weeks later, on February 12, he struck an even tougher note. All functionaries evacuated from the East were ordered to report within a week to "the district leaders of their present place of residence." Anyone failing to do so would be "considered a deserter and dealt with accordingly."

On January 30, 1945, the twelfth and last anniversary of the Thousand-Year Reich, Bormann announced with pathos in his voice that now, at the height of danger, each Party comrade must "give his very best in performance and dedication." Collections of money, textiles, shoes and junk were no longer important at this point, nor for that matter was the evacuation of endangered areas. All that mattered now was "to organize intellectual and physical resistance." This was followed two days later by a ("Secret!") threat to the high-level Party officials, warning them to be sure that Party orders were strictly obeyed. "Anyone who fails in this respect, be it only through negligence, will be ruthlessly taken to task." On February 23 he became more explicit: "Whoever neglects his duties" or "exploits his official position to his own advantage and to that of his family" will be subject to severe punishment, as will "whoever abandons comrades entrusted to his care, whoever tries to disassociate himself from the NSDAP, whoever flees at the enemy's advance and refuses to fight." Exclusion from the Party and a court-martial would be the inevitable result. The Reich Minister of Justice had announced these Draconian measures on February 15. Bormann stepped them up by giving the Gauleiters court jurisdiction. They decided on the life or death of the defendants while being bound themselves by Bormann's orders that anyone who refused to fight must be hanged.

The Gauleiters received the instructions almost simultaneously with an invitation to join the Reichsleiters and unit leaders on February 24 to commemorate the founding of the Party in 1920. This time the traditional ceremony was to take place not in Munich but in the Reich Chancellery. In Bormann's invitation they read that their only chance of survival was to fight and thus bring about victory by force. It offered neither logic nor comfort, but they hoped that Hitler might show them a silver lining somewhere on the horizon.

The Reich capital gave them an ominous welcome with fires still burning from the air raid of the night before. Bormann's office advised them to wait in the bomb-scarred restaurants around the government buildings until they were called. When they gathered in the badly battered Reich Chancellery, they were asked to leave their coats and pistols. As long as they were still among themselves, they were able to talk freely. One of the participants, Gauleiter Rudolf Jordan of Dessau, later described it: "Harsh words are being said; there is criticism of the Führer's being isolated in the bunkers of headquarters, and Bormann's name is mentioned as the probable stage manager." When Bormann finally appeared, he announced the day's program with instructions: a speech by the Führer but no questions and no consultation, not even during lunch, for "the Führer is in the midst of important, not to say vital, conferences and must not be distracted."

They were shocked at the sight of their aged, trembling leader. His voice sounded tired and his slogans failed to excite them, although he promised them a fleet of new submarines and improved new jet fighters which would soon wipe the German skies clean again and bring a turn in the war. This time they knew that he was lying to them, for they were in charge of the defense industries in their provinces. In the silence of general gloom, one trusted follower was heard to sigh "Oh, my God" as the Führer went out of the door. When, during lunch, Hitler began one of his monologues and it seemed impossible to prevent some guest from turning to his Führer with questions and reports, Bormann stepped in. Slipping Hitler a note, he made him break up the party, and as he followed him out of the room, he said, "Goodbye then, until two weeks from now!"

If, as Jordan related, the Party leaders referred to Bormann as the "stage manager of Hitler's isolation," it was because they resented the fact that they were being denied access to the Führer. But it never dawned on them that under the Party clerk's management the permanent staff was steadily diminishing. They noticed that the head of the Reich Chancellery, Reich Minister Hans Heinrich Lammers, was fading farther and farther into the background, but they never learned that it was Bormann who had pushed him there, nor how he had done it. An exchange of letters between the two, written in the last phase of their relationship, provided the final kick by which the Party man pushed aside the government official.

At home, on January 1, 1945, Lammers had drafted a humble handwritten, ten-page letter to his colleague, whom he addressed as *Du*. He had trouble, especially with the beginning; the first page of his draft became almost illegible because of all the corrections. He made his secretary retype the whole thing and two days later had it delivered "in person," with the request for a receipt, at his headquarters near Ziegenberg. In it he extended to "dear Bormann all best wishes . . . for your important work on the Führer's and the nation's behalf as well as for your own personal well-being and that of your family." For himself Lammers hoped "that our hitherto pleasant cooperation in office and our friendly personal relationship may remain the same as it has been all these years." But "to my infinite regret our official and personal relations seem to have become strained . . . for reasons I have no way of knowing and which I can only guess at."

Over two months before, Lammers had been sent home from Hitler's entourage and for more than three months he had not been allowed to report to the head of state. Now he was being "pressured from all directions about a large number of urgently awaited Führer decisions." By the same token, he had "been informed of Führer decisions . . . in which I have had no part whatever, but for which I am supposed to bear the responsibility. . . . If I am to be further left out in this manner . . . I would appreciate it if you, dear Bormann, would at your earliest convenience request a brief meeting for me with the Führer." Hadn't they often enough reported to the Führer together and compared notes in the past? During the twenty days Bormann had spent in Berlin in late November and early December of 1944, Lammers waited in vain for a heart-to-heart talk, but even his telephone calls went unanswered. He was told that Bormann was not in. Had something offended him? Lammers could not find anything in himself that might have caused a rift in their relationship and was convinced that "a frank discussion and an honest meeting of minds" would clear everything up.

Bormann replied instantly and in terms so friendly as to defy any suspicion. "If you were here, we could meet more often and talk things over, and there would be none of these unintentional misunderstandings." He had never pretended not to be in when Lammers called. If he had not called from Ziegenberg yet, it was because, due to the bombings, the lines were constantly out of order. Lammers scribbled sarcastic remarks on the margin of the three-page letter, for the written reply said not one word about his actual request.

Sixteen months later, in April 1946, defendant Lammers was reminded of his letter during the Nuremberg Trials. On this occasion he corrected himself: in actual fact his relations with Bormann had never been all that good, but in a New Year's message, unfriendly remarks were generally avoided. In any case, nothing happened, for he was no longer needed at headquarters, and Bormann's promise that he would "ask the Führer as soon as possible when he can see you," was nothing but a sop. As Lammers himself said, he had been "given the slip." The Committee of Three had turned into a twosome in which Bormann had the say and Keitel had none. In the last days of the war, the unemployed minister went south with Hitler's permission and joined Göring at Obersalzberg—which almost became his undoing. When Bormann labeled the Reichsmarschall a traitor, Lammers was placed under house arrest on Bormann's orders.

Anybody who could influence Hitler in any way was an annoyance to Bormann—supposedly because such people were diverting the Führer's attention from the larger issues, but actually because they might tell him what Bormann was trying to conceal from him. This included a lot, from intrigues against his rivals for Hitler's favor to reports on the broken morale of the German people or the damages caused by bombs. Once, when Goebbels sent a number of aerial photographs of devastated areas to the Reich Chancellery, Bormann returned them with the comment that the Führer's confidence should not be undermined by such pictures. The Gauleiters' reports on the effects of the war also went straight from Bormann's desk into a file cabinet.

One Hitler confidant was a particular nuisance to Bormann because he could neither control him nor order him about. Photographer Heinrich Hoffmann played no role in the Party, except for the fact that back in the early days he had covered parades and rallies and earned the privilege of photographing where no one else in his profession was admitted. This suited Hitler because it enabled him to censor Hoffmann's photographs and prevent publication of all pictures in which he did not like the image of himself. Hoffmann on his part profited from having a monopoly on photographs depicting Hitler in more or less private settings or in particularly attractive poses.

It was through Hoffmann that Hitler had acquired his mistress, Eva Braun, who was an employee at his studio. But that was not the reason for the close relationship between the two men. It went back further than that, to the early twenties, when beer-hall patriotism became fashionable among the privileged circles of Munich and Hoffmann, who was witty and entertaining, found a grateful public in Hitler and his followers at the coffeehouse tables. He advanced to being court jester and was summoned whenever the dictator was in the mood for light gossip from Munich and juicy little anecdotes about the upper levels of the Party Organization. On such occasions Bormann was asked to send a telegram and prepare a pass—instructions he resented every time.

In September 1944 Bormann thought of a way to banish Hoffmann. During one of Hoffmann's visits to the Wolfsschanze, Bormann solicitously remarked that he looked ill and suggested that he see Dr. Theodor Morell, Hitler's personal physician. Hoffmann had no objection, particularly since he had recommended the doctor to Hitler some years before. The checkup had no immediate result, but two weeks later Hoffmann, who had meanwhile returned to Munich, was informed over the telephone by Morell that although he was not actually sick himself, a bacteriological test had shown that he was a carrier of paratyphoid bacteria of the dangerous B type. Hitler therefore no longer wished to see him, and Bormann had given the Munich Department of Health orders to call for the photographer the next day and place him in quarantine in a sanitarium.

Doubting the findings of the checkup, Hoffmann left for Vienna to obtain a second opinion from a doctor friend of his son-in-law, Baldur von Schirach. The Viennese doctor sent Hoffmann to a bacteriological specialist in a Wehrmacht hospital. The tests turned out to be negative. The information was immediately forwarded to Bormann, but Hoffmann waited in vain for a reply. Instead, the Vienna Department of Health sent word that instructions had been received from Führer Headquarters to have Hoffmann placed in quarantine as a carrier of a dangerous communicable disease.

Only the medical certificate plus family protection saved him from these drastic measures.

In December a detective from Hitler's escort came to see Hoffmann with orders "to interrogate all persons connected with your case and, if necessary, to arrest them." In order to avoid a bureaucratic hassle over the bacteriological tests in the Wehrmacht hospital, the photographer's stools had been sent to the labs as those of a twenty-six-year-old infantryman, Heinrich Hoffmann. These details fit the description of Hoffmann's son. Bormann was sure he had come upon a fraudulent maneuver: no doubt junior had sat on the can for his father. To avoid further consequences, Hoffmann was obliged for a while to produce his stool daily under SS supervision. No pathology was found. Again the reports went to Bormann, but headquarters continued to be closed to Hoffmann.

Early in April, just a few weeks before the end, which was already in sight, Hoffmann went to Berlin of his own accord. Whether he was motivated by a feeling of friendship or whether he simply did not want to miss out on a chance to take pictures of historic importance is hard to say. At the Reich Chancellery, Hitler voiced concern that he might end up by contaminating the entire headquarters. Bormann furiously snapped at him, "Who told you to come here? You'd have done better to invent death rays to bring down the planes." But eventually Hitler invited Hoffmann for a talk in his bunker living room, called for a bottle of champagne and asked him to spend the night. He did not want to hear about his illness. The next evening he asked Hoffmann to take Eva Braun back to Munich. When she refused, Hoffmann saw no further reason to stay. While he was taking leave of Hitler, the air raid sirens started wailing. Hitler told him not to leave during the attack, but Hoffmann felt "like a mouse in a trap. Bormann might bar the last exit at any moment. If he had his way, I would never get out of the Reich Chancellery alive." He took his small suitcase and ran panic-stricken through the devastated, smoke-filled streets to the Reich Postmaster General's office. There, waiting with an automobile ready to leave for Bavaria, was his old friend from Munich, Reich Postmaster General Wilhelm Ohnesorge.

Hoffmann's son later told the author that in his opinion Morell was not in on the plot. It is conceivable, because the bacteriological test was performed not by him personally but by an institute from which Bormann would have been able to order a positive result. Besides, the encounters between the Führer's personal physician and his Secretary were always marked by the kind of reserve that conceals dislike. Since Hitler with his stomach cramps and his fear of cancer felt safe only with Morell, there was nothing Bormann could do. For a while he may even have hoped to win over the fat, always slightly messy-looking medic, for he did not object when the 60,000-marks-a-year physician acquired pharmaceutical factories and used his position to increase their production. By order of the Führer, every soldier at the Russian front was compelled to carry a bag of Morell's "Russla powder" in his pocket or face severe punishment. Morell had convinced Hitler that the powder would prevent and destroy body lice, which plagued the troops and carried spotted fever. As a joke, soldiers would push their lice into the bags to prove that the creatures actually thrived on the powder.

On Hitler's orders, Bormann had to get Morell a professorship, and when the doctor requested an electronic microscope, the Secretary to the Führer was instructed to procure that for him too. Bormann personally did not put himself in his care. Once when he was ill—which seldom happened—and Hitler sent his personal physician to his quarters, Bormann accepted the medication but did not take it. He later sent it to his wife with instructions to pass it on to an aquaintance.

When in the fall of 1944 Hitler stayed in bed with a stomach ache for a few days, Bormann wrote home on September 30 that the Führer "is still convinced that Morell's is the right treatment." On October 4 he reported to his wife that Hitler's staff physicians Karl Brandt and Hans Karl von Hasselbach felt Morell's therapy was wrong. "Not being a medical man," Bormann wrote, "I cannot judge that." There were also other reasons why, at the time, he considered it inexpedient to get into a hassle with Morell. In fact, he did not get rid of the doctor until April 21, 1945; on that day Hitler sent his personal physician and a large part of his entourage out of Berlin to the South. There Morell was captured by the Americans, interned in a camp and interrogated endlessly. He died behind barbed wire, reduced to half of his former considerable weight.

As he had done in the Hoffmann intrigue, Bormann used Morell to bring disgrace on Hitler's staff physician Karl Brandt. For some time the surgeon had belonged to the team of Reichsleiter Philipp Bouhler, with whom he had organized the secret mass murder of mental patients. He was also a friend of Bormann's enemy Albert Speer. This fact alone made Brandt undesirable. When in January 1944 Bormann suspected Brandt of aiming for the office of Reich Minister of Health, Morell became worried. With Speer in charge of industrial production and Brandt as Reich Commissar —or even Minister—of Public Health there would be a sharp eye kept on the pharmaceutical industry, which did not suit Morell, who was about to procure for himself the exclusive rights to the German production of penicillin.

With support from Speer, Brandt did try to become Reich Commissar in August. Hitler had already approved the idea. Bormann had on his side an old aquaintance from the days of the Relief Fund, Leonardo Conti, the Berlin physician who had meanwhile ascended to the rank of Chief Physician of the Third Reich and who shared Brandt's ambition. On August 14, 1944, Bormann wrote to his wife that he had had a bad day; Conti had been supposed to see Hitler and bring charges against Brandt, but the Führer not only refused to see him but also furiously declined to listen to Bormann's arguments that Brandt was "an ambitious climber and mischief-maker" with whom he, Bormann, would not sit at the same table. Nor did Bormann get anywhere when he put pressure on the Führer by asking to be relieved of his post and sent to the front—a maneuver which held no risk whatever, since Hitler could not do without his Secretary, and the ex-gunner had never had any military training. A few days later the Führer's ill humor had evaporated; on August 26 Bormann was able to report home that Hitler was being particularly nice to him.

But Bormann did not give up that easily. On September 15 he called Conti to the Wolfsschanze, and the two conferred with Morell. The next day the fat doctor had his patient "A"—Hitler's code name—all to himself for at least an hour. During the following two days the three conspirators talked again. All they lacked was the proper provocation to start hostilities. Brandt supplied it by asserting that Hitler was slowly being poisoned by the strychnine compound Morell had prescribed. He made this remark on October 4. On October 10 Bormann triumphantly wrote to his wife: "Brandt will no longer be staff physician." Hasselbach was fired too. Hitler would not allow any criticism of Morell.

The new staff physician was the surgeon Ludwig Stumpfegger, who had held this position on Himmler's staff and who, like Brandt, had a record of medical crime. The Reichsführer SS was delighted to put him at the Führer's disposal, believing that this would give him one more confidant at headquarters, but here he was mistaken; Stumpfegger very soon switched over to Bormann's side.

In addition to his victory, Bormann wanted revenge. It came late, not until the second half of April 1945. At that time Brandt and his wife appeared again at the Führer bunker in Berlin to take leave of Hitler. The family was advised to take refuge at Obersalzberg. But Brandt, certain that he would be held responsible for the euthanasia crimes after the defeat, wanted to fight and die. Before he did, he wanted to be sure that his wife and son would be safe. He took them to Eisenach, from where he hoped they would reach the advancing Americans. But the commandant of the city had Brandt arrested as a deserter. When this was reported to Hitler, he ordered Bormann to find out whether Brandt had taken along the secret documents on the newly discovered nerve gas called Tabun. If so, Brandt should be court-martialed. The documents were quickly found and Brandt's innocence established, but Bormann let him be sentenced to death nevertheless. He felt that if the deserter argued he had "only done his duty," this in itself was proof that he had never been a loyal follower of the Führer's. Brandt was held in custody by the Gestapo, but Himmler did not have the sentence carried out; he thought that the doctor's international contacts might come in handy. It was left to the Allies to hang Brandt after the Nuremberg medical trials had found him guilty.

While Brandt was under Gestapo house arrest in his Berlin villa, Speer tried to save him; it was partly on his behalf that he came to the concrete bunker under the Reich Chancellery for a last talk with Hitler. He was venturing into the lion's den, for this was Bormann's last chance to destroy a man he had persecuted for many years with concealed but all the more relentless hatred. If during those last years Hitler had declared the man who was probably his most able minister fair game, Bormann would not have hesitated. As it was, he never achieved anything but a partial curtailment of Speer's powers.

Their mutual antagonism had started as guerrilla warfare at the time when Speer as the Führer's architect had drawn the plans for the face lifting of Berlin. The conflicts multiplied after February 1942, when Fritz Todt died in a plane crash and Speer became his successor as Minister for Armament and Munitions. By the fall of 1944 Bormann with the help of the Gauleiters had so sharply reduced the Speer ministry's prerogatives that the minister was obliged to make an all-out effort not to become just a part of the scenery. In the provinces, the Party controlled industrial production, taking workers away from their jobs—to repair bomb damages, build fortifications or be drafted into the Wehrmacht or the Volkssturm. Speer was no longer able to reach the scheduled target of defense production. On September 21, 1944, at the Wolfsschanze, he presented Hitler with a memorandum protesting against the Party's criticism and interference and requesting that his authority be newly defined. Without even reading it, Hitler passed it on to Bormann; Speer should settle the matter with him and with Goebbels as Minister Plenipotentiary for the Total War Effort.

A few hours later he was called into Bormann's bunker. The Secretary to the Führer received him "in his shirt sleeves, suspenders stretched across his heavy torso." Goebbels, on the other hand, was neatly dressed as usual. The clothes were significant for the part each was playing in the scene: "in his boorish way," one defied any criticism of the Party and would not tolerate any attempt to influence Hitler directly; the other operated with threats and cynical arguments. In the end Speer had to submit to the new twosome; the minister was obliged to bow to the Party. Moreover, his authority inside the ministry itself had been undermined; his closest collaborators, two old-time Party hacks, Saur and Dorsch, had switched to Bormann.

Since Göring's responsibilities had also been clipped in the economic sector, Speer occasionally confided in him. Bormann never failed to find out about these meetings very quickly. "Right now neither of the two likes Goebbels," he sneered in a letter to his wife early in November, "and they like me even less. In their eyes I am incapable of compromising, a stubborn Party man. And, like an idiot, I bring everything to the Führer." A few days later Speer was obliged to defend himself against Party gossip; it was said that during the Gauleiters' conference at Posen in August he had boasted about using exaggerated production figures to deceive Hitler. In an open letter he proved to the Gauleiters that such deception was impossible, since it was not he but the Wehrmacht that provided the figures. He sent his comments directly to the addressees without letting them be distributed, as usual, through the Party Chancellery.

Toward the end of 1944, when Speer tried to keep up the supplies of coal and gas despite the air raids, which constantly threatened and disrupted the railroad system, it became painfully evident how weak he was in comparison to the Party. On December 29 he asked Bormann for the Party's support in enforcing the emergency fuel restrictions for households. He complained that individual Gauleiters had "held up or diverted coal trains destined for other districts." Bormann played dumb. On January 20 Speer warned Bormann that the Gauleiters were confiscating coal trains at random, distributing the coal inside their provinces as they pleased. As a result several defense industries had been forced to close. "I would be grateful," he wrote obsequiously, "if you would instruct the Gauleiters, making sure that even in cases of extreme need they refrain from taking advantage of passing coal trains."

According to Speer, in the first days of February 1945 Hitler, Bormann, Goebbels and Ley often sat late at night in closed session, conferring about how to stop the advance of enemy forces into the Reich. Evacuation plans and ways to immobilize and destroy areas which could no longer be held were drafted. Speer tried to hold up the demolition, arguing that the Führer envisaged only a temporary loss of territory. At first Bormann, who still had hope for an ultimate victory, agreed with this argument. He could not believe, he wrote to his wife, "that fate should have allowed us and the Führer to walk this road to glory only to let everything turn to ashes now."

Bormann's office was in the badly damaged Reich Chancellery, which was now without heat, electricity or water. By the middle of February his letters began to sound more and more pessimistic: "There are times when I am without hope, because the German soldier is no longer persevering the way he used to and the way he could . . . Right now we are groping in the dark." And later "We haven't seen the worst. The most critical months are yet to come."

On March 18, 1945, Speer arrived at headquarters, where growing despair was taking a toll of everybody's nerves. He brought with him a new memorandum which stated that the war was lost and there was no point going on with it; further destruction of public utilities, transport systems, food supplies and industries would deprive the Germans of their chance to survive and make a new start.

Hitler did not read the memorandum right away, but suspecting what it might contain, reacted with ominous coldness. Bormann had flown to Obersalzberg for a few days. Speer immediately took off again for the western provinces, to prevent, if possible, the worst destruction. Thus there was no argument. But none would have had any effect, even under the most favorable circumstances. Hitler's course was set. His Nero Decree, which committed the Wehrmacht and the Gauleiters to a "scorched earth" policy wherever territory had to be abandoned, had already been drafted and would be issued the next day. Since the German people had proved itself to be the weaker of the fighting powers, Hitler stated in this order, and since the best had been killed in the war, the inferior elements that remained deserved no consideration.

At 2 A.M. on March 20, Bormann returned to Berlin and immediately went into conference with Hitler. Three days later his amendment to the Nero Decree emerged from the Gauleiters' telex machines. Since the Wehrmacht had been balking at the demolition orders, the Gauleiters were now given the responsibility. Bormann further ordered that cities and villages threatened by the enemy's advance should be evacuated to the last inhabitant, and where no transportation was available, people in the East and West should head for the center of the Reich on foot. Had this totally unprepared-for operation been carried out, practically all the people would have lost their possessions, and many of them their health and their lives. When the Wehrmacht protested that the stream of refugees would block the highways, Bormann decided that in that case they would have to use the back roads. "Together with Speer," General Guderian wrote later, "the military authorities tried to stop this insane order." Speer found support inside the Party Chancellery with State Secretary Klopfer, but because it was Speer's idea, it was high treason in Bormann's eyes. Had Bormann had his way, Speer would have been court-martialed even before he visited the Führer bunker for the last time.

During one of Speer's last trips to the West, Hitler, in a flash of his former benevolence, sent his chauffeur Erich Kempka with him. Bormann would not have minded at all if both the minister and the driver had been killed by strafing planes. As Kempka tells it, he had long been on Bormann's blacklist because he was "the last of the staff of old faithfuls" who was "allowed to enter the chief's office and private quarters without orders or special summons." Once when, as a result of Bormann's chicanery, Kempka applied for active duty at the front, Hitler refused to let him go, saying that he trusted him with his life, which was more important than "the constant bickering of Herr Bormann." Bormann's tricky strategy failed to work with, of all people, the most harmless man in the Führer's entourage.

On all larger issues, however, his influence on Hitler during the last phase of the Third Reich was stronger than that of any other man. Even though his lack of imagination and intellectual capacity prevented him from providing his Führer with any original thought, his fanaticism could still drive Hitler to the most radical decisions, and being the perfect apparatchik, he could phrase the orders even more sharply and execute them more ruthlessly. There is only one case known where Bormann helped to prevent an inhuman act.

In mid-February, British and American air squadrons bombed Dresden, which had hitherto remained undamaged. The city was largely destroyed. The extent of the loss of life has been debated for several decades. In any case, the first reports that reached the Reich Chancellery estimated 40,000 victims. Hitler was so outraged by this terror attack that he swore to have one captured airman shot for each victim. Goebbels supported the plan and instructed his department chief Hans Fritzsche to prepare for the mass murder by a news and radio campaign. But Fritzsche refused to have any part of it. His arguments gave Goebbels second thoughts, but in order to convince Hitler, Bormann had to be brought around. Goebbels and State Secretary Werner Naumann finally succeeded in persuading Bormann because Fritzsche cleverly held out the prospect of negotiations with the British for an exchange of 50,000 prisoners of war. This finally made an impression on Hitler as well; he saw a chance to create suspicion among the Allies and at the same time to replenish his declining divisions.

Of course, nothing came of it, and at some point the powerless dictator's rage against the enemy's air force was bound to explode. It happened during a military briefing in mid-March when Bormann reported that an American bomber crew which had parachuted to safety had been protected by German soldiers from being lynched by the public. Hitler ordered—as Bormann had surely expected—that all bomber crews captured in the past few weeks and those shot down in the future should be handed over to the SD and executed by SS firing squads. But now even Kaltenbrunner refused to go along. He and the Wehrmacht jointly decided to ignore the order. It was left to Bormann's Gauleiters to perform their own local justice. Here and there this was actually done, and after the war those executors of Bormann's orders paid for their murders with their lives before the Allied courts of justice.

In the last phase of the dying regime, Bormann's Party apparatus began to crumble rapidly. How far the deterioration had already gone, and with how little heroism the Nazi big shots were willing to fight for the destiny of the German people, was brought home to him in a grotesque episode of corruption that took place between Düsseldorf and Arnhem. In September 1944, British paratroopers had landed in the Dutch city and turned it into a combat zone. The population had been forced to evacuate their homes in haste. Referring to one of the Führer's sweeping statements, Bormann ordered that Germans from cities on the Rhine and the Ruhr, which had been struck particularly severely by bombs, should be furnished with household goods and textiles from the supplies left behind by the citizens of Arnhem. The Gau Düsseldorf promptly dispatched a task force to Holland consisting of six political leaders, three-hundred transport workers and a fleet of trucks. For three months they ransacked the abandoned city, enriching themselves and living it up behind the lines.

Hitler made use of this incident to remonstrate with Bormann on the bad morale of his troops. He wrote: "Unless this is acted upon at once, there will be the utmost damage to the prestige of the Party." Barely concealing his *Schadenfreude,* he added: "No one here knows to what extent Gauleiter Florian [Friedrich Karl Florian of Düsseldorf] is going to cover up for the incident. I have instructed the Düsseldorf security police to immediately search the homes of everybody involved."

With a "special Party Chancellery task force to strengthen the Party in areas close to the front" Bormann tried to regain a better grip on the political leaders. All through the second half of February his aides drew up plans and drafted memos and announcements. Their boss was hard to please. He wrote his criticism on the margins of their drafts—the necessity for the action and their specific duties should be more convincingly impressed on the Gauleiters, for "after the many failures of the Volkssturm operations . . . they are fed up to the teeth." After numerous corrections, which allowed him to squeeze in a few popular slogans about endurance and such, his instructions were sent out on March 6, 1945. They obtained for him a small crew of slave drivers and executioners to be assigned wherever morale and determination were crumbling.

To justify his action, he told the Gauleiters: "The enemy's invasion of Reich territory has caused crisis situations in certain areas which must be counteracted by every available means. Certain towns and villages have been abandoned by the able-bodied population without a fight" and have fallen "undefended into enemy hands." It often took just one energetic man to reverse a critical situation. But for war-connected reasons, the Party agencies were not always manned by "people who . . . themselves set an outstanding example of determination and valor." In such cases "fanatical, dynamic National Socialists" must step in. Each of the provinces still unoccupied by enemy forces should make at least five experienced leaders available for the operation. The nature of their duties was illustrated by the fact that each of them was to be assigned "one officer, one NCO and one enlisted man"—a sufficient quorum for a court-martial in an emergency.

In mid-March these superpatriots arrived at the Olympic Village in Wusterhausen near Berlin for a brief training course. They were drilled by men from the Party Chancellery. Being a bad speaker, Bormann wisely refrained from addressing them, restricting himself to supplying them with written maxims and pithy phrases. "You have all the powers you need to perform your duties. With skill and unwavering faith in victory we must stand up to the enemy and inflict heavy damages on him . . . Our aim is no longer orderly evacuation but the successful defense of every bit of territory. Every town, every village along the front line must be turned into an impregnable fortress. Strengthen all those who are faltering, stand up to every weakling with the necessary toughness, and punish without hesitation all army deserters and those who neglect their duties." By this pointless action, thousands lost their lives in the last weeks of a war that had long since become hopeless.

The Werewolf, organized as a secret partisan organization, turned out to be a total failure. At the Nuremberg Trials, several defendants attributed its creation to Bormann. Both prosecutors and judges voiced strong suspicion that this of all responsibilities should be blamed on an absentee. But their doubts were unjustified, for on March 10, 1945, Bormann had sent an open letter marked *"Geheime Reichssache"* to the Gauleiters "regarding special missions behind enemy lines." Under the code name "Werewolf" all volunteers ready for action should apply; they were to attack enemy supply lines and raid storage depots, destroy lines of communication and help "prepare airborne landings, etc." Goebbels supported the operation; a Werewolf radio station spread heroic tales which, almost without exception, were invented to scare the enemy and boost the courage of the Germans. There were a few pointless and unproductive scattered acts—barbed-wire road blocks were erected on supply routes, and a few sniper shots were fired —the only result being that the occupying forces ruthlessly shot hostages wherever they suspected the presence of Werewolves.

Needless to say, in those last weeks it was hard to find National Socialists willing to give their lives for Führer, *Volk* and Fatherland. Even the Gauleiters had ceased to believe in the success of such operations. They were staking their last hope on a miracle weapon which, under the seal of strict secrecy, Bormann's commissars told them would be launched at any moment. No one knew better than Bormann that no such weapon existed.

22

Two Bodies on the Bridge

During the last months of the Third Reich, Bormann achieved what he had been striving for over the past decade: he got his Führer more and more to himself. On February 2 he moved with a minute staff from the Party Chancellery's official residence into the Reich Chancellery, and when, two weeks later, its ruins became uninhabitable, he and Hitler's entire entourage went underground into a quadrangular labyrinth of cellars, garages, connecting passages and chambers. Now he was closer to his god than ever before, and closer than any other man of rank and influence.

Early in February the Führer and his Secretary began to draw up a sort of testament, leaving it open as to whether it was intended for posterity or as a document they would use at some future time. One of them took down what the other offered in justification of his policy. So far their manuscripts have been printed only in a French translation; they were found in the crates of files that Bormann had evacuated to the southern Tyrol during the last days of the war.

Ever since they started on their writing project (which, with interruptions, lasted until April) Bormann knew that Hitler regarded military defeat as almost inevitable and that his constant prophecies of the Asian hordes being annihilated on German battlefields were really nothing but fantasies. He also knew that disaster could be headed off only by a miracle, which was what Hitler's gambling instinct had banked on throughout his entire political career. Now they were waiting for it under a ceiling of almost three feet of concrete and behind six-foot concrete walls.

Prematurely senile, Hitler believed in the miracle only when he became fogged in by the rhetoric of his own monologues. Sharp-witted Goebbels, now a frequent though not yet a permanent guest in the bunker, was less hopeful and was preparing for his heroic exit into world history. Only Robert Ley, the third of the last paladins, still trusted in the kindness of fate with the fanatical mindlessness of a sectarian preacher. According to his letters to his wife, realist Bormann had growing doubts that a disaster could be averted, but if his hectic activity was to make any sense at all, he, too, had to believe in miracles, trust in Providence and the Führer's genius, and rely on the logic of Christian Morgenstern's* paradox that "What must not be cannot be." He focused all his energy on making time for the miracle to happen. Since time could be gained only by blood, the Germans must be made to continue fighting.

Late in February 1945, Hitler Youth officer Griesmayr sent him a manuscript entitled "What's the Score in the War?" and since it expressed his own thoughts better than he himself could have formulated them, he thought it would be appropriate to show the political leaders the right way. With apparent candor, the author wrote that for the first time "the present crisis" had caused crippling terror, open criticism and numb despair among wide circles of "the medium- and low-ranking leadership." This represented more of a threat than the Bolshevist advance. Logically, any National Socialist no longer able to believe in victory should commit suicide. The crisis could be overcome if every Party functionary were determined to go down with flying colors. "The ruthless liquidation of cowardly superiors is not only an act of justice but one of wisdom." And: "In times of emergency, it is better to shoot one weakling too many than a hundred too few."

This mixture of promises and threats appeared to Bormann to be the right medicine for the corps of functionaries. The text was to be printed "quickly" —in his instructions Bormann used the word four times—and sent to all Reichsleiters, Gauleiters, Kreisleiters and members of the Reichstag. Prior to that, however, "some of the unacceptable criticisms which unintentionally cause rifts" must be eliminated, including the statement that "in all emergency situations . . . a capsule of poison . . . is part of the requisites of heroic people." At this point Helmuth Friedrichs, who was in charge of Party affairs in the Chancellery, wrote in the margin: "Nope! Not necessarily!" Bormann had another reason to eliminate the paragraph. No one needed to know that the regime's elite would use this device as a last resort to weasel out of all responsibility.

During the days when this vest-pocket brochure was rolling off the presses, Hitler tried to stop the course of destiny in another way. In an attempt to bolster the morale of the troops, he went to the front for one last time. He did not have far to go, barely sixty miles; the Red Army had reached the Oder at Frankfurt. On that March 13 he told the officers and generals of the Ninth Army: "We still have things that need to be finished,

*Twentieth-century German poet, noted for his satirical verse.—*Tr.*

and when they are finished, they will turn the tide." Since Bormann knew there was no such chance, he did what he could to prolong the war; night and day, without interruption, he conferred with the Reich Minister of Justice and the chief public prosecutor on faster methods of bringing subversives to the gallows; with the generals of the armed forces operations staff on how greater Nazi fanaticism could be instilled into the troops; with Robert Ley, whom he sent as an itinerant preacher first to the army and then to the Tyrol, where he was supposed to organize gray-haired riflemen into a fighting force.

Bormann himself was unable to muster the confidence and heroism he demanded from his Party comrades. When late in March the Red Army advanced on Vienna and even the SS Leibstandarte could no longer hold the front, he advised his wife to do what he had so often forbidden his functionaries to do. Military leadership down there was so bad, he wrote her on April 2, that she should be prepared for the worst. "At the first sign of danger to the Gau Salzburg," he ordered, "women and children should immediately be moved from Obersalzberg to the Tyrol." A fleet of private cars, trucks and buses was especially assigned for the escape. But twelve hours later he had regained his self-control. "There is no danger," he wrote Gerda. "Vienna is 330 kilometers away, and the Americans at Heidelberg are 460 kilometers from where you are. We must wait and see what happens."

Vienna fell on April 13. Shortly before, Bormann had instructed the Gauleiters by radio: "Reichsleiter Baldur von Schirach will join the troops at his last military rank." Schirach, who ranked as an army lieutenant, knew what else was in store for him, since as Gauleiter of Vienna he had refused to lay the city in ruins. He reported to the command post of the Sixth SS Panzer Army under the command of Bormann's enemy Oberstgruppenführer Sepp Dietrich. Dietrich had already taken precautions and reinforced his command post with machine guns. "I have set up a hedgehog defense," he explained to Schirach, "just in case Adolf tries to get me for not having defended Vienna." The two Party old-timers were in the same boat.

Bormann's letter of April 2 to his wife is the last one that has been preserved (later ones were presumably lost). In it he once again accused the man whom for months now he had held responsible for the military catastrophe: Reichsmarschall Hermann Göring, officially still the Führer's successor, head of the Luftwaffe, the Reich Defense Council and the Four-Year Plan and thus of the entire economy, Reich Minister, Ministerial President of Prussia, and holder of many other offices, titles and medals. Bormann had come to an understanding with him in the first weeks after Hess's flight to England; the Reichsmarschall would have declined a wholehearted alliance with the functionary who was then still in an inferior position, as beneath his dignity. But recent years had destroyed all his glory from within. Only a façade remained of his former power structure, and the head of the Party Chancellery now had greater authority than anyone else to act in the Führer's name.

Bormann had been determined for a long time to get back at Göring for a variety of things, from the disdain he had shown him in the first years of his Party career to the Reichsmarschall's innumerable attempts to incite other big shots against him. The true reason for their antagonism ran still deeper, however. There were no two greater opposites among the regime's entire elite than these two men. Both were ruthless and unscrupulous, but where one had the mannerisms of a Renaissance prince with his splendor of uniforms and affectations of a patron of the arts, the other had the bigotry of the petty bourgeois; one was a loud-mouthed demagogue, the other an inflexible bureaucrat; one an unprincipled condottiere, the other a primitive fanatic. The days were over when Bormann trembled before Göring.

Since the army, the Luftwaffe and now even the Waffen SS had failed, Bormann was convinced that only the Party could save Germany. However, in this hour of need, it hardly proved itself the blood brotherhood of idealists it pretended to be. Bormann had to keep reminding its corps of leaders that according to the law of "caught together, hanged together," they had their backs to the wall and their only chance was to fight to the end. In a decree issued on April 1, Bormann impressed this on his Party comrades (see the Appendix, page 412). By now his pronouncements were nothing but a shrill fanfare of worn-out slogans strung together; in retrospect, they reflect the despair of a hunted man at the end of his tether rather than the confidence they were supposed to inspire. He talked of a "crucial hour of personal sacrifice" and the fight which must be conducted with "extreme tenacity and ruthlessness." "*Ein Hundsfott* [a scoundrel]"—he quoted Frederick the Great—"who leaves his Gau during an enemy attack . . . who fails to fight to his last breath, will be dealt with as a deserter. There is only one motto now: Win or die!"

That day, under his ceiling of concrete in Berlin, the "telex general" no longer had the means of communication to convey this message to all of his followers by the usual method. He was obliged to have it broadcast over the radio stations still in operation. But his entreaties had as little effect as his threats. Words were no longer worth anything, and he had nothing else to offer. Twelve days later he ordered that every city must be "held and defended to the bitter end." Whoever failed or resisted would be executed. And three days later, on April 15—American forces had just occupied Chemnitz and Bayreuth—he reminded the Gauleiters in another open letter (see the Appendix, page 412) that they would have to "deal with any situation instantly if necessary, and with extreme ruthlessness! . . . The faint-hearted, the incompetent must immediately be replaced by men of action . . . The true leaders," he announced in his confused way, "have burned all their bridges and are totally prepared."

Most of the Gauleiters no longer paid any attention to such outbursts. They were at the front, in an exposed position. Not, to be sure, the actual front, where shots were fired, but at the Party front, where they were supposed to act as bloodhounds, chasing people to death and ruin. Gauleiter Karl Wahl of Augsburg, who for years had been on bad terms with Bormann, now threw the orders bearing his signature into the wastebasket without reading them. The Gauleiter of Bayreuth was to regret his casual attitude; he was shot as a defeatist on Bormann's orders. Gauleiter Rudolf Jordan, in charge of Magdeburg-Anhalt, was sharply reprimanded by Bormann in a telephone call late at night because he and his staff happened to be not in Dessau, the capital of his Gau, but in a village on the Elbe where the American forces had dug in on the west bank. Jordan argued that he was closer to the enemy than the Wehrmacht generals. Nevertheless, Bormann ordered the Gauleiter back to Dessau so the people could see that he believed in victory.

Needless to say, Bormann never allowed any of the Gauleiters near Hitler. Gauleiter Wahl discovered that a number of jet fighters of the Me-262 type were parked, poorly camouflaged, ready for takeoff in the vicinity of the Messerschmitt plant. Since he knew that the Luftwaffe was in urgent need of this particular type of aircraft, he sent the plant's production engineer to headquarters, and since Wahl, in by-passing Bormann, had notified the military adjutant of the visitor's arrival, he received a visitor's pass signed by Hitler. For two days the engineer waited around in Berlin. Then Bormann sent him home with the message that because of the pressure of heavy workload, Hitler was unable to see him. Wahl thereupon decided to go to Berlin himself and enlighten Hitler, via Bormann, on the state of the war and on conditions among the people. He was planning to take the Gauleiter of Stuttgart, Wilhelm Murr, with him. But Murr was about to leave his capital and make off toward the South. "You ought to know," he warned Wahl, "that there is absolutely no point in trying this with Bormann, and besides, we would never leave Berlin alive." Dreading Bormann's revenge as much as the conquerors' punishment, Murr fled all the way to Vorarlberg, and there bit into his cyanide capsule.

Wahl received orders from Bormann to defend Augsburg to the last stone, and in case the city could no longer be held, to continue the fight with the Munich Gauleiter Paul Giesler, who was also Supreme Defense Commissar for South Germany. When Bormann again radioed him to hold out, saying that things were moving in "foreign relations" and that it was only a matter of hours, Wahl put his foot down. He told Giesler on the phone: "I no longer believe in that Bormann stuff. . . . As far as I am concerned, the war is over. Augsburg is about to fall, which is my downfall too." He saw to it that the city surrendered to the Americans without a fight.

The Draconian orders did not apply to Erich Koch, Gauleiter of East Prussia and Bormann's friend. When Königsberg, his provincial capital, was turned into a pile of rubble and the commandant capitulated with the sad remains of his division, Bormann announced that the Wehrmacht general involved had been sentenced to die on the gallows for having abandoned the fight behind the back of the Gauleiter, who happened to be absent. In truth, Koch had made off, just in time, for the port of Pillau, where a heavily laden, seaworthy ship was waiting for him. He later surfaced in Schleswig-Holstein, where the war had never reached. Equipped with false identity papers, he lived there in a village until 1950 under the name of Berger. He was exposed and extradited to the Poles, sentenced to death as a mass murderer but never executed. Bormann also provided most of the other Gauleiters with false identity papers. If the enemy swept over their territory, they were supposed to go underground and organize partisan groups. Bormann deliberately gave them Jewish-sounding names. Thus Gauleiter Rudolf Jordan turned into Richard Gabriel.

At headquarters, April 12 unexpectedly turned into a day of hope. A radio message intercepted from a U.S. news agency reported the death of President Franklin D. Roosevelt: the miracle which, by the sudden death of the Russian Empress had once saved Frederick II from total defeat, apparently was coming now to Frederick's admirer, Hitler. In his order of the day to the Wehrmacht, he predicted a turn in the war "now that destiny has removed the greatest war criminal in the world from this earth." Bormann regarded the event as important enough to call his Gauleiters that very night. He predicted there would be "a total reversal in the attitude of the Western powers toward the Soviet offensive in Europe." Now, at last, they would realize that Hitler had been their natural ally against the onslaught of Communism. The announcement of the death was "the best news we have had in years. . . . Tell all the men, the most dangerous man of this war is dead."

But at 5 A.M. on April 16, a murderous barrage of shell fire erupted all along the Soviet front on the Oder and the Neisse, during which half a million artillery shells plowed through the German positions. Enemy tank troops and motorized infantry crossed the Oder on both sides of Frankfurt. On April 18 and 19 Bormann noted in his journal: "Extensive battle action at the Oder front." And on April 20 he wrote: "Not exactly a birthday situation unfortunately."

Hitler did not really want to see any well-wishers, but his closest followers sent Gruppenführer Hermann Fegelein to see his sister-in-law Eva Braun, who persuaded her lover to accept handshakes and brief congratulations in the first minutes after midnight. In the afternoon the elite of Party and Wehrmacht assembled for the official birthday reception in the garden of the Reich Chancellery adjoining the bunker. Once again they were assured, although this had long since become absurd, that at the end of all the trouble the Germans would be victorious. Göring turned up in the bunker during the military briefings. Fed up with Hitler's remonstrations over the failure of the Luftwaffe, he had not visited headquarters for a long time. Now he had a special reason to appear. In the event that the Reich was divided by enemy forces, Hitler had assigned separate operational staffs for the North and the South. With American forces advancing into Saxony, this now seemed imminent. Göring, still the potential deputy head of state, had been assigned the South. He had come to take his leave. "My Führer, you probably won't mind if I leave now for Berchtesgaden." His fleet of cars was already at Karinhall, ready to go.

For the past weeks, Hitler and Bormann had also repeatedly discussed the idea of a retreat to the South. During the military briefings on February 24, Hitler had been asked whether his Berghof should still be artificially fogged in each time enemy planes were sighted over German territory. The stocks of chemicals were running out. "It is one of our last resorts," he had replied. "Nothing will happen to the bunker"—by which he meant the comfortable shelters built into the rock under Bormann's auspices—"but the whole site will be gone. If someday Zossen [seat of the Armed Forces High Command] is smashed up, where would we go?"

In April 1945 Zossen, fifteen miles south of Berlin, was still more or less intact, but it was threatened by the Soviet advance no less than the Reich's capital. Bormann felt that he had almost won his boss over to a move to the South. He indicated to the secretaries that the Führer's birthday would mark the end of their stay in Berlin. He had already sent some domestic staff to the Berghof with orders to get the house ready for the move. But as he had done so often, Hitler held up the decision; in cases such as this, he would always wait for an event to make his decision inevitable and then chalk it up as an act of fate.

He had not much time left now. American forces had already reached the Elbe, and the Red Army was sweeping westward across the Oder and the Neisse. One could almost predict when they would join up, divide the Reich in half and cut off all surface connection with Obersalzberg. Moreover, U.S. General George Patton's tank troops were advancing deep into Bavaria, and on April 20 the French occupied Stuttgart. There was no refuge in the West or Northwest. The Rhine and the Ruhr were surrounded by the British, who also stood outside Bremen and Hamburg. Bormann had every reason to urge that headquarters be shifted now lest they be trapped inside Berlin. He had also succeeded in having orders issued to Erich Kempka to prepare for the journey. Already there was a list of cars—private automobiles, trucks, buses, cross-country and armored vehicles—and of the people they were to take.

Understandably, Bormann was anxious to leave for Obersalzberg. There he had his wife, his children, his home and an air-raid shelter safer than the bunker of the Reich Chancellery. He would no longer have to camp in emergency quarters but would have his own area with ample room for normal office routine. Goebbels, with whom he was now sharing his

Führer, would not be able to follow him there because, as Gauleiter of Berlin, the Minister of Propaganda was obliged to stay and be trapped inside the Reich's capital. Besides, Bormann the military amateur believed that in the high Alps, between the South Tyrolean Dolomites and the Zugspitze, the remainder of the Nazi regime would be able to hold out for a long time with relatively little effort. And if the enemy's coalition should disintegrate, the Alpine Redoubt would most likely be besieged by the Western powers, with whom negotiations would be easier than with the Russians. If all was lost, the impassable mountains would offer better chances to get away and fade from sight.

In the early afternoon of April 20 Bormann announced to the secretaries that the departure was scheduled for two days hence at the latest, probably earlier. They might as well start packing their bags. Hitler's valet, Heinz Linge, and his cook were also advised to get the boss's wardrobe and food supplies ready for departure. But by evening Hitler had again changed his mind. He told his secretaries: "I must make a stand here in Berlin or die." He would therefore reduce his staff: the two older secretaries should go South. "Reichsleiter Bormann will tell you everything else." He would follow as soon as possible.

Nothing came of the departure by car because the Russians were already shelling the southbound autobahn. "Ordered departure of advance party to Salzburg," Bormann wrote in his notebook on April 20, the word "advance" obviously indicating that he was still counting on a general exodus. The next day's entry said: "Puttkamer takes off with majority of staff." Admiral Karl Jesko von Puttkamer, naval adjutant at headquarters, was something of a senior officer in the traveling party. At 2 A.M. they boarded aircraft at Gatow Airport, where Hitler's planes were kept; flying in the daytime would have been suicidal. Apart from the secretaries, the passengers were the stenographers, Dr. Theodor Morell, who had meanwhile been dismissed as Hitler's personal physician, and other staff members, including those from the Party Chancellery.

Bormann kept only his personal secretary, Else Krüger, and his aide, Wilhelm Zander, with him. On his orders the heads of most government agencies and the ministers also left Berlin that night. He instructed them to take the northern route because it had become impossible to get through to the south.

The fugitives who had hoped to find refuge in the Alpine Redoubt they had heard so much about were in for a disappointment. It was just a put-on, invented by Bormann and embellished by Goebbels with the promise that here the counteroffensive was being prepared with new and formidable weapons. During the night of April 21 Helmut von Hummel, Bormann's deputy at Obersalzberg, radioed to Berlin that he was having trouble finding accommodations for all the people that kept coming down. Helmuth Friedrichs radioed from the Party Chancellery in Munich that because of acute food shortages, Gauleiter Franz Hofer of the Tyrol was closing the borders of his province to any further influx.

Many years later, in the search for Martin Bormann, one of these many radiograms led to an absurd misunderstanding. On April 22, at 9:21 A.M., Helmut von Hummel received this message at Obersalzberg: "Agree to proposed *Übersee* [Overseas] transfer south. Reichsleiter Bormann." Soviet journalist Lev Besymenski, a Bormann biographer, interpreted this as an indication of a prescheduled escape to South America via Italy. The correct explanation is simple. As mentioned earlier, "Übersee" was the code name for those sections of the Party Chancellery that had been evacuated from Munich to Straubing on the Übersee, a Bavarian lake; their files were to be saved from the advancing Americans and evacuated to the southern Tyrol, where alternate quarters had already been prepared.

At the military briefings on the afternoon of April 22, Hitler finally decided against moving to the Alps. The day before, he had ordered SS Obergruppenführer (Lieutenant General) Felix Steiner to utilize all his forces to divert the Russians from Berlin. The Luftwaffe was supposed to join this effort with every aircraft at its disposal. But the regiments Hitler was shuffling around existed only in fragments, and there were practically no aircraft left at all. Steiner therefore thought it wiser to leave the doomed Reich's capital to its fate and lead his troops westward to the relative safety of American captivity. When Hitler learned that Steiner was ignoring his orders to attack, he screamed in a fit of anger, which unnerved all those who witnessed it, that he was surrounded by treason, deceit, corruption and failure. Since he could no longer fight, he would stay in Berlin and commit suicide. This meant that Bormann was defeated, and Goebbels, who at least aspired to historical immortality by some sort of Götterdämmerung climax, had won. Nor could anything change Hitler's mind now, much as Bormann and the generals encouraged by him tried.

On April 23, when Speer came to the bunker for the last time, Bormann saw one final chance for his plans. Outside Hitler's door he intercepted the man whom he had always fought and systematically discredited, and with unusual friendliness and familiarity asked for his help, since the Führer had always listened to him. Couldn't Speer persuade Hitler that it was "high time he took over command in South Germany? These are the last hours when it will be possible."

Hitler actually did ask Speer for his opinion, and Speer told him that there was no point in moving to Berchtesgaden, since the fall of Berlin would mean the end of the war in any case. If Bormann had had his way, the man who had offered this advice would not have left the bunker alive, especially since, during the conversation, Speer had made it clear that he had sabotaged the Nero Decree and prevented demolition wherever possible. But Hitler had now entered his wistful, resigned phase. Under his protection, Speer was able to stay in the bunker and witness how Bormann, in a burst of activity and with masterly intrigue, toppled the only man who, in name at least, still stood between him and the Führer of the German Reich.

During the military briefings the day before, Hitler, in a fit of unrestrained fury, had actually announced his resignation. He shouted that he had no more orders for the Wehrmacht, Göring should continue the war and conduct the negotiations with the enemy since he was better suited for this anyway. Bormann had been instructed to draft a message to this effect and have it flown to Berchtesgaden. Later, however, he had obviously once again succeeded in changing Hitler's mind. The message was never sent—understandably; Bormann could not expect much good if Göring became head of state.

But he could not prevent the incident from being reported to the Reichsmarschall, for General Eckard Christian, the liaison officer of the Luftwaffe at headquarters, had been present, and Göring's chief of staff, General Karl Koller, had had it confirmed by General Alfred Jodl. The news convinced Göring that his hour had come. On April 23 he radioed to the Reich Chancellery, asking whether Hitler agreed that he "take over at once the total leadership of the Reich, with full freedom of action at home and abroad as your deputy . . . If no answer has been received by 10 P.M., I shall have to assume that you have been deprived of your freedom of action" and shall "act for the good of our people and Fatherland." Visibly outraged, Bormann emerged with the text from the radio room, but Hitler hardly reacted at first. If his Secretary had thought the Führer would now board a plane and take off for the reckoning, as he had done in the Röhm affair, he was mistaken. Even Bormann's argument that this marked the beginning of a coup d'état left Hitler cold.

Soon thereafter another message came from the radio room, a telegram from Göring to Ribbentrop advising the Foreign Minister to proceed to Obersalzberg should the appointed deadline pass without a reply from Hitler. This, to Bormann, was proof of treason; now he could at least get Hitler to annul the decree on the succession and stop Göring from all further action. Bormann was authorized to draft the text of the radiogram. It accused Göring of treason, but assured him at the same time that no further action would be taken against him if he resigned from all his offices for reasons of ill health. "He can still negotiate the surrender," Hitler decided.

Göring's resignation arrived an hour later, but Bormann was not satisfied. He argued that since every little traitor was condemned to death, the people's fighting morale would suffer if exceptions were made in cases of government and Party leaders. He ordered the SS detachment at Obersalzberg to keep Göring under house arrest together with General Koller and Reich Minister Lammers. This order was followed up by another: "After our death, the traitors of April 23 are to be shot."

Strangely enough, the space for this eventful day remained blank in Bormann's journal, although it marked the fall of the last obstacle that separated him from the number two post in the country. Not until April 25 did he note: "Göring expelled from the Party." Since expulsion from the Party was the step just before a death sentence, he had obviously won Hitler over. Göring knew what was in store for him. Shortly before his arrest he told General Koller, who had just arrived at Obersalzberg by plane, "Bormann is my mortal enemy. He is just waiting to do me in." Now Koller was equally threatened, for he was the best-informed witness once the so-called treason was investigated. Directly afterward he received an order from Hitler over Bormann's radio line, summoning him to the Reich Chancellery without delay. With a number of excuses he postponed his takeoff. He later learned from the new head of the Luftwaffe, Robert Ritter von Greim, that no such order had ever been issued. "It seems a rather sinister story to me," Greim said. The Luftwaffe's General Staff officers also doubted that their chief would survive a visit to Führer Headquarters.

The state prisoners Göring and Lammers, and Reichsleiter Philipp Bouhler, who had joined them, were able to remain at Obersalzberg only briefly. On the morning of April 25, 318 British four-engine planes bombed the "sacred mountain of the Germans" in waves. It had not been fogged in, and in the bright spring sun, the buildings stood out clearly in the snowscape of the alpine valley. Most of them were heavily damaged; Bormann's and Göring's villas were totally destroyed. Having been warned in time, almost all the inhabitants were in the air-raid shelters. On this day Bormann's notebook lists three brief entries, one underneath the other, and since he always entered them only at the end of the day or later, their order is revealing. The first triumphantly reports Göring's expulsion from the Party. The second reads: "First massive attack on Obersalzberg." Not one word about the fate of his wife and children or his lost home. The third entry is underlined and reads: *"Berlin surrounded!"* Nor is his family ever mentioned again in the diary.

It is conceivable that the air raid saved the family's life. Adolf Martin Bormann later testified that as far as he knew, his father had sent a wire ordering his mother and the children to kill themselves with poison as soon as the *pater familias* declared the situation to be hopeless, but that Helmut von Hummel had not relayed the message. Hummel indirectly confirmed this to the author; considering the multitude of wires in those days, he could not remember exactly, but he thought it was conceivable.

Shortly before the air attack, Gerda Bormann had received several sealed courier pouches from her husband. They contained notes on Hitler's table talks, the last protocol of the late-night conferences, some of Hitler's watercolors, and among other papers and valuables, her and Martin's recent correspondence. Gerda was obliged to add all this to the personal luggage she had to take with her. Although a convoy had long before been assigned for the evacuation, in the present chaos it was no longer available. Gerda, her brother Hermann Buch's wife and fifteen children boarded a bus whose windows had been blasted by bombs and drove across the snowy alpine passes to Bolzano, where Gauleiter Franz Hofer of the Tyrol had prepared space for the Party Chancellery files and shelter for the family. At Wolkenstein, a remote alpine village on the Grödner Valley road about thirty miles east of Bolzano, the Bergmann family, as they now called themselves, had their quarters. They had no need to fear they would be betrayed by the almost entirely German-speaking population, who, thanks to the persecutions they had suffered from Italian Fascists, had become strong nationalists.

U.S. intelligence eventually found them, but by that time Gerda Bormann was a very sick woman. A doctor from Bolzano diagnosed cancer of the uterus, and as a last resort, recommended an operation which in those days could be performed only in Munich. Her sister-in-law appealed to the American city commandant of Bolzano to allow the patient to take the train that went from Italy to Munich once a week. The officer refused: "This is not a train for Nazis, but for people who have suffered under the Nazis." Gerda Bormann died on April 26, 1946, almost exactly a year after her escape, in the field hospital of an internment camp at Bolzano, where she was buried. A Catholic priest ministered to her during her illness and assumed the care of her children. They all asked to be baptized in the Christian faith; one of the girls became a Protestant, the others Catholics.

Adolf Martin Bormann entered a seminary and went to the Congo as a missionary but later left the order, married, and lives in the Federal Republic of Germany. During the time of his priesthood he said, "If my father were alive, he would never get in touch with me, for he hated the Catholic Church even more than he hated Bolshevism." And his younger brother Gerhard observed, "Certainly, our father would gladly have shot Adolf Martin." Gerda Bormann's legacy ended up in the possession of François Genoud, a Swiss citizen who lives in Geneva. For reasons hard to explain, he has not published the correspondence between Gerda and Martin in German, which means that all the passages quoted from it suffer from having been translated into English from the German via the French.

In Bormann's diary, the space for April 26 remained blank; perhaps because the inmates of the Führer bunker, accustomed to disastrous news, found this a day of faint hope. Coming up from Bohemia, units of Field Marshal Ferdinand Schörner's army group advanced some distance north toward Berlin, and General Walther Wenck's army had turned around at the Elbe and was fighting its way toward Potsdam. Attacks on the Russian encirclement of Berlin were to be launched from the north. Hitler exhorted the last of his faithful followers; once he had won the battle of Berlin, everything would again look different. He expected a lot from SS General Steiner's two tank divisions—or whatever was left of them. But toward evening of the next day, General Jodl, chief of the Wehrmachtführungsstab (Army Operations Staff), reported that the tanks had been ordered to move north, i.e., away from Berlin, because the Red Army was advancing rapidly in pursuit of the Germans who were fleeing through Mecklenburg into British-American captivity. Bormann's entry of April 27 starts accusingly: "The divisions on the way to rescue us are being stopped by Himmler-Jodl!" It is followed by a pledge: "*We* shall stand firm and die with the Führer: faithful unto death." Then the condemnatory remark: "There are those who believe they must act '*out of superior* insight,' they are sacrificing the Führer, and their disloyalty—damn them—equals their 'sense of honor'!"

Bormann had always suspected that Heinrich Himmler was determined to rise from the ruins of the Third Reich like the mythical phoenix from the ashes. But he did not yet know about the actual betrayal Himmler had been working on since mid-February 1945: his conspiracy with Count Folke Bernadotte, the vice-president of the Swedish Red Cross. Urged by Walter Schellenberg, Himmler had met with the count on several occasions, the last time on April 21, to discuss the ouster of Hitler, who was sick and therefore incompetent.

Bormann, being suspicious by nature, was certain he was on the trail of an SS plot. Two days earlier, on April 25, Hermann Fegelein had been sent to Steiner to urge him to start the requested attack, but since he had not been able to achieve a satisfactory result, he was now convinced that Berlin would fall. Being determined to survive, he moved, on April 26, from the bunker of the Reich Chancellery to a private apartment and late that night implored his sister-in-law Eva Braun by telephone to get herself out of the inevitable disaster. But by that time Bormann—on Hitler's orders—had a search party out to look for him. Agents from the Security Service found Fegelein dressed in civilian clothes in the company of a young woman, his packed suitcases and their contents—jewelry, gold pieces, watches, Swiss-franc notes and over 100,000 marks—leaving no doubt about what he had in mind. He was arrested and brought back to the bunker.

The next day, April 28, when the news from Radio Stockholm reached the bunker that Himmler was negotiating with the Western powers for the surrender of the German armed forces, the SS conspiracy was complete in Hitler's and Bormann's eyes. Steiner, Fegelein, the Reichsführer were all a gang of traitors. Eva Braun tried to appeal on Fegelein's behalf. But Bormann only poured oil on the fire: his drinking companion of many a night was going to die. Without a court-martial, Hitler ordered his execution by a firing squad, and shortly before midnight the sound of automatic pistols crackled in the courtyard of the Reich Chancellery.

The reckoning with Himmler had to be canceled; he had joined Grand Admiral Karl Dönitz, who was now supreme commander of all the armies in the North with headquarters at Plön in Holstein.

The new chief of the Luftwaffe, Robert von Greim, was still in the bunker; he was ordered to leave in a training plane, a hedgehopper, and arrest the Reichsführer. In his diary Bormann summed up the dramatic events in two sentences: "High treason—unconditional surrender is announced abroad. Fegelein busted—cowardly, tried to leave Berlin in civilian clothes." Bormann remarked to Hitler that he had always known that people don't wear their loyalty on a belt buckle but in their hearts. He telegraphed Admiral von Puttkamer, who had flown to Munich: "Instead of issuing urgent orders and appeals to the troops assigned to our rescue, those responsible are silent. Loyalty seems to have turned to disloyalty!" Hitler's verdict on Himmler said: "Never shall a traitor succeed me as Führer." If there was ever to be a succession at all—which Bormann in his determination to survive still believed—the number of candidates by now had shrunk to a minimum. But a note on this same April 28 shows that Bormann would not give up: "Our RK [Reich Chancellery] is turning into a pile of rubble; the world now teeters on the razor's edge."

In bitter street fights, the Red Army was advancing deeper and deeper into the heart of the city, narrowing the ring around the Führer bunker and pounding it with ever-increasing shell fire. Soviet tanks were appearing south of the Potsdamer Platz, just a few hundred yards away from headquarters. General Wenck's army was the last chance of survival, but as it approached from the west, it was no longer able to progress against the superior force of Soviet tanks in the vicinity of Potsdam.

Together with the Chief of Staff, Hans Krebs, Bormann sent Wenck an urgent telegram late that night. Himmler was planning to surrender the Germans unconditionally to the Western plutocrats. "Only the Führer can bring about a turn of the tide." This required "immediate contact between us and the Wenck army." But the general did not have the necessary tanks; he incorporated into his own the remains of the Ninth Army, which had fought its way from the Oder, by-passing Berlin, and headed back toward the west.

The night Himmler's defection was announced, Bormann and Generals Krebs and Burgdorf were seeking solace in a few bottles. But the alcohol merely removed their inhibitions. Burgdorf went from arguing into noisy vituperation. He asked what on earth he had ever committed himself for and why the Wehrmacht had gone to war "with a faith and idealism unique in human history." "They died for you, for your life of luxury, for your thirst for power," he charged. Millions of people had been sacrificed while "you, the leaders of the Party, enriched yourselves on public property. You have splurged and feasted, amassed enormous riches, stolen country estates, built castles, lived off the fat of the land, cheated and suppressed the people." Bormann tried weakly to defend himself; he at least had never enriched himself. He forgot or suppressed the fact that the Party had made him what he was and that his air-raid shelter at Obersalzberg housed supplies so vast that after the guards departed, the looters waded up to their ankles through flour, sugar and other foodstuffs.

With little hope of a rescue operation left, Hitler decided on the night of April 28 to get married and to dictate what he intended to leave to posterity. In his political will he expelled Göring and Himmler from the Party and appointed Dönitz Reich President, Goebbels Reich Chancellor and Bormann Party Minister. In his personal testament he appointed the "most loyal Party comrade, Martin Bormann," executor of his will and authorized him "to make all legal and final decisions." Both wills were signed by Bormann as witness. Göring speculated later at Nuremberg that Bormann might even have been their co-author. Around midnight on April 28, while the testaments were being transcribed from shorthand into typescript, an official from the municipal administration of Berlin, summoned by Goebbels, married Adolf Hitler and Eva Braun. Together with Goebbels, Bormann officiated as a witness.

Bormann now considered himself the actual heir of the Third Reich—justifiably so, for the Führer was determined to commit suicide, as was Goebbels, and with Bormann's help the entire elite of the NSDAP had been demoted during the past few months. Still frantically busy, he hardly took time out to celebrate. Copies of the documents, the only proof of his new powers, had to be taken out of Berlin. A major was instructed to take one carbon copy to Bohemia to Field Marshal Ferdinand Schörner, a second messenger was to reach Field Marshal Albert Kesselring, the commander of the armies in the South, and Bormann's adjutant, Wilhelm Zander, was ordered to proceed to Plön. All were given covering letters from Bormann. To Dönitz he wrote: "Dear Grand Admiral! Since all divisions have failed to arrive and our position seems hopeless, the Führer dictated the enclosed political testament last night. Heil Hitler! Yours, Bormann." The couriers never reached their destinations.

No one among the regime's elite could have suited Bormann better than Dönitz as the future head of state. The admiral had no political following to speak of. In the Party, he did not even figure as a dark horse; if he wanted to make use of it, he would have to depend on Bormann. He was also a stranger to the workings of the government. He would always need a man experienced in administration and well versed in political strategy to pull the strings in the background. If it were possible to maintain a government as Hitler had conceived it, the new Party Minister would be even more indispensable now than before.

On the night of April 29 Hitler once again asked Jodl by radio what had happened to Wenck, and what about those other units in the vicinity of Berlin that had been assigned to his rescue. For hours there was no reply. Bormann smelled more treason. He radioed to Plön, no longer over the relay station of the Wehrmacht High Command (code name "Teilhaus"), but over the Gauleiter of Mecklenburg's radio station. The text read:

Dönitz:

> Our impression grows daily stronger that the divisions in the Berlin theater have been standing idle for several days. All the news we receive is controlled, suppressed or distorted by Teilhaus. As it is, we can only broadcast through Teilhaus. The Führer orders you to proceed at once, and mercilessly, against all traitors.
>
> Bormann

And an added postscript: "The Führer is alive, and is conducting the defense of Berlin."

These phrases deserve analysis. The address in itself is unusual; it suggests that Hitler himself may have sent the message. Without actually mentioning his name, Keitel, chief of "Teilhaus," is counted among the traitors. There is not even a hint of Hitler's imminent suicide; Bormann had to keep him alive and in office as long as possible, for his own was only a borrowed authority.

During the early-morning hours of April 30, a message came from Keitel that nothing could be expected from the relief armies. To Hitler's question, SS Brigadeführer Wilhelm Mohnke, who was in charge of the defense of the Reich Chancellery, replied that he could not hold the area beyond May 2. That did it. Bormann and Otto Günsche, Hitler's personal adjutant, were summoned into the holy of holies and learned that the double suicide was planned for that afternoon and what should be done with the bodies. About twenty faithful followers, called in by Bormann, shook hands with Hitler and heard him murmur something unintelligible before he retired to his bedroom. When Hitler woke up around noon, he called his chief pilot, Hans Baur, and ordered him to take Bormann to Plön, since he had "a number of instructions from me" which it was extremely important for Dönitz to know.

At 3:30 P.M. Bormann, Günsche and Heinz Linge were waiting for the pistol shot outside Hitler's living room, but it was drowned out by the heavy gunfire. When Günsche finally opened the door, Hitler and his wife were dead. Goebbels and Hitler Youth leader Artur Axmann arrived on the scene. Dr. Ludwig Stumpfegger certified the deaths. Wrapped in a blanket, Hitler's bleeding body was carried out by Linge and Stumpfegger; Bormann carried Eva Braun's. Erich Kempka, the Führer's chauffeur, took it away from him. "Eva used to hate Bormann," he said later, justifying his act. "She had been on to him and his power play for a long time. She should not have remained in Bormann's arms for one more step." When the corpses turned to charcoal in the blaze of nearly fifty gallons of gasoline, Bormann stood under cover in the entrance to the bunker with his arm raised. Then Goebbels, for the moment still senior official, called him in to the military briefing with Generals Burgdorf, Krebs and Mohnke.

The new Reich Chancellor, long determined to die with his family, had no desire to rule. Bormann, on the other hand, wanted to survive and continue at the levers of power. He referred to Hitler's final orders, which Goebbels had to respect. The purpose of the briefing was to combine the widely differing aims of the two last paladins into a joint plan. They finally solved the problem by agreeing that there must be a way to negotiate with the Russians for a brief cease-fire and obtain safe-conduct for Bormann through the enemy's lines. This would give the little doctor his end of the world and the fat Party functionary his new beginning. Krebs, who years before had been military attaché in Moscow and had once received a demonstrative bear hug from Stalin in the railroad station, was to go over and negotiate with the enemy. Mohnke was instructed to establish contact through an emissary with a white flag.

As far as Dönitz was concerned, Bormann intended to manipulate events so that he could not be eliminated. At 5:40 P.M. on April 30, while Hitler's body was still smoldering, he sent an ambiguous message to Plön:

> Grand Admiral Dönitz:
> In place of the former Reichsmarschall Göring, the Führer appoints you as his successor. Written confirmation is on its way. You will immediately take all such measures as the situation requires.

The text gave the impression that Hitler was still alive. "Written confirmation" referred to the copy of the will which Wilhelm Zander might or might not deliver at some time.

Surprised by his nomination—he had seen Himmler as the successor—Dönitz addressed a telegram to Hitler, asserting his devotion.

Shortly before midnight on April 30, word arrived at the bunker that the emissary was with the staff of a Soviet division and that General Krebs was expected there. In the early hours of the morning, at 3:50 A.M., Krebs climbed out of a Soviet jeep at General Vasili Chuikov's headquarters and presented three documents, typed on the Führer's typewriter: an authorization to negotiate signed by Bormann, a list of the Reich's new executive officers as designated in Hitler's political testament, and a letter to Stalin, drafted jointly by Bormann, Goebbels and Krebs. It informed the Moscow dictator of the advantages he would gain if he helped an anticapitalist, antiplutocratic government of National Socialists to power. This would necessitate, however, that Bormann travel to Plön to see the new head of state, lest the reactionary elements in the new government come to an agreement with the Western powers.

Krebs enlarged on these arguments in personal conversation. It was to the Kremlin's advantage that there be only one German government at the moment—namely Reich Chancellor Goebbels and Party Minister Bormann —with its seat in Berlin and thus exclusively at the disposal of the Soviets for discussions. The Russians were the first to be told of Hitler's death, which was being kept secret to prevent another government from being formed. Should this happen, Stalin would forfeit his advantage, but it inevitably would if the Russians refused to grant a cease-fire and insisted on surrender. What would happen then had already been proved by Himmler, who had tried to make a pact with the Western powers. But at 10:15 P.M. a telephone message from Moscow rejected these proposals.

Krebs made one last attempt. If unconditional surrender of the fortress of Berlin was what the Russians demanded, the new government needed at least a head start: certain persons it would indicate by name must not be treated as prisoners of war by the Red Army. With a small escort, Bormann would travel to Plön, where his contacts with the Soviets would make him indispensable. Chuikov rejected this proposal also. When Goebbels and Bormann heard the meager result of the negotiations over a telephone line that meanwhile had been established, they told Krebs to return. He left Chuikov's headquarters exhausted after nearly twelve hours of talk.

While Krebs was negotiating and Goebbels was devoting the last hours of his life to his children, Bormann continued to play his game. At 7:40 on the morning of May 1 he sent Dönitz another wire: "The testament is in force. Coming to you as soon as possible. Till then you should in my opinion refrain from public statement." Shortly after 11 A.M. the text was on the admiral's table, but all that Dönitz could gather from it was that Hitler was no longer alive. The first telegram had authorized him to act on his own, but since the wording was so vague, he suspected that Bormann was setting a trap for him. In order not to be considered a traitor, he had to be sure that Hitler was dead. He ordered that all witnesses who could be reached in the Führer bunker be questioned and their testimony radioed to him. The order did reach Bormann but he never acted on it.

Just before 2 P.M. Krebs was back at the Reich Chancellery. Bormann reproached him for not having made the advantages of a cease-fire suffi-ciently clear to the Russians. He was sure he could negotiate a better result over the telephone. But the line had been shot to pieces. He ordered General Mohnke to have it restored at once and began to shout when Mohnke told him that he would not send any soldiers to their death for such a thing. The SS general coldly retorted that he alone would decide where his men were going to be assigned. Bormann gave in; for the first time he realized how little he had inherited of Hitler's authority. And it occurred to him that he had no friends among the SS officers in the bunker; they had already agreed among themselves to arrest him if he should try to slip away. Goebbels no longer paid attention to Bormann's plans either. He insisted that Dönitz should now learn the whole truth and dictated a radiogram, which was sent at 2:16 P.M. Whether he liked it or not, Bormann had to sign after Goebbels. It informed Dönitz that Hitler had already been dead for twenty-three hours and that the senders had been appointed members of the new government. But Dönitz had no intention of having his team chosen for him, and he was by no means prepared to make Party comrades Goebbels and Bormann his ministers. He gave orders to have them both arrested should they turn up in Plön. Then he announced over Radio Hamburg, the only radio station still available, that Hitler had died at the head of his troops.

On the afternoon of May 1, the alliance of the two shadow ministers came to an end. Goebbels, Chancellor-without-a-Reich for a day, drafted his justification for posterity. Party Minister Bormann found himself a bag made of oilcloth and sewed it into the blouse of his gray SS uniform that bore the Obergruppenführer insignia. Inside he put the original of the late Führer's personal will and a carbon copy of his political testament. They gathered for a farewell meeting in a small group that included Magda Goebbels and Artur Axmann. General Hans Baur was summoned, and Goebbels urged him to escort Bormann to the airfield at Rechlin, and—should this still be possible—to fly him to Plön. Dr. Stumpfegger arrived; he had taken it upon himself to poison the six Goebbels children. That took place at 6 P.M. The parents died two and a half hours later.

During the afternoon Mohnke had prepared for the breakout at night. As the senior official, Bormann insisted on taking the lead, which he was granted, since everybody was certain he would not be able to perform it anyway. Mohnke announced that soldiers, civilians and women should exit from the "Citadel" (the Reich Chancellery's code name) in ten mixed successive groups and first try to leave Berlin toward the north, using the subway tunnels to get away from the enemy. He suggested to Bormann that they break out together in the first group, but Bormann opted for the third, insisting that Baur and Dr. Stumpfegger should also be assigned to this group. Mohnke interpreted this as a sign of cowardice, but it may also have been clever calculation; if the advance party found a weak spot in the enemy encirclement and managed to get through, the next groups would be able to use the gap. Moreover, the third group was led by Werner Naumann, State Secretary in the Ministry of Propaganda, who was an experienced soldier and had been earmarked for Minister of Propaganda on the list of Cabinet ministers Hitler had left. He might be a possible ally in a joint meeting with Dönitz.

But Bormann was no longer as self-assured as he had acted that afternoon. Up to this moment the ruler of the Chancellery had remained a stranger to the war. Early in April he had still boasted to his wife that if it was his destiny, he would go to his death proudly holding his head high "like the old Nibelungen in King Attila's hall." For days now, the enemy had been shelling the bunker. The wounded were crowding the cellars. Corpses were lying outside in the ruins. Bormann was not a soldier by nature and had no talent for the role of tragic hero; he simply wanted to survive. But his confidence of success was sinking by the minute. He missed his Führer, whose promises had buoyed up his spirits. His drinking companions, Krebs and Burgdorf, emptied their last bottles before they shot themselves. Nobody missed him, nobody cared about him. He had no orders to give, and if he had, there was no one left to obey them. With Baur's help he drew a picture of the Big Dipper with the North Star to help orient himself in the nights when he would slink through Brandenburg and Mecklenburg on his way to Schleswig-Holstein.

How meek he had become was witnessed that night by Hans Fritzsche, Goebbels' department chief who, with a number of his colleagues in the basement of the adjoining Ministry of Propaganda, had decided to go to the Russians with a white flag and offer to surrender Berlin. This would have made the breakout a violation of martial law. Fritzsche said he would consider delaying his action if Bormann would immediately disband the Werewolf. During a pause in the shelling they met in the garden of the Reich Chancellery, and without protest, Bormann accepted the request. As Fritzsche related later, he summoned "a few men in SS uniform and in civilian clothes" and gave the required order.

Soon after dark the first group got ready to leave. Among them was Bormann's secretary, Else Krüger. He had seen little of her in the last two weeks; whatever there was to write, he had typed himself. When she said goodbye, he said, "I shall try, but there isn't much use now." In his diary he noted: "Escape attempt!" As the word suggests, he doubted that the attempt would succeed. Mohnke was the first to climb out through a basement window of the Reich Chancellery; followed by his group, he ran across the Wilhelmsplatz toward the subway entrance. Every twenty minutes another group followed.

They stumbled along the tracks in the darkness of the tunnels. They hardly dared use their flashlights, for the Russians, too, were roaming through the tunnels and lurking on the subway platforms. Behind the Friedrichstrasse S-Bahn station, the tracks dip down underneath the river Spree. Here the tunnel was closed by a watertight bulkhead. The Mohnke group climbed upstairs and snaked its way north through the rubble. Most of them were captured on May 2.

The Naumann group lost its way and reached the Friedrichstrasse station only after a lengthy detour. At the Weidendamm Bridge nearby, they ran into a group of soldiers and decided to join forces and break through to the north along Friedrichstrasse and Chausseestrasse. An antitank block separated them from the Russian line. Baur was trying to sneak off sideways through the ruins, but Bormann caught him. "Stay with us, Baur. You may get yourself shot. I still need you." Heavy infantry and mortar fire made it seem impossible to get through. Toward midnight Erich Kempka appeared on the battle scene with a group. Bormann felt the breakthrough could be achieved with the help of tanks—and lo and behold, three tanks and three armored cars were rattling up in their direction. Kempka stopped them.

During the hearing of the International Military Tribunal at Nuremberg, Kempka described how the tanks rolled slowly toward them, and how he and Dr. Stumpfegger moved ahead and took cover behind the first, Bormann and Naumann stepping alongside its turret. The tank was hit; it exploded and all of them were blown off to the side by the blast. Wearing a leather coat over his SS uniform, Bormann collapsed in the blaze, obviously dead. But Kempka never saw the body. Since Kempka himself not only survived this encounter but managed to get through all the way to Berchtesgaden, the court could not establish conclusive evidence that the defendant was no longer alive.

In actual fact, he survived the explosion unhurt. During the next attempt to get through to the north, he lost sight of Baur. The wounded Luftwaffe general was picked up by the Russians and for many years presumed that his companion had been killed in the attempt. Bormann, however, had taken cover in a shell crater. There he came upon Axmann, his adjutant Günter Weltzin, Dr. Stumpfegger and Goebbels' adjutant, Günther Schwägermann. Werner Naumann also joined them.

What happened next, presumably around 3 A.M. on May 2, was described by Axmann in his testimony late in the fall of 1945, but nobody would believe him. Only the historian H. R. Trevor-Roper, who as an intelligence officer interrogated many National Socialists after the war, called this the most likely version. At the Friedrichstrasse S-Bahn station, the group, numbering about ten men by now, entered the roadbed and walked west along the tracks. On the embankment they tore the insignia off their uniforms and threw away their weapons. Axmann, an experienced army soldier —he had lost his right arm in the war—noticed how uncertain Bormann felt. At times he would rush ahead of the group as though he could not get away fast enough. Without interference they approached the Lehrter Bahnhof S-Bahn station. They discovered just in time that Red Army soldiers were standing on the platform. The quick getaway split the group. Bormann, Naumann, Schwägermann, Axmann, Weltzin and Dr. Stumpfegger jumped down from the roadbed into Invalidenstrasse, landing right next to a Russian outpost. The Russians took them for stragglers from the Volkssturm, offered them cigarettes, started talking to them in broken German —"*Voyna* [The war] kaputt, Hitler kaputt"—and marveled at Axmann's artificial arm.

This was too much for Bormann's jittery nerves. Together with Stumpfegger he headed east, toward the Charité Hospital at ever-increasing speed. They did not get far. At the Sandkrug Bridge (today an East German checkpoint) they ran into Russians again. The others noticed that the breakaway had made the soldiers suspicious. They sneaked off in a westerly direction toward Moabit along Invalidenstrasse. Naumann and Schwägermann vanished in the underbrush of a fairground. Axmann and Weltzin turned back only after they heard tanks rattling up ahead. Returning to the Lehrter Bahnhof S-Bahn station, they saw in the dim light of dawn two men lying on the bridge at Invalidenstrasse which crosses the tracks of the Lehrter Bahnhof freight depot. They recognized Bormann and Stumpfegger. Apparently both were dead, but there was no sign of blood or injury. Axmann knew that the bunker elite had been issued poison capsules. He presumed that both had used them to kill themselves.

A little earlier, Bormann and Stumpfegger might have been in his situation. Perhaps they could have gotten away. Axmann succeeded and was even able to make his way down to the Alps. But Bormann and Stumpfegger gave up. Both had reasons for not wishing to fall into Russian hands alive.

Weltzin was the only one who could have confirmed Axmann's report, but he died in Soviet captivity. Naumann was able to confirm Axmann's version only up to the talk with the Russian outposts. The investigators and judges doubted the story because the reports of Kempka and Baur had Bormann die an hour earlier, and each in a different place. A news flash from Radio Prague I, on May 7, 1945, completely confused the situation. That day the radio station was still in German hands, since Field Marshal Schörner was holding Bohemia. The station announced that in Berlin, together with Hitler and Goebbels, Reichsleiter Bormann, State Secretary Naumann, Generals Krebs and Burgdorf had "died in battle, as loyal Germans."

Thus it is not surprising that the search for the missing Secretary to the Führer began soon after the end of the war, and since it was unsuccessful, continued for more than a quarter of a century. The Soviet secret service might have been able to solve the mystery much earlier. Since May 1945 it had had in its possession an imitation-leather pocket diary which on its first page listed Bormann as its owner, with his addresses and telephone numbers. And there is no doubt that the daily entries, from the beginning of the year to May 2, were made in Bormann's hand, as were the addresses and telephone numbers on the pages in the back.

According to the Soviet account, an officer of the Fifth Army pushing into Berlin handed in the notebook, reporting that it had been inside the leather coat of a dead German who had been found next to a disabled tank. By now we know better. Perhaps the officer had been casual in wording his report. Perhaps the Soviet secret service was napping and recognized the importance of the discovery too late. Perhaps it took the diary for a ruse —Bormann stuffing his notebook into the coat of a dead man before going underground. Besides, a Bormann living underground suited Soviet policy for Germany as proof that in the Western world a Fascist network may, without interference, pursue its conspiratorial aims. But meanwhile it has been proved that in the early hours of May 2, 1945, at Invalidenstrasse in Berlin, Martin Bormann committed suicide.

Postscript:

How I Found Martin Bormann

I learned for the first time on May 1, 1945, a few hours before his death, that there was a Reichsleiter Martin Bormann and that he was one of the Third Reich's leading figures. I was nineteen years old, and after being wounded as a war correspondent I had been assigned to the Reichssender Berlin (Berlin's national radio station). The broadcasting studio was in the section of the capital that the Red Army had not yet captured. The broadcasting crew worked under ground, protected from Soviet artillery by heavy concrete ceilings. That night the monitor service reported that Radio Hamburg was spreading the news that Hitler had been killed in action and succeeded by Dönitz as Reich President. Although we were only a few miles away, we had no idea of the events taking place inside the Reich Chancellery.

At that time the broadcasting studio had an acting military commander. When we started wondering whether or not the war was going to continue, he straightened us out: "There can be no question of an end to the war. The Führer has now opened the way for us to negotiate with the Americans and the British so that we can jointly march on Moscow." No one was thrilled at the prospect. But what else could the commander say, since he was sheltering in his post two rather prominent representatives of the regime, SS General August Heissmeyer and his wife, Gertrud Scholtz-Klink, the Reichsfrauenschaftsführerin [leader of the National Socialist Women's Organization]. That his sentiments were right on target was proved shortly afterward by a phone call from Central Command: "We are not going to surrender but will break out at midnight via Spandau and Nauen, heading for Hamburg. The sortie will be led by Reichsleiter Bormann."

The name surprised everyone. "Hey, what's this?" one Berliner asked.

"Have all them generals died with the Führer? Who the hell is Bormann?" The Reichsfrauenschaftsführerin clued us in: "He is the Führer's closest confidant, his Secretary." I was not the only one to find it strange that a secretary of all people should lead us into the last battle. It was the first time I had ever heard his name.

As I know now, the Secretary did not lead me. I was lucky; I managed to get out of Berlin and was at Nuremberg as a journalist in 1946. Immediately after the trials of the surviving Nazi elite had ended, I visited Hans Fritzsche, who had been acquitted and released from custody. From him I heard about Bormann for the second time. Fritzsche told me that on the night of May 1, 1945, he had requested Bormann to dissolve the Werewolf. Surprised, I asked how this unknown man could have had that much power. Fritzsche replied, "In a way, the man had more power than Hitler." He promptly illustrated this by another story. The half-Jewish wife of the owner of an Augsburg printing press was to be deported to the East. To prevent this, Fritzsche called on Bormann, warning him that it might cause considerable commotion in the printing office, since the woman was very popular with the employees. Fritzsche suggested that the deportation be postponed until after the final victory. Bormann agreed, and with a few lines written on a scrap of paper, stopped it.

Years later, when I was researching subjects of contemporary history as an editor on *Stern* magazine, I came upon Bormann and his activities more and more often. He had meanwhile become a permanent feature in the German and international press, a kind of "Flying Halberstadt man" who, like the "Flying Dutchman," roamed all over the world but could never be tracked down.

Among other occasions he was sighted:

In July 1945 on a train in Schleswig-Holstein by the author Heinrich Linau;

in 1947 in Australia by Joseph Kleemann, Secretary of the International Seamen's Union;

in 1950 in Africa by a Danish journalist, in Argentina by a British, and in Spanish Morocco by a German colleague;

in 1951 in Chile by Paul Hesslein, former member of the Reichstag in the Weimar Republic;

in 1952 in Rome, disguised as a Franciscan padre, by a former employee of the NS Ministry of Armaments.

This went on, year after year, with ever new and fantastic stories. As a precaution, the Chief Public Prosecutor of the Berlin District Court opened a preliminary inquiry in 1959 against Bormann on suspicion of collaboration in the euthanasia operation, of the persecution of the Jews, and of multiple murders in the "scorched earth" plan. Two years later the case was passed on to the Public Prosecutor's Office at the Frankfurt Court of Appeals, and the Hessian government put up a reward of 100,000 D-marks for any "information that might lead to the discovery, whereabouts and arrest of the accused." More than anyone else, Frankfurt's Chief Public Prosecutor Fritz Bauer was convinced there had to be fire where there was that much smoke, and when in 1960 Adolf Eichmann was kidnapped from Argentina by the Israeli secret service, he stepped up the search for Bormann all the more energetically, since during his interrogations Eichmann had supposedly indicated that Bormann was still alive.

The large reward on the one hand and the press honoraria for sensational Bormann stories on the other launched countless new hunters on the elusive Reichsleiter's trail. In January 1964 Erich Karl Wiedwald, then thirty-eight years old, offered *Stern* magazine a Bormann story. He claimed he had escaped with the Secretary to the Führer from besieged Berlin. Bormann was now, he claimed, living with other ex-Nazis in the jungles of Brazil on a huge plantation, protected by trigger-happy bodyguards. He even promised to arrange a meeting. Two *Stern* reporters flew to Brazil and duly waited in vain for weeks to make contact. Years later Wiedwald was obliged to admit at a court hearing in Frankfurt that he had made up the story.

At *Stern*'s editorial office, the hoax spurred interest in the mysteriously vanished Bormann. I was asked where I would look for him. "Certainly not in South America," I said. "In fact, I would start the search in the place where he was last seen." That same day I flew to Berlin.

Artur Axmann had often given me information on contemporary history. I also knew his testimony to the Allied secret services on the Bormann case. Together we went to the Lehrter Bahnhof. He showed me the place where he had seen Bormann and Dr. Stumpfegger lying lifeless—he purposely did not say "dead," for "I am not a medical man"—on the bridge, and he described in detail what had happened prior to that. Since Axmann had known both men well, there was no question of his having made a mistake in identifying the two people. I also was certain he would not tell a lie to protect Bormann from further persecution, should he still be alive, for the two had been bitter enemies.

If at one time two bodies were lying on the bridge, I said to myself, somebody must have removed them. There is in Berlin the "German Office for Notification of Next of Kin of Wehrmacht Members Killed in Action." It helped me, as it had on previous occasions, quickly and unbureaucratically. Bormann was not listed there, but Stumpfegger was. The files contained a notarized copy of a letter which the head of Post Office 40 (Lehrter Bahnhof) had sent, registered and accompanied by eleven photographs, on August 14, 1945, to Frau Gertrud Stumpfegger, Nursing Home, Hohenlychen:

Dear Frau Stumpfegger:
On May 8 of this year, members of the Post Office found on the railroad bridge at Invalidenstrasse the body of a soldier, killed in the

battle of Berlin. According to identification found on the body, it was Ludwig Stumpfegger. Since it must be assumed that the deceased was your husband, I regret to inform you of this sad fact and would like to express my sincere sympathy to you on your tragic loss. Your husband was buried, together with several other soldiers killed in action, on May 8 on the site of Alpendorf (formerly Landesausstellungs-park) [National Expositions Park] at 63 Invalidenstrasse, Berlin NW 40. The pictures found on the body are forwarded to you herewith as per enclosure . . .

Most of the employees in the Parcel Post Office knew nothing at all. A few vaguely remembered that some of their colleagues had buried dead soldiers at the end of the war. The incident was by now almost two decades old, and whoever had worked there at the time had been too old to serve in the Wehrmacht. All the same, it turned out that four postal workers had been assigned by the Russians to bury the dead, and one of them, Albert Krumnow, was still alive. He led me to the spot where the dead had lain. It was exactly where Axmann, too, had seen them, but during the succeed-ing days they had obviously been robbed of their belongings. Krumnow told me that the taller of the two bodies had been clad only in new white underwear and that the other, stouter one had been in a gray army uniform without any insignia of rank. Someone had made off with the boots. On the orders of a Red Army soldier, he and his colleague had carried the dead on a stretcher to the exposition ground nearby and had buried them there in a pit.

On this occasion I also learned that Krumnow had already been ques-tioned about this incident by the Berlin police on behalf of the Frankfurt Public Prosecutor's Office. I was having government competition. Obvi-ously it would be best to join forces, but the judicial authorities' traditional distrust of journalists could be overcome only if I could offer new material. This I was able to produce when, on the twentieth anniversary of the end of the war, my *Stern* colleague Kurt Wolber and I published a series on "The Last Hundred Days" of the regime, in which we used Axmann's report on Bormann's death. Subsequently a reader—Herbert Seidel—wrote from Berlin. He described how, as a fifteen-year-old boy, he had rummaged through the freight cars at Lehrter Bahnhof early in May looking for food, and on that occasion had passed by the two bodies on the bridge at In-validenstrasse. Like Krumnow, he had also been struck by the fact that the bodies had not shown any injuries.

If it were possible, I said to myself, also to track down the people who took the clothes, other objects or even papers, there might be a chance to prove that besides Stumpfegger, Bormann too had died on this spot. But I could not get any further without official help.

At the Frankfurt Court of Appeals, First Public Prosecutor Joachim

Richter was in charge of the Bormann case. I found him unbiased and ready to cooperate if it would serve the cause, a man whom I could trust and who proved a friend even in tough situations when I was being attacked for the work I was doing. (Unfortunately he never read this report, for he died in the spring of 1977 shortly after his retirement.) I came to him just in time; a few days later he was going to dig for the remains of the two dead men on the spot Krumnow had described. It was to be done inconspicuously, and the press was not to get wind of it. Since my investigation had already proceeded this far, I was the only one authorized by Richter to be present. But by the second day of the digging, at least forty reporters showed up. They became witnesses to a total failure; we did not find a thing because structural changes in the area had misled Krumnow in his search for the burial place. Seven years later the remains of Bormann and Stumpfegger were found about thirty-six feet away.

Richter and I agreed that we were on the right track. We were a team now, and we were not going to give up. Defying the rules of his office, he told me about the testimony of Willi Stelse, a toolmaker who had worked in a plant near Lehrter Bahnhof and had also seen the bodies. At the time, Stelse testified, a French slave laborer had appeared at the plant one day in a leather coat—postwar loot—and a colleague had seen him pull out of one of the pockets a diary, bound in imitation leather, which according to a handwritten entry had once been the property of Reichsleiter Bormann.

Ever since then, Richter had searched in vain for the colleague—Stelse vaguely remembered that his name was Bruno Fechner. Now it was my turn to try. On my next fact-finding trip to Berlin, I picked up the Berlin telephone book. None of the listed Fechners fit the case. I finally looked through the entire letter *F* listing and found a Bruno Fechtmeier who lived in the immediate vicinity of the place where the bodies had been found and, of course, also close to the plant. He confirmed that he had seen Bormann's diary and reported that a foreman at the plant by the name of Ernst Ott had pocketed and kept the little book.

Now the Frenchman, supposedly called Maurice or some such name, had to be found, and foreman Ott had to be asked what had happened to the diary. Richter appealed to the French police to trace the former, but they were unsuccessful. *Stern* reporters traced Ernst Ott to North-Rhine Westphalia; he had left his family in Berlin and moved there with his girl friend, Inge Schwandt, but he had recently died in an accident. However, Inge Schwandt knew the whole story. She and her boyfriend had given the notebook to her father, a long-time Communist whom the Russians had appointed deputy mayor of Berlin Center. "You can be sure you'll get a huge food package for that," her father had promised.

In the summer of 1945 Ernst Ott and Inge Schwandt were summoned to Soviet headquarters at Karlshorst, questioned for two days and actually given the lucrative reward. Moscow journalist Lev Besymenski was finally allowed to use the diary in his book on Bormann, which was published in 1974.

But Joachim Richter already had copies of a few pages of the diary in 1965; they had been put at his disposal by the East German judicial authorities. He allowed me to copy the address part, which led my *Stern* colleague Armin von Manikowsky to an important discovery. He remembered that in *The Bormann Letters,* which had meanwhile been published, a mistress of Martin's was referred to by just the letter *M.* Now he found at the top of the list of addresses the name Manja Behrens, her private phone number in Dresden, and the phone numbers of the theater where she performed.

It seemed to me that this provided sufficient evidence that the corpse on the bridge had been Martin Bormann's. We also had adequate proof as to when and how he had died. All that was missing was the body itself, but neither the Public Prosecutor's Office nor *Stern* magazine was able to have the Berlin site of several thousand square yards completely dug up. However, the Berlin authorities assured me they would let me know if for any reason excavation should be undertaken on the location.

In November 1965 Rolf Gillhausen, *Stern* magazine's assistant editor in chief, decided the time had come to publish the results of the investigation. They appeared under the heading "Bormann Is Dead." They were supposed to put an end to a legend, but they turned out to be the beginning of a witch hunt. Simon Wiesenthal, the professional Nazi-chaser living in Vienna, who on previous occasions had discovered various Bormann traces all over the world, announced at a press conference that he had always known *Stern* magazine was a Nazi publication and Jochen von Lang a long-time Nazi trying to protect Bormann, who was alive, from further persecution. Joachim Richter also got into trouble; sometime before, his superior, Frankfurt Chief Public Prosecutor Fritz Bauer, had received a letter from Adolf Eichmann's son Horst Adolf indicating that Bormann was secretly living in Argentina. Bauer considered this a likely version. He reproached me, saying that my report was irresponsible as long as the corpse was missing. In retaliation I asked him to search for Dr. Ludwig Stumpfegger, who, as an SS physician, was proved to have conducted human experiments on Soviet prisoners of war. Bauer flared up: "That's nonsense. You know as well as I do that the man is dead." It was not the moment to ask him where he was hiding Stumpfegger's body.

If I wanted to refute all the critics, I had to find Bormann's corpse. But where? Maybe his body, like those of so many soldiers killed in action, had been moved away. Three of my reporter friends, Dieter Heggemann, Cornelius Meffert and Gerd Baatz, helped me with the search whenever they were in Berlin. We walked through a great number of Berlin cemeteries, went through the casualty lists, interviewed cemetery custodians. My efforts became known even in East Germany. Once, when I had something to do there in the press office of the Privy Council chairman, I was asked by the official in charge of the West German press whether I would give him a chance to talk with me at lunch. Over Hungarian goulash in the Haus der Intelligenz he told me what was on his mind. "You are jeopardizing your career. Bormann is not dead. We have proof that he is being financed in South America by West German Chancellor Kiesinger." I was not anxious for those proofs.

As long as the corpse, or rather what was left of it, had not been found, Bormann would continue to make his ghostly appearances all over the world. Simon Wiesenthal announced he had photos of the ex-Reichsleiter, now living in Argentina. Reinhard Gehlen, the former chief of West German intelligence, stated in his memoirs that even during the Third Reich, Bormann had been an agent of Stalin's, had of course defected at the end of the war and had since died in Moscow. Erich Karl Wiedwald also reappeared, with an improved version of his story, and published a book in Holland.

On behalf of *Stern* editor in chief Henri Nannen, I was allowed to participate in the demystification of the last and most beautiful of all Bormann legends. A British and an American mass-circulation magazine had come out with a series entitled "Bormann Is Alive." The author was Ladislas Farago, a former member of U.S. Naval Intelligence. He maintained he had found out that before the end of the war Bormann had shipped precious metals, foreign currency and art works valued at $200 million to Argentina by submarine, and chaperoned by emissaries of a Catholic bishop, had left for Rome after the collapse. There he had met Evita Perón, who had offered him asylum in Argentina, provided he transferred a large part of his riches to her. At the time, he called himself Ricardo Bauer. Farago had been able to produce not only a photograph of this man but also certificates by Argentina's political police, according to which Bauer actually was Bormann. The fanciful Farago had borrowed the name—Bauer, Ricardo—from the head of the Berlin Document Center whose name was Richard Bauer; he was a German who had emigrated and returned to Germany as an American. Meanwhile Bauer had also become a friend of mine and helped me wherever possible.

I met Farago in London. I had brought along a professor of anthropology from Hamburg University and the son of Hitler's photographer, Heinrich Hoffmann, who had often taken pictures at Hitler's headquarters and of course knew Bormann. The anthropologist was to examine the shape of the skull in Farago's Bormann photos. But the Hungarian immediately dissociated himself from his pictures; he had not taken them himself but had obtained them from the Argentinean secret service. Neither Hoffmann nor the anthropologist could detect any resemblance to Martin Bormann. *Stern* magazine's South America editor, Hero Buss, found the explanation soon after. The photographs depicted a schoolteacher living in Argentina. Buss also exposed the validity of the secret-service certificates. With the help of a $50 bribe, he had the Argentinean secret police provide him with written proof that Ladislas Farago was actually Martin Bormann. After that the Bormann hunters gradually lost interest in concocting new fairy tales.

Nevertheless, the case kept bugging me. Yet I almost missed my last chance of finding Bormann. One day Herbert Seidel, a former member of the Hitler Youth, sent me a clipping saying that excavation was shortly to begin on the site where I still assumed Bormann's remains to be. I alerted my Frankfurt friend, Joachim Richter. He reacted promptly and informed the Berlin police and building authorities. Their workmen eagerly set to it, hoping to earn the 100,000 D-marks that had been put on Bormann's head. Being ignorant of legal matters, they did not know that only the live head was worth that much.

Lo and behold, they soon came upon two skeletons—in a strange position, the skull of one next to the feet of the other. To Richter and myself this was the first indication that we had reached our goal. Krumnow had told us that during the transport "the little fat one" had fallen off the stretcher again and again until finally they had decided to carry the two bodies in this position. And not wanting to touch the already decomposing flesh, they had dumped the load into the pit just like that.

The final word was left to the experts of forensic medicine. That they were successful I owe to another friend, the British historian David Irving. One day when he asked me how I was coming along with my Bormann search, I had to admit: "If we ever find him, it is quite possible we may not be able to identify him. We have no record of his teeth." During his next stay in the United States, Irving went to the National Archives in Washington and there found Bormann's dental chart as recorded by Professor Hugo Blaschke of Berlin, who had treated the teeth of the entire Nazi elite and made the drawings of them for the Allies after the war. It confirmed that we had found the right skull. Dental technician Fritz Echtmann and Blaschke's assistant, Katharina Heusermann, were also able to recognize the work they had done on Bormann's teeth. Moreover, Bormann's height of 170 cm, recorded in his questionnaires, coincided with the skeleton's measurements. It was even easier to identify Stumpfegger, since the Berlin Document Center had the results of a medical examination SS physicians had conducted. Finally, the chief pathologist of the Munich police department, Moritz Furtmayr, reconstructed the heads and faces of the two deceased from the skulls. We compared his work with photos of Bormann and Stumpfegger. There could no longer be any doubt.

After the case was closed, the Frankfurt Public Prosecutor's Office put Bormann's remains at the disposal of his family on condition that they were to be buried only, not cremated. It is, after all, not entirely impossible that they may be needed again as evidence at some point. So far, Bormann's children have not accepted those conditions. For the time being, therefore, the Secretary to the Führer reposes in a cardboard box in the vault of the Frankfurt Public Prosecutor's Office.

Appendix

DOCUMENTS

Part A
Excerpts from Final Report* of the Frankfurt State Prosecution Office under File
Index No. Js 11/61 (GStA Ffm.) in "Criminal Action against Martin Bormann on
Charge of Murder" dated April 4, 1973†

Prefatory Note:

The complete dossier consists of the following:
a) Judgments and decisions in other court cases, guide indices for documents and
other exhibits (in special carton).
b) 8 special volumes on personal data and concrete accusations lodged against the
accused.
c) Special volume on excavations on 20/21 July, 1965.
d) As of this date [of writing], 34 volumes of documents relating to the search [for
Bormann].
e) As of this date, 10 volumes of criminal prosecution documents.
f) Special volume re [Ladislas] Farago.
g) Special volume (bound in green) on Axmann.
h) Green loose-leaf notebooks from office of Berlin Chief Police Commissioner
regarding excavation of skeletons on December 7/8, 1972.
i) As of date of writing, 2 special volumes on skeleton finds.
k) [Germans don't use *j* in alphabetizing] 1 Leitz correspondence file with Document Center data documents on the accused.
l) Card index (classified according to: witnesses—white cards; alleged places where
the accused had resided—red cards; informants—blue cards).
m) 2 notebooks listing expenses.
n) Blue portfolio on facial reconstructions.
o) Loose-leaf notebook summation with closing remarks together with appendices.

*This Final Report was written by First State Prosecutor Joachim Richter, who pursued the
search for Martin Bormann for over a decade on behalf of the Frankfurt State Prosecutor's
Office. On account of the cooperation furnished in the clarification of the "Bormann Case,"
the Hessian Minister of Justice, Karl Hemfler, granted the author the right to first publication
of this Final Report. (Editor's note.)
†The Final Report has been abridged by the author for the edition in English translation.

Table of Contents [unabridged] of Summation (of Final Report) with Exhibits

III. Preliminary Proceedings Search [for the accused] and Preliminary Examination

In 1959 the Chief Public Prosecutor of the Berlin District Court initiated Preliminary proceedings against the accused, as substantive information had come in to the effect that Martin Bormann was still alive. This proceeding 3 P (K) Js 248/60 was filed together with a Letter of Transmittal dated May 24, 1961 (Vol. I, sheet 96 of the foregoing record) with the local authority and on July 2, 1961, in accordance with Par. 145 GVG [Gerichtsverfassungsgesetz, Law of Judicial Organization] and was simultaneously accepted for action by the office of the State Prosecutor (Vol. II, sheet 130–131 of the Records).

The accused was charged at this time with complicity in murder in the "Euthanasia" crime and in the Jewish persecution, as well as attempted murder in the "Scorched Earth" policy. The charges are found—summarized in their entirety—in the Arrest Warrant of the Frankfurt-am-Main Court dated July 4, 1961-Gs 4388/61 (Folder Volume II, sheet 147 of the Records). The proofs offered in evidence consist almost exclusively of documents.

The locale of jurisdiction derives from the "Euthanasia" crime having been perpetrated in Hesse, specifically in the Hadamar death camp near Limburg; the persecution of Jews also took place in Hesse, i.e., in Frankfurt-am-Main, and finally the Hitler headquarters at which the accused regularly served from December 16, 1944, to January 16, 1945, was located in Ziegenberg near Bad Nauheim.

The proceeding concentrated at first on the search for the accused, as indications had been forthcoming that he had escaped from Berlin and had survived the war, such reports originating both from within the Federal Republic and from many parts of the world. Following his alleged escape from Berlin he was said to have been seen in several places in Germany, in Argentina, Australia, Bolivia, Brazil, Chile, Colombia, Denmark, Ecuador, Guatemala, Great Britain, Italy, Canada, Cuba, Mexico, Austria, Paraguay, Peru, Switzerland, the Soviet Union, Spain, South Africa, Surinam, Venezuela and the United States.

No claim is made for the completeness of the foregoing list.

With concurrence of the Hessian Minister of Justice (Decree dated November 13, 1964-III (IV) 901/61-) (Sheet 75 of the Report Book) an award of 100,000 DM (one hundred thousand Deutsche Marks) was authorized for information concerning the person, residence, and leading to the extradition and arrest of the accused.

A press release was thereupon distributed, dated November 23, 1964 (Exhibit 5 of this report [deleted]).

In the March 1965 number of the English-language edition of *Reader's Digest,* pages 74–77, there appeared an article entitled "World's Most Wanted Criminal" by Blake Clark, the subject being the accused. This article made reference to the reward that had been posted. The end of the article reads literally: "If you know or have seen a man whom you believe to be Martin *Bormann,* call the nearest West German embassy."

Reader's Digest is published in all the languages of the world.

With respect to this appeal the [West German] Foreign Office issued a directive dated June 4, 1965, to all diplomatic and consular offices representing the Federal Republic of Germany. The Foreign Office was supplied with copies of a fingerprint chart, copies of the text of the Arrest Warrant, and a photograph of the accused taken around 1939.

All leads offering even a semblance of seriousness were pursued within the German Federal Republic through the Special Commissions in the Offices of Criminal Prosecution of the various district governments. Insofar as these leads dealt with foreign countries, the Foreign Office was asked to check the information through the diplomatic offices representing the German Federal Republic. All the information, whether originating at home or abroad, proved false.

The possibility was considered that the accused might be arrested in South America. The governments of Argentina, Brazil and Chile do not recognize a simple judicial action, i.e., an arrest warrant, as sufficient grounds for suspending the statute of limitations. They insist on a court decision to open Preliminary Examination, otherwise a request for extradition encounters the objection that statute of limitations has expired. Therefore, on April 25, 1968, a motion was entered to open Preliminary Examination against the accused. Preliminary Examination proceedings were initiated on the same day (Volume IV, sheet 396 ff. of the Record).

The examining judge concentrated all his efforts mostly on the search for the accused. All judicial investigation measures carried out to this end failed. Since the purpose of a Preliminary Examination, namely the procurement of evidence on which to base a decision whether the trial should proceed or the accused declared immune from prosecution (Par. 190, Section 1, StPO) could not be established, on October 14, 1971, the termination of the Preliminary Examination was petitioned. The examining magistrate granted this petition with a Court Order dated December 13, 1971 (Vol. IX, sheet 1470 of the Record).

IV. Reasons for the (unsuccessful) Attempted Disinterment on July 20/21, 1965, at the Ulap Fairgrounds in Berlin

---

Along with the continuing search for the accused based on the various leads, information was developed concerning the movements of the accused immediately following the breakout from the Reich Chancellery on the evening of May 1, 1945. From this it was concluded that contrary to what Hitler's chauffeur Kempka maintained, the accused did not lose his life in the explosion of a German tank at the Weidendamm Bridge but survived this explosion unharmed, and then, in the company of witnesses Dr. Naumann, State Secretary in the Ministry of Propaganda; Schwägermann, Adjutant to Goebbels; Dietrich, chief liaison officer of the Reich Youth Leader of the NSDAP to the Reich Propaganda Ministry; Reich Youth Leader Axmann and his adjutant Weltzin (died on October 16, 1945, in Russian captivity); as well as with Dr. Ludwig Stumpfegger, Hitler's last personal physician in the Führer Bunker, he walked along the railroad tracks from the Weidendamm Bridge to the Lehrter railroad station. This is confirmed unanimously by the judicially interrogated witnesses aforementioned, Dr. Naumann, Schwägermann, Dietrich and Axmann in the Preliminary Examination proceedings. The whereabouts of Dr. Stumpfegger at first remained unexplained.

This group broke up at the Lehrter railroad station. Witnesses Dr. Naumann, Dietrich and Schwägermann initially concealed themselves in the bushes south of Invalidenstrasse and then moved on in a westerly direction, managed to hide for several days in the area then used for industrial purposes west of the Lehrter railroad station and with difficulty reached the areas occupied by the Western Allies. The accused went with Dr. Stumpfegger along Invalidenstrasse in a northeasterly direction to the Sandkrug Bridge, the witness Axmann went with Weltzin southwest in the direction of Alt-Moabit. The witness Axmann also succeeded in making his way out of Berlin, first to Mecklenburg, and later to Lübeck. In the vicinity of the Moabit Criminal Court witnesses Axmann and Weltzin encountered Russian tanks, which forced both to retrace their steps.

1. *Axmann*

In his interrogation of April 17, 1970, by the examining magistrate (Vol. V sheet 743 ff. of the Record, especially sheet 745) the witness Axmann continued his account as follows:

"As we passed the bridge over the railway tracks on the way back, we saw two men lying at the bridge's end in the direction of the Stettin railroad station. During our withdrawal the fire had become more intense. We knelt down beside both bodies and recognized without question Martin Bormann and Dr. Stumpfegger. Both were lying on their backs and both had their arms and legs outstretched sideways. Dr. Stumpfegger lay in this position some 2 to 3 meters behind Martin Bormann. I spoke to Bormann, ran my hand over him and shook him back and forth somewhat, and noticed no breathing. Moreover both men were wearing the overcoats they had been wearing previously. In view of the battle situation I previously described, it was not possible to conduct a closer examination to verify to what extent death had actually occurred in the two persons. In any event, they gave an impression of lifelessness. I could see no signs of wounds or bullet marks. I was also unable to detect any external changes around the mouth that could have suggested that they had taken poison. At any rate, I did not open the mouth. I also observed no striking odor, such as prussic acid or strong smell of bitter almonds. The examination and observations I have just described here refer to Bormann. I removed no object of any kind from their clothing. The time when this occurred I would estimate at somewhere between 1:30 and 2:00 in the morning, it could have been 2:30—May 2, 1945—in any case, it was still dark, though the terrain was illuminated by fires burning all around. This explains how I was able to recognize Bormann's face beyond any doubt. There were no bodies other than these two lying in the immediate vicinity of that bridge. As far as I can recall, Bormann's eyes were closed, at any rate not wide open."

The witness Axmann expressed himself similarly earlier in an interrogation by Professor Dr. Kempner in Nuremberg on October 10, 1947. The interrogation ran verbatim as follows:

Q: And where did Goebbels get his poison, later?

A: I assume, from the Führer's personal physician.

Q: Who was that?

A: That was Dr. Stumpfaecker.*

Q: What became of him?

A: I saw Bormann and Stumpfaecker lying on the Invaliden Bridge in Berlin. As I stood before them, they gave no sign of life.

Q: You assume, then, that Bormann is dead?

A: In my interrogation in Oberursel I indicated that around 2:30 in the morning I was standing in front of these men, with my companion.

Q: Who was that?

A: That was Welzin. [Also misspelled in Nuremberg Court Record, should read Weltzin. (German editor's note.)]

*Misspelled in the Court Record of the International Military Tribunal (German editor's note).

Q: Is he still alive?

A: I also heard that he had died in Russian captivity.

As was found in various interrogations in the course of the Preliminary Examination (i.e., Erna Axmann, Ilse Fucke-Michels, *née* Braun, Wilhelm Gause, Liselotte Gause, *née* Schmidt) the witness Axmann had already told the same story in conversational recounting of the events in Berlin and in connection with his interrogation on October 11, 1962, by the Berlin Criminal Police (Sheet 3 ff. of Special Volume "Excavations in Berlin 1965").

2. *Correspondence from WASt*

In a letter dated January 16, 1963, the German Office for Notification of Next of Kin of Former Wehrmacht Members Killed in Action (WASt) in Berlin-Borsigwalde wrote the Central Office of the Land Court System in Ludwigsburg that Dr. Stumpfegger had been found dead on May 8, 1945, by employees of Post Office 40 (Lehrter Railroad Station) "on the bridge over the R.R. tracks on Invalidenstrasse" and was buried on the same day on the grounds of Alpendorf in Berlin NW 40, Invalidenstrasse 63 (Exhibit 9 of this report [deleted]). A map of the grounds in question may be found in Folder Volume V, sheet 770 of the Records . . .

3. *Krumnow*

In the investigation to find those employees of Post Office 40 who had been involved in these burials, Postal Clerk Albert Krumnow was contacted, and in his interrogation by the police on April 24, 1963 (Special Volume, "Excavations in Berlin"), he stated among other things the following:

"Around May 8, 1945—I now no longer recall on what day exactly—we were ordered by the Russians to remove bodies lying on the railroad bridge on Invalidenstrasse and bury them. At that time I personally went to the bridge and found two male corpses. One of these two corpses was a German Wehrmacht soldier, while the other was clad only in underpants and undershirt. I still remember that with the corpse dressed only in underwear, there was something about a pay book [*Soldbuch*] which indicated that it belonged to an SS doctor. I saw no SS uniform items anywhere in the immediate vicinity of the body. My colleagues Wagepfuhl and Loose and another named Paul Stelze and I were just ordered to bury the two bodies. For this purpose we dug a grave on what used to be Ulap fairgrounds (Alpendorf) and buried the two German soldiers properly, as we were told. My colleague Wagepfuhl took the pay book along for safekeeping."

In his judicial interrogation during the Preliminary Examination the witness Krumnow (who died on November 5, 1970) (Vol. IV, sheet 510 ff of the Record) among other things made known the following:

"A few days after the fighting stopped in Berlin—it could have been May 5, 6 or 7, 1945—I went to the office where I worked, Berlin Post Office NW 40 near the Lehrter railroad station.

. . .

"I don't remember anymore if it was on the first or second day that I was on the bridge that takes Invalidenstrasse over the tracks of the Lehrter Central Railroad Station, on the sidewalk to the north, on the side that leads to the Sandkrug Bridge, where I saw two men's bodies.

. . .

"On that day Russian soldiers around the Lehrter station ordered me and a few fellow workers to come along and remove the bodies lying where I described.

"One of the bodies was that of an unusually tall man. From the military identification we found on this man, we figured it was the body of a Dr. Stumpfegger from Hohenlychen. This man no longer wore a uniform, but was dressed only in underwear. The ID just mentioned had been underneath the body. The other body was that of a smaller man. This body was dressed in an army uniform. No insignia or collar patch was on the blouse, and there were no shoulder straps. There was also no insignia of rank on the blouse. The boots were no longer on. We could not tell whose body this one might be. Neither body showed any visible wound. There were also no bandages in sight. Neither was there any trace of any kind of wound or bleeding. As I recall, there were no signs of decomposition to be seen. With the help of a stretcher, which we found in our post office, we then carried both bodies to the grounds where the Weigmann freight forwarding company is now located. I think I recall that this forwarding firm had the place back in those days. A Russian soldier told us that this was where we were to bury the two bodies. This Russian soldier designated a particular place on the Weigmann forwarding company grounds where we were to dig the grave. As I remember, in that courtyard there were four trees that formed a square. The place for the grave was about in the center of the square. Accordingly we dug a grave. The group of trees forming a square I just mentioned was situated about opposite the entrance to the forwarding firm; although more toward the commuter train station [S-Bahn] than the entrance. As for what sort of trees they were, I don't know. I can only assume that they were deciduous trees. The digging was not hampered in any way by roots. As I recall, the grave was dug to a depth of 1/2 to 3/4 of a meter."

4. *Osterhuber/Müller*

In the course of an interrogation of the accused's sons Martin and Gerhard in Freising on March 30, 1965 (Vol. 16, sheet 2827 ff. of the Search Records) by Attorney General Metzner and myself, Gerhard Bormann said that some time around 1958 he was told by a police officer of the Land Police in Freising that a certain Sebastian Osterhuber, formerly a detective on Göring's staff, knew something about the death of the accused. Osterhuber, who died in the interim, is supposed to have said that he saw the accused, after he sustained a wound in his neck, attempt to take a potassium cyanide capsule. Osterhuber is supposed to have dashed the capsule out of his hand, and the accused took the second capsule before he could be stopped. Osterhuber then saw the accused fall down dead. This police officer was identified. He was Officer [Polizeimeister] Karl Müller, who made the following statement in his report dated April 19, 1965 (Vol. 17, sheet 2951 of the Search Records):

"As a result of the reorganization of the Bavarian Land Police I was transferred on April 29, 1960, to the Land Police Station of Freising. From this date I began eating lunch daily in the Hackerbräu Inn in Freising. Once, Herr Sebastian Osterhuber sat at my table. He introduced himself as an air-raid official and formerly an officer, staff officer, I believe. In a conversation with Herr Osterhuber I mentioned that Bormann's youngest son, Gerhard Bormann, was working as a truck driver at the asylum in Birkeneck. The conversation inescapably turned to what had happened to Martin Bormann.

"Then Herr Osterhuber stated that he knew for certain that Martin Bormann was dead because he personally saw his dead body in Berlin. I can't remember now whether Osterhuber said anything about how Bormann met his death, but I don't think he did, because if he had, I would surely still be able to recall it. What I cared about at the time was to have Gerhard Bormann find out about Osterhuber so he could talk with him. When I asked about that Herr Osterhuber told me Gerhard

Bormann should look him up, and he would tell him about his father's death. Soon after, I told Gerhard Bormann about Herr Osterhuber."

Osterhuber died on May 22, 1962, in Freising. He was a detective and a member of the Reich Security Service, and, according to a statement by retired Police Counselor Kiesel, former chief of personnel of the Security Service (Vol. 18, sheet 3172 of the Search Records), he was employed as an air raid warden from July 12, 1965 [date must be an error—*Tr.*] (Vol. 19, sheet 3340 of the Search Records) to the end of April 1945 in the Government Quarter of Berlin, in which capacity he was directly subordinate to Major General of Police Rattenhuber, now deceased. In the fall of 1944 Osterhuber was a member of the Veesenmayer Escort Command in Hungary (Vol. 27, sheet 4951 of the Search Records). In Osterhuber's application for prisoner-of-war indemnification dated January 21, 1955 (Vol. 18, sheet 3145 ff. of the Search Records), it is stated that he had been Military Police Commissioner at OKW [Wehrmacht High Command] since 1939 and was taken prisoner by the Russians on May 2, 1945, in Berlin, whence he escaped in the middle of May 1945.

5. *Excavations of July 20/21, 1965*

In the spring of 1965, thorough investigations were initiated on whether any disinterments had meanwhile taken place on the grounds of what was formerly known as Alpendorf (also called Ulap Fairgrounds), which the witness Krumnow had indicated as the place of burial. These investigations revealed that no disinterments had taken place (Vol. 18, sheet 3161 of the Search Records). In view of the result of this investigation and in consideration of the fact that up to that time all reports that the accused was still living had proved to be of no substance, on July 20 and 21 digging was done on the grounds designated by the witness Krumnow. If in the course of the digging two skeletons were to be discovered, one relatively short and one tall—it had since become known that Dr. Stumpfegger had been strikingly tall—and glass splinters found between the teeth of the skulls, a high probability would exist that they could be identified as the accused and Dr. Stumpfegger. Identification by teeth would have been difficult as no dental chart for either individual was known to exist at that time. It is true that several dental technicians, Echtmann and some nurse assistants, had been located who had been employed in the office of the by then deceased dentist Professor Dr. Hugo Johannes Blaschke, who had treated prominent National Socialists.

The digging was unsuccessful (Vol. 20, sheet 3589 ff. and sheet 3621 of the Search Records).

V. Appointment notebook of the accused

Immediately following the excavation, the witness Stelse reported voluntarily to the Berlin Criminal Investigation Division. He had passed by Invalidenstrasse during the time between May 2 and 8, 1945, to reach his place of work, the firm Solex-Vergaser [Solex Carburetor Co.] in Heidestrasse. He reported having seen two dead bodies on the bridge over the tracks, dressed only in underwear. He told this to his colleagues at work. One of them, identified by *Stern* magazine as Bruno Fechtmeier (the witness Stelse could only recall it as Fechner, which turned out to be wrong) immediately said that near the place where the two dead bodies lay, someone had found a notebook wrapped in wax paper, presumably a sort of pocket appointment book, belonging to the accused. According to the Soviet journalist Besymenski, this notebook is in the custody of the Attorney General of the Soviet Union (Vol. VIII, sheet 1276 of the Records). In response to an international request for legal aid by the examining magistrate dated October 13, 1971 (Vol. VIII, sheet 1347 of the Records), which asked for an attested photostatic copy of the complete text of this appointment book, the Soviet Foreign Ministry answered by verbal note dated November 17, 1972, that all original documents concerning charges against Martin Bormann were with the records of the proceedings against the major Nazi war criminals conducted at Nuremberg. The Soviet authorities concerned had no other materials on Martin Bormann on hand.

A transcript of excerpts apparently from this notebook was sent to the local authorities in 1964 by the Public Prosecutors in the German Democratic Republic (Vol. II, sheet 1847–1849 of the Search Records). This is a translation from Russian back into the original German (Exhibit 10 of this report [deleted]).

According to a statement by the witness Fechtmeier, this notebook was found in a leather coat that a French slave laborer, employed in the Solex-Vergaser firm, had brought to the firm's cellar in the beginning of May 1945 following an expedition to find food and drink. According to the researches of *Stern* magazine, the individual involved was Maurice Lachoux, by then a French Justice Department employee living in Paris. As Lachoux refused to give the *Stern* reporters any information on the circumstances of his finding the leather coat, an International Request for Legal Aid, dated January 11, 1966 (Vol. 23, sheet 4257 ff. of the Search Records), was sent to the French examining magistrate of the proper jurisdiction asking for an interrogation of this witness in order to bring any possible clarification on where this coat had been found—i.e., on the Invaliden Bridge—and whether it had been taken from a dead body. In this interrogatory, dated April 27, 1966 (Vol. 28, sheet 5179 in the Search Records), the witness Lachoux declared that during the time he was in the cellar of the Solex firm he never heard anything about any leather coat that had been brought in from the outside.

It was therefore impossible to determine whether this notebook of the accused had actually been found in a leather coat. The fact remains that this notebook must have been found in the vicinity of the Invaliden Bridge.

VI. Further Search [for the accused] in Germany and Abroad

As the excavations of July 20/21, 1965, had failed and the witnesses Dr. Naumann, Schwägermann, Dietrich and Axmann of the previously described group had succeeded in escaping from Berlin, the search for the accused was resumed both within Germany and abroad, especially as reports that the accused was still alive were coming in, partly from informants, partly in the press. In at least fifty cases the Foreign Office in Bonn was asked to have offices of [diplomatic] representation of the Federal Republic verify reports originating from the countries where they were stationed. In addition, correspondence was conducted with foreign informants, in some individual cases personal contacts were developed with these informants when on their own initiative they sought out the Public Prosecutor's office of the Frankfurt-am-Main Superior Land Court (i.e., Verloop from Surinam, Gray from England). Besides, the German diplomatic offices abroad reported information that had come in directly to them, which in most cases could be checked out on the spot—invariably with negative results.

All leads from domestic or foreign sources were further checked by the special commissions of the Land Criminal Investigation offices, and all proved false.

1. *Leads from Simon Wiesenthal*

Among the numerous press reports that repeatedly maintained the accused was still alive and was living in South America, special notice was taken of those from the chief of the Document Center of the Association of Jews Persecuted by the Nazi Regime, Simon Wiesenthal in Vienna. In the Italian illustrated magazine *Epoca*, No. 1029, dated June 14, 1970 (Vol. VI, sheet 811 in the Records) an interview on this line was published, according to which the accused had lived a year before in Dribura, a German "colony" in the State of Rio Grande do Sul, which borders on Paraguay. The pastor of this colony, moreover, was named "Himmler." In a report from United Press International dated March 13, 1968, which appeared in the *Neue Zürcher Zeitung* issue of March 15, 1968 (Vol. VI, sheet 913 of the Records) it stated that Simon Wiesenthal had asserted in an interview with [the Swedish newspaper] *Dagens Nyheter* that the accused was still alive and that his—Wiesenthal's—co-workers had tracked him down in the "Waldner Kolonie" in the southern part of Brazil on the Paraguay border. Further information that came through Mr. Wiesenthal—especially the recent material—contained predominantly anonymous and frivolous-sounding letters.

The interview published in *Epoca* was evidently also run in the Brazilian illustrated magazine *O Cruzeiro*. The German embassy in Rio de Janeiro promptly reported on October 9, 1970 (Vol. 33, sheet 6287 of the Search Records) as follows:

"In the enclosed interview with Simon Wiesenthal, printed in the illustrated magazine *O Cruzeiro*, several errors have been noted. The alleged domicile of Bormann should read 'Ibirubá.' It is on the Argentine border and has roughly 4,000 inhabitants. The pastor there is named H*ü*mmler."

The office of the Elective Consul in Ijui (Consul Honscha) sent the embassy the following opinion (*ibid.,* sheet 6288):

"1. Prior to receiving the letter of reference I had spoken with my son Hartmut, who lives in Ibirubá, about the interview with Simon Wiesenthal printed in *Cruzeiro*. My son found the statements made in it senseless and impossible.

"2. A family I know that has lived in Ibirubá for years confirmed my son's opinion.

"3. Yesterday, while visiting Ibirubá, I learned that the Catholic priest of that parish, Pastor Hümmler, had sent in a written protest to *Cruzeiro*.

"It is commented that regarding the name of the pastor of the parish, *O Cruzeiro* had made a special point that the man's name was Himmler."

Regarding the UPI report of August 13, 1968, reference will only be made to the judicial interrogation of the witness Wiedwald, on December 17, 1969 (Vol. IV, sheet 557 ff. of the Records), and on January 12, 1970 (Vol. V, sheet 590, especially sheet 595 of the Records). Wiedwald, the informant in the story by Antony Terry that appeared in the beginning of January 1968 in *Der Spiegel* on the Waldner Colony, is a fraud, who—after I requested the examining magistrate to place Wiedwald under oath—finally admitted that he traveled to South America for the first time in 1964 with journalists from *Stern*. Because of the repeated interviews with the witness Wiesenthal, on my initiative, through the route of an International Legal Aid request, he was finally interrogated under oath on September 29, 1970, by the Criminal Investigation Division of the Provincial Court in Vienna in the presence of the examining magistrate (Vol. VII, sheet 965 ff. in the Records). Insofar as it is of interest here, his statement is as follows:

"It is true that until very recently I have made statements to several journalists regarding the conjectural whereabouts of Martin Bormann. In this representation

I could admittedly only make statements on a locale of residence where in my opinion Bormann could conceivably have been some time ago. In other words: at no time during a questioning—and that goes for my interrogation today—could I or can I say how I might be in a position to represent with certainty that the accused was at this particular place. I ask that it be recognized that my conjectures were not without certain reasonable grounds.

. . .

"The hypothesis that Bormann is living in a certain Camp Waldner in South America is in my opinion completely false. I know that this view—that Bormann lives there—is being put forward by a certain Wiedwald. I have also come to know this man. What he asserts regarding Bormann is preposterous, therefore I have placed no value on any collaboration with this man whatsoever.

. . .

"This being premised, I can say regarding the abovementioned piece by Gorney, and on the basis of my own verification of the more select information at hand, that during my conversation with the aforementioned writer I was convinced that the accused might in fact have stayed in the small town of Maréchal Rondon in the first months of 1968.

"According to the information I had at that time, there is in the vicinity of this small town another one called Ibirubá. Many Germans live in both places. In the latter there is a hospital. The head of this hospital is a German, Dr. Seiboth. I was told that this Dr. Seiboth had performed a surgical operation on the accused. I emphasized explicitly that the informant is personally known to me and that I could not doubt his credibility. In any event, this information appeared to me so trustworthy that I promptly passed it on verbally to Prosecutor General Bauer when he stopped here in Vienna, shortly before his death."

Neither in the Search Records nor in the dossier is any note by Prosecutor General Bauer to be found.

(Vol. VII, sheet 967 of the Records):

"In May of this year I had a conversation with the Italian journalist Lazzero Ricciotti. This conversation led to the publication in the June 14, 1970, issue of the Italian magazine *Epoca.* I was not familiar with the text of this article. I did get to read the German translation of this piece. In this particular version a large part of the interview is given, and the other part of the article has information from another source, presumably from a dossier of earlier published stories about Bormann. In contrast to the article in *France Soir,* here at least some of the reservations are included that I expressed during the interview. In the interest of accuracy I wish to point out that the name of the town is given incorrectly. The place in question is not called Dribura, but rather Ibirubá. The essential difference between what I said and what was published lies chiefly in the fact that things I mentioned as being believable were presented in the article as facts."

2. *Lead from Lev Besymenski*

In connection with the interrogation of September 29, 1970, the witness Wiesenthal also supplied some photocopies of "documents" from which could be judged what quality of information he had been getting. Among these photocopies is a secret telex message addressed to the witness Dr. von Hummel, who acted to a degree as the private secretary to the accused at Obersalzberg, sent from Berlin on April 22, 1945, and received at 9:21 A.M. The text is as follows:

"Hummel, Obersalzberg. I agree to suggested removal Overseas South."*

*The original reads: *"Bin mit vorgeschlagener Übersee Süd Verlagerung einverstanden."*—Tr.

Photostatic copies of this and other telex messages irrelevant to this matter were given over to the Records (Folder Vol. 50, sheet 5581 of the Search Records) on September 15, 1967. Also in his book, *On the Tracks of Martin Bormann*—published by Dietz-Verlag in Berlin in 1965 and distributed in East Germany—which consists preponderantly of highly emotional propaganda directed against the [Bonn] Federal Republic, he quotes this telex message verbatim and tacks on the evaluation comment (page 254 of his book):

"This document is of extraordinary significance. It confirms once again our thesis of the escape to South America."

Investigations as early as 1966 revealed unequivocally that the words *"Übersee Süd,"* which Besymenski interpreted as "Overseas South," as well as *"Übersee/Hohensee,"* referred to the Party Chancellery of the NSDAP, which had been moved out to Schloss Steinach near Straubing. The address on this telex reads: Übersee Office Postal Address: NSDAP Office Übersee Straubing/Donau [on the Danube], P.O. Box 99."

More precise information is found in the record file NS 6/original text 241 from Sammlung Schumacher/368 of the Federal Archives in Coblenz (cf. also Vol. 27, sheets 4975–4980 of the Search Records). As the witness Dr. von Hummel declared under oath in his interrogation May 3, 1966 (Vol. 26, sheet 4811 of the Search Records), the word *"Südverlagerung"* was commonly used in reference to shipments [of files] to South Tyrol. Besymenski's deduction is completely false.

3. *Lead from Gehlen*

In the fall of 1971 Major General Reinhard Gehlen (Ret.), last chief of the Foreign Armies East section of the General Staff and subsequently first chief of the Federal Intelligence Service [of the German Federal Republic], published his memoirs. In them he also mentioned the accused. In the highlight quotes that appeared in the press it was stated that the accused had died in the Soviet Union some two years previously. In his interrogation on September 21, 1971, by the examining magistrate, in which I participated, the witness Gehlen declared under oath that he and Canaris, in their search for an apparent security leak in the top echelon of military command, which was passing important German command decisions immediately to the enemy, had considered the accused as a possible source of the leaks. Furthermore, this witness among other things declared under oath verbally (Vol. VIII, sheet 1313, 1314 of the Records) as follows:

"Not until reports became known of statements made to American agencies concerning Bormann's fate was some renewed attention paid to the Bormann matter. According to my recollection it was either in 1946 or 1947 that a source—reliable beyond a doubt—made known to me that Bormann had been seen in a motion picture that played in an East Berlin movie house and dealt with a sports spectacle. Bormann was among the group of Russians shown watching the event—Soviet dignitaries as I recall—and the accused was recognized with certainty. I should mention in this connection that it is known to me that the source in question, from whom this information comes, had been in a position to see the accused face to face prior to May 2, 1945. This recognition report was then passed on to the American office charged with receiving such information. I would like to add that there are no written records on hand concerning this matter. The written records of the Intelligence Service were destroyed from time to time, at set intervals.

"Following the establishment of the Federal Republic I had occasion to brief either Federal Chancellor Adenauer or State Secretary Globke on the Bormann matter. I had learned from a source, again of the utmost reliability in my opinion, that on the Russian side a plan was being considered to spread the rumor throughout the world that Hitler was still alive, and it was further being contemplated to permit the surfacing of Bormann, Hitler's plenipotentiary political heir, allegedly at that time in Russian custody, all for the purpose of rallying together a unified—that is, National Communist—Germany.

"I recall that the Federal Chancellor decided at the time that there were no political measures to be taken in this matter. In any case, some sort of position along this line remains in my memory. It goes without saying that the Intelligence Service received numerous reports on the supposed whereabouts of Bormann. These reports I always looked upon with skepticism, then as now, because the reliability of the informants seemed to me inadequate. Only in the two cases described were there no grounds for reasonable doubt of reliability on my part.

"When I am asked today about the alleged death of the accused I say that I have never maintained that the accused died some three or four years ago. Personally I must assume that Bormann, to a degree of probability bordering on certainty, died some time after when the above-mentioned concept of a National Communist Germany first became known. For my part I have never maintained, and cannot state today, that I had even a single source of information that was in any sense certain."

For reasons of security, the witness Gehlen did not reveal the identity of the two sources. Given the manifest inadequacy and poor quality of both items of information, there was no need to try to compel him to do so. The Soviet journalist Besymenski, mentioned earlier, and by this time accredited Bonn correspondent of the Soviet newspaper *Novoye Vremiye* (New Times), in the course of a conference with the examining magistrate in Bonn on September 11, 1971, at which I was present, commented on the above-mentioned revelations of Gehlen's "only that some satirical remarks could be made about them" (Note of the examining magistrate dated September 13, 1971, in Vol. VIII, sheet 1276 of the Records). In my written notes I put down on September 12/20, 1971, that Besymenski held Gehlen's version on Bormann here reported to be absolutely false, and that, moreover, he had no information of any sort to give us on the survival of the accused, on which point I had queried him pointedly and precisely.

4. *Lead from Ladislas Farago*

At the end of November 1972 there appeared in the *Daily Express,* billed as a sensational disclosure, a serialized account by Ladislas Farago which, taken as a whole, gave the impression of a collection of all the sensational reports on Martin Bormann that had appeared up to that date. In two conferences, on December 4, 1972, and January 10, 1973, he described secret intelligence service reports prepared for the Argentinean President in 1963. He also claimed to have in his possession over 200 photographs and a four-minute motion-picture film on Martin Bormann. In the January 10, 1973, conference—which took place after the finding of the skeletons and at which I was present—he was questioned as to the authenticity of the contents of his documents, and he answered that there was no reason for him to assume that the Argentinean authorities were deceiving themselves. When queried on his forthcoming book on several Nazi higher-ups then in preparation, he declared that very little would appear in it on Martin Bormann, and none of what had run in the *Daily Express* on Martin Bormann. In addition, he declared himself prepared to make available photostatic copies of original handwritten letters by Martin Bormann allegedly in his possession, and of the doctor's statement on an alleged hospitalization of Martin Bormann in a clinic or sanatorium. This request was made of Mr. Farago because in the Search Records there is an original letter in Martin Bormann's own hand, and he—as mentioned above—had two ineradicable scars on his body from surgical operations. In a letter dated January 17, 1973, Farago promised anew to send the source documents requested and previously promised. Enclosed in his letter was a photostatic copy of a dental chart of the accused's jaw that appeared in the *American Dental Association News* issue of January 1, 1973, executed by Professor Reidar F. Sognnaes, who had been working for years on the identification of Hitler by dental techniques and who also possesses material on Martin Bormann's dental structure (Exhibit 11 of this report).

The source documents adverted to by Ladislas Farago have up to this writing not arrived. The discovery of the skeletons on December 7 and 8, 1972, render it unnecessary to go into the obviously worthless serial reportage from the *Daily Express.*

VII. Further Investigations concerning the Ulap Fairgrounds in Berlin

1. *No disinterments from the Ulap fairgrounds*

As already mentioned, prior to the excavation of July 20/21, 1965, careful investigations had been initiated to determine if any disinterments for transferral to cemeteries had occurred on the grounds where the digging was being done. No leads were developed. Despite that, in the beginning of 1966 all available records were examined of the Erich Schroedter Funeral Service Partnership, 1 Berlin 21, Ottostrasse 7, for the years 1945 and 1946, as this firm conducted all the exhumations and transferrals during that period. From the Ulap Fairgrounds (Invalidenstrasse 63–68) there were no records of any such exhumations. There were, however, exhumations from other street numbers of Invalidenstrasse (i.e., opposite the entrance to Ulap, No. 56a) as well as from Alt-Moabit (south of Ulap) that is, in places adjacent to the area still presumed to be the burial site. This led to a formal conclusion that the grave in which the witness Krumnow buried two bodies had not been dug up, perhaps because, situated where it was on the grounds, it had not been recognized as a grave at all (cf. Vol. 23, sheet 4102 of the Search Records).

As in several instances—the most recent being immediately after Gehlen's disclosures in the fall of 1971—a certain Horst Schulz from Berlin asserted that the accused and Dr. Stumpfegger had been buried in the cemetery for military personnel killed in action in Berlin 21, Wilsnackerstrasse, I asked the burgomaster of the Tiergarten borough of Berlin for the records of the Office of Planting and Landscaping [*Gartenbauamt*] on the War Veterans' Memorial Cemetery on Wilsnackerstrasse and asked the Schroedter firm for additional records of their transferrals to cemeteries. The Schroedter firm no longer had any such records available. The records of the borough burgomaster for Berlin-Tiergarten show no mention of transferrals from the Ulap fairgrounds (cf. Vol. IX, sheets 1506–1525 of the Records).

2. *No further burials on the Ulap fairgrounds*

Before the skeleton finds of December 7 and 8, 1972, evidence came to light that in the last days of the war at the end of April 1945, executions by firing squad of individuals the Gestapo arrested in connection with July 20, 1944, were carried out. Some of the victims had been condemned by the People's Court (Vol. 23, sheets 4128–4138 of the Search Records). For clarification of this question, which appeared important at the time because it could initially not be excluded that additional bodies might be buried on those grounds, the investigation records 3 P(K) Js 167/60 of the Prosecutor General of the Berlin Supreme Court were taken in evidence (Vol. II, sheets 229–230 of the Special Volume "Skeleton Finds"). In the concluding remarks of this proceeding, dated January 13, 1969, which the Prosecutor General of the

Berlin Supreme Court had temporarily taken in hand in accordance with Article 145 GVG (P [K] Js 1/68) (Vol. VII, sheets 129–141 of these records), it is to be concluded that the first group of prisoners shot on the Ulap fairgrounds in the night of April 23, 1945 (Schleicher, Bonhoeffer, John, Perels, Nieden, Sierks, Marks and Kuenzer), were buried on May 5 or 6, 1945, in a bomb crater on the Dorotheen City Cemetery in Berlin 65, Clausewitzstrasse 126. The second prisoner group shot on the Ulap fairgrounds that same night (Professor Albrecht Haushofer, von Salviati, Moll, Munzinger, Stähle, Jennewein, Sossimow), of which the mechanic Herbert Kosney was the sole survivor, were buried in a mass grave after May 13, 1945, in the Kleiner Tiergarten [*Small Zoo*]. This excludes the possibility of misidentification.

VIII. Preparations for Renewed Excavations on the Ulap Fairgrounds in Berlin

1. *The dental chart of the accused*

Along with a letter of transmittal dated July 15, 1971 (Vol. VIII, sheet 1236 ff. of the Records), I sent the examining magistrate a description of the teeth of the accused, which Professor Dr. Hugo Johannes Blaschke, since deceased, the dentist who treated prominent Nazis, reconstructed from memory for the Military Intelligence Service Center Headquarters for the United States in the European theater. This description (translation in sheet 26 of the green dictation pad of the Chief Police Commissioner of Berlin on the skeleton finds) was sent to me by Jochen von Lang, editor of *Stern* magazine (Exhibit 12 of this report). The original is in the National Archives in Washington. The dental chart matches the drawing by Professor Reidar F. Sognnaes sent by Ladislas Farago with his letter of January 17, 1973 (cf. Exhibit 11 of this report).

2. *Communications to the Chief Police Commissioner of Berlin*

In a letter dated September 8, 1972 (Vol. 34, sheet 3468 of the Search Records), Jochen von Lang, editor of *Stern* magazine, who since 1965, for professional and personal reasons, had been interested in clarification of the whereabouts of the accused, and with whom an agreeable, purposeful collaboration developed, sent a photostat of a report in the Berlin newspaper *Der Tagesspiegel* dated August 13, 1972, telling of forthcoming plans to construct an institutional building complex on the former Ulap fairgrounds on Invalidenstrasse ("Ulap" was, incidentally, an acronym for the "Universal Exhibition Park" [Universum-Ausstellungs-park]). Construction was due to commence in 1972. The grounds were, however, not yet vacated by the commercial tenants in the old houses marked for demolition, and furthermore, the terrain was considered so poor for construction purposes that a complete change of soil was necessary.

With transmittal of a photocopy of the construction drawing which had been on hand in the Preliminary Examination Records (Vol. IV, sheet 504 of the Records) since October 1969, I requested the Chief Police Commissioner of Berlin, in a letter dated September 11, 1972 (Vol. 34, sheet 6470 ff. of the Search Records), to get in touch with the construction authorities concerned through the Construction Commissioner [*Bausenator*] and to ask to be informed promptly when construction was to begin so this opportunity might be used to dig with special care in the supposed area of the grave. The Berlin Police Commissioner took the required steps and got in touch with the architect in charge of this project. The word was passed on to watch especially for skeletal bones in the course of the excavations, and in the event such bones were unearthed, to suspend the operations.

IX. The Skeleton Finds of December 7 and 8, 1972, on the Ulap Fairgrounds in Berlin

On December 7 and 8, 1972, two skeletons were discovered on the Ulap fairgrounds—some 12 to 15 meters distant from the excavation site of 1965—by two workers performing operations concerned with moving electric-power conduits as part of the preparations for construction. The architect, who had been advised by the request dated September 11, 1972, from this office, notified the Criminal Investigation Department of the Police immediately upon the finding of the first skull, and they conducted a systematic search and found both partially incomplete skeletons of different size. The skeletons were relatively well preserved. One skull, later designated as No. 1—had been damaged on the parietal area by the steam shovel. The skeletons were sent for safekeeping to a nearby morgue. In Skull No. 1, found on December 7, 1972, the teeth were well preserved. In Skull No. 2, found on December 8, 1972, the teeth of the lower jaw were nearly all present, though several front teeth of the upper jaw were missing. As expected, in the jaws of both skulls (cf. IV, 5, above), glass splinters were found and placed in safekeeping. On December 19, 1972, among the secured bone fragments and earth of Skull No. 2, two additional teeth were found from the lower jaw and one from the upper jaw belonging to this skull, which could be replaced in the jaw, as they fit perfectly. On March 12, 1973, in the immediate vicinity of where the skeletons were found, a gold bridge over three teeth was found by chance.

The accused's son Martin (born on April 14, 1930) gave the information in response to a query that his father had broken his collarbone in a fall from a horse in 1938 or 1939, though he did not know if it was the right or left one. The accused's son Gerhard (born on August 31, 1934) also told me that at the beginning of the war in 1939 his father had been thrown from a horse while riding on a country estate north of Berlin that belonged to the Party Chancellery, and broke his collarbone. The Document Center materials on Dr. Ludwig Stumpfegger (born on July 11, 1910) were obtained from the Berlin Document Center, for inclusion with the evidence. Among these papers is a medical examination form from the Head Office of Race and Resettlement of the SS, dated November 11, 1939 (Exhibit 14 of this report) which contains precise data on height (190 cm), head circumference (58 cm) and skull type (long), and includes a dental chart. Dr. Ludwig Stumpfegger himself supplies the information that in 1923 he suffered a broken left forearm which had healed completely.

1. Dentition of Skull No. 1

The dentition of Skull No. 1 was examined by the Berlin Police Dental Clinic. Chief Medical Councillor Dr. Matschke executed the expert-witness statement dated January 4, 1973 (Exhibit 15 of this report) and concludes—based only on the dental chart of skull No. 1 and the dental chart from 1939, i.e., without reference to any other circumstances—as follows:

"In summary it can be stated that except for the wisdom teeth, strong similarities exist between the skull find and the dental chart from the Archives, to the effect that an indentification of the discovered skull as belonging to Dr. Stumpfegger is possible with probability bordering on certainty."

The witness Echtmann, who worked as a dental technician in Professor Dr. Blaschke's office, is unable to furnish any concrete information regarding the dental work on this skull. There are indeed no reasons to believe that Dr. Stumpfegger was ever treated in that office.

2. *Dentition of Skull No. 2*

The dentition of this skull was also examined by the Police Dental Clinic in Berlin. Similarly, on January 4, 1973, Chief Medical Councillor Dr. Matschke executed an expert-witness opinion on this set of teeth on the basis of a dental chart she herself executed from Skull No. 2 and the dental chart by Professor Dr. Blaschke (Exhibit 16 of this report). This expert opinion closes as follows:

"In summary it may be asserted that except for a few fundamental discrepancies, which could have arisen from error on the part of the attending dentist, great similarities and in addition unequivocal instances of identical coincidence between our findings on the skull and the report and dental chart of Dr. Blaschke are on hand, so that an identification of Skull No. 2 as being that of M. Bormann is not to be excluded as a possibility."

The dental technician Echtmann, who was shown Skull No. 2, made the following statement on December 12, 1972:

"Regarding Skull No. 2 I can say that the dental work that is there was done in Dr. Blaschke's office. I refer here to the technical work. The items in question are the two bridges and the crown.

"The material used in part for the tooth restoration—Palapont—a synthetic material from the Kulzer firm, was then in the first stages of being introduced in dental practice.

"I was also shown the dental chart reportedly executed by Dr. Blaschke. Regarding that I would say that it is indeed very possible that Dr. Blaschke might have been mistaken with respect to the bridge with the window crowns, and also that this bridge was not placed as indicated in his drawing, in the upper jaw, but rather in the lower jaw.

"I can once again say unequivocally that the dental work was done in Dr. Blaschke's office and also that I performed this work myself."

The witness Katharina Heusermann, on March 19, 1973, gave the following statement:

"I was employed from April 1936 to May 1, 1945, as chief assistant to Professor Dr. Blaschke. I am a trained medical-technical dentist's assistant. I assisted Professor Blaschke whenever any prominent National Socialists were treated, including Martin Bormann. Records of dental work done on this accused and Hitler's whole entourage no longer exist.

. . .

"As far as I can recall, the accused had no removable dentures. I cannot recall anything further from memory.

"I have been shown the lower jaw of the undamaged skull. The bridge from lower right lateral incisor to lower left lateral incisor installed on the lower jaw obviously is work that was done according to Blaschke's technique. Both window crowns on the left and right lower lateral incisors are typical of Professor Blaschke's work. The other bridge lower right over 2nd bicuspid to 2nd molar is not typical of Blaschke. Then I was shown the upper jaw of the same skull. The gold crown on the upper right 3rd molar (wisdom tooth) is also work done according to Blaschke's technique, and this because the shape is elegant, not squat.

"From memory I know nothing of a bridge on the upper teeth. If it is a window crown with a tab, that could also be Blaschke's technique.

. . .

"Then I was shown the dental chart that Blaschke executed from memory. Blaschke forgot to put in the good-looking gold crown just described on the upper right 3rd molar (wisdom tooth). Besides, he forgot the bridge on the lower jaw from lower right to lower left lateral incisors. The bridge is missing that was also noted as missing in Dr. Matschke's expert opinion. These teeth must have been severely loosened by paradentosis already during the accused's lifetime. According to the technical work that can be seen on the jaw, it was done by Dr. Blaschke's technique. I definitely assisted in this work. Whether Martin Bormann is the patient that was treated I cannot swear. I rather think it was. Echtmann's statement of December 16, 1972, was read to me and discussed with me. As far as I can judge, this statement is entirely accurate."

The bridge found after the skeletons on March 12, 1973, was shown to the dental technician Echtmann. On March 22, 1973, he made the following statement:

"The recently found bridge that has been shown to me was executed in the office of Dr. Blaschke. I would say that I made this bridge. It is one I made at the beginning of my employment with Dr. Blaschke.

. . .

"It is made of 20-karat dental gold. The missing incisor was provided for with an artificial tooth made of Pontopin to serve as support in the middle. The central and lateral incisors are window crowns which Blaschke favored in his practice. Judging from the crowned teeth, they must have been affected with paradentosis.

"The bridge only has to be put in place on the dental chart to see that it fits perfectly."

Chief Medical Councillor Dr. Riedel of the Berlin Police Clinic, who had examined the skulls jointly with Dr. Matschke, issued the following statement on March 13, 1973:

"The bridge that was found, 2 half-crown,*1 porcelain center support and 1 half-crown, is unquestionably to be considered a missing prosthesis from Bormann's skull. The alveolus 1 in the skull had healed over. Should the recently found prosthesis fit in the empty alveoli of the lateral and central incisors, the chain of proof would be complete."

Dr. Mühn, Staff Dental Surgeon (oral surgery) at the Munich Federal Military Hospital, who was asked for an opinion on whether the bridge fitted skull No. 2, issued the following expert opinion on March 31, 1973:

"The bridge here before me fits the configuration of the skull. The configuration of the roots of the supporting teeth corresponds with those of the alveoli of the skull.

"It was established that the shape and distension of alveolus 12 fits the root configurations of tooth 12 in this bridge.†

. . .

"The shape of the palatine portion of alveolus 21 corresponds to tooth 21 in the bridge. *In situ* the center lines of both rows of teeth are the same. The bite marks present in the bridge unequivocally match the imprint of the opposing teeth.

"On the basis of the above-described similarities, the bridge in question is to be considered a dental prosthesis from the skull of M. Bormann."

3. *Expert opinion of court-appointed physician on the identification of the skeleton find*

On March 31, 1973, the Director of the *Land* Institute for Forensic and Social Medicine, Medical Director, later Senator Dr. Spengler, executed the forensic medical-expert testimony on the identification of the skeletons (Exhibit 17 of this report).

a) According to the anthropometric measurements from the average dimensions of the hollow cylindrical bones of the two skeletons, which differ in size, Skeleton

*Refers to the three front teeth affected.—*Tr.*.
†This report uses a different dental nomenclature.—*Tr.*

No. 1 indicates a body height of 190–194 cm and a head circumference of 57–59 cm. The skull is classified as a typical "long [dolichocephalic] skull." These measurements match the medical examination form (Exhibit 14 of this report) with data recorded on Dr. Ludwig Stumpfegger.

On the basis of the same type of examination, Skeleton No. 2 indicates a body height of 168–171 cm and a head circumference of 55–57 cm. The skull is classified as a "round [brachycephalic] skull." The body height fits the data in the extract from the SS Register of Prominent Members, 170 cm.

b) According to x-ray examinations by Dr. Schöldgen, recognizable alterations may be seen on the radius and ulna of the left forearm of skeleton No. 1 (Exhibits 20 and 21 of this report), which probably reflect an old fracture in the lower third of the forearm. This tallies with information supplied by Dr. Stumpfegger regarding a broken left forearm. On Skeleton No. 2, both by macroscopic observation and per x-ray examination by Dr. Schöldgen (Exhibits 20 and 22 of this report) a defective knit may be seen following a fracture of the right collarbone in the center third. This confirms the information supplied by the two sons of the accused.

c) Since a scar appears over the left optical torus on the forehead in photographs of the accused, Skull No. 2 was examined accordingly. No observable injury to the bone could be found. This does not exclude the possibility of a bleeding injury having been sustained accidentally by the accused to his forehead during his lifetime.

d) Photomontage of profile photographs of both skulls with profile photographs of the accused and of Dr. Ludwig Stumpfegger, which were superimposed upon each other, indicates complete congruence of the skulls and shape of the faces (Exhibits 23 and 24 of this report).

4. *The result of the forensic testimony*

The expert witness, on the basis of examinations in a), b) and d)—i.e., without reference to examinations of the jaw and other circumstances—concludes that Skeleton No. 1 is with highest probability identical with the person of Dr. Ludwig Stumpfegger.

With respect to Skeleton No. 2, the expert witness concludes that skull and skeleton alone appear with highest probability to be identical with the person of the accused. In the event that the anthropometrically determined size relationships of Skeleton No. 2 coincide with the height, head circumference and head shape and the typical prosthetic dental work on the set of teeth in this skull can be dentally verified, "the identity of Skull No. 2 and Skeleton No. 2 with the person of Martin Bormann can be proved with a probability bordering on certainty." These assumptions are made—with exception of the head circumference. In addition, however, are the conclusions discussed in IV. 1 to 4 and No. V of this report.

5. *The glass splinters*

The glass splinters found in both jaws—as expected based on the hearsay evidence of Osterhuber (cf. IV.4) were examined by the Criminal Investigation Division KD C (KTU-Chemistry) of the Office of the Chief Police Commissioner of Berlin. The result of the investigation was that because of the thickness and shape of the splinters, they could be the shattered remains of ampoules or phials. There was no evidence of potassium cyanide, as it degrades in the atmosphere and is easily soluble in water.

The attempt to find material for comparison in Germany or abroad remained without success. The only item placed at my disposition, a capsule made of synthetic material dating from the World War II period, sent me by a private individual in Berlin, was obviously one put together privately by a chemist for the use of his immediate family. There was, moreover, no reason to search further for material for comparison, as it was possible to trace the chemist Dr. Albert Widmann, who until the war's end served in the Technical Criminology Institute (KTI) of the Reich Police Office—as chief of the Chemical Department of the KTI. In answer to a query on this matter his letter dated February 15, 1973, stated the following:

"On orders of our Department Chief Nebe, Reich Director of Criminal Investigation, Brigadier General of Police and SS Gruppenführer, self-destruction devices were developed and manufactured. They were intended for distribution to German agents. It might have been 1943 or 1944, when approximately 950 of these devices were ordered by the Reich Chancellery, for distribution to the senior leadership. For that reason the filling operation was supervised personally by Senior Criminology Secretary Karl Sacks. The self-destruction devices were given over to the courier from the Reich Chancellery by me. They were obviously in fact distributed, as they were used.

. . .

"Our Department Chief Nebe gave the order to manufacture self-destruction devices that were infallibly effective. Potassium cyanide tablets, according to his statement, were disapproved from the medical end, for the reason that in cases of subacid stomach, and with diabetics due to synthesis of cyanohydrin, they may fail to function. This gave a clear directive for production of the self-destructor. As an effective agent anhydrous hydrocyanic acid was used as a filler. For stabilization, 2 percent oxalic acid was added. For this reason the liquid is still in perfect condition today. It has neither polymerized, colored brown nor turned resinous, as was the case with the Polish ampoules. The dosage per ampoule was an even cubic centimeter. The lethal dose on inhalation, as I recall, is around 8 mg. The hydrocyanic acid was made from pure sodium cyanide. This work was done by a prisoner, Dr. Kramer, who was a chemist. Manufacture of the hydrocyanic acid and loading the ampoules was done in a small building in the RKPA plant in the Sachsenhausen concentration camp. Supervision was by Senior Criminology Secretary Sacks and Hauptscharführer Gerhard Maier. There were no accidents. Some 3,000 to 4,000 were made. We made the glass ampoules to fit the containers. The diameter was 9 mm, and the total length after annealing about 35 mm. The bottoms of the ampoules were flat. The annealed top was tinted blue for reinforcement. Ampoules that had been tested for hermetic seal in a vacuum were marked with a small red spot on the blue.

"As containers for the self-destructors, spent infantry rifle cartridges were fashioned into small cases. The cartridge cases were cut away on a lathe below the narrowing point.

"Their length came to about 41 cm. The 9-mm-long caps were also made from cartridge cases. The caps were simply pushed down over the cases. The total length of the self-destructor therefore came to about 46 mm, the diameter about 11 mm.

. . .

"It should be added that we probably received 1,000 empty ampoules from the Army Medical Center, each at three different times. I do not know which lot went to the Reich Chancellery."

The witness Hanna Reitsch (cf. Gerhard Boldt: *Die letzten Tage der Reichskanzlei,* Rowohlt-Taschenbuch, 1964, p. 122) confirmed the statements of Dr. Widmann in her interrogation on February 20, 1973. Among other things she reported:

"The description of the cartridge case agrees completely with the account given by Dr. Widmann on page 2 of his letter of February 15, 1973, in the indentation, beginning with '*Zur Aufbewahrung . . .*' and ending at '11 mm.' I know this so precisely because I sewed the capsule inside the cartridge case myself into the lining of a uniform skirt. That was how I came to measure the size in comparison with my little finger, then immediately measured it.

"When Hitler gave me the capsule, he said that I was free to use it. General von Greim had asked for capsules for himself and me. Hitler further said words to the effect that we should not be put to any disadvantage with respect to the other people in the bunker."

The dentist Dr. Kunz, who served since April 23, 1945, as dental officer in the Infirmary bunker of the Reich Chancellery (cf. Lev Besymenski, *Der Tod des Adolf Hitler,* Christian Wagner Verlag, 1968, pp. 79–84) stated on February 21, 1973:

"I only know about the capsules that were on hand in the bunker; however, I do not know what the ampoules that were supposedly inside them looked like. Therefore I can say nothing about the glass, the color and the shape of the capsules on hand in the bunker. I was given to read the last passage but three in what Dr. Widmann wrote on February 15, 1973. I should like to comment that the containers that I saw in the possession of Frau Goebbels and Eva Braun might easily have been made from an infantry-rifle brass cartridge case. The total length might have been about 46 mm. I myself had no such container in my possession. Besides, I never had one in my hand.

. . .

"I do not know if Dr. Stumpfegger had any capsules in his possession. Frau Goebbels had several in the jacket of her suit. I am convinced, however, that it was Dr. Stumpfegger or Frau Goebbels or both who gave the Goebbels children poison."

The glass splinters were examined by Dr. Widmann. He was able to verify that they were all of a cylindrical vault-shape so they could be placed around the flat bottom of an ampoule in their original position, and that this swelling out of the glass splinter fits an ampoule with approximately 9 mm diameter. As no splinters were found with blue lacquer—for this was applied for safety to the annealed end of the prussic acid ampoules—Dr. Widmann came to the following conclusion:

"Strictly speaking, the present find permits only the conclusion that the glass splinters in safekeeping are the remains of an ampoule of the same size as that from which the self-destructors were also made, and they are *not* the remains of a variety of ampoule that was not actually used."

Thus it may be concluded with probability bordering on certainty that these glass splinters originate from self-destructors which, according to statements by Hanna Reitsch and Dr. Kunz, personnel in the bunker in the Reich Chancellery had the opportunity to obtain. In the published autopsy findings on the Goebbels family and on Eva Braun, published in the book by Lev Besymenski, a further reference may be made. Glass splinters of a thin-walled ampoule were found in the teeth of these bodies.

6. *The motives for suicide*

Nothing more than conjecture can be made on the motives that drove the accused and Dr. Stumpfegger to commit suicide—for suicide it unquestionably must have been, since neither Axmann nor Krumnow noted any wounds on either body, and the glass splinters were found in the teeth.

As unanimously testified by all witnesses interrogated during the Preliminary Proceeding and the Preliminary Examination, and as is evident from the last wireless messages sent from the Reich Chancellery, the accused was at that time by no means weary of life, but rather, was eager to reach Dönitz in northern Germany. The situation for both individuals must have been hopeless, particularly for the accused, who had spent the war only in Hitler's headquarters and lacked any combat experience. It may be assumed that now that he became aware of the fact that if taken prisoner, he might be brought before an Allied tribunal as "Secretary to the Führer" he may well have imagined what their verdict might be.

Dr. Ludwig Stumpfegger, according to the Document Center papers, appears to have had some combat experience. Nevertheless, he might also have recognized that if taken prisoner, a bitter fate awaited him. He was Obersturmbannführer (Lieutenant Colonel) in the Waffen SS and Hitler's personal physician. He must probably have feared that as former Adjutant to the Reich Physician of SS and Police, Major General of the Waffen SS and president of the German Red Cross, Professor Dr. Karl Gebhardt, who was condemned to death by the Nuremberg "Doctors' Trial" on August 20, 1947, and executed, he might be held responsible for complicity in cruel and often lethal medical experiments on concentration camp inmates, POWs, and other individuals (cf. Telford Taylor, *The Nuremberg Trials*). Added to this, the awareness might have supervened that he could be accused of the murder of the Goebbels children.

Nevertheless, these are conjectures only, on motives for suicide which seemed to merit some thought.

X. Plastic Facial Reconstruction as Supplementary Verification

Partly as a means of cross-checking, and also out of concern to neglect no possibility for obtaining information that would lead to the identification of the skeletons, the Office of the State Prosecutor of the Supreme District Court of Frankfurt-am-Main commissioned Kriminalhauptmeister (Chief Pathologist) Moritz Furtmayr on February 5, 1973, to have expert testimony procured according to the method he had tried out and employed of plastic reconstruction of a face from the basis of the skull. Kriminalhauptmeister Furtmayr had previously indicated in a letter from the Bavarian District Criminal Office in Munich dated January 29, 1973, in reply to previous specific questioning, that in the case at hand, in which— given the press reports that had meanwhile appeared—it was no longer a question of unidentifiable remains—he could give an absolutely objective expert opinion. As a result, the Bavarian District Criminal Office wrote on February 14, 1973, as follows:

"The procedures developed by Herr Furtmayr, which he is willing to perform with the two skulls for purposes of expert testimony, are recognized juridically by the Court of superior instance. Herr Furtmayr has opportunity during duty hours to carry out sequences of tests to verify his procedure."

Furthermore, explicit reference was made to Kriminalhauptmeister Furtmayr as a specialist for identification of persons by plastic facial reconstruction over the skull in the supplement to Bavarian District Criminal Journal No. 40, dated October 5, 1972.

In order to maintain objectivity, Kriminalhauptmeister Furtmayr performed all his work in his office until March 6, 1973, under supervised conditions, so that it could be verified that he was not modeling after the photographs spread before him. Moreover, he included both skulls in a series of five skulls on which he was to model the faces.

Kriminalhauptmeister Furtmayr was not informed of the contents of the forensic medical-expert testimony, except for what appeared in the press from the interview given by Dr. Spengler. Also, he was not given access to the Document Center papers on the accused and Dr. Ludwig Stumpfegger.

The results of the plastic facial reconstruction was received in a portfolio with an accompanying report from Kriminalhauptmeister Furtmayr dated March 28, 1973, the conclusion of which reads:

"Both skulls were then included in a series of a total of five skulls, in order to ensure the greatest possible degree of objectivity to the plastic reconstruction of the soft-tissue parts of the face picture in the actual execution.

"Finally both plastic faces underwent a further modeling for detail. In this procedure, pains were taken to refrain from bringing artistic considerations to bear on the execution of the face, as the faces by themselves, in objective, straightforward form, offer a large amount of testimony value, and in that way can serve for cross-checking by comparison in the establishing of identity."

This comparison cross-check shows in the photographs of the reconstructed faces for Skull No. 2 (Martin Bormann, Exhibit 25 of this report) and Skull No. 1 (Dr. Ludwig Stumpfegger (Exhibit 26) a far-reaching resemblance to the photographs, especially of the accused (cf. Exhibits 7 [deleted], 18, 19) and of Dr. Stumpfegger (Exhibit 27), and furnishes unequivocally a verification of what has already been determined about the two skeletons. With the reservation that this is a new procedure still only in the testing stage, not yet to be ranked equally with fingerprinting, the purpose of the verification has been achieved.

XI. Result

Although nature has placed limits on human powers of recognition (BGHZ Vol. 36, pp. 379–393—NJW 1962, 1505), it is proved with certainty that the two skeletons found on the Ulap fairgrounds in Berlin on December 7 and 8, 1972, are identical with the accused Martin Bormann and Dr. Ludwig Stumpfegger.

The accused and Dr. Ludwig Stumpfegger died in Berlin in the early hours of the morning of May 2, 1945—sometime between 1:30 and 2:30 A.M.

XII. Further Measures

1. The search for Martin Bormann is officially terminated.
2. Since Preliminary Investigation has taken place, the concerned court shall promptly be advised of a motion to declare the case closed, by court decision based on proof of death of the accused. This court decision appears necessary because a death certificate, which would make this decision redundant, is unavailable.
3. The concerned court shall be advised of a motion to withdraw the arrest warrant dated July 4, 1961, to remove the otherwise still present possibility of action due to mistaken identity against some individual with the same name.
4. The offer of reward is to be withdrawn.
5. The Foreign Office is to be instructed on the outcome of the case? so the Decree of June 4, 1965 (-V4-88-537-), can be rescinded and replaced by one informing the diplomatic and consular offices representing the Federal Republic in foreign countries that the Office of the Chief Prosecutor of the Supreme District Court of Frankfurt-am-Main is no longer seeking information on an allegedly still-alive Martin Bormann. The aforementioned foreign representation offices of the Federal

Republic may notify informants bearing such information immediately.

6. The domestic and foreign press is to be advised of the outcome.

7. After the court order to be petitioned takes effect, the skeletons are to be released to next-of-kin for burial. In view of the fact that the skeletons must remain carefully preserved for the purposes of scientific research and recent history, cremation of the remains is explicitly prohibited.

8. All records, search records, special volumes and handwritten notes, following expiry of the mandatory waiting period according to the Records Ordinance, shall be transferred to the proper department of the Hessian State Archives to be made available as research material of historic value.

[signed] Richter

[First Prosecutor Joachim Richter]

Exhibit 11 Dental Chart of the accused by Professor Reidar F. Sognnaes

DENTAL STATUS OF HITLER'S DEPUTY
MARTIN BORMANN 1945

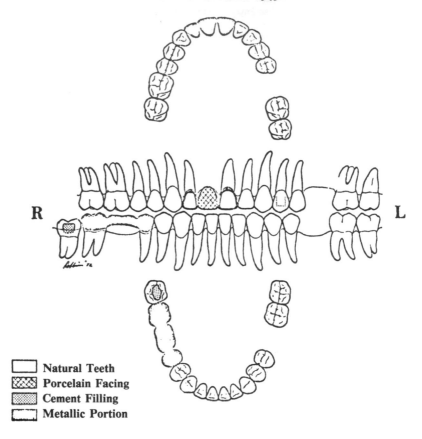

R   L

☐ Natural Teeth
▨ Porcelain Facing
▨ Cement Filling
☐ Metallic Portion

Above is the first publication of the 1945 dental status of Martin Bormann, Adolf Hitler's wartime deputy who disappeared at the end of World War II. The chart above may help track down Bormann, who in recent days has reportedly been traced to Argentina. It was diagrammed by Reidar F. Sognnaes, professor of anatomy and oral biology at the School of Dentistry, University of California at Los Angeles. The data was taken from documents in the US National Archives based on 1945 interrogations of Hugo J. Blaschke, dentist for both Hitler and Bormann. Dr. Sognnaes has had access to those documents during the past year and used them to prove finally that Hitler did die in Berlin as the war ended and that the Russians found his remains. It is possible that Dr. Sognnaes's information, which will be published in full in *The Journal of the American Dental Association,* can be used to help identify Bormann, dead or alive, even if the dentition has altered considerably in the past 28 years.

American Dental Association News, January 1, 1973

Exhibit 12 Dental status of the accused by Professor Dr. Hugo J. Blaschke

Blaschke states that he treated Martin BORMANN regularly from 1937 to 1945, for the last time in March 1945. During that period BORMANN was not treated by any other dentist. Source states that despite the non-availability of X-ray pictures (see last two paragraphs of Appex I) he remembers BORMANN's dentition in detail.

Description of Martin BORMANN's Teeth

Upper Jaw, seen frontally

The upper right central incisor was missing. It had been lost about 1942. Since the gap had to be closed immediately, temporary window-crowns were made for the upper left central incisor and the upper right lateral incisor. The missing tooth was replaced by a procelain facet on a golden back part.
Since all upper incisors were more or less loosened by paradentosis, a bridge-support was planned extending from cuspid to cuspid. As, however, the loosening of the incisors progressed slowly, the temporary arrangement proved satisfactory and the bridge was never made.

Lower Jaw, seen frontally

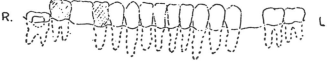

The lower right 3rd molar has not broken through all the way, and therefore occupies a lower position than the 2nd molar. It has an iodoform filling in the pulp cavity. A large cavity on its masticating and labial surfaces is filled with cement.

Color of Teeth

(NOTE: The color symbols used are those of the S. S. WHITE color ring for dentist.)

Upper right central incisor:	"6"
Upper right lateral incisor:	"6"
Upper right cuspid:	"G"
Upper right 1st bicuspid:	"G"
Upper right 2nd bicuspid:	"G"
Upper right 1st molar:	"G"
Upper right 2nd molar:	"G"
Upper left central incisor:	"6"
Upper left lateral incisor:	"6"
Upper left cuspid:	"G" and "K"
Upper left 1st bicuspid:	"17" or "18"
Upper left 2nd bicuspid:	"G" (?)

Upper left 2nd molar:	"G"
Upper left 3rd molar:	?
Lower right central incisor:	"6"
Lower right lateral incisor:	"6"
Lower right cuspid:	"G"
Lower right 1st bicuspid:	"G"
Lower right 3rd molar:	"17"
Lower left central incisor:	"6"
Lower left lateral incisor:	"6"
Lower left cuspid:	"G"
Lower left 1st bicuspid:	"G"
Lower left 2nd bicuspid:	"C"
Lower left 2nd molar:	"G"
Lower left 3rd molar:	?

Exhibit 14
Medical examination form filled out on Dr. Ludwig Stumpfegger

---

Head Office for Race and Resettlement SS
Medical Examination Form
  (for use on both male and female subjects)
Name: Stumpfegger, Ludwig   No. 84119   Status
Born in Munich on July 11, 1910 *legitimate*   *unmarried*
                       illegitimate   married
                                   widowed
                                   divorced
Residence: Berlin **Street and Number** Hospital, [address illegible]
Born a twin? No   Fabeck
           (If yes, name and address of twin sibling)
The examination of an SS-member and his future wife may only be done by an SS physician.

1. Permission for Disclosure
a) I herewith release

SS Untersturmführer Loderhose M.D.
as well as my former physicians vis-à-vis the Head Office for Race and Resettlement from the physician's obligation to confidentiality, and I empower the Head Office for Race and Resettlement to use the data supplied for purposes of marriage counselling.
b) I undertake under oath that I will answer all questions asked by the SS-physician to the best of my knowledge and conscience.
Place: Berlin   **Date:** 10.11.39
                    Signature: L. Stumpfegger

2. Past History of Family
(Information to be supplied: 1) attained age, 2) cause of death if known, 3) precise data on chronic diseases, i.e., endocrine disturbances, allergies, alcoholism).

Children (including illegitimate) of the subject: none
Father   62   living   none
Mother   51   living   none
Siblings: brother   28   living   none
Children of siblings   (left blank)
Paternal grandfather   62   unknown
Paternal grandmother   85   weakness of old age
Maternal grandfather   68   cirrhosis of the liver
Maternal grandmother   80   sclerosis of the arteries

3. Past Medical Treatment
(Supply names of physicians, hospitals—exact dates and addresses)
1923   fractured left forearm. Completely healed.
1936   torn cartilage. Removal of meniscus, inner side of right knee in
          Hohenlychen. Fully functional. No complaints.
Name and address of family physician: SS-Oberführer Prof. Dr.
                                             Gebhardt
                                             Clinic, Hohenlychen

4. Personal History
Birth: normal   **Bedwetting?**   no
Learned to walk   at age 1   **Convulsions?**   none
Learned to talk   at age 1 1/2
Childhood diseases: Measles
Subsequent illnesses: nothing special
Physical development and activity: normal
Mental development (schooling, career training, delinquency if any)
                                    normal
Character development: [o.B.—*Ohne Belästigung,* "no defects"]
Noteworthy special giftedness: [left blank]
Venereal diseases: none
Which?   ./.   **When:**   ./.
Menstruation: **Last menses?**
Births (year of births, character of parturition, health and development of the child)
Miscarriages (time—factor)
        (give accurate data)
Alcohol consumption, smoking: nonsmoker
Relationship to surroundings: in good order
Complaints: none
Special remarks: none

5. General Findings of Examination
Age   29 1/2 years
Height   190 cm   **Height seated**   92 cm   **Weight**   85 kg
Chest circumference   92/103 cm   **Head circumference**   58 cm
Shape of skull   long
        Body build: muscular-athletic   rotund   *slender*   weakling
        Bearing and stride: *trimly erect*   relaxed   notably poor
        Musculature: *powerful*   medium   inadequate
            vaulted
        Ribcage: *well-arched*   barrel-shaped   flat-sunken   deformed
        Belly: *flat/firm*   fat   loose-hanging

Tissue tonus: *elastic* flabby
Skin color: *pink-white*   ivory-colored olive-brown
Color of eyes: *blue* gray greenish 1 brown d. brown
Color of hair: light blond *dark blond* brown brown/black red
Type of hair: straight *smooth* long-wavy closely wavy curly
Is Mongolian fold present on eyes? *no* (pronounced, hinted at)

(Underline which applies)

Type of body build (Kretschmer classification) [left blank]
Preponderant racial component: Nordic with ./. admixture

Dentition	upper right	*Dental Chart*	upper left
	../. ..		./..
	87654321		12345678
	87654321		12345678
	..K.		K.
	lower right		lower left

Key to Dental Chart
/   carious   K.   tooth capped
•   filled   W   wisdom tooth not yet in
O   missing   S   pin-tooth [Stiftzahn]
+   root   Br   bridge
k   artificial   Pl   palate plate
Dentition needs care? yes *no*
Skin character   vigorous
Hair growth   normal   **Moles, birthmarks**   none
Mucous membranes   good blood circulation   none
Extremities: o.B. [no defects]
Spinal column   o.B.   **Thorax** o.B.
Skull and face   narrow
Eyes: o.B.   **Pupils** react **Wall-eyed or cross-eyed?**   no
Visual acuity   **R without glasses**   6 meters   **R with glasses**   [blank]
Visual acuity   **L without glasses**   6 meters   **L with glasses**   [blank]
Able to distinguish colors? *yes* no
Ears o.B.   **Whisper heard R** 6 meters **L** 6 meters
Speech impediments   yes *no*
Nose: o.B.
Oral cavity: o.B.
Thyroid gland: o.B.
Swelling of lymphatics: none
Lungs: diaphragm moves well   breathes noiselessly
Heart: Clear tones
  Pulse: 72 regular   **Blood pressure:** 120/85
Stomach organs: o.B.   **Disposition to hernia:** none
Reproductive organs: o.B.
Reproductive capability: present
Capability to bear children: [left blank]
        Pelvis (rickets, pelvic anomalies, if necessary measure and enclose diagram)
                [left blank]
        Any disorders or changes of uterus and adnexa (examine if necessary)
                [left blank]

Urinalysis

    Urine: *clear* cloudy   Reaction: *acid* Albumen ./. Sugar ./.

Blood: o.B.   Wassermann reaction, if any? ./.

    Reflexes: Abdominal wall

Babinski: negative   **Cremaster reflex** o.B.   **Patellar ligament**

Coordination: o.B.   **Romberg** negative   **reflex:**   o.B.

Motility: o.B.   **Pupil reaction** good on L and R

Sensitiveness: o.B.   **Nystagmus** none

Psyche: o.B.   **Strangle reflex** present

                              Achilles tendon reflex o.B.

Degree of talent   normal

Does the subject of the examination make a credible and frank impression?   yes

6. Is further examination by a specialist or supplementary examination necessary?
    no

    By whom? ./.

7. Examination by Army Medical Service in: March 1938 Classification: acceptable 1

8. Summary judgment on suitability for marriage:

    a) Total impression: *good* average mediocre bad

    b) Is perpetuation in racial/national sense desirable? very desirable

    c) Are any conditions present that would affect medical opinion to contraindicate advisability of entering into a pregnancy?

    d) Is the subject now pregnant?

Place   Berlin, SS-Hospital, Fabeckstrasse 62   Date 10.11.39

                       [signed] Loderhose

                  Physician's signature

                                            Stamp

SS rank   Untersturmführer SS Medical Squadron V.-T.

Command   [rubber stamp] Chief physician of Kramen Battalion I

Exhibit 15

Expert dental opinion on Skull No. 1 (Dr. Stumpfegger)

Z B s t   Berlin, January 4, 1973

                                         6579

To:

I A—KI 4—

Re: Identification of Dr. Ludwig Stumpfegger and of Martin

        Bormann,

        Skeleton finds of December 7 and 8, 1972;

        2 expert opinions

        Reference: Letter of December 18, 1972—OB. No. 733/72—

  We herewith submit the expert opinions regarding Dr. L. Stumpfegger and M.

        Bormann. 4 enclosures

                                   [signed] Dr. Matschke

                                   Chief Medical Councillor

A. For identification in the case of Dr. Stumpfegger, the following is at hand:

Skull No. I Dr. Stumpfegger

1. A dental chart made by the undersigned of Skull No. 1.
2. A dental chart taken from the results of a medical examination by the former Head Office of Race and Resettlement of the SS done in 1939.

It should be mentioned that the dental chart of Skull No. 1 made in our office coincides in essential points with the dental chart of Dr. Stumpfegger made available to us from the Archives.

This chart was done in 1939. It should therefore be taken into account that in the period 1939–1945 the following additional changes might have occurred:

In upper jaw: a filling in upper right cuspid
a filling in upper left central incisor
a filling in upper left 2nd bicuspid (carious already in 1939)
a crown on upper right 1st molar (already filled in 1939)

In lower jaw: a crown on lower right 2nd molar (already filled in 1939)
a filling in lower right 1st bicuspid lower left 2nd molar missing (already filled in 1939).

All other fillings and the crowns on lower right 2nd bicuspid and lower left 1st molar there are identical. The dentition gives an impression of good care. The fillings are preponderantly gold and there are gold crowns, which would be in keeping with the position and age of the individual whose skull this supposedly is.

The only discrepancy in the data in Dr. Stumpfegger's 1939 chart are the wisdom teeth. In this chart they are neither marked with the key sign (0), missing, nor the key sign (W wisdom tooth not through yet).

Our examination of the skull shows wisdom teeth retained in the bone $\frac{8/8}{8}$, while upper left 3rd molar shows no trace, which, however, could be definitely determined by x-ray.

It is entirely possible that in an examination at that time, wisdom teeth were considered of minor importance and were therefore not taken into account, with only the teeth that were actually visible marked on the chart.

In summary, it can be stated that with the exception of the wisdom teeth, great similarities have been established between the skull find and the chart from the Archives, to the effect that an identification of the found skull as belonging to Dr. Stumpfegger is possible with a probability bordering on certainty. [signed] Dr. Matschke, Chief Medical Councillor

---

Exhibit 16
Expert dental opinion on Skull No. 2 (Martin Bormann)

B. For identification purposes in the Bormann case the following items are at hand:
Skull II M. Bormann:
1. Dental chart executed by undersigned of Skull II, taking into consideration all fillings, crown and bridge prosthesis, and missing teeth.
2. A report of attending dentist Dr. Blaschke (drawn up from memory after 1945) with a drawing of a dental chart of the upper and lower jaw.

Only false teeth and missing teeth are drawn in.

For purposes of comparison or identification, conclusions may be drawn only on the basis of the crowns and bridges here at hand and the gaps in the dentition.

The following comment is to be made:

Fundamental discrepancies are to be found in that the crown on upper right 3rd molar and the window-crown bridge from lower right lateral incisor to lower left lateral incisor with central supporting members made of synthetic material are not shown in Dr. Blaschke's chart. The fact that Dr. Blaschke drew this chart from memory suggests that the possibility of error is not to be excluded. Thence there are also small discrepancies in the missing teeth as drawn by Dr. Blaschke and those missing from skull II which may be similarly explained.

The gap in the dentition in the lower jaw at lower left 1st molar is enlarged by the absence of lower left 2nd bicuspid. In the gap of missing teeth in the upper left jaw, it is not upper left 1st molar that is involved, but rather upper left 2nd bicuspid.

In the case of the aforementioned teeth, the alveoli have healed over, i.e., bone formation has taken place. Therefore the teeth must have been lost during [Bormann's] lifetime.

In Dr. Blaschke's report it says that due to severely loosened front teeth in the upper jaw, a bridge from canine to canine had been planned, but that when upper left central incisor was lost in 1942, this gap was immediately remedied with a 3-element bridge, consisting of 2 window crowns on upper right lateral incisor and upper left central incisor with a central element of porcelain facet with a gold back part installed as a temporary solution. The bridge is not to be found in the skull, as all teeth from upper right 1st bicuspid to upper left cuspid are missing. From the condition of the bony alveoli at this date, except for upper right central incisor, it may be concluded that during [Bormann's] lifetime these teeth had in fact been severely loosened, and (this is in agreement with Dr. Blaschke) had fallen out only after death had occurred.

This is further confirmed by the fact that at the discovery site, teeth upper right 1st bicuspid, upper left cuspid and upper right cuspid were found at a later date.

In contrast with the well-preserved neighboring alveoli, the skeleton find confirms the upper right central incisor lost in 1942 mentioned by Dr. Blaschke, the alveolus of which was subject to a fairly long healing process (no empty alveolus). Here, too, there is agreement with Dr. Blaschke.

The possibility of the bridge drawn in by Dr. Blaschke and mentioned by him is therefore not to be excluded.

In one of the photographs of Bormann made available from the Archives, one may in fact observe a notable discrepancy between the color of the teeth on each side and the color of the porcelain facet, even though black-and-white photographs cannot be adequate for use as evidence.

One could introduce as further proof supporting the identification the similarity of construction of the window-crown bridge present in the lower jaw of Skull II— a technique no longer in common use today—and the window-crown bridge mentioned by Dr. Blaschke in his report and indicated in the dental chart he drew. Here the statement of Dr. Blaschke's former dental technician that the dental prosthesis still in the skull is work from Dr. Blaschke's office, performed by him as dental technician, can prove of value.

Items favoring unequivocal identification are: a) the 3-member bridge in the right lower jaw lower right 2nd molar to lower right 2nd bicuspid, which is indicated on Dr. Blaschke's chart and is also present in the skull; b) the more deeply recessed wisdom tooth lower right 3rd molar, which both in Dr. Blaschke's report and as found in the skull has a temporary filling.

The indication of the position of the filling on the masticating and labial surfaces in the chart is identical with the position of the temporary filling in our skull findings (occlusal—buccal).

In summary, it can be stated that apart from a few fundamental discrepancies that could be ascribed to an error on the part of the attending dentist, great similarities and also unequivocal agreement exist between our skull findings and the report and dental chart by Dr. Blaschke, so that an identification of Skull II as that of Martin Bormann is not to be dismissed. [Signed] Dr. Matschke, Chief Medical Councillor

---

Exhibit 17
Forensic expert medical opinion of Dr. Spengler

Land Institute
for Forensic and Social Medicine,

Berlin	1 Berlin 21, January 31, 1973
Office of the Director	Invalidenstrasse 52 (at
GeschZ.	Lehrter RR. Station)
	Telephone 35 01 41 Ext. 286
To: Chief of Police, Berlin	Inter office: (988)

        Department I A
        1 Berlin 42
        Tempelhöfer Damm 1-7
Re: Skeleton discoveries, December 7 and 8, 1972 in Berlin 21
        Invalidenstrasse 59
        here: Identification Dr. Ludwig Stumpfegger
        Martin Bormann
Ref.: Your letter of December 18, 1972
        Gesch. Z.: I A - KJ4 - OB 733/72

Forensic Expert Medical Opinion on Identification
of Skeletons
    In order to identify the above-named individuals, two partial skeletons and two skulls (known as Skull 1 and Skull 2), held in safekeeping at the Berlin morgue, were subjected to a) anthropometric examinations to extrapolate head and body measurements of the two individuals
b) x-ray examinations
        1) of the forearm bones for signs of fracture
        2) of the collarbones for signs of fracture
c) examination of Skull 2 for injury to the bone on the forehead over the right eye
d) photographic comparisons of profiles of Skull 1 and Skull 2 with profile photographs of Dr. Stumpfegger and Bormann.
    The expert opinion additionally makes reference to the results of a medical examination of Dr. Ludwig Stumpfegger by the former Head Office of Race and Resettlement of the SS in 1939.
Re a), macroscopically the skeletal bones can be separated into two partially incomplete skeletons of differing body size.

Average size of skeletal bones	*Skeleton 1* (large)	*Skeleton 2* (small)
Femur (thighbone)	52.0 cm	45.3 cm
Tibia (shinbone)	43.1 cm	37.7 cm

Humerus (shoulder to elbow)	36.7 cm	31.5 cm
Ulna (forearm opp. thumb)	28.5 cm	23.9 cm
Radius (forearm, thumb side)	26.8 cm	damaged

Calculating anthropometrically from average dimensions of the hollow cylindrical bones, the following body dimensions result:

	Skeleton 1	*Skeleton 2*
Height	1.90–1.94 m	1.68–1.71 m

	Skull 1	*Skull 2*
	(dolichocephalic)	(brachycephalic)
Circumference	51.9 cm	49.8 cm
Diameter lengthwise	17.4 cm	16.2 cm
Diameter horizontal	14.3 cm	14.7 cm

Skull 1 was damaged on left parietal bone in the course of excavation on December 7, 1972. Typical dolichocephalic skull with high steep forehead and narrow facial bones. The dentition, preserved almost intact, shows dental work.

Skull 1 Circumference would make a head circumference of 57–59 cm.

Skull 2 is undamaged. Brachycephalic skull with a receding, wavy, convexly rising forehead and short, abruptly descending back of the head. The dentition is missing in places and shows typical dental repair in the lower jaw,· a bridge from the 1st canine over windowed yellow metal crowns to the 2nd canine.

Skull 2 Circumference would make a head circumference of 55–57 cm.

Re b) By macroscopic observation, no pathological-anatomical findings are visible on the left forearm bones of Skeleton 1 (large). However, x-ray photographs show noticeable changes in the radius and ulna, which probably were caused by an old fracture in the lower third of the left forearm. (See x-ray findings of Dr. Schöldgen.)

Re c) On Skull 2 on the forehead over the prominence above the right eye there are no changes in the bone that can be detected by pathologic anatomy. Skull 2 has experienced no bone injury worthy of mention. These negative findings with respect to the bone do not, however, exclude the possibility that during lifetime a bleeding wound of the skin (laceration or cut) might have taken place accidentally.

Re d) The enclosed profile photographs of skulls 1 and 2 superimposed by photomontage over the profile photographs of Dr. Stumpfegger and Bormann show perfect agreement of skull and face shapes.

(When the photographs are examined, the difference created by the skin of face and head—hair as well as tissue—must be taken into consideration.)

On the basis of the examinations described in a), b) and c) together with the interpretation of the medical examination results from the former Head Office of the Race and Resettlement of the SS, Skull 1 and Skeleton 1 (large) are with highest probability identical with the person of Dr. Ludwig Stumpfegger.

The forearm fracture suffered by Dr. Stumpfegger in 1923—completely healed— has been verified by x-ray of the skeletal bones.

The body height, calculated anthropometrically from the skeletal bones as 1.90 to 1.94 m, matches the body height given in the medical-examination result as 1.90 m. The same goes for the head circumference, given as 58 cm on the examination form.

The skull shape (dolichocephalic) and the racial classification "Nordic" correspond with the findings from examination of Skeleton Skull 1.

Skull 2 and Skeleton 2 (small) demonstrate with highest probability an identity with the person of Martin Bormann.

According to reports I have received, Bormann suffered a broken collarbone as the result of a fall from a horse. The collarbone fracture has been verified both macroscopically and by x-ray examination of Skeleton 2 as defectively healed.

Insofar as the anthropometrically extrapolated measurements of Skeleton 2 match the body height of 1,68 cm to 1,71 cm, the head shape with essential characteristics (brachycephalic) as well as the head circumference of 55–57 cm match those of Bormann, and the typical dental prosthetic and dental-technician work on the jaw of Skull 2 can be verified by a dentist, the identity of Skull 2 and Skeleton 2 (small) can be certified with probability bordering on certainty as belonging to Martin Bormann.

[signed] Dr. Spengler
Medical Director
Chief of the Institute

Exhibit 18
Photograph of the accused

Exhibit 19
Photograph of the accused

Exhibit 20
Radiological expert opinions on portions of the skeletons
of Dr. Ludwig Stumpfegger and the accused

K.-J. Schöldgen, M.D.   1 **Berlin 42**   5.1.73
Specialist in Radiology   Tempelhofer Damm 138
                                                          Telephone 7 52 77 45

Dear Colleagues:
    The x-ray examination gave the following results:
    Skeleton photographs of left forearm bones, both sides, of Dr. Stumpfegger,
Ludwig:
    Slight deformation of the distal third of the left radius with structural bulge of
the marrow area and thickening of the periosteum in comparison with the radius
of the right side.
    Also in the left ulna in the distal third there is a somewhat denser structure
observable in comparison with the other side.
    Opinion: On the basis of comparison of both forearm bones this is probably a
            condition following fracture of the distal third of the forearm with
            noticeable changes in the radius.

                                                          [signed] Schöldgen

K.-J. Schöldgen, M.D.   1 **Berlin 42** 5. 1. 73
Specialist in Radiology   Tempelhofer Damm 138
                                                          Telephone 7 52 77 45

Dear Colleagues:
    The x-ray examination gave the following results:
    Skeleton photographs of the right clavicula from two angles
    Reference Bormann, Martin:
    In the middle third of the clavicula periosteal span, a pronounced twist with
complete bony regrowth, with the periosteum substantially thinned in this region
and in places entirely missing.
    The structure of the bone is perfectly straight in the proximal and distal region;
then some areas appear somewhat strand-like.
    The bony span in the area referred to is relatively dense.
    Opinion: In the clavicula designated as from Bormann, Martin, there is absolute
            evidence of a defective healing after fracture of the clavicula in the
            middle third.

                                                          [signed] Schöldgen

Exhibit 21
X-ray photograph of the left forearm of Dr. Ludwig Stumpfegger's skeleton

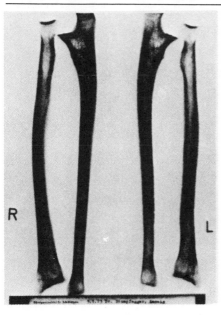

Exhibit 22
X-ray photograph of the collarbone from the skeleton of the accused

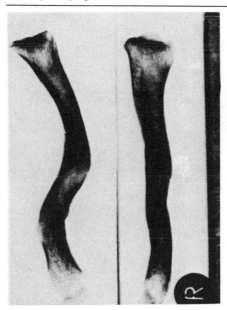

Exhibit 23
Photomontage of Skull No. 2 with photograph of the accused

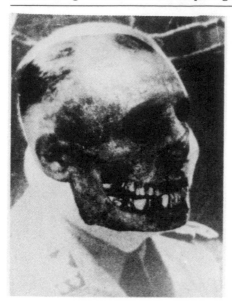

Exhibit 24
Photomontage of Skull No. 1 with photograph of Dr. Ludwig Stumpfegger

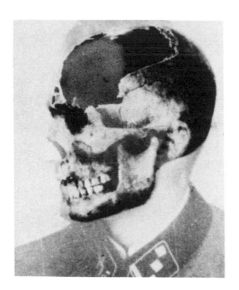

**Exhibit 25
Plastic facial reconstruction of
Skull No. 2 (Martin Bormann)**

**Exhibit 26
Plastic facial reconstruction of Skull
No. 1 (Dr. Ludwig Stumpfegger)**

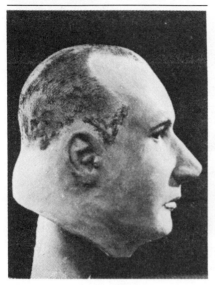
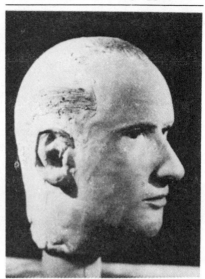

**Exhibit 27
Photograph of Dr. Ludwig Stumpfegger**

DOCUMENTS

Part B

Select documents, each reproduced in its entirety, from October 5, 1932, to April 1945.

The documents* referred to in the text were supplied by the following archives and institutes unless they were made available to the author from private sources:

Bayerisches Hauptstaatsarchiv, Munich
Berlin Document Center
Bundesarchiv, Koblenz
Bundesarchiv—Militärarchiv, Freiburg
Deutsche Dienststelle (WASt), Berlin
Deutsches Zentralarchiv, Potsdam
Geheimes Staatsarchiv der Stiftung PreuBischer Kulturbesitz, Berlin-Dahlem
Hessisches Hauptstaatsarchiv, Wiesbaden
Imperial War Museum, London
Institut für Zeitgeschichte, Munich
Institut für Zeitgeschichte, Vienna
Institute of Contemporary History—The Wiener Library, London
National Archives, Washington
Zeitgeschichtliches Bildarchiv Heinrich Hoffmann, Munich-Hamburg

*The complete collection of source material for this book comprises several thousand documents, whose authenticity the [German] publisher and editor vouch for. It would be beyond the scope of this book to include all of them here; therefore, only some of the most important were included in this documentation. (Ed's. note.)

Letter dated October 5, 1932
Martin Bormann "To the Private Secretary to the Führer, Herr
Rudolf Hess" (cf. text, page 60).

Martin Bormann   **Munich,** October 5, 1932

To:
Private Secretary to the Führer, Herr Rudolf Hess
currently in Dachau

Dear Herr Hess:
It is only because of the pressure of events that I bother you on your vacation. The following, however, *has* to be said, in my opinion. You and the Führer must be made aware of the attitudes that prevail on the outside.

Let it be clear at the outset, as you already know, anyway, that I have nothing against the SA. Nor do I have anything against Röhm personally. As far as I am concerned, someone in faraway India can fool around with elephants, and in Australia with kangaroos, I couldn't care less. For me and for all true National Socialists, the only thing that counts is the Movement, nothing else. Anything or anybody useful to the Movement is good; whoever does it harm is a louse and my enemy. The Movement and only the Movement is paramount.

But the things that have been coming to light in sworn statements in the hearing as undisputed facts—Röhm's diversionary tactics no longer impress any thinking person—knock the bottom right out of the barrel. One of the most prominent leaders in the Party is complaining to an equally prominent leader of the opposition, and is insulting and reviling his own Party comrades, who are also leaders, calling them *Schweinehunde.*

Every SA man, every ordinary Party member has it drummed into him as one of the first and most elementary rules, as the Chief himself says in the Foreword to the *Member's Handbook:* "Never forget, wherever you may be, that you are the representative of the National Socialist Movement, and of our whole philosophy. *The stranger judges the Movement by the impression he gets of you.* So be a National Socialist in everything you do and are! *Always remain a good example* to your comrades."

Every SA man, every ordinary Party member has it drummed into him, and this was especially important in the Röhm case, that he must cover for his comrades and leaders even when mistakes are made, right to the end—and then the most prominent SA leader of all goes ahead with flagrant betrayal and slander.

If the Führer still stands by this man after that performance, then I and countless other people don't understand him anymore, and there simply *isn't* any way of understanding. In his office the Führer has three pictures of the Great Prussian. What would have happened to one of Old Fritz's generals if he had carried on like that???

Let it not be said that the past services performed by Chief of Staff Röhm outweigh faults of that sort. The harm that R. has caused by his example—"the stranger judges the Movement by the impression he gets of you"—cannot be outweighed by any amount of past services. To say nothing of the question: *What* services?? Take a good look at all the orders Röhm issued—you won't find a single *basic* innovation since Pfeffer's time. The Movement grew, and the SA along with it; the mission stayed the same from the beginning, except for one single task, and I'll get back to that. The hard work, the General Staff work that had to be done, was performed by General Hörauf, who got the cold shoulder!

They say Röhm is quite a personality, a "brain." One can certainly be of two minds about that. Besides, an accurate yardstick for judging a person is the quality of his co-workers. Brains? Take a look at the former Deputy Chief of Staff, Major Fuchs, and the present Deputy Chief of Staff, "Major and Gruppenführer" Hühnlein, and you will get some idea of how little gas there is in the tank, or ever could be. I am convinced that the post of chief of staff could be filled by any SA leader with an understanding of people and a talent for organization (Lutze). I was never much of a soldier myself, but I'd bet my boots that even I could manage it. Take a look at the SS. You know Himmler and you know Himmler's capabilities.

People praise Röhm's loyalty to the Chief. To put it bluntly, many a dumb Private Kaczmarek was a loyal soldier, and at the same time a complete blockhead and not worth much as a soldier. Loyalty by itself is not enough and cannot be a decisive consideration. To say nothing of the fact that genuine loyalty to the Führer would hardly allow anything like the Mayr business to come about. And if the Chief wants to return Röhm's loyalty and wants to keep him on for that reason, then the question arises which is more important, loyalty to the Movement or loyalty to Röhm. One is almost tempted to think of the Kaiser's fateful Nibelung loyalty toward Austria, which the Chief knows well enough about.

It is said that the attitude against Röhm springs from the general resentment of the political leaders toward the SA. An outrageous insinuation, because as I said before, every man with the true spirit of a fighter eagerly welcomes the growth and flourishing of the SA. And after all, all of us old Party members were once plain SA men. In the Political Organization, from top to bottom, there is no bad feeling being fomented against the SA, as is the case the other way around. Who is only too eager to call our political leaders *"Bonzen"*? Not the political opposition, but our own SA leaders—even though most of the political leaders are putting themselves on the line every bit as much as the SA. Personally I would rather be out in the field as an SA leader than be stuck behind a desk day after day, pushing papers around from morning to night. Furthermore, who spends more money, and more freely? Certainly not the man who collects the dues and knows how reluctant most Party members are about paying up.

It is said that the SA stands behind Röhm. The SA stands behind the leader Hitler appoints for it, no more, no less. It is doubtful that R. was the object of any great *love* on the part of the SA.

But what is essential and of decisive importance is the following: Does the Führer know how many Party members have dropped out of the Movement because of acts of terror? Obernitz, who from the viewpoint of the top SA leadership was the person most successful in carrying out the orders in question, or having them executed by others, told me that SA lieutenants had refused to carry out such orders for him, Party members had told him that they had voted for National Socialism for the last time, etc. This order included a mission which, as far as Röhm was concerned, failed totally. Does the Führer know that the opinion is widely held in Party circles that Röhm was thoroughly duped by Schleicher?

Does the Führer know about the "no confidence" attitude of Party members toward the elections? Does he know that a large number of SA men take the position that the best thing to do would be to vote Communist? When the Röhm correspondence was made public and the Führer let it be known that Röhm was to stay on as Chief of Staff, many Party members shook their heads. The idea of subjecting the Movement to the same trial by ordeal in the present situation seems to me extremely dangerous. There is practically no confidence in a victory in the Reichstag elections;

the majority of the Party members, including the SA, are disappointed as a result of the exaggerated hopes aroused by responsible leaders (Röhm, Goebbels) in connection with the first Reich presidential election and the election of July 31. Trust *in the Führer* still exists, and this must be preserved, for if it were ever lost, the Movement would be if not permanently done for, certainly knocked out for the moment. *Certainly countless people will lose confidence in the Führer if the Führer continues to keep a man who betrays his comrades to a political enemy, asks for and gets damaging material to use against them.*—We mustn't consider our Party members for dumber than dumb. [Bormann's original wording reads "dumber than they really are."] Röhm's public statements don't impress anyone anymore; the Party membership has gradually gotten wise to his line. Don't you think that most of the readers of today's statement by Röhm will ask right away: "Well, if Bell and Mayr made false sworn statements, why should they—that would be handing us the case on a platter—not be indicted and prosecuted for perjury? Why does Röhm merely make a so-called sworn deposition which he could never be prosecuted for even if it turned out to be false? Why, etc.???" No, Herr Hess, our Party membership is not being taken in by that kind of thing anymore, and anyone who still thinks so is grossly deceiving himself. Besides, the answers from the other side won't be long in coming, and it will go on and on, and the Movement is exposing itself needlessly to these attacks and suffering the most grievous harm from them. And moreover, if, as Reiner says, the interview is supposed to have been recorded on discs, there might be some surprises coming out of that, too. And *we* have to stand by with our eyes open and see the Movement get hurt by such unbelievable things, all because we won't withdraw the weakest point in our front, but instead hold on to it whatever the cost. And in the process the Führer's image is being systematically undermined by the most malicious allegations. God's mercy protect my own brother, if he were to do only a fraction of the things against the Party that have been perpetrated by Röhm. Taking all this into consideration, I find the Chief's attitude completely incomprehensible. If I or some other Party members fail to understand political decisions, well and good, we don't know enough about the circumstances and conditions, the Führer is the Führer, he'll straighten it all out in the end. But this is a question of the grave damage the Movement is suffering because of the behavior of one of its members.

Heil Yours,
[signed] Martin Bormann

Letter dated May 27, 1933
Martin Bormann "To the Deputy Party Leader, Herr Rudolf Hess"
(cf. text, page 66).

Martin Bormann   **Munich,** May 27, 1933

To the Deputy Party Leader, Herr Rudolf Hess
Berlin

Dear Herr Hess:
   Reich Party Treasurer Schwarz has already told me twice that the management of the Relief Fund is getting to be too much for him, and a simpler procedure for the computation of dues must be introduced—namely, deductions from the local groups [Ortsgruppen] are not to be made according to the number of names in Relief Fund records, but rather according to the rating of the local groups in the card index

of the Treasury. In other words, this will be the job of the Relief Fund card index and the Relief Fund bookkeeping, and all that's left will be the Accident Section. Herr Schwarz places no value on my opinions, I am just the employee in the Treasury who has to toe the mark and do as he is told.

In view of this I ask you once again to employ me elsewhere, in the *Political* Organization. I do not want to work in the Treasury any longer. Had I known that things were to take this turn, I would have put in this request as soon as the Relief Fund had been set up, a long time ago. For, to me, the job of running the Relief Fund is no longer a challenge and therefore no longer offers any satisfaction. What has to be done now can be managed by Stabsleiter Geisselbrecht or Card Index Manager Kirchbauer, and if the anticipated phasing-out goes through, then Accident Section Manager Wehse can handle it.

May I ask you to say nothing to Reich Party Treasurer Schwarz concerning my request for employment in the Political Organization; he would not understand and would break with me immediately and completely.

With Hitler-Heil!
[signed] Martin Bormann

Handwritten letter, March 30 (presumably 1935)
Martin Bormann to Reich Peasant Leader Richard Walter Darré (cf. text, page 84)

National Socialist German Workers' Party
The Führer's Deputy
[Nazi Party Insignia]

Stabsleiter

Munich, Briennerstrasse 45
Tel. 34901
53844
[written in] now in Berlin, March 30
[illegible squiggles]

Dear Darré:

This evening I went home with joy in my heart over the substance of our conversation, since God knows present conditions demand close cooperation between National Socialists. To bring this about it is necessary, however, for us to assess the situation, first very thoroughly and then on a day-to-day basis, for if we don't, then despite the basic attitudes we both share, there could be one situation or another in which we could handle people or affairs at cross-purposes. For instance, it could happen that you may feel the same way about a certain person that I do, but for the sake of expediency you might want to stroke him as the ant strokes the aphid while I am doing the very opposite!

I have no more use for half-assed measures than you people do, hence this letter. If you [changed from *Sie* to *Du*] agree with me and are going to be in Munich next week, we could get together at the Tegernsee or meet at my house. In any case, I will be in Berlin Wednesday and Thursday.

Regards to your wife!
Heil Hitler!
Yours,
[signed] Martin

Handwritten letter dated April 15, 1936
Martin Bormann to his office colleague Heinrich Heim (cf. text, page 70)

Martin Bormann   **Munich,** April 14, 1936

Dear Herr Heim:
Many thanks for your letter. My compliments: you write in a terrific style, really great! That's why getting letters from you is such pure pleasure.
I am not going to write you at any great length. First, the work on the East is taking too much of my time, and second, you'll be here soon anyway. You can always write your letter to Herr Schwarz after having a conference with me. I put the thing through for various reasons: first I pointed out your long years of work in my office and your accomplishments on behalf of the Relief Fund (memorandum). Second, your self-sacrificing work in Frank's office. Third, because I felt your high [Party] number was as incongruous as it was embarrassing, and because in addition I did not want my successor(s) to draw false conclusions about you. Fourth and finally—hold on to your seat—I fixed it so you will be given the rank of Oberregierungsrat [senior state counselor]. It wasn't easy, but I'm stubborn. It does not make any difference to *us* whether as our lawyer you are in or out of civil service. But I believe it is important for you because you never use your elbows for yourself, only for others, and something must be done to take care of your future. No objections: *The Führer has appointed you!* And when I am no longer around and you don't want to stay any longer, you can get yourself pensioned off any time.
One thing more—I must ask you not to say anything to anyone about the Party number or the reasons for your getting civil-service rank. What I have done for you does not go for others who would take off for somewhere else right away.
Best regards from my wife, the children, and myself.

Heil Hitler!
[signed] Martin

Letter dated October 10, 1939
Rudolf Hess and Martin Bormann "To the Reich Minister for Church Affairs, Hans Kerrl" (cf. text, page 131)

National Socialist   [Nazi emblem]   German Workers' Party

Copy

The Führer's Deputy   Munich, October 10, 1939
                                            Brown House
                                            Bo/Fu

To: The Reich Minister for Church
    Affairs Hans Kerrl
    Berlin W 8
    Leipziger Strasse 3

According to information I have received, you are planning to publish a work in the near future in which, among other things, you comment on the concepts of *"Weltanschauung"* and "religion." Your proposed publication impinges on the domain of the Party in the strongest possible way; according to your own statements, the antithesis you have developed, *"Weltanschauung* and Religion," is also intended to show where the line is to be drawn between the Party's jurisdiction and the area that should be reserved for the churches.

I consider it wrong to publish such a work whose purpose it obviously is to criticize and condemn the Party; in any event, in my opinion the Führer must decide whether the book may be published. Also, I take for granted that you will send me the draft of your work for an opinion.

F.d.R.d.A.   Heil Hitler!
Signature illegible   [Signed] Hess

Letter dated December 19, 1939
Martin Bormann "To Reichsleiter Party Member Dr. Goebbels (cf. text, page 131)

National Socialist   (Nazi emblem)   German Workers' Party

                                        Carbon copy

The Führer's Deputy   Munich 33, December 19, 1939
                                                                    Brown House

Stabsleiter

To: Reichsleiter Party Member Dr. Goebbels
Munich
Karlstrasse 20

Re: Book by Church Minister Kerrl, *Weltanschauung and Religion*

I have before me the Christmas catalogue of the Gsellius Bookstore. On page 75 there is an announcement of *Weltanschauung und Religion,* the book by Reich Minister Kerrl publication of which, as is well known, the Führer has prohibited.

I am also informed that almost all Lutheran bookstores have included Party Member Kerrl's book in their catalogues and are promoting its sale. I do not consider it right that a book whose publication has been prohibited by the Führer should be advertised anywhere, particularly as Reich Minister Kerrl some time ago sent the Führer's Deputy advice that he had instructed the publisher to cease his preparations for printing the book.

Heil Hitler!
[Signed] M. Bormann

**Letter dated September 24, 1940
Martin Bormann "To the office of the Gauleiter of Franconia,
Attn. District Leader Zimmermann"**

National Socialist   [Nazi emblem]   German Workers' Party

The Führer's Deputy   Currently in Berlin, September 24,
                                             1940

Stabsleiter

                                Bo-An

                                                             Personal

To: Office of the Gauleiter of Franconia
      District Leader
Attn.: Zimmermann
Nuremberg
Gauleiter Headquarters of the NSDAP

I was shown your letter of September 13, 1940, by Party Member Hoffmann. The committee that was functioning in Neuendettelsaus [Editor's note: correct spelling is Neuendettelsau] is under the control of Reichsleiter Bouhler, and is acting on his orders.

As I once again verified yesterday, notifications of relatives are being phrased differently; of course there might be one or two cases in which two families living close together have received letters with the same wording.

Obviously, advocates of Christian *Weltanschauung* will be speaking out against the committee's measures; it must be equally clear that all Party offices give their support to the committee's work whenever necessary.

                                             Heil Hitler!
                                             [Signed] M. Bormann

Handwritten marginalia illegible

Letter dated November 20, 1940
Martin Bormann "To Reich Minister and Chief of Reich Chancellery
Dr. H. H. Lammers"   (cf. text, page 152)

National Socialist   [Nazi emblem]   German Workers' Party

Berlin—Wilhelmstrasse 34   Handwritten marginalia illegible

The Führer's Deputy

November 20, 1940

III/09—Ku.

2610/0/102

Registered mail

To: The Reich Minister and Chief
of the Reich Chancellery
Dr. H. H. Lammers
Berlin W 8
Vosstrasse 6

Re: Introduction of Penal Code Regulations in the Incorporated Eastern Territories

Following the introduction of German penal law in the incorporated Eastern territories in accordance with the decree of June 6, 1940 (Reichgesetzblatt I S.844), the Reich Minister of Justice, in connection with the introduction of further penal code provisions, sent me drafts of the following decrees with a request for endorsement:

1. Decree on the implementation and amendment to the decree on the introduction of the German penal code in the incorporated Eastern territories (File No. 9170/2 IIa² 1291.40).

2. Decree on the introduction of German extradition law in the incorporated Eastern territories (File No. 9351/1—IIa³ 529/40).

3. Decree on the introduction of the law on the use of weapons by forestry and game-warden officers as well as officials of the Fisheries Service and fishery wardens in the incorporated Eastern territories (File No. V b² 1636).

4. Decree on the implementation of the law on expiation of sentences and the decree on maintenance of criminal records in the incorporated Eastern territories (File No. 4240—IIa⁴ 948.40).

Regarding the last two drafts I have already told the Reich Minister of Justice that under no circumstances are the provisions in these decrees to be applied to non-Germans, and also that I would find it more practical if the governors [Reichsstatthalter] were empowered to promulgate decrees to the same effect. This would have the advantage that the governors would be able to suit the scope and enforcement of their decrees to the particular requirements of the situation.

Regarding the introduction of the right to use weapons for forestry, game and fishery officers, the Reich Minister of Justice has already replied that he cannot go along with the suggestion of granting power of decree to the governors. [Translator's note: mistake in text here, I'm sure. Reads *his* suggestion, should read *my* suggestion.]

Meanwhile, my expressed objections to the abovementioned decrees have become stronger—except for determination by the governors of the manner and timing of promulgation—in yet another fundamental direction.

According to reports I have received, it is already becoming obvious that it had been a mistake to introduce the German penal code in the Eastern territories. The Poles are already starting to take advantage of the introduction of these laws, in that they are lodging complaints against German officials for alleged arbitrariness, requisition, etc. Since the suspension of drumhead courts-martial there has been a noted increase in incidents of insubordination, i.e., assault on police officers and refusal to work on a major scale.

It seems to me that the German penal code, by reason of its total basic attitude and objective, is inappropriate to the special circumstances of the East.

I am even convinced that the wholesale application of the penal code in the East goes a long way toward abridging the freedom of action of government offices and officials, who must find themselves impeded by the numerous provisions in the penal code providing protection of the individual against excesses of the administration.

Recognizing this danger, the Reich Minister of Justice made provision in Article 1, Section II, Paragraph 1 of the decree on juridical regulations governing penal law practice in the incorporated Eastern territories to the effect that only those torts be prosecuted whose prosecution would be in the public interest. However, in each case so tried, the matter is one way or another made the object of a judicial review, surely resulting in delays and inconveniences, which move the "perpetrators" to proceed in the future with more caution.

Still more dangerous, however, is the possibility that the Poles might seek protection from these procedures and the juridical provisions fashioned for the protection of the accused and thereby not inconsiderably strengthening their position. With all the good will in the world, not every judge will feel free, amid all these difficulties, to assume responsibility, and above all, have enough presence of mind, to arrive at decisions that are keyed to political objectives.

I would therefore like to see it avoided that the danger conjured up by the introduction of the [German] penal law should be reinforced by the similar introduction of other laws from the penal code in the Eastern territories.

I should like to point out in this connection that the Führer's remarks on the presentation given by Gauleiters Bürckel and Wagner on September 25, 1940, give fundamental support to my position. The Führer emphasized that in the Eastern territories the Gauleiters must also have freedom of action. They are responsible to him alone for the accomplishment of their assigned missions. At the present moment, introducing Reich law in the new territories means making the work difficult, if not impossible, for the men charged with bringing about the new order. In these territories it will be necessary to create all the preconditions first, so that bit by bit the situation becomes such that introduction of Reich law will be possible. These conditions, however, cannot be brought about simply by introducing Reich law. Only when the Gauleiters have assimilated the new territories with the original Reich can one think of introducing Reich law. The Führer stressed further that there is only one report he will demand from his Gauleiters after a ten-year period—namely that their district is German and pure German. He is not going to ask what methods they employed to Germanize their districts, and it is all the same to him if at some time in the future it might be established that the methods for the conquest of this area were ugly or other than juridically impeccable.

Now, it is possible that the amendment to the decree on the introduction of the penal code to the incorporated Eastern territories may not represent a formal introduction of Reich law, since it brings with it a whole new set of circumstances. Basically, however, the same considerations apply to it as to the other draft decrees. The Reich Minister of Justice has what is in itself a commendable motive in wishing to close a loophole by this decree that has remained open despite related provisions in the penal code and the law against malicious gossip. Regardless of the fact that the sentences in paragraphs 2 and 3 of the draft still seem too lenient to me despite subsequent tightening, the Poles will find ways and means to get around these statutes so that new penal laws will necessarily follow. It will never be possible to set down formulations that cover all possibilities.

If contraventions against Poles who have committed offenses against public order are punished according to the German penal code, then this punishment is still only discharged within the framework of this penal law. The special character of the work in the incorporated Eastern territories, however, makes it mandatory to make each case a step toward the realization of the set objective by appropriate increase in the severity of methods of punishment employed for the purpose of inspiring more terror, since every action in the Eastern territories must serve to assist the responsible Gauleiters in the execution of the Führer's orders.

In my view, that will only be possible if the application of German penal law in the Eastern territories as it has so far been employed is suspended and a special penal law is drafted for Poland.

This penal law could limit itself to a certain few regulations, which should be so formulated as to cover as closely as possible all offenses against public order by Poles.

Together with this special penal law, a corresponding criminal procedure must be created as well, making possible rapid and efficacious court action. As for the provisions for the protection of the accused and/or indicted, created according to the criteria prevailing when the penal code came into existence in 1870, which provisions are still essentially on the books, extensive restraint should be exercised. Likewise the adherence to rules requiring formalities, such as observance of reprieves, etc., is to be dropped. Special preconditions for issuance of arrest warrants, orders for confiscation and search are similarly just so much more interference.

A penal procedure of this sort must furthermore be over and done with at a single-court level. It seems insupportable to me to permit a Pole to take a case against him up through a series of higher courts and possibly even right up to the Reich Supreme Court.

Apart from the obvious increased severity in comparison with corresponding penalties imposed on Germans, the penalties set down for this policy are to be used unequivocally for the purpose of terrorizing [the Polish population] and for the furtherance of the political objectives set for the Eastern territories.

In this connection, the Poles' insensitivity toward prison sentences in their present form must be borne in mind. Along with the option of death sentences, consideration should be given to the introduction of corporal punishment and the creation of other measures with perhaps more of a police character.

In the event that this special penal law for Poles is to be administered by the officials of the Justice Department, then consideration should be given to the possibility that the courts operate in this situation as much as possible in procedure and objectives as did the police drumhead courts, which, according to reports before me, worked very well and unfortunately were dropped as a result of the introduction of [German] penal law in the incorporated Eastern territories.

Only thus will it be possible to avoid the dangers inherent in the introduction of [German] penal law in the Eastern territories.

In reference to my letter of October 21, 1940-2610/0/103 in answer to your letter of September 26, 1940-Rk. 14371 B on the question of introducing civil-law provisions in the incorporated Eastern territories, I therefore ask you also, in view of the application of German penal law in force in Poland, to bring about a decision by the Führer.

The Reich Minister of Justice has received a copy of this letter.

Heil Hitler!
by authority
[signed] M. Bormann

Handwritten marginalia illegible

Circular letter dated December 7, 1940
Martin Bormann to "Reichsleiters, Gauleiters, Organization Chiefs"
(cf. text, page 152)

COPY
National Socialist German Workers' Party

The Führer's Deputy
Stabsleiter

Munich 33, December 7, 1940
Brown House
Dr. Kl./Ra.

Circular Letter
(Not for Publication)

Highly confidential

Re: Construction of Houses of Prostitution for Foreign Workers

The growing necessity for bringing in ever increasing numbers of foreign workers is endangering German blood. Prohibitions and threats of punishment are of only limited effectiveness, and because of political considerations they cannot be promulgated in all cases. The Führer has therefore directed that special houses of prostitution be established for workers from other countries, if possible in all localities where they are employed in large numbers.

By circular notice dated September 9, 1939, the Reich Minister of the Interior and Chief of the German Police ordered the establishment of special houses for prostitutes, directing in this connection that general racist principles are to be taken into consideration. Implementation of the necessary measures is the responsibility of the local criminal police headquarters and stations concerned.

Communities are directed to support these police measures and to charge all expenses involved to indirect police disbursement accounts. I am negotiating with the Reich Labor Minister on the matter of the proportion of the expense that can be charged to the employers.

I request the Gauleiters to give special attention to the question of establishing bordellos for foreign workers. Bordellos of this character must be set up rapidly in every locality where foreign workers are employed. In case difficulties arise, I request an immediate report.

Heil Hitler!
[signed] M. Bormann
For authentication
Signature
Secretary for Criminal
Affairs

F.d.R.
[Signed] Dr. Klopfer

Circular Letter dated May 15, 1941
Martin Bormann "To all Reichsleiters, Gauleiters and Organization Chiefs" (cf. text, page 161)

National Socialist German Workers' Party

Party Chancellery   Kreisleiters advised

Personal. Strictly Confidential.   Führer Headquarters, 5.15.41
                                               Bo/Si

To all Reichsleiters,
Gauleiters and Organization
Chiefs

Dear Party Member Zimmermann:

The work of the Party Chancellery will go on operating as before, but now under the supervision and protection of the Führer himself. I shall of course keep the Führer abreast of all important issues and I will similarly pass current information to Reichsleiters, Gauleiters and organization chiefs on the Führer's decisions and views; a large proportion of the circulars sent out by me in the past two years emanated as a consequence of my activities in the Führer's office anyway.

Since I belong to the Führer's most personal staff, I am to continue to accompany the Führer at all times. While the war is on, this has the disadvantage that at times it will be impossible to reach me except by telephone or letter. On the other hand this circumstance has the great advantage that in wartime, too, all important affairs of the Party, the Reichsleiters, Gauleiters and organization chiefs can be presented to the Führer on a day-to-day basis.

Moreover, my associates, Party Member Friedrichs and Party Member Klopfer, are always available in Berlin or Munich for consultations.

If anyone says now, as happened a few days ago, that he won't have anything to do with the lower echelon, then I must insert a very personal observation and ask for a little more fairness toward myself and my men.

Since 1933, when I was given the job of coordinating and executing the collaboration of the NSDAP in laws and ordinances, and when I was given the additional duty of passing on the current political guidelines to the various Party offices, when I was given the difficult task of bringing about a unified attitude throughout all the NSDAP offices, each involved with countless matters, I have worked like a horse! Indeed, more than a horse, since a horse has its Sunday and its night's sleep, and in the past years I have scarcely ever had a Sunday off and precious little night's sleep. In spite of that I could not have done all that work by myself; rather, I had to have my co-workers. For that reason I have asked the Gauleiters over and over again to make their best and most capable men available to me; the better the men the Gauleiters send me, the better the work that can be accomplished in central headquarters. For the most part my men have also had to work hard in the past years, and they have spared themselves as little as I have. What is more, I am of the opinion that we did a very respectable and useful job. Anyone who thinks otherwise should tell the Führer at once who he thinks could do my job better than I can. It seemed to me necessary to inject this personal remark.

Additionally, I will in the future always notify Reichsleiters, Gauleiters and organization chiefs whenever the Führer is staying in Berlin. The Führer would welcome it very much if Reichsleiters, Gauleiters and organization chiefs who are in Berlin at such times would come to lunch or dinner in the Reich Chancellery residence, after first notifying the Führer's Adjutant's Office (tel. 12 00 50).

Heil Hitler!
[signed] M. Bormann

By special delivery, receipt requested

Office Staff Memo dated June 4, 1941
Martin Bormann to his closest associates Gerhard Klopfer and
Helmuth Friedrichs (cf. text, page 162]

PERSONAL!

Memorandum for Party Members Klopfer and Friedrichs

The Reichsmarschall is currently at Obersalzberg. Through General Bodenschatz I requested a meeting, which took place today. I spent 1½ hours in Landhaus Göring; first the Reichsmarschall had a long conversation with me on the construction I had done at Obersalzberg, then on political problems. The Reichsmarschall stressed repeatedly that he was aware that a lot of people (Dr. Frick, etc.) thought they could by-pass the Party; of course he, the Reichsmarschall, was not one of them; rather, it was his wish that collaboration by the Party with the drafting of government laws and ordinances should remain at the same level of intensity as hitherto. The Reichsmarschall is aware that, for example, there is a desire to by-pass the Party in personnel evaluation, awards of the *Kriegsverdienstkreuz* [War Merit Cross], etc., with reference to the point that Gauleiters are also Reich governors [Reichsstatthalter].

For my part I informed the Reichsmarschall that several Reichsleiters had sought the Party's collaboration in drafting laws, ordinances, etc., for their own domains; this the Reichsmarschall rejected as completely unworkable; also, in his opinion the Party Chancellery should continue handling these matters as before, as a central headquarters.

I also asked the Reichsmarschall several times always to send for me immediately if he had anything in mind with respect to the Party, when he received complaints, etc. Of course we must continue to work closely with the Reichsmarschall's departments.

In closing, the Reichsmarschall declared that he had full confidence in me and was convinced that we would be able to work together excellently.

[signed] M. Bormann

Führer Headquarters, June 4, 1941
Bo/Si

Telex dated June 29, 1941
Martin Bormann to Gerhard Klopfer

Carbon Copy

Telex

June 29, 1941
Secret!

Reichsleiter Bormann to Ministerial Director Dr. Klopfer, Munich
Very urgent, immediate action!

Gruppenführer Heydrich informs me that on invitation of the president of the German Academy, Ministerial President Siebert, General [Karl] Haushofer is to participate in the June 30, 1941, conference in Strassburg as senator of the German Academy and as member of the Select Council of the German Academy. Gruppenführer Heydrich tells me that apparently Ministerial President Siebert places great value on Haushofer's participation.

In Haushofer's position I would long since have resigned all public offices on account of the perhaps involuntary participation in the affair of May 10, 1941. General Haushofer apparently has no such intention. It is therefore necessary that we point out to Ministerial President Siebert that it is known to all Gauleiters that the two Haushofers are to be regarded as the brains behind the May 10 incident, and therefore their appearance in public is not desired.

Please call on Ministerial President Siebert *immediately* and instruct him accordingly. Of course you must stick closely to the facts.

The premiere of the play *Augustus,* written by Professor Albrecht Haushofer, will take place on July 4, 1941, in the Residenz-Theater in Munich.

Please call on Gauleiter Adolf Wagner and let him know that Haushofers, father and son, were both involved in the affair of May 10; R.H. [Rudolf Hess] discussed with both the theoretical possibility of reaching an understanding by personal conference with the right people. Because of the so-called reality dream [*Wahrtraum*] which was followed by another, similar one, R.H. ended by firmly believing in the success of his undertaking.

Cancellation of the play *Augustus* is surely not possible, but wide publicity is not desirable.

[signed] M. Bormann

Circular letter dated April 2, 1942
Martin Bormann to "Reichsleiters, Gauleiters and Organization Chiefs"
(cf. text, page 165)

National Socialist   [Nazi emblem]   German Workers' Party

Party Chancellery

The Chief of the Party Chancellery   Führer Headquarters
April 2, 1942

Circular No. 49/42
(Not for Publication)

Re: Area of Responsibilities of the Party Chancellery

In the implementation directive of January 16, 1942 (Reichgesetzblatt I, p. 35, Exhibit 1), to the Führer decree of May 29, 1942,* regarding the position of the Chief of the Party Chancellery *(ibid.),* the jurisdiction of the Chief of the Party Chancellery vis-à-vis the top-level agencies of the Reich is made clear. This provides me with an occasion to summarize once again the directives to date regarding the domain of the Party.

The Party Chancellery is an office of the Führer. He uses it to run the NSDAP, leadership of which he resumed totally and exclusively on May 12, 1941.

The Chief of the Party Chancellery is entrusted by the Führer to handle, in accordance with his basic instructions, all internal Party planning and all vitally important questions for the preservation of the German people within the Party's purview, as well as to adapt all suggestions from Reichsleiters, Gauleiters and chiefs of organizations to overall political exigencies. Instructions and guidelines for the general political leadership tasks of the Party are issued either through the Führer himself or by his orders through the Party Chancellery to the Party, its organizational units and its affiliated organizations.

Establishment of the political line to be followed by the Party, its organizational units and affiliated organizations is a prerogative the Führer has retained for himself. In my capacity as his special assistant in that department I am to keep him abreast of the status of the Party's work at all times and acquaint him with all important circumstances relevant to decision making in Party matters. It is therefore necessary that as Chief of the Party Chancellery, I be kept up to date on the development of the Party's work, as well as of plans and intentions with political implications by the Reichsleiters, Gauleiters and organization chiefs, and that I participate from the start in the elaboration of basic questions involving Party policy. Conversely, it is my intention to keep Reichsleiters, Gauleiters and organization chiefs always up to date on all the Führer's decisions, directives and wishes; I believe that precisely in this way the effectiveness of the NSDAP will be increased and the unity of its attitude in all basic political questions can be guaranteed.

Furthermore, by the Führer's decree of May 19, 1941, based on the Law for Safeguarding the Unity of Party and State, I as Chief of the Party Chancellery have been appointed to represent the Party vis-à-vis the senior authorities of the Reich. The following powers are thereby once again conferred, by authority of the decree for implementation of the Führer's decree of January 16, 1942 (RGB1. 1942, p. 35) on the position of the Chief of the Party Chancellery:

1. Participation in legislation of the Reich and the *Länder* [federal states], including the preparation of Führer executive orders. The Chief of the Party Chancellery thereby represents the viewpoint of the Party as effective protector of the National Socialist *Weltanschauung* (Führer Executive Order of July 27, 1934, and April 6, 1935).

The Chief of the Party Chancellery is to receive prior notification from the senior Reich agencies of preparatory work on Reich laws, executive orders and instructions of the Führer's, regulations of the Ministers' Council on Defense of the Reich, as well as regulations issued by the senior Reich agencies, including implementation instructions and directives for execution. The same goes for concurrence with laws and regulations of the *Länder* and regulations issued by Reich governors.

*The correct year—1941—is given in the left margin.—Ed.'s note. Hereafter, Reichgesetzblatt is referred to as RGB1.—*Tr.*

2. Participation by the Party in personnel matters concerning the officials and Labor Service leaders whose appointment the Führer has retained as his prerogative (Führer Executive Order dated September 24, 1935, RGB1. I, p. 1002, and July 10, 1937 RGB1. I, p. 769). The participation of the Party in personnel evaluations of other government employees has been turned over to the Gauleiters by the Führer's executive order supplementing the executive order of March 26, 1942, on the appointment of officials and the abolition of the status of government officials (RGB1.I, p. 153).

3. Guarantee of the Party's influence upon the autonomous government of corporations in the [newly acquired] territories (Section 3, Paragraph 5 of the First Executive Order on Promulgation of the Ostmark [Austria] Law of June 10, 1939, and Section 2, Paragraph 5 of the First Executive Order on Promulgation of the Sudeten Gau Law of June 10, 1939).

Since all powers have been transferred to me which were conferred upon the previous Führer Deputy by all the laws, executive orders, ordinances and whatever other regulations enacted to date, all previous rulings also remain in force with regard to dealings of Party offices with senior Reich authorities and senior authorities of *Länder* comprising several Party districts. Accordingly, the Party's participation in legislation and personnel processing of government officials by the senior Reich authorities is to be done exclusively through the Party Chancellery. Also, suggestions and proposals for legislation coming from the Party, its formations and affiliated organizations may only be transmitted to the senior Reich authorities concerned by the Chief of the Party Chancellery.

Direct communication between senior Reich agencies and senior authorities of *Länder* that include several Gaus on the one hand, and offices of the Party, its formations and affiliated organizations on the other, is, as before, inadmissible in the future in matters of basic and political questions, especially those connected with preparation, amendment or promulgation of laws, executive orders and regulations, as well as the processing of personnel files of officials.

These conditions were laid down by the Führer explicitly to guarantee a *unified* representation of the Party. They are therefore to be complied with absolutely. For my part, I have given instructions to inform the offices of the Reich leadership at regular intervals on pending legislative work by special conferences, to receive suggestions and proposals from these offices at the conferences, and to enlist the Party offices concerned in the processing of all individual questions to the fullest extent.

[signed] M. Bormann

f.d.R.:
[signed] Friedrichs

Memorandum dated January 12, 1943 [unsigned]
Party Member Tiessler, liaison between Martin Bormann and
Joseph Goebbels, noted "Copy for the Minister [Goebbels] through
Party Member Gutterer" (cf. text, page 229)

COPY FOR THE MINISTER
through Party Member Gutterer

Re: Increased Anti-Bolshevik Propaganda

Reichsleiter Bormann was informed by me on the Minister's remarks regarding the conduct of total war, and he welcomed them enthusiastically.

In this connection the Reichsleiter especially emphasized to me the following lines of thinking:

At the start of the Russian campaign we featured Bolshevism and its consequences on the broadest scale, in domestic as well as foreign propaganda. Reichsleiter Bormann, however, is of the opinion that we have slackened off in this area as time has gone on. In his opinion it is necessary to give more insistent emphasis on our struggle against Bolshevism seen as the struggle for all Europe. In connection with the struggle for Europe even those peoples (not the governments) must be named that face us as neutrals or even as enemies. The Reichsleiter referred to our adversary's bent to crush all Christianity, something that should be repeated at every opportunity. We must to the same degree exploit the first-class propaganda possibilities offered us by Bolshevism and its manifestations. While the British and the Americans day after day depict to the neutrals (Spaniards, Swedes, etc.) how a victory by the authoritarian states would be a triumph of godlessness, we have not made enough use in recent times of the opportunity to portray what a victory for Bolshevism would mean to Swedes, Spaniards, etc., as well as to each individual fellow countryman [in Germany].

By means of first-class news and picture documentation it would be easy for us to make clear to the neutrals the consequences of Bolshevism, as they have proved out for the past twenty years.

We wage this war not only for ourselves and our children; rather, in the struggle against Bolshevism our whole culture is at stake. What this means should be represented in detail repeatedly with a new variation each time, in order that every German, Spaniard, Frenchman, Swede get the message. We are fighting for Goethe, Schiller and Kant, but just as much for Shakespeare, Milton, Corneille, Calderon.

Over and over again, using fresh examples, it must be made clear to the individual nations that the whole culture they have accumulated to date would be destroyed if the Bolshevik chaos were to prevail.

But we are fighting not only for the cultures of each one of the European nations, but also for the great men of their past. What—to take just one example—would happen to the image of Napoleon if Bolshevism were to win? The hero of the French would become a bloodthirsty murderer of nations.

Selecting from these viewpoints, every week the European press as well as radio should deal with a particular new side of Bolsheveik, all concentrating together on a special point. Each week a new chord should be struck on the necessity of fighting Bolshevik. The theme can take so many forms that it could always be structured as something new, colorful, interesting to everyone.

In domestic policy, each and every citizen in all walks of life should have it made clear to him what his fate would be in the event of a Bolshevik victory. Here, too, one should use individual examples and add on to them continually with new material. Each individual must have the condition of life possibly awaiting him portrayed in terms of his own immediate existence.

The propaganda sources against us used by the English, etc., are so scanty that they partly have to be built up around a V. By contrast, we have in the Bolshevik chaos quite another set of propaganda possibilities, a steam roller we can set in motion with a new aspect of it showing each time.

No signature

Berlin, January 12, 1943
Ti/Ge

Office memorandum dated January 26, 1943
Martin Bormann to Helmuth Friedrichs and other staff members

Distribution illegible

Führer Headquarters, January 26, 1943
Bo/Kr.
("Received" stamp February 1, 1943)

Office memorandum for Party Member Friedrichs, III S and III D.

Re: Christianity

From a conversation that took place with the Führer:
The missionaries who came to Germania to spread Christianity were political commissars.

•

The Roman state was destroyed by Christianity; the so-called religion of Paul revolutionized the slaves and the subhuman elements of Roman society.

•

Christianity is in every age characterized by its cultural effects: the Roman artists, the Roman state, created the finest works of art; the so-called works of art made by the Christians of those years that have been preserved in the catacombs show Bolshevik-futuristic traits.

•

The whole magnitude of the contrast between barbarism and Christianity is revealed in the hygiene both inspired:
We still to this day wonder at the Roman aqueducts and baths! In contrast, Christianity suppressed every form of sanitation made necessary by nature; a man became a saint by living in his own excrement.
Even today it is forbidden for nuns to bathe undressed. They take their baths just like children in schools run by the "Englische Fräulein,"* in a long chemise.

•

How would the world look if Christianity had not come and scientific discovery had not stopped for around 1500 years?

•

The extent to which Christianity destroyed the so-called barbarian culture is something we can hardly imagine today.
Something similar might have happened if Thomas Münzert† had established himself and his doctrine.

•

---

*Translated as "English Sisters" in Payne, *Life and Death of Adolf Hitler,* p. 347: ". . . a convent school kept by the English Sisters, so named because English nuns had founded the convent in the eighteenth century." Eva Braun went to school there.—*Tr.*
†A German religious enthusiast and rabble-rouser, contemporary and adversary of Martin Luther.—*Tr.*

What we need are history books by National Socialist scholars who possess a strong realistic sense and therefore do not come up with completely idiotic hypotheses.

[signed] M. Bormann

Office memorandum dated May 8, 1943
Martin Bormann to his co-workers Gerhard Klopfer and Helmuth Friedrichs

---

Illegible handwritten distribution list

Führer Headquarters, May 8, 1943
Bo/Kr.

Office Memorandum for Party Member Dr. Klopfer and Party Member Friedrichs

Reich Minister Dr. Lammers told me today following the conversation that took place with the Führer on the reduction of meat rations that the title "Secretary to the Führer" has already made quite a stir.

I answered Dr. Lammers that this was completely incomprehensible to me, as in fact I have been acting for years as Secretary to the Führer for all practical purposes; as Dr. Lammers knows, I used my personal letterhead in that capacity and this inevitably gave rise to repeated misunderstandings; I was confronted with accusations that I was mixing in things which were none of my business and which I had patently not been ordered to do by the Führer.

I told Dr. Lammers that I had already made clear that no new office or new set of duties had been created. Nothing at all would be changed in the current administration of the office.

Dr. Lammers answered that people were trying to alarm him, saying that now Dr. Lammers had become superfluous. The Reichsmarschall told Dr. Lammers that in the future he was to hold his thumbs on his trouser seams when he got a letter from me as Secretary to the Führer. Dr. Lammers answered that if the receiver of the letter had any objections, he could always take his objections to the Führer along with my letter.

Dr. Lammers then showed me the draft of a circular letter to the top government agencies, with the contents of which I declared myself to be in concurrence.

In closing, Dr. Lammers emphasized that Reich Minister Dr. Goebbels especially appeared not to be at all pleased by my appointment as Secretary to the Führer.

[signed] M. Bormann

Memorandum dated January 29, 1944
Martin Bormann on "Safeguarding the Future of the German People"
(cf. text, page 276)

Führer Headquarters
January 29, 1944

Note Re: Safeguarding the Future of the German People

1. During the night of January 27–28 the Führer had a conversation with us on the problem of our future as a people. The upshot from this and earlier discussions and reflections is here recorded:

Our racial situation will be *disastrous* after this war, for our people is now experiencing the second massive bloodletting within a span of thirty years. There can be no doubt that we will win the war militarily, but we will lose it racially unless we make drastic readjustments.

The loss of blood is not something that just happens once; rather, it has its effect year after year, way into the distant future.

A single example:

How many more children would have been born during this war if it had been possible to give our front-line soldiers leave from the army entirely or more frequent home leave?

We are shown what frightful political consequences a war can have by the Thirty Years' War: at its start the German people numbered over 18 million, and by the time it ended, a mere 3 ½ million. The consequences of this spilling of blood have not yet been made up and compensated for to this day, for we lost that world leadership which at the beginning of the Thirty Years' War the German people seemed first in line to assume by predestination; our dismemberment as a state persisted until 1870, and as a people, looking at the big picture, until 1933; the sectarian religious disunity is not yet mended to this day.

2. On previous occasions I have pointed out again and again the condition that will prevail after the war is over: we must hold before our eyes the population map of Europe and Asia as of 1850, 1870 and 1900 and 1945: *The Asiatic peoples are multiplying at a much faster rate than the* Nordic peoples, some of whom are not increasing their population at all any more. If this ratio persists, then it will do our Nordic peoples no good at all if we win this war, for in a hundred years at the latest, they will still be overwhelmed by the tremendous masses of Asiatic peoples. The present struggle is already made infinitely difficult by the waves of ever fresh masses of troops the Russians are able to keep throwing in.

3. As the Führer stressed, after this war we will have 3 to 4 million women who either no longer have husbands or will not get any. The drop in the birth rate resulting from that would be impossible to put up with for our people: how many divisions—the Führer emphasized—would we be short in twenty to forty-five years and beyond that!

4. The future and life of a people are the more secure, the higher the birth rate of that people.

The calculation of many parents to keep down the number of their children in order to assure the future of those children already born is basically wrong-headed: the reverse is true! With sufficient insight all women, therefore, who have *one* child, should insist that not only they themselves but all other women have as many children as possible, since these children's future is that much more secure, the greater their number. This is a completely cool-headed calculation.

5. Now, it is a fact that women who find themselves without a man after this war cannot have children by the Holy Spirit but only by men who have survived. Increased propagation by the individual man is—obviously from the standpoint of the good of the people—only desired in the case of a portion of these men. Good men with strong character, physically and psychically healthy, are the ones who should reproduce extra generously, not the ones warped in body and mind.

6. If the dead of the past world war and the present war are not to have died in vain, we must secure the victory with all means at hand. Every woman whose husband or brother or father or other relative was killed in one of these struggles must wish that! This means that every woman must wish that *every* healthy woman capable of doing so after war's end will have as many children as possible, to secure the victory and to secure the future of our people and the future of her own grandchildren.

7. Now, government regulations alone, particularly in this ticklish area, serve no purpose whatever. Here only a very serious conviction borne along by the Movement can lead to the required attitude. The question is too serious for wisecracks and cheap jokes; here what is truly at stake is the safeguarding of the future of our people.

8. After this war we cannot command women and girls to have babies. What is called for is the most intelligent enlightenment possible—and here the much overused superlative is used advisedly.

9. This [enlightenment] must in my opinion not be carried out by men who might too easily be considered personally interested parties, [sexual] profiteers. In my opinion only older men should be allowed to speak on this theme, and above all, our women's organizations must perform the necessary job of enlightenment.

10. These needful actions involve not only convincing the women who have lost husbands or will never get one, but what is needed first of all is the enlightenment of the old folks, the mothers and fathers, who grew up among quite different attitudes in the past.

11. Still more necessary is the enlightenment of the wives, who in many cases turn into fanatical [advocates] of respectability only after their marriage.

12. When we reflect on what is necessary to bring this so vitally important problem for our people to a successful solution, then we must make the situation clear for the individual case. At first many women—want of logic is something women are born with—will affirm the appropriateness [of the new order of things], but in the individual case, applied to their personal lives, they will fanatically reject it.

13. The public, i.e., general, enlightenment [campaign] can, for obvious reasons, only get under way after the war. To mention only one reason: we cannot yet appeal today to the women whose husbands might become casualties in the future, and also out of consideration for our soldiers we cannot begin our enlightenment campaign; that would assume that we would have to get this line of thinking across to our men now serving as soldiers, but not every soldier will readily accept the prospect of his wife or bride bearing children by another man after his own death.

14. Meanwhile *we* must be fully cognizant of the steps that can be taken while the war is still on, and of those to be introduced immediately after war's end.

15. We must begin immediately to remove all impediments to the attainment of our objective: in particular, the point is to orientate contemporary poets and writers. New novels, short stories and stage plays based on marriage and divorce are no longer to be permitted, and by the same token [we will allow] no poems, writings, motion pictures that treat the child born out of wedlock [*unehelich*] as of diminished worth, as a bastard.

(The word *"unehelich"* must, as I pointed out long ago, be expunged [right out of the language]. The prefix *"un"* generally denotes something to be rejected. Examples:

ehelich [in wedlock, legitimate]	*unehelich* [illegitimate]
Frieden [peace]	*Unfrieden* [strife]
Ehre [honor]	*Unehre* [dishonor]
frei [free]	*unfrei* [in bondage]
sympathisch [likable]	*unsympathisch* [unpleasant]
appetitlich [appetizing]	*unappetitlich* [unappetizing]
hold [lovely]	*unhold* [unfriendly]
Heil [salvation]	*Unheil* [ruin]
Glück [luck, happiness]	*Unglück* [disaster]
Glaube [faith]	*Unglaube* [infidelity])

In other words—we must begin right away to reject anything that presents this problem in a way that partly or fully harms the future of our people! Neither on the stage nor in the world of literature can we allow conflicts between a "lawful wife" and her "unlawful rival" to be introduced anymore.

On the contrary, we must cleverly and unobtrusively point out that, for instance —as has come to light in tracing ancestry—many family trees of famous scholars, artists, statesmen, industrialists and soldiers show evidence of children born out of wedlock. To put it another way: how many famous men who performed the greatest services for our people would not have been born if their mother or female forebear had not brought her child into the world.

16. Now, the antipathy toward illegitimate children undoubtedly has a reason behind it, which we—more precisely *we of all people*—must recognize.

No more than anyone else, we don't want our sisters or daughters to have children casually by just any man, or first by one and then by another. What we should strive for is to get the women in our country who are unable after the war to get married in the way that has prevailed up to the present to commit themselves to a man who really suits them and have children by him.

When I observe that in animal husbandry only animals that can tolerate each other are bred to each other, then I must hold to the rules that govern all mammals in the case of humans too: if I want children with a pleasant disposition who are never disturbed, then I must let it be known that only people who really suit each other should beget children.

In other words, we must not wish that a woman—even by means of so-called remote conception—should get children from just any man; it is much more desirable that only people who are really attached to one another should conceive children.

17. Conclusion: It is desirable that wherever possible, women who do not have or find a husband after the war enter into a marriagelike relationship which will produce as many children as possible.

It is of course possible that not all such relationships will last through a lifetime; rather, it is natural, as many marriages also are terminated in divorce after long or short duration. Moreover, I am convinced that two people who are bound together in friendship but do not see each other all that often can stay together for a lifetime more easily than others; this is particularly true when the bond is strengthened by children of love and friendship.

18. As I mentioned above, any defamation directed at relationships that are desirable from the viewpoint of the people must be stopped. Whoever insults a woman who has children without a husband (in the current sense) must be severely punished. Whoever—this will hit many pastors—speaks out against propaganda that is for needs of the people is likewise to be punished severely.

19. In many cases the resistance on the part of married women will be due to *material* considerations: for the sake of her own children, the wife would not want to share her income or her husband's inheritance with another woman and her children.

This is understandable! But since the people and the state want to secure their future, they must use every means, hence also material means, to ensure the greatest possible increase in numbers of births; hence the state must provide adequate subsidies.

20. Should the state fail to do so, the most important capital would be irretrievably lost: the productivity of many age groups consisting of millions of women.

21. Many women and young girls would be glad to have children—many children, in fact—if they only knew that they would be taken care of for the rest of their lives. They do not want to have children and then find that one day, because the father of these children dies, becomes impoverished or leaves her, she and her children are left unprovided for, having to depend on the mercy and compassion of charitable institutions.

22. It is quite obvious that women who work at a job and have children should be paid more proportionately, and further, that such women should be allocated housing commensurate with the number of family members in the household.

23. After the war I would like to have this kind of housing built in Sonnenwinkel for female employees of the Party Chancellery who have children born to them.

24. The number of state-run boarding schools (public schools—boarding schools, upper classes of elementary schools with boarding, and preparatory schools, upper schools with boarding and preparatory schools) must be increased considerably so that all women with any reason for not being able to bring up their children part or all of the time can let them be brought up without difficulty in the state-run boarding schools. This should be the case for [both] boys and girls.

These state boarding schools are also needed because the best and most capable men are usually real wild ones in their youth and cannot be controlled by their mothers alone.

25. Meanwhile, these women should not have to wait until their children are of mandatory school age before they can send them to state boarding schools; rather, according to Führer decree the NSV [National Socialist People's Welfare, *National-sozialistische Volkswohlfahrt*], as pointed out earlier, should build the best maternity homes and also the best children's homes, where children can be raised from infancy to school age. The upbringing in these children's homes must be far better than it can be in the general run of family households. *This* is the great task for the future for the NSV!

26. We must—for the sake of the future of our people—get a regular motherhood-cult going, and in it there must be no difference between women who are married in the hitherto normal way and women who have children by a man to whom they are bound in friendship! All these mothers are to be honored alike.

(Obviously this would not be the case, for instance, for those asocial elements who don't even know who the fathers of their children are.)

27. When two people go to the registrar's office to make their intended union for life known to and legitimized by the state, this [act] has chiefly the following purposes:

a) The marriage partnership, together with the progeny, is placed under the protection of the state and its powers and its codes of civil and criminal law.

b) Both partners are thereby aware that one is obligated to the other, and that one is not free to leave the other for no good reason.

c) Moral security: Extramarital relations are taboo according to hypocritical bourgeois attitudes. Marital sexual relations are, however, considered respectable beyond any question!

d) Material security: A man who gets a divorce must take care of his wife as long as she is not at fault.

28. These statements illustrate what inhibitions we must eliminate and what preconditions we must create in order to attain the increase in births needed for survival:

1) For mothers who have not been married in the hitherto acceptable way we must also create a quite similar encompassing moral as well as material security. That includes among other things that the children must in every case get their father's name without any difficulty.

2) Additionally: On special petition, men should be able to enter into a binding marital relationship not only with one woman, but also with another, who would then get his name without complications, and the children automatically getting the father's name.

3) The idea of a man letting himself be sued for nonpayment of alimony ought to be an exception; any man who behaves that way without a compelling reason deserves to be disgraced for it, because in general, his conduct is outrageous.

4) As I mentioned before, it is necessary that we abolish the terms for relationships currently in use, having a more or less disreputable overtone, and forbid them. Instead, we must coin good, positive-sounding terms. We must also think about what to call the relationship between a woman and a man whom she cannot marry in the usual sense; we must think about what the children of such a friendship union are to be called, etc.

The more felicitous the designations we come up with, the easier it will be for us to get rid of the existing inhibitions. But these inhibitions must be eliminated, for otherwise all the sacrifices of the previous war and of this war will be in vain because our people *must* [inevitably] fall victim to the coming onslaught. In twenty or thirty or forty or fifty years we will be lacking the divisions that we absolutely need if our people is not to perish.

5) After the war, childless couples and single men must be taxed much more severely than hitherto. The taxes on bachelors imposed up to now will seem like child's play compared to the tax burdens to be laid on them in the future.

The revenue from these bachelor taxes will serve to support the mothers who have children, i.e., for the material support of our efforts on behalf of the coming generation.

I ask you to give close attention to the entire problem and then let me have your opinion.

[signed] M. Bormann

Circular letter dated May 30, 1944
Martin Bormann to Reichsleiters, Gauleiters, to Reichsleiters, Gauleiters, Organization Chiefs, Kreisleiters (cf. text, page 261).

SECRET
Circular Letter 125/44—Secret
(not for publication)

Re: Justice Exercised by the People against Anglo-American Murderers

In the last few weeks, low-flying English and American fliers have repeatedly strafed children playing in open squares, women and children at work in the fields, farmers plowing, vehicles on the highways, trains, etc., and have thus murdered defenseless civilians—particularly women and children—in the vilest manner.

Several instances have occurred where crew members of such aircraft who have bailed out or have made forced landings were lynched on the spot immediately after capture by the outraged public.

No police or criminal proceedings were lodged against the citizens involved.

[signed] M. Bormann

Circular letter dated May 30, 1944
Helmuth Friedrichs to all Gauleiters and Kreisleiters

Re: Circular Letter 125/44—Secret

The head of the Party Chancellery requests that the local group leaders [Ortsgruppenleiter] be informed of the contents of this circular letter orally only.

[signed] Friedrichs

Circular letter dated April 5, 1945
Directive from Martin Bormann

Office of the   Schliersee, April 5, 1945
Supreme SA Leader
G.Z.: FO No. 11 150

Re: Conduct of Party Leadership in Areas Where the Enemy Has Penetrated

To: *Group Leaders*

Following below, Groups are herewith informed of a directive of the Führer to the Party Chancellery dated April 1, 1945.

The Chief of the Supreme
Directorate
Jüttner
Obergruppenführer

April 1, 1945
The Chief of the Party Chancellery

Directive

By the Führer's command I hereby direct:
National Socialists! Party comrades!
After the collapse of 1918 we dedicated ourselves with life and limb to the struggle to justify the existence of our people.
Now the crucial hour of personal sacrifice has struck:
The danger of renewed slavery faces our people, demands our ultimate and supreme effort.
From now on the following is in force:
The struggle against the foe who has penetrated into the Reich is to be waged everywhere, with extreme tenacity and ruthlessness.
Gauleiters and district leaders, other political leaders and formation leaders will fight in their own Gau and district, win or die.
A scoundrel who leaves his Gau during an enemy attack without express orders from the Führer, who fails to fight to the last breath, will be dealt with as a deserter.
Raise high your hearts and overcome all weaknesses!
There is only one motto now: Win or die!
Long Live Germany! Long live Adolf Hitler!

[signed] M. Bormann

Circular dated April 15, 1945
Martin Bormann to Reichsleiters, Gauleiters and Organization Chiefs
(for this and previous Bormann circulars to the Party, cf. text, page 317)

National Socialist   [Nazi Emblem]   German Workers' Party

Party Chancellery

The Chief of the Party Chancellery Führer Headquarters, 4/15/1945

Circular Letter 211/45

Re: Action Duty of Political Leaders

Party Comrades:
The Führer expects you to deal with any situation in your Gaus instantly if necessary, and with extreme ruthlessness!
Rally your district leaders around to the same stance too. Now one sees the difference between leaders and the feckless! Now it shows what each Gau and district, unvarnished, is made of! Master is only he who can achieve mastery; the faint-hearted, the incompetent must be immediately replaced by men of action! Every man radiates only so much faithful confidence and so much unshaken hope as he has within him. The strong radiates strength, the laggard and weary only perplexity and doubt. The true leaders have burned all their bridges and are totally prepared. They are the only ones we can rely on, for only they are capable of resurrecting the spirits of the ones who yield and hesitate. Let every political leader clearly understand: the honor of each individual is worth only so much as his steadfastness, his preparedness and his actions.

[signed] M. Bormann

List of Interviews

Artur Axmann, head of the Hitler Jugend, with the title Reichsjugendführer
Friedrich Bergold, Martin Bormann's defense attorney at the Nuremberg Trials
Adolf Martin Bormann, eldest son of the Secretary to the Führer
Albert Bormann, NSKK commander, Hitler's adjutant and Martin Bormann's brother
Sepp Dietrich, SS Oberstgruppenführer (General) and the first commander of the Leibstandarte Adolf Hitler (bodyguard regiment)
Karl Dönitz, Grand Admiral and named Hitler's successor in the Führer's last will, with the title Reich President
Alfred E. Frauenfeld, Gauleiter of Vienna
Hans Fritzsche, section chief in the Ministry of Propaganda
Franz Halder, General and Chief of Staff
Heinrich Heim, ministerial counselor on Bormann's staff
Ilse Hess, wife of Rudolf Hess, Hitler's Deputy
Heinrich Hoffmann, Jr., son of Heinrich Hoffmann, Hitler's photographer
Rudolf Jordan, Gauleiter of Saxony-Anhalt
Karl Kaufmann, governor and Gauleiter of Hamburg
Robert M. W. Kempner, U.S. assistant prosecutor at the Nuremberg Trials
Otto Kranzbühler, Karl Dönitz's defense attorney at the Nuremberg Trials
Heinz Linge, SS Hauptsturmführer (Captain) and Hitler's valet
Wilhelm Mohnke, SS Brigadeführer (Brigadier General)
Hanni Morell, wife of Hitler's personal physician, Theodor Morell
Werner Naumann, State Secretary in the Ministry of Propaganda
Henry Picker, who recorded *Hitler's Table Talks*
Karl Jesko von Puttkamer, Rear Admiral and Hitler's naval adjutant
Hanna Reitsch, German test pilot
Hans Ulrich Rudel, Colonel in the Luftwaffe
Gustav Adolf Scheel, NS Studentenführer, later governor and Gauleiter of Salzburg
Baldur von Schirach, head of the Hitler Jugend; governor and Gauleiter of Vienna
Henriette von Schirach, wife of Baldur von Schirach

Richard Schulze-Kossens, one of Hitler's adjutants

Lutz Graf Schwerin von Krosigk, Minister of Finance

Lord Shawcross, British Chief Prosecutor at the Nuremberg Trials

Otto Skorzeny, SS Sturmbannführer (Major) and Mussolini's rescuer

Albert Speer, Minister for Armaments and War Production

Felix Steiner, SS Obergruppenführer (Lieutenant General)

Otto Strasser, Gregor Strasser's brother; early Nazi organizer, later head of the "Black Front"

Ehrengard von Treuenfels, wife of Bormann's employer Hermann von Treuenfels

Karl Wahl, Gauleiter of Augsburg

Walther Wenck, General, commander of the Twelfth Army

Karl Wolff, SS Obergruppenführer (Lieutenant General) and head of Heinrich Himmler's personal staff

Wilhelm Zander, SS Standartenführer (Colonel) and personal consultant to Martin Bormann

Hans Severus Ziegler, Deputy Gauleiter for the Gau Thuringia

Bibliography

Albrecht, Gerd, *Nationalsozialistische Filmpolitik.* Stuttgart, 1969.
Altner, Günter, *Weltanschauliche Hintergründe der Rassenlehre des Dritten Reiches.* Zürich, 1968.
Aronson, Shlomo, *Reinhard Heydrich und die Frühgeschichte von Gestapo und SD.* Stuttgart, 1971.
Der Aufstieg der NSDAP in Augenzeugenberichten, Ernst Deuerlein, ed. Düsseldorf, 1968.
Auschwitz, Zeugnisse und Berichte. H. G. Adler, Hermann Langbein and Ella Lingens-Reiner, ed. Frankfurt a.M., 1962.
Bauer, Fritz, *Die Kriegsverbrecher vor Gericht.* Zürich, 1945.
Besymenski, Lew, *Auf den Spuren von Martin Bormann.* Berlin, 1965.
———, *Der Tod des Adolf Hitler.* Hamburg, 1968.
———, *Die letzten Notizen von Martin Bormann.* Stuttgart, 1974.
Bibliographie zur Geschichte des Kirchenkampfes 1933–1945, Otto Diehn, ed. Göttingen, 1958.
Bibliographie der Gauleiter der NSDAP, Günter Plum, ed. München, 1970.
Bollmus, Reinhard, *Das Amt Rosenberg und seine Gegner.* Stuttgart, 1970.
Bormann, Martin, *The Bormann Letters. The private correspondence between Martin Bormann and his wife (Gerda Bormann) from January 1943 to April 1945.* Ed. with an introduction and notes by H.R. Trevor-Roper. London, 1954.
Bracher, Karl Dietrich, Sauer, Wolfgang, and Schulz, Gerhard, *Die national-sozialistische Machtergreifung.* Köln, 1960.
———, *Die Auflösung der Weimarer Republik.* Villingen, 1964.
———, *The German Dictatorship: The Origins, Structure, and Effects of National Socialism.* Paperback, Prager, 1970.
Bross, Werner, *Gespräche mit Hermann Göring während des Nürnberger Prozesses.* Flensburg, 1950.

Broszat, Martin, *German National Socialism, 1919–1945.* Paperback, ABC-Clio, 1966.

————, *Nationalsozialistische Polenpolitik 1939–1945.* Stuttgart, *Vierteljahrshefte für Zeitgeschichte,* No. 2 (1961).

————, *Der Staat Hitlers.* München, 1969.

Buchheim, Hans, *et al., Anatomy of the SS State.* Walker & Co., 1968.

Bullock, Alan, *Hitler. A Study in Tyranny.* Harper & Row, 1964.

Conway, John S., *Nazi Persecution of the Churches.* Weidenfeld & Nicolson, London, 1969.

Daim, Wilfried, *Der Mann, der Hitler die Ideen gab.* München, 1958.

Darré, Richard Walter, *Um Blut und Boden,* München, 1940.

Delarue, Jacques, *The History of the Gestapo.* Morrow, 1964.

Deutsch, Harold C., *Conspiracy Against Hitler in the Twilight War.* University of Minnesota Press, 1968.

Deutsche Geschichte seit dem Ersten Weltkrieg. 3 vols.

    Vol. I: Heiber, Helmut, "Die Republik von Weimar"; Graml, Hermann, "Europa zwischen den Kriegen"; Broszat, Martin, "Der Staat Hitlers."

    Vol. II: Gruchmann, Lothar, "Der Zweite Weltkrieg"; Vogelsang, Thilo, "Das geteilte Deutschland"; Petzina, Dietmar, "Grundriss der deutschen Wirtschaftsgeschichte 1918–1945."

    Vol. III: Benz, Wolfgang, "Quellen zur Zeitgeschichte." Stuttgart, 1971–1973.

Der Deutsche Widerstand gegen Hitler. Walter Schmitthenner and Hans Buchheim, ed. Köln, 1966.

Diehl-Thiele, Peter, *Partei und Staat im Dritten Reich.* München, 1969.

Diels, Rudolf, *Lucifer ante portas.* Stuttgart, 1950.

Dietrich, Otto, *Das Buch der deutschen Gaue.* Bayreuth, 1938.

————, *Auf den Strassen des Sieges.* München, 1939.

————, *12 Jahre mit Hitler.* München, 1955.

Dönitz, Karl, *Memoirs: Ten Years and Twenty Days.* Greenwood, 1976.

Dollinger, Hans, *Die letzten hundert Tage.* München, 1965.

Domarus, Max, *Hitler. Reden und Proklamationen 1932–1945.* München, 1965.

Domber, Yves van, *Ik leefde met Martin Bormann.* Amsterdam, 1969.

Ehlers, Dieter, *Technik und Moral einer Verschwörung.* Bonn, 1965.

Ehrhardt, Helmut, *Euthanasie und Vernichtung "lebensunwerten" Lebens.* Stuttgart, 1965.

Eyck, Erich, *A History of the Weimar Republic,* 2 vols.

    Vol. 1: *From the Collapse of the Empire to Hindenburg's Election.* Harvard University Press, 1962. Paperback, Atheneum, 1970.

    Vol. 2: *From the Locarno Conference to Hitler's Seizure of Power.* Harvard University Press, 1963. Paperback, Atheneum, 1970.

Fabry, Philipp Walter: *Mutmassungen über Hitler.* Düsseldorf, 1969.

Facsimile-Querschnitt durch das Schwarze Korps. Helmut Heiber and Hildegard von Kotze, ed. München, 1968.

Faschismus-Getto-Massenmord. Compiled by the Jewish Historical Institute, Warsaw. Tatiana Berenstein, Artur Eisenbach, *et al.,* ed. Berlin, 1961.

Fest, Joachim C., *The Face of the Third Reich: Portraits of the Nazi Leadership.* Pantheon, 1970.

Fest, Joachim C., *Hitler*. Harcourt, Brace, Jovanovich, 1974. Vintage paperback, Random House, 1975.

———, Hoffmann, Heinrich, and Lang, Jochen von, *Adolf Hitler*. München, 1975.

Finker, Kurt, "Die militaristischen Wehrverbände in der Weimarer Republik," *Zeitschrift für Geschichtswissenschaft, No. 14* (1966), 357–377.

Frank, Hans, *Im Angesicht des Galgens*. München, 1953.

Führer befiehl . . ., Albrecht Tyrell, ed. Düsseldorf, 1969.

Gamm, Hans-Jochen, *Der braune Kult*. Hamburg, 1962.

Geiss, Josef, *Obersalzberg*. Berchtesgaden, 1958.

Gersdorf, Ursula von, *Frauen im Kriegsdienst*. Stuttgart, 1969.

Gessler, Otto, *Reichswehrpolitik in der Weimarer Zeit*. Kurt Sendtner, ed. Stuttgart, 1958.

Goebbels Diaries Nineteen Forty-Two–Nineteen Forty-Three. Trans. by Louis Lochner. Reprint of 1948 ed. Greenwood, 1977.

Goebbels, Joseph, *Vom Kaiserhof zur Reichskanzlei*. München, 1936.—*My Part in Germany's Fight*. Reprint of 1935 ed. Fertig, 1977.

———, *Wetterleuchten*. München, 1939.

Graml, Hermann, *Der 9. November 1938*. Bonn, 1962.

Granzow, Klaus, *Tagebuch eines Hitlerjungen. 1943–1945*. Bremen, 1965.

Grebing, Helga, *Der Nationalsozialismus*. München, 1964.

Gruchmann, Lothar, "Hitler über die Justiz," *Vierteljahrshefte für Zeitgeschichte, No. 12* (1964), 86–101.

Gründler, Gerhard E., and Manikowsky, Armin von: *Das Gesicht der Sieger*. Oldenburg, 1967.

Halder, Franz, *The Halder Diaries: The Private War Journals of Colonel General Franz Halder*. 2 vols. Westview, 1977.

Hallgarten, George W. F., *Hitler, Reichswehr und Industrie*. Frankfurt a.M., 1955.

Hanfstaengl, Ernst, *Zwischen Weissem und Braunem Haus*. München, 1970.— *Unheard Witness*. New York, 1957.

Heiber, Helmut, *Hitlers Lagebesprechungen*. Stuttgart, 1962.

———, *Joseph Goebbels*. Berlin, 1962.

———, *Die Republik von Weimar*. München, 1966.

Henkys, Reinhard, *Die nationalsozialistischen Gewaltverbrechen*. Stuttgart, 1964.

Hillgruber, Andreas, *Staatsmänner und Diplomaten bei Hitler*. Frankfurt, 1970.

Hitler, Adolf, *Mein Kampf*. Paperback, Houghton Mifflin, 1962.

Hitlers Weisungen für die Kriegsführung 1939–1945. Walther Hubatsch, ed. Frankfurt a.M., 1962/München, 1965.

Hockerts, Hans Günter, Die Sittlichkeitsprozesse gegen katholische Ordensangehörige und Priester 1936–1937. Mainz, 1971.

Höhne, Heinz, *The Order of the Death's Head: The Story of Hitler's SS*. Paperback, Ballantine, 1971.

———, *Canaris*. Gütersloh, 1976.

Hölzle, Erwin, *Die Revolution der zweigeteilten Welt*. Reinbek, 1963.

Höss, Rudolf, *Kommandant in Auschwitz*. Stuttgart, 1958.

Hoffmann, Heinrich, *Hitler Was My Friend*. London, 1955.

Hoffmann, Peter, *The History of German Resistance 1933–1945*. MIT Press, 1976.

Honolka, Bert, *Die Kreuzelschreiber*. Hamburg, 1961.

Horn, Wolfgang, *Führerideologie und Parteiorganisation in der NSDAP (1919–1933)*. Düsseldorf, 1972.

Irving, David, *Hitler's War*. Viking, 1977.

Jacobsen, Hans-Adolf, *Der Zweite Weltkrieg*. Frankfurt a.M., 1975.

———, *Decisive Battles of World War II: The German View*. J. Rohwer, ed. Deutsch, London.

———, "Kommissarbefehl und Massenexekutionen sowjetischer Kriegsgefangener." In Hans Buchheim, *et al., Anatomy of the SS State*.

Jäckel, Eberhard, *Hitlers Weltanschauung*. Tübingen, 1969.

Jäger, Herbert, *Verbrechen unter totalitärer Herrschaft*. Freiburg, 1967.

Jordan, Rudolf, *Erlebt und erlitten*. Leoni am Starnberger See, 1971.

Der Kampf um Berlin 1945 in Augenzeugenberichten. Peter Gosztony, ed. Düsseldorf, 1970.

Kater, Michael H., *Das "Ahnenerbe."* Unpublished M.S. thesis, Heidelberg, 1966.

Kempka, Erich, *Ich habe Adolf Hitler verbrannt*. München, 1950.

Kempner, Robert M. W., "Blueprint of the Nazi Underground." In *Research Studies of the State College of Washington*, Vol. XIII (1945).

——— "The Nuremberg Trials as Sources of Recent German Political and Historical Materials. In *American Political Science Review*, No. 44 (1950), 447–459.

———, *Eichmann und Komplizen*. Zürich, 1961.

———, *SS im Kreuzverhör*. München, 1969.

———, *Das Dritte Reich im Kreuzverhör*. München, 1969.

Kersten, Felix: *Totenkopf und Treue*. Hamburg, 1952.

Klönne, Arno, *Hitlerjugend*. Hannover, 1960.

Kogon, Eugen, *The Theory and Practice of Hell*. Farrar, Straus, 1951.

Koller, Karl, *Der letzte Monat*. Mannheim, 1949.

Kordt, Erich, *Wahn und Wirklichkeit*. Stuttgart, 1947.

Krausnick, Helmut, "Legenden um Hitlers Aussenpolitik." In *Vierteljahrshefte für Zeitgeschichte*, No. 2 (1954), 217–239.

Krebs, Albert, *Tendenzen und Gestalten der NSDAP*. Stuttgart, 1959.

Krummacher, Friedrich A., *Die Weimarer Republik*. München, 1965.

——— and Lange, Helmut, *Krieg und Frieden*. München, 1970.

Kühnrich, Heinz, *Der KZ-Staat*. Berlin, 1960.

Lange, Karl, *Hitlers unbeachtete Maximen*. Stuttgart, 1968.

Lewin, Ronald, *Rommel*. Batsford, London.

Liddell Hart, B. H., *The German Generals Talk*. Paperback, Morrow, 1971.

Lohalm, Uwe, *Völkischer Radikalismus*. Hamburg, 1970.

Lüdde-Neurath, Walter, *Regierung Dönitz*. Göttingen, 1951.

Mann, Klaus, *Der Wendepunkt*. München (n.d.).

Manvell, Roger, and Fraenkel, Heinrich, *Dr. Goebbels*. Simon & Schuster, 1960. Paperback, Mentor Books, New American Library.

———, *The Men Who Tried to Kill Hitler*. Coward-McCann, 1965.

———, *Hermann Göring*. Simon & Schuster, 1962. Paperback, Mentor Books, New American Library.

———, *Heinrich Himmler*. Putnam, 1965. Paperback, Mentor Books, New American Library.

McGovern, James, *Martin Bormann*. London, Barker, 1968.

Medizin ohne Menschlichkeit, Alexander Mitscherlich and Fred Mielke, ed. Frankfurt a.M., 1960.

Meier-Benneckenstein, Paul, *Grundfragen der deutschen Politik*. Berlin, 1939.

Meldungen aus dem Reich, Heinz Boberach, ed. Neuwied, 1965.

Meissner, Otto, *Staatssekretär unter Ebert—Hindenburg—Hitler.* Hamburg, 1950.

Milatz, Alfred, "Das Ende der Parteien im Spiegel der Wahlen 1930 bis 1933." In *Das Ende der Parteien 1933,* Erich Matthias and Rudolf Morsey, ed. Düsseldorf (1960), 743–793.

Mitscherlich, Alexander, and Mielke, Fred, *Doctors of Infamy.* Schuman, 1949.

Mommsen, Hans, "Beamtentum im Dritten Reich." *Vierteljahrshefte für Zeitgeschichte,* No. 13. (1966).

Müller, Hans, *Katholische Kirche und Nationalsozialismus.* München, 1963.

Müller, Klaus-Jürgen, "Reichswehr und 'Röhmaffäre.'" In *Militärische Mitteilungen,* No. 1 (1968), 107–144.

Müller, Klaus-Jürgen, *Das Heer und Hitler.* Stuttgart, 1969.

Müller, Willy, *Das soziale Leben im neuen Deutschland unter besonderer Berücksichtigung der Deutschen Arbeitsfront.* Berlin, 1938.

Der Nationalsozialismus. Dokumente 1933–1945, Walter Hofer, ed. Frankfurt a.M., 1957.

National Socialism, US Dept. of State. Div. of European Affairs, ed. by Raymond Murphy, *et al.* US Gov. Doc.Progr.Ser. 1976.

Neufeldt, Hans-Joachim, Huck, Jürgen, and Georg Tessin, *Zur Geschichte der Ordnungspolizei 1936–1945.* Koblenz (Bundesarchiv), 1957.

Neurohr, Jean F., *Der Mythos vom Dritten Reich.* Stuttgart, 1957.

Nürnberger Prozesse (Blaue Reihe) (Amtlicher Text. Deutsche Ausgabe), Vols. 1–42. Nürnberg (Internationaler Militärgerichtshof), 1947–1949.

Nürnberger Prozess. Internationale wiss. Konferenz aus Anlass d. 20. Jahrestages d. Beginns d. Nürnberger Hauptkriegsverbrecherprozesses. Berlin (Staatsverlag d. DDR), 1966.

O'Donnel, James, and Bahnsen, Uwe: *Die Katakombe.* Stuttgart, 1975.

Papen, Franz von, *Memoirs.* Dutton, 1953.

Picker, Henry, *Hitlers Tischgespräche im Führerhauptquartier 1941–1942.* Bonn, 1951.

Picker, Henry, and Hoffman, Heinrich, *Hitlers Tischgespräche im Bild.* Jochen von Lang, ed. Oldenburg, 1969.

Raeder, Erich, *My Life.* U.S. Naval Inst., 1960.

Reichhardt, Hans-Joachim, *Die Deutsche Arbeitsfront.* Unpublished M.S. thesis, Berlin, 1956.

Reichsführer! Briefe an und von Himmler, Helmut Heiber, ed. Stuttgart, 1968.

Reimann, Viktor, *Goebbels.* Doubleday, 1976.

Ribbentrop, Joachim von, *The Ribbentrop Memoirs.* London, Weidenfeld & Nicolson, 1954.

Ribbentrop, Annelies von, *Deutsch-englische Geheimverbindungen.* Tübingen, 1967.

Röhm, Ernst, *Die Geschichte eines Hochverräters.* München, 1928.

Rohe, Karl, *Das Reichsbanner Schwarz-Rot-Gold.* Düsseldorf, 1966.

Rommel, Erwin, *Krieg ohne Hass.* Lucie-Maria Rommel and Fritz Bayerlein, ed. Heidenheim, 1950.

Rosenberg, Alfred, *Letzte Aufzeichnungen.* Göttingen, 1955.

Das politische Tagebuch Alfred Rosenbergs aus den Jahren 1934/35 und 1939/40. Göttingen, 1955.

Rosenberg, Alfred, and Härtle, Heinrich, *Grossdeutschland, Traum und Tragödie*. München, 1970.

Rosenberg, Arthur, *Geschichte der Weimarer Republik*. Kurt Kersten, ed. Frankfurt a.M., 1971.

Rothfels, Hans, *The German Opposition to Hitler. An Appraisal*. Greenwood, 1976.

Ruge, Wolfgang, *Deutschland von 1917 bis 1933*. Berlin, 1969.

Schacht, Hjalmar H., *Confessions of the Old Wizard*. Greenwood, 1975.

Schaumburg-Lippe, Friedrich-Christian Prinz zu, *Dr. G., Ein Portrait des Propagandaministers*. Wiesbaden, 1963.

Schellenberg, Walter, *The Labyrinth*. Harper, 1957.

Schenck, Ernst-Günther, *Ich sah Berlin sterben*. Herford, 1970.

Scheurig, Bodo, *Free Germany. The National Committee and the League of German Officers*. Wesleyan University Press, 1969.

————— *Verrat hinter Stacheldraht*. München, 1965.

Schirach, Baldur von, *Ich glaubte an Hitler*. Hamburg, 1967.

Schlabrendorff, Fabian von, Offiziere gegen Hitler. Zürich, 1946. The Secret War Against Hitler. Pitman, 1965.

Schmidt, Paul, *Hitler's Interpreter*. Macmillan, 1951.

Schwarz, Albert, *Die Weimarer Republik 1918–1933*. Konstanz, 1968.

Schwerin von Krosigk, Lutz Graf, *Es geschah in Deutschland*. Tübingen, 1951.

Secret Conferences of Dr. Goebbels: The Nazi Propaganda War, 1939–1943. Willie Boelcke, ed. Dutton, 1970.

Siewert, Kurt, *Schuldig?* Bad Nauheim, 1968.

Smith, Bradley, *Heinrich Himmler. A Nazi in the Making 1900–1926*. Stanford, 1971.

Speer, Albert, *Inside the Third Reich*. Macmillan, 1970. Paperback, Avon, 1974.

—————, *Spandau*. Macmillan, 1976. Paperback, 1977.

Spiegelbild einer Verschwörung (The Kaltenbrunner Reports). Stuttgart, 1961.

Springer, Hildegard, *Es sprach Hans Fritzsche*. Stuttgart, 1949.

Die SS-Henker und ihre Opfer. Auschwitz 1940–1945. Frankfurt 1963–1965. Internat. Föderation d. Widerstandskämpfer (FIR). Wien, 1965.

Steinert, Marlies G., *Die 23 Tage der Regierung Dönitz*. Düsseldorf, 1967. Hitler's War and the Germans: Public Mood and Attitude During the Second World War. Ohio Univ. Press, 1977.

Stephan, Werner, *Joseph Goebbels*. Stuttgart, 1949.

Strasser, Gregor, *Kampf um Deutschland*. München, 1932.

"Studien zur Geschichte der Konzentrationslager," *Vierteljahrshefte für Zeitgeschichte*, No. 21 (1970).

Taylor, Telford, *The Nuremberg Trials, War Crimes, and International Law*. Carnegie Endowment, 1949.

Toland, John, *The Last Hundred Days*. Random House, 1966.

Trevor-Roper, Hugh Redwald, *The Last Days of Hitler*. Macmillan, 1962.

—————, "Hitlers Kriegsziele," *Vierteljahrshefte für Zeitgeschichte*, No. 8 (1960), 121–133.

—————, "Hitlers Testament," *Der Monat*, No. 4 (1961), 36–47.

Unbestrafte Kriegsverbrecher. István Pintér and László Szabó, ed. Budapest, 1961.

Das Urteil im Wilhelmstrassen-Prozess. R. M. W. Kempner & Carl Haensel, ed. München, 1950.

Das Urteil von Nürnberg. München, 1961.

Die Verfolgung nationalsozialistischer Straftaten im Gebiet der Bundesrepublik Deutschland seit 1945. Bonn, 1964.

Vogel, Georg, *Diplomat unter Hitler und Adenauer.* Düsseldorf, 1969.

Vogelsang, Reinhard, *Der Freundeskreis Himmler.* Göttingen, 1972.

Vogelsang, Thilo, *Reichswehr, Staat und NSDAP.* Stuttgart, 1962.

———, *Die nationalsozialistische Zeit.* Frankfurt a.M., 1968.

Vogt, Martin, "Zur Finanzierung der NSDAP zwischen 1924 und 1928. In *Geschichte in Wissenschaft und Unterricht* (1970).

Volz, Hans, *Daten der Geschichte der NSDAP.* Berlin, 1939.

Wahl, Karl, *Patriot oder Verbrecher.* Heusenstamm, 1973.

Von Weimar zu Hitler. 1930–1933. Gotthard Jasper, ed. Köln, 1968.

Whiting, Charles, *The Hunt for Martin Bormann.* New York, 1973.

Wilmot, Chester, *The Struggle for Europe.* Greenwood, 1972. Paperback, Watts, 1974.

Wulf, Joseph, *Das Dritte Reich und seine Vollstrecker.* Berlin, 1961.

———, *Martin Bormann—Hitlers Schatten.* Gütersloh, 1962.

———, *Aus dem Lexikon der Mörder.* Gütersloh, 1963.

———, *Presse und Funk im Dritten Reich.* Gütersloh, 1964.

Zipfel, Friedrich, *Kirchenkampf in Deutschland 1933–1945.* Berlin, 1965.

Zmarzlik, Hans-Günter, *Der Sozialdarwinismus in Deutschland als geschichtliches Problem, Vierteljahrshefte für Zeitgeschichte,* No. 11 (1963), 246–273.

Index

424 · *Index*

About the Author

Born in 1925, JOCHEN VON LANG is an editor on the German news magazine *Stern,* for which he has written extensively about German history. Two of his best-known pieces, which were serialized in the magazine, are "The Last Hundred Days of Hitler's Reich" and a report on Auschwitz, "Assassins Are Like You and Me." He is the writer and producer of the German radio program "Eyewitness Reports" and has produced some notable documentary films, including one called "Nuremberg Prosecutor." He wrote the book *Adolf Hitler: Faces of a Dictator* and edited *Hitler: A Collection of Informal Photographs.* As *The Secretary* describes, he was influential in establishing the facts of Martin Bormann's suicide, and it was his search for Bormann's remains that first kindled his interest in the man and his role in the Third Reich. *The Secretary* has been a best seller in Germany.